CONSUMER SOCIETY

LORNE TEPPERMAN & NICOLE MEREDITH

ROCK'S MILLS PRESS
Oakville, Ontario
2021

Published by

Rock's Mills Press
www.rocksmillspress.com

Contents

EACH CHAPTER CONCLUDES WITH
DISCUSSION QUESTIONS, A QUICK QUIZ,
SUGGESTIONS FOR FURTHER READING,
AND A LIST OF KEY TERMS.

CHAPTER EIGHTEEN **The Future of Consumerism**

Chapter One
The Dance of Desire

Learning Objectives

After reading this chapter, you will be able to:

- ✓ Picture four types of consumers as a basis for common patterns of consumption.
- ✓ Consider buying behaviour as social communicative behaviour
- ✓ Understand the conditions that make a consumer society and shopping possible.
- ✓ Identify the historical drivers of conspicuous consumption.

begin this book with a look at four familiar figures: Angelyn, Anton, Tamara and Donald. You probably know people just like them. They are typical members of our consumer society.

Angelyn is down to earth and mainly buys things she needs for her family. Her goal in buying is to achieve sufficiency: enough of the things her family needs. The things she buys are things she has bought many times before, though she doesn't keep a large stock of such things at home. She doesn't know what's in fashion or in style, and never spends more than the family can afford. Angelyn and her family like to save money, so they watch for bargains, make and follow a budget, and discuss and plan their purchases, taking advice from friends and workmates.

Yet, despite this modest profile, Angelyn and her family feel confident about themselves and their possessions. They are secure and happy at work, at school, and at home and have strong values, goals, and ambitions. Generally, Angelyn and her family lead a quiet, comfortable life. They are not very aware of the social class they belong to and don't really concern themselves with displaying their belonging in that class. Their only fear, if they have one, is losing their stability and security because of shifts or injustices in the external world such as the COVID-19 pandemic, job loss, or other unforeseen hardships.

Then there's Anton. Anton buys what we'll call "treats": things that help him feel full and assuage the feelings of emptiness, depression, and anxiety he struggles with. Many of the things Anton buys he has bought before. In fact, he has a stock or surplus of many things at home, and out of embarrassment, he hides this surplus stock in closets and the basement. Often—maybe most of the time—he feels insecure and unhappy at work and at home.

As a consumer, Anton doesn't know much about what is in fashion or style, yet he often manages to spend more than he can afford, even though he is always looking for bargains. He has a hard time controlling his buying behaviour and buys a lot of things on impulse. He rarely manages to save money and his uncontrolled buying occasionally gets him into trouble with family, friends, and workmates. Anton even risks long-term harm through financial self-destruction and bankruptcy.

Anton has weak and uncertain values, goals, and ambitions; he's adrift in a world that feels threatening. Anton has occasional problems with drinking and drugs. Although he buys his treats to try to make himself feel better—a form of so-called "retail therapy" known as compensatory buying—it doesn't actually make him feel complete or full, at least not for long. He is swallowed up by recurrent feelings of emptiness and dreads the possibility of debt and bankruptcy.

Tamara, for her part, is a confident and purposeful buyer. She buys "tickets": things that other people she knows—friends, neighbours, family members, or co-workers—own and enjoy. In large part, this is how she knows what is in fashion or in style; that is, because she sees other people consuming these goods and services. Buying what others have helps Tamara feel confident in herself and her possessions. As a result, she is generally secure and happy at work and at home.

Though she wants to fit in and be fashionable, Tamara she doesn't spend more than her family can afford. Her family exercises control over their buying, and under Tamara's leadership, they make and follow budgets. Together, they discuss and plan purchases with family, friends, and workmates.

Tamara and her family are secure and happy at work, school, or home. They all have strong values, goals, and ambitions, which they discuss and share. They are very aware of the social class they belong to—the middle class—and regularly tell others about their newest acquisitions because they want to be recognized for their class position and accepted by others in their class. Tamara's biggest fear, if she had one, would be a failure to receive acceptance from her neighbours, friends and workmates. More than anything, Tamara wants to fit in and even be popular. She dreads rejection and unpopularity.

Finally, there's Donald, who is driven by a need to excite envy, admiration, and jealousy in the eyes of others. He loves to buy "trophies": things that no one else—whether a friend, neighbour, family member, or workmate—already owns. To achieve this distinction, Donald must follow what is in fashion and pay attention to what other people own. And though he has a good income, he always spends more than he can afford, with the result that he never manages to save money.

Yet Donald always feels insecure and unhappy, whether at work or at home, never comfortable in his own skin. He has a hard time controlling his buying behaviour and he buys impulsively. This impulsiveness sometimes gets him into trouble with family, friends, and workmates. The criticism he receives is only partly offset by his pleasure in telling others about what he has bought and how much better he is doing than other people in their class or community. Donald wants to be "high class"—in fact, he wants to be the classiest person around. Other than this goal, he has weak, uncertain values and ambitions; he's all about showing off and making a spectacle of his life. From time to time, Donald wrestles with anxiety and depression; he doesn't drink but he has obesity and eating issues. His biggest fear is that he will encounter ridicule and indifference from the people he is trying to impress, and

Tickets are purchases meant to gain admission to a select group, such as a golf club membership.

that he will go bankrupt again, limiting his chances of buying more stuff.

Now, let's dig into the kinds of consumer goods that our four consumers tend to buy. First, "basics" are common products—usually low-cost items—that the buyer needs: a loaf of bread or a bar of soap, for example. The purchase of these necessary products has no important meaning either for the buyer or for people witnessing the purchase. By contrast, treats are often (though not always) more expensive than most basics. What distinguishes them is that, by definition, they are special and do not satisfy any fundamental human need. A treat may be an occasional (inexpensive) ice cream cone, for example. Or it may be a (more costly) trip to Galway, Ireland to visit relatives. In each instance, the treat is meaningful to the buyer; it satisfies some personal desire and maybe even helps them feel better about themselves or the cards they've been dealt in life. However, it may not mean anything to other people or change the buyer's status in their eyes. Thus, it has no social meaning or content.

Third, tickets are goods or services that are purchased to gain admission to, or maintain membership in, an institution or social group. They are the "cost" of joining and belonging to a community. Examples might be a golf club membership, a current model car, a donation to the local synagogue, a winter holiday in Antigua, or hosting a periodic house party. Ticket-buyers want attention for this purchase to gain acceptance from other people in the group. They want to spend the right amount and, certainly, they don't want to spend too little. If anything, they are likely to discuss the bargain they got.

Finally, trophies are lavish social expenditures—spectacles—designed to astonish others.

Their goal is to surpass and even diminish group membership. Suppose that last year the wealthy Jones family invited 300 guests to a New Year's party, served a buffet banquet, and featured an internationally known musical group. As a trophy purchase, this year the Smith family will invite 400 guests to their New Year's party, serve a sit-down ten-course banquet, and feature three internationally known musical groups, plus a circus troupe.

In the course of this book, you will read about theorists who discuss each of these kinds of purchases. For example, we will see that Thorstein Veblen, who studied the conspicuous consumption of the leisure class, is interested in trophy spending. A wide variety of writers, such as David Riesman, Erving Goffman, and Jean Baudrillard, have been largely interested in ticket spending. That is, they have written about social emulation, mass society, and consumer society. Some writers, like George Orwell in *Down and Out in London and Paris* or Barbara Ehrenreich in *Nickel and Dimed*, have been primarily interested in basic spending. Finally, people who write about shopping as an addiction—for example, Gerda Reith in *Addictive Consumption* or Benjamin Barber in *Consumed*—have been mainly interested in treat spending. We will have much more to say about all of them in the course of this book.

That leaves several bodies of writing we will have to wrestle with throughout this book.

Top to bottom: Veblen, Orwell, and Baudrillard

For example, we will consider the writings of Horkheimer and Adorno and of the **Frankfurt school**. They view many types of consumer spending as symptomatic of cultural degeneration: a loss of human integrity and taste that accompanies the rise of a capitalist "cultural industry." At the other extreme is a body of writing by marketing researchers, who focus on how best to convince consumers to buy what they are selling. We will try very hard to find a place for these bodies of thinking as well.

One thorny topic we will return to repeatedly is **materialism**. Materialism is typically defined as a preoccupation with, or belief in the supreme value of, money and material goods to the virtual exclusion of all else. Some authors associate materialism with compensatory spending—the use of spending to make up for a sense of low self-worth.

In that vein, materialism is a form of treat buying. Other authors (for example, Horkheimer and Adorno) see much or all of ticket spending and trophy spending as evidence of a type of materialism—a cultural pathology, if not a personal pathology. We will try to figure out where materialism falls in this story of consumer behaviour as well.

Defining Our Terms

We start each chapter in this book by defining some of the key terms we use throughout that chapter and others. In this introductory chapter, we'll start with two terms that appear throughout this book: consumer society and consumerism.

A **consumer society** is a society where consumption—buying goods and services—is a significant part of daily life. Most people in a consumer society are not like Angelyn; they own or aspire to own more than the "basics." Wants, rather than needs, are the primary motives for most buying in Canadian consumer society.

Consumer societies are peopled by consumers. By **consumers**, we mean the end-users of products and services. Merely buying something does not make you a consumer. The people we call consumers buy for personal use, not for resale.

A key feature of every consumer society is consumerism. **Consumerism** is a way of life that centres on buying things, sometimes at the expense of other concerns (Shaw and Aldridge 2003; for an extended discussion, see Searle 2008, Lindsay 2010). As well as a pattern of behaviour, consumerism is also an **ideology**: a belief system with wide-ranging social, economic, and political implications. It is political in the sense that it influences people's confidence in public institutions and ideas about their government. People tend to think their society is doing well if they are reasonably comfortable and healthy, with hopes of further gradual improvement. **Capitalism**, through consumerism, promotes an illusion of comfort, well-being, and gradual improvement by giving us almost limitless freedom in what we can buy (if we have the cash).

Consumerism supports capitalism so effectively *because* consumerism is a way of life. It is not an afterthought tacked onto our society after other social patterns had been established (Douglas and Isherwood 1996). It is the foundation of our most important rituals, habits, and activities. Consumerism structures the way we shape our identities, spend our time, set our goals, and plan our lives. In these ways, consumerism shapes the form and content of our society.

Because it is so foundational, consumerism props capitalism up without us even noticing most of the time. Consumerism focuses on the rewards that "treats," "tickets," and "trophies" bring—be it emotional fulfilment (however fleeting), a feeling of belonging, or a sense of superiority. By fulfilling our personal yearnings, consumerism legitimizes capitalism, painting it in a favourable light. After all, if it weren't for capitalism, we wouldn't have all those nice things to buy that make us feel so good.

How This Book Is Organized

In the balance of this chapter, we provide additional introductory information about our consumer society. The next four chapters are about *agents of socialization*: the people and institutions that teach us how to communicate our cultural and social ambitions by using consumer goods.

The middle section of the book examines *four social categories and the consumer behaviour associated with each*. First, we discuss the ways rich and poor people spend their money. Then, we discuss the ways men and women spend their money. Third, we discuss the ways older adults—seniors—and youth spend their money. Finally, we discuss *citizens of the Global South* and *immigrants to North America*. Throughout these discussions, we take an **intersectional approach**. We recognize that many factors influence a consumer, including their income, sex, age, country of origin, ethnicity, and more. By recognizing the interplay of these factors, we also recognize the many social groups consumers try both to identify with and distance themselves from.

These discussions show that people orient their buying to **reference groups**: people they want to copy, attract, or impress. Thus, buying is socially communicative. It is also a demographic process in the sense that is about different "types" of people—people with different social goals, identities, loyalties, and histories. They all spend their money in different ways. If there were room (and we wanted to), this book could contain hundreds of such chapters, each detailing the spending pattern of a particular social demographic. Consider the chapters on income, gender, age, and birthplace to be merely illustrative of a larger pattern. This larger pattern, a secondary theme of this book, is the matter of social identification and distancing, or inclusion and exclusion.

We will end our story of consumer society with what some fear will be the end of consumer society: perhaps, the collapse of the current world system through climate change or otherwise. In the final chapter of this book, we will consider the prospects for the consumer society, including its possible demise, after less than 300 years of existence. Before that, as preparation, we will discuss some of the ways people today break the rules of consumer society, resisting it, protesting it, and undermining it wherever possible. This in turn brings us to a discussion of unresolved issues, including the link between consumerism (on the one hand) and environmental destruction and global inequality (on the other).

A Love-Hate Relationship with Consumerism

As becomes increasingly clear throughout the book, anyone who thinks about consumer society at length develops a love-hate relationship with the topic.

Most people love the treats, tickets, and trophies (not to mention the basics) a full-fledged consumer society makes possible. Many people, far from criticizing it, think consumerism is natural, normal, and good for humanity. Consumerism contributes to economic growth, they say, which raises our standard of living and pulls people out of poverty. Some suggest the consumer societies we see in many developed Western nations promote affluence, equality, and free choice.

However, many people also hate the hucksterism, misinformation, exploitation, and environmental destruction the consumer society seems to require. In the chase for material comfort, social status, and power, too many people become obsessed with consumption. To make more money and gain more possessions, they seem willing to sacrifice anything, including human rights, human lives, and the environment. For example, some say the current climate crisis is the fault of capitalism and what Allan Schnaiberg (1981; for a fuller statement, see Gould, Pellow and Schnaiberg 2015) memorably called a "treadmill of production." As we will see throughout this book, mass consumption is associated with the globalization of environmental threats such as deforestation, pollution, global warming, and loss of biodiversity.

In short, some people love consumerism, some people hate it, and a lot of people both love and hate it at the same time. For that reason, in the course of this book, we will consider a few critical questions:

1. What are the social and cultural causes of consumerism?
2. Do people have a natural wish to shop or do marketers, advertisers, and capitalism trick them into it?
3. Does consumerism produce cultural, social, and moral decline?
4. Do some people in our society have an excessive preoccupation with consumer goods?

In answering these questions, we will see that consumer behaviour is **social behaviour:** that is, behaviour that is intended to communicate with and, often, influence other people. Specifically, consumer behaviour is largely a form of human communication. We will argue that, as consumers, people want to signal their membership in groups. They want to copy other members of the group to which they belong, or to which they want to belong. They also want to signal their separation from other groups to which they don't belong, or don't want to belong. Consumer buying helps people send these messages and signal these ambitions.

To send these signals, many consumers—like ticket-buying Tamara—use material goods as communicators. British sociologist Mike Featherstone (2007; for a more recent discussion, see Featherstone 2018) was just one thinker who advanced this idea. He noted that material goods do more than just fulfill the purpose they were designed to serve; we also use them to tell others about ourselves. Clothes, for instance, don't merely cover our bodies and keep us warm; they send a message about our income, profession, and taste.

Marketers and advertisers, as discussed in a later chapter, know this. They try to persuade us to buy by promising their particular goods or services will help us send the messages we want to. The question is: How much buying can marketers and advertisers take credit for? Conversely, if we decide that consumerism is bad, how much blame do they deserve? What part do marketing and advertising play in the buying choices we make?

Sociologists use the idea of agency to help answer this question. **Agency**, for sociologists, refers to an individual's ability to make their own decisions, freely and independently. Some say consumers have little agency in our consumer society. These observers stress the many factors that can influence consumer behaviour and potentially reduce consumer agency, from childhood socialization to formal education to gender identity. Some even consider advertising and marketing as being akin to a form of brainwashing that compels people to buy excessively.

In this book, we present consumerism as a deeply social activity. In fact, we can view it as a mutual seduction or dance of desire. On one side of the dance floor are consumers. They want to buy the things they value. On the other side are sellers. They want consumers to consume so they can make a profit. Both are (often) knowing, voluntary participants in these acts of mutual seduction. In other words, we argue that consumers make their own choices, at least to a degree. They are voluntary participants in the dance of desire; no one is holding a gun to their heads. That said, consumption doesn't happen in a vacuum, without persuasion and even deception. As we will see, many social forces are at work, strongly influencing the things and ways we consume.

The Lonely Crowd was a pioneering analysis of social conformity that has influenced subsequent researchers in their understanding of the nature of consumerism.

The Lonely Crowd

The love-hate relationship with consumerism is nothing new. More than 70 years ago, soon after the end of the Second World War, increasing numbers of intellectuals were writing worried books about consumerism and mass conformity. One such book, *The Lonely Crowd* (1950), is a classic work of American sociology, and representative of the thinking of scholars who have viewed consumer behaviour as a sign of almost mindless social conformity. (For recent reflections on this book and related issues, you might look at Costa et al. 2019; Schwartz 2017; Hastings 2016).

In *The Lonely Crowd*, Harvard researchers David Riesman, Nathan Glazer, and Reuel Denny identify three main types of people, whom they call **tradition-directed**, **inner-directed**, and **other-directed**. Without delving into the history of these human types, it is sufficient to note that in 20th-century North America, people became more other-directed, more concerned with how their neighbours were living their lives. North Americans wanted to win social approval—in essence, they became more like Tamara, eager to fit in, to be a part of the community. And just as much, they wanted to enjoy the new material prosperity. These other-directed people lost sight of themselves as they pursued social acceptance and material well-being. This rise in other-directedness thus coincided with the rise of consumerism and materialism.

At nearly the same time, Canadian-born sociologist Erving Goffman was publishing his classic work, *The Presentation of Self In Everyday Life* (1956). Here, Goffman urged us to think of all social life as a theatre, with scripts, props, rehearsals, front stages, and backstages. Life in this dramaturgical world is nonpolitical and aimed wholly at gaining, keeping, and influencing an audience of observers. Life, in Goffman's eyes, is the ultimate version of "other-directedness." However, unlike Riesman and his collaborators, Goffman did not assume this orientation was unique to mid-20th-century America. It is, he claimed, an essential feature of all contemporary social life. We will talk further about Goffman's ideas in a later chapter, where we consider self-presentation and impression management.

Accounts of mid-century life in Canada like *Creeping Conformity: How Canada Became Suburban, 1900–1960* by Richard Harris (2004; for a more recent discussion of suburbanization, see Keil 2017) reach similar conclusions. Before the 1920s, Harris argues, working-class Canadians were community-oriented and, though they valued consumer goods, they also valued thrift. They were a little more like Angelyn, buying just the basics. As the century went on, and especially beginning in the 1950s, prosperity increased and with it, the popularity of consumerist lifestyles. The effects, Harris says, could be seen in Canadian suburbs. Houses and the properties on which they rested grew steadily in size, as suburbanites came to think that "bigger is better."

Today, seven decades after the publication of *The Lonely Crowd,* cultural critics continue to note similar themes. North Americans continue to value material comfort and ease, perhaps to a worrisome degree. Some Americans even confuse material plenty with well-being. They consume plentifully because, from their other-directed perspective, doing so will bring them approval, acceptance, and social worth. They crave "the good life," to be attained by owning the newest and best gadgets in the neighborhood. As a result, as Scranton (200) points out, for nearly 150 years, American business and industry have been driven by a popular desire for "endless novelty."

Why might all of this be worrisome? Excessive consumerism, and a desire for endless novelty, can be seen as embodying a political agenda, as a means of (unconsciously) perpetuating a status quo that's unfavourable to most people. Critics suggest the promise of material plenty entices consumers to value capitalism, even when capitalism is unfair or exploitative.

How exactly do consumerism and capitalism prop each other up? Well, as we said, consumerism is deeply social and it highlights two central elements of social life. First, people like to join communities and copy their fellow community members. Second, people like to exclude each other and compete with people from other communities. As a result, some people may become unhealthily preoccupied with consumer goods in their efforts to "get ahead," "show up," or shame others. Caught up in the rat race—and occasionally enjoying rewards like belonging and inclusion—many people come to feel content with the status quo. They approve of (or at least quietly tolerate) capitalism because it's framed as the key to material comfort and social admiration. They become less likely to resist, revolt, or rebel against social injustice.

In this and other ways, they prop up a highly unequal capitalist economy and society. To better understand how consumerism and capitalism prop each other up, we first need to understand where they came from and how they evolved into the versions we see today.

The Conditions for Consumer Societies

Many social, economic, and political factors gave rise to the perfect storm from which consumer societies evolved. The Industrial Revolution, the transformation in manufacturing processes that began in Britain around 1760 and spread throughout Europe and, eventually, the entire world, is often seen as the most important of those factors. And it is true that you can't have a consumer society without **mass production**. For people to consume on a massive scale, massive quantities of consumer goods need to be available for them to buy. Mass production was enabled by an intellectual, social, legal, cultural, and political climate that encouraged experimentation and innovation; and a growing entrepreneurial spirit, spurred by growing social mobility. City building helped too, as vast numbers of agricultural workers moved to growing industrial cities in search of factory work. The result was widespread and growing (if unequally shared) prosperity.

This coffee and tea service was manufactured in Josiah Wedgwood's factory in England around 1775, and is now on display at the Victoria and Albert Museum. A process called transfer printing made it possible to produce high-quality ceramics at a low cost, thus encouraging the emergence of a mass market for these goods.

But the Industrial Revolution was not the sole or even the most important impetus behind the creation of the consumer society. Even more crucial—and perhaps most important of all—was the role played by consumer demand. As 18th-century ceramics entrepreneur Josiah Wedgwood could attest, mass production emerged in response to an existing demand for goods. Consumer desires were present and growing even before breakthroughs in technology and manufacturing made new kinds of commodities available to the masses on a larger scale. What drove that demand? Some say the answer is social striving and emulation (for a recent discussion of the role of social emulation, see Goodin 2018). People emulate or imitate those they admire and want to be like (e.g., the peasantry emulated the aristocracy by buying Wedgwood's wares). They aim for upward social mobility, or at least try to create the illusion of belonging to a higher social class by buying "high-class" goods.

So, when it comes to mass production, the supplier does not thrive because he invents new ways to produce more products faster. He thrives because more consumers want those products and, increasingly, can afford them. From this perspective, demand—not supply—is a necessary precondition for and stimulant to the growth of mass production. Once the pursuit of luxury became possible for an ever-larger portion of the population, it became an engine for growth and a motive for mass production.

Second, you can't have a consumer society without **mass consumption**: the purchase and use of standardized, mass-produced products. You need many consumers with money to spend. People typically have money to spend when they live in societies with a high and growing standard of living. To achieve this high standard of living, nations often invest in public spending, state wealth redistribution, and minimum wage laws.

However, you don't need large numbers of wealthy people to have mass consumption. Today, we see growing mass consumption in the Global South, even though these countries have only rudimentary social safety nets, and their populations do not have large discretionary incomes. In part, that is because consumer goods—even necessities, like food—become more affordable when mass produced. Mass production thus helped boost the standard of living for even the poorest of the poor. They could start participating in mass consumption using their new (if modest) discretionary income.

Third, you can't have a consumer society without **mass communication**. Mass consumption requires large-scale advertising and marketing, and the spread of these practices to hundreds of countries. We'll expand on these topics in later chapters. For now, note that different types of mass communication aim at different goals. Some simply tell consumers that a given product or service exists. Greater awareness can mean that more consumers who want or need these goods and services can buy them. But as we will see, mere awareness isn't always enough to get consumers to buy advertised products. The purpose of mass communication when it takes the form of advertising is to *persuade* consumers to make a purchase. Advertising is designed to make consumers believe that consuming particular products will bring particular rewards: beauty, fame, popularity, glory, and various other desirable social outcomes.

However, mass communication is not the same thing as brainwashing. Remember: consumers have (varying degrees of) agency. Many ignore or discount these advertising messages. Mass media messages do not, by themselves, determine consumer's thoughts, values, or actions. They are only one factor of many that enable and promote a consumer society.

Fourth and finally, you can't have a consumer society without **mass distribution**. Today, products and services that were once only available to a small segment of local consumers can now be ordered for delivery straight to the doorstep of a consumer on another continent.

These four critical developments—mass production, mass consumption, mass communication, and mass distribution—all had foundational effects in the creation of consumer society. The result of all this was an activity we are all familiar with—shopping.

A Short History of Shopping

For consumers to shop, there need to be several conditions in place. First, there must be a surplus of products to buy. For example, hunter-gatherers—typically, nomadic people who live from hand-to-mouth—don't have a material surplus of food or anything else to sell, so there is no buying in such societies. To have a surplus, you need a detailed division of labour in which people produce different kinds of things for use or trade. For instance, humans have made tools for hundreds of thousands of years, but it was only in the last 10,000 years or so that there have been people who *specialize* in making tools and spend the bulk of their time doing so. Specialization tends to standardize and improve the quality of the products made, but more importantly, it increases the quantity of products, and lowers the price of each unit.

Shopping also assumes a common understanding of private property and personal ownership. Hunter-gatherers typically share everything they capture or find, so there is no private property, hence no shopping. There must also be something equivalent to money: a basis for the exchange of anything for anything else. Hunter-gatherers historically didn't have money with which to buy things, even if they had things to buy.

Only with the so-called Neolithic Revolution—the development of agriculture—did humanity begin to meet these key conditions for shopping to exist in even the most basic form. The origins of agriculture date to somewhere between 7,000 and 10,000 years ago. The resulting increase in food production resulted in the creation of the first cities as well as greater specialization of labour.

Eventually, money emerged—perhaps around 3,000 years ago—and this allowed people to buy land and build personal wealth. Soon, people could even collect money from faraway buyers they'd never met. With the creation of military empires controlling large geographical areas, long-distance shopping (and therefore commerce) through shipping became possible.

After the fall of the Roman Empire, long-distance travel and commerce dwindled in Europe. But around 1400, travel over land and on the Mediterranean Sea began to pick up again. There were many reasons for this, and a classic source on this topic is historian Henri Pirenne's *Medieval Cities: Their Origins and the Revival of Trade* (2000 [1925]). Markets also began to expand, especially in growing cities like Venice and Genoa. Increasingly, merchants reached out to even larger, more distant groups of buyers, and manufacturers wanted to produce more goods more cheaply. As a result, people could shop much farther from home.

In the late 17th century, luxury markets emerged. Again, there were several conditions that led to this development. For one, imperial expansion had opened new markets in many parts of the world. New consumer goods became increasingly available, including tea, coffee, tobacco, metal ware, china, inexpensive ornaments, and cloth for furnishings and fashion.

Second, social and cultural changes made it more acceptable for people to desire and demand these products. Prior to this change, excessive spending was seen as a vice—at least for poor people. There were even "sumptuary laws" in place designed to curb it. These laws prevented people in the lower social classes from legally obtaining goods used by the upper classes. In reality, these laws were not aimed at discouraging the "immoral" behaviour of excessive spending; they were meant to preserve traditional social distinctions. Just like today, rich people signaled their status by distancing themselves from the poor. How could the upper classes *show* their social superiority if anyone could buy the same goods and services they did?

In the late 17th century, all of that started to slowly change. As trade expanded, a city-based bourgeois class emerged. This **bourgeoisie**—a class of business owners, entrepreneurs, and other employers—wanted to shake off restrictions on lending and other business transactions. They thought that easier banking could promote commerce and help their trading businesses succeed.

A few people—especially those with the most status to lose—continued to question the morality of luxury spending. But in 1714, Bernard de Mandeville's *Fable of the Bees* noted that consumer spending could lead to economic growth that benefitted everyone. Burgeoning capitalists increasingly felt justified in pushing luxurious wares. And in 1776, the controversy over Mandeville's fable was resolved when Adam Smith published *The Wealth of Nations*. There, Smith argued that trade produces prosperous, polite, and refined people. Consumption, at least for Smith and the bourgeoisie, was no longer considered a vice.

That said, these developments played out differently for men and women. The male industrialist could claim to be doing God's work when producing wealth. He could also argue that he was rejecting the frivolities of consumerism by choosing the sober black businessman's suit. Women, on the other hand, were open to criticism for their supposedly uncontrolled and indiscriminate desires. Women allegedly pined for the silly baubles and trinkets of Smith's "productive labour" (Donohue 1999).

In this setting, women were also objects of prominent display. Newly wealthy industrialists did not have the social status granted by inherited wealth, land, or title, so they had to mark their new social status by displaying their wives. Specifically, their wives were expected to equip their homes with commodities that reflected admirable wealth and authority. By the late 19th century, marketing experts were using language such as "Mr. Breadwinner" and "Mrs. Consumer" to describe this gendered division of (consumer) labour (Donohue 1999).

The Galerie Vivienne, seen here in this panoramic view, is one of Paris' famous covered passageways and a forerunner of the modern-day shopping mall. It first opened in 1823. The concourse featured a wide variety of shops, including wine merchants, a bookstore, tailors, and cobblers. Declared a historical monument in 1974, the Galerie remains a busy shopping area today.

Modern shopping came of age in the mid- to late 19th century. That's when mass production, mass consumption, mass distribution, and mass communication all took on recognizably modern forms. As capitalism and modern state-building started to take off in northwestern Europe and North America, so too did shopping. The international trade exhibitions that followed London's Great Exhibition of 1851 opened consumers' imaginations to new and spectacular products. By the end of the 19th century, shops and shopping had expanded dramatically. Shopping districts developed. The great department stores of New York, Paris, and Berlin emerged as fantastic "cathedrals of consumption," as sociologist George Ritzer (1999, 2007) called them, bolstering and stimulating consumer demand. Shopping became a social activity, an opportunity to see others and to be seen.

Eventually, indoor shopping malls developed, to a large degree supplanting shopping streets, shopping arcades, and department stores. Indoor shopping malls have been especially important for Canadians, protecting us from the winter cold.

From the beginning, shopping was a social activity. A classic work of social history by Walter Benjamin ([1940], 1999) on the so-called Paris arcades describes how *flaneurs*—men of leisure out for a stroll—wandered the covered shopping areas, savouring the products on sale and the shoppers out to look at them. The *flaneur* became a familiar figure associated with urban modernity, someone who had come to enjoy the anonymity, alienation, and beguiling confusion of city life. The *flaneur* "consumed" the city, absorbing its crowds and their (consumer) behaviours.

Department stores remain important today and embody the four revolutions we mentioned earlier: production, consumption, transport, and communication (Belisle 2011). However, since the Second World War, indoor malls have gradually joined, and sometimes replaced, department stores, arcades, and shopping streets as meccas of consumer activity. And in turn, indoor malls have also begun to decline, for several reasons, including rising rents, the advent of so-called "big box" stores in suburban and exurban "power centres," and, of course, the rise of online shopping. Having shed many of the overhead costs that burden bricks-and-mortar retailers, large online commerce companies can sell goods in greater volumes and often at lower prices than their competitors (Pappas et al. 2017). As market researcher and *Forbes* contributor Pamela Danziger (2018) put it, "buying something—anything—is faster, easier and infinitely more convenient done online."

Box 1-1
Eaton's
A Classic Canadian Merchandiser

The T. Eaton Company Limited, founded by Timothy Eaton in 1869, was at one point the largest department store chain (and indeed retailer of any kind) in Canada. Before the First World War, some Eaton's stores boasted over 100 departments. (The postcard to the left shows the Toronto store at Yonge and Queen Streets in 1923; it was demolished in the 1970s to make room for the Eaton Centre.) Eaton gave his department managers great autonomy. In a way, it was as if the store were a cluster of independent shops, each with their own staff. Meanwhile, by 1920, Eaton's operated "buy-offices" all over the world. These offices sourced exotic products for the stores back in Canada. One of Timothy Eaton's goals was to, in effect, bring the world to Canada. For Eaton, it was important that the stores become "local interpreters of international trends to Toronto" (Penfold 2016).

Eaton also realized that almost half the Canadian population lived in rural areas, far from his department stores, and in response developed a pre-Internet version of Amazon: the mail-order catalogue. The company issued its first 34-page catalogue in 1884, and began to open catalogue offices across Canada. If some Canadians couldn't come to Eaton's, Eaton's would come to them. The catalogue was a hit, providing a selection of goods otherwise unavailable to rural Canadians. Canadians bought everything from clothing to farming implements from the Eaton's catalog (Library and Archives Canada).

The COVID-19 pandemic that began in 2020 caused new troubles for traditional retailers with physical locations, while boosting the fortunes of many online retailers. Many brick-and-mortar stores were forced to close for significant periods of time. Even when they re-opened it was often with physical distancing restrictions. Although grocery stores remained open (and saw increased profits), in this segment, too, online commerce made gains, as many people felt safer ordering groceries online rather than venturing into a store to buy them. Some who hesitated to try online shopping in the past did so for the first time, putting aside security concerns and forgetting they preferred to select their own products from the shelves. It may well be that we will see long-term changes in consumers' shopping habits as a result of the pandemic.

If they are to survive (and COVID-19 may mean many won't), malls must realize they no longer have a monopoly. Variety, ease, convenience, and other factors make the experience of buying online better for many consumers. What malls can offer, Danziger (2018) suggests, is a shopping *experience*. "Experiential retail" describes in-person shopping experiences, in brick-and-mortar retail spaces, that may include anything from interactive art displays to live music, lounges, or virtual reality. Consumers need no longer set out for the mall with the intention of shopping; they can go just to experience something—and then shop when they get there. Similarly, pop-up shops—retail stores open only for a limited period—can help malls feel fresh, as though there's always something new on offer. However, COVID-19 could also wipe out this singular advantage malls have over online shopping. If consumers do not feel safe when close to each other, it will take a very impressive "experience" to draw them into a mall.

Conspicuous Consumption

As we will learn at greater length in the next chapter, shopping is a form of **conspicuous consumption**. To understand this term, think about consumer behaviour as a display of sacrifices. People who make—and show they *can* make—the most significant sacrifices gain the most social respect and status from others. These sacrifices can come in many forms: some are related to financial status, while others may be related to health or personal reputation. In every instance, people must give up something important to get something else they value.

That is because our consumer society values what is most challenging to get—what requires the most sacrifice. All commodities are evaluated in this way. In his classic work *The Philosophy of Money* (1907; English translation, 1978), sociologist Georg Simmel points out that objects—whether gumdrops or gold—have no inherent value. Instead, we assign value to them. And, as a society, we collectively agree on those values. A **market** is the mechanism through which we reach and display this agreement.

Economic life is all about the exchange of sacrifices. The commodity needing the greatest sacrifice is the one that is hardest to get and, therefore, the most highly valued. Whoever gets it is often the most widely admired for his or her sacrifice. What's more, that person is often copied or imitated. In short, people make sacrifices to gain possessions that others will view as admirable symbols of status. By showing off their possessions, people send a message about who they think they are and what groups they want to join. Our possessions also help people distinguish themselves from the kinds of people they don't want to be mistaken for: people unable or unwilling to make similar sacrifices.

Social researcher Thorstein Veblen was among the first to examine the idea of conspicuous consumption in his classic text, *The Theory of the Leisure Class* (1899). His book, though more than a century old, still helps us understand the connection between class, status, and consumption today. *The Theory of the Leisure Class* is about class divisions in late 19th-century America. It uses historical research and observation to analyze how the **leisure class**—what we might call the "one percent" today—promoted economic inequality during the early industrial period.

This leisure class had evolved gradually over time. But it wasn't until the early days of industrialism that the leisure class as Veblen defined it began to flourish. At that point, it began amassing massive personal and corporate wealth. People in the leisure class made money from land, investments, and by exploiting the lower classes. Titles of honour, prestige, and a dignified social image were reserved for them. They used conspicuous consumption to show where they stood on the socio-economic ladder. They bought goods for the sole purpose of flaunting their wealth, consuming in ways that no one in the working or even middle classes could afford to emulate.

Quickly, competition developed among members of the leisure class. Those at the top set the standard for consumption. They defined how much, and what kinds of, consumption one needed to remain a member of the class. These standards were revised upward, making it hard for families to maintain their place in the social order. Thus, there was a constant need to buy more, to relieve the fear of social downfall. Members earned higher repute through increasingly lavish feasts, acts of gift-giving, and luxurious entertainment. These visible acts determined one's place among neighbours and fellow class members. The more friends and enemies one had, the better. These were signs that someone had enough wealth and social clout to be envied and emulated.

Box 1-2

Conspicuous Consumption
by Rich and Ambitious People

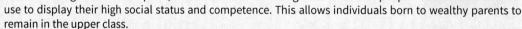

Besides wealth, the leisure class lay claim to possessing more taste and sophistication than anyone else. And they are able to teach their children how to develop elegant taste as well, thus passing along cultural capital. Cultural capital, which we discuss at length in later chapters, includes all the knowledge and skills that people use to display their high social status and competence. This allows individuals born to wealthy parents to remain in the upper class.

According to Canadian humorist (and economist) Stephen Leacock, seen here in a photograph from 1913, possessions displayed in tasteful moderation can be more useful in establishing one's identity and enhancing personal satisfaction. To be a successful consumer, one must exercise restraint. As a result, when newly rich people enter a market with their gaudy desires, they drive out the people with old money who prefer simple yet elegant goods. This then forces the old-money people to seek out new and more expensive goods that are unattainable to new-money individuals.

Conspicuous consumption is a defining feature of the leisure class. Two others are conspicuous leisure and conspicuous waste. Conspicuous leisure consists of idling in public, like the flâneurs of Benjamin's time or the Kardashians of ours. It is time spent visibly and pointedly not working, and it marked a critical distinction between the upper and lower classes. Industrial workers had to work long hours every day to survive; members of the leisure class did not have to work at all.

Conspicuous waste combines the needless spending of money (conspicuous consumption) and wasting of time (conspicuous leisure). Such waste was a way of showing membership in the leisure class. Consider, for example, the extravagant parties Jay ("The Great") Gatsby threw for hundreds of people in his mansion. A great deal has changed since Veblen wrote *The Theory of the Leisure Class*. However, his theories underpin our central argument in this book. Veblen may have been the first to note that conspicuous consumption sends messages about the elite's distance from groups to which they do not want to belong.

Disenchanting and Re-enchanting the World

Although the desire for status is an important reason why people buy consumer goods, it is not the only one. They also buy to enjoy **enchantment**, however momentary. By enchantment, we mean a temporary cessation of everyday rational and instrumental thought, and a feeling of transport beyond routine concerns and activities. Émile Durkheim meant something like this when he compared so-called "profane" everyday life with what he called the sacred feelings and activities associated with religious faith. But why this desperate need for enchantment through buying?

Max Weber in 1918.

Foundational sociologist Max Weber proposed that modern life, with its emphasis on reason, science, and the rule of law, has become **disenchanted**. For him, no social institution is more typical of modern life than the rational, bloodless bureaucracies in which so many consumers have to work. Perhaps because our world seems so disappointingly dull to so many, consumers have come to crave enchantment through shopping.

During COVID-19-induced lockdowns, some consumers' worlds became even duller than usual, resulting in even greater cravings for such enchantment. Many people worked from home, making it difficult to preserve a sense of work-life balance. Others were laid off, with little to keep them occupied. All felt stressed and overwhelmed, grappling with an uncertain future. As a result, some turned to consumption to quell boredom or enjoy a dose of "retail therapy." And some consumed substances that they thought would make them feel better. For example, alcohol sales increased across Canada as physical distancing kept people at home (Alexander 2020).

In order to sell products, businesses must find ways to enchant (or re-enchant) consumers. But what kinds of buying can enchant us, and how is this to be performed? George Ritzer says businesses have glamorized everyday life and created fantasies out of grim realities, bedazzling consumers with spectacle. People no longer go to church to see such displays; shopping malls, movie theaters, and marketplaces became the new "cathedrals of consumption." Familiar settings where consumers are used to buying things are re-developed and therefore "re-enchanted," making them livelier and more enticing (but for a different interpretation, see Musial 2019).

This means creating consumer spectacles, and to do this, Ritzer says businesses use two techniques: **simulation** and **implosion**. Through simulation, they breathe a sense of reality into things that don't exist, like Chicken McNuggets, sold by McDonald's. These are made-up creations, not "real" food. But by making them *seem* like food, McDonald's got consumers to buy them, and other fast-food franchises followed suit.

Implosion, on the other hand, meets consumer wants and needs by bringing multiple product providers together in one place. A gigantic shopping mall, for example, brings together a wide range of products and brands, allowing consumers to buy items and foods from around the world, all in one convenient location. We see implosion at its finest in Las Vegas, where tourists can visit miniature "cities" and other "natural wonders" just by walking down the Strip.

Time is Money is Time

At various points in this book, we will shift gears slightly and talk about time. That is, we will talk about how people spend their time, not their money. There are several reasons for this.

First, like the spending of money, the spending of time is a way that people signal to one another who they are and what groups they want to belong to. That's because different sections of the population spend time in different ways.

Second, most adults in western society sell their time for money: that is, for wages or salaries or fees. So, the notion that we can convert hours into dollars is a far from radical notion. Most of us are familiar with the expression "time is money," and we are taking that idea seriously here.

Third, people who do not have a lot of money tend to have much more time than they have money. That would include several of the demographic segments we discuss below—poor people, young people, seniors—as well as the unemployed and underemployed. How they consume their time tells us as much about their lifestyles as how they spend their money. This leads us to the development of a new concept: **time poverty**. We will discuss time poverty below in the chapters on low-income people, women, and low-income societies.

Fourth, people with money often use some of that money to buy the time of other people, whether as nannies, childcare providers, housekeepers, drycleaners, launderers, and so on. In this way, they gain more time which they use for leisure or to earn more money.

Finally, as we will discuss in the final chapter, we may be entering a **share economy** in which cash transactions play a smaller part and barter or exchange of services will play a greater role. For all these reasons, it seems appropriate to discuss the ways people consume time in our consumer society.

Final Thoughts

In this chapter, we have begun to discuss consumer behaviour and consumerism. People have been studying this topic since at least the beginning of the 20th century.

Is consumerism a problem in and of itself that we should be concerned about, or can we leverage it for good? In this chapter, we saw that consumerism may benefit us by helping people to improve their material comfort and standard of living. Consumerism is a pillar of our capitalist society that fuels the desire for material comfort and social acceptance above all else. On the other hand, for some social critics, consumerism is a social menace. It leads people to become content with the status quo, desperate to fit in instead of willing to speak up for their own rights or those of others. They are hungry for plenty because owning plenty fills a void and gives their lives meaning. They are hungry for novelty, because novelty distracts them from their emptiness.

Second, the rise of the Internet has made shopping easier by enabling online shopping. However, some suggest such ease and convenience cause problems, including shopping addiction, which we discuss in a later chapter. Online shopping makes it easier for people to spend recklessly and/or for emotional reasons. Finally, we noted that the social habits of competitive consumption magnify our natural desire to join groups and exclude others from those groups. In later chapters, we explore the ways people learn to do this. The agents of socialization, or teachers of desire, that we discuss in coming chapters often teach us to consume in ways that show we belong to distinct social groups.

Overall, in this chapter, we have argued that consumer behaviour is human communicative behaviour. It is a willing dance of desire between consumers and producers—also, a way that people send signals about themselves. Does this passion for buying in our society signal a deep loneliness—a deep need for attachment and meaning? Are more consumers in our society like Angelyn and Tamara, using consumer goods for practical and social purposes? Or like Anton and Donald, using consumer goods for remedial and psychotherapeutic reasons? By the end of this book, we will have come closer to answering these questions. In the next chapter, we discuss the culture of consumption that breeds these various types of spending.

Discussion Questions

1. Harvard researchers David Riesman, Nathan Glazer, and Reuel Denny identify three types of people whom they call tradition-directed, inner-directed, and other-directed. What do you identify as? What traits do you have that would make it seem otherwise? Do you think most people around you identify the same way as you?

2. Today, we have mass consumerism because of mass production. While this has improved our lives significantly, we have also run into issues surrounding increased materialism. Do you think this trade-off is worth it? Why or why not?

3. Conspicuous consumption is a form of materialism we use to signal our status via what we buy. Think of the last time you used consumerism as a way to signal status? Did it work?

Quick Quiz

1. For consumerism to be successful, which of the below is required?
a. Mass production
b. Mass consumption
c. Mass distribution
d. Mass communication
e. All of the above

2. Who published *The Wealth of Nations*, pointing out that consumption might not be such a vice after all?
a. Bernard de Mandeville
b. Adam Smith
c. Thorstein Veblen
d. Walter Benjamin
e. George Ritzer

3. What is conspicuous consumption?
a. Purchasing goods in a secretive manner
b. Purchasing expensive goods
c. Purchasing an unnecessary amount of goods
d. Purchasing goods for the sole purpose of flaunting wealth
e. Purchasing goods for their functionality

4. *The Theory of the Leisure Class* helps explain the connection between:
a. Class and production
b. Class and consumption
c. Class and wealth
d. Class inequality
e. Class and life expectancy

5. Bringing multiple product choices and providers together to meet consumer wants is known as:
a. Commodification
b. Consumerism
c. Implosion
d. Simulation
e. Determinism

The answers to the Quick Quiz are provided at the end of the book.

For Further Reading

Motivational Complexity of Green Consumers by Johanna Moisander
Moisander looks at the challenges that environmentally conscious consumers face in today's marketplace.

Work, Consumerism and the New Poor by Zygmunt Bauman
This book explores how "being poor" has shifted meaning from being unemployed to being a flawed consumer. This brings to light differences in how poverty is experienced.

"Marketing and Consumerism: A Response to O'Shaughnessy and O'Shaughnessy" by Andrew V. Abela
The paper looks at the connection between consumerism and personal wellbeing. It analyzes the correlation between the rise of consumerism and the rise of modern marketing.

Key Terms

Conflict theory
Frankfurt school
Functionalism
Macrosociology
Mass communication
Mass consumption
Mass distribution
Mass production
Microsociology
Objectivity
Social Structure
Sociological imagination
Sociological perspective
Symbolic interactionism

Chapter Two
The Culture of Desire

Learning Objectives

After reading this chapter, you will be able to:

- ✓ Analyze consumer behaviour as both a product and producer of culture.
- ✓ Draw connections between cultural values and patterns of saving and spending.
- ✓ Understand how and why today's debt culture evolved.
- ✓ Identify links between consumer culture and capitalist ideology.

In the last chapter, we saw that consumer behaviour is a dance of desire. Consumers—the buyers in this dance—want to be satisfied, excited, and enchanted with their purchases. Their partners in this dance—manufacturers, retailers, marketers, and advertisers—want to attract, seduce, and enchant potential buyers, to gain the greatest possible profit.

But how do buyers and sellers learn the steps to this dance of desire? And why do the dance steps change over time, in keeping with new reasoning on both sides of the dance floor? The answer lies with **socialization**: the process of learning to do these dance steps, and the focus of the next several chapters. And to understand socialization, we must understand **culture** and the "culture of desire" in which we live.

Defining Our Terms

To start, let's review some definitions of terms we will turn to again and again in this chapter and throughout this book.

First, **culture** is the collection of beliefs, values, norms, language, material objects, and behaviours shared by members of a particular community. Culture is also about the signs and signals people use to communicate with one another, and the values, norms, and beliefs that underlie these communications.

Cultures vary across geographic location. "Geographic location" can refer to a regional political division, such as country or province or state. Alternatively, it can refer to a regional cultural division, such as "small-town culture" or "inner-city culture." Cultures also change over time—from one century to the next, and even one decade or year to the next. Because culture is dynamic, we know it is socially constructed. People are not born knowing their culture; they need to learn it.

There are two main aspects of culture. **Material culture** includes all the physical objects we create and consume: the clothes we wear, the cars we drive, the restaurants we visit, and so on (Riello 2017; Lawrence 2017; Whitfield 2018). **Nonmaterial culture** includes all the aspects of culture that do not exist physically, such as values, beliefs, philosophies, conventions, and ideologies. Social researchers sometimes refer to non-material culture as **symbolic culture** because its main ingredients are symbols (Gao 2018; Withers 2017). Our values and beliefs about consumer products are part of our nonmaterial culture. They influence what we want to buy and how we use our purchases.

In sum, culture is a filter through which we see and understand the world (Inglehart 2018; Storey 2018; Pieterse 2019). For its part, a **consumer culture** is largely a material culture where people, often unconsciously, strive to gain consumer goods largely because they symbolize power and status. Consumption, in consumer cultures, is thus a key basis for status differentiation, personal identification, and perceived happiness (Samiee 2019; Sherry and Fischer 2017; Kilbourne et al. 2017). The consumer culture is made possible by the existence of our consumer society. This is a society in which consumer goods are widely available, thanks to the processes of mass production and distribution we discussed in the last chapter. So, the consumer society gives people what they want; it makes all those goods available for us to buy. And the consumer culture justifies our doing so.

Consumer culture is a large part of **popular culture**. Popular culture consists of the everyday practices, values, and desires of ordinary people, often as depicted in the media (Storey 2018; Ross 2016; De Groot 2016). In earlier centuries, popular culture was thought of as **working-class culture**, in contrast with the high culture of the elite. **High culture,** for its part, is typically influenced and promoted by the upper classes (Alexander 2018; Gans 2017; Berger 2018). It consists of activities they think sophisticated: reading works of literature they judge intellectually stimulating, for example, or viewing works of art they consider aesthetically valuable. We will have a lot to say about high culture in relation to what is called cultural capital in later chapters.

Today, we think of popular culture as the culture shared by large swaths of the population, regardless of their socioeconomic status. For example, a low income retail worker and middle income professional may both listen to the same country music. That said, there are multiple popular cultures to enjoy at a given time. These are rooted in subcultures—for example, black popular culture or teenage popular culture—that branch out from mass popular culture.

The study of popular culture typically involves the study of mass media. As we note in a later chapter, mass media include all the forms of communication that reach a wide audience. People in the media industry often say they simply give the public what they want. In this sense, mass media content mirrors the popular culture, and in so doing, helps to perpetuate it. This cultural perpetuation, like all consumer behaviour, is voluntary when people have agency. Consumers do indeed demand and consume mass media, even media that they themselves admit is mindless entertainment (for example, "guilty pleasures").

Just as the broader culture is a product of people's actions and wishes, so too are popular culture and the mass media. They all reflect important social forces as well as cultural traditions. First, popular culture reflects the power of the state. Since the 17th century, the state has shaped popular culture—for example, by creating and emphasizing the significance of certain holidays and celebrations. A second influence on popular culture is mass production and consumption. As noted earlier, consumer choice started to grow in the 18th century and that trend has continued ever since. Increasingly, consumers have choices in housing, home decoration, clothing, reading material, and more.

Third, today, we enjoy new forms of leisure: for example, "self-care." Marketers have commodified every form of pampering and relaxation, from facials to yoga to aromatherapy. As a direct result, increasing numbers of

Novel forms of leisure activities such as massage therapy represent the expansion of consumerism into whole new realms in contemporary Western society.

ordinary people have organized their leisure time to make room for these pampering products and services. Fourth, the growth of new urban centres has also come to shape and dominate popular culture. By the mid-20th century, Canada already contained large, built-up city districts with dense populations. In the biggest, most prosperous regions, new urban identities and cultures emerged, in which the masses took part. The entertainment district in each town gave all of us new forms of theatre, music, and spectacle.

Fifth, commercialization erupted everywhere and shaped popular culture. Today, we all continue to influence mass entertainment; we show our likes and dislikes by buying certain movies, books, magazines, and music and not others. Taken together, we represent a massive amount of buying power. **Commercialization** describes the **commodification** of goods, including cultural goods. In short, commodification means attaching a price tag to goods and services that were previously given freely or in casual exchange or were not exchanged at all. Commercialization means stressing the importance of profitability above all other concerns. Even news media become commercialized: indeed, most magazines, newspapers, and journals are forced to commercialize. To attract and keep a large paying audience, they often need to focus on sex, violence, and scandal, not more esoteric or spiritual items.

The Study of Consumer Cultures

In this chapter, we introduce another perspective from which researchers study consumer cultures: critical theory. **Critical theory** is an approach to social and cultural analysis that reflects the influence of philosophy and psychoanalysis. It typically focuses on social inequalities in wealth and power and criticizes the social order (How 2017; Poster 2019; Corradetti 2017).

Early critical theorists included Max Horkheimer, Theodor Adorno, Erich Fromm, and Herbert Marcuse. They were neo-Marxist social theorists and philosophers originally associated with the *Institut für Sozialforschung* (Institute for Social Research). This Institute, established at Frankfurt University in 1923, was driven into exile by the Nazis in 1933. It operated out of Columbia University in New York City after 1936 but returned to Frankfurt in 1950, where it continues to produce research today.

Critical theory's greatest contribution has been to promote socially critical interdisciplinary research on popular culture. Critical theorists recognize that no single discipline can adequately study the cultural complexity of the modern world. To address this problem, the Frankfurt School usefully combined philosophy, psychoanalysis, Marxist theory, sociology, and economics.

How can we systematically study a vast, abstract topic like consumer culture? One approach is by looking at the ways people spend their money. Statistics Canada (2017) reported that in 2016, Canadian households spent most of their income on three kinds of things: shelter (29.0 percent), transport (19.2 percent), and food (14.1 percent). In other words, Canadians spent nearly two-thirds of their household income on what we can call **necessities**.

Spending on transportation, and especially on private cars, has been an ongoing major expense of Canadian families. A century ago, few understood the cost to our environment that this

Box 2-1
Cars and Canada
An Environmental Issue

After the First World War, Canada experienced its second wave of urbanization. The automobile, meatpacking, farming, and small-scale consumer goods sectors developed. The result was that primary industries exploited the local coal, forests, metals, oil, and gas resources. Perhaps most of all, the automobile industry changed the type of resources that companies needed. Following Henry Ford, the car industry adopted a mass production, assembly-line structure. Companies built cars at an unprecedented pace.

Between 1918 and 1923, Canada was the world's second-largest vehicle producer. Lower costs made automobiles more affordable for ordinary people. More consumers bought cars as suburbs developed outside of city centres. The increased number of major streets and highways further simplified commuting. Life improved with this new form of personal transport. But under the weight of this new industry, carbon dioxide levels rose and the climate began to change.

The production of cars and roadways put a toll on the environment. New roadways led to the emptying of rural areas. As developers and companies built new homes and factories, industry encroached upon animal habitats and agricultural land. The rising number of cars also increased greenhouse gas emissions. Today, Canadian greenhouse gas emissions are enormously higher than in 1919. While there are many reasons for this, the impact of cars is among the most significant. New technology may help manage the problem, but new environmental standards will struggle to keep pace with population growth and increasing consumer demand for vehicles. We are still coming to grips with what these dangers mean for the Earth.

transportation convenience would bring. Now this consumer-related problem is a major concern.

Cars and transportation aside, spending patterns vary from one household to another. For example, compared to couples with children, one-person households tend to spend a higher proportion of their income on shelter, but a smaller proportion on transport. Consumption patterns also vary from one province to another, in part because of regional disparities in the cost of living in Canada. Canada is a large country, but 90 percent of its population lives within 160 kilometres of the U.S. border. Our major population centres are well-connected to transport infrastructure and this keeps down the cost of consumer goods. In contrast, many remote communities, including the entire territory of Nunavut, lack any connection to a year-round road system (CBC News, 2012). People and goods must be flown in. As a result, some consumer products may cost two or three times what they do in southern Canada (Battle and Torjman, 2013).

As with the costs of transportation, we also see regional disparities in the costs of housing. Canadians in Ontario and British Columbia spend proportionally more on shelter than Canadians elsewhere. This is because the costs of housing are higher in those provinces, especially in and around major cities like Toronto and Vancouver. In Newfoundland and Labrador, Canadians spend just 23.7 percent of their household income on housing, compared to 30.9 percent and 30.0 percent in Ontario and British Columbia respectively.

That said, people in the northern territories also face high housing costs. Nunavut's population is growing much faster than the rest of Canada (ISP, 2018) and the supply of housing cannot keep up. It is not profitable for private companies to build low-income housing in Nunavut, so half of the housing there is publicly owned (Battle and Torjman, 2013). Of the public housing that does exist, half is over 30 years old and much of it is in poor condition (Frizzell, 2018).

Inuit who live in Nunavut are especially vulnerable to these problems. A government report observed that many Inuit cannot access satisfactory public or private housing. They are forced to live in illegal plywood shacks or house their families in single rooms in overcrowded homes. Overcrowding also poses serious health risks to this population: as a result, Inuit are 300 times more likely than an average Canadian to develop tuberculosis (Minogue, 2017). The disproportionately high cost of shelter, in turn, contributes to the disproportionately high incidence of tuberculosis. In turn, poor health means that fewer can work and buy necessities for their families.

No matter where they live, people's income affects their spending. Canadian families in the bottom 20 percent of the income distribution spend the highest proportion—35.1 percent—of their income on shelter. By comparison, families in the top twenty percent spend the lowest proportion: 27.3 percent. The most impoverished Canadian families also spend proportionally more on food than other income groups. And they spend the smallest fraction of their income on transport compared with people in higher income groups.

Access to private transport is also a need, but one can survive without it, although in a limited way. A car alone—not including maintenance, insurance, parking fees, and fuel—is a big expense. Low-income households may save money by relying on public transit or bicycles. However, in expensive cities like Toronto and Vancouver, many low-income neighborhoods are in suburbs distant from downtown, with underdeveloped transit connections (Allen and Farber 2019). That makes it difficult for suburban residents to access job opportunities and social supports.

To sum up, most Canadians' expenses—about 62 percent—fall into the categories of shelter, transport, and food: the necessities of life. Missing from this account are other crucial resources. Education, out-of-pocket health care expenses, communication (e.g., telephone and Internet), clothing, and personal care items are also vital for most of us. Then there is spending on items that are vital for recuperation from work: namely, entertainment, travel, and other leisure. After spending on all of this, some households are still able to save money for future purchases: for example, to buy a house, send a child to college, or afford to retire. However, many cannot save for these things.

That said, Canadians consume both necessary and non-necessary items in different ways. Where transport is concerned, some Canadians drive themselves to work in new BMWs while other Canadians take public transit or carpool. In these and other respects, Canadian spending patterns vary by income, gender, age, and other critical social features we will discuss in this book.

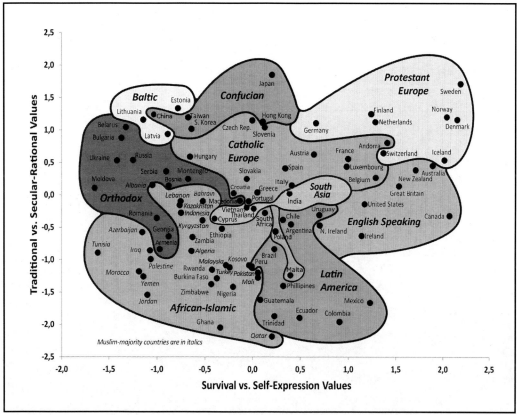

A pictorial representation of world cultural values, based on the World Values Survey. This figure illustrates the survey's 2017 findings. Note Canada's location, at the lower righthand side of the English-speaking domain.

The Influence of Values on Spending

All spending and saving reflects our cultural values. As discussed, people's values vary from culture to culture. Our North American cultural values include and are influenced by consumerism, individualism, and secularism, as is evident in the figure above, which compares Canadian values to those of other nations.

By **individualism**, we mean giving priority to personal autonomy and minimizing government involvement in the economy and personal life. Individualism also means a strong commitment to the notion of personal responsibility for success and failure. These beliefs have contributed to the widely held myth of the "self-made man." This individualistic outlook is even stronger in the U.S. than in Canada and is often contrasted with a collectivist outlook. **Collectivism**, as the name suggests, gives a higher priority to the collective good over individual liberty and choice (Triandis 2018; Nabi et al. 2019; Kyriacou 2016).

We saw just how strongly people hold these values in the spring of 2020. Americans took to the streets in over a dozen states to protest lockdown and stay-at-home orders aimed to reduce the spread of COVID-19 (BBC News 2020). They staged parades, blocked roads, honked their horns, and otherwise tried to draw attention to what they saw as excessive state intervention that was hurting people, businesses, and the economy, and infringing on their civil liberties. In Colorado, hundreds of these protesters came up against healthcare workers staging their own counter-protest by standing in intersections, wearing their scrubs, to block the parades.

Photographs of the meeting capture an iconic stare-down representing conflicting interests. On the one hand is our capitalist free market economy, represented by a woman brandishing a homemade sign reading "Land of the Free" from her pick-up truck. On the other hand are human lives, represented by a scrub-donning healthcare worker blocking her path.

Although protests against COVID-19 lockdowns attracted far more participants in American states like Colorado and Michigan, such protests occurred in Canada as well. Above, protestors gather at Queen's Park in Toronto on April 25, 2020.

By **secularism**, we mean a separation of everyday, earthly affairs from religion or the afterlife. Max Weber meant something like secularization—the growth of secularism in modern industrial societies—when he referred to the disenchantment of the modern world. The secular world is a world without supernatural interventions, though not without spiritualism or morality (Zuckerman and Shook 2017; Berg-Sorensen 2016; Taylor 2017).

When we say North American culture is "secular," we mean that it is more secular than other cultures, such as the "African-Islamic cultures" identified in the figure on page 29. Similarly, although our culture values individualism in general, no North American is self-reliant. Nor do all North Americans want to abolish social safety nets. Individualism and secularism are expressed in many ways, some less obvious than others. The values of consumerism, individualism, and secularism that we discuss in coming pages are themes in our culture, not unbreakable rules by which every North American leads their life. That said, our culture is permeated by these values.

Cultural Drenching

When Celia Lury, in her book *Consumer Culture*, says consumer products are "culturally drenched" in our society (2008: 53) she means that we have taken meaningless consumer objects and given them meaning. For example, a Tesla automobile doesn't just serve the practical purpose of transporting you from one place to another; it also sends a message about your identity and goals. It tells people you're up-to-date on the latest auto technology, that you are engaged with protecting the environment, and can afford this expensive, electricity-powered vehicle. In this way, consumer goods—here, a Tesla—help us compete for status and membership in communities.

Consumption also helps us live out the other values we just mentioned: individualism and secularism. Our individualistic culture means we assign people responsibility for their position in society, even if systemic factors limit their choices. Some see people who live in costly housing as having earned their reward and think poorly housed people should have made better choices. Our cultural attitudes survive because they affirm the notion that our capitalistic economy is just; and capitalism is supremely individualistic.

As for secularism, our laws leave us free to embrace any religion we like, or none whatever. Lacking a strong belief in the afterlife, many of us view happiness in material, not spiritual or ethical, terms. Many are eager to live "the good life" while they can. They crave immediate satisfaction and pleasure, and often use money to get it—for example, by buying a fancy pair of shoes or ordering a $6 latte.

Many or most people use consumer goods to communicate their identities. Consumer goods make it easy for us to communicate information about ourselves, as full-fledged members of our culture. We use consumer goods to express our gender, class, ethnic, age, and regional identities, and to identify ourselves as members of various subcultures. Doing so, however, leads many of us into debt.

Debt Culture

An acceptance of widespread debt is one sure result of our consumer culture. In effect, then, our consumer culture is also a **debt culture**. Thirty-nine percent of Canadians say they feel overwhelmed by debt (Media/Corps, July 17, 2017). Fully 26 percent of this debt is mortgage debt, followed by credit card borrowing (18 percent), car financing (17 percent), and line of credit balances (16 percent).

To put it in the simplest possible terms, people take on debt when they spend more than they earn. Every month, 50 percent of Canadians spend their full pay cheques or more (Media/Corps, July 17, 2017). Some of this is because of luxury buying, about which we will say much more in a later chapter. Even people who are poor often overspend on luxury goods, for reasons we will explore later. Some who overspend are unemployed or underemployed and, therefore, least able to deal with debt.

In the mid-20th century, when *The Lonely Crowd* was published, a new generation was just starting their families. This generation had come of age during the Depression and the Second World War—a 16-year period of deprivation (Williams 2004). They had sacrificed their personal comfort to bring their countries to victory. After the war, they (rightfully) expected a better standard of living. Governments fulfilled these expectations by giving them credit with which to build their new lives. The American Veterans' Authority (VA), for example, provided loans to veterans' families that allowed them to purchase new homes with a minimal down payment and a hefty mortgage (Hyman 2012: 97).

The new, wealthy postwar lifestyle was financed not only by public investment but also by private lending. In the new shopping malls and department stores that quickly sprang up, consumers made large and often unaffordable purchases on credit. They bought luxuries like television sets through small consumer loans they took out at individual stores. The credit manager of one American department store bragged that his biggest problem with customers was their "tendency to overbuy" (Hyman 2012: 106).

Later, banks entered this market, expanding the breadth of financial services they offered through credit cards and lines of credit (Williams 2004). Many houses built then were federally insured, and banks were happy to provide mortgages for them. In these early days, small businesses were flexible with their middle-class customers. They used delicate language when demanding payment, so as not to drive customers away (Hyman 2012:103). For their part, some consumers were earning enough money by this time that they could confidently buy expensive refrigerators, cars, and houses, sure they could be able to pay off their loans over time.

Of course, poverty still existed, but thanks to the rapid rise of a well-off middle class, many remember the postwar period as a time of great prosperity and optimism in North America. Much of the new wealth was made possible through the expanded access to credit we have mentioned. However, debtors now became "more completely and complexly [bound]" (Williams 2004:12) to the institutions that lent money to them. To pay off their debts, workers would have to commit to their boring, routinized jobs. Debt allowed people to buy more but it also shackled them to particular jobs and particular lives.

Children of these postwar borrowers, the Baby Boomers, were born into this high standard of indebted living. As a result, they came to expect comfort and pleasure from life. However, when they entered adolescence and adulthood in the 1970s, economic growth slowed. Companies sent manufacturing jobs overseas to countries where wages were lower, and the costs of things like housing and tuition all rose. It was then, during the period from the late 1960s to the early 1980s, that credit cards became widely available. Instead of encouraging careful borrowing, credit-card companies promoted and normalized debt in North American culture.

Consumers who paid off their credit card debt each month did not amass interest charges and were therefore not profitable (Williams 2004; Santos et al. 2019). For banks, therefore, the ideal credit card user was someone who could *not* afford to pay their bills each month. Most of them would eventually pay off their debts but, meanwhile, their unpaid balances would accrue interest charges. People understood that going into debt was a bad thing, so lenders had to improve the image of credit-card debt, to encourage people to borrow more. So, they expanded their offerings so people could even pay household bills and insurance with credit cards (Williams 2004: 35). In this way, people gradually began to live with, and even expect, large amounts of personal debt from month to month. Debt came to be seen as a cash-flow problem.

It is still too early to say how our views on debt might change in the aftermath of the CO-VID-19 pandemic (or if they will change at all). What we do know is that many people who were struggling to make ends meet before the pandemic found themselves under even greater financial pressure. We can assume, from the experience of past recessions, that many people will lose their jobs, their homes, and their savings.

The New Culture of Debt

Caught between cultural pressures to spend and economic limits, Baby Boomers spent the most and saved the least of any generation before them (Nye 2003, cited in Williams 2004). But they are far from the only people going into debt. Today, there are at least two reasons different types of consumers go into debt. First, some consumers simply earn too little money to pay their bills. As in the past, low-income earners continue to resort to "borrowing for groceries as well as cars," Lears (2006) explains. So, they accumulate debt by buying things they need but cannot currently afford, including food, shelter, and transport.

Second, people add to their debt by buying costly but unnecessary consumer goods and services. This luxury spending shows your other-directed neighbours that you've "made it," at least, in the eyes of onlookers who do not know how much you borrowed to finance the flashy purchase. Today, wealthy people are not the only ones buying designer shoes or vacations at five-star resorts. Since the mid-20th century, it has become normal for middle-class families to use credit to buy consumer products previously considered luxuries (Hyman 2012:116; also, George et al. 2018). This habit has continued, and ordinary people still buy luxury items, on credit if necessary, to show they're also "successful" and have "good taste."

In addition, the Baby Boom generation soon began to see the lifestyles of their parents as the norm for adults. So, they spent beyond their means to show they had "grown up" (Williams 2004). The marketing of financial services tapped into this desire for comfort and pleasure set by the postwar middle class. To this day, the North American middle-class lifestyle is "artificial," kept alive mainly through financing on credit. If middle-class people did not have easy access to credit, it would be clear that they have less buying power than the generations that came before them (Williams 2004: 53).

Luxury spending by middle-class people is even more marked in the U.S. than in Canada. There, spending on personal luxury goods rose 5 percent between 2014 and 2015 to about $73 billion (Nielsen 2015). Today, four in 10 Americans are "aspirational" luxury consumers: they value luxury products, but don't buy them often because they can't afford them. When they do buy them, it's a way of rewarding themselves for hard work. We see this pattern among Baby Boomers, many of whom feel they have too little time to themselves and need occasional pampering. They spend their money with the goal of making the most out of what little time they have.

Why does North American culture value debt-driven luxury spending? That is, why have we learned to reward ourselves with consumer products? To answer this question, let's step back about 50 years and look at a classic work on spending and buying. This book is by a scholar whose work you'll see mentioned repeatedly in the coming chapters, Jean Baudrillard.

According to sociologist Jean Baudrillard, every consumer good—every item we buy—is a sign that sends signals to others. For so-called "foodies," certain kinds of purchases signify the buyer's taste and discernment.

Baudrillard's Symbols and Signs

Two decades after the publication of *The Lonely Crowd*, French sociologist Jean Baudrillard wrote a classic book on consumer behaviour aptly titled *The Consumer Society* (1970). This is a book about the culture of consumer societies, which is why we discuss it here (for other, more recent reflections on this topic, see Baudrillard 2018; Habib 2018; Gane 2017).

In the simplest terms, Baudrillard proposes that whenever you buy a car, a sweater, or a snow shovel—whatever you buy—you are buying a **sign**. Every consumer good is a sign that sends signals or messages to other people. They help us belong to groups we want to join, mark our distance from other groups, and show off our position in the social hierarchy.

For Baudrillard, signs are objects, behaviours, or events that stand for something else. A stop sign is the classic example. It stands for a command to drivers to "stop your car behind the line and make sure no other drivers are coming before you start moving again." But the object itself—a painted piece of wood or metal with letters on it—has no inherent meaning. A red octagon *in itself* doesn't tell drivers to stop their cars; it's been given this meaning by people in our culture.

Signs give our world and our relationships meaning. They also help us share our thoughts and ideas—that is, to have social lives. Religion once provided this sense of shared meaning and social connection. But religion has, in general, lost its hold on mainstream Canadian secular culture. It no longer gives most people a sense of community and purpose.

Instead, advertisers today try to appeal to the senses: they try to excite us with emotionally charged words, images, sounds—and Baudrillard's signs. They try to make people feel they understand the world around them. People crave this understanding because they cannot be certain others share their view of reality. But for Baudrillard, all of these signs have come to shape—even create—our world. This media-constructed world is what Baudrillard calls our **hyperreality** (for recent treatments of the idea, see Cross et al. 2018; Canning 2019; Bang et al. 2019).

In our hyperreal world, signs overwhelm us. According to Baudrillard, things themselves take a back seat to signs. Signs, not things, confer reality and significance. The stop sign is no longer a post topped by a red octagon; it's a symbol of one of many traffic laws, and of the power of the state. Deviating from our shared understanding of this sign—that is, failing to stop in front of it—can send a range of messages. It may boost teenagers' rebellious personas in front of their friends or shore up privileged drivers' sense of being "above the law." In short, Baudrillard's hyperreality is a simulated reality. It is made up of signs, not real things.

Box 2-2

Signal Sending by Women and Men

In 2017, following several high-profile lawsuits in Canada and beyond, the province of British Columbia banned employers from obliging women to wear high heels—traditional symbols of femininity. Many of the female complainants who raised this issue worked active jobs such as waitressing, where wearing high heels threatened their health and safety. Everyone understood the gendered meaning of high-heeled shoes and women were protesting the safety and health consequences of being forced to wear them.

Despite the significance we assign them, the consumer items we use to distinguish men and women—clothes, makeup, hobbies, and so on—are culturally arbitrary. They have no inherent connection with the things they symbolize. There is no reason women should wear perfume (or high-heeled shoes) and men should not. Or take the arbitrary meanings of colours. In the early 20th century, pink was considered a "strong" colour. This made pink suitable for baby boys, while blue was thought a more "delicate" colour that suggested femininity. Now, the symbolism has been completely reversed, even though nothing about the colours themselves has changed (Maglaty, 2011).

Marketers use these arbitrary cultural symbols to sell us things we don't need. In doing so, they exploit the insecurities (for example, feeling "unmanly") that make us feel a need to express gender in our product choices. For instance, some brands develop two separate lines of razors and sell the pink ones to women at a markup. In one notorious case, a large company known for producing razors extended this strategy beyond personal-care products. It created a line of pink and purple pens with a "slender barrel to fit a woman's hand," marketing them under the brand name "For Her."

Hyperrealities and Spectacles

If you surround people with signs of things, rather than the things themselves, the result is a **spectacle**. Consider Las Vegas, a city built for legalized gambling in the middle of a Nevada desert. Along its famous "strip," you encounter many extravagant hotels, including the Venetian, where Italy's waterways have been re-created so visitors can take gondola rides both inside and out. In every possible sense, this is a spectacle—a visually striking display, something eye-catching, dramatic, unusual, notable, and entertaining. It is all of those things because it is absurd. Creating a Venetian lagoon in the middle of a dessert is something so outlandish, expensive, and hard to do that it must mean something. What it shows is a wish to flaunt wealth and surprise the observer.

Thus, by spectacle, we mean a cultural obsession with appearances and visual surprise. Of course, visual surprise and appearances don't always confer reality or signify something, therefore, aren't always signs. However, most humanly constructed spectacles are intended to both surprised and convey meaning. Several scholars other than Baudrillard have written on this subject. First, Marxist Erich Fromm proposed that commodification had led people to be less concerned with "being" and more concerned with "having." Second, French Marxist critic and activist Guy Debord took it one step further in *La Société du Spectacle* (1967). "Having," he said, has been replaced by "appearing" (for extensions of this thinking, see Mihailidis and Viotty 2017; Kellner 2019). In late-capitalist society, we are not driven to produce things or even own things. We are driven by concerns about how our things make us *appear*. Las Vegas wants to be a "wonder of the world" and Sheldon Adelson, creator of the Venetian, wants to appear to be a person of insight and creativity. The absurd thing itself—a vast canal in the middle of a desert—has no meaning beyond this.

AT CALGARY STAMPEDE 1919
Nº 1011

Box 2-3
The Calgary Stampede
Making a Spectacle of Canadian Consciousness

Today we live in a fantasy world of appearances, spectacles, and consumerist events. In Canada, one of the oldest of these is the annual Calgary Stampede. A particularly exciting Stampede in 1919 unfolded over several days and was attended by 57,000 people (CTV News 2019). Organizers referred to it as the "Victory Stampede" for the ways in which it celebrated Canada's success in the First World War and supported returning veterans. This Victory Stampede also introduced the Indian Village as a way of incorporating Indigenous peoples into the event.

Indian Village, which survives today, is now known as Elbow River Camp. In 1919, the federal government was still trying to extinguish Indigenous cultures and assimilate Indigenous peoples into Canadian culture. This was the era of the residential school system where children were forcibly removed from their families and banned from speaking their mother tongue or engaging in traditional practices. The Stampede's decision to include the Indigenous community in the event was an important one. The Stampede was to be a place where Indigenous people could (appear to) celebrate their own traditions. The organizers encouraged Indigenous peoples to wear traditional outfits and display their culture.

In 2019, one hundred years after that momentous Victory Stampede, the Stampede hit a record attendance for a single day (Smith, 2019). From 1919 when it plainly celebrated Indigenous culture, to 2019 when it broke attendance records, the Calgary Stampede remains an event that Canadians enjoy. They like the way it brings diverse people together.

For Debord, a concern about appearance is not mere vanity. We are condemned to image-consciousness in a society that has substituted secular spectacle for God. The spectacle we seek is the illusion that our fragmented, alienated life is whole; it's what we believe in when our religious beliefs have been devalued. For Debord, spectacle is the idea that appearance is enough in and of itself. The consumer market is no longer seen as a means to an end, but an end in its own right.

A third scholar to write on the topic is Mike Featherstone (1993; also 2017). Like Baudrillard, Featherstone suggests that pictures and signs have blurred reality, resulting in what he calls the **simulation world**—much like Baudrillard's hyperreality. In this simulation world, people are increasingly concerned with visual displays and public spectacles. Values formerly defined by ethics and truth are now replaced with values defined by aesthetics and appearances.

The postmodern view that there is no "truth" about reality fits naturally with the idea that everyday life is a simulation or hyperreality. Postmodernism holds that we can't know anything for certain. Our culture is a sea of signs and images that we, as people, can merely interpret. In a simulated hyperreality, there is no objective reality, just individual perspectives on the countless signs we encounter daily. Your personal feelings about, or reaction to, the Venice of Las Vegas are the ultimate measure of this spectacle's worth.

If Baudrillard were writing today, the Internet and social media would surely figure in his discussions of hyperreality. His hyperreality consisted largely of physical objects that signify some other meaning, creating a simulated world in which nothing is as it seems. When he wrote, Baudrillard had no way of knowing that, by the second decade of the 21st century, our culture would be dominated by an invisible World Wide Web. This invisible realm would have its own signs and meanings (for example, emojis or emoticons). It would be populated by fake news, self-proclaimed influencers, and unlimited possibilities for self-presentation.

So perhaps material objects are no longer as necessary for signal-sending as they were in Baudrillard's time. Consumers today can send signals through the digital hyperreality even faster and (perhaps) more effectively than they can by buying and displaying, say, a new car. Online environments—especially social media—allow them to craft personas for themselves, putting their bodies, homes, pets, families, work, and lives on display for the world to see. Consumers can Photoshop themselves to perfection, fabricate glamorous lifestyles, and communicate instantly about their latest (real or imaginary) purchases. Then, they can send all of these signs to thousands of people who would have never received them in the pre-digital world.

Never was this digital hyperreality more important for identity formation than during the coronavirus lockdowns, when most social interactions occurred online, while people physically distanced at home. Apartments and home décor were on display while you "met" with your co-workers on Zoom. And instead of "being seen" at a popular bar or nightclub, "outings" with your friends consisted of virtual drinks. Many people took to capturing this in a screenshot, to share with the rest of the virtual hyperreality by posting it to social media.

Finally, Baudrillard might have seen the Internet as a postmodernist playground. Social media, chat rooms, and online discussion boards allow anyone with WiFi to weigh in with their perspective. The channels themselves—Twitter, Facebook, Instagram, YouTube, and the like—are under pressure to protect vulnerable groups, while simultaneously upholding freedom of speech.

So far, the Internet is a world of representations and appearances largely without clear rules or sanctions. Yes, these platforms do specify terms and conditions; and whenever posted content do not adhere to these rules, the platform can take down pictures, demonetize videos, or even delete certain profiles. While these platforms grant many accounts the freedom to display a lot of things, there are certain limits to what's put out to see. Yet, government efforts to exercise control over hate speech and inflammatory disinformation on Facebook and elsewhere have been largely unheeded.

How Consumerism Structures the Social Hierarchy

Social interaction, in today's hyperreality, means using our shared system of signs to define ourselves and others. According to Baudrillard, we rate other people above or below us based on the objects they own and their sign value. Even socially advantaged people are prisoners of this system, obliged to follow its rules as much as people with less status and power.

To repeat, much of our spending goes toward necessities, such as food. Businesses recognize these needs and develop products to meet them. As well, marketers make us feel we "need" things that are certainly not necessities. For example, they may make us feel the "need" for a diamond bracelet. Beyond that, even through so-called necessities in life such as food and water, a lot of us still try to display our status by choosing certain brands over others. For example, consumers buy fresh, locally farmed organic produce (instead of canned alternatives) or drink Fiji water (rather than tap water). In these ways, marketers still make us feel the need to signal our status even when we're choosing our necessities.

Consider how these processes played out during the COVID-19 outbreak. Amid lockdowns and stay-at-home orders, online shopping became an important way for people to access genuine necessities. Grocery-store delivery services, for example, where you order your foodstuffs online and have them dropped at your front door, were overwhelmed and unable to take new orders for weeks at a time. As time went on, however, shopping habits evolved in interesting ways. First, retailers ranging from online shopping giants like Amazon to local businesses like Pusateri's in Toronto were accused of profiteering. They had drastically marked up prices for hand sanitizer, Lysol wipes, and other hygiene products that were suddenly in huge demand. Then, after the panic-buying of toilet paper subsided, consumers cleared warehouses of at-home workout equipment, games, puzzles, and other goods to entertain themselves while in lockdown. Roughly two months in, hair clippers and hair dye became the latest hot commodities. These goods are hardly necessary. In fact, we might have thought consumers would opt to do without them, given that they were not expecting to be venturing out into public for at least the next few weeks.

So, our consumer culture creates false problems, like the "need" to be thin, or the "need" to cover your roots. Then, it uses advertising to sell us false solutions, like juice cleanses and chemicals that change your hair colour. On a larger scale, advertising also reminds us of our need to feel fulfilled and happy. And it aims to convinces us we will feel those ways if we buy certain things. Thus, consumption is an emotional experience for many. In his book *The Romantic Ethic and the Spirit of Modern Consumerism* (2018), British sociologist Colin Campbell says this is an evolution of Romanticism. Romanticism is a worldview originating in the late 18th century that encourages individuality, imagination, and dissatisfaction with the modern world. According to Campbell, Romanticism leads people to think they can find creativity and beauty—and the resulting pleasure—in commodities. They seek enchantment and find it today in material possessions, by attaching emotional significance to consumer products.

Campbell says these Romantic emotions run so high that people can feel pleasure by just imagining consumption. Often, fantasizing about buying the car you've dreamed of can bring more pleasure than having and using it. So, the Romantic worldview supplies a set of this-worldly rewards that are as enchanting as a medieval vision of heaven.

A second scholar, sociologist Zygmunt Bauman, takes these ideas even further in his book *Consuming Life* (2007). For Bauman, consumption isn't just something we daydream and fantasize about; it's at the core of who we are (see also Jacobsen and Poder 2016; Rattansi 2017). Baumann draws on the work of philosopher Louis Althusser, who developed the idea of interpellation. **Interpellation**, according to Althusser, is one of the ways we form our identity. Think of it like a wave. When someone waves at you, they're saying they know who you are. And by waving back, you are, in some sense, accepting their identification of you. You're admitting you see them and confirming you are who they think you are.

For Baumann, interpellation is our culture waving at you. It's putting you in your place—telling you who you are—by "waving" you down in social interactions. According to Bauman, the consumer society tells us we need to admit we are consumers and, therefore, subject to the whims of change and fashion. Consuming is the main thing we expect to do, as members of this society.

Even though they are wrong to think this, people feel punished if they fail to make an effort or if they consume the "wrong" way. Our fellow citizens expect us to consume particular goods at a high level to establish and then preserve standing in our community. In some circles, buying the "wrong" garment or tickets for "tacky" forms of entertainment can knock members down a rung. If there are repeat offenses, such buying may even lead to exclusion from the group altogether. Consumption is thus the industrial production of social differences. It is a tiered system in which some buy plenty of expensive objects and others, few or none.

Featherstone (1993; 2017) points out that this system also demands repetition. The "paper chase" in capitalist societies continually forces people high up in the social hierarchy to buy new goods. If they don't, they lose their coveted position as fashion or taste leaders. In a desperate attempt to keep up appearances and maintain power, many high-status people buy constantly.

At first blush, these ideas may seem pessimistic (Davis 2011). For Baudrillard, advertising is like brainwashing that robs people of their agency: they buy goods just because someone has made and advertised them. Baumann has been accused of making humans seem like mindless robots, responding without agency to the waves and invitations of a fickle culture. In some contexts, for some consumers, that conclusion may be justified. But we aren't entirely passive victims. People are still responsible, at least in part, for what they choose to buy and not buy. People give themselves over to the endless cycle of consumption because they think it is "the good life," and there is nothing they want more. In that sense, we don't choose to live in a culture that values material prosperity over all else. However, few people question or try to change it, or imagine alternatives.

This seemingly mindless behaviour makes consumerism **ideological**: an unseen set of values and beliefs people use to make sense of their lives and worlds. When it comes to consumerism, one of those beliefs is that buying things leads to happiness. Because of this outlook, many people organize their lives to allow even more buying. They chase credentials and skills, so they can get high-paying jobs, so they can buy more things that cost more money, more often.

Of course, everyone needs to buy the basics we discussed earlier: food, shelter, and so on. There is nothing wrong with aiming for an education or well-paying career. Our point is that almost everything you do in life has been shaped subconsciously by the consumer society and its cultural values, whether you realize it or not. In this sense, the ideology of consumerism justifies capitalism. By giving people a sense of achievement, meaning, and happiness, consumption gives us the satisfaction we crave. And by supposedly satisfying us, consumerism removes the need for social conflict or social change.

Distinctly Canadian Values

The fact that people care—even obsess—about the signs of success says a lot about what we value. In Canada, buying forms a big part of our social and cultural life. We spend most of our waking hours working for money, and then we spend most of our money on consumer products. That it is not uncommon for people to go into debt to buy a fancy car, for example, reveals a lot about what our culture has taught us to consider important.

The world values map (see page 29) shows that, compared to other countries, Canada has a largely individualistic and secular culture. As discussed earlier, that means many Canadians put themselves first, before thinking about the good of the community. We are not as individualistic as some countries, however. For example, in Canada, one finds such collectivist features as universal healthcare and relatively high taxes, contrasting in the United States with individualist features like private healthcare and lower taxes. But neither are we as collectivist as some countries. A small fraction of Canadians lives in multi-million dollar mansions, while many—even middle-income earners—can no longer afford to buy homes at all.

Although Canadians subscribe to many different religions, few would willingly sacrifice their earthly comforts for the promise of a rewarding afterlife. Finally, many Canadians are more concerned with efficiency—with getting things done—than with examining the purpose of this efficiency. Our dedication to efficiency and this-worldly pleasure contributes to widespread materialism. We think about ourselves, often refuse to postpone immediate pleasure for future rewards, and rarely question the status quo as much as we might. So we buy consumer goods and gadgets that we've been told will solve our problems and make us feel great.

Beyond individualism, secularism, and materialism, what makes Canadians Canadian? Canadians have long struggled to answer that question. Many feel we lack a shared cultural identity. To a degree, the federal government has tried to create one with multiculturalism, if only to distinguish "us" Canadians from "them" Americans.

Some businesses have capitalized on our failure to voice a national culture. They have set out to define one for us, with their brand at the centre of it all, of course. No one has been more effective on this front than coffee-and-donut chain Tim Hortons. Today, plenty of people say Tim Hortons is one of Canada's defining features—part of our national identity. The chain managed to

make consuming everyday goods (coffee and donuts) a "Canadian" cultural habit (Cormack 2008). Similarly, sponsors of the 1976 Montreal, 1988 Calgary, and 2010 Vancouver Olympics all sought opportunities to link Canadian culture to consumption.

The Tim Hortons coffee-shop chain has become emblematic of Canadian culture, despite the fact its current parent company, Restaurant Brands International, is controlled by a Brazilian investment firm, 3G Capital.

In some cases, such efforts go awry. Think of Hudson's Bay Company mittens, scarves, and sweaters—consumer products many people consider classic icons of Canadian identity. These products take us back to a time when that identity was defined by European settlement, colonialism, and the start of a long and oppressive history with Indigenous peoples (Fresco 2015). In effect, and perhaps unconsciously, we have defined ourselves, as a nation, based on that still unresolved history.

This handful of examples suggests Canadians have always had trouble defining their national sense of self. For better or worse, consumption is so engrained in the culture that many use commercial products like Tim Hortons as patriotic symbols and adopt Drake as a Canadian icon. Today, at least some would say Canada has defined itself, as a nation, based on iconic striped blankets, cheap coffee, and a currently popular singer.

The Culture Industry

Admittedly, our culture pushes us to consume. However, culture is itself a victim of consumer society, in the eyes of some theorists.

Max Horkheimer and Theodor Adorno, whom we introduced earlier as critical theorists, put this idea forward in their foundational book *Dialectic of Enlightenment* (1944). They suggest capitalism, as an economy and a philosophy, commodifies and corrupts culture. The result is not a real culture, but, rather, what they call the **culture industry**. Mass production under capitalism, according to Horkheimer and Adorno, creates a mass culture characterized by uniformity, repetition, and homogeneity (Keltie 2017; Kellner 2017; Moore 2019).

Within this culture, even art becomes clichéd and formulaic. Good art makes you think about the world and your place in it, they say. It questions convention, critiques authority and power. But the culture industry makes art just another form of production. It puts art on the assembly line, making it standardized and easily copied to ease its mass distribution. It smooths away the rough edges and removes the challenges we associate with real art. On this, Horkheimer and Adorno would have agreed with Lury, who said (in *Consumer Culture*) that today we consume art just like any other consumer product. Even art has its own market, including its own supply, demand, inflation, and competition.

German philosopher and social critic Walter Benjamin, in *The Work of Art in the Age of Mechanical Reproduction* (1935), claims that reproduction robs artworks of their "aura." By this he meant their authenticity—their uniqueness in time and space. Certainly, reproduction robs artworks of their exclusivity (i.e., their exclusive ownership by a museum or art patron). As well, it robs photographed paintings and sculpture of a third dimension, and recorded music of the ambient noise of the concert hall. Benjamin may have meant more than this by the word "aura," as he was given to mystical thinking. In whatever sense he meant them to interpret the word, Benjamin influenced other cultural critics like Horkheimer and Adorno, who argue that creative art can inspire outrage and even social change, perhaps in part through its aura.

By contrast, mass-produced art reproduces and justifies the status quo. Consider movies: patently fake reproductions of real life. Commercial (e.g., Hollywood) films are intended to distract us from the hardships of life under capitalism. A dramatic, scary, funny, or romantic film tem-

Canadian musician Drake is an example of the "self-made man" archetype that is nearly ubiquitous in our culture.

porarily distracts you from your responsibilities and troubles. By distracting and entertaining us, movies help us cope with the drudgery of life in a capitalist society. They are the new opium of the masses, replacing religion for this purpose.

The same is true of other products of the culture industry. As Marx pointed out, under capitalism, workers need something to ease their sense of alienation and give their lives meaning. Without religion to provide this ease and contentment, instead they can buy a 40-inch flat screen television and watch reruns of game shows until they fall off to sleep. In this sense, cultural products reinforce our ability to carry out the labour we must do to pay our bills.

Advertisements for some mass-produced cultural products are more manipulative. They misinform us by deliberately creating mass mythologies, for example by disguising inequality and stressing the role of individual responsibility. Stories of "self-made men" have been staples in our culture almost forever, depicting people who "started from the bottom." They include the rags-to-riches character Jay in Fitzgerald's Jazz Age novel *The Great Gatsby* and aforementioned Canadian rapper, Drake.

Horkheimer and Adorno's ideas, compelling as they are, reveal a tension we grapple with throughout this book. On the one hand, we (the authors of this book) agree that consumer culture manipulates people. As we discuss in later chapters, consumers are influenced powerfully by the stories they read, the music they listen to, the movies they watch, and the people they follow on social media. Our cultural values of individualism and materialism are consistently on display, as with the "self-made man" narratives just mentioned. No wonder many people consider themselves failures if they are not rich or famous. No wonder they seek solace in materialism and overconsumption.

On the other hand, Horkheimer and Adorno display a tendency of some cultural critics to paint a toxic picture of capitalist consumerism and to characterize all consumers as puppets or robots. Many of us—not least, marketers, advertisers, and economists—would dispute this representation of our culture and its members. We think we have agency and some measure of free will. True, we should be concerned with the "brainwashing" potential of mindless entertainment. But should we feel guilty and manipulated every time we watch a movie?

We propose a more balanced view. While keeping in mind Horkheimer and Adorno's insights about the dangers of mass production and mass manipulation, we should also remember the benefits. In particular, the culture industry—thanks to commodification, standardization, and mass distribution—has opened a formerly exclusive world of art and music to the masses. It has given ordinary people, earning ordinary pay cheques, a chance to enjoy some of the beautiful and entertaining goods and services previously reserved for a wealthy elite.

Final Thoughts

In this chapter, we began unpacking answers to some of our key questions. First, we noted the dangers of consumerism, especially for people without much money. We discussed the seductive opportunities provided by loans, mortgages, and credit cards, all of which make it easy for people to consume, even to excess. In some contexts, for some consumers, these opportunities are necessary and useful. For example, few can afford to buy a house outright. Mortgages give them the means to make such an investment, and many consumers responsibly pay them off. Other consumers must borrow money to cover basic needs, such as groceries.

However, as we also discussed in this chapter, other consumers take great risks when presented with these opportunities, resulting in massive debt. For example, they buy flat-screen TVs on credit and when they cannot pay off their cards, they begin accruing interest charges they are even less able to pay off. So, consumer culture is seductive, and it can lead people into financial danger.

Why might people consume in such dangerous ways? We saw that these luxury purchases are often communication tools. They send out messages about our prosperity, "good taste," luxurious lifestyle, and other qualities we want to portray. The reason many people go into debt over these luxury items is precisely because they cannot afford them. The messages they are sending about prosperity and luxury are dishonest and artificial, like a great many Instagram selfies. So, for some consumers in some contexts, the increased opportunities for buying can lead to risky behaviour, including overspending.

Then, we tried to explain the heavy demand for consumer goods in our society. As we saw, the ways Canadians spend their incomes reveal a great deal about our cultural values. We spend on necessities including food, shelter, and transport, of course. But in our consumer culture, even the types of food, shelter, and transport you buy send messages: they are what Lury called "culturally drenched" purchases. Consumer goods are in high demand largely because they help us communicate who we are and who we would like to be. And it is our culture that has awarded such communicative power to otherwise mundane consumer goods.

Our culture also teaches us that consuming feels good. We learn, from a young age onward, that buying goods and services can fill a void, solve a given problem, or lift our spirits. From this perspective, we don't just see a heavy demand for consumer goods in our society. We see a heavy demand for relief, pleasure, and happiness. Again, as Marx might have said, consumerism is the opium of the modern masses.

This need to moderate our spirits through buying is, also, a response to the high degree of inequality in our society. People lower on the income ladder are made to feel like losers. Our unequal society has taught us that consumption signals your status in the social hierarchy. So, wealthy people engage in conspicuous, luxurious consumption and lower-income people go into debt trying to copy them. From this standpoint, social inequality and the desire to display success create a heavy demand for "communicative" consumer goods.

For better or worse, consumerism is part of our learned culture. Even the essence of our culture—what it means to be "Canadian"—has been reduced to consumer products such as donuts and scarves. Our culture is what Featherstone described as "aestheticized," saturated with signs and signals that we have been socialized to understand, despite their lack of an intrinsic meaning.

As consumers, we all help to uphold this Baudrillardian hyperreality: this spectacle, fantasy, or romance. We send one another signs and signals through consumption, and we invent new ways of sending signs and signals, such as emojis. Consumers help shape their culture, just as their culture shapes them. That means we also take part in perpetuating the inequality mentioned above. To some degree, we all play the game of consuming to signal status in our social hierarchy. And by playing this game, we perpetuate the envy, jealousy, indebtedness, and sense of deprivation that is so common in our society.

In this chapter, we have focused on culture broadly: namely, on our consumer capitalist culture. But within our consumer capitalist culture exist smaller subcultures. The cultural world of poor people is different from that of rich people. The cultural world of an urban Italian Canadian is, in many ways, different from the cultural world of the rural Inuit. The cultural world of a woman is different from that of a man, just as the cultural world of a teenage girl is different from that of her mother or grandmother.

All of us live in different subcultures, but all are under the umbrella of the capitalist consumer culture. This means that different groups of people consume in different ways, depending on how they were raised and what values they're striving to achieve through consumption. In later chapters, we will unpack the consumption habits of some of these different groups.

Discussion Questions

1. The concept of a "culture of desire" is about ways of thinking and behaving in a consumer society. Think about how the culture of desire impacts your everyday life. What are some societal values that influence how you choose what to buy?

2. According to Baudrillard, we rate people above or below us based on the objects they own and their sign value. Think of a time a consumer good another person had influenced what you thought about them.

3. Horkheimer and Adorno believe that capitalism corrupts culture. Consider the role of the market economy in your own life. Make a list of the pros and cons. Compare your list with another classmate. How do your lists vary? What might this comparison suggest about market capitalism?

Quick Quiz

1. What is popular culture?
a. A way of looking at the world only accessible to people in their twenties
b. All the cultural artifacts or media content produced for mass audiences
c. The spread of affluence and purchasing power within national populations
d. Luxurious items that are desired by everyone
e. Sophisticated objects and activities of the upper class

2. Horkheimer and Adorno argue what about capitalism?
a. It is the best thing that has happened to the world since the steam engine
b. It plays a valuable role in creating good consumer culture
c. It stimulates the economy
d. It leads to opportunities for everyone
e. It corrupts culture

3. What is cultural drenching?
a. To take objects that had no inherent meaning and give them one or many
b. Buying the most relevant cultural items to fit in
c. When one culture has significant influence over another
d. How a culture changes over time
e. The way social media influencers change spending habits

4. What did Baudrillard focus on?
a. The prevalence of religion
b. The ills of globalization
c. Symbols, hyperreality, and postmodernism
d. The Fordist economy
e. Marxism

5. What is true about post modernism?
a. It is identical to modernism
b. It was studied by Adorno and Horkheimer
c. Its primary concern is social inequality
d. It was adopted around the time of the industrial revolution
e. It denies or resists universal truths, ideas, activities, narratives, and definitions

The answers to the Quick Quiz are provided at the end of the book.

For Further Reading

Consumer Culture by Celia Lury
In this milestone book, Lury writes that consumption is more than a strictly economic act; it encompasses both cultural and social forces.

The Cultural Industries by David Hesmondhalgh
The Cultural Industries considers the role of cultural industries in creating meaning within society. It traces the commercialization and the rise of these industries through the centuries.

The Rules of Art by Pierre Bourdieu
Bourdieu explores the role of art and structural relations through art in its three states. In the process, he considers the history of literature and art.

Key Terms

Aestheticization
Commercialization
Commercialized popular culture
Consumer culture
Frankfurt school
Hyperreality
Mass consumption
Material culture
Popular culture
Postmodernism
Spectacle

Chapter Three
Learning the Culture of Desire

Learning Objectives

After reading this chapter, you will be able to:

✓ Show how people learn about consumer culture and their role within it.

✓ See how class background and parenting styles relate to consumer habits.

✓ Understand why some consumers learn to be more materialistic than others.

✓ Evaluate why consumers' saving and spending habits vary.

As noted, we are not born with an innate knowledge of culture. We learn it over time, from many people and many experiences. This learning process is called **socialization**. Socialization describes the way people internalize the norms, values, and ideologies of their culture.

For some theorists, socialization is all about social integration. Socialization teaches people how to fit into our consumer society. Like a sculptor, society (through socialization) molds people into whatever shape it needs them to take. In our case, socialization molds them into motivated consumers who will prop up our capitalist economy.

For other theorists, socialization is about power and control. It allows a more powerful social group to teach less powerful groups their "place" in society while convincing them that this place is inescapable. For example, through socialization, we learn to blame poor people for their misfortunes and to praise rich people for their successes. Socialization is so powerful that many poor people come to internalize these ideas. They feel ashamed and responsible for their own poverty. They feel more driven to compensatory spending to deal with this shame and sense of inadequacy.

Either way, socialization in a consumer society teaches people that capitalism and consumerism are right.

As we will see, socialization varies according to gender, class, and birthplace. People of "different kinds" are socialized differently, to prepare them for the different roles they will play in life and the different opportunities and rewards they can expect. Socialization continues throughout life, changing us as long as we live. As a result, people learn to consume differently as teenagers than as pre-teens, and differently as older adults compared to middle-aged people.

Throughout life, key people and institutions help in socialization. These agents of socialization include family, peers, schools, and mass media. We touch on each of these agents of socialization throughout this book.

Defining Our Terms

Let's begin once again by defining some key terms.

First, people need to learn how to use commodities as signs, signals, symbols, or social markers. A **social marker** is any characteristic or attribute (e.g., a way of speaking, a personal possession) that reflects or identifies a person's status in society. These are called "markers" because they signal (or "mark") a person's social standing in relation to other people (Pitts and Gallois 2019; Sebastian and Ryan 2018).

Learning to read and display social markers is a key part of learning self-presentation. **Self-presentation** means taking conscious control of the impression we create in social situations (Leary 2019; Schlosser 2020; Yang and Brown 2016). It is one type of **impression management**: the effort to control how you are perceived by others. The distinction between these two ideas is subtle: chiefly, impression management means controlling the information others have about you, so that you will not be humiliated or stigmatized. Self-presentation means projecting positive information about yourself, as well as hiding negative information (Bolino et al. 2016; Ward 2017; McFarland et al. 2019). A Canadian-born U.S. sociologist, Erving Goffman, popularized these ideas in his classic book *The Presentation of Self in Everyday Life* (1959), mentioned in chapter 1.

As people develop their self-presentation skills, they also develop their **personal identity**: their subjective sense of who they are (Noonan 2019; Starmans and Bloom 2018). Developing a personal identity starts early, as children come to recognize that they are different from their parents and other family members. This formation of a distinct identity grows out of social interaction and reflect the roles people get to play. The more varied the roles they play, the more complex their identity will be. As a result, a personal identity will often contain many parts: a gender identity, ethnic identity, sexual identity, and class identity, among many other elements.

While growing up, people also develop a **consumer identity**: a distinctive way of consuming that is influenced by their age, sex, social class, and other characteristics related to consumption. A person's consumer identity is the lens through which marketers view a person and predict his or her (consumer) behaviour (Black and Veloutsou 2017; Grewal et al. 2019; Hackley et al. 2019).

Related to the ideas of personal identity and consumer identity is the idea of self-concept. **Self-concept** refers to what people think they are and how they see themselves, as opposed to their actual personality characteristics (Rosenberg, 2017; Adam et al, 2018). It is shaped by past, present, and desired future experiences. People want to have a positive self-concept, and to have it affirmed by others. Consumer goods help to influence the way others see a person and, therefore, their reaction to that person. This reaction, in turn, influences their self-concept for better or worse. As people grow up, they learn how to use consumer goods to send messages about their personal identities and self-concept.

Development of Personal Identity

Social researchers think the process by which people develop personal identity is the same means by which they internalize (or learn) their culture. That is, children are not born with a sense of themselves, any more than they are born already speaking English. The early American sociologist Charles Cooley was the first to stress the importance of socialization in the development of a personal identity, putting forward the theory of the **looking-glass self**. According to Cooley, social environment molds identity. People form their self-images in response to the ways other people treat them. They see their own actions as either living up to, or disappointing, the expectations of their parents, friends, or teachers. More likely than not, they tailor their behaviour to gain the most approval from others who view them, since this raises their self-image.

In short, the ways we think and feel about ourselves reflect the ways others think and feel about us. We behave in ways designed to gain a favourable response from the people who matter most to us. Nowhere is our search for approval more obvious than in social media. There, everyone from your mom to a total stranger on the other side of the world can signal that they "like" you with the tap of a screen. We take selfies to invite likes and comments from strangers telling us we're attractive, fit, or well-dressed.

Like Cooley, foundational sociologist George Herbert Mead (1934) wondered how we learn to think like this. The answer, he proposed, is through **internalization**. Children internalize the rules, norms, and values that others model or impose on them. They become committed to these rules, so they feel guilt or shame when violating them. For this to happen, people need to learn

Charles Cooley and George Herbert Mead are among the scholars who have studied the formation of personal identity.

how to "take the role of the other": that is, to try to understand the other person's view. That way, we are most likely to do and say what we need to in order to get the responses that we want.

Mead viewed taking the role of the other as a vital first step in understanding other people and thinking about your own relationship to them. It is also an essential step in coming to see yourself as others see you. Usually, we do come to see ourselves as we think that others see us: as pretty or ugly, smart or dumb, and so on.

From this insight, Mead proposed the idea of the **generalized other**, a person's sense of how the larger social group expects them to act (for extensions of this, see Otnes 2017; Zavestoski and Weigert 2016; Timmermans 2018). According to Mead, we develop our identities with this generalized other in mind. We judge ourselves—our appearance, social value, and morality—as we think the generalized other would judge us. So, the generalized other is based on societal expectations and standards, and also on the individual's subjective sense of what they think they're expected to do.

Infused with this generalized other, we learn to use consumer goods to send messages about who we want people to think we are. In today's world of global markets, we have a world of choice in the way we craft our message (Marten, Southerton, and Scott 2004: 168; see also Martens and Scott 2017). That means you must know yourself, your community, and the variety of available goods that might best express yourself to your community. In learning all of this, you may seek help from advertising, the media, and influencers, all of which will guide you through that sea of choices.

As we become more confident of who we are and who we want to be, we become more skilled as shoppers. Self-perceptions and consumer choices often develop at the same time. Self-realization and identity-building happen gradually, through our consumption choices. We may think we will look fantastic in that yellow sweater, but other people's reactions may eventually convince us otherwise.

As children get older, they broaden and deepen their knowledge of shopping. They learn where and how to buy certain things, and how to compare the quality of similar products: how to judge which package of socks is the best deal, for instance. They learn shopping **scripts**, such as when to pay and what help to ask for from salespeople. They come to understand that prices reflect the imagined value of products, and develop defenses against deceptive advertising. They also learn to connect the symbolic meanings of products with their social role models (Chaplin and Lowry 2009; Chaplin et al. 2016). For example, they learn to associate a particular brand of sneakers with one or another basketball star. So, they view some sneakers as cool, classy, and worth a lot of money and other sneakers as not. In this way, children also learn a **consumption constellation**—a collection of products, brands, or activities that, taken together, achieve or present a social role (for example, "cool guy" or "player"). These are Baudrillardian signs that only have the desired effect when combined in a knowledgeable way.

As they develop their shopping skills, children also gain more influence over family purchases, with older children having more control than younger ones. We will say more about this in a later chapter. When they reach adulthood, they will have been socialized into much more skilled and motivated shoppers with product and brand loyalties that can persist through life. Of course, social class will influence what kinds and amounts of socialization a person receives, as we will see. Someone who comes from a poor family can't do a lot of shopping or can't see as many "role-model" shoppers, so their consumer identity would be weaker than that of kids who come from wealthier families. Kids with more experience and practice in shopping are likely to become more self-assured shoppers.

In short, our consumer identities don't reflect innate, "wired" shopping impulses. They are all learned in (somewhat) the same way you might learn baseball or video games. As shoppers, we act the ways we do because we have learned and internalized cultural values and consumer skills. Throughout childhood and adolescence, people continue to develop and refine their views about which products are cool and which are not.

But exactly how does all of this learning occur? The answer is largely through the process of imitation.

Imitative (Social) Learning versus Developmental Learning

According to the social learning theory developed by psychologist Albert Bandura (1977; also, Bandura 2019), we learn through **conditioning**, which involves both reward and punishment. We learn to copy others who receive the rewards we want and our society values.

But socialization is more than a game of Monkey See Monkey Do. We interpret what we see before we mimic it. And our agents of socialization help us with that interpretation. If we value their opinions, we take their views and advice seriously. If they tell us to ignore or avoid a behaviour we have seen, we are less likely to copy it. On the other hand, if they approve and praise what we have seen, we are more likely to copy it. Observations and interpretations shape our views, then are translated into words and actions.

But observation and imitation are not the whole story. Bandura noted that if people simply copied what they saw, they wouldn't know what to do when they faced a situation they hadn't seen before. Instead, socialization teaches us to learn from our observations: to generalize from what we have learned and apply these general rules to new situations.

When we are young, we make a lot of mistakes when trying to do this, but over time we improve. In part, that's because we have seen the results of making mistakes and have become more cautious. Also, as we get older, our judgment improves. This improvement is a normal part of aging, unless we have been deprived of social interactions and nurturing relationships.

So, we become better observers and interpreters as we age and develop. That's why a second approach to socialization highlights the importance of passing through developmental stages. In 20th-century scholarship, various **developmental theories** were discussed, studied, and revised (Weiss 2017; Capuzzi et al. 2016; Kail and Cavanaugh 2018). These included famous formulations by Sigmund Freud, Erik Erikson, Jean Piaget, and Abraham Maslow, to name just a few. They differ in important ways, but they also have key similarities. Before continuing, let's consider three common aspects of these developmental theories.

First, all of these theories connect social and psychological (and even moral) development to biological aging. They recognize that certain psychological developments commonly occur around certain ages. Increasingly, with the development of brain science, we have come to understand the physiological bases of these developments, and how they connect to biological aging.

Second, these are all sequential theories. They see certain kinds of developments as occurring before other types of developments are possible. No one learns to run before they walk. No one learns to buy things before they understand the purposes and meanings of the things they buy. In studying development, we need to understand the stages and their connection.

Third, these are all stage theories. They view developments as depending on carrying out or resolving earlier developments. You simply cannot advance to developmental "stage n+1" until you have performed the developmental tasks of "stage n." Though developmental theories differ in the stages they identify, they all assume that people pass through them in a (roughly) age-graded sequence, and that these stages are more or less universal.

Primary socialization refers to the learning that takes place in the earliest years of a person's life, between birth and ages 4 or 5. It happens within our family homes, mostly thanks to the efforts of our parents (Frønes 2016; Shklyar 2016; Garcia-Alexander et al. 2017). From them (as well as from our siblings), we learn deep-rooted cultural values, identities, and consumer behaviours. This primary socialization has a massive impact on the things we grow up to value, as well as whether we grow up to be "materialistic," which we discuss in greater depth below.

The socialization that occurs after earliest childhood is called **secondary socialization**. It's the way we learn about the specific roles, norms, attitudes, skills, and beliefs that help us through various social situations. Different social roles—for example, as friend, pupil, teammate, girlfriend, and so on—need different kinds of knowledge and skills, and we get them through secondary socialization. In other words, secondary socialization teaches us how to behave outside the family—in school, say, and later, on the job. It shows us how to "dress for success," how to talk to clients, customers, or patients, and how to present ourselves professionally to the outside world.

Secondary socialization is a critical part of our development, as it helps us interact successfully with others as adults. However, some might say secondary socialization has a less significant effect than primary socialization, especially when it comes to shaping our self-image or sense of competence.

Primary socialization also teaches us many things that shape our consumer behaviour. One is **future orientation**, or a tendency to consider how our present behaviour can shape our future. In a sense, future orientation is a skill that we develop throughout life by observing the lives of family members, peers, and colleagues. This trait helps us become better shoppers because it inculcates notions of planning, saving, and information use that are all important for consumer success. Most generally, a person with strong future orientation would agree strongly with the following statements:

> *I think about how things can change in the future and try to influence those things in my every-day life.*
>
> *I often work on things that will only pay off in a couple of years.*
>
> *I am ready to sacrifice my well-being in the present to achieve certain results in the future.*

That same person would disagree strongly with these statements:

> *I am only concerned about the present because I trust that things will work themselves out in the future.*
>
> *With everything I do, I am only concerned about the immediate consequences (in the next couple of days or weeks)* (Webley and Nyhus 2006: 147).

One study (Webley and Nyhus 2006; see also Agnew et al. 2018) showed that we can predict an adult's future orientation by studying how they were socialized as children. For example, the adults who are most future-oriented are likely to have grown up with parents who earned money, had a bank account, were thriftier than average, and discussed financial decisions with their children.

Our primary caregivers, usually our parents, provide most of our early socialization. Parents also play a key role in mediating the impact of mass and social media. For example, they may limit their children's screen time, censor the media content they allow children to view, and teach them about media literacy. They may also choose—or not choose—to buy their children smartphones, tablets, laptops and other devices. Increasing numbers of children and teens today are digital natives, having never known a world without the Internet and social media. Often, they are the ones teaching their parents how to use these technologies. When parents don't know how to filter, censor, or oversee their children's access to media, it becomes hard for them to control their primary socialization.

In some ways, these new technological agents of socialization are helpful. For example, they expose young people to a much wider range of thoughts, opinions, beliefs, and groups of people than they would otherwise meet. This exposure may help them develop more open, accepting views of the world around them. But in other ways, there are risks. To use a common example, children can now easily and instantly access an unlimited amount of free Internet pornography. Repeatedly viewing this graphic content may socialize children to think that violent, degrading forms of sex are normal and desirable. Other results of this digital socialization may include poor mental health, including anxiety, depression, and feelings of loneliness, reduced self-esteem, and

Studies have shown both benefits and risks associated with young children's exposure to social media.

even increased thoughts of suicide. Some studies suggest these results are caused by—not just correlated with—use of social media.

In sum, primary socialization, whatever its source, has the most significant impact on the values, norms, and beliefs we'll hold for the rest of our lives. So, parents need to do a good job parenting, and we know a lot about the different effects of parenting styles.

Evidence that has gradually piled up since ground-breaking research by Baumrind (1966, 1967; Gittins and Hun 2019) shows the best parenting is **authoritative**: loving and firm, with equal parts affection and close supervision. Parents who adopt this style of parenting raise children who have better-than-average health, self-esteem, and academic performance. These children are also less likely to get into trouble with the law.

Other parents neglect, threaten, or bully their children. Still others spoil them and let them live without any rules at all. These other approaches often have harmful results. Children subjected to these kinds of parenting are found to do more poorly in school; they have poorer mental and physical health and have fewer friends.

Parenting styles also influence whether a child will grow up to be **materialistic**. Materialistic people view money, material possessions, and comfort as the best possible outcomes of life. They put these results first even if it means sacrificing social and ethical goals. They are a lot like the "other-directed" people whom Riesman described and criticized.

The Cause of Materialistic Values

In the very first chapter, we noted materialism is a "thorny" topic in discussions of consumer behaviour. That's because the term has a long history. Today, as mentioned, it often carries negative connotations; "materialistic" people are thought to be superficial, with misguided priorities. That wasn't always the case, however.

For our purposes, "materialism" first arises in scholarly discussions in the 19th century, when Karl Marx declared himself to be a scientific and dialectical materialist. In doing so, he pitted himself against the then-dominant German school of idealist philosophy. The idealist school held that ideas control and shape the world. In opposition, Marx proposed that ideas themselves have social and economic roots; in fact, ideas are mere superstructure—flotsam floating on the ocean of economic necessity and class relations. People, in his eyes, develop ideas that help them make sense of, justify, and, in some cases, control the economic world in which they live. Thus, the ideas of any historical period, far from controlling the world, are pale reflections of power relations in that period. At most, they are the tools that dominant classes—the capitalist owners of the means of production—use to justify and perpetuate their control.

Within this materialist approach, all ideas—including ethical, moral, legal, political, and even spiritual ideas—are of secondary social importance. In fact, from this perspective, religious or even spiritual ideas are ideological: used by the ruling class to secure domination over the rest of society. As Marx said, they are opiates (or pain-killers) for the alienated masses. Only by stripping them away, and confronting our material realities, can we begin to achieve something resembling social justice. For materialist social critics like Adorno and Horkheimer, C. Wright Mills, and David Riesman, this end goal of social justice required a just distribution of material resources, not the abstract ideas of piety and purity, right and wrong, touted by idealists. People should be aware of their class interests and fight for class justice, according to materialists.

When we use the term "materialistic" in this book, we mean people who are not idealistic or spiritual, but neither are they class conscious. They have no political insight or desire for social justice—in fact, they do not have any goals beyond gaining comfort and social belonging. This kind of materialism—and related materialistic values, such as an admiration for success and wealth—have probably always existed in all societies. For example, the conspicuously consuming leisure class that Veblen described no doubt included a fair share of people with such characteristics. Mass prosperity and the rise of mass consumerism in the 20th century allowed this mindset to spread and permeate deeper into society. Everyone was encouraged to think this way, while paying lip service to God and freedom. Liberal political theories of the market and the State assumed such materialistic desires were "natural" and saw no reason to limit them.

That said, some people are more selfishly materialistic than others. Many theories have been put forward to explain how some people become so materialistic, in the sense we have defined. One is **social learning theory**, associated with the work of psychologist Albert Bandura (for an updated version, see Akers and Jennings 2016). In this model, agents of socialization (parents, peers, celebrities, and social media influencers) encourage children and teenagers to hold materialistic values. They do so by modeling materialistic goals, attitudes, and motives for children to copy. That being said, many people who see their parents model materialism do not become materialistic (or, at least, *as* materialistic) themselves. Conversely, many people who do *not* witness materialistic modeling *do* become materialistic.

That is why other social researchers have put forward a competing **compensation theory**. This theory proposes that people become materialistic when they have low self-worth, the result of a damaged self-image (Norberg et al. 2020; Koles et al. 2018). Such people spend money and buy possessions to compensate for these feelings. This theory arises out of psychodynamic psychology, associated with Sigmund Freud and such disciples as Alfred Adler, who developed the idea of the "inferiority complex." People with feelings of inferiority or inadequacy are desperate for social approval. Often, they develop "compensatory" or remedial lifestyles to make themselves briefly feel better. (Others use drugs, alcohol, or sex for the same reason.)

Parents and peers are the people who most shape our confidence and sense of self-worth when we are young. Unsupportive, harsh, and severely critical parents and peers can undermine our self-esteem from childhood onward. The impact of unsupportive parents and peers becomes especially obvious in adolescence, when young people become aware of and concerned about the opinions of others. Increasingly, they come to base their views of themselves on how they think other people see them. If your parents and friends tell you that you're a loser—unattractive, unpopular, and unintelligent—you'll likely come to see yourself in these ways.

Both social learning theory and compensation theory aim to explain why some people become materialistic. Both theories are supported by evidence, and both plausibly explain materialism. However, each makes a different prediction. If social learning theory is valid, teens with materialistic parents and peers will be more materialistic than other teens, regardless of their self-image or the support they receive from parents. If compensation theory is valid, teens with unsupportive parents will be more materialistic than other teens, regardless of the materialism of their parents and peers. Each argument is believable, so what do the data say?

To find out, Chaplin and John (2010) collected data from 50 boys and 50 girls aged 12 to 18. They asked these youth if they agreed or disagreed with various statements, including:

"I feel good about myself" and "I am happy with the way I look." Answers to these (and other) questions measured participants' self-esteem.

"My mom makes me feel special" and "My mom puts time and energy into helping me." Answers to these questions measured parental support.

"My friends like me for who I am" and "My friends get mad at me." Answers to the questions measured participants' peer support.

"My mom would love to buy things that cost a lot of money" and "My mom thinks the more money you have, the happier you are." Answers to these questions measured how materialistic participants' parents were.

"I would love to buy things that cost lots of money" and "I think when you grow up, the more money you have, the happier you'll be." Answers to these (and other) questions measured the adolescents' materialism.

Chaplin and John's results supported compensation theory, not social learning theory (see also Chaplin, Shrum, and Lowrey, 2019). In this study, the adolescents with the most materialistic views had the lowest self-esteem and reported the least support from parents and peers.

Self-esteem played a far larger part in predicting materialistic views than did parental values. So, according to this study, low self-esteem promotes materialism, and materialism is an effort to compensate for low self-esteem.

To generalize from this study, adolescents with low self-esteem buy things to feel better about themselves. Perhaps adolescents with low self-esteem also post about their purchases on their social media profiles. Doing so may be one way that adolescents with low self-esteem seek approval from a large audience. That is, if they show off their latest purchase online, perhaps they will receive affirming likes, comments, and followers.

Of course, this is just the result of one study and more work is needed to prove the general applicability of this principle to people of all ages and social backgrounds. That said, the results of this study suggest that negative socialization—poor parenting—can have negative social effects. In this case, the effects are compensatory buying, sometimes to excess, as we see among people with a so-called shopping addiction.

We will discover in the course of this book that materialism is treated in at least three different ways in the consumer literature. One body of literature, of which Chaplin and John's work is a part, argues that materialism is a reaction to low self-esteem. This psychological problem is often found among adolescents and it results in large part from competition and social comparison. Often, it disappears naturally with maturation, though parents and peers can make the problem better or worse. Donald, our trophy seeker in chapter 1 of this book, is someone who has never shaken loose this adolescent need for approval through buying. Recent examples of work in this vein are found in Gentina et al. 2018; Jaspers 2018; Kim et al. 2017; Lenka and Vandana 2015; Martin et al. 2019; Richins 2017; and Wang et al. 2015).

A second, sizeable body of research shows that materialism as we have defined it is correlated with psychiatric symptoms of depression and neurosis. Materialistic people like Anton in chapter 1 of this book are often addicted to shopping or hoarding and cannot control their need for material acquisition. Their materialism problem is to be solved, if solved at all, through psychotherapy. Recent examples of work in this vein are found in Gornik-Durose and Boron 2017; Muniz-Velasquez et al. 2017; and Ruvio et al. 2013).

Finally, a third body of literature, of which David Riesman's work is a part, sees materialism as a social and cultural, not psychiatric or developmental, problem. Materialism here is the result of a society gone wrong: a society that has placed all its faith in personal ownership, material prosperity, and technological progress. It is also a society where people are desperate to fit in, like Tamara in chapter 1, and not to stand out. It is a society marked by economic competition, not cooperation, even though the economic competition rewards only a few and disappoints the majority. This problem is not to be solved by psychotherapy or social maturation; it may require a more fundamental revision of society. Recent examples of work in this vein are found in Rabie 2018; Rai et al. 2018; Song et al. 2020; and Zhong et al. 2016).

Thus, for example, in a survey of 2702 participants, Zhong et al. (2016) found that living in a wealthy neighborhood increases material desires while decreasing happiness. Their results showed that, after controlling for age, gender, and population size, a higher neighborhood socio-economic status (SES) increased a person's desire for material consumption and produced more impulsive buying and less saving. Interestingly, individual SES predicted the reverse pattern. In other words, status envy (induced by the social environment) led people to act in materialistic ways.

We will have more to say about all of these themes in later chapters. Note, before we continue, that all of these findings are consistent. For example, the Chaplin and John finding fits well with Riesman's theory of other-direction and Zhong et al.'s theory of status envy. Socially insecure people seek personal confirmation by appealing for the approval of others—in this case, through the purchase and display of material goods. Yet consuming proves to be a false cure: it does not permanently relieve feelings of low self-esteem. Researchers Sweeting, Hunt, and Bhaskar (2012: 802) looked at reports of materialistic values in almost 3,000 secondary-school students. They found that materialistic values deeply influenced all of these teens. However, the researchers found no evidence that "modern consumer goods promoted happiness." In other words, buying things didn't make people feel better for long. This "lonely crowd," with all its possessions, still felt lonely.

This finding agrees with much research on contentment, happiness, and life satisfaction. As Myers (2000) reports, income (and the things money can buy) has a limited influence on happiness once people have the basic necessities of life (see also McMahan et al. 2016). Among people who live above the bare subsistence level, extra money (and the things it can buy) contributes relatively little, if anything, to happiness. Among middle- and higher-income people, money is unimportant when compared with good family relations, a satisfying job, and a purposeful life (provided to some people by religious faith; Sander 2017).

Far more reliably important for happiness are people's social relations and their sense of purpose. Diener (1985: 263), in an early, well-known comparison of average-earning and wealthy people, found that "the wealthy group more often mentioned self-esteem and self-actualization and less often mentioned physiological and security needs." (See also Biswas-Diener and Wiese 2018.)

Overall, the findings on happiness show that material possessions are unimportant in the face of low self-esteem. Self-esteem is rooted, mainly, in childhood experience and primary socialization. Therefore, we need to look carefully at parenting and the ways it prepares children for adult life in a consumer-oriented society.

Preparing Children for their Place in Society

In 2003, American sociologist Annette Lareau published a now-classic analysis of the effects of social class on parenting styles. Through participant observation of children ages 9 to 11, Lareau identified two central parenting "philosophies," which varied mainly by social class: concerted cultivation and natural growth.

Middle-class parents tended to engage in what she called "concerted cultivation." This involved efforts to hone their children's talents and skills through a series of organized activities: music lessons, ballet, and language training. These parents were also very involved in overseeing their children's experiences in structured institutions, such as schools. They taught their children to be assertive and to use opportunities to their personal advantage.

By instilling a sense of confidence, persistence, and right from a young age, these parents prepared their children to climb the ladder of success. These "cultivated" children often succeeded in school because their parents (plus private tutors, coaches, and others) had taught them time management, organization, discipline, and multitasking.

By contrast, poor and working-class parents adopt what Lareau called the "natural-growth style" of parenting. They avoided scheduling their children's lives the way middle-class parents did. Instead, they let their children follow their interests in their own ways. These parents also reacted passively to authority. For instance, they did not examine or challenge teachers as the middle-class parents did. By what they did and didn't do, lower-income parents implicitly taught their children to go along with what the authority figures said.

Lareau suggested that both of these parenting approaches have benefits; both provide children with tools to use in adulthood, but they provide different tools. The working-

Middle-class parents hone their children's talents by enrolling them in organized activities like ballet classes, swimming lessons and so on.

class style of parenting often produces better-behaved and more creative children. The middle-class style produces children who are ready to compete aggressively in institutional settings, like schools and bureaucratic workplaces.

Ten years later, Lareau revisited all the families she had studied earlier (Lareau, 2017). The children were now between 19 and 21 years old. Interviewing them, their parents, and their siblings a second time, she found that differences between the middle-class children and lower-income children had widened with age. The middle-class children continued to benefit in distinctive ways from parental involvement. Their parents had continued to intervene in their lives, even after they had moved away from home. Many parents even intervened in their children's college careers.

The most significant difference was in the maturity of the two groups. Lareau found the lower-income children had matured more rapidly. While the middle-class children still seemed young, full of large dreams and big hopes, the lower-income children had grown up. By their early twenties, many had been working for years and some even had children of their own. In these lower-income families, parents had quickly come to see their grown children as "grown-ups," a view the young adults themselves shared.

Of the two groups, the ambitious, middle-class young adults were more educationally and occupationally successful. Many were on the verge of obtaining professional jobs. By contrast, the poor and working-class children had obtained only working-class jobs. In part—though only in part—these differences could be credited to the parenting styles Lareau identified. Neither group of parents had shown more love, care, or nurturing than the other. However, the middle-class parents had given their children a class advantage. From the start, they had taught their children how to get ahead in a competitive, capitalist society. They taught an approach to life that helps to perpetuate the class structure and increases one's chance of success in it (see also Lareau and Jo 2017).

Thus, good middle-class parenting can produce children with skills useful in climbing the social hierarchy, earning a high income, and taking part easily in the consumer society. Children raised in this way are likely to enjoy both a high income and a strong desire to consume—as celebratory, rather than compensatory, behaviour. For these children, consumerism is mainly a form of social communication. The happiness that comes from it is likely a result of better integration into a desired community, a more fulfilled sense of purpose, and a more secure and comfortable family.

Box 3-1
Etiquette and Netiquette

Attentive parents are also concerned with teaching their children something about good manners: rules of proper behaviour, of which etiquette is an important part. By **etiquette**, we mean rules of behaviour that are widely considered polite, proper, and genteel. The early American sociologist Bertram Doyle (1937; see also Herzfeld 2018) correctly asserted that etiquette was a sign of high social status. When people of all social classes strive to uphold such decorum, it shows they all agree on the meaning of these signs. It also shows our culture deeply values the high social status that proper etiquette represents.

Today, the rules of etiquette and good behaviour are far less obvious than they once were. The Internet has opened a new world of social possibilities and, in turn, a new world of "netiquette" (Holmes 2011; also, Bodinger-deUriarte 2019). In Doyle's 20th-century world, etiquette meant knowing your place in the social hierarchy. It taught you to humble yourself to people at the top. But today, social networking sites like Facebook, LinkedIn, Instagram, and Twitter let people connect in more egalitarian, lateral relations. Though there are still social rules to be learned and followed online, you can invite almost anyone to be your "friend" or to "connect" (depending on their privacy settings). Nothing, including netiquette, prevents you from tweeting or following Meghan Markle (now more properly known as Meghan, Duchess of Sussex) or the Dalai Lama.

That said, you wouldn't consider all the people you contact your friends—you might not even consider many of them your equals. People today must decide whether to connect with people of much higher or lower social status, knowing others will be able to view their list of friends, followers, or connections. That said, a huge social media following can boost your social status. Perhaps it can even earn you money and complimentary products, as it does for influencers. By becoming an online influencer, an ordinary person has a shot at climbing the social ladder online. Having done this, they get to sit at the top of the digital hierarchy and be paid for telling their followers what to buy, eat, wear, and do.

In short, we are devising and learning new rules of netiquette that will guide our digital interactions, influencing how we relate to each other in the real world. This has a clear application to modern consumer behaviour, especially online behaviour.

Applying These Ideas to Consumer Behaviour

The study of **consumer socialization** largely focuses on the ways that consumers develop preferences and learn buying behaviours. It includes studying the role of family, friends, and media in teaching young people the "rules of consumption."

Let's start with family influences. In the first known study of this topic, Moore and Moschis (1978) asked high-school students to complete questionnaires that revealed family influences on the development of various consumer competencies. The researchers went on to distinguish two types of communication within families: socio-oriented communication and concept-oriented communication. **Socio-oriented communication** stresses the importance of preserving pleasant family relations, even if it means avoiding certain topics. **Concept-oriented communication** stresses the importance of discussing varied and strongly-felt topics, even if it stresses family relations.

Crosstabulating these two types of communication with the frequency of communication gives us four family patterns. They are:

Laissez-faire communication: rare communication between parents and their children;

Protective communication: rare communication that stresses the importance of obedience to parents;

Pluralistic communication: frequent communication that encourages an open exchange of views; and

Consensual communication: frequent communication that preserves family harmony.

Moore and Moschis' data showed that adolescents from pluralistic families, with frequent open communication, knew more than other adolescents about consumer-related matters and available products. They were better prepared to detect fakery in advertising and to manage a family budget. By contrast, children from a socio-oriented family—whether protective or consensual—were likely to have less knowledgeable and more materialistic views. They were also more likely to buy consumer goods for social (or communicative) rather than for practical purposes.

The researchers also found that families influence their children's spending by example, as well as through direct communication (Moschis and Churchill 1978; also, Moschis 2017). For example, different parents set different rules around watching TV. Parents were gatekeepers to other agents of socialization, including mass and social media. The more television (and television advertisements) a child viewed, the more likely that child was to develop materialistic inclinations. However, more media consumption also promoted the mastery of more consumer information and better consumer skills.

The data showed that interactions with peers also condition the interest of children in consumer goods and services. In adolescence, peers teach one another social motives for buying, and even materialistic values. Often, peers make one another more aware of goods and services in the marketplace, and how to buy them. This greater awareness may result in more focused and more skillful media consumption.

All of this is to say that both family and peers are key agents of socialization. By comparison, schools contribute less to adolescents' learning of consumer skills, for several reasons we will explore in a later chapter. Other students provide most of the consumer socialization at school.

However, many students may not be ready to grasp complicated ideas about consumerism. A teen's cognitive development will also influence his or her mastery of consumer skills. Young people gain more advanced consumer knowledge as they age and develop cognitively (Ward and Wackman 1974; also, Lindquist 2016). But from an early age onward, social learning teaches them simple consumer attitudes and values, like what to admire and what to buy.

Growing up in a wealthier family may help adolescents to learn the consumer role better and faster, because wealthy families have more opportunities for buying (Moschis and Churchill 1978; Moschis 2017). Children in wealthy families may also have more to spend: bigger allowances or access to a credit card. Within the same social class, boys and girls learn different aspects of the consumer role. For example, boys learn more about consumer items that entertain, while girls learn more about social markers that aid self-presentation (for example, cosmetics and clothing). We will examine the effects of income, gender and age in later chapters.

Saving and Spending

Why do people save their money, and what kind of socialization leads them to do so? One study (Canova et al. 2003; but see also Tang et al. 2018) looked at the ways that consumers explain and justify their saving habits. They found 15 goals that influence how people spend or save. Some were concrete ones, like saving to buy something or to take a vacation. Some of these goals might be considered materialistic. But others were abstract, psychological goals like saving for self-esteem and self-gratification.

That said, people are often unaware of why they act as they do. When answering questions in a study, many people try to rationalize their behaviour to display intelligence and social desirability. For example, it's possible that people who *said* they save to build self-esteem really save to support their love of shoes. In short, we can't necessarily tell from consumers' self-justifications whether their saving is materialistic or not.

Though we don't always know their motivations, we *do* know that people's saving and spending patterns vary socially and demographically. Many people learn to save early in life, typically from their parents. They learn to open a bank account, pay off their credit cards, and build habits of thrift. In this way, parents' behaviour can impact their children's economic behaviour, both while they are still young and when they grow up (Webley and Nyhus 2005; Agnew et al. 2018). For many, saving grows out of personal, family, and community values learned and practiced from an early age.

Another aspect of such socialization involves opportunities to spend. Some children never have a chance to decide whether they are going to save or spend. Either their family income isn't high enough for them to have access to money of their own, or they aren't trusted with money. As adults, they suddenly have the responsibility of managing their own finances, but have no experience learning the results of spending or the rewards of saving.

On the other hand, parenting practices like giving children allowances may promote saving, allowing them the opportunity to practice financial management on a small scale, with limited risks. One study found that children who receive more money from their parents save more money—and save it more regularly (Furnham, 1999; Fenton-O'Creevy and Furnham 2019). Another revealed that teenagers who know about and feel positively towards saving are more likely to know about and feel positively towards pensions and life insurance (Furnham and Gloletto-Tankel 2002; Gerhard et al. 2018).

Parents can also help their children understand the benefits of saving. They might discuss how saving for the future can make that future less stressful and more enjoyable. Robust retirement savings may reduce the stress of that transition and make the prospect more exciting (Ellen et al. 2012). People who have such an understanding instilled in them from a young age, and who can picture their retirement positively, are more likely to save. They want to take action now to bring about the future state they have been taught to value. By contrast, fear of the future doesn't motivate people as much. So, parents who underline the negative effects of being unprepared for retirement may not successfully inspire their children to save.

Studies show that parents can play an important role in helping children learn about saving and managing money.

People who are usually careful with their money—even frugal—are sometimes sent into a tizzy of spending by important changes in their life situation. Of these, few are more important or potentially costly than courtship. In societies with a high ratio of males to females, men save less and spend more (Griskevicius et al. 2012). Some say this is because there is more competition for mates. With a scarcity of possible partners, people expect men to spend more money during courtship, such as paying for dinner and buying expensive engagement rings.

Yet this spending strategy can backfire. Good savers are, in fact, more attractive mates than chronic spenders (Olson and Rick 2014). For one, savers will likely provide a more stable, secure future. Saving also signals greater self-control, which many see as a desirable quality in a partner.

Other psychological factors can also derail saving habits. For example, stressed consumers save more, yet they also increase their spending on products they see as necessities (Durante and Laran 2016). Likely, they want to gain control in an otherwise uncontrollable environment, though they may not be aware of this motivation or able to state it in words. For example, many families spent large amounts of money stockpiling supplies of toilet paper and canned goods in the early days of the COVID-19 pandemic.

Others trick themselves into spending. For example, people who use multiple bank accounts, debit and credit cards, and other sources of money may delude themselves into thinking they have more money than they do. People with only one bank account are less likely to exaggerate the amount they have saved (Mishra et al. 2012). They also find it harder to justify their spending.

Finally, people's motivations to save or spend can stem from the way it makes them feel. Perhaps unexpectedly, spending on others makes people happier overall (Dunn et al. 2008; Aknin et al. 2020). We feel better when we buy things for our friends, family members, or colleagues than when we buy things for ourselves. Anticipating these feelings of happiness, altruistic spenders may save not for things like their own futures, but to give gifts to others.

All of that said, some consumers today are shifting towards thrift, through a combination of conserving and reusing what they already have (Flatters and Willmott 2012). For example, they recycle more, buy used goods, and teach their children the harms of excess consumption and waste. Marketers have tapped into this trend. Many know consumers are eager to support brands with green mandates and corporate social responsibility campaigns that champion environmental sustainability. More brands are advertising their recycling initiatives or energy-efficient manufacturing. Even though this segment of consumers wants to spend less, marketers are keen to attract them and encourage them to buy more.

Buying at "environmentally friendly" stores has become a growing trend in recent decades, one we will discuss in more depth later. For now, note that this consumption choice can sometimes feel like an obligatory action to avoid backlash from other consumers due to the rising concern for climate change. These consumers avoid fast fashion brands like H&M and buy from sustainable clothing stores like Reformation. For those who can afford it, shopping sustainably has become a way for many consumers to show their level of awareness about current environmental issues; also, a way to flaunt their ability to shop at expensive sustainable alternative stores.

In short, people vary in their beliefs about spending and saving. Some see money as evil, or at least, as the root of all evils. Others see it as a neutral instrument for exchange, without any moral or social meaning in its own right. Others still—typically, materialists—see money as a positive good, the symbol of success and social value. For this last group, money is a way to get everything you want out of life. More than that, it is proof that you have not lived your life in vain.

Social Roles and Social Learning

Socialization goes on throughout our lives, teaching us how to be informed consumers in every role we play. Being an "informed consumer" means knowing as much as you need to know about the items you are buying or thinking about buying: for example, where the goods were made, how they were made, perhaps even how the workers were treated where the goods were made. Only by being an informed consumer can one become an "ethical consumer," for example; we will say more about this in later chapters.

Being informed is critical, because we pass through dozens of different roles in life. For example, we enter and leave the roles of student, employer, parent, or grandparent. These social roles, and many others, carry different expectations and identities. They also influence the ways we spend money. Consider, for instance, the difference between the ways that parents and nonparents spend money, or the ways that employed and unemployed people spend money.

Box 3-3
Student Debts Change Spending Patterns

Student debt stops people from being able to spend on what would be expected of people their age. Growing numbers of young people are holding off on buying houses, cars, and other "adult" purchases that their parents might have bought at the same age.

Today, the average Canadian undergraduate owes about $28,000. Although the situation is not as bad as in the U.S., accumulated student debt still limits graduates' career choices. Consider the case of a McMaster University student who paid her tuition using money from student loans. By the time she graduated, she had amassed a total debt of over $150,000 and had to declare bankruptcy. What's more, bankruptcy does not eliminate government-guaranteed student loan debt in Canada unless you graduated more than seven years ago. Filing for bankruptcy ruined her credit score and prevented her from borrowing any money to start her own business.

Years after graduation, many of those with outstanding student loans still cannot afford to marry and start a family. When one graduate and his partner married, they were still in debt and could not afford the down payment on a home. They had to stay in a small old apartment that had once belonged to the student's mother-in-law. No wonder they felt hesitant about having children (Sagan 2014).

From a social perspective, reduced spending power because of student debt also depresses retail sales and economic growth. Today, many graduates cannot afford to buy cars, homes, or even new clothes for work. If debtors cannot afford to repay their loans, an economic crisis may follow (Moloney, 2019). With rising tuition and living costs, student loans will only make adulthood more expensive.

When people change roles, their group memberships, goals, and identities change too. As a result, alterations in their spending patterns usually follow. So, how do people learn to spend in new ways? How do they learn to regulate their spending, so it fits their new role? And, returning to our central concern, how do they learn to spend in a way that communicates their group membership, their identity, and their ambitions?

To choose one concrete example, roles often influence the foods we buy and eat. We eat and drink every day, but our abilities to prepare food and drink vary depending on what we have learned. As we take on different roles and new needs emerge, we learn to buy, prepare, and consume new food in new ways. For example, teens may not learn how to cook until they leave home to go to university. Without parents to prepare food for them, they have to learn to feed themselves. Similarly, people who become parents often need to adjust their own meal preparation habits. They can no longer skip breakfast or stop by a bar for a beer and a slice of pizza on their way home from work. They have a baby who must be fed particular food at particular times.

Our demographic attributes—gender, age, income, and birthplace, among others—influence the roles we assume. Women (as daughters, wives, and mothers) have traditionally been assigned responsibility for domestic chores. Most learned how to cook as they grew up—and expected to cook for their families. But with more women entering higher education and paid work, gender roles have blurred and family cooking arrangements with them. Now, men as well as women are expected to learn how to cook (for themselves and others). A woman who doesn't know how to cook—or chooses not to—sends a social message. So does a man who does know how to cook and takes on the responsibility of cooking for his dependents. Our learned behaviours send messages, whether purposefully or not, about our roles and status. Some display these behaviours pointedly, to show others who they want to be seen as.

Experience with different kinds of food is part of what social researchers call cultural capital: the intangible resources that set privileged people apart. Cultural capital is a collection of knowledge, behaviours, and skills that display high socioeconomic status and distinguish the top social classes from the rest. It includes having "good taste." People display their cultural capital by doing high-class activities, like going to the ballet or playing tennis at country clubs. We will have much more to say about cultural capital, and how it passes from parents to children, in a later chapter. For now, consider the excerpt from a menu in an expensive restaurant below. As they grow up, people with cultural capital will feel confident ordering appetizers from this menu. In effect, the menu items are social markers, and being able to order them confidently is part of an effective self-presentation. A consumer's confidence and know-how (or their confusion in response to such a menu) tell dining companions about their social origins and ambitions.

APPETIZERS

Daily Soup
PRICED ACCORDINGLY

Fois Gras Terrine
Sea salt brioche, pickled grapes, and maple jelly with a sour cherry glaze
TWENTY-EIGHT DOLLARS

Oysters Daily
On the half shell with red wine mignonette, horseradish and lemon
PRICED ACCORDINGLY

Ontario Tomato Salad
Buffalo mozzarella, arugula, capers, artichokes, lemon, and artisanal Italian anchovies.
Pine nut Paremesan crumble and extra virgin organic olive oil
TWENTY-THREE DOLLARS

Ricotta Ravioli
Late summer vegetables, basil oil, warm tomato butter
TWENTY-SEVEN DOLLARS

Though intangible, cultural capital can be expensive to acquire. You need knowledgeable parents, devoted teachers, opportunities that make for exciting life experiences, and, most important of all, time and money (Farkas 2017; O'Shea 2016). To acquire cultural capital, people may have to attend costly private schools and take part in expensive extracurricular activities. There they may learn soft skills like good manners, how to interact with authority figures, and how to network effectively.

In turn, cultural capital affects their educational, occupational, and even marriage prospects (DiMaggio 2019). The more cultural capital you have, the better your chances of getting a good education, landing a good job, and marrying "up." That's because people with cultural capital usually also have social capital (that is, good contacts) and financial capital (that is, money).

Cultural Capital and Tasteful Consumption

One of the more important kinds of socialization we will discuss in this book is the teaching of taste. Tasteful consumption is the continuing display of cultural capital. When people of the elite classes consume in public, they show their high-culture preferences and their worthiness of high social rank. Demonstrating one's taste is slightly different from what Veblen called conspicuous consumption because, even though it is public behaviour and displays class position, it is not supposed to be showy or flashy. It is aimed not so much at outdoing other people (like conspicuous consumption) but at showing you belong.

Thus, wealthy people have learned to be good at what researchers Berger and Ward (2010) call inconspicuous consumption: tasteful spending that only people with wealth and cultural capital would recognize. In this situation, self-presentation must be subtle and understated. Knowing insiders—people with old money and lots of cultural capital—can decode subtle signals, such as small and discreet logos. These distinguish "classy" purchases from the "flashy" buys of newly-moneyed people with less taste and cultural capital (Makkar and Yap 2018; Lee 2017; Wu et al. 2017; Jack 2018).

For example, cheap sunglasses may have no logo on them, while moderately expensive sunglasses (priced from $100 to $300) sport well-known, easy-to-see logos. Expensive sunglasses ($300 and up) are likely to have a subtle, "classy" logo that is hard to see. Only those with taste and a wide knowledge of consumer products would be able to spot it. And they learn to detect and interpret such cultural symbols of "classiness" through the same socialization we have been discussing throughout this chapter.

Final Thoughts

In this chapter, we began exploring the process of socialization through which we learn our consumer culture. Through primary socialization, families play an important role in teaching us how to consume. Parenting style and family communication habits help shape the ways we think about consumption, advertising, saving, and budgeting. And they contribute to making us more or less materialistic, and more or less likely to consume for social as opposed to practical purposes. As we saw, even the seemingly simple rules parents set around screen time can influence children's buying skills, consumer awareness, and degree of materialism.

Mainstream North American culture is a consumer culture. Most of us learn to put a high value on material consumer objects and spend much of our time working to earn enough money to buy these products. In this chapter, we've learned the reasons we come to value material objects so deeply.

Lifelong socialization imbues us with consumer wants from the moment we're born until the day we die. We learn about and internalize consumerist beliefs, values, and behaviours through social interaction and comparison. We learn to see ourselves (and others) largely through our possessions. And since we want to look good to the world, we use symbolic consumer goods to communicate our identities and goals. In this way, consumer goods help us compete for status and membership in communities.

In this chapter, we also tried to understand the heavy demand for consumer goods that we see in our society. We decided there is a significant social ingredient to this desire to own and display consumer goods. Consider Cooley's theory of the looking-glass self, which holds that people develop a picture of themselves by comparing themselves to others and seeking favourable responses. According to Mead, we also internalize the expectations others have for us, coming to expect certain behaviours from ourselves just as they might do.

These ideas help explain why people feel the need to display their "selves" to others. We need signs—such as consumer goods—to prove to others and ourselves that we are living up to expectations. For example, we learn we need a sharp suit to show that we have "made it" in the work world. We lease a BMW because we know that doing so will send the desired message of success in our capitalist consumer culture; leasing a Hyundai or a Hummer would send a different message. Through the process of socialization outlined in this chapter, we learn about these different signs, including how to choose, buy, and use them.

Does consumerism cause problems we should be concerned about? In this chapter, we introduced compensation theory, which suggests that some people—materialistic people—consume to relieve their feelings of inadequacy. Parents can create such feelings in their children if they do not provide love and attention, or if they are emotionally abusive. Social media may also contribute to a negative self-image, if users receive unsolicited, hateful comments from strangers. Agents of socialization—whether parents, peers, or the media—also teach us how to manage these feelings of low self-esteem. Often, they teach us, wrongly, that consumption makes people feel better; among people who consistently need to feel better, this belief may breed materialism.

Some consumers chase the brief good feelings they get from "retail therapy" (perhaps even to excess as is the case with "shopaholics," whom we discuss in later chapters). However, in the long run, their purchases do not have the intended effect. People who consume in the hopes of gaining happiness and inclusion often find themselves unhappy and excluded (Skivington et al. 2016).

This poses a social problem because our economy is geared to sell people material possessions with the implied promise they will, indeed, bring happiness. People are socialized to think that buying and happiness are, and should be, associated. They buy to belong and to signal their belonging, yet may never truly feel they do belong.

Materialism and even "shopping addiction" may not necessarily be "bad." However, they are problems we should try to address, since they are (at least sometimes) indicators of deeper insecurity and unhappiness. They may signal that people have low self-esteem or feel inadequate and lonely. Some have been socialized to think that consumption is the solution to these feelings; but since it isn't, we, as a society, may want to develop and present alternative solutions to unhappiness. For example, we might teach people to parent their children in ways that build self-esteem, which may leave them less likely to seek solace in material things.

Discussion Questions

1. In this chapter, we discussed how personal identity is a social product. How is your identity shaped by society at large?

2. How is the "consumption constellation" present in our everyday lives? What does the author mean by "they are Baudrillardian signs that only have the desired effect when combined in a culturally knowledgeable way"?

3. What are some of the ways demographic features influence the roles we assume? How has this trend changed throughout the years?

Quick Quiz

1. What is a feature that reflects a person's status in a society?
a. Cost to influence ratio
b. Impression control
c. Social marker
d. Personal identity
e. Self-concept

2. What is an individual's self-concept?
a. How others view them
b. Their objective characteristics
c. How they see themselves
d. Their family background
e. How the individual is expected to act

3. Which sociologist emphasized the importance of socialization for the development of a personal identity, or what he called your "self"?
a. Charles Cooley
b. Jean Piaget
c. George Herbert Mead
d. Erving Goffman
e. Max Weber

4. What is compensation theory about?
a. Distribution of resources that is fair to both relational partners
b. A person will act in a certain way because they are motivated to select a specific behavior over others due to what they expect the result of that selected behavior will be
c. An individual's background and life trend are tied with their consumption tendencies
d. An individual can make decisions on behalf of another person or entity
e. People become materialistic when they have low self-worth, the result of a damaged psyche

5.   Which is a definition of laissez-faire communication?
a.   Rare communication of any kind between parents and their children
b.   Rare communication that emphasizes the importance of obedience to parents
c.   Frequent communication that encourages an open exchange of views
d.   Frequent communication that preserves family harmony
e.   Daily conversations about stress and family concerns

The answers to the Quick Quiz are provided at the end of the book.

For Further Reading

The Commodification of Childhood: The Children's Clothing Industry and the Rise of the Child Consumer by Daniel Cook

This book presents a study into the historical formation of children as consumers. It examines changing norms about childhood as reflected in dress codes. Cook charts the rise of industries that cater to children over the 20th century.

The Meaning of Things: Domestic Symbols and the Self by Mihaly Csikszentmihalyi and Eugene Rochberg-Halton

This extensive and innovative study accounts for the transactions between people and objects within their homes. The research is underpinned by a belief that domestic objects are identity symbols. Results shed light on processes of identity formation in relation to family, life course, gender, and the uses and meanings of objects within the home.

Subculture: The Meaning of Style by Dick Hebdige

This book provides a classic account of the role of consumption within youth subcultures. Young people who are participants in subcultures are identified as skilled consumers who use everyday consumer objects as a means to challenge and subvert dominant social norms. Codes of dress and personal style become arenas for creating meaningful personal identities and for upsetting conventional codes of behavior and appearance.

Key Terms

Commodities as social markers
Consumer identity
Identity
Individualism
Lifestyle
Self-presentation

Chapter Four

Teaching the Culture of Desire: Families

Learning Objectives

After reading this chapter, you will be able to:

✓ Analyze how parents contribute to their children's consumer socialization .

✓ Show how family members influence each other's consumption habits.

✓ Note the ways homes and their furnishings signal families' identities and aspirations.

✓ Consider how families ritualize consumption.

As we began to explore in the last chapter, families are among the most important agents of socialization. They are the first of many groups to teach us the culture of desire. We will discuss three other agents of socialization—schools, peers and the media—in later chapters. For now, though, we will focus on families and their role in raising us to be consumers.

As we will see, family members—including children—communicate with one another through and about consumerism. Many families consume together, as a unit; for example, they may do one grocery run that feeds everyone, or save up for a new family car. Equally, families signal to each other and to other families their identity, their aspirations, and the groups to which they belong (or want to belong). Family members use material goods to illustrate their identities and roles to each other. For example, some teenagers choose clothing that they know their parents will disapprove of in an effort to signal their independence. And, perhaps unintentionally, parents may reveal their division of labour through their purchases. Those who do the grocery shopping, for example, may signal their responsibility for meal preparation, while those who purchase power tools indicate their responsibility for home maintenance.

As a whole, families also use possessions to send signals to other families: the home itself, home furnishings, the car, the front lawn, the barbecue, and the patio furniture. They use these material goods to tell others the "type" of people and family they are—or, at least, want to be taken for. With all of this collective signaling going on, it is no wonder that most families raise children who are knowing and skillful consumers.

Defining our Terms

To start, what counts as a **family**? For many years, social scientists used anthropologist George Murdock's oft-cited definition (1949: 1): a family of people lived together; had some sort of economic relationship; had one parent of each sex; and had one or more children. However, that definition excludes many groups we consider families today, including childfree married couples, single parents and their children, and same-sex married couples (for more on definitions of family, see Gavriel-Fried and Shilo 2016; Woodhouse 2017; Tam et al. 2017).

An alternative definition is that used by market researchers and census-takers. They focus on **households**—people living under one roof. This definition may also fall short: many families maintain ongoing family relationships while living in separate homes—for example, divorced parents who share custody. A third approach defines family in socio-economic terms. That is, families provide emotional, financial, and material support to each other, transmit cultural values, and help each other develop. Fourth and finally, Canadian family law and policy includes families that are structurally diverse—i.e., made up of members who differ among themselves—but similar in their processes—i.e., the ways they live life together (Kronby 2010).

These many definitions show it is difficult today to make generalizations about families because they are so diverse. Yet we can still identify some common processes. First, families display dependency or interdependency. Many family members are intimate with one another, in the sense that they understand one another and often care about one another deeply. Second, all families contain members who communicate with one another. Families display a division of labour, and members negotiate what tasks are to be done and who will do them. Members exercise influence over one another and bargain when decisions are to be made.

Third, families provide some protection to their members. In our culture, parents and other relatives are supposed to keep children safe; spouses are supposed to protect one another; and adult children are supposed to protect their parents, especially as they grow old. In reality, however, family members often fail to protect each other enough, and worse, some people neglect, exploit, or abuse family members. Others overprotect.

Fourth, families have a distribution of power. There are significant differences in power, strength, age, and social resources among members. Ideally, the more powerful family members protect the less powerful ones. However, these imbalances in power have meant dominant males (typically, fathers) have traditionally been "in charge" of families. As mentioned, such power dynamics come into play when purchasing decisions need to be made.

Whatever their form, all families play a critical role in what researchers call social reproduction. **Social reproduction** is the process through which a society continually recreates its social order, relations, and structures of dominance across time and space. This includes the teaching of social norms and values we discussed earlier. It also includes policy and legislation as well as institutions, which work to maintain the status quo (Federici 2019; Jarvis et al. 2016; Gimenez 2019). In different ways, families transmit values such as patriotism, internationalism, anti-racism, and respect for nature. By passing these values on to their children, families help support their continuation. This status quo is continually under pressure through resistance and transgression. For the most part, however, social reproduction helps to ensure that people continue to believe in values that promote social stability, obedience, and acceptance of the dominant ideology.

Families are also crucial for the production and reproduction of the labour force. By this, we mean the ways families support and care for each other within the home so that they can work for pay outside of the home. Family members—especially mothers—also typically assume primary childcare responsibilities, meaning they raise the next generation of workers. These patterns are culturally specific and vary over time and by location. For example, it is more common today than two generations ago for fathers to share domestic and childcare responsibilities somewhat more evenly with mothers.

Through these same processes, families also help transfer class position from one generation to the next. They do this, in part, by teaching their children their taste and values, which are often tied to social class. For example, a child who grows up in an upper-class family may visit art galleries and museums, or even have highbrow art in their homes. While they attend the symphony and become well-versed in the tastes of the upper classes, their working-class counterparts may be holding down part-time jobs and learning the value of a strong work ethic. Neither set of tastes or values is inherently superior. But learning and living by them means children from different classes will likely continue to fit in with the same classes as they age. This preparation for class membership is also gendered: that is, different for boys and girls, as we see in Box 4-1 on the next page.

Also related to the learning of class membership is the transmission of ideology. For social researchers, an **ideology** is a system of beliefs that are disseminated, reinforced, and reproduced

Box 4-1
The "Gibson Girl"
Trendsetting Woman of the 1900s

In the late 1800s and the early 1900s, society looked to the iconic "Gibson Girl" for fashion inspiration. The Gibson Girl was a fictional character created by the American graphic artist Charles Dana Gibson. Through his drawings, he created what society deemed the "ideal" woman. Gibson portrayed the Gibson Girl as "a member of upper-class society, who was always perfectly dressed in the latest fashionable attire" (Bulo 2017). She was independent and athletic, yet fragile and feminine. She wore long elegant dresses, bustle gowns, and shirtwaists. The Gibson Girl's choice of clothing illustrated her wealth—it was a means of Veblenian conspicuous consumption. Women who did not belong to the upper classes, yet still aspired to the Gibson Girl's "look," could turn to popular magazines such as *The Delineator*, which advertised stylish dress patterns that could be ordered by mail. They would then sew their dresses by hand. The Butterick Pattern Company, the textile company behind *The Delineator,* sold their patterns in specialty stores across Canada. They also had a manufacturing centre in Toronto. As a result, Canadian women of all social classes were able to recreate the look of the Gibson Girl.

almost invisibly (Seliger 2019; Bershady 2017). These beliefs bind groups of people together and guide their actions, for the most part without their being aware of it. The **dominant ideology** consists of the ruling ideas in society: those that are widely seen as natural and inevitable. Marxists suggest that the dominant ideology usually serves the interests of the ruling class. As you may imagine, the dominant ideology shapes views of poverty, welfare, crime, drug addiction, and even educational choice (Riley 2019; Codd 2017; Reinarman and Duskin 2017).

Ideology is often used—especially in the media—as a negative term. Sometimes it is equated with false consciousness, taken to mean that only certain types of people are hampered by ideology, which makes them unable to think for themselves. But this view is itself ideological. It sets itself up as somehow non-ideological: the "normal" or "common-sense" view of things, compared to an abnormal or distorted ideological view. The notion of a non-ideological position is a myth—or, perhaps, a wish. In reality, ideology is part of everything we think, see, and do.

Another feature of families often noted by researchers is that they have a typical **life cycle**: a sequence of typical transitions (see for example Rapoport and Rapoport 2019; Shannon et al. 2020). The six main **stages of family life**, based on demographic data, are outlined below. At each stage, people have different needs and interests. That makes these categories useful for marketers and advertisers, who need to be able to define the markets for the goods and services they're promoting (Freitas 2018; Shannon et al. 2020; Dupont 2018; Moschis 2019).

1. Young single people. The first stage of family life occurs when people are young, single, and no longer living in the parental home. Typically, this family, though often without much money, has few financial burdens. Marketers tend to focus on their interests in fashion, leisure, basic household items, cars, equipment, and holidays. Financial-services marketers increasingly target this group while they are still students and as they gain their first jobs, hoping to build a lifelong relationship with them as their financial needs grow.

2. Young couples without children. Newly married couples who are childfree are typically better-off than singles, since they pool their incomes. Marketers often focus on their initial purchases of starter homes, household goods, holidays, and financial services.

3. Full nesters. This category is typically split into two stages, often referred to by using Roman numerals. Full nesters stage I includes couples with children under six. They tend to have low levels of disposable income and savings, usually because of mortgage commitments, or because one parent—often a woman—has taken time off work to bear and raise children. Marketers therefore tend to focus on selling financial services to this group, especially credit products such as cards, loans, and overdrafts. In addition, this group spends most of their disposable income on their children, making them ideal targets for baby products and clothes, as well as children's toys and books.

Full nesters stage II includes couples whose youngest child is age six or older. Usually, if the job market is strong, they enjoy an improved financial position. Perhaps they've earned pay increases. Both parents have likely returned to work, since their children are old enough to attend school full-time. Children continue to absorb a significant amount of household spending. Marketers therefore focus on promoting clothes, bicycles, sports gear, musical instruments and lessons, and activity-oriented holidays to these families.

4. Couples with dependent children. Also known as "full nesters stage III," these are older married couples with dependent children, perhaps in full-time higher education or working their first jobs. The financial position of this group typically continues to improve but improvements may be undermined by the financial demands of their children's education. Typically, these are dual-earner families who focus on saving for and spending on schooling and related costs. Marketers often promote updated furniture, luxury goods, boats, timeshares, and exotic holidays for members of this group.

5. Empty nesters. Then come the so-called empty nesters, who can also be divided into two subgroups. Empty esters stage I comprise older married couples who are still working, but whose children are no longer living with them, having moved to the first stage of the family cycle. Empty nesters stage I have mortgage payments that have become less onerous, so they have a high degree of savings and disposable income. Marketers hone in on this group as perhaps the wealthiest of all target markets. Their interests include unique travel experiences, possibly a second home in a foreign country, sophisticated leisure, top-end cars, expensive home improvements, and self-education.

Empty nesters stage II are, like those in stage I, older married couples with no children living at home. The difference is that this group is retired. They experience a significant cut in income in turn and are heavily dependent on pensions and savings. As a result, they are often concerned with budgeting and no longer support their children financially. Marketers focus less on this group, due to their reduced disposable income. However, they remain a popular target market for financial-services providers and companies selling medical devices and products.

6. Solitary survivors. In later stages of life, we find the solitary survivors. Solitary survivors stage I comprises people who are still working, but may have divorce and maintenance costs to bear. Their income is still adequate, but they may sell their family home and purchase smaller accommodations. They are worried about security and increasing dependency. They spend a little on hobbies, pastimes, and specialist holidays designed for singles. This group is not a top target for the marketer.

Solitary survivors stage II (retired) comprise people who have experienced a significant cut in income and require increasing amounts of care, especially medical, and special attention and security. They may depend on other family members for personal and financial assistance, in the same way their children were once dependent on them. This group is no longer a target of marketers, but their relatives may be, especially for financial services, such as insurance, and also for medical services.

At different stages of the life cycle, family members may want and buy different products and services, and they also have different levels of disposable income. People also pass through these stages at different ages, in different marital statuses, and at different phases in their careers.

Finally, companies that specialize in specific products or services may target a segment *within* one of the six stages. For example, a boutique spin studio may focus on the first stage: young single people. Then, they may segment further still, targeting single women between the ages of 20 and 25 who live within a five-kilometre radius of their studio and are seeking a more intense workout experience.

Units of Production and Consumption

Over time, families have evolved from "units of production" to "units of consumption." In the 19th century, most people worked in agriculture and lived on family farms. There, all family members helped to produce food for survival or sale. The family was a **unit of production**. Today, on the other hand, few people work in agriculture, and few people work in family-controlled businesses (farms or otherwise). Most people work outside the home to support themselves and their family members. Most family life is devoted to childcare, sociability, and consumption, not commercial production. Thus, the family today is a **unit of consumption**. That means one of its important duties is teaching children how to consume—especially, steering them toward responsible consumer habits and away from irresponsible ones. For example, parents can:

The small family farm, once a common sight in rural Canada, represents a time when families were most often units of production as well as units of consumption. This photograph was taken in Ontario in 1905.

Allow their children to influence family purchases—or not. In turn, children may learn they have a say over how money is spent. Or they may grow up with no understanding of money, thinking items and services magically appear in their home.

Go shopping with their children: a practice called **co-shopping** (Keller and Ruus 2014). Co-shopping allows children to experience and observe consumerism firsthand. They learn which stores to patronize, what products are considered "desirable," and how to interact with salespeople. In one study (Drenten et al. 2008), researchers observed preschoolers while they pretended to shop for groceries in a simulated grocery store. They saw that young children mimicked the shopping patterns they'd seen adults follow. They even displayed peer-to-peer consumer socialization, advising each other on how to shop correctly (see also Fung and Cheng 2017).

Monitor and control their children's media exposure—or not. Children may learn some media literacy skills from their parents, or may be kept from consuming ads that target adults. Others may be exposed to content they don't understand.

Often, these decisions are influenced by parents' choice of the various parenting styles we discussed in the last chapter (Rose, Dalakas, and Kropp 2003: 373; also, Mikeska et al. 2017), as the following table indicates.

Parenting style	Characteristics	Child influence on purchases	Co-shopping with parents	Controlled media exposure
Authoritative	Warm, restrictive	High	High	High
Permissive	Warm, nonrestrictive	High	High	Low
Authoritarian	Cold, restrictive	Low	Low	Low
Neglectful	Uninvolved, unrestrictive	Low	Low	Low

Source: Based on research by Bertol et al. (2017), Rose et al. (2003), and Carlson and Grossbart (1988).

The ways parents teach their children to shop are crucial because research suggests parents are more significant agents of socialization than schools, peers, and the media (Pinto, Parente, and Mansfield 2003). By way of illustration, one study (Pinto et al. 2003; but see also Letkiewicz et al. 2019) showed that the more information parents gave children about credit, the lower were their college kids' outstanding credit-card balances. Information from media, schools, or peers, on the other hand, had no significant influence on students' credit-card balances. Parents have significant teaching opportunities and responsibilities. By educating their children, parents can help protect them from future financial problems.

How Children Try to Influence Purchase Decisions

As we have seen already in this chapter, children quickly become knowing and competent consumers. They learn to shop at ever-younger ages and, before they have money of their own to spend, influence their parents' consumption choices.

In the beginning, young children mainly pester and nag their parents (Buijzen and Valkenburg 2008; Dikcius et al. 2019). This coercive behaviour typically increases until they reach early elementary school. Then, it starts to decline, and is replaced by more mature approaches as children come to understand who, when, where, and how to ask for items.

At this point, children start trying to show their parents that they are knowledgeable about the product they want (Flurry and Burns 2005; Calderon et al. 2017). Some promise to reward their parents with good behaviour if they purchase the product or threaten bad behaviour if it seems they won't. They also time their requests carefully, asking for things on special occasions like birthdays and Christmas. Financial constraints factor into their purchase requests too, so they often ask for inexpensive items, reasoning that their parents are more likely to say "yes" to affordable purchases. Finally, children are aware that parents will purchase products that benefit them too, so they try to reason with their parents and point out how they will also be able to make use of the purchase.

Parents, for their part, come to see their children's consumer requests as part of a natural parent-child interaction (Nash 2009). And they are more often persuaded to buy when their children have rational conversations with them, as opposed to pestering. Of course, pestering still works in some situations. That's why so many stores display child-friendly items near the cash registers at the front of the store. One study in Melbourne, Australia found that four out of five supermarkets displayed chocolate, gum, and other sweets at checkout (Dixon et al. 2006). In only seven percent of checkout lanes were these goodies placed beyond the reach of children. Perhaps this is why many parents avoid shopping for food with their children. They find the experience stressful and exhausting (see also Vohra and Soni 2016).

As they learn, grow, and acquire new skills, children sporadically try new approaches when shopping. Sometimes they ask nicely, while other times they beg and plead, get angry, try to bargain, sulk, display affection, ask outright, evoke guilt, or try to con their parents (Williams and Burns 2000; Carillo et al. 2018). Parents use just as many tactics to sidestep these requests. They may bargain, stall, flat-out refuse, distract their child, or have a lengthy discussion with the child. Many parents think these strategies help soften the refusal and ease their child's sense of disappointment. Indeed, children often accept refusals without incident. Both they and their parents seem to know they are playing a bargaining game of sorts. Children know they'll only win so many times, so they eagerly accept their successes when they happen.

Some tension occasionally emerges between parents and children but dissipates rather quickly. Again, both parent and child seem to recognize that such tension is part of the game. Children avoid damaging their relationship with their parents as part of the game; doing so would simply hurt their chances of winning the next round.

Both parents and children also recognize the need to strike a balance between purchases and refusals. They need to make sure everyone in the family is satisfied. One child can't get everything he asks for, while another gets nothing. The parent realizes the child who is left out won't stand for it. And even the spoiled child knows their luck will eventually run out. So, all parties see the value of balance and fairness. As a result, this bargaining game perpetuates the status quo, making sure all family members have a chance to exert their influence. For parents, this means there's a time to say "no" and a time to say "yes" to each child.

Usually, the game also involves weighing the pros and cons of a desired product together, as a family. Especially around certain family rituals where gift-giving is customary, like birthdays and Christmas, parents will explicitly ask their children what they want. They encourage their children to want and request products, just as much as children use these special occasions as excuses to ask for things (Clarke 2008; Holiday et al. 2018). Together, they also think about how suitable the gift is—for the child and the occasion—and question what they know about it. For example, they may read product reviews. Purchase requests are not unilateral. Many parents tolerate—and perhaps even help create—a family environment where children feel free to ask for whatever they want.

In sum, children are consumers: they want material goods, and they aren't afraid to ask for them. They also use a variety of tactics to get the goods they want. Though research varies, many scholars agree that "pester power" may not be as common or influential as it once was (Gram 2011; Page et al. 2019). Parents and children today seem to engage in more advanced negotiation. They build a habit of negotiating for things and then buying them. Many families seem to look at consumption like a long term game, with some rounds won and some lost. To keep everyone happy, the family members realize they need to preserve long-term relationships. So sometimes parents give in to requests, and children accept refusals at other times.

The outstanding question is: when do parents give in, and when do children accept defeat? Below, we review the factors that play into these decisions.

Box 4-2

Back-to-School Shopping
A Stressful Time for Parents

Ninety-four percent of Canadian parents involve their kids in back-to-school shopping (Newswire 2019). For kids, it's exciting and fun. However, 53 percent of Canadian parents experience financial stress during the pre-school shopping season. Another 39 percent say that it takes months for them to pay off these bills (Lowestrates.ca 2017).

Part of the problem is that tablets and laptops are often required for school. Sara Skirboll, a shopping and trends expert, claims that "Canadians are spending more on back-to-school than ever before—more than parents in the U.S. and more than they did on gifts for the holidays" (Lowestrates.ca 2017).

What's more, kids ask for the trendiest products to help them fit in. One mom says, "Coming up with the money … kids always want what others have … it's crazy expensive" (*Ottawa Citizen* 2019). Another parent, Zenith Nieva from Waterloo, Ontario, says he only buys his two boys the necessities. "If they want something more than that, they have to cover [it] with their own money" (Global News, 2019). Still others try to hold a conversation with their child about financial literacy to help them understand financial limits. But for those families with children too young to earn their own money, or not mature enough to understand financial stress, the back-to-school shopping season can feel overwhelming.

Factors Affecting Children's Purchasing Influence

Whether they coerce or converse, children are more likely to convince their parents to buy certain *types* of products. Not surprisingly, they have more influence on the purchase of products that directly relate to them—say, a new T-shirt for their first day of school (Ramzy et al. 2012).

Children are also likely to convince their parents to buy products that will be used by the whole family—for example, a movie they will watch together (Isin and Alkibay 2010; Boghani et al. 2016). On the other hand, children usually have less sway when it comes to products parents are buying for themselves. These would include the parents' own clothing, home décor, and technology, as well as big-ticket items like a new family car.

The older a child, the more influence he or she has in this process. That's because parents feel more confident in the decision-making abilities of older children. However, data suggest that, over time, children have become more influential at younger ages. Decades ago, parents might not have trusted their six-year-old to help make a purchasing decision, but they may today, depending on the purchase.

There are two plausible reasons for this shift. First, in most families with children today, both parents work outside of the home. With both parents absent during the day, younger children are relied on to make or influence purchase decisions. Second, children may have greater access to consumer goods, and information about consumer goods, at younger ages than they did in the past. Some young children today have extensive wardrobes, iPads, and "play rooms" dedicated to housing their toy collections. Having been consumers from birth, perhaps children are developing consumption skills at earlier ages.

Children's influence on purchasing varies around the world. For example, Egyptian children reportedly have more influence, at younger ages, than American children (Ramzy et al. 2012). Several factors account for this. First, children in Egypt tend to take on adult responsibilities at a younger age than American or Canadian children. Their parents are more likely to see them as "grown-ups" and thus deserving of a greater say in family purchases. Second, Egyptian parents may indulge their children more than American parents. That is, they may be more inclined to buy their children what they want. Finally, Egyptian children may have more technological expertise than their parents. These parents may need to rely on their help when purchasing products such as computers, cell phones, home Internet, tablets, or speakers. They may also turn to their children for support with online shopping, credit card activation, online bill payments, and the like.

At the other end of the spectrum, Japanese mothers reportedly allow their children less influence in consumer decision-making than American mothers (Rose 1999; for comparison, see Mandrik et al. 2018). In general, they control their children's consumption more. Many do not think their children will mature until they are older, and do not think they can be trusted to make independent purchasing decisions. American mothers, by contrast, encourage and expect their children to become independent consumers earlier.

In both countries, communication style can influence consumer behaviour (Rose et al. 2002; Gentina et al. 2017). Remember from earlier that *concept-oriented* communication means having rational discussions about buying. It encourages children to develop independent consumption views. By contrast, *socio-oriented* (or consensus-seeking) communication encourages deference to parental standards and typically results in increased dependence. Because many parents in Japan do not think their children are mature enough to make independent buying choices, they tend to use socio-oriented communication styles. It's therefore difficult to say whether Japanese children are indeed less competent consumers or if their parents have obliged them to exercise less competence.

As a final example, consider ethnic differences in Canada. One study looked at the differences between Chinese-Canadian and Caucasian-Canadian consumers (Kim et al. 2008). It found that Chinese–Canadian children had more purchase influence, for certain products. But both sets of children were equally influential when it came to deciding on the purchase of durable goods. Chinese-Canadian and Caucasian-Canadian children also displayed different buying preferences. Chinese-Canadian children made more practical choices. They were confused by excessive choice, were less impulsive buyers, and did not participate in conspicuous consumption as much as Caucasian–Canadians.

Family type also plays a role. For example, children have more influence when there are fewer relationships to negotiate (Tinson and Brace 2008; Tomic and Lekovic 2017). Consider a single parent with only one child. That child only has to convince the one parent that a desired product is a good buy. She doesn't have to convince her parent that other siblings will benefit from the purchase, or that the other parent will be pleased. So, child influence is potentially much greater in this simple family. But child influence is typically much less in complex families—for example, in blended families where there are stepparents and stepchildren present. In these families, parents have to take into account many more consumers' needs and wants.

Different siblings may exert different amounts of influence in a given family, since parents view their children differently (Kerrane and Hogg 2011; Bettany and Kerrane 2018). Try as they may to treat their children equally, many parents still see them differently. Children who are viewed more favourably can succeed with more relaxed influence strategies. By contrast, children held in low regard may need to adopt much more devious or confrontational strategies.

Box 4-3
The Influence of Siblings Is Greater than You Think

Toronto sisters Jyoti and Kiran Matharoo did everything together: they wore the same styles throughout high school, went to the same fashion program at college, shopped together, went to social events with each other, and planned a fashion line together. They were exclusive and called themselves the "anti-social socialites" (Kimball 2017). Eventually, when they both started dating wealthy men, the sisters continued shopping together, but at designer stores such as Dior and Louis Vuitton.

The Matharoo sisters show how siblings influence one another. Younger siblings use older siblings as role models. Older siblings use younger siblings to confirm that they are still fresh and on the cutting edge. For the Matharoo sisters, the love of shopping, luxury, and materialism played off one another.

By contrast, the influence that a parent has on a child only goes so far. Parents teach children how to behave in formal situations. However, siblings influence each other's informal behaviour. Siblings teach each other how to dress and how to look cool. They help each other fit in. According to one survey, people have more positive memories of shopping with siblings than with mothers because of the lack of parental criticism (Minahan et al. 2010). When siblings get along and spend time together, like the Matharoo sisters, it is easier for them to influence each other's shopping.

Some family members may form strategic coalitions to boost their influence. For example, children may form an alliance with one of their parents, or with some of their siblings. Sometimes, "weaker" family members unite to counter the influence of a "stronger" family member. For example, they may recruit other siblings to help them strengthen their influence. In some cases, these group efforts simply coalesce; everyone involved wants the family to purchase a given product, so they band together to get it. In other cases, such cooperation may not be willingly granted and may require bullying.

Finally, family income also plays a role. Some low-income parents fear their children will be ridiculed or stigmatized if they show up to school "looking poor." They make sacrifices so they can buy their children brand-name clothes and backpacks, for example (Hamilton and Catterall 2006; Ghanem et al. 2017). Sometimes, it's the parents' own self-consciousness that motivates this buying behaviour, and other times, it's their children complaining that they will be made fun of. Either way, these parents may limit spending on themselves so they can spend more on their children. Others work extra shifts or get a second job so they can afford to meet their children's consumer wants.

In short, there is no single, simple story to describe children's influence processes. Families have different cultural environments, different power structures, and different compositions (e.g., numbers and groupings of siblings, by age.) Different socialization tendencies may also exist within the same family, varying with the ages, birth orders, genders, or personalities of the children in question. Children, therefore, have different opportunities to form coalitions with siblings and/or their parents to influence family purchase decisions.

Homes and Home Furnishings as Identity Signals

As units of consumption, families buy homes and furnish them in ways that bring comfort but also signal family status.

Homes and home furnishings commonly send messages about a family's identity and their aspirations (Hepworth 2002; Highmore 2019). This is only true, however, for the aspects of home life that families choose to share with others. For example, the well-maintained façade of a house—its so-called "curb appeal" — may send a message of middle-class success to neighbours living on the street or passersby from the broader community. Within the house, furniture, art, and décor tell people who have been invited inside something about the family's style and taste. Some families only welcome guests into certain areas of their houses (such as the living room and kitchen, for instance), cultivating those spaces with consumer goods that project a certain image. Other areas (such as the bedrooms and basement) may be off-limits. Guests are not invited to spend time in those spaces and they remain private and personal.

These personal spaces, however—and the consumer goods that fill them—are full of messages, too. As Daniel Miller puts it (in Clarke 2001: 14), "[I]n industrialized societies, most of what matters to people is happening behind the closed doors of the private sphere." Some people think of their homes as their private oases: places where they may be fully "themselves," free from the observations and judgments of others. Some may shape these spaces with consumer goods that help craft their own personal identities (see also Johnston 2018). They use private furnishings to remind themselves who they are, deep down.

People who live alone—for example, single adults—can make these purchases most freely. When couples move in together, people must compromise on the goods with which they outfit their homes. And when children are thrown into the mix, they often want spaces in which to express themselves as well. Some families allow their children to decorate their rooms as they wish. In other families, members of several generations share the same home. Grandparents, for example, may want to have a say in the family's kitchen renovation, the new sofa being purchased, or whether the new flooring should be carpet, hardwood, or tile. Sometimes, then, homes reflect the tastes and identities of multiple family members from several generations.

In our consumer society, home furnishings and homes themselves are meant to send signals to others about such matters as class, social status and wealth.

But at least some people, some of the time, are aware that guests may stray into private spaces intended only for family members. For example, during large dinner parties in large homes, the hosts may invite guests to use bathrooms other than those on the main floor designated specifically for guests. Some homeowners *want* guests to wander through their bedrooms and other "private" spaces, so those guests can see even more evidence of their refined taste.

Single adults also realize they will, at times, share their private spaces with others. Romantic partners, friends, and visiting family members may spend time in their apartments. These adults therefore craft their homes to tell these different visitors something about themselves. Perhaps they refuse to clean before their parents come over, to send a message of newfound independence and a disregard for the rules they had to live under in their parents' home. And perhaps they tidy and arrange these spaces in different ways when they are entertaining friends rather than dates.

The famed Italian tenor Enrico Caruso was presented with a special phonograph by the Victor Company on the occasion of his wedding in 1918. Sociologist F. Stuart Chapin would later classify phonographs as cultural possessions in his discussion of home consumer goods.

With that in mind, let's turn to some of the many consumer goods with which people outfit their homes. Early American sociologist F. Stuart Chapin (1928) was perhaps the first of many social scientists to study the role of homes and home furnishings as signals of social class. In his attempt to measure social class, he listed and categorized the many goods he found in various homes. Chapin filed these goods under two main headings: cultural possessions and material possessions (Chapin 1928: 100–101). He classified "books, newspapers, periodicals, telephone, radio, musical instruments, sheet music, phonographic records, phonograph, etc." as cultural possessions. If we were doing the same exercise today, we might remove "phonograph" from the list and add video-game consoles and the set-top box that streams Netflix.

On the other hand, Chapin defined material possessions as "household equipment." These included furniture, cooking utensils, cabinets, appliances and other goods that presumably have practical uses. But of course, these material possessions are "cultural," too. A British family's kitchen is likely stocked with forks and knives, while a Chinese family will keep chopsticks on hand. Many families update their furniture every so often as fashions change and new, stylish items come on the market. For example, the 1990s saw a swing towards more "modern" furniture (Leslie 2003; 2017). Traditional, ornamental furniture went out of fashion as consumers started distancing themselves from "excessive" 1980s furniture styles, sought simple, clean designs, and moved to lofts and condominiums in increasing numbers. So, cultural shifts in esthetics are reflected in our "household equipment" (Leslie 2003).

And, to Chapin's central point, even these material possessions signal a family's social class, making them cultural signs. For example, a lower-income family may opt to keep the builder's-grade appliances their newly purchased home came with, while a higher-income family will install luxury-brand ones. When they have visitors over to admire their newly upgraded home, they will expect their visitors to recognize the new Wolf rangehood (for example) as a Baudrillardian sign of wealth, status, and taste.

Since Chapin's time, many social researchers have studied home furnishings and come to similar conclusions. People furnish their homes in ways that reveal their social class position and their social aspirations. As Amaturo et al. (1987) report in a classic study of 100 Italian city homes, home furnishing styles tend to fall into two main categories. These are the functional items Chapin labelled material possessions or household equipment, and the goods families use to flaunt their status. Armaturo et al. found such ostentatious furnishing especially common in homes where the families were upwardly mobile or aspired to upward mobility (on this, see also Edwards 2017).

The use of home furnishings to express mobility aspirations is mirrored in, and perhaps influenced by, advertisements for such furnishings. In an early study, Belk and Pollay (1985) carried out a historical analysis of advertisements appearing in popular U.S. magazines between 1900 and 1980. They found that advertisements increasingly used themes that promoted luxurious home products. The ads also began depicting "consumption as an end in itself": something to indulge and take pleasure in, rather than a way to secure those pieces of "household equipment" that could enhance your family's well-being (see also Lavy et al. 2016 for a discussion of the portrayal of home gentrification.)

Box 4-4

The "Smart Kitchen"
The Future of Kitchen Technology

Many appliances we consider "standard" today only became widely available a few decades ago. For example, a majority of American families didn't have refrigerators until 1944 and it wasn't until the 1990s that more than 50 percent of U.S. families owned a dishwasher.

Today, cooking is easier and less time-consuming. But younger Canadians are cooking less. In our busy culture where dual-earning couples are the norm, many have turned to food delivery services like Uber Eats and Foodora. Before the COVID-19 outbreak, 54 percent of Canadians ate out once a week or more (Statistics Canada 2019). We can't yet say how (or if) the pandemic will have a lasting impact on cooking habits. But soaring sales of breadmakers suggests many people spent their days in lockdown in the kitchen.

Plenty of companies are working on "smart" gadgets: devices that make cooking easier to control and more efficient. Homeowners can control Wi-Fi-enabled appliances through their smartphones. Although these gadgets make certain aspects of cooking easier, they are also expensive. To really change Canadians' cooking habits, these products would need to be convenient as well as efficient, affordable, and multipurpose.

As mentioned, houses themselves, in addition to the furnishings inside them, are also used to signal social status (Gram-Hanssen and Bech-Danielssen 2004; Gram-Hanssen and Darby 2016). Consider the process of urban gentrification, in which middle-class people take over poorer areas and reconfigure them in their own image (Bridge 2007). They invest significant amounts of money in renovating—or even tearing down and rebuilding—existing homes and converting them into larger, flashier houses. Meanwhile, their "takeover" pushes the former lower-class residents out of the neighbourhood. In so doing, the middle class not only secures more space and comfort for their families; they also send a signal about social class, reminding those they displace that they are more powerful.

This brings us to a discussion of the relevance of social class in buying decisions—a topic we will discuss at length in another chapter. There is little doubt that class *aspirations* influence people's buying behaviour; we have seen this repeatedly. What is less clear is whether class *position* also influences people's buying behaviour, and if so, in what ways. In a much-cited paper, Henry (2002) considers whether higher-income people tend to buy for "expressive" (i.e., esthetic or symbolic) reasons while lower-income people tend to buy for "functional" or practical reasons. Using survey-data, Henry (424) confirmed that, as you trace consumption up the income ladder, people make more "expressive" purchases and are less concerned with the functionality of those purchases. Older working-class men are especially likely to prefer functional goods, while young professionals, both male and female, are especially likely to prefer expressive, esthetically pleasing goods.

On the other hand, a similar study by Creusen (2010: 31–32) fails to find such consistent or impressive results (likewise, Thompson et al. 2018). Creusen wonders whether occupation, income, or education is the best predictor of class-based buying behavior.

As is the case with other types of consumer behaviour, people may not consciously choose home furnishings to send signals to others. Socialization is not (always) an explicit or conscious process. Often, socialization teaches us to behave in ways that seem natural and normal but in fact, reflect the cultural values we have been discussing. Some consumers certainly *try* to send signals through their homes and home furnishings; but for others, their values, ideals, beliefs, assumptions, and socioeconomic status are simply *reflected* in their homes (Clarke 1991: 73; also, Valadez-Martinez 2019). For example, the host who tours her houseguests through her newly renovated master bathroom is consciously sending a message about her wealth, status, and taste. But the barista renting the only studio apartment he can afford may unintentionally communicate his precarious employment status and paycheque-to-paycheque lifestyle. Or he may consciously outfit the space with eclectic furniture and alternative artwork to distance himself from traditional middle-class aspirations.

Though they are often aware of the ways that outsiders will view their home, some consumers choose home decorations that are personal and private (Woodward 2003; Paavilainen et al. 2017). These consumer choices, some research finds, can be influenced by what's important to the family in question. Those with strong "family values" tend to emphasize comfort, relaxation, and protection (Madigan and Munro 1996; Mackay and Perkins 2019). They select consumer goods that suit these priorities. On the other hand, families that are concerned with "respectability" will maintain high housekeeping standards and select up-to-date technology and décor.

Others still see furnishings as a means of establishing a family identity within the home: a sense of who they are and what they care about. As mentioned above, many couples design, decorate, and arrange their household interiors together. They deliberate on how their shared spaces will be used and laid out: how the decorations, furniture, functional items, personal goods, and more will be placed within those spaces. Those spaces, routinely updated and rearranged, come to reflect their "shared identity" and the way their relationship has developed over time (Gorman-Murray 2006; 2018).

Home decorating can also contribute to an individual identity. For example, some women today continue to express themselves through the goods with which they adorn their homes (Gram-Hanssen and Bech-Danielssen 2004), and as the traditional gendered division of labour becomes somewhat less rigid, men increasingly express themselves in the same way. Young single men, for example, sometimes express their identities through so-called "bachelor pads." And some scholars have suggested that the move towards "modern" furniture could have been driven in part by men's growing interest in decorating their homes in somewhat spare, masculine ways (Leslie 2003).

The New Household

What happened to that traditional gendered division of domestic labour and how have these changes coincided with changes in family consumption?

For one, the solo male breadwinner is largely a thing of the past. In 1976, there were roughly 1,487,000 single-earner families with a stay-at-home parent in Canada (Statistics Canada 2017). By 2015, that number had dropped to 493,000. The gender of stay-at-home parents had also changed: "Families with a stay-at-home mother declined by 1,025,000, whereas those with a stay-at-home father increased by 32,000" (Statistics Canada 2017).

These role changes influence parents' behaviour as consumers (Li, Haws, and Griskevicius 2018). Family breadwinners, regardless of their gender, are typically more future-focused: they are less likely to consume to achieve immediate outcomes. On the other hand, family caregivers are usually more present-focused. They often consume in ways that do yield immediate outcomes, by buying services or products that benefit them in the short term. These caregivers spend the most time with their children and tend to do a great deal of housework. Likely, they see and feel the benefits of these short-term gains more than breadwinners.

In her book *The Sociology of Housework* (1974), British sociologist Ann Oakley explains that all of the women she studied hated housework. Yet they felt responsible for the home and their children. Even today, most married women work a "second shift": they come home from day jobs to a list of household chores. They feel pressured to take responsibility for the household, whether they hold a paid job or not (for an update of Oakley, see Kan and Laurie 2018.)

Women (and their families) use household objects in ways that reflect this gender inequality. For instance, studies by Martin Hand (2007a, 2007b) show that mate-

Television commercials from the 1960s and 1970s frequently portrayed housewives in dresses and high heels busily mopping floors and cleaning sinks. Today such images are re-created to ironic effect, as above, but the fact remains that in our society women are still responsible for a disproportionate share of housework, even if they work outside the home.

rial goods like stoves and fridges don't just serve practical functions. These products help people live up to cultural expectations as well. Their purpose and uses change accordingly over time and across different households.

Take the freezer as a case in point. For working parents with children enrolled in a variety of extracurricular activities, it can be challenging to prepare healthy meals from scratch every day. Freezers simplify meal prep. Parents can cook in bulk and freeze several portions for use later in the week. But when children leave the home (say, to go to university), some parents no longer feel the need to do this. Perhaps the freezer does not get used as much, or gets repurposed for other needs (say, storing frozen desserts). In other households, parents may feel strongly about feeding their family the most nutritious food. One mother in Hand's study grew her own produce and froze it. This let her always cook with healthy ingredients without having to shop every day. So, like many other consumer products, household "equipment" is used and valued differently in different households.

These domestic consumer products help people carry out family life as they think it should be. In our culture, mothers often feel pressed to feed their families nutritious food and keep up a family mealtime routine. But most women today are also expected to work for pay outside of the home. Freezers can help them do both. Dishwashers, washing machines, and dryers also make it easier to keep the family functioning. Thus many families try to make use of these technological "necessities," even in small rental apartments. Homeowners, for their part, expand and modify their houses to make room for the latest appliances.

Such renovations don't just boost productivity; they also send a message about our identities to friends, family, and other guests who visit our homes. Many families in Hand's study said they wanted "guest washrooms" that overnight visitors could have all to themselves (2007: 676). Even if they only hosted guests a few times a year, they were willing to spend large amounts of time and money designing their homes around those rare visits. By putting friends and family up in a "spare bedroom" complete with its own bathroom, these families showed they could afford more than the bare minimum. They signaled they had surplus funds, enough to build more living space than they needed every day.

Hand also studied kitchen renovations. We no longer use kitchens just for food preparation. When we have guests over, everyone knows the party's in the kitchen. Over time, as kitchens have become spaces for socializing, more families have renovated theirs to make them more spacious. Now, breakfast bars are not only for eating breakfast and islands are not only additional counter space for food preparation. These features also enlarge a home's entertainment space, allowing guests to admire and comment on the appliances, upgraded cupboards, lighting, and other features that signal the homeowner's status.

As cultural practices change gradually over time, so do our homes. We renovate them to show how well we're living up to the latest expectations. People learn, through observation and study, how to use their homes to show off their cultural savvy. Some children, for their part, watch parents spend their hard-earned money on "spare" bedrooms and bathrooms that get used only once a year. They come to think such housing surplus is necessary. Other children watch their parents struggle to pay the rent on a tiny apartment without enough bedrooms for everyone who lives there year-round. In short, children learn about the consumption of housing early in their lives.

Family Practices and Rituals

As mentioned above, though many women still feel pressured to cook, the traditional daily ritual of a family meal is reportedly becoming less common. Reliable statistics are hard to come by, but according to one poll by NPR, the Robert Wood Johnson Foundation, and the Harvard School of Public Health (in Braider 2019), 46 percent of those surveyed said eating together is hard to do on a regular basis, and fewer than half the parents surveyed said they had eaten together six or seven nights out of the previous week.

This change in family eating patterns has worrisome consequences. A review of the literature by Harrison et al. (2015: e96) finds "frequent family meals are inversely associated with disordered eating, alcohol and substance use, violent behaviour, and feelings of depression or thoughts of suicide in adolescents. There is a positive relationship between frequent family meals and increased self-esteem and school success." In other words, regular family meals predict good behaviour and mental well-being among family members.

Why does the seemingly simple ritual of eating together have such significant consequences? Socialization teaches us much more than how to nourish ourselves. The old ritual of eating together also teaches us about family solidarity, and helps families reaffirm their social connection. Family dinners are full of bonding opportunities. At family meals, people have a chance to tell (and re-tell) their favourite family stories, share their day-to-day experiences, discuss their plans, get into arguments, and then resolve them. Around the dinner table, family members use nicknames, inside jokes, and terms of endearment that reinforce their connection (Fiese, Foley, and Spagnola 2006). In these ways, family members strengthen their emotional bonds during mealtime gatherings. And when such bonding is recalled at a later time, it gives us a sense of belonging: that we have a safe refuge waiting for us in the family home.

As to the consumer goods that serve as props for these bonding occasions, some people have definite ideas about what constitutes a family dinner. However, these ideas vary somewhat from one family to another, and depend on the occasion. In a study of ideas about domestic dinner in suburban Norway, Bugges and Almas (2008) found a variety of social and cultural conventions that frame eating practices (see also Makela and Neva 2019). In interviews, young mothers identified three distinct models for "proper" dinners: traditional, trendy, and therapeutic. A proper dinner can be traditional, like mom used to make. It can be trendy and stylish, including new and fashionable foods. Or it can be therapeutic, made only from healthy ingredients. Thus, a family dinner is only "good" or "bad"—done "right" or "wrong"—in relation to the model it intends to follow.

Family meals also provide an opportunity for generational continuity. Dishes, recipes, and blessings pass down from one generation to the next. Jokes, arguments, and topics of conversation are repeated or continued from one meal to the next, reinforcing family identity. Rituals around preparing the food remind people of their respective roles in the family, as well as family traditions. For example, the mother may be responsible for the grocery shopping and cooking, the children accountable for setting the table, and the father for cleaning the dirty dishes. This division of labour helps people feel like they all have a place in the family. Each member has a role and responsibility that contributes to the group's functioning.

Even leftovers can be part of the ritual. Family members often have an unspoken agreement to save those leftovers, store them, and reheat them for the next day. This routine may even draw members of the family closer together (Cappellini 2009; 2016). People usually eat leftovers to save time and money. Instead of picking up fresh ingredients every day and preparing each meal from scratch, they cook in bulk. Often this strategy is part of a family's collective effort to be thrifty and save up for their shared desires—say, for a family vacation.

Leftovers can also build family bonds because there's a shared sacrifice involved. Families often eat leftovers after a festive or ritualized event such as Christmas or Thanksgiving. During the lead-up to these special events, family bonds are forged and tested in different ways. For example, mom may not have time to make breakfast every morning in December because she's too busy shopping for Christmas dinner. So, the rest of the family fends for themselves. And when mom is exhausted on December 26 from entertaining the entire extended family, the children agree to eat leftover turkey.

Of course, not every family participates in these rituals. To some degree, family dinners are, increasingly, an aspirational ritual. Many families cannot and/or do not wish to prepare and eat their meals together. For example, parents who do shift work may not be home at dinner time and the children may cook (or order in) their own meals. Other families prefer to eat their meals in front of the TV, on their way to work, or even alone, in their bedrooms. As mentioned, frequent family meals carry some benefits and protect against negative outcomes. But that does not mean that people who do not eat together are doomed to a life of pathology and poor health. Family mealtimes are beneficial because they provide opportunities for social bonding. However, some families find other ways to bond socially.

In short, different families have varying (and particular) rites and rituals that they perform before, after, and during mealtimes. Typically, they have many other rites and ceremonies associated with bedtime, homework, extracurricular activities, vacations and holidays, and other occasions. Some of these rituals, such as gift-giving on birthdays and holidays, introduce children to consumption. Sharing in these rituals gives family members a sense of belonging and purpose, by displaying and reinforcing their role in the family.

By teaching us to think such rituals are normal and natural, our families also teach us how to be consumers. Childhood socialization teaches us how to be thrifty, how to outfit our homes, and what foods to buy. It teaches us how we're expected to contribute to a household, depending on our age and gender. And it teaches us to connect some of our most precious family memories— birthdays, reunions, religious holidays, and more— to rituals of consumption.

Two-Way Socialization

Parents don't just socialize children; children also socialize their parents. For example, many parents think their children are technology experts (Lobo and Brennan 2011; Sharma and Panackal 2018). Parents may turn to their children for advice when it's time for them to buy a computer, phone, TV, and the like. And, because males are often perceived to be more knowledgeable about technology than females, parents are generally inclined to seek their son's opinion in particular.

Another example of parent-child buying behavior is the shopping relationship between mothers and daughters. Mothers teach their daughters to buy certain types of products, but daughters also teach their mothers (Gavish et al. 2008; Getina et al. 2018). Many mothers say they deeply value their teenage daughters' opinion about the clothes they buy. Often teenagers serve as trendsetters for their parents. At the same time, many mothers are role models for their adolescent daughters. So mothers and daughters frequently shop together for fashion items in the same stores. As well, many adolescent daughters occasionally borrow their mothers' clothes, jewelry, and shoes.

Box 4-5
Teenage Daughters Influence their Mothers

The "Mini-Me" trend of mothers and daughters wearing matching outfits started when celebrities like Kim Kardashian, Beyoncé, and Victoria Beckham, and their respective daughters, posed in identical designer outfits. More affordable clothing brands jumped on board. Stores such as H&M now sell outfits that fit both mother and daughter.

Mothers have more control over what their daughters wear when they're young. As their daughters grow older, they develop their own sense of style, influenced by what they see celebrities wearing in the media and what their classmates wear at school. Eventually, teenage daughters come to have a significant influence on what clothes and products their *mothers* buy—a sort of "reverse socialization" (Pappas 2011). Mothers who care about fashion and want to look hip and cool are likely to copy what their daughters wear.

Presumably, these mothers are trying to use clothing to project the appearance of youth our culture values so much. Of course, many teenagers want their mothers to dress nicely—but not in the same type of clothes they themselves wear. Adults also have plenty to say about these "20–40 mums": women in their forties who dress as if they are 20.

Parents and children may also reinforce each other's shopping preferences. For example, they may respond similarly to price discounts and other promotions (Schindler et al. 2014). Young adults and their parents may also hold similar preferences for particular kinds of transactions: say, coupons over advertised discounts. Perhaps this is because of socialization: after all, parents have taught their children to consume in these particular ways.

Such two-way socialization is more likely to happen in some families than others. Children who are seen as knowledgeable are more likely to influence their parents (Watne and Winchester

2011; Baia 2019). Some parents see their children as "experts" on certain products and services (though not others) and are therefore willing to learn from them. In other words, reciprocal socialization happens in families that allow it. Parents who see their children as immature or irresponsible are much less likely to learn from them.

Similarly, two-way socialization happens more often in families that communicate often and effectively (Martin 2013). For example, some families shop together, interact with each other while shopping, and enjoy the time they spend together shopping. These families are more likely to influence each other's purchases than those who don't shop together and interact less often at home. Indeed, some children and teens actively try to hide their shopping habits and purchases if they think their parents will disapprove.

Those who do shop together explicitly try to influence each other's purchases. One study found that different "types" of mothers try to shape their children's consumption in different ways (Neeley and Coffey 2007; but see also Lee et al. 2020). First, "diva mothers" pay close attention to advertisements and encourage their children to buy the latest trends. On the other hand, "struggler mothers" resent media and marketing influences. They think advertising makes their children crave products they cannot afford and do not need. Third, "balancer mothers" use marketplace influences, such as advertising, as educational opportunities. They have the financial means to buy their children the things they want but urge their children to study advertisements so they can become more independent consumers. Fourth, "protector mothers" mistrust outside influences, including the media and advertising. They focus on, and encourage their children to focus on, educational, psychological, and emotional goals, not commercial ones. These mothers accordingly express strong attitudes against advertising and consumerism more generally.

All "types" of mothers have some degree of influence on their children's—especially their daughters'—perceptions of themselves and their bodies. In our culture, we hold particular ideas about physical beauty, such as slender figures for women. Unsurprisingly then, many mothers and daughters discuss their bodies and dieting at length. Through these interactions, mothers socialize their daughters to accept or reject these ideas about beauty. Then, as daughters grow up, they begin to socialize their mothers in turn (Ogle and Damhorst 2003; Ogle et al. 2017; Ogle and Park 2018). For example, both mothers and daughters may validate each other's appearance by saying things like, "No, you're not fat," or "You're just fine the way you are." At other times, they may encourage each other to stick to their weight-loss goals. Mothers and daughters thus shape each other's attitudes towards their bodies, and the actions they take to change them.

In many cases, mothers are more heavy-handed in socializing their daughters (Ogle and Damhorst 2003; Ogle et al. 2017; Ogle and Park 2018). Indeed, some mothers push hard to instill specific ideas, attitudes, and behaviours in their daughters. They want them to be slim so they will be accepted, or they want them to feel confident and not care what others think about their appearance. In trying to impart these values, mothers often model certain attitudes or behaviours themselves. They may purposefully strike up a conversation about weight loss, for example, or avoid purchases and other behaviours they know would send their daughter the wrong message.

In sum, family socialization is often reciprocal. Our parents shape us and we shape them. In this way, people learn and refine their consumer behaviour over the course of time.

Final Thoughts

In this chapter, we learned that consumers are raised, not born. Everyone in our culture is socialized, from birth, to be a consumer, because it is impossible not to consume when you live in our consumer society. This socialization begins in a child's family, and for many decades this family continues to exercise an influence over buying behaviour.

Children begin to learn about consumer behaviour through observation and by participating in their family's shopping decisions. However, the right to participate in these consumer activities varies widely, from family to family, country to country, culture to culture, and according to the age of the child and the item to be purchased. It also varies with the child's position and power in the family.

Some families socialize their children to be more materialistic consumers than others. Different "types" of parents (e.g., authoritative versus neglectful) make different decisions about their children's introduction to consumption, with some allowing co-shopping, purchase influence, and media exposure. These decisions shape the type of consumers their children will grow up to be. So, there is a heavy demand for consumer goods in our society because we learn, as children and throughout our lives, to make such demands.

Some parents might say that learning process brings out the worst in their children. Plenty have experienced children pestering them to buy the latest toy or treat. Parents who have experienced the wrath of a toddler denied—especially in public—would say that such behaviour is undesirable and antisocial. That said, as we saw in this chapter, many children's consumer behaviour matures quickly. By the time they are around seven, many turn to more grown-up tactics in pressuring their parents to buy. Tantrums are still thrown, to be sure, but many children eventually learn that calm, rational requests are more effective in getting them the products they want, much of the time.

Perhaps part of the reason some think that people are unhealthily preoccupied with consumer goods is that this preoccupation is lifelong. As we saw in this chapter, people are socialized to consume from birth. As children, we learn to signal our personal and family identities, status, and aspirations through consumer goods (albeit to different degrees and in somewhat different ways, depending on factors such as income). To gain the goods that send these signals, we learn to work harder, be more ambitious, and make sacrifices. These qualities, though admirable, can be taken to extremes. Sometimes, we value them at the expense of other things that are valued in our culture, such as kindness, family loyalty, and social sensitivity. So our cultural preoccupation with consumer goods, which starts in our childhood family, may be unhealthy if it distracts us from other pursuits for our entire lives.

Discussion Questions

1. There are six stages of family life. Each group has its specific needs and interests. What are some examples of needs and interests that characterize each stage? How might marketers use this knowledge in creating advertisements?
2. Think about how household technology has changed the everyday lifestyles of families. In what ways has technology brought the family closer together? In what ways has it distanced family members?
3. In this chapter, we learned that children have a certain amount of influence on their parents' purchasing decisions. In some cultures, children have more influence compared to other cultures. What are some characteristics of different cultures that determine how much influence a child has on their parents?

Quick Quiz

1. What is social reproduction?
   a. Processes a society uses to maintain and transform its social order, formations, and relations
   b. The constant changing of social norms in a society
   c. The responsibility that parents have in socializing their children
   d. The reproduction of social inequality
   e. The reproduction of social trends in a population

2. Without class consciousness, we are likely to suffer from _____.
   a. Social reproduction
   b. Privatism
   c. False consciousness
   d. Consumerism
   e. Social disorganization

3. What is co-shopping?
   a. When people shop at co-operative associations
   b. When people are assisted by sales clerks in stores
   c. When customers own shares in a store that they are shopping at
   d. When parents go shopping with their children
   e. When people go on bus trips to visit factory outlet malls

4. What are the three distinct dinner models for "proper" meals?
   a. Traditional, modern, and therapeutic
   b. Conventional, popular, and therapeutic
   c. Traditional, popular, and innovative
   d. Classic, simple, and innovative
   e. Traditional, trendy, and therapeutic

5. What are the four types of mothers who try to shape their children's consumption in different ways?

a. Dramatic mothers, Struggler mothers, Harmonious mothers, and Protector mothers

b. Materialistic mothers, Traditional mothers, Balancer mothers, and Protector mothers

c. Diva mothers, Conflicted mothers, Balancer mothers, and Defensive mothers

d. Diva mothers, Struggler mothers, Balancer mothers, and Protector mothers

e. Dramatic mothers, Conflicted mothers, Equal mothers, and Defensive mothers

The answers to the Quick Quiz are provided at the end of the book.

For Further Reading

The Fall of Public Man by Richard Sennett

In this book, Sennett explores the decline in public culture and the rise of privatism. He analyzes the consequences created by this imbalance.

The Polish Peasant in Europe and America by Florian Znaniecki and W.I. Thomas

Using personal documents, The Polish Peasant in Europe and America studies Polish immigrants and their families between 1918 and 1920. It reports the immigrant children's role in teaching their parents skills such as reading and writing.

The Sociology of Housework by Ann Oakley

Oakley interviews housewives in London and discovers their attitudes towards housework. She learns about their daily lives and the struggles they face in balancing their responsibilities.

Key Terms

Family

Household

Stages of family life

Unit of consumption

Unit of production

Chapter Five
Teaching the Culture of Desire: Schools

Learning Objectives

After reading this chapter, you will be able to:

✓ Assess the role of schools in socializing students to consume responsibly.
✓ Critique school uniforms as a commodification of school disorder and poor performance.
✓ See how consumption in school cafeterias impacts health and academic outcomes.
✓ Consider the neoliberal evolution of education into a consumer product.

Like families, schools can play a critical role in raising the next generation of consumers. They are particularly critical agents of socialization in that they bring together large groups of peers for prolonged periods of time, giving youth ample opportunities to observe, imitate, and influence one another's consumption habits.

In principle, schools could be the most important agents of consumer socialization. That is because, historically, schools have been the institutions with license to intervene in the lives of young people. For over a century, governments have used schools to supervise, control, and indoctrinate—as well as educate—young people. As institutions in the public domain, schools are subject to state, political, and communal influence in a way that families and media are not. Importantly, schools have been used to promote a wide range of civic, religious, and public health concerns over the years.

More recently, as we will see, some have sought to discipline young people through the use of school uniforms, while others have sought to correct social inequality through breakfast and lunch programs. And, as we will also see, schools have not been slow to market themselves as consumer products in the public realm. In this way, they have taught consumer values by example. Increasingly, schools have been held out, and have held themselves out, as instruments of upward mobility for less-advantaged people and, for this reason, deserving of great personal and family sacrifice.

So, in view of all this school activism, it is surprising to find how little they have engaged in the formal teaching of consumer behaviour and its dangers. In this chapter, we will look especially at secondary and post-secondary schools. We will ask what schools explicitly and intentionally teach their students about consumer behaviour. Then, by examining three specific cases—school uniforms, school lunches, and school tuition costs—we will ask what schools implicitly and unintentionally teach their students about consumer behaviour.

Defining Our Terms

We might begin by remembering the origins of the word "education." It comes from Latin roots meaning "to lead out of." The clear implication is that education is meant to lead people out of ignorance and into knowledge. This is the intended and stated role of schools—or, as theorist Robert Merton called it, schools' **manifest function**.

Today, however, many take a narrower, more practical view. Many see the manifest function of schools as teaching information and skills that will prepare students for adult work and active citizenship. In other words, schools develop children's human capital. **Human capital** includes skills like the ability to read, write, and carry out numeric calculations (Goldin 2016; Lim et al. 2018; Marginson 2019). People with more human capital not only have more skills, but also have the academic credentials and workplace experiences that such skills make possible. They are more likely than other candidates to get jobs, keep jobs, and rise into well-paying, secure positions.

Over time, human capital has become more and more necessary for occupational success. Today, it also encompasses a larger variety of skills than it did in the past, so people need more formal education to become economically independent. These human capital skills are especially critical in what has been called an information society and a knowledge economy. An **informa-**

tion society is dominated by information technology and focused on jobs in knowledge industries (Martin 2017; Bradley 2017). Arguably, all modern societies can be considered information societies because of their reliance on information for communication and control.

Our information society is fueled by what some call the **knowledge economy**. The knowledge economy uses knowledge as the primary tool to produce new economic benefits and increase existing ones (Unger 2019; Hadad 2017; Gandini 2016). Examples of knowledge-economy companies include Facebook, Google, Amazon, Uber, and AirBnB. Sociologist Daniel Bell (1980) noted that in transitioning to an information society and a knowledge economy, our workforce transitioned from manual (or blue-collar) work to office (or white-collar) work. The knowledge economy has thus redefined the skills and abilities that are valued (and demanded) in the workforce. Today, we value above all the ability to use information, problem-solve, and innovate, as opposed to the ability to, say, lift and move heavy objects.

Knowledge industries need smart, highly-educated workers. Knowledge workers are educated to a level where they can be independent and flexible decision-makers, as well as experts in their specialized fields. The most highly trained of these workers are often clustered in certain key locations, like research universities and high-tech industrial parks such as those in Silicon Valley. Schools are expected to provide the human capital that will prepare people for work in our knowledge economy.

Second, however, schools also play an unintended and unstated role, but one that is no less important: what Merton would call their **latent function**. The latent function, or hidden role, of schools today is to connect young people socially. This connectedness provides them with what Pierre Bourdieu, James Coleman, and others called **social capital**.

Unlike the "hard skills" of human capital, social capital includes social, non-economic resources people use to pursue economic and cultural capital (Dubos 2017; Rogošić and Baranović 2016; Engbers et al. 2017). That is, people use their social capital to find jobs and improve their careers, among other things. A classic study of middle-level managers in the Boston area by Mark Granovetter showed how valuable social capital can be (1970; see also Granovetter 2018). He found that people's job opportunities are improved significantly when they have a large network of acquaintances who are not kin or close friends. Many people start building such networks in college, secondary school, or even primary school, and continue expanding them in the workplace.

Social networks are patterns of personal relations among individuals based on face-to-face interaction or mediated communication (Borgatti et al. 2018; Fracassi 2017; Hurlbert et al. 2017). They consist of friendship or support links between people who are connected by family, neighbourhood, workplace, recreation, and, today, the Internet. Anthropologist Alfred Radcliffe-Brown first introduced the idea of social networks in 1940. Traditionally, anthropologists and sociologists focused on kinship and friendship networks, because these were the most common in small, preindustrial communities. However, the arrival of the Internet stimulated the exploration of the concept of network societies. We will have more to say about social networks, online relations, and virtual communities in later chapters.

In schools, students gain friends as well as acquaintances: peer groups and reference groups. Both are important for socializing young people into consumer roles. A **peer group** is a collection of people who share a common characteristic (Kelly 2017; Braun and Bierman 2019; Ellis et al. 2018). Typically, it's a small group of friends with shared interests, activities, and values. In the school context, members of peer groups belong to the same age group and are in the same academic grade. We will talk more about peers and peer groups in a later chapter on young people as consumers.

A **reference group** is a group that a person uses as a standard in forming opinions, attitudes, or patterns of behaviour. These groups set standards that people use as positive or negative models (Singer 2017; Fernandes and Panda 2018; Hayakawa and Venieris 2016). People often copy the behaviour of a positive model—for example, a friend or celebrity they respect. They avoid copying, and express contempt for, the behaviour of a negative model—a person they hold in low regard.

Peer groups and reference groups play an important role in the socialization of young people.

People also use reference groups as a basis for judging their own social standing. They measure their own appearance, income, or skill against the norms of a group to which they belong or aspire to belong to. These comparison groups play an important role when people evaluate their lives. Feelings of deprivation, for example, mainly arise when people compare themselves to others who are obviously living superior or easier lives.

As children grow, they begin looking outside their family home to their peers for guidance. In doing so, they position and define themselves in comparison to other group members. These reference groups help them to decide, for instance, whether to actively take part in, question, or object to our consumer society. More concretely, they help young people decide what to buy, how to dress, and how to act with members of the opposite sex.

Finally, some social researchers have called attention to another latent role of schools: their ideological role in preparing young people for a life of obedience, subordination, and inequality. From this perspective, schools prepare most people—especially lower-income students—to be passive citizens, willing workers, and eager consumers. Some sociologists propose that most of the effect schooling has on occupational and earning attainment is a result of the social traits it builds, not the cognitive human capital it teaches. These are traits like the ones Annette Lareau studied and we discussed in an earlier chapter: the ambition, competitiveness, and self-confidence instilled in children by middle-class parents, to name a few.

These social, non-cognitive variables have a huge impact on students' academic outcomes. Research shows that, in evaluating student performance, primary and secondary school teachers look for two things. They look for mastery of the course materials—cognitive performance. But they also look for good work habits, class participation, effort, and organization—non-cognitive or social performance. These good work habits prove to have a stronger effect on grades than mastery of the material (Farkas 1996; see also Garcia 2016; West et al. 2016; Smithers et al. 2018). As a result, variations in grade attainment across gender, ethnicity, and income groups can be largely attributed to these social skills.

Such **social skills** also affect workplace success. As mentioned, research suggests that social, non-cognitive abilities are more important than cognitive skills in achieving success on the job. Employers look for and reward workers who show energy, reliability, collegiality, and trustworthiness—qualities learned as children at home and in school. Bowles and Gintis (2002; see also Carlson 2019; Posselt and Grodsky 2017) find that only 20 per cent of the effect of schooling on earnings reflects cognitive skill (as measured by an IQ test, for example). The implication is that nearly 80 per cent of the "school effect" on income is a result of social, non-cognitive traits.

Schools as Teachers of Responsible Consumption

Schools—both secondary and post-secondary—have made relatively few efforts at consumer education. Ideally, schools should teach children how to consume responsibly: that is, in ways that maximize their well-being. This need for school-based consumer education has been widely recognized for decades.

For example, in 2013, the Office of Consumer Affairs (an agency of the Government of Canada) produced a literature review titled "Programs in Consumer Studies/Sciences." It recognized that little progress had been made in consumer education to date. Thirty years prior, Kroll and Hunt (1980) had highlighted the field of consumer studies as "an emerging discipline," and thought consumer studies would evolve into a field of its own, with unique elements setting it apart from other fields. However, by 2013, only the University of Guelph and Laval University had developed programs devoted to studying consumerism.

In 2012, Canadian researcher Chris Arthur worried about the role of "consumer education" as a response to what he called the "neoliberal crisis." Arthur saw the teaching of consumer subjects—especially, financial literacy—as an effort to shift blame for increased economic turmoil and inequality onto ordinary citizens. Said another way, he thought it was part of an attempt to make individual consumers responsible for their financial welfare, despite the "constantly changing financial marketplace."

Whatever its purpose, consumer education had not gotten far in Canada by 2016, when Sue L.T. McGregor reported on the results of a cross-Canadian survey of courses loosely considered "consumer education." She found 64 secondary-school courses that taught material related to consumption, most of them courses in home economics and family studies, social studies, math, and business. Nearly three-quarters of the consumer material taught in these courses had to do with resource management. Nearly three-quarters of these courses were not offered until senior high school. Further, courses and approaches varied greatly across different regions, subjects, and grade levels. The problem, McGregor suggested, was a lack of political will: a lack of desire to educate students consistently across Canada on matters of consumer behaviour.

In the years that followed, media increasingly called for and reported steps towards more student consumer awareness and financial literacy. In the *Financial Post*, reporter Garry Marr (2016) surveyed Canada's national financial literacy programs, calling for more action. On Global News (2017), Laurel Gregory reported "Canadian kids need to learn about debt and financial literacy." Gradually, the provinces took action. Charlene Rooke reported in *The Globe and Mail* (2017) "[h]ow B.C. children are learning financial literacy from K to 12." Geoff Johnson (in the *Times Colonist*, 2018) reported that "[f]inancial literacy [was] on new B.C. curriculum." In July 2019, the Ontario government introduced a new Grade 10 Career Studies curriculum that would include some information on financial literacy. For example, it would ask students to think how they would fund their first year of life after completing high school.

In short, there has been an explosion of talk about consumer education, and plans in several provinces, especially British Columbia and Ontario, to do something about it. However, so far, very little has, in fact, been done.

Where consumer education has been introduced, the research is at best mixed as to whether it has any positive results. Pinto (2017) identified some of the key conceptual and organizational difficulties that beset the planning of such courses in Canada. Teaching young students about stock markets, mortgages, long-term savings, and other complex topics has been ineffective in the past, Pinto notes. Instead, financial literacy courses must be suitable for the age group being educated. They must teach students about topics that are immediately relevant to them and use illustrative activities that help them apply their learning.

Furthermore, the question remains as to what consumer education should actually consist of—skills students would find useful in navigating a consumer society (e.g., financial literacy), or a critique of the consumer society and its deleterious social and environmental effects, with a view to encouraging students to consider whether there are other, better ways of organizing society. A pioneer in this area, George Moschis (1979; see also Moschis 2019), wrote a classic article on this subject four decades ago. According to Moschis, school programs in the 1970s that tried to teach consumer behaviour were not succeeding. He called on educators to re-evaluate the content of consumer education materials and the goals of consumer education in general.

For Moschis, materials and practices designed to teach adolescents how to be effective consumers should stress socially desirable consumer choices. These may include comparison-shopping and rational ways of making decisions. They should show students how to find and use suitable sources of consumer information. Students should learn about their legal rights as consumers, he said, and learn how to budget and manage their finances. Finally, educators should know the greatest need for consumer education exists among adolescents from lower-income families and target their efforts suitably.

For Moschis and many others, consumer education is part of what one might call "practical education." As early as the 1940s, educators were thinking about how to make curricula more relevant to "the real world." Consider, for example, the Canadian Research Committee on Practical Education. In the postwar era, they sought to develop a high school curriculum that taught Canadian youth consumer information, thus setting them up for future success as consumers and workers (Rollwagen 2016).

A team at Purdue University in the U.S. similarly tried to re-imagine consumer education in the 1970s and 1980s (McGregor 2015). They recommended three types of teaching. Type I would teach instrumental consumer skills in the private sector—that is, it would teach students what to buy, how to comparison-shop, and when and where to purchase. Type II would teach students how to make wise consumer choices in the public sector—for instance, how to buy health care, housing, public transportation, insurance, and recreational services. Type III would provide a political backdrop to all of this, by explaining the rules, laws, and policies that influence the conduct of firms in the private sector.

Finally, Danes et al. (1999) suggested financial planning courses that would help students learn how to consume responsibly (see also Deenanath et al. 2019). Students would learn how to use credit cards and savings accounts carefully. In addition, they would study the effects of consumption that bring about climate change. As curriculum documents in Ontario and elsewhere show, these objectives persist today.

But how well are schools performing these tasks today? Often, the answer is, not well. Some schools and provinces don't try at all; consumption does not figure in their curricula. Others try

---

Box 5-1

Financial Literacy in School Curricula

Most teenagers follow the example of their family and friends in making decisions about how they spend their money. Yet this information from close-to-home can lead to bad spending habits. Young people need to acquire financial literacy. BMO reported that millennials are held back by bad spending and saving habits (BMO Wealth Management 2017). The report noted that many millennials stated that non-financial matters were more important than saving money for the future (Global News 2017).

Many Canadians, of all ages, subscribe to finance-related fallacies: 51 percent of respondents in a recent survey thought that they would pay no interest on a cash advance as long as they paid off the credit card balance in full by the due date (Global News, 2017). Moreover, 20 percent thought banks could issue credit cards without the customer's prior approval.

As noted, Canada has recently started to create financial literacy programs to deal with a growing consumer debt problem (*The Globe and Mail* 2019). In Ontario, the revamped career studies course focuses on helping students learn how to budget, understand taxes, and set aside money for the future (CTV News 2019). But even with the new curriculum, it will take time for students to make use of their newly acquired knowledge in everyday life.

to teach students to be prudent consumers but haven't put in much time and effort (Benn 2004). As a result, schools are still not an important source of consumer socialization, compared to peers, families, and media.

In Quebec, Lachance and Legault (2007; see also Deb and Lodh 2016; Zolkeplee et al. 2018; Kiełczewski et al. 2017) compared how different agents of socialization affect the consumer behaviour of students. According to the students themselves, the strongest influencers are peers. Most students crave acceptance and approval from their friends, so they pay attention to their peers' views. Media are the second most influential agents of socialization, mostly by affecting students' attitudes about available consumer products. In third place are parents. Lachance and Legault point out that most of the youth they studied still live with their parents, and parents still exerted a big influence because they were always around.

Lachance and Legault found that schools did little to teach consumer skills, according to the youth they interviewed. Some college courses focused on related skills, like budgeting and comparing prices before purchasing. However, college instructors spent little time in class teaching students about credit and over-consumption, or how to be critical of advertising. In other words, schools still put a low priority on teaching students about responsible consumption.

Easy access to credit and stagnating incomes in most Western countries have made financial literacy even more important today.

The Importance of Financial Literacy

Yet responsible consumption may be even more important today than it was forty years ago, when Moschis first put forward his recommendations. Today, more and more young people have credit cards and go into debt because they don't know how to use these cards responsibly. They may not understand interest charges, and few may have learned to budget or save a portion of their earnings. Second, many youth don't understand how to invest money. Few parents, let alone students, have started saving for their retirement. This is especially true of people with lower incomes. In short, there is a lack of financial literacy in Canada and schools are doing little to improve matters.

Financial illiteracy is especially common among older adults, racialized populations, and people with less-than-average levels of education (Lusardi and Mitchell 2011a). It is also common among low-income earners who are financially vulnerable: precisely the people with the greatest need to understand saving, credit cards, and retirement planning (Martin 2007; Martin et al. 2017). Finally, studies find that girls and women have less information about financial topics than boys and men, and less confidence in their financial judgment. Research by Danes and Huberman (2007; see also Amagir et al. 2019) suggests this gendered ignorance can be reduced with a suitable curriculum.

Even slight improvements in financial literacy have noticeable effects on the likelihood a person will plan for retirement. That said, like any other knowledge, financial knowledge decays with time. One study found that even significant learning opportunities, involving hours of teaching, no longer affected spending or saving behaviour just twenty months later (Fernandes et al. 2013). So, though consumer education is valuable, it needs to be revisited and updated regularly.

Ideally, then, consumer and financial education needs to start early, in primary and secondary schools, and continue through college and into the workplace. Some research suggests that higher education courses on this subject have measurably valuable results. For example, college students who took a seminar on financial responsibility finished the course with more financial knowledge and more responsible attitudes toward credit (Borden et al. 2007; Wagner 2019). They say they also plan to engage in significantly more effective financial behaviors and fewer risky financial behaviors in future.

Four problems beset the large-scale adoption of consumer literacy courses. First is the problem of demonstrating, with compelling data, that these courses are useful enough to warrant curriculum change. Largely, the problem is methodological. Most of the studies done to date, being non-experimental, have a limited ability to draw strong conclusions about cause and effect (Hastings et al. 2013). Of the few studies that have used experimental methods, the evidence that financial education improves financial results is still inconclusive; more research is needed.

A second problem is that many teachers may be not be motivated to teach this material or trained in how to teach it well. Some jurisdictions have no clearly defined standards of excellence for financial-education effectiveness or teacher preparation (McCormick 2008; Compen et al, 2019). A third problem is that most financial literacy courses are consumer products themselves. At the college or university level, they cost students hundreds or even thousands of dollars in tuition. People on a tight budget may be reluctant to take such courses.

A fourth, larger problem with consumer education is unclarity about its scope. Researchers today propose an ever-increasing number of educational goals, especially around the ethical and environmental effects of consumerism. For example, some suggest consumer education today must not only teach practical skills (like comparison-shopping and financial literacy). In their view, it must also help students critically analyze the consumer society (McGregor 2015). Such courses, they say, should prepare students to stand up for the environment, for exploited workers, and for themselves. In short, consumer courses would help young people confront the moral and ethical implications of consumption (McGregor 2015). By contrast, other commentators would see these goals as falling outside the scope of basic teaching on consumer issues.

In part, that is because most high school students, and even many postsecondary students, still rely on their parents financially. They don't see how consumer skills apply to them when they aren't earning a significant income or making many costly consumer choices. Until they have significant buying decisions to make, they don't see the need to learn about responsible consumerism. On the other hand, some adolescents may feel they already know what they need to about good consumer behaviour (Batat 2009; 2019). This may be true for students who have jobs and pay for a lot of their own things, but it is not likely true for a majority.

In short, educators are far from figuring out what consumer education should contain and how it can best be delivered to people at different educational levels.

The Debate over School Uniforms

One type of school-related consumption has received much attention in the past 25 years, and that is the issue of school uniforms. Uniforms have been required in European schools for centuries. There, they were considered a mark of distinction, signaling the status of children from high-standing families who could afford costly private schools, and marking them off from lower-status children. However, North American schools tended to reject uniforms, until recently.

Some of those in favour believe uniforms foster regimentation and that regimentation improves student performance and school safety. Baumann and Krskova (2016) analyzed the Organization for Economic Co-operation and Development's (OECD's) Program for International Student Assessment data. They focused on several aspects of school discipline—noise levels, class start time, students listening well, students working well, and teacher waiting time—in five geographic regions. The results showed differences in school discipline across the five regions, with eastern Asia showing the highest levels of discipline. This region was also the most likely to require school uniforms.

In this research, then, a high degree of student discipline was apparently correlated with the wearing of uniforms. Students listened better, and their teachers had to wait less time for them to quiet down. They also worked harder and, in turn, performed better academically. With this in mind, the authors recommend educators keep uniforms where they are already in use and consider introducing uniforms where they are not.

Others in favour say uniforms help children from different socioeconomic backgrounds feel like equals. As mentioned, clothes are often Baudrillardian signs: they can signal the type of person you want to be taken for and help you craft your personal image. Children from lower-income households may not be able to afford clothing that sends peers the signals they want to send. Even children from higher-income households may not have much say in the clothes their parents buy them. For all of these students, uniforms may be a blessing because they take clothing differences out of the picture.

If all students are required to wear the same clothing, they all send more or less the same signals with that clothing. In that sense, uniforms "level the playing field" for students of different economic backgrounds (Bodine 2003b; Jones 2017). True, uniforms are still expensive, placing an initial financial burden on low-income parents. However, the one-time expense may be easier to bear than the constant pressure of having to update a child's wardrobe with the changing trends in "fast fashion." So perhaps students who wear uniforms are less likely to exclude or be excluded

Research suggests adoption of school uniforms may result in lower financial stress for parents as well as helping make students from varying financial backgrounds feel more equal. At the same time, when students attending elite private schools wear uniforms, a clear signal is sent that they belong to well-off families capable of affording private school tuition and fees.

on the basis of their clothing and (in turn) economic background. And those same uniforms may help relieve the financial stress placed on parents.

Clothes are not, of course, the only consumer goods that send signals about students' socio-economic status. When schools were closed and classes were held online to help slow the spread of COVID-19, the playing field changed. With students expected to "attend" class by videoconference, their homes were visible in the background—large, comfortable bedrooms in some cases, or perhaps a home office or media room. Others were in cramped apartments. For those students, the option to hide their real surroundings with virtual backgrounds may have helped.

Before COVID-19, even those who were required to wear uniforms could display their wealth (or lack thereof) through many other consumer items. For example, some students are driven to school in expensive cars, or show up driving their own cars. Others walk, bike, or take the bus. Some do their homework on pricey laptops, while others trek to the library to access WiFi. Uniforms may force students to *dress* the same, but they do not strip away the signals sent by the many other consumer goods youth flaunt.

Supporters of school uniforms also note that non-uniform clothing can signal group membership within the school. For example, teenage gang members may wear their clothing in particular ways, such as rolling up a pant leg; or they may wear particular colours. By showing these signals at school, gang members can incite rivalry and even violence (see Lumsden 2001). School uniforms eliminate these signs of gang membership and, therefore, reduce the outbreaks of group conflict (Boutelle 2007; Dussel 2005; Malcolm 2017).

Finally, school uniforms may prepare students for their future in the work world. As mentioned earlier, wearing uniforms tends to regiment students and, in that way, train them for on-the-job regimentation and obedience as adults. In this way, it gives them valuable job "skills" at a young age. It also forces children to distinguish themselves by their actions, not their outward appearance.

On the other side of the debate, researchers, educators, and parents question such regimentation. Indeed, school uniforms have a long history, so we know a lot about their effects. In early 20th-century Argentina, for example, educators assigned white smocks as school uniforms to advance an agenda of Hygienism, underpinned by "ideals of moral and racial purity" (Dussel 2005; Chacko 2019). And in North America, Indigenous children were forced to wear uniforms in school, including Canada's notorious residential schools. Uniforms were considered a means of rigorously keeping their "unruly bodies" in line. These uniforms aimed to lessen the individuality of what were then considered undisciplined minority groups. Detractors of school uniforms suggest that, today, uniforms and dress codes build on this history of disciplining and suppressing young, unruly populations of students. They do not teach students to be autonomous, to regulate their own appearance, or control their self-presentation.

Box 5-2
The Catholic School Effect

The "Catholic school effect" is a presumed improvement in students' academic performance some have claimed to observe in Catholic parochial or private schools. School reformers have been quick to ask why this might be the case.

Within the Catholic school literature, school uniforms have never been asserted as a primary factor in producing the Catholic school effect. Nevertheless, public school administrators are beginning to consider uniform policies as a way to improve the overall school environment and student achievement.

As it turns out, uniforms have a spurious connection with good behaviour and high achievement in Catholic schools. Brunsma and Roquemore (1998), using educational data from the United States, write, "Catholic schools and uniforms go together in most people's minds, and in fact, they are the sector which utilizes uniform policies the most (65.4%)." Yet, these authors, in comparing Catholic with non-Catholic schools, and within the Catholic group, schools where uniforms are and are not worn, conclude that the effects of uniform wearing (for example, on absenteeism) are weak or non-existent. They conclude that the so-called 'Catholic school effect' "is not associated with whether the students wear uniforms or not; it is more likely due to the social relations fostered in Catholic schools."

Attempts by James Coleman (1987, 1988) to explain this "Catholic school effect" in terms of social closure—i.e., dense network connections among the parents of students, hence, closer monitoring and supervision—are challenged in a later study. Here, Morgan and Sorenson (1999) find the opposite effect in public schools. In Catholic schools, dense networks among parents somewhat increase student achievement; in public schools, they do not. In fact, these authors conclude that in the public system, "horizon expanding schools foster more learning than do norm-enforcing schools."

In effect, sociologists have been unable to explain the "Catholic school effect" fully, but school uniforms likely do not play a key role. If anything, school uniforms merely signify a *desire* to regulate student behaviour—to create and enforce norms—more closely than in public schools. Thus, uniform-wearing in Catholic schools, and the good behaviour that allegedly accompanies it, is probably a result of the teachers' and parents' commitment to enforcing discipline; uniforms are mere symbols of that commitment.

For their part, students may resist uniforms. As mentioned, some support uniforms because they reduce other students' ability to signal their wealth and class status through their clothing. However, students can easily find ways around such restrictions on their self-presentation. An untucked shirt may signal rebelliousness and a colourful manicure, scarf, or hair dye can replace a designer T-shirt as a symbol of social status.

Some schools have extra rules, on top of their uniform policies, that stipulate the sorts of accessories, hairstyles, and jewelry students are allowed to wear to school. But sometimes, students see these policies as rules that were made to be broken. And not even these added rules can always blot out (unintentional) status signals. Uniforms that are too small, visibly aged, stained, or tattered may give away students' low income status. The signal they send then is that their family does not have money to replace the uniform regularly. So, while many teachers and parents thought uniforms would limit competition and distraction, students themselves often did not agree. When it came to reducing clothing costs, most parents said they thought uniforms had achieved this goal, but a few said their clothing costs had increased.

People opposed to student uniforms also point to research that refutes the claims of improved academic achievement cited above. Brunsma and Rockquemore (1998) claim uniforms have "a negative effect … on student academic achievement." Though Bodine (2003a), after reanalyzing the same data, found a positive correlation between uniforms and academic achievement, other studies showing "no effect" continue to surface (Firmin et al. 2006; see also Edwards and Marshall, 2018). In a later study, Yeung (2009: 847) brought econometric tools to bear on whether, and to what degree, school uniforms affected student achievement. He found no significant association between school uniform policies and school achievement (on this, see also Fisher et al. 2019). At most, teachers and students could agree that uniforms helped them dress more "modestly."

Beyond this, the research leaves some central questions unanswered. Are uniforms good tools for educating youth to become responsible consumers, where many students who wear uniforms no longer have to conspicuously consume as much compared to their counterparts? For example, does wearing uniforms and saving money on clothes affect children's ability to save in the future? Or does it make them less experienced consumers compared to public school students who presumably get more practice shopping, evaluating product quality, comparing their options, looking at prices, and so on? We don't know the answers to these questions yet.

Detractors of school uniforms have tended to question the findings of increased order and safety cited above. Generally, it is only teachers and not students who think uniforms reduce gang presence in their school (Wade and Stafford 2003; Lee at al. 2018). As for the effect on self-esteem, students who did not have to wear uniforms expressed a higher view of themselves than students who did have to wear them. And opinions of the "climate" at school did not vary, among students or teachers, whether the schools required uniforms or not.

In an early but convincing summary of the evidence, Wilkins (1999; also see Jones 2017) finds no support for, or merit in, school uniforms. Below are her objections to some of the points made by uniform proponents:

- *Easier identification of students versus non-students:* Perhaps requiring all students to carry a school ID would help solve the case of the mystery person out of uniform.

- *Diminishing class distinction:* If students are to be prepared for the outside world, they need to prepare for a world full of inequalities, injustices, and inflexible social divisions.
- *Decreasing bullying:* Bullying has deep roots and will never stop just because children are dressed the same. Bullying has been going on forever in British uniformed schools.
- *Improving self-esteem:* Students cannot develop positive self-esteem when they cannot express themselves as individuals and are forced to dress like everyone else around them.
- *Increasing sense of belonging:* This sense of "belonging," based on school uniforms, may result in an "us and them" mentality that regards students of all other schools as rivals.

In short, commodifying the problem of school disorder and/or unsatisfactory performance by imposing school uniforms may not have the desired effect. The results of research on this topic, as we have seen, are mixed.

School Lunch and Breakfast Programs

Another school-related consumer issue, and an attempt to level the social playing field, has to do with food consumption at schools.

Some low-income students rely on the free food provided by meal programs in their schools. And, like uniforms, such meal programs have sparked a debate about the benefits and costs, and how those costs should be shared. The intended or manifest goal of these meal programs is to improve nutrition and, thereby, academic performance among low-income students. However, the outcomes (and perhaps latent goals) may be just as important: namely, influencing food choice and food waste among lower-income people, and the learning of healthy food consumption choices.

In the United States, the National School Lunch Program was established by an act of Congress in 1946. The program served 4.8 billion meals in 2018.

Usually, in our society, people are responsible for feeding themselves and their dependents, using money they have earned. Yet, food insecurity affects one in eight Canadian households, meaning they struggle to put food on the table (PROOF 2019). One in six Canadian children under the age of 18 goes to school hungry. Such food insecurity predicts poor academic performance and the development of poor social skills (Jyoti et al. 2005; Seshradi and Ramakrishna, 2018). Hunger reduces a child's ability to learn (Taras 2009; Rajendran and Chamendaswari 2019), because hungry children have less energy and must struggle to concentrate.

School lunch and breakfast programs were developed to solve these problems. School officials thought that by providing the nourishment needed to study, school lunch and breakfast programs would improve academic performance, especially among lower-income children. However, as with the research on school uniforms, the research on these programs' effectiveness is inconclusive.

Some studies find these programs have succeeded. For example, meal programs have been found to boost attendance and encourage students to arrive at school on time (likely because they don't want to miss their free breakfast) (Taras 2009). They also improve cognitive functioning and academic performance among otherwise undernourished students (Taras 2009). Other studies, however, find no effect on students' attendance or academic performance (Mhurchu et al. 2013).

Detractors often point to the food from these programs that goes to waste. "A Harvard Public Health Study revealed 60 percent of fresh vegetables and 40 percent of fresh fruit are being thrown away [in school lunch programs]" (HFCIS, 2015). Another study looked at meal consumption in two Boston middle schools receiving funding from the National School Lunch Program (Co-hen et al. 2013: 114). Students in this program did not get the rec-ommended levels of nutrients from their lunches. In part, that was because the students threw out the equivalent of 26 percent of the total food budget each year. Less than 85 percent of the free lunches were consumed in full. Byker et al. (2014: 406) find that kindergar-ten and pre-kindergarten pupils were especially likely to waste the food. These young children threw out fully 43 percent of the food and drinks served them. Vegetables, main entrees, and milk made up the greatest amount of waste.

However, alternatives like for-profit student cafeterias may be even worse for student health. Students of all incomes, including low-income children, buy food from such cafeterias when they are available. Their schools may not offer free breakfast and lunch pro-grams, or low-income children may feel ashamed to take part. And, while various choices may be available to them in the cafeteria, stu-dents of all income levels often make nutritionally poor choices.

In recent years, many schools have removed the once ubiquitous "pop machine" from their hallways in favour of vending machines dispensing healthier beverages.

For example, on a typical day, 18 percent to 33 percent of infants and toddlers in one study consumed no vegetables in their school cafeteria (Birch 2007; see also Gross et al. 2019). In rejecting their vegetables, children are often imitating their parents, who model faulty eating behaviours for their children. If parents regularly con-sume calorie-dense fast food, their children learn to do the same (Scaglioni et al. 2018). When children have not developed a taste for healthy eating at home, they often seek out the same non-nutritious foods in school cafeterias.

Income plays a major role in this problem. Many students have a hard cap on their lunch money; their parents may only provide them with (say) five dollars in cash each day for lunch. If they have to choose between buying unhealthy junk food that fills them up and healthy food that doesn't keep them feeling full for long, they will usually choose the high-calorie junk food. One study—which conducted focus groups with teens from low-income families—also confirmed that many students find healthy foods unappealing. They value healthy eating in principle but say that their schools are failing to make healthy choices look and taste good, and also failing to make them widely available (Evans et al. 2006; Lucas et al. 2017).

Some schools have set up policies to control the types of food that can be sold on their prop-erty. For example, they may not allow fast-food companies to operate on school grounds and may ban the sale of soda pop in their on-site vending machines (Woodruff et al. 2010; Woodruff 2019). These policies may help, but children and teens still have access to such foods when they bring their own lunches from home. For example, one study asked students in grades 6, 7, and 8 in southern Ontario schools (Woodruff et al. 2010: 421) to complete a food behaviour questionnaire. These schools all had formal policies restricting the sale of junk food. Nonetheless, 46 percent of students in this study said they drank sugar-sweetened drinks at lunch. They must have brought these drinks from home, since they could not them buy at school.

In the U.S., a comparable study drew even more worrisome conclusions about the quality of lunches that students bring from home (Caruso et al. 2015: 86). Compared with those provided through the National School Lunch Program, "lunches brought from home contained more sodium and fewer servings of fruits, vegetables, whole grains, and fluid milk. About 90 percent of lunches from home contained desserts, snack chips, and sweetened drinks, which are not permitted in reimbursable school meals."

Renewed attention is being paid to free school meal programs during the COVID-19 pandemic. Though they may not solve issues related to student nutrition, with schools closed, children who would usually rely on these programs to eat are going hungry.

In sum, educators and legislators have been unable solve the problem of nutritional inequality, despite publicly funded school lunch programs and public health campaigns. It's true that the organization and funding of these programs has differed between the US and Canada—also, that they have varied somewhat from state to state and province to province. In all cases, they have run into similar problems of uptake: students are often reluctant to eat, and willing to waste, the food that has been provided.

At school, in what they wear and what they eat, many young people continue to consume in ways that teachers and parents might dislike or disapprove of. When it comes to food, many students buy meals that lack nutritional value or bring such meals from home. As for clothing, students—whether they are required to wear school uniforms or not—continue to find alternative ways to signal their family income, social status, and identity. Such consumption becomes a problem when certain students are marginalized, excluded, or denied opportunities because of their appearance or their lunch choices. Programs to monitor and support healthier types of consumption, at least on school grounds, have so far been largely unsuccessful.

Schooling Itself as a Consumer Product

It may be a while before students at any level receive a solid, clearly stated, and well-taught consumer education from their own teachers. However, schools—as commodified products themselves—already teach young people a lot about consumer behaviour. This is especially true of private schools and elite colleges, and it is increasingly true of public research universities.

Before the Second World War, Canada's universities were small and mainly given over to liberal arts education, with some professional training added in (for a discussion of the liberal arts tradition, see Marber and Araya 2017; Telling 2018; Nishimura and Sasao 2018). Over the last fifty years, however, public research universities have come to dominate postsecondary education in

Canada and elsewhere. They have largely replaced liberal arts colleges in educational and cultural importance, and they have made possible mass postsecondary education. However, as their name suggests, these institutions are concerned more with research than with educating students.

In Canada, tuition rates are essentially uniform across public institutions (with a small degree of variation) except for "market-rate" programs in law, medicine, or business. However, those fees have greatly increased in recent years. For example, it is no longer possible—as it was forty years ago—to pay for a year's tuition with the earnings from an average summer job. At the same time, educational credentials are more and more important for gaining social status and a good job.

Although buildings at large research universities such as the University of Toronto may boast a traditional—sometimes even medieval—appearance, the emergence of these schools as the dominant force in higher education is largely an artifact of the last fifty or sixty years.

This places enormous pressure on students and their families to come up with significant sums of money.

Postsecondary education has become a global market. Students with enough money, or (sometimes) with high enough grades, can choose from top universities across the world. They "shop" for the best choice, reading up on the different schools online, taking campus tours, and meeting with faculty. In exchange for expensive tuition fees, they get degrees, connections, and maybe even work opportunities. In this sense, research universities sell what Australian researcher Marginson calls "positional goods" (2007: 1; see also Marginson 2018). These are goods that show off cultural capital and set up graduates for occupational and financial success. Because there are far more students than these elite research universities can ever accept, their positional goods become highly valued.

These changes in higher education, in Canada and elsewhere, have occurred mainly because of neoliberalism (Gledhill 2018; Springer et al. 2016). This political ideology, which emerged after 1980, calls for free-market funding of education. When neoliberal ideas are widely held, domains that, at their core, aren't mainly about making money nonetheless adopt money-making, business-oriented thinking. When it comes to education, neoliberalism favours making students pay their own way, on the assumption that only they will benefit from their education. This approach usually drives tuition up. Many students graduate with tens of thousands of dollars in debt and a degree that proves useless in today's job market. Some young adults from poor and even average middle-class families can't afford postsecondary education at all.

Education costs are also growing because formal education is being commodified (Ball 2018; Meadows 2019; Leher and Vittoria 2016). The capitalist approach to schooling treats knowledge as an object, like bricks or onions, to be bought and sold in a marketplace (Schwartzman 2013). People measure the value of knowledge by comparing the cost of a degree with the earnings the degree supposedly provides over a lifetime. Computer science students earn a lot after graduation, so they visibly gain from an investment in higher education. History and philosophy students earn a lot less after graduation, so their investment in higher education was foolish and not to be subsidized by public funds.

Post-secondary institutions now function like other for-profit organizations in a consumer society. They now prioritize financial performance (almost) above all else—this applies to the whole system, not just research universities (Campos, 2015; Cai and Heathcote, 2018; Mumper and Freeman, 2005, 2011). And there are other interesting parallels to for-profit organizations. One is the tremendous growth in the size of university bureaucracies, which far outstrips enrolment, and the adoption of private-sector titles for executives and compensation levels in many cases (for a discussion of these issues, see Hattke et al, 2016; Chatterji et al, 2014, and Paradeise and Thoenig, 2013). Another is the emphasis on satisfying the consumer (student) and the use of consumer surveys to guide organizational priorities (on these issues, see Bienen, 2012; Gallego et al, 2009; Estemann and Claeys-Kulik, 2013; and Altundemir, 2012).

No less important is the effort to reach out to new markets when the existing one is saturated or in decline. In the last case, faced with declining domestic enrolments and sometimes overbuilt systems, school administrators may chase international students as a new source of revenue. This has happened to Ontario's community colleges, for example. They have ended up with some programs that are now 90 percent international students and now worry about how drops in international enrolment will affect them (see also McCartney and Metcalf, 2018; Lincoln, 2018).

Like other profit-seeking organizations, faced with a decline in the market for their product, post-secondary schools sought new markets. They did this even though, unlike private-sector companies, they were created to serve a particular public good, not simply to expand into whatever market is available. These and related issues are being discussed internationally, as the competition for foreign students expands continuously (on these issues, see Cantwell, 2019; Stein and deAndreotti, 2016; Hegarty, 2014; and Robertson, 2011).

Under neoliberalism, higher education is a commodity developed to meet a consumer demand (Carter, 2020). Complicating matters is the fact that while employers need well-educated workers, those employers no longer want to invest in training and skills development. They want students—the workers of the future—to shoulder the cost of their own education and training. With a dollars-and-cents mentality dominating education today, colleges and (especially research) universities now run like corporate entities in the private sector. They aim to generate revenue and post a surplus, even at the expense of educational quality (Mohamedbhai 2008; Lam 2020). Increasingly, universities model their approach on the "basic economic formula: get the maximum and give the minimum" (Larrasquet and Pilnière 2012: 209).

On this matter, McPherson and Purcell (2018: 34) write:

Across many institutions, more attention is paid to faculty research than to faculty teaching. Relatively little focus on measuring and observing teaching performance takes place, except for student questionnaires, which are generally a weak indicator of performance.… The reality is that the main occupation of the majority of college faculty is teaching undergraduates, yet faculty often get very little initial training, ongoing support, or recognition for this central work. Further, the growing number of "contingent" faculty—an international trend—allows institutions to save money by relying more heavily on short-term, part-time instructors who are paid less, have few benefits and negligible job security, and often lack a voice in governance. Even more concerning, they often have scant time and opportunity to engage with students.

Do higher-end universities provide most students with value for money spent? Should students pursue a degree in computer science, history, or philosophy? Or would it be more rational to learn a trade like plumbing, where wages are high, there is a shortage of labour, and the cost of training is relatively low? One analysis comparing the financial status of doctors and plumbers shows that the plumber has a higher net worth until age 41. Admittedly, this is a U.S. scenario, and bigger student loans in the U.S. and the (much) bigger doctor's earnings in the U.S. likely balance off against each other. Still, it would appear that a good-paying trade is likely a better financial choice than all but the highest-paying careers requiring post-secondary education.

Along slightly different lines, Abel and Dietz (2014) carried out an economic analysis of the costs and benefits of a higher education. Their analysis reveals that the benefits of a bachelor or associate degree "still tend to outweigh the costs, with both degrees earning a return of about 15 percent over the past decade." The research findings are not all positive, however. The reason a university degree is still a good financial investment—even if not as good as in the past—is because wages for people *without* degrees have decreased. That means you're still better off getting a postsecondary education than not. It also means the opportunity cost of going to school has been lowered. Students are no longer missing out on significant earnings by staying in school, because their working peers are not earning as much as they once were.

As to whether graduates of high-prestige private colleges (such as the Ivy League schools) benefit in proportion to the high tuitions they have paid, the answer is inconclusive. No doubt, an education at one of the most prestigious private colleges provides valuable credentials, cultural capital, and social capital (or social contacts). In recent years, however, articles in *The New York Times* and elsewhere have spoken out for the benefits to be gained from less expensive, top-tier public American universities. These include the University of Michigan, the University of California at Berkeley, and the University of North Carolina at Chapel Hill. These are similar in quality to Canadian universities, some of which—like the University of Toronto, McGill University, McMaster University, and the University of British Columbia—rate highly in international measures of quality.

At the same time, what we decide about the value of education depends on how we define and measure the desired outcomes. Are we concerned only (or mainly) with social and cultural capital, or with salaries after graduating? Are we equally interested in the perceived quality of education a student receives, or a person's life satisfaction after graduating? Some research finds that attending a prestigious college may provide many social contacts but does not affect graduates' future job satisfaction (Kim et al. 2016).

Despite the uncertain worth of a costly education, commodification continues, even at the primary and secondary schooling levels. One example is the upgrading of primary and secondary schools or "academies" by political leaders looking to gain repute for their "charter schools." Some of these leaders use selected urban schools to show how they are revitalizing their cities. They rebrand selected schools and try to attract the children of professional families. In so doing, they hope to attract and keep these families in the downtown core, effectively gentrifying the neighbourhood.

The adoption of school uniforms is sometimes part of the rebranding. This rebranding also involves treating middle- and upper-income parents as sought-after customers. One tactic is to make these parents think they'll be able to influence the school once their children are admitted (Cucchiara 2008; Cucchiara and Horvat 2017). Many teachers and tutors commodify themselves too, especially among high-income families seeking to send their kids to prestigious universities. These teachers advertise themselves in terms of how many students they sent to an Ivy League school, or the average SAT score of their students. The higher these numbers are, the higher the pay they receive for training the children of affluent families. This may be an especially big trend in Asian countries, where affluent students attend additional schools and training sessions to prepare them for college admission.

Throughout the whole process, middle- and upper-income parents are catered to, while low-income and minority parents are ignored. These examples, drawn from the United States, may suggest where Canadian education is heading in due course.

Such school marketing sometimes requires the spread of less-than-honest information about the school and the community. "Desirable" parents are purposely misled, limiting their ability to make good choices based on evidence of the school's effectiveness. Instead, many schools use emotional themes and images, implying that only the best kinds of students grace their competitive hallways (Lubienski 2007; Lubienski and Lee 2016; Jessen and DiMartino 2016). These promotional strategies aim at attracting high-performing students, not spreading benefits to lower-income or less successful students in the community.

For example, some schools that include the words "American School" in their name are run under the Canadian, British or other school system and most of the teachers are from countries other than the United States. These schools are branded as American schools to local parents who may be more familiar with universities in the United States. This association of local high schools with a certain country or university (usually, in the United States) is deemed highly desirable by local high-income families.

However, many educators view such marketing with suspicion and think it's dishonest. "Impression management" (Symes 1998) is not usually what educators strive for in their classrooms or professional lives, some will say (see also Drew et al. 2016). On the other hand, some think they may help to attract top students and offer them the most relevant programs. As well, many post-secondary schools rely on the higher tuition paid by international students to meet their expenses.

This reliance means finding ways to attract the favourable attention of international students looking for schools abroad. Therefore, schools increasingly market themselves digitally and provide customer service online to compete more effectively (Gomes and Murphy 2003; Royo-Vela and Hünermund 2016).

All this shows that education has become a commodity that is used for social signaling. It is sold in both the local and global marketplace, to consumers all over the world. It yields credentials that symbolize success and ambition. It is an important part of the wars to amass and display cultural capital.

Most important, the credentials gained from higher education are used to signal membership in an exclusive upper echelon of society. Postsecondary institutions build prestige by being selective, which in turn allows them to ratchet up prices. The problem is, postsecondary education is a precondition for many jobs today. The commodification of education therefore contributes to income inequality. Unaffordable tuition fees keep low-income students from rising through the socioeconomic ranks of society and speeds the higher-income students on their upward trajectory.

Box 5-3
Marketing Education

Our economy values high-skilled labor in knowledge industries. The data show that "[e]mployment in STEM [science, technology, engineering and mathematics] occupations grew by 10.5 percent, or 817,260 jobs, between May 2009 and May 2015, compared with a 5.2 percent net growth in non-STEM occupations" (BLS, 2017). Postsecondary education is essentially required for one to obtain a good job in this labour market. Universities have also benefited as suppliers of labour. "On average, undergraduates pay 40 per cent more in tuition than they did 10 years ago" (Global News 2016).

Like large private-sector corporations, universities want to grow their revenues. So, they market themselves towards people who will pay the most. But people will only pay a lot if the school is demonstrably and recognizably excellent. One way for a school to make money is to admit top students and help them get high grades. As well, these schools publicize the activities of their most productive and eminent faculty members. Essentially, universities manipulate public impressions to maximize profits.

The pressure to excel puts pressure on kids and faculty members alike. Such competition emphasizes efficiency, accountability, and test-taking, not learning. This may make sense for a widget maker or a software company, but for a school, whose primary job is to educate people, the outcome can be problematic, and may include students with mental health problems. These practices also marginalize poorer families, who do not tend to be as academically successful as wealthier kids. Global News reported that "60 percent more Toronto students have private tutors—in wealthy areas most of all" (2013).

Final Thoughts

As we have seen throughout this book, people consume as part of their efforts to craft a desired social image. In this chapter, we looked at school uniforms, which seemingly reduce students' opportunities to craft their own image. On the one hand, with everyone dressed the same, wealthier students can't show off their privilege with expensive, branded clothing, and poorer students are less likely to be ridiculed or excluded for wearing the only clothing they can afford. On the other hand, uniforms are still consumer products. They are still an expense that lower-income families may not be able to bear. Students may therefore reveal their class status through the quality, age, and fit of their uniforms, as well as through their accessories and grooming. In other words, uniforms do not eliminate students' ability to use consumer goods to cultivate and display their identities. What's more, as consumer goods, uniforms often reflect our social norms and values. For example, by obliging female students to buy skirts as part of their uniforms, schools may reinforce traditional gender roles and contribute to their sexualization.

We also discussed the efforts to level the playing field among lower- and higher-income students by providing lunch programs in elementary schools. We noted that it may be easier to find the money for such programs than it will be to teach new eating habits to children who have been raised on a low budget.

Finally, we noted that schooling itself can be considered a consumer product or service. People exchange money for skills, knowledge, and a label they can use to secure employment. Just like other consumer products—say, clothes or a car—people use their education to send messages about themselves. Graduating from Princeton sends a different message than graduating from community college. Further, graduating from Princeton is possible only for a small segment of the population—for the most part, those who can afford the tuition or whose parents have the social and cultural capital to negotiate their acceptance. In turn, the perks of such an education are also reserved for a small minority.

In this way, the neoliberal transformation of schooling into a consumer product helps perpetuate status and income inequality. It ensures that only those who can pay have access to the "products" that get people ahead in our society. We will discuss the problem of class advantage and class inheritance further in chapters to come.

Discussion Questions

1. In this chapter, we talked about how popular culture is continually evolving and forever in flux. Why might this be? What forces in society shift and change popular culture to contribute to this "ever-evolving" system of change?

2. The North American cultural value set is made up of three central tenets: consumer behaviour, individualism, and secularism. Think about other cultures that you are familiar with. How do their buying patterns reflect their own cultural value sets? Are they different from that of the typical North American values, or do they just vary in specific small ways? Discuss.

3. Celia Lury used the phrase "culturally drenched" to refer to the multiple meanings that are attached to the goods we buy and sell on the consumer market. Take the most meaningful device or object in your life and list all the ways in which that object has been culturally drenched. Consider the cultural values that underlie the meaning that has been attached to it.

Quick Quiz

1. What is consumer culture?
a. The anthropological study of how people acquired things
b. The economical overview of income inequality
c. A culture where goods are available to few, but everyone works for an income
d. A culture where goods are available to all and people work to pay for the goods
e. A culture where goods are distributed by the government

2. What is material culture?
a. All the signs and symbols that make up a culture
b. The luxury goods available to the rich but not to the poor
c. The ways people bought and sold goods in the pre-industrial era
d. A form of branding and marketing that speaks to people's subconscious desires
e. All the objects made and used in any society

3. What is commercialization?
a. Anything that is made
b. Ideas and creative outlets fostered in a society
c. Government incentivization
d. The stage of a new product where a decision is made to produce and distribute it
e. The early stages of engineering an object where the mechanical processes are worked out

4. What did the Frankfurt School support?
a. Capitalism
b. Critical theory
c. Anarchy
d. Liberalism
e. Neo-liberalism

5. What is socialization?
a. A specific diet that one follows
b. A way of schooling kids where they are not allowed to use modern technology
c. The removal of a person from a society
d. Making someone a social outcast in a group
e. The ways people internalize norms and ideologies of their societies

The answers to the Quick Quiz are provided at the end of the book.

For Further Reading

The Adolescent Society by James Coleman
Sixty years ago, athletic ability, coolness, and social maturity (e.g., knowing how to talk to girls) determined a boy's position in high school's social hierarchy. How much has this changed?

Schooling in Capitalist America by Samuel Bowles and Herbert Gintis
Forty-five years ago, this book showed that nearly 80 per cent of the financial benefit of schooling for individual graduates is a result of learning social skills like obedience, diligence, and sociability. How much has this changed?

The Rules of Art by Pierre Bourdieu
Bourdieu explores the role of art and structural relations through art in its three states. In the process, he looks at the history of literature and art.

Key Terms

Human capital
Ideologies
Information society
Knowledge economy
Peer group
Reference group
Social capital
Social networks

Chapter Six
Teaching the Culture of Desire: Media and Advertising

Learning Objectives

After reading this chapter, you will be able to:

✓ Evaluate how advertising helps people understand the symbolism of consumer goods.

✓ Trace the historical evolution of advertising.

✓ Consider which channels and tactics are most trusted among different consumer segments.

✓ Engage with common criticisms of advertising and debates around its effectiveness.

The last major agent of socialization we discuss in this book is the media. We consider how advertising tries to socialize people and influence them to buy in particular ways. We ask whether advertising is successful in these efforts, and, if so, what makes it effective (or ineffective)? As well, does advertising (of certain kinds, or of any kind) produce any negative side effects—any results that harm people?

As we will see, there is extensive research on how advertising is *supposed* to work and on its harmful side effects. Much less information is publicly available on advertising's effectiveness: how well it works, and why. No doubt companies safeguard research they have commissioned on their own advertising campaigns. They do not want to share their knowledge with competitors. They may also be reluctant to let customers see these studies.

So, with these questions in mind, we will start by describing what advertisers are trying to do, and how they are doing it.

Defining Our Terms

The media, marketing, and advertising are all about **communication**. Communication is the passing on or exchange of information and news. It is a universal social activity: no society exists without it (Berger et al. 2018; Gulbrandsen and Just 2016; Van Ruler 2018).

 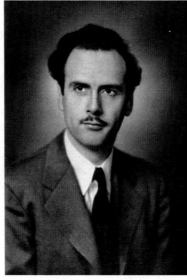

Harold Innis (left) and Marshall McLuhan (right) were two prominent communication theorists of the twentieth century. Both taught at the University of Toronto.

Forms of communication vary from one society to another with population size, dispersion, and available technology. Two Canadian theorists—Harold Innis and Marshall McLuhan—famously showed the **medium of communication** changes as societies become larger and more complex. A **medium** is a means of communication, such as print, radio, or television. As societies grow, communication typically shifts from a reliance on spoken communication to a reliance on written communication, then from written communication to communication mediated by technology such as radio, television, and computers (Leppaniemi and Karjaluoto 2005; Yu et al. 2017; Ahamat et al. 2017).

The sign of good television

When this symbol shines out from a television screen, it identifies, for viewers and advertisers alike, the network where they're most likely to find what they're looking for:

...where 6 of television's 10 most popular shows* are broadcast

...where average ratings are higher than on any other network*

...where television's solid-success package programs come from...shows like Mama, Toast of the Town, Studio One, Suspense, Burns & Allen, Talent Scouts

...where the new hits will *keep* coming from: I Love Lucy, Frank Sinatra, Corliss Archer, See It Now, An Affair of State, Out There, My Friend Irma

...where 89 national advertisers...including 15 of America's 20 biggest...are profitably doing business today."

"This is the CBS Television Network"

This advertisement from the December 1951 issue of *Fortune* magazine marked the introduction of the famous CBS "eye" logo. Television networks and newspapers, the dominant mass media organizations of the twentieth century, have now been joined and, to a large degree, supplanted by a later generation of social media and Internet giants, including Google and Facebook.

Mass media include all the techniques and institutions that communicate rapidly and simultaneously to large, geographically remote, and socially distinct audiences. In other words, the mass media consist of large organizations that use technology to share information with large numbers of people. Taken together, the media have great economic, political, and social influence (Russo and Simeone 2017; McCluskey et al. 2016; Brito and de Freitas 2019).

According to C. Wright Mills in his classic work *The Power Elite* (1956; see also Dandaneau 2019; Ross 2017), the mass media have two important sociological characteristics. First, they allow a few people to address many. And, second, the audience typically has no easy and effective way of answering back. Mass communication is, for Mills, a one-way process. As we will see, mass communication has changed with the rise of online interactive communication. Such communication typically takes place through media such as websites, which not only send content out to an audience but also let audience-members engage with and respond to that content. For example, consumers can often leave their comments at the end of an online news article (on mass communications, see also Paxson 2018; Sterling et al. 2016; Denis et al. 2016).

Media research—or media studies—has expanded enormously since the 1960s. Within this discipline, there are at least four sub-disciplines (Hartley 2019; Ott and Mack 2020). First, some researchers study how biases emerge in the media and what effect they may have on the audience. For instance, they may look at racial stereotyping or violence in television programs aimed at children. Second, some researchers study the influence of the media in promoting certain values, beliefs, norms, and lifestyles. Third, some explore how media may affect democratic politics through agenda setting. This includes studying the distortion of news, the deflection of public attention from social problems, and the use of television advertising in political campaigns. Fourth, some researchers study patterns of media ownership and control. For example, they may note that more and more media outlets are being integrated into a few large corporations. They look at cross-media ownership and its consequences.

In recent decades, the entertainment and information businesses have also converged with the telecommunications industry. This convergence is driven by a wish to reap the rewards of **media synergy** (Dong et al. 2018; Huang and Li 2016). Though media synergy takes many forms, it is mainly concerned with connecting more people with more media content through integrated systems and providers. For example, a network may simultaneously promote a performer or author across various media, entertainment products, and leisure goods. It may use product placements in TV shows to coincide with newspaper and online advertising.

Another form of media synergy occurs when previously distinct hardware items converge. Popularly known as "multimedia," such technology allows still and moving photos, sound, and text to share the same (digital) format (Qin et al. 2019; Danaher 2017; Wang et al. 2016). Finally, media synergy occurs through new technologies of distribution. The key development here is fibre-optic cable. Because it can transmit such large amounts of data, fibre-optic cable has created a so-called "information superhighway" along which mass communications can travel.

Debate about the social and cultural implications of this new media landscape often focuses on issues of democracy and access. Proponents say developments such as pay-per-view and media subscriptions allow consumers to have more say in what they watch and hear. Similarly, new forms of interactivity through digitalization and the Internet allow consumers to access the media in their own preferred way. The Internet also offers previously marginalized groups new opportunities to organize, communicate, and share an identity.

On the other hand, critics have pointed to the increasing gap between the so-called "information-rich" and "information-poor" people in the new media universe. New technologies are not equally accessible to everyone, especially those who cannot afford to pay for them (Ayeh 2019; Yu et al. 2016; Marcella and Chowdhury 2019). Similarly, they may not be available to people who live in remote or rural regions with limited Internet access. Linked to these issues of accessibility are issues of social marginalization, which occurs when groups do not have opportunities to access information and express themselves through these media. The growing concentration of media ownership is not likely to improve this problem. So, in one sense, modern media provide more social and cultural diversity in their range of products. However, this diversity is not available to everyone, nor is social diversity reflected in the management of media corporations themselves.

Marketing means promoting and selling products and services. This involves identifying target audiences through research and finding the most effective ways to bring them a product or service (Armstrong et al. 2018; Hastings and Stead 2017; De Mooij 2018). There is no one accepted model of marketing that is shared across all organizations. In part, that is because markets are changing rapidly; they are increasingly complex and globalized. No single approach has emerged so far that adequately masters the dynamism (and often irrationality) of global markets. Customer patterns are also changing all the time, defying any simple analysis of tastes and buying patterns.

As noted above, marketing has many subsets, including advertising and sales promotion. These two marketing subsets, which we will describe in greater depth shortly, usually conform to an overall **marketing strategy**. That is, they work together to achieve shared objectives. These wider objectives include increasing sales, attracting new customers, and defending the product from competition, to name just a few examples (Kingsnorth 2019; Morgan et al. 2019; Palmatier 2018).

To achieve these objectives, a marketing strategy typically includes a series of planned choices. Marketers decide which parts of the market to focus on and how to compete within that target market. They base their strategies on a thorough analysis of the target market and careful consideration of how the product or service is positioned to reach that target. **Positioning** is another core element of a marketing strategy. It shows the potential consumer how a service, idea, or product stacks up against a competing product (for example, Neirotti et al. 2016; Rodríguez-Díaz et al. 2018).

Finally, marketing strategies include **tactics**: specific actions that marketers will take to achieve their objectives. For example, a marketing strategy may require building trust among consumers by highlighting the expertise of the company's staff. One objective of this may be to increase sales by 15 percent. The target market may be suburban mothers aged 25 to 30. By presenting their seasoned staff as carefully trained experts, they can stand out against competitors who, say, employ teenaged volunteers. To carry out this strategy, marketers may choose a tactic of YouTube how-to videos that showcase their staff's superior skill and experience.

Another element within a larger marketing strategy is **sales promotion**: a direct inducement to buy. Sales promotions are typically tactical and they offer potential customers incentives for buying. They may include contests, exhibitions, gifts, free products, price discounts, loyalty points, celebrity approvals, and money-back guarantees, to name a few (Van Heerde and Neslin 2017; Yang and Mattila 2020; Aghara et al. 2018).

The Language of Advertising

Advertising is another crucial part of a marketing strategy. It is also a form of communication, and it capitalizes on media synergy through the use of many different media at the same time.

Specifically, an **advertisement** is any communication that promotes ideas, goods, or services that has been paid for by an identified sponsor (Hackley and Hackley 2017; Clow 2016; Percy 2016). At the least, advertising creates awareness of a product. It also creates confidence in the product and, if effective, a desire to buy the product. Effective advertising is both emotional and rational: both a form of entertainment and a way of conveying useful information.

The two basic elements of advertising are the message and the medium (on this, the classic statement was by Marshall McLuhan, 1964; also, Heydon 2017). The **message** is the key idea that an advertiser wants to leave with consumers. *X deodorant makes you smell good. Y automobile will be fun to drive. Z restaurant will give you delicious food for a low price.* As mentioned above, the **medium** is the means of communication. Newspapers, television, cinema, radio, and outdoor billboards are all media that carry advertising (for theories around medium and message, see Meyrowitz 2019; Strate 2017; Mawhinney and Kochkina 2019).

Then, there are at least three types of tools advertisers use in their work. First, **psychographics** focus on the psychological factors in an advertisement that motivate people to want a product. For example, they may show a celebrity using the advertised product (Pitt et al. 2020; Mittal 2016; Pitman et al. 2018). Second, **demographics** looks at the "kinds of people" who are most likely to be interested in the product (Lees et al. 2016; Gajanova et al. 2019; An et al. 2018). For instance, older adults are often the best targets for medications and health-related products, as opposed to teenagers. Third, **sociographics** focuses on the role of networks and communities of users in promoting a given product (see, for example, Contandriopoulos et al. 2018; Hogan et al. 2019). They encourage the viewer to see himself or herself as part of a group of loyal customers.

The promotion of specific goods and services is what typically comes to mind when we think of advertising. However, there are other kinds of advertising as well. First, **institutional** or **corporate advertising**, also known as **image advertising,** promotes an organization's image: how it wants consumers to think about the company, whether reliable, exciting, popular, or unique. Such advertising increases consumers' trust and faith in a given company and, in turn, its products. Second, **location** or **place advertising** is advertising by communities, cities, states, or even countries intended to promote particular travel destinations. For example, the "I Love New York" campaign was designed to attract tourists and businesses and to revitalize the image of this once-maligned city. Finally, **classified advertising** is used for the sale of goods, services, and jobs, originally through newspapers or other periodic publications. Today, classified ads appear primarily through online services like Kijiji and eBay (Abdallah 2018; Kaizer et al. 2016; Turna et al. 2018).

As one might expect from this potpourri, advertising has multiple goals and approaches. Some aim at promoting products and services, and these have usually dominated the advertising of consumer products. Some aim at increasing the use of existing products and services or encouraging repeat buys. Others aim at setting up, reinforcing, or extending existing product recognition, awareness, value, and esteem. Still others aim at reaching new markets and buyers.

Each example listed so far focuses on selling to a consumer. These types of advertising are designed to encourage buying by ordinary people. They directly push a product or try to create a positive impression of the product, so consumers become more likely to buy it later. But advertising can also be used to promote ideas, organizations, and causes. Charities use advertising to persuade people to give money to a worthy cause. Businesses use advertising to recruit new employees. Politicians use advertising to gain votes and support for their platform, or to tear down their opponents.

To achieve any of these goals, advertising often uses signs, words, and images to create spectacle, fantasy, and enchantment in the buyer's mind. By **enchantment**, we mean to connect this view of advertising with that of sociologist Max Weber, who, as mentioned, famously equated rational, modern, bureaucratic societies with "disenchantment." As discussed in an earlier chapter, **disenchantment** describes how, according to Weber, societies lost the excitement of magic and superstition as they grew more secular and rational (for elaborations of this, see Josephson-Storm 2017; Loia 2019; George 2016).

Box 6-1
The Many Approaches to Advertising Women's Fashion: Enchantment, Comparison, Comfort

Advertisements do not always highlight the usefulness of the product or service they're promoting. Often, the "meaning" they promote is symbolic and mainly helps to "enchant," not inform, the consumer.

For example, advertisements for women's clothing play a huge role in upholding or undermining popular conceptions of womanhood. Phillips and McQuarrie (2010) find that many such advertisements try to "enchant" consumers into buying (on this, see also Lien and Chen 2013).

Their research revealed that women engage with fashion advertisements in several different ways. First, some women treat fashion magazine advertisements as pages from a catalogue. They scan the advertisements, carefully inspecting the goods detail by detail. These women are focusing on the product, not the advertisement. They're not immersed in the experience—they are not "enchanted." Second, by contrast, other women look at fashion advertisements to make themselves feel better. For example, a particular advertisement helps them feel happy (or not). Women who read the advertisement this way respond to the product according to their mood. They buy goods that make them feel happy. Third, other women want to be enchanted. They look for stories—even fairy tales—in advertisements. The effective advertisements "transport" these women out of their boring, every-day lives to a far-away place of novelty.

Some advertisements play a much more ominous role. For example, in a classic study of the reading and buying patterns of "working men's wives," sociologists Rainwater and Coleman (1963) found that some magazines were aimed at unsettling and then comforting their female readers. Their reading audience was poorly educated women who, often, feared losing the affection (also, support and income) of their working-class husbands. Stories in the magazine (often about "other women" and sexy love affairs) played on such fears. Advertisements in the magazine suggested ways that wives might make themselves and their homes more appealing, to prevent the feared husband-loss. The solutions suggested weight loss, cheap and delicious menu items, and ways to spruce up the home for not much money.

Weber thought such rationalization and disenchantment was unavoidable, given the growth in scale and complexity of organizations. He even recognized its benefits, including the rise of science and the secular state. At the same time, however, Weber was concerned that with rationalization came a reduction in the importance of belief and ritual. Such disenchantment challenged traditional ways through which societies had found meaning and developed a collective identity. As we will see, some advertising today aims to fill this void and "enchant" consumers. To give just one example of how this can play out, consider advertisements for women's clothing.

A related notion is **fantasy**, by which we mean any process or product of pure imagination. Fantasy is any image or account that contrasts with "reality" and the known world: for instance, leprechauns, sea monsters, unicorns, and the like (Johnsen and Sørensen 2017; Žižek 2018; Fitzpatrick 2019). This term has been used in many different senses. First, fantasy describes many kinds of fiction, including melodrama, romance, and science fiction. Second, the term fantasy is also used in psychoanalytic theory to mean the content of dreams that represent repressed desires. Fantasies, for psychoanalysts, let us safely explore our wishes and dreams. Psychoanalysts Sigmund Freud and Jacques Lacan both studied fantasy in their work. Where Freud saw fantasy as conflicting with reality, Lacan thought fantasy is at once both a defence against and a necessary support for reality.

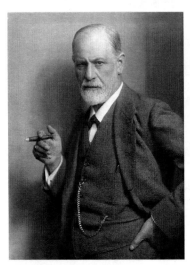

Although pioneering psychologist Sigmund Freud viewed fantasy as being in conflict with reality, enchantment and fantasy have proven powerful tools in the service of modern advertisers.

A field that, with psychoanalysis, has been important in plumbing the depths of fantasy is semiotics. **Semiotics** or **semiology** is concerned with the ways in which people create, decode, and transform signs and meanings. It is often used to analyze literary works, to understand how they carry meaning and stir emotion. However, the scope of semiotics goes beyond spoken or written language to other kinds of communication such as cinema, advertising, clothing, gesture, and even cuisine.

A semiotic approach is useful in the study of advertising because it helps to reveal the underlying power of an image or idea. That is, it shows why a particular advertisement is or is not powerfully appealing (Chandler 2017; Jones 2019; Metro-Roland 2016).

Advertising is part of what has been called the **cultural economy** (Spence and De Beukelaer 2018; Montgomerie 2017; Grodach et al. 2017). This is the part of an economy made up of **creative** and **cultural industries**. These industries focus on creating and profiting from intellectual production. Besides advertising, they include fashion design, computer game design, music, art, and creative services for businesses (O'Brien et al. 2017; Wang et al. 2020; Boccella and Salerno 2016). Recall that Adorno and Horkheimer argued that the culture industry ruins artistic production through standardization, reducing art to a tool that trivializes human creativity and that perpetuates the status quo.

In his influential book *The Hidden Persuaders* (1957), Vance Packard identified the various ways advertising can affect prospective customers. He explored advertisers' use of consumer motivational research and other psychological techniques to manipulate expectations and induce a "need" for products. Packard identified eight "compelling needs" that advertisers promise products will fulfill. According to Packard, these needs become so intense that they essentially force people to buy products to satisfy them (along similar lines, see also Schudson 2013; Wänke 2016; Köcher et al. 2019; Powell 2018).

Some advertisements, for example, promise the product will bring you comfort, happiness, and safety. Others promise the product will show that you deserve your coveted place in society. Some advertisements promise the product will help you to find, win, and keep a loved one. Others promise the product will help you stay young and vigorous longer.

Consumers today still long for these benefits and advertisements still promise them. To some, Packard's analysis seemed dramatic—even sensationalistic—and at the time some reviewers criticized him for this. Some felt he was over-dramatizing the danger and harm associated with advertising. However, much more recent analyses express similarly intense concerns. For example, Leiss et al. (2018) describe some of the ways we can view advertising:

- It is a mirror that reflects society's current vision of material well-being.
- It is a means of selling products, often with the result of promoting environmental destruction, encouraging obesity, or other unwanted results.
- It reproduces capitalist social relations, making the dominance of the ruling class appear natural by distorting the material relations of capital.
- It gives goods meanings they otherwise lack, shaping and fueling our identities as consumers.

In short, advertising's intended role in the marketplace is economic—to sell goods—but its cultural role is much broader. It shapes our desires and the meanings we give to everyday life. It does so by transforming and creating new meanings for consumer goods, drawing on a trove of symbols and ideas. Mass marketing shapes not only consumerism (our decision to buy certain goods), but also our culture, social lives, politics, and economy—in fact, every part of our society.

The Evolution of Advertising

How did we get here? How did advertising evolve into this meaning-making industry that touches so much of our lives?

In the late 19th century, agrarian values were beginning to decline, to be replaced with new urban marketplace values. These included new values around consumption, individuality, and competition. Commercial advertising began to appear on signs and in newspapers. Only a few media were in wide use then, and they were all put to use.

This early advertising had at least two effects. The first was to unify people. Amid the chaos of many social changes, mass commercial imagery helped unify or homogenize people's views, beliefs, and lifestyles (Ewen 1976; see also Nadler and McGuigan 2016). For newcomers to North America, advertising helped shape a national identity centered on consumption. It told people what to wear, eat, and buy. A second effect was to intensify the craving for luxury and personal improvement. People increasingly looked to new ways to improve and transform themselves: to help them get better jobs, find a mate, and make themselves more socially acceptable.

In the 19th century, most advertisements struck a tone of respect for the products they were promoting. Advertisers treated consumers as rational people and appealed to their desire for reliable, effective, and well-priced products.

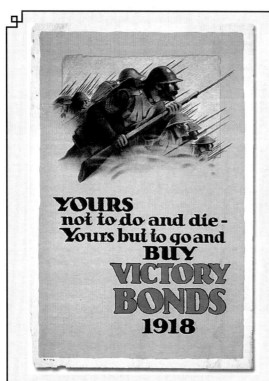

Box 6-2

Victory Bonds
Selling Canadians a Better Tomorrow

A century ago, Victory Bonds played a key role in helping Canada finance the cost of fighting the First World War. Between 1915 and 1919, the government raised over $2 billion (the equivalent of more than $46 billion today, adjusted for inflation) through bond sales. The sales campaigns used poems, images, and messages urging people to show their patriotism.

After the war ended, the 1919 campaign changed its slogan. The theme "Bring Him Home" suggested that the funds raised would be used to support the return and reintegration of soldiers and would serve as a "bridge between war and peace."

Only after the First World War did this tone changed. From roughly 1925 to 1945, in what Leiss et al. (2018) call its "iconology phase," advertising came to focus on the symbolic qualities of a product, rather than its usefulness. Increasingly, advertising played on social themes such as personal identity, self-presentation, and social acceptance.

Edward Bernays, a nephew of psychoanalyst Sigmund Freud, is sometimes called the founder of modern advertising. Bernays famously claimed that consumers are mainly driven by motives unknown to and concealed from themselves. The advertiser must look beneath seemingly rational, self-proclaimed goals to tap the real motives behind buying. Appealing to the rational minds of customers is bound to be less effective because unconscious desires (like the sexual desires that Freud insisted were enormously important) are the true drivers of human action. Sex sells; so do fantasy, enchantment, heroism, and the desire for popularity and acclaim.

By the 1960s, advertising had entered the "totemism phase," depicting more varied lifestyle possibilities and products (Leiss et al. 2018). Products became **totems** in the sense that they came to symbolize whole systems of social meanings. Products were also used more explicitly in advertisements to signify group membership. The display of a surfboard and surfers alongside a particular drink or item of clothing, for instance, would suggest youthfulness. The product on display was for people who were young (or young at heart), adventurous, energetic, and sexually active—or aspired to these qualities.

According to Leiss et al. (2018), today we live in the "*mise-en-scene* phase" of advertising. Advertisers see consumers as individuals and subgroups, rather than as a homogenous group. This view is reflected in the strategies of market segmentation and audience targeting that advertisers use today. It is expected that different gender, age, income, and cultural groups may want different products—or at least different *benefits* from the same products. Different people have varying views of themselves and of the groups they want to belong to.

Though advertisers make an effort to target niche groups, many consumers continue to purchase mass-produced products from big brands like Canada Goose and Lululemon (for other examples, see Balderas-Cejudo et al. 2019; Daniels and Spencer 2019; Ferreira and Castro 2020). Consumers claim to want to preserve their identity and individuality. To meet that desire, some advertisements position particular goods to make them look like a way to stand out from the crowd. Many automobile advertisements promote the idea that a particular car will take you to unique places while giving you unique pleasure doing so. But, of course, you are hardly demonstrating your unique identity by buying the same car as tens of thousands or even hundreds of thousands of other consumers.

The Internet, social media, and mobile communication platforms all play key roles in this new advertising landscape. Google and Facebook dominate the Internet advertising marketplace because they provide access to millions of people who provide personal information about their interests and wishes. They give advertisers the golden key to market segmentation.

Using these data, advertisers serve up content they know particular consumers are looking for, enticing them with advertisements customized according to their likes, interests, past searches, and more. Increasingly, the advertisements people see on their social media channels, in their email inboxes, and in their Google search results have been personalized: tailored to their individual consumer preferences, demographics, and psychographics. This personalization gives advertisers much greater power than ever before to place the right content in front of the right person.

As a source of unlimited personal data, Google and Facebook also contribute to the increasingly widespread surveillance of consumers (Maulana 2019; Plangger and Montecchi 2020; West 2019). This surveillance has increased in both scope and speed throughout the 21st century. Its goal is to separate consumers into ever smaller, more homogeneous groupings. With these smaller groups in mind, marketers (and politicians) can tailor more personalized and effective persuasion (Ognyanova et al. 2018; Buhr et al. 2017; Fletcher 2017).

Which Advertising Types and Channels are the Greatest Agents of Socialization?

For media to act as agents of socialization, people must consume them. As advertising has evolved, different generations have come to pay attention to different types and channels of advertising.

Like earlier generations, millennials still watch traditional TV, but they spend more time than older generations consuming content on game consoles and digital streaming devices. Nearly one-quarter of millennials' total video viewing time is reportedly spent on these TV-connected devices, compared to just 6 percent for consumers age 35 and over (Nielsen 2017). Millennials are more likely to consume entertainment on services such as Netflix; older generations use these services too, but consume more traditional (network and cable) TV than millennials.

Millennials also consume their fair share of digital advertisements while watching TV and they are less likely to change the channel during commercial breaks than older viewers (Nielsen 2017). However, millennials are media consumption multi-taskers. For example, a millennial may watch TV while *also* engaging with other devices, such as their laptop and smartphone. While they are less likely to change the channel during a commercial break, Millennials are often the viewers least engaged with TV programming. When a commercial break begins, they are likely to check their social media feeds and email until the programming resumes. As a result, they have the lowest ad recall, compared with other viewers. The average recall of TV advertisements among Gen Xers aged 35 and over is roughly 48 percent, but only 38 percent—10 percentage points lower—among millennials (Nielsen 2017).

Consumers of all ages now often have the opportunity to skip digital advertisements entirely. YouTube, for example, usually requires users to view only five seconds of an advertisement before allowing them to skip ahead to their desired video content. Other channels, however, do not allow such "skipping," in the hopes that consumers will engage with their advertisements if they are forced to. Sometimes, the strategy works. Roughly 51 percent of millennials aged 15 to 24 said they were willing to view advertisements if it meant they could access free content (Nielsen 2017).

People of all ages typically find the so-called traditional media—including newspaper, radio, and television—most trustworthy, and Millennials are no exception (Rody-Mantha 2018). They consider advertisements that appear in newspapers to be the most trustworthy of all, followed by radio, "out of home"—outdoor advertising that reaches consumers when they are not at home—and, finally, television advertisements. They also consider "new" digital media trustworthy, rating email promotions highest on this front. Millennials are more willing to trust social media advertising than their older counterparts (Genoese 2016; Dharmesti et al. 2019; Wang et al. 2018).

These trends have accordingly influenced the strategies that marketers use to reach millennials. For one, most marketers now know they need to appear genuine, socially conscious, and "alternative" if they want to appeal to millennials. The millennials' desire for ethical consumption (or at least its appearance) has also led to the emergence of "ethical marketers," who supposedly put corporate social responsibility front and centre. We will have more to say about them later.

Cause-related marketing campaigns have also emerged as a popular strategy (Guerreiro et al. 2016; Pracejus et al. 2020; Howie et al. 2018). These appeals link a product or brand with a socially worthy cause. For example, Bell Canada's "Bell Let's Talk" event raises awareness of mental health initiatives. It also raises awareness of Bell itself, and creates the impression that Bell is socially conscious. As well, many marketers have begun to show more diverse people in their advertisements (for example, Campbell's Soup ran an advertisement showing a gay couple feeding their son). This implies that they endorse and promote socially worthy goals of inclusion and equality.

Appeals to rational self-interest also appear in digital advertising. Consumers are still encouraged to consider what products can do for them personally—to consider how products, as totems, can represent their group membership and social connectedness. One result of this is the formation of communities around various products or organizations (such as the Lululemon bag, which signals membership in the Lululemon "community"). We will discuss brand communities in the next chapter.

To repeat an earlier point, advertising is a form of social communication. As social communication, advertising has changed society in several important ways. First, it has increased the power of large corporations by helping them reach ever-larger numbers of people. Second, it has concentrated this communicative potential in the hands of a few gigantic institutions (for example, Facebook and Google). Third, it has changed how people interact and socialize with one another online. Fourth and finally, advertising has become a means through which we approach politics, social problems, and even personal problems.

Box 6-3
The Cheerios Effect

If you have ever poured Cheerios into milk, you have seen the "Cheerios effect" in action. In science, the Cheerios effect is the mutual attraction of floating objects, due to surface tension. Toronto agency Cossette launched its Cheerios campaign in 2014. They used the "Cheerios effect" to represent a "human desire to connect." Tapping into widespread concern about isolation, these advertisements featured stories about diverse people coming together—an appealing message of unity in multicultural Canada.

Jason Doolan, marketing director of General Mills Canada, emphasized that he wanted his advertisements to "be relevant" to consumers. He felt that cause-based advertising could help achieve that goal. Doolan also considered another Cheerios ad a great success. It addressed the link between dieting and self-esteem—a cause many care about, but which some struggled to connect to the Cheerios brand.

Responses to the "Cheerios effect" campaign were similarly mixed. Some thought the message had been stretched too far: they found it hard to equate human connection and solidarity with cereal clumping. So, cause-related marketing no doubt appeals to many consumers, but it is hard to pull off effectively.

For these and other reasons, historian Stuart Ewen (1976; see also Guarneri 2017; Ha 2019) has called people who run the advertising industry "captains of consciousness." These captains shape how we see the world and manipulate our needs, to make us want to buy particular goods and services.

Effectiveness of Media and Advertising

Even in the earliest mass media studies, in the 1930s, researchers were worried about the potential power of new media technologies. Adolf Hitler's successful use of radio for propaganda, for example, was a lesson in the possible dangers of the new media. Some started to fear that mass media would enable a new and dangerous form of mind control, with a tiny elite of communicators dominating huge, passive audiences. However, more recent studies of the media show their effects are complex, hard to predict, and depend on many factors. These include the audience's class, values, beliefs, emotional state, social context, and even the time of day.

In other words, researchers have come to realize how hard it is to *prove* that mass media or advertising work as desired. We face an interesting riddle: the survival of an activity—a costly activity—that does not predictably achieve its stated goal of selling products. Advertising's persistence in the face of mixed results suggests that it must achieve an unintended or latent goal, perhaps one that is ritual or aesthetic. In a review of books on the history of advertising, Canadian historian Paul Rutherford (1988: 104) touches on this challenge. Reiterating there is no clear evidence that advertising works (but for a later examination of its effectiveness, see Rutherford 2018), he suggests instead that advertising is "best seen as a cultural phenomenon whose social significance, and perhaps social power as well, is far greater than its economic significance or its impact on the marketplace." Perhaps, he infers, "advertising has become the chief means of shaping common sense in the so-called First World." It provides entertaining myths and messages to live by, whether selling products or not, and is "a sometimes amusing, sometimes enlightening form of art."

In the marketing industry, this uncertainty is one of the more enduring frustrations, as well as one of the more enduring criticisms professionals face. In an age when businesses of all types demand measurable results for every investment, marketing and advertising remain hard to assess with agreed-on metrics. Until recently, no one has been able to say with certainty whether an advertisement *made* a consumer do or buy what the advertisement promoted.

In fact, many marketers would deny that advertising ever has the ability to compel buying. They recognize the complex web of factors that drive consumers' behaviour. Yet, because they cannot guarantee results, marketers are routinely accused of being unpredictably effective and financially unaccountable. For their part, some marketers are frustrated with what they see as an obsession with analytics and sales. People who got into the industry because they wanted to be creative and experimental often feel they are doing work that focuses only on making profits.

One way that marketers try to ensure they are making a good investment is through advertisement pretesting (Rossiter and Percy 2017; O'Keefe 2018). Before launching an advertising campaign, they may try it out on test groups to assess its impact, the emotional reactions it elicits, and whether people remember it afterward. Marketers also post-test their advertising. Often, they do this through a customer survey or recall test, in which each respondent or test group is asked about what advertisements he or she has seen recently. Or they may use recognition tests, in which each respondent is shown the advertisement and asked if they recall it and what it meant to them.

Another evaluation technique is sales testing. This approach measures the sales or order growth that followed (and presumably resulted from) an advertising campaign. This is a less reliable test because, generally, advertising works more on shaping opinions than on immediate buys.

Nevertheless, marketers do their best to connect their advertising to changes in sale volume. Doing so may include measures of the impact of the campaign on revenues compared to advertising expenses. Alternatively, they may measure the number of new leads resulting from a campaign or the number of new customers gained thanks (at least in part) to the campaign. Or they may simply measure the percentage increase in sales after a campaign, compared with the period immediately prior.

Offer redemption is often the simplest method of evaluating a campaign (see, for example, Kirkman 2019). It measures the uptake of a special offer promoted in the advertising, such as a lowered price, a special package, or a coupon included in the advertisement. These methods give easy measures of the interest in an offer or a product, following an advertisement.

The growing availability of **big data** has raised new challenges and provided new opportunities to measure advertising effectiveness (Gordon et al. 2019). "Big data" are large data sets that, when analyzed by computer, reveal patterns, trends, and associations in human behavior: for example, buying patterns and consumer preferences.

 Ideally, a measurement of advertising effectiveness would draw on randomized controlled trials (RCTs). In the past, this has rarely been possible. Instead, marketers have typically relied on uncontrolled observational methods to estimate their advertisements' effectiveness. For various reasons, these more casual methods are not reliable, as shown by a study Gordon et al. (2019) carried out using data from 15 U.S. Facebook advertising experiments. A series of randomized experiments and observations yielded different results for the traditional and big data methods, even after controlling for demographic and behavioral variables. It's clear that, increasingly, marketers will have to rely on these new, more data-intensive methods.

That said, even big data studies do not always lead to similar conclusions. On the one hand, Lewis and Rao (2015a: 1941) used big data to carry out 25 large field experiments with major U.S. retailers and brokerages. These ad campaigns had reached millions of people and cost $2.8 million. The sales data showed that individual consumers' buying habits changed quickly and unpredictably. Given the amount spent on each individual consumer, it wasn't obvious the advertising had paid off in higher sales.

On the other hand, another study using big data reported the "positive, sizable, and persistent" impact of online and offline advertisements on a retailer's profits (Lewis and Reiley (2014: 263). Revenue, they said, was seven times the cost of the advertisements, making these advertisements well worth the expense. Another randomized field experiment on three million consumers similarly found that online display advertisements increased sales by 3.6 percent, compared to a control group (Johnson et al. 2017: 43).

Yet another study looked at advertising for movies (Elberse and Anand 2007; Karray and Debernitz 2017). It also found an impact on revenue. However, the effect of advertising varied strongly across movies of different "quality." Returns on advertising may be high for well-received movies, but estimated returns on advertising for the average (or poor) movie are often negative. This finding supports research that has examined the relationship between a film's acclaim by critics and commercial profitability. Most researchers have found a positive connection between reviewers' assessments of a movie and box-office success, controlling for other possible effects on success. In other words, even a massive (and massively expensive) advertising campaign may not be able to turn a pig's ear of a movie into a silk purse.

Huang et al. (2015) remind us that movie advertising can be tricky. Films are often—if not always—advertised before they are released. Marketers want to drum up excitement to ensure consumers flood into the theater on opening day. For that reason, they spend most of their advertising dollars on pre-release advertisements. But it's hard to know whether these advertisements are working. After all, there are no sales data yet. Instead, they have to rely on consumer surveys after the opening day, and these can be expensive.

Another issue is the effectiveness of different media. Many advertisers are reluctant to shift a large fraction of their advertising budget to the Internet because they still view television advertising as most effective. The data are divided on this question. By studying 20 advertising campaigns across various industries, Draganska et al. (2013) found that Internet advertisements perform just as well as television advertisements. Considering differences among media formats, brand recall for Internet advertisements proved as good as that for television ads. On the other hand, Bollinger et al. (2013) studied the effect of television, online banner advertisements, and Facebook exposures on buying. They found that both TV and online exposure creates goodwill, which increases household spending on a product. By contrast, Facebook exposure—another kind of online advertising—has an insignificant effect on buys.

Online word of mouth (OWOM) represents a powerful new tool for marketers.

Because timing is so important, firms across many industries release new products in stages, launching separate advertising campaigns at each stage (Bruce et al. 2012a). In this way, both advertising and **word of mouth** (**WOM**) can play a role. Examining the theater-to-video sequential distribution of motion pictures, one study found that spending more on advertising was effective at the earlier stages. Then, there was more time for consumers to absorb the advertisements, and advertising effects could operate in tandem with WOM. Along similar lines, Moon et al. (2010) found that high advertising spending on movies, coupled with high ratings from both professional critics and viewers, maximized revenue.

Precisely *what* these advertisements and reviews say can be just as important as how many of them there are. Gopinath et al. (2014) compared **online word of mouth** (**OWOM**) with traditional advertising. They found that only positive OWOM recommendations had a direct impact on sales, and this impact increased over time. Contrast this with the influence of attribute advertising (i.e., what the product does) and emotion advertising (i.e., what it makes you feel). The influence of this advertising usually decreased over time (see also Chae et al. 2017; Fay and Larkin 2017; Seiler et al. 2017). Also, consistent with prior research, the researchers find that attribute advertisements wear out a bit faster than emotional ones. **Wearout** refers to the decline in an advertisement's effectiveness over time. Marketers may use different versions of advertisements, with different themes, to minimize this problem (Bass et al. 2007; Chae et al. 2019; Chen et al. 2016; Woelbert and d'Hombres 2019).

Similar principles apply to **celebrity endorsements**. Negative comments from a celebrity can be harmful to an advertising campaign (Amos et al. 2008; Knoll and Mathes, 2017; Pradhan et al. 2016). On the other hand, positive comments from celebrities who are seen as trusty, expert, and attractive can increase approval of a product and plans to buy it. Attractiveness and reliability are always desirable in celebrity endorsements; expertise is only necessary for some products. For example, people will be more swayed by a race-car driver endorsing automobiles and motor oil.

Lovett and Staelin (2016: 142) compare three ways firms can communicate about their brands: through **paid media** (advertising), **earned media** (unpaid news coverage), and **owned media** (brand websites and other owned content). They also consider the roles these advertising types play in reminding us, informing us, and increasing enjoyment of the brand. Stated most simply, they find advertising calls people's attention to a product and makes them think about it, often in a positive way. But advertising may not be able to direct attention as narrowly as marketers would like. It may put the viewer in the mood to buy a car, but not necessarily to buy the car advertised.

In fact, some advertisements may unintentionally promote rival products. In one study, display advertising was used to influence what customers searched for online: it made them search for the advertised brand, but information about competitors also appeared (Lewis and Nguyen report 2015: 93). As a result, the display advertisements increased searches for the advertised brand by 30 percent to 45 percent, but they also increased searches for competitors by up to 23 percent.

Last, even as advances are made in measuring traditional advertising, new challenges are on the horizon. As mentioned, media no longer work just one way. When consumers can interact with media, it becomes hard to isolate the impact of a single advertisement (Pavlou and Stewart 2000; Bang et al. 2019). With that in mind, marketers will need to figure out how to account for the ways people choose which advertisements to watch (rather than skip) and how they interact with those advertisements (if at all).

In short, marketers can wish that advertising has the desired effect, but often, researchers are far from being able to prove it or measure the impact. Advertising probably does have measurable (and increasingly, well-measured) effects on sales, but it is usually difficult to get the data needed for such measurements. It is also difficult to disentangle the welter of influences that go into making an advertised product a commercial success or a commercial failure.

Criticisms of Advertising

Despite the uncertainty about its effectiveness, advertising has been criticized for decades. But before we examine that criticism, let's first consider the praise advertising has also received. Some have claimed that advertising promotes and diffuses innovation throughout society and stimulates new product development. Many of the great modern inventions and innovations—such as cars, telephones, cameras, record players, air travel, electrical appliances, and computers—have relied on promotion through advertising. And because it is an aspect of market competition, advertising contributes to lower prices and helps prevent monopolies. Beyond that, advertising gives people information about products and issues of interest. Sometimes, advertising is even an entertainment in its own right.

However, criticisms of advertising are more numerous than words of approval. First, some say advertising puts consumers at risk because ads are not always fair, honest, and truthful. Some governments attempt to rectify this, but the controls they put on advertising vary. Some countries provide light advisory control (for example, forbidding cigarette advertising), while other countries (like China) censor advertising extensively. Some countries allow unsubstantiated claims for certain products ("Product X improves your health") whereas others do not. Some countries allow the use of exaggeration ("Product X is the best mouthwash you can buy") while others do not. For example, in the UK, the beer company Carlsberg had to modify its claim to be "the best lager in the world" with the word "probably."

Internet-based advertising has complicated things even more for regulatory authorities. Goods and services ordered online from other countries are not necessarily subject to national quality and safety controls. For example, drugs that are sold over the counter in one country may be available only by prescription in another. People may see them advertised online, order them remotely, and receive them through the mail, bypassing local rules and controls. Quality assurance for goods and services advertised on the Internet can thus be sketchy.

Some claim that the media, and especially advertisements, prey on people's gullibility and self-consciousness. They make people feel like they have a horrible problem, like body odour, then offer them a product that allegedly solves the alleged problem, like a perfect deodorant (Goldman, 1992; Tsai et al. 2019).

For instance, there's a huge market for "anti-aging" products among middle-aged North American women. Marketers tap into these women's insecurities around wrinkles and stretch marks. They sell them products that will supposedly "erase" those lines and "take off" 10 years. Advertisers focus on specific demographic groups like this because advertisements are expensive. Marketers don't want to waste their money advertising to people with limited buying power or little likelihood of buying the product on offer. The trick is figuring out what will appeal to the needs, vanities, and insecurities of particular slices of the population.

A second criticism is that advertisements may produce what Presbrey (1929; see also Beard 2017), long ago, called "national homogeneity." Marketers are selling consumers the same products over and over, packaged in different ways. To impress consumers, they make their message sound professional, glamorous, or research-based—whatever they think will best resonate with their audience (Stanfield and Stanfield 1980; but see also Watkins 2018). Consumers waste their money and throw away perfectly good products, believing the new product will make them professional, glamorous, or whatever other outcome the ad promised.

A third common criticism is that advertising distorts the economy and our culture. From this perspective, advertising aims to convince us that consumption is the only worthwhile source of satisfaction and happiness in life. Advertising creates false needs to manipulate people into buying. It convinces people to buy nonessential goods—Baudrillardian signs that are used to signal status, at best. In effect, advertising directs people's attention away from real-life concerns towards fantasy goals and fantasy worries.

Fourth and finally, advertising locks in the status quo. Stuart Ewen, who characterized advertisers as the "captains of consciousness," famously also calls advertising the "surface fluff" of capitalism (Ewen 1976: 80). By that, he meant that advertising hides the darker realities of capitalism, including the class struggle between corporations and consumers. By locking people into con

---

Box 6-4
Dove: Capturing the Rise of "Real Beauty"

For much of the 20th century, media fed on women's insecurities. For example, Listerine's 1927 advertisement campaign used the slogan "Often a bridesmaid, never a bride." It was among the first of many companies to portray a sad woman whose physical imperfections—bad breath, skin blemishes, and dandruff—kept her from finding love. Today, advertisers continue to assure women that buying particular clothes, makeup, skincare products, and so on will make them attractive enough to win a mate.

In the 1970s, feminists started criticizing this approach. The movement aimed to encourage women to love themselves and honour their bodies. Eventually, marketers caught on. Dove's 2007 "Campaign for Real Beauty" in Canada featured women of all shapes, sizes, ages, and races. Instead of "become more beautiful," Dove's campaign asked women to "embrace the attributes that already made them beautiful." This campaign was a huge success. Dove's sales increased from $2.5 billion to over $4 billion. Since then, more advertisements have used women with "everyday" looks to capture "real beauty." Today, marketers love to point out when their women are "Photoshop-free" and represent a range of the dimensions of diversity.

---

sumerism—by ensuring we continue to believe that buying things is the only way to be happy—advertising locks workers into jobs they hate and obedience to the demands of the capitalist boss.

Advertising as Propaganda

Advertising a political candidate or a political party is not different from advertising deodorant. Both the commercial and political product rely on enchantment, mythmaking, and some measure of misinformation.

In their examination of fascist German filmmaking, Adorno and Horkheimer noted that media can spread political propaganda as well as commercial fantasy. In so doing, they can spread misinformation and drum up support for dangerous—even deadly—ideas and movements. When marketers spread distorted or made up stories to serve a political agenda, we call it "propaganda."

Voters today have an increasingly difficult time sourcing reliable information about the candidates and parties for whom they should cast their ballots. Fake news, for example, can include intentionally misleading content shared via traditional or new media. Instead of persuading voters to support a given candidate by sharing information about their platform, spreaders of fake news might dishonestly smear an opponent. The role of targeted advertising in fair elections has also been questioned. Targeted ads are ads that are strategically placed in front of specific audiences. For example, misinformation about a particular candidate or party could be targeted to reach voters likely to support that candidate or party.

French philosopher and sociologist Jacques Ellul tackled the issue in his 1962 book *Propaganda: The Formation of Men's Attitudes* (see also Tal and Gordon 2016, for an appreciation of this work). There, he focused on hidden political messages the masses may not even be aware of. For Ellul, propaganda isn't easily recognizable. It blends in with our culture and infiltrates all mainstream institutions including schools, businesses, and governments. For that reason, Ellul says every modern state is drenched with propaganda (along similar lines, see Jowett and O'Donnell 2018; Mackenzie 2017; Benkler et al. 2018).

Although we live in a democracy, Ellul says our government does not follow public opinion; it leads it. It does not trust regular citizens to competently decide important state matters. Instead, governments take over and make all the decisions, but to avoid public backlash, they let citizens think everything was their idea. Governments use propaganda to convince people that democracy is alive and well. Elected officials give speeches, go on tours, and appear on the media to create the impression that public opinion is still important to them. Government leaders communicate dumbed-down messages designed to resonate with the public. They even play on the public's fears and cater to their wants.

Why do people accept government (and other) propaganda? For one thing, they get to feel like they are actively influencing their country's future. Political propaganda, for Ellul, makes people think *they* were the ones who got their government to decide what they did.

Second, Ellul calls propaganda the "true remedy for loneliness" (147). If you buy into propaganda, you join a huge community of others who think the same things. You embrace a collective ideology and share ideas with people who agree with you. Most important, propaganda gives you an outlet for your frustration and anger. Adorno and Horkheimer used Hitler's scapegoating of the Jews as an example. Recall that Hitler blamed the Jews for all of Germany's problems. He successfully convinced his followers to direct all their fear and rage towards this hated group. Scapegoating is still used by politicians today, for similar purposes.

Ellul links propaganda, like mass consumption of every kind, to a standardized message that tells people what they need and want to hear. People buy useless stuff in great profusion because they've been told, again and again, to want that stuff. Such propaganda serves the capitalist ideology. It's even more effective when it's concentrated. If news agencies, the press, and other media outlets all trumpet the same message, it's easier to standardize that message and beat people over the head with it.

Though Ellul focuses on political propaganda, his argument has many obvious links to consumerism. For one, in our consumer society, every politician serves capitalism. All political propaganda must uphold the economic system our society is based on. Second, the same principles used in political propaganda apply to advertising—a form of propaganda in itself. As we have seen, myths, images, stories, and ideologies are all part of selling a commercial product, just as they are part of selling a political candidate or platform.

Viewers and Viewership as Commodities

Advertisements reflect the collaboration of several key players, each with their own interests. Media owners want advertisers to buy (properly, "rent") advertising space at a high rate per page or per second of exposure. Advertisers want consumers to buy the advertised product or feel good-will towards the advertised brand. Finally, for advertisements to mean anything, there must be consumers to target.

All of these players interact through what Sut Jhally (2005) calls (in the book of the same name) the codes of advertising (for a discussion of codes of advertising applied to women consumers, see Butkowski and Tajima 2017). He says media owners and marketers turn consumers into unpaid workers (on this, see also Ravenelle 2019). Media owners have access to millions of people who spend hours every day watching their television shows or listening to their radio stations. It is this time spent watching or listening that the media sell to ad companies. The cost of an ad is based on the number of people who will see or hear it.

In effect, ordinary people work without pay for media owners, who profit from their viewership. While they unwind after work in front of the TV, or seek news updates on the radio, consumers are unwittingly generating huge profits for media corporations. Jhally compares the unpaid labor we do watching TV in our living rooms to factory work. However, while factory workers get a small share of the profits that they produce for factory owners, viewers get none of the profits they produce for media owners. That makes media the perfect tool of capitalist exploitation (Jenkins et al. 2018).

The Corrupting Influence of Advertising

Yet another criticism that has been leveled at advertising—whether political or commercial—is that it corrupts what is "good." It takes authentic traditions and genuine sentiments and packages them into commercial, commodified products. In this sense, some say, it transforms anything and everything into a profit-making opportunity.

Perhaps the most popular subject of this criticism is Christmas. Advertising, critics propose, has made people think about this holiday in a new, commercial way. Today, Christmas isn't (much) about the Christian values many associated with the holiday centuries ago. Instead, it's about shopping and gift-giving. Christmas has been dubbed "the most important consumption festival in the United States" (Hirschman and LaBarbera 1989; Miller 2017; Batinga et al. 2017). The same is true in Canada.

In his book, *Unwrapping Christmas* (Miller 1995; also, 2016), Daniel Miller notes that today people celebrate Christmas all around the world (for a multicultural follow-up to this book, see Feller 2019). True, some Christians still stick close to tradition, attending midnight mass on Christmas Eve, for example. But many non-Christians also put up trees, decorate their homes, host family dinners, and exchange gifts. What's more, Christmas has become a *season*. "The holidays" include not only December 25, but also most of December leading up to it, Boxing Day, New Year's Eve, and January 1. Arguably, the season kicks off with the supreme shopping day of the year, Black Friday, near the end of November.

Box 6-5

One Hundred Years of Christmas with Eaton's

Eaton's mail-order catalogue encouraged Canadians to make Christmas gift-giving a convention. Images in the catalogs portrayed Christmas as a special time to spend. Early catalogues suggested gifts that were small and practical, such as handkerchiefs, pencils, pocketknives, silverware, and sewing baskets.

The real indulgence in holiday spending was for children. Across the country, each Eaton's store had its own Toyland during the Christmas season, complete with an in-person Santa Claus. For decades, Eaton's sponsored the Santa Claus Parade that wound its way through the centre of Toronto (a photograph of the 1918 parade is reproduced above). Children looked forward to reading the catalogs and dreaming about the gifts they might receive.

The national chain of Eaton's stores closed in 1999, but Toronto's Eaton Centre continued the legacy of Christmas at Eaton's. Christmas is still a time for family, but it is also a time for shopping—the biggest shopping season of the year. Today, the Eaton Centre's approach to Christmas stresses "last-minute holiday shopping." Every store in the Eaton Centre uses Christmas to cultivate the culture of materialism and only secondarily, the culture of "time with the family."

This holiday season comes with lots of buying. People are buying not only gifts, but also trees, ornaments, turkeys, candles, garlands, and wreaths. Marketers tell us these purchases serve a higher purpose: this money is spent in the "Christmas spirit," to celebrate our loved ones. The goods we buy for Christmas are thus given moral worth. They may be foolish trappings, yet we come to think they have emotional and spiritual meaning. Christmas buys (supposedly) help us show our loved ones how important they are to us.

It's hard not to notice this confluence of consumerism and marketing at Christmas time. But perhaps the media are not wholly to blame. Christmas has historically been a season of feasting, drinking, and excess (Nissenbaum 1996; Weinberger 2017). The media alone did not make consumers treat this season as a buying and spending frenzy.

Long ago, Christmas may have been about bringing families together. But, according to Miller, the holiday is now about materialism, capitalism, profit-making, and marketing. Advertisers latch onto popular stories like Rudolph the red-nosed reindeer to sell us goods we don't need. As well, advertisers socialize our children to see the materialism in Christmas. Even their "letters to Santa"—lists of consumer goods they long for—are featured in newspapers and on social media and read out loud on talk shows.

Christmas, as marketers frame it, is made for people with money to spend. They're encouraged to spend it freely, because they're spending "for family." As Miller puts it, Christmas gift-giving is just "an excuse for greed." And it's not just gifts; every instance of spending is seen as a family bonding ritual. Families spend quality time together at Christmas markets, where they buy seasonal paraphernalia. Then they decorate the tree with all the overpriced ornaments they bought. All shopping during this season happens in the name of family unity.

Final Thoughts

So far in this book, we have repeatedly noted that consumerism is a social and communicative behaviour. This chapter shows that advertising is a way of communicating persuasively with consumers and a way of equipping them to communicate with one another. As a key feature of our consumer culture, advertisements help shape the conversation about goods and services. They both reflect our views on our consumer society and help perpetuate them.

Many critics think advertising is harmful in many ways. Some point out that large corporations do the most advertising and reach the most people. This means the power that comes with mass influence concentrates in the hands of a few. Others highlight how the media has affected our political system. This includes the debate around fake news, and the way that accusations against political candidates spread like wildfire across multiple channels.

The research we reviewed in this chapter suggests some of these critiques are justified. However, we will likely never be able to show that advertising *causes* these problems, much less that it is their main or only cause. Instead, advertising is one of many factors that supports capitalism by encouraging consumers to buy.

In the next chapter, we continue this discussion about marketing with a focus on brands and branding. Nothing shows the power of modern advertising as clearly as the power of successful brands to inspire, compel, and bewitch consumers.

Discussion Questions

1. In this chapter, we talked about the prevalence of advertising in society. Advertising has evolved and influenced the public in significant ways. Besides the economic factors, why is advertising so important in our lives? Consider how individuals advertise themselves with social media.

2. While some goods are purchased for their utility, others are purchased for symbolic meaning. Based on the three reasons identified in the text, think of something you recently bought primarily for symbolic value. Which of the reason(s) had the most impact on your purchasing decision and why? How much do you think advertising and mass media shaped/changed how you perceive the value in goods today?

3. Different people trust word-of-mouth (WOM) information for different reasons. It might be because of the influencer's expertise or one's relationship with the influencer. Think of influencers you follow, or the times you purchased something a friend suggested. What are the factors you took into consideration before buying something through WOM?

4. Craig J. Thompson used stories of heroes and villains as part of "enchantment" to make consumers buy products to feel heroic. Take some of your favourite childhood stories or heroes. Think of examples in advertisements that drew on these narratives. Then, consider how they transformed into products/ideas you consumed.

5. One critique on the dangers of media and advertising is that games portraying realistic violence may spark "real" violence or aggression in players. How do you see this argument in your own experience, or those you know? Why do you think virtual fantasies focus on a theme of violence/ deviance? Think about the social factors that play into its popularity and consumer's desire.

Quick Quiz

1. How is communication defined in the text?
a. The study of how information is transmitted through various means
b. The exchange of ideas and values in society
c. The imparting and exchange of information and news
d. The means of connecting people and places
e. The means of sending or receiving information

2. What are mass media?
a. Spreading academic information into the population
b. Communication that conveys information using many mediums simultaneously
c. Communication that conveys information simultaneously to large numbers of people
d. The transformation in media that developed large mediums of communication
e. Communication targeted to the majority population of a society

3. What is the cultural economy?
a. The part of the economy made up of creative and cultural industries
b. The careful management of culture as wealth
c. The cultural resources of a country or region
d. The part of economy concerned with culture
e. An economy centreed on culture

4. Which of the choices below best defines the function of advertising?
a. It is a marketing strategy
b. It persuades consumers to buy something they don't need
c. It promotes an idea, good, or service, paid by a sponsor
d. It builds awareness and recognition of a product
e. It promotes consumption in creative ways

5. What are the two basic aspects of advertising?
a. The content and method
b. The scope and reach
c. The message and medium
d. To persuade and inform
e. The market and audience

6. What form of communication was Marshall McLuhan referring to when he said that "the medium is the message"?
a. Written communication using bold language
b. Oral communication through WOM
c. Communication using pictographs
d. Communication using pictures and words
e. Communication using popular symbols

7. What did C. Wright Mills in *The Power Elite* (1956) see as a key sociological characteristic of mass media?
a. It dominates the mental life of modern societies
b. It is a one-way process
c. It is bureaucratic
d. It creates propaganda
e. It shapes the power structure of society

8. Which theorist is responsible for the concept of "commodity fetishism"?
a. Jean Baudrillard
b. Karl Marx
c. Sigmund Freud
d. Daniel Miller
e. Max Weber

9. Which is NOT one of the "compelling needs" Vance Packard identified that advertisers promise products to fulfill?
a. Emotional security
b. Ego gratification
c. Creative outlet
d. Reassurance of self-worth
e. Status attainment

10. What does Daniel Miller see as the major concern about the celebration of Christmas today?
a. Hedonism
b. Materialism
c. Secularism
d. Feminism
e. Social isolation

The answers to the Quick Quiz are provided at the end of the book.

For Further Reading

Social Communication in Advertising: Consumption in the Mediated Marketplace by William Leiss
A classic text for understanding how culture and commerce meet. The fourth edition is updated with current issues arising in the new media era.

The Mass Media in Canada, Fourth Edition by Mary Vipond
The Mass Media in Canada considers how the five largest mass media in Canada were shaped and how they in turn shaped society.

How the World Changed Social Media by Daniel Miller et al.
Analyzing the ethnographic work of nine anthropologists, *How the World Changed Social Media* offers insight into how social media have been transformed to impact politics and gender, education and commerce.

Media, Society, Culture and You by Mark Poepsel
Media, Society, Culture and You takes a historical approach, covering a range of topics in media, communication, culture, and social institutions. This helps us see how the "new" issues of media had their origins.

Key Terms

Advertising
Advertising effectiveness
Communication
Creative industries
Cultural economy
Enchantment
Fantasy
Marketing
Marketing strategy
Mass media
Sales promotion
Semiotics

Chapter Seven
Brands: The Struggle for Consumers' Desire

Learning Objectives

After reading this chapter, you will be able to:

✓   Understand how and why brand advertising emerged.

✓   List factors that may contribute to brand loyalty.

✓   Consider the consequences of mass publishing and the "democratization" of new media.

✓   See consumers as advertisers, via word of mouth and brand communities.

In past decades, most advertisements urged consumers to buy particular products. Today, most ads promote brands, not just products.

Why this momentous shift from simple, straightforward product promotion to this more abstract idea of brand promotion? There are many reasons, but one is what marketers describe as an "attention deficit." Impossibly large numbers of products and services exist in our consumer society. Every day, countless advertisements bombard consumers. Marketers know this and purposely try to make *their* advertisements "cut through the noise" and attract attention. The result is an ever-louder noise of advertising that, it seems, wearies at least some consumers.

One response is the emergence of "branded content." As we will see, branded content gives audiences the media information they seek. Less often does it annoy and interrupt them with information about something they do not want and did not ask for. By shifting to branded content, brands are trying to address the advertising avoidance of millennials and generation Z. For many, branded content is a way to rebuild trust, foster goodwill, improve reputation, and enhance corporate credibility.

In this chapter, we ask whether this increasing focus on brands has enticed more consumers to buy. Has the shift improved customer loyalty? Has this change benefited consumers by, for example, allowing them to base buying decisions on the recommendations of fellow consumers? Or are consumers now just subjected to even more subtle, manipulative forms of advertising disguised as emotional stories and heart-warming messages?

Bovril, a paste made of beef extract, was first produced in 1870 by John Lawson Johnston, a Scot living in Canada, and became extremely popular in the UK by the end of the 19th century.

Defining Our Terms

A **brand** is a trade name that is used to identify a manufacturer or a specific family of products (Keller 2020; Bronnenberg et al. 2018; Pike 2016).

The sale of branded products is said to have begun in the UK at the turn of the twentieth century. Some brands, such as Bovril and Horlicks, date from even earlier—from mid-Victorian times. Manufacturers introduced brands to distinguish their goods from those of their competitors. As consumers became more sophisticated, manufacturers placed more emphasis on promoting their brands directly to consumers, rather than just to distributors.

The manufacturers' rationale was (and, in general, continues to be) that by investing in their brands, they build up a brand image. **Brand image** is the impression consumers have of a brand's "personality" (Cheung et al. 2019; Wang et al. 2019; Kim et al. 2017). This idea of a brand image developed over time, in part through advertising, and is validated (or not) when the consumer experiences the branded product for themselves. Manufacturers think consumers will respond to a positive brand image by asking for generic goods by their brand names. To give a classic example, instead of saying they need to buy "tissues" (a product), well-trained consumers will say they need to buy "Kleenex" (a brand).

Before the widespread adoption of branding as a business practice, many products were sold as staples in bulk. But in the late nineteenth and early twentieth centuries, products came increasingly to be packaged, labeled, and promoted. This added a source and identity to the product (Bastos et al. 2012).

Today, packaging, labeling, and promotions often bear a brand's **logo**. A logo is a sign, letter, or symbol that represents a company or brand (Brasel and Hagtvedt 2016; Machado et al. 2018; Bresciani and Del Ponte 2017). It visually identifies the brand and triggers people's memory of it. Logos are typically displayed on buildings, signs, advertising, vehicles, uniforms, and websites. The average urban dweller sees an estimated thousand logos a day. To compete effectively, a brand needs a logo and other visual identifiers that are distinctive, easily recognizable, and memorable.

Logos are expected to elicit two responses from consumers. First, they are representative. A logo stands in as a symbol for its brand. For example, the familiar logo of Shell Oil—an open clamshell—helps you immediately identify a gas station as a Shell Oil gas station. Second, a logo can trigger a reaction in a consumer, by serving as a sign of the brand's identity. **Brand identity** is a set of distinctive features that a brand tries to suggest. It may call to mind the brand's history, philosophy, mission, business practice, or difference from competitors. So, ideally, when a consumer sees a logo, they react to its associated brand identity. Thus, the stylized representation of a shell is supposed to call to mind the brand's origin (shells originate in maritime regions, as does some of Shell's gasoline) and its business (oil comes from the fossilization of ancient, primitive materials). More to the point, perhaps, the original Shell company sold not only kerosene but oriental seashells and chose the latter as its symbol.

From this example alone, it's clear that logos do not always trigger reactions related to brand identity. The mere sight of the Shell Oil clamshell does not make the company's origin story spring to mind for every consumer. That doesn't necessarily make it (or the logos of many other companies that are merely representative) "bad." Especially given how many brands and logos consumers see every day, it is a feat in and of itself to get your logo recognized—to have consumers understand it signals your company.

Many brands invest heavily in explaining and justifying their logos, and it takes a while for the logo to sink in. People need to see a logo repeatedly before they automatically associate it with the brand (and maybe even with its identity). Often, brands introduce their logos during advertising campaigns. The resources needed to develop and entrench a logo explain why it's such a big deal to "re-brand" and develop a new one.

As mentioned, major brands create **branded content**. Branded content is content that is paid for or produced by a company to market that company's products (Lou and Yuan 2019; Lei et al. 2017; Hardy 2018). It aims to entertain, provide information, or educate; most important of all, it calls positive attention to the brand or the manufacturer. Thus, branded content is not advertising

---

Box 7-1

Branded Content

We briefly discussed Dove's 2013 Real Beauty campaign in the last chapter. Dove thought that too few women saw themselves as "beautiful." So, to spread their brand message—"beauty is for everyone"—they had women describe themselves while a sketch artist drew what he heard. Then, Dove had strangers describe the women while the sketch artist drew. The process was captured in a series of videos that showcased the dramatic differences between the two portraits. This branded content campaign was intended to help Dove showcase their values.

The strategy worked. The campaign was the most-watched branded content of the year it appeared and the third most-shared video. It went viral, spreading awareness to vast numbers of people at no extra cost to Dove.

Branded content is part of a brand's effort to make itself heard in a saturated market. Increasingly, it is aimed at millennials, whom some marketers see as impervious to traditional advertising. Branded content is thought to capture their attention and make them feel like the brand shares their views and values.

---

in the traditional sense, though it typically includes references to things related to the brand, such as logos, products, and brand values.

Many brands also respond to market saturation through the use of **influencer marketing** (Lou and Yuan 2019; Lagrée et al. 2018). **Influencers** are (seen as) trusted subject-matter experts with extensive contacts. Through their large social networks, they shape (or influence) the opinions of others about a particular topic (Khamis et al. 2017; De Veirman et al. 2017; Himelboim and Golan 2018). Often, influencers use their social media channels to promote a brand, product, or service to a particular target market. Typically, they receive payment from the brands they promote.

Brands, just like consumers, use influencers to associate themselves with certain types of groups and distance themselves from a different realm of influencers (and their followers). Brands choose influencers who represent their brand values—those who showcase lifestyles and voice opinions that align with the brand's. That's why brands often scramble to denounce and distance themselves from influencers who find themselves embroiled in scandal or who voice opinions that a brand's customers might find off-putting.

Some influencer content closely resembles paid advertisements and clearly recommends the purchase of a given product or service. However, much of their advice is less direct. It appears directly alongside, and looks similar to, regular content produced by ordinary people. An influencer's paid Instagram post may show up in a consumer's feeds right after their mother's or best friend's post. Unlike a traditional advertisement, it may lack high-quality Photoshopped imagery, a well-placed product, brand logo, or a clear call to action. For example, the sofa being promoted may appear in the background of a photo, and the brand's account may be tagged, allowing consumers to easily see where it came from.

However, some of this is starting to change. Rules are tightening to ensure influencers reveal when they are being paid for their content. For example, they may have to include markings such as "#ad" or "paid partnership" in their posts. As well, consumers are starting to catch on. They are beginning to see influencer marketing as just another kind of advertising. Many are happy to receive product recommendations in this way. However, others are annoyed that ads by influencers are interrupting their enjoyment of content from friends and family. And, as more and more brands use influencer marketing, this new marketing noise becomes just as loud and irritating as the traditional advertising noise.

Brands, for their continued success, depend on customer loyalty. **Customer** or **consumer loyalty** is the ability to keep customers from switching to competitors' products. However, gaining and keeping customer loyalty is difficult. To build customer loyalty means, at the least, delivering a product that meets customers' expectations and ensuring that customers feel valued (So et al. 2016; Luo et al. 2016; Kiseleva et al. 2016). When consumers are dissatisfied, they shop around for alternative products and brands. This is bad news for the brands that have been jilted. Research shows it can be up to six times more expensive to gain a new customer than to keep an existing one. What's more, happy customers tend to give positive word-of-mouth recommendations that improve a company's competitive position and lower marketing costs. Finally, satisfied customers are often less sensitive to price rises, giving a product higher profitability.

To build and preserve customer loyalty, brands often rely on **loyalty marketing** (Kumar 2019; Tanford et al. 2016; Berezan et al. 2017). This is a technique for gaining and keeping customers, giving them incentives to buy again, and persuading them not to switch to a competitor. **Loyalty programs** are one aspect of this, offering rewards to frequent customers, such as frequent flyer or hotel guest programs (Dorotic 2019; Brashear-Alejandro et al. 2016; Bijmolt and Verhoef 2017).

In the end, most customer loyalty depends on **customer** or **consumer satisfaction**. Consumer satisfaction is a consumer's belief that a product or service has met or exceeded his or her needs and expectations (Powers et al. 2018; Razak et al. 2016; Meesala and Paul 2018). To keep customer satisfaction high, many brands carefully monitor the quality and effectiveness of their customer care. Often, they do this through customer surveys, feedback cards, or online ratings and reviews. Sometimes, employees are rewarded for delivering excellent customer service with incentives such as bonuses.

The Value of Intangible Assets

Companies amass two types of assets: tangible and intangible. Tangible assets are properties of a company that people can touch and see. They include the company's real estate, factories, machinery, and inventory of products. Tangible assets are extremely valuable and important to a company's survival.

Today, however, intangible assets have gained almost equal importance. Intangible assets are properties of a company that people cannot touch or see. They include the company's image, identity, and brand. Unlike tangible assets, these intangible assets do not lose value as people use them. In fact, the more a brand is used—the more people talk about it, share its content online, and sport its branded merchandise—the stronger it becomes. And one of the most important brand assets is brand personality. **Brand personality** includes all of the characteristics or traits that consumers associate with a given brand (Davies et al. 2018; Matzler 2016; Rauschnabel 2016; Papadimitriou et al. 2019). For example, a brand may want to be seen as passionate, creative, disciplined, agile, and collaborative (Keller and Richey 2017). However, promoting a brand personality is not as simple as declaring that your brand is passionate or creative. Consumers want to see evidence of that passion and creativity repeatedly over time.

Often, consumers associate brand personality with the employees and representatives of the company that produce the brand. Their words and actions—whether helpful or unhelpful, friendly or surly—largely define how consumers see the brand's personality. Therefore, many companies have changed the way they train their staff to make them seem more helpful and friendly, for example.

In *Brand Society: How Brands Transform Management and Lifestyle*, Martin Kornberger (2012, 2017; also, Kornberger et al. 2017) shows that human relations departments in many industries try to convince employees to "live the brand." If that brand is fresh, edgy, and innovative, staff must learn to embody those qualities. Or if it's welcoming and inclusive, specialized training and recurring seminars are needed to make sure employees "bring the brand to life."

When brands behave in ways that contradict their proclaimed brand personality, consumers may turn against them. For example, consumers (especially millennials) increasingly reject brands that display unethical or environmentally dangerous practices, or that mistreat and exploit their workers. In these cases, many consumers judge these brands to lack compassion or good ethics. The result may be a boycott that devastates a brand's bottom line. We will discuss this further in a later chapter.

In short, consumers expect brands to "walk the talk." If advertisements or branded content declare a brand's commitment to certain values, consumers want to experience those values firsthand when they shop for and use the brand's products (Moore 2007; Brown 2016). For example, the Apple brand is all about simplicity and ease of use. These values are reflected in its clean, simple logo and advertisements. But if customers bought a MacBook and discovered it was impossible to use, with all sorts of excessively complicated features, their view of the brand would crumble.

In this sense, there are two parts to every brand. The first is how marketers *want* the brand to be seen; the second is how consumers actually see a company. Their experiences with the company, the way they interpret the brand's story, and how they use the product to shape their lifestyle all contribute to branding. In this sense, a brand is just as much about its consumers' lifestyles and identities as it is about the slogan an advertising executive made up to promote it (Spicer 2010; 2017).

A brand's tangible attributes—its products and services—are supposed to give concrete form to its immaterial attributes (Arvidsson 2005; Carah and Brodmerkel 2020). Using the products and services should make consumers feel the emotions and lifestyles the brand claims to embody. Viewed this way, a brand is an ideology, a memory, and a life experience (Holt 2007; von Loewenfeld and Kilian 2016). Branding has "symbolic and expressive functions" (Moore 2007). It gives meaning to everyday goods and services. Consumers then use these products to express who they are. They buy products that hold meanings they value, an approach sometimes called **purpose branding** (Holt 2015, 2016).

TOMS Shoes are a great example of this. Under their One for One model, whenever a customer buys a pair of TOMS shoes, the company donates a pair to someone in need. Customers who value the brand's reputation around doing good become loyal patrons. In this way, brands distinguish themselves from the competition when, chances are, several companies offer more or less the same product.

Deciding Between Brands: The Art of Standing Out

Every grocery, drug, and convenience store has an aisle full of soaps to pick from. Branding is the marketers' effort to make you pick *their* soap. It's about trying to influence people's choices when they are trying to choose between products that, in utility and price, are almost identical. How, precisely, does that decision-making work? What makes people choose one brand over another? There are several factors.

One is fame. Big, well-known brands can boost the buyer's personal identity and show others the sort of person you are. If you buy a bag from, say, Burberry, you become a member of a worldwide community of Burberry consumers (Holt et al. 2004; Parsons et al. 2017). You don't enjoy the same feeling of being "part of the club" when you buy an unlabeled purse from an anonymous seller in a backstreet market.

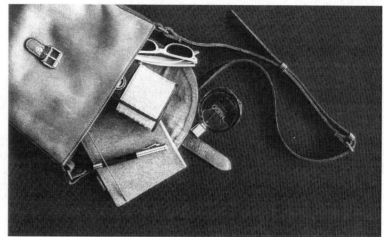

Consumers use prominent brands to boost their sense of personal identity. Brands are also often viewed as a guarantee of product quality.

Sometimes, branding implies better quality. Many people think branded products are simply better than generic or unbranded ones. For example, they'll opt for Gay Lea butter instead of No Name. They're even willing to pay more for branded items. Marketers spend time and money building these positive perceptions of their brands. For example, when brands have loyalty card programs, a cultivated corporate reputation, and programs designed to boost their in-store image, estimates of their quality increase (Calvo-Porral and Lang 2015).

It's hard to evaluate a product's quality when it's all packaged up on the shelf, or when looking at it online. But if you know the brand, you feel a little safer about what you are buying. You know what quality to expect. This is known as **reputation value** (Holt 2004; see also Ledikwe and Klopper 2019; Bratu 2019). Brands can build a reputation for being great or for being awful. When consumers compare two similar products, the tipping point may be one brand's reputation.

Similarly, good brands keep consumers coming back for more. In her widely read book, *Brands: The Logos of the Global Economy* (2006), Celia Lury says brands build customer attachment and loyalty. People come to know and love their brand of choice (on this, see also Paterson 2017). Sometimes, when consumers are faced with making a product choice, they opt for brands they have tried before or even just recognize. It feels more comfortable than risking hard-earned money on a brand you've never heard of. For the same reason, branding helps companies branch out into different products they weren't initially known for.

Consider Oral-B, best known for dental hygiene products like toothbrushes and floss. They also produce other items people like to use in their bathrooms, including nightlights. When people are in the market for a nightlight, they are more likely to choose the Oral-B branded version than one of the other choices. They've come to trust and rely on the Oral-B brand, whereas they may not know the other brands at all.

Box 7-2

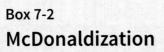

McDonald's is one of the most successful and resilient brands of all time. (The McDonald's restaurant pictured above, the oldest one still operating, opened in 1953 in Downey, California.) The chain sells hamburgers and other fast food, like hundreds of other companies. But its market share is significantly larger than that of its competitors. It owes part of its success to its branding, which guarantees the same selection of predictable food at any location in the world. McDonald's can deliver on that promise thanks to a process that social researcher George Ritzer (2009) called McDonaldization (on this, see also Ritzer 2017, 2018; Possamai 2018).

Ritzer explains that the chain developed a production model that's predictable, efficient, measurable, and controlled. It broke each production task down into logical, predictable parts until food preparation was no different from an automobile assembly line. Other fast-food restaurants—and companies in other industries—have succeeded by following the chain's lead, with mixed results.

McDonaldization has some negative features, Ritzer explains. For one, just like the original factory workers of the Industrial Revolution, McDonald's employees don't get to be creative. Many do the same monotonous task over and over, dipping baskets of french fries into a deep fryer or punching orders into a cash register. Over time, their physical, mental, and emotional health may suffer. Ritzer says it's a lot like the bureaucracies Max Weber criticized. Weber's classic analysis described them as "cages," where people's humanity is trampled on. Working in a fast-food restaurant like McDonald's is just as deadening and dehumanizing as working in the largest, most impersonal bureaucracy.

Finally, some brands need to focus on the *people* behind them. Branding is not exclusive to products and companies. People sometimes seek to brand themselves, too. That is, they aim to project a consistent image and identity for themselves through their aesthetic, online presence, work they do, or cause they believe in (Marwick et al. 2010; Whitmer 2019). People have been branding themselves for decades, as celebrities, movie stars, sports idols, or politicians. Today, **self-branding** is especially common on social media, where even ordinary people can craft the self-images they want to be known for (Chen 2013).

Commercial brands try to tap into this personal-branding trend and market their products as ways to authenticate consumers' personal brands. Companies develop a **brand genealogy** to help consumers make these mental connections (Holt 2007; 2018; also, Cantone et al. 2017; Testa et al. 2017). A brand genealogy is a storyline that appeals to consumers. Marketers rely on such stories because they are easily understood, and consumers can even relate them to their personal lives. They use brief, suggestive storylines that create a quick relationship between the brand and consumers.

As we cultivate our personal brands, we turn ourselves into advertisements for consumer products. As foundational figure Judith Butler (1987; also see for commentary, Maclaran 2018) has said, people perform gender. Along similar lines, today, people perform their entire selves for others to consume online. Many people seem to feel a constant need to document their hard work, comfortable life, or cool, trendy taste. And just like corporate branding, continuously pushing out content about ourselves builds, reinforces, and authenticates our personal brand over time (Khamis et al. 2017; Gandini 2016; Duffy and 2017).

The Politics of Personal Branding

Consumers can build their own personal brand thanks in large part to our relatively new power as publishers. You'll recall from the last chapter that control over mass media has traditionally been concentrated in the hands of the privileged few. Social media changed that, granting publishing power to the masses. Today, anyone can "talk back" to the media and create their own content. To explain why this is politically significant, we need to return to critical theorists Theodor Adorno and Max Horkheimer, whom we introduced earlier.

They explained that media helped early capitalism take root and keep it grounded in our culture today. The capitalist culture is like a factory, churning out standardized and predictable—i.e., branded—goods. According to Adorno and Horkheimer, mass media bloat consumers with easy, familiar pleasures, making people feel satisfied and tranquil, even if they hate their job or struggle to put food on the table. It keeps us glued to the couch, instead of questioning capitalism or standing up against it, as Marx recommended.

In this analysis, the bourgeoisie not only rule capitalist societies economically; they also control the arts and the media. They own broadcast corporations, newspapers, and film production companies, for instance. This control over the media helps them control consumers. Mass entertainment turns consumers into passive followers of capitalism. For Adorno and Horkheimer, the social role of the American film industry is not so different from the German film industry under fascism. Both create media meant to appeal to the masses, funded and delivered by a few powerful institutions. And both target a passive, almost hypnotized audience.

Adorno and Horkheimer want us to recognize that other media can be equally sinister. Like the German fascists, North American media owners have an agenda, too. Their own biases show up in the programming they fund. Their economic and political motives surface in our TV shows, movies, music, and magazines. Quiet compliance with capitalism is in their best interest. So, as discussed, they lull consumers into apathy with mind-numbing programs. Or, like Fox News in the U.S., they may try to oust governments they disagree with by airing programs that report on bad news, stir up unrest, and create feelings of crisis.

Finally, the media persuade us to think like consumers about education, politics, religion, and everything else. In other words, they work alongside families and schools to integrate us into a system of passive consumption. In that sense, capitalism and the media feed each other. Think of the music we pay to download, the magazines we buy, and the cable networks we view. Media content, itself a consumer product, is a good we pay for, thus supporting the capitalist economy. And capitalism also supports the mainstream media. Without the capitalist owners of the means of media production, there wouldn't *be* any media for us to consume.

What Adorno and Horkheimer could never have predicted was the Internet. The Internet—at least, ideally—lets anybody and everybody *create* their own media and share it with mass audiences (McQuarrie, Miller, and Phillips 2012). It lets ordinary people produce and disseminate their own, personally-branded content.

However, the Internet hasn't leveled the playing field. Despite the differences between traditional media and the Internet, capitalism prevails in both. While the platforms are depicted as "opposites," both function to dominate and filter media content. Some people still have a louder voice than others, even in the new media.

Take aspiring fashion influencers as an example. They can become bloggers or social media stars, if they have the right cultural capital (McQuarrie, Miller, and Phillips 2012; Corciolani et al. 2020). In their field, cultural capital means showing off their unique style and aesthetic consistently over time—in short, it means self-branding, as discussed above.

At first, fashion bloggers act like every other consumer on the Internet. They're just another commentator among millions. They comment on other blogs, share other people's content, and have conversations with their followers. But as these bloggers build their audiences, they stop interacting with followers, avoid answering specific questions, ignore suggestions for posts, and refuse to address issues raised in comments. (As we will discuss shortly, they begin by building "communities" around their personal brand, but those tight-knit communities eventually deteriorate into more casual "brand publics" (Arvidsson and Caliandro 2015)). Thus, like traditional media, Internet bloggers work to focus content and promote selective ignorance about the products available.

Once they've made it big, fashion bloggers enjoy economic and social rewards. Brands send them free clothes, make-up, and jewelry to model. Many also get paid every time they model those products. Others enjoy paid sponsorship of their blog content or paid writing assignments for other publications.

So, even though their audiences may be regular, everyday consumers, these bloggers gain status in the fashion industry that no regular consumer would ever enjoy. Consumers see bloggers as real people showing them how to wear fashionable items, using themselves as models. The blogger's "ordinariness" creates the illusion that a consumer could trade places with them—that they, too, could become fashion insiders. But it is indeed an illusion. The new influencers take part in mass media and support capitalism even when the Internet promises an equal base for everyone to voice their opinions. The new media is less democratic than we would like to believe. For example, not everyone has access to the Internet. That means not everyone has the opportunity to become a highly paid fashion influencer or otherwise use the new publishing power opened to the masses.

What's more, many people are not seizing this new ability to "talk back" at the media to challenge the capitalist status quo. Some are indeed engaging in meaningful conversations online—for example, the explosion of dialogue around anti-Black racism following the murder of George Floyd in May 2020. But others have joined the conversation with the goal of profiting by peddling consumer products to their loyal brand communities. There is nothing wrong with finding new ways to make a living in our capitalist economy. But the point here is that (at least some) consumers have used their new publishing power for profit, reinforcing the media's role in propping up capitalism.

Finally, mass publishing has not "rounded out the conversation," as some predicted. As mentioned, concentrated mass media ownership means content is biased. It means media support the views and causes that are good for a handful of wealthy, powerful owners. But if everyone's a publisher, social media should (in theory) become more representative, full of a diverse range of viewpoints, instead of only those that perpetuate the status quo. As we shall see, however, new and emerging media are anything but representative or unbiased.

Fake News and False Advertising

In 1929, Milton Handler published one of the earliest, most prescient academic discussions of false and misleading advertising, concluding:

> Newspaper censorship can weed out the blatant frauds. The Better Business Bureau can effectively work from without. But the solution can only come from within. A new business psychology must be bred. A regard for truth and a dislike for falsity must be learned. The buyer must learn to demand useful and truthful information. Here is a task for the educator and missionary. Here is the opportunity of the trade associations. The lawyer can do little (Handler 1929: 51).

Today, more than 90 years later, we are still beset by false advertising (Rhodes and Wilson 2018; Poddar et al. 2019), both in the commercial and political domains. Many would say the problems are even worse, as a result of both a darkening political climate and the rise of social media. Today, "fake news" poses significant problems in both politics and merchandising (Lazer et al. 2018; Tandoc et al. 2018). Large-scale purveyors of fake news allegedly include Facebook and Fox News Channel.

People have assigned various meanings to this term (Tandoc et al. 2018). What we mean here by **fake news** is information that is both factually inaccurate and intentionally deceptive. Typically, fake news is promoted by a combination of market segmentation and social media curation (Spohr 2017; Shu et al. 2017). Taken together, these processes put listeners and viewers into bubbles of prepared content and reduce their likelihood of encountering competing facts and interpretations, thus strengthening people's existing biases.

Fake news is hard to detect and regulate online because, for one, it is crafted to seem real. It doesn't always stand out as blatantly false. What's more, existing methods of detecting fake news in the traditional media, such as fact-checking, cannot be applied quickly or comprehensively online. That's because, every second of the day, countless users are producing endless content.

So, once again, we see the Internet has not levelled the media playing field and given everyone access to valuable and reliable information. Like the traditional media dominated by elites, digital content—even that created by average consumers—is apt to be biased and, often, has an agenda.

The most infamous example was the alleged use of fake news to influence the 2016 American election. Allcott and Gentzkow (2017: 232) guessed that "the average U.S. adult read and remembered one or more fake news articles during the election period, with higher exposure to pro-Trump articles than pro-Clinton articles." Shao et al. (2017) analyzed 14 million messages spreading 400,000 claims on Twitter, during and following the presidential campaign and election. These researchers found evidence that social bots played a crucial role in spreading fake news. These automated accounts often launched false claims, targeting influential users with the clout to spread them far and wide.

Curbing social bots could curb the spread of fake news. But controlling those bots will prove difficult, given how easy they are to set up and how quickly they operate through automation. What's more, much of the massive disinformation campaign was encouraged and paid for by the Russian government.

Though it seems apparent that fake news was spread during the election campaign, some have continued to debate how much—if at all—such news influenced voters' decisions. This debate reminds us of the market research on advertising, discussed in the last chapter. There is little (if any) concrete evidence to prove advertising *causes* consumers to purchase the advertised product or service, yet marketers spend vast sums on advertising. Similarly, studies like Spenkuch and Toniatti's (2016) question the degree to which political advertising is effective.

Nonetheless, political candidates and parties spend heavily on advertising during election campaigns. Marketers and politicians alike remain convinced they must brand and advertise themselves to succeed. And political branding (Lindblad 2019; Grimmer and Grube 2019; Pich and Newman 2019) is not so different from commercial branding. In both cases, a product is on offer. Buyers need information about it and receive that information from the media. And in both cases, the use of social media increases the risk of the spread of misinformation—fake news.

Even traditional media can misinform the public with *false claims*. In one study, Faerber and Kreling (2014) measured the distortion and outright lies in advertisements for pharmaceuticals.

Misleading claims omitted or exaggerated information, made lifestyle associations, or expressed opinions (not facts), while false claims were factually false or unsubstantiated. Analysis of television ads revealed a high degree of deception: of the most common claims in advertisements for prescription and non-prescription drugs, fully 57 percent were potentially misleading, and 10 percent were false. Only one-third of claims were objectively true.

If this level of deception exists in a heavily regulated industry like pharmaceuticals, one can imagine the amount of deception in other, less regulated fields, like politics. Below we consider the implications of fake news and false advertising for consumers seeking reliable information.

Box 7-3

How Ads Shape the Political Landscape

Social media has radically altered the way political messages are distributed and who sees them. In the Canadian federal election of 2019, political parties used Facebook, Twitter, and Instagram to garner the attention of the electorate. According to *Maclean's* magazine, "The Liberals spent as much as $148,947 on 2,592 ads in the first seven days of the campaign, including $92,685 on 1,991 ads purchased by the party, $50,662 by 73 candidates who spent more than $100 and as much as $5,600 by 56 candidates who spent less than $100." Increasingly, it seems candidates must "pay to play."

A CBC analysis reviewed 35,000 political ads on Facebook for the election in 2019. It found that a person's location will determine which ads are seen. According to the CBC study, most Facebook ads in Alberta and British Columbia discussed the oil and gas pipeline controversy. In Ontario, the ads focused on education cuts by the Conservative premier. In Alberta, the largest sponsor of ads was the Canadian Taxpayers Association. In B.C. it was the Canadian Energy Pipeline Association, and in Ontario it was three teachers' unions. Like advertisements for consumer goods and services, advertisements for politicians and their platforms are targeted, catering to the specific issues different voters care about.

Political parties in Canada, like elsewhere, use slogans to brand and distinguish themselves from one another. The Liberals used "Choose Forward" while the Conservatives went with "It's time for you to get ahead." The NDP told its followers the party was "In it for you," and the Green Party went "Forward Together." The Green Party further distinguished itself through a series of ads showing children standing in front of a white background, holding signs. This provided a stark visual contrast to ads from other political parties, which often highlighted the party's leader. While the Green Party seemed to want to highlight the future, other parties were more interested in focusing on the present.

The Power of WOM

Consumers are increasingly inclined to trust each other's recommendations as opposed to the claims made in advertisements (Hallem et al. 2018; Fritz et al. 2017; Riefler 2020), making word-of-mouth (WOM) information ever more critical.

Work by pathbreaking social researchers Elihu Katz and Paul Lazarsfeld (1966) showed that most people seek help from others to assess information from the media before acting on it (see also Balaji et al. 2016; Huete-Alcocer 2017). Typically, we do this by seeking the opinions of people we respect. Katz and Lazarsfeld called them opinion leaders. Today, they're more often known as the influencers already mentioned. These influencers help us decide what information to notice and what to ignore, who to vote for and who to vote against, what to buy and what to avoid (for an appreciation of Lazarsfeld's research, see Jerabek 2016).

WOM is essential when it comes to assessing products that are expensive and hard to evaluate from a distance (Litvin, Goldsmith, and Pan 2008; 2018)—things like foreign vacations or luxury hotels. People want to know whether they will enjoy a particular cruise, tour, or resort before they spend thousands of dollars. This need for reliable information makes WOM from people with firsthand experience valuable, and today we're better able to get that information than ever before. The Internet conveniently shows us the likes and dislikes of thousands of people just like us.

The widespread use of social media has heightened the importance of word-of-mouth (WOM) endorsements of products and services, with many companies devoting substantial resources to monitoring and responding to online reviews.

Think about the advertisements you've seen on Facebook or reviews you've read on TripAdvisor. You can quickly count how many thousands of people gave an airline a thumbs-up or left a nasty complaint. In these ways, you hear opinions you would not have, had you relied solely on your immediate friends and family for advice. Research shows that both buyers and sellers pay a lot of attention to the reviews that goods and services receive (Ifrach et al. 2013).

People trust WOM information for different reasons (Safdar et al. 2018). Some people focus on non-social factors, such as the rater's knowledge of and expertise on the thing they are recommending. Others concentrate on the rater's personal experience with the issue under discussion. Still others focus on social or personal factors, such as their relationship with the rater. People evaluate WOM information just as they evaluate information from advertisements and the mass media. They weigh all of these types of information carefully before making the (more or less) autonomous decision to consume.

Some raters and influencers use tactics reminiscent of those deployed by advertisers. On social media, influencers establish what feels like a personal, one-on-one relationship with consumers. Consumers "follow" their social media channels, "like" their posts, write comments on them, and perhaps even chat with them through direct messages. Many influencers address their followers as though they share personal ties. They open their videos with greetings like "Hey guys!" and refer to followers as part of a "family."

All of this makes **sponsored content**—paid content disguised as WOM—appear more trustworthy than traditional advertisements (Ikonen et al. 2017; Zhao et al. 2017). One study (Hutchinson 2019) found that 51 percent of social media users surveyed thought "content posted by other consumers is more authentic," 48 percent found it more relatable, 37 percent thought it was unbiased, and 29 percent bought a product after seeing it on an influencer's channel.

Box 7-4

The Evolution of Branding in the 21st Century

In a collection of essays titled *What is a 21st Century Brand? New Thinking from the Next Generation of Agency Leaders* (Kendall, 2015), branding professionals explore how the industry has evolved. First, they note that brands used to be longer-lived. They were built on one-way communication, with messages and calls to action exclusively from the producer to the consumer.

Today, you could say the reverse is true. Brands continuously change in response to consumer ratings and needs (see also Habib and Patwardhan 2019; Patwardhan et al. 2019). They do not only reflect the company's wants and needs; they are developed using careful market research and designed to add value for consumers. People want to know what the brand will do for *them*. They want to know how it will help them solve their problems and fulfill their wishes.

Second, today's consumers are also savvier. Branding is no longer about clear messaging alone. It relies on subtle signals and hints because marketers know that many consumers resist advertising. Marketers also know branding is a language of its own. If the marketer is careless, a brand can send unwanted signals unintentionally, or the messages may be misread or interpreted wrongly. In short, branding today takes more care and sophistication than in the past.

Some think that influencer marketing may have lost its peak power. Many followers and consumers today expect sponsored content, just like they expect TV commercials and magazine advertisements. Because of this, sponsored posts and WOM by influencers are no longer garnering the same audience interaction they once did. Young audiences in particular are increasingly skeptical of influencers. On the other hand, marketers are aware of the power of user-generated content and WOM recommendations. In response, they invest in programs designed to elicit ratings and reviews, and also strategize about how to get free recommendations from regular consumers (Evergreen and Sabarre 2019; Goulart, Sztejnberg and Giovanardi 2017). WOM, they think, can complement traditional advertising by allowing people to hear about a product from multiple sources (Hogan, Lemon, and Libai 2004; Fay et al. 2019).

In sum, consumers today are powerful communicators. Online ratings, reviews, and blogs allow them to play a critical role in shaping other consumers' impressions of available brands. This is hugely important because, as noted earlier, media-literate consumers are skeptical of advertisements and even branded content. They are increasingly likely to trust and believe their fellow consumers rather than marketers.

Some observers view this change as a sign that consumers' power has increased at the expense of marketers. Others like Lury disagree. In her book *Brands: The Logos of the Global Economy* (2006), she argues that marketers have more power than we realize. It's true, she says, that brands can't exist without consumers. They are brought to life only when consumers interact with them. Marketers listen to consumers' responses and reorient brands accordingly. They want us to believe they are at our service, making things that will improve our lives.

But Lury says it's the opposite. Brands don't cater to our wants. Instead, consumers are at the mercy of what brands want to sell us. To explain, she cites management consultant Peter Drucker who points out that marketing "does not start out with 'who is the customer?' but 'what do we want to sell?' It is aimed at getting people to buy the things you want to make" (2004: 60). (For more on Drucker's vision, see Minchin and Alpert 2017).

From this perspective, all that "power" consumers supposedly wield through WOM recommendations is actually just free labour. Consumers work on behalf of brands. Just as media owners sell the unpaid labour of their viewers to advertisers, marketers use the unpaid immaterial labour of consumers to build their brands (Farrugia 2018; Steinhoff 2019; Rose and Spencer 2016). When shopping for, comparing, and buying branded products, consumers review the values, experiences, and lifestyles associated with those brands. They also discuss their favourite and most hated brands. If marketers ensure their customers have excellent experiences with their brands, they'll enjoy free promotional labour in return. That labour is invaluable (Arvidsson 2005; Aakhus et al. 2017; Kaplan 2020). We know our friends and family aren't getting paid to tell us how great their new vacuum cleaner is, so we are more willing to believe these unpaid WOM testimonials than we are to believe paid advertisements.

If consumers had real power when it came to influencing brands, they would be able to vote with their money and WOM. They could buy and recommend brands offering the best version of a given item. Trademarks, according to Lury, keep that from happening. When producers trademark their logos or designs, they prevent other companies from making similar products. Lury suggests that trademarks help brands build monopolies, but they also stop progress. Improved products that better serve consumers' wants and needs can't be developed if innovators will be slapped with lawsuits for trying.

The Deterioration of Brand Communities

Brand communities are groups of people organized around their loyalty to a particular product or brand (Muniz and O'Guinn 2001; Li et al. 2019). They are not new. There have been brand communities of Harvard alumni, Yankee fans, and Apple users for decades (in the first two cases, for centuries). What is new is the multiplication of such communities through social media and their greater importance in marketing and sales. Thanks to digital media, brand communities can also be geographically dispersed. They may take various forms, from a Facebook group to an influencer's Instagram following, to a live group chat on a video game (see also Black and Veloutsou 2017; Coelho et al. 2018; Hollebeek et al. 2017). They also do much of the unpaid marketing work mentioned above, including WOM recommendations (Schroeder 2017).

Brand communities are a logical extension of the basic social processes we discussed at the beginning of this book: namely, the desire people have to form groups and exclude members of rival groups. In a world of "lonely crowds," people seek meaning wherever they can find it—even in the products they buy. They are hungry for association, for belonging and approval, and brand communities fulfill these needs (Arvidsson, 2015). Take the Lululemon brand community as an example. Everyone involved with retailer Lululemon is part of the brand community they have dubbed the "sweat collective." The idea is that when you shop at Lululemon, you aren't just buying workout wear; you're joining a community of like-minded people who are all committed to living a lifestyle of health and wellness.

To help you make this mental leap, Lululemon tries to entrench their brand values in many ways among both their employees and their customers. According to the *New York Times*, on a walk through Lululemon headquarters, you see a yoga studio, a meditation space, a 553-square-foot greenery wall, and a kombucha café. Working at Lululemon is like living in a yogic bubble. In this sense, they strive to authenticate their brand, showing consumers that the people peddling leggings and tank tops "walk the talk."

Lululemon intentionally works to extend the "sweat collective" through a multi-tiered ambassador program. Elite and community ambassadors alike work to keep the brand alive, whether by publishing branded content on social media, teaching Lululemon exercise classes, weighing in on retail store design, or collaborating on products. Lululemon is one of the few brands that manages to make a free bodily process—sweating—into something that unites its brand community.

Consumer communities can help create brand value, strengthen customer loyalty, and spread the word about products. As we have seen, social media and WOM have a significant impact on how a brand is viewed and valued, allowing consumer communities to form around and champion the brand. Hassan et al. (2016; see also Alkon and Guthman 2017; Barnaud et al. 2018; Steinert-Threlkeld 2017) propose there are at least four ways this process works on social media:

Defending the brand. First, all brands receive negative comments and complaints against them online. Consumers can help protect brands against these attacks and mitigate their negative impact. For example, consumers may step in to blame uncontrollable features, the complainer's own actions, or a third party. Or they may point out that competitors' brands are even worse.

Reassurance. Consumers can communicate real-life stories to reassure others about the brand's abilities to satisfy consumers and to correct their own shortcomings. In doing so, they are substantially increasing the value of the product. People are more likely to trust the assurances of other people, instead of those from the company itself.

Amplification. Third, consumers can promote the brand by recommending it to others, displaying brand-related items in public space, and taking part in brand-sponsored events. Members of Facebook communities can then enlarge the impact of these brand-related events by posting pictures or commentaries about the occasion. Such posts encourage others to attend events and celebrate the brand.

Reminiscing. Finally, consumers who are passionate about a brand will engage in a much more emotional relationship with it than other consumers. They may even crave the brand or feel lost when the brand is unavailable. Many consumers make emotional disclosures where they reminisce about the brand and express loss when they cannot have it.

Marketers think brand communities are valuable for generating WOM and keeping customer loyalty, so they invest in building and strengthening these communities. For example, they host events and celebrations, cultivate Facebook groups, and offer special treatment to loyal members (Schau et al. 2009; Lin et al. 2019). At in-person events and through online discussions, people can build relationships with other fans of the same brand. Mingling with one another strengthens community consciousness and also the brand's identity (Hollebeek et al. 2017). Such events also celebrate and revive a brand connection, reminding customers of the reasons they liked the brand initially.

As discussed in an earlier chapter, Tim Hortons built its brand loyalty by making customers think that nothing is more Canadian than grabbing a Timmies. "What pops into my mind when I think of Tim Hortons is Canada. It's distinctly Canadian" (Friesen 2018). The company undertakes numerous initiatives to perpetuate this view of their brand as a symbol of Canadianness. During hockey events, Tim Hortons donuts have been transformed into the logos of the Toronto Maple Leafs, London Knights, and Windsor Spitfires. On Remembrance Day, one store in Calgary even

pulled off poppy-shaped donuts (Canadian Press, 2017). The Tim Horton Children's Foundation gives kids from low-income families a chance to go to summer camp. When Canadian singer Shawn Mendes came to Toronto for a concert, Tim Hortons partnered with Mendes to create coffee cups with his picture on them, surrounded by maple leaves. And in Toronto's financial district, Tim Hortons opened its first "Innovation Café," meant to attract millennials. All of these initiatives exemplify the work marketers do to entrench their brands.

Such is the identification of Tim Hortons with Canada's national identity that in the 2019 federal election campaign, Andrew Scheer, then leader of the Conservative Party of Canada, held a campaign event at a Tim Hortons restaurant. Scheer posted this picture and wrote on his Flickr account: "Jumped behind the local Timmies counter to serve coffee in Oakville. Great to hear directly from everyone here over a cup of coffee with David Sweet and Conservative Candidates Terence Young, Nadirah Nazeer, Sean Weir and Jane Michael. Conservatives will help you get ahead instead of just getting by."

Some research confirms marketers are right to spend time and resources building these brand communities. People who engage with brand communities on social media end up spending more on those brands (Goh et al. 2013: 88). People are more likely to buy something other consumers post about than something they see marketed by the company. What's more, involvement in a brand community increases brand loyalty (Munnukka et al. 2015; Laroche et al. 2012; Royo-Vela and Casimassima 2011). Consumers are more likely to stay loyal to a brand if they chat with other brand-community members and attend branded events (Brodie et al. 2011; Leckie et al. 2016).

On the other hand, some think social media tend to *disrupt* brand communities (Holt 2015). When people come together on platforms like Facebook and Twitter to discuss brands, their interactions are fleeting and unstructured. Such platforms merely gather thousands—even millions—of one-time comments, images, stories, and experiences; they don't necessarily create a united feeling of community among lovers of the brand.

In this sense, social media may be more likely to facilitate the development of **brand publics**, as opposed to brand communities (Arvidsson and Caliandro 2015). Brand publics differ from brand communities in three ways (Arvidsson and Caliandro 2015, 2016; see also Todd and Soule 2020; Raymond 2018). First, brand communities are preserved by interaction. Members communicate with one another, either face-to-face, on the phone, or online, and these interactions create social bonds, which are the basis of communities. Brand publics, on the other hand, are preserved by mediation. Members don't find one another naturally. Often, a brand itself will bring them together. For example, the brand will launch its own Facebook page, hoping fans will "like," share, and comment on the content.

Second, members of brand communities and brand publics communicate for different reasons. Brand community members want to discuss and deliberate about the brand. They want to know what others think about the brand's latest product or most recent scandal. In brand publics, by contrast, communication is about making a statement or voicing your view. For example, members of brand publics post Instagram selfies showing off their new Swarovski earrings. They want "likes" as well as comments about how beautiful *they* are—not how pretty their new earrings look.

Third, brand communities give members a sense of identity and meaning. Members feel distinct from non-members; they feel like they belong. In brand publics, on the other hand, members do not shape their identities around the brand. They don't belong to anything; they have simply visited a discussion venue. The explosion of digital content and social platforms thus poses both a challenge and an opportunity for brands and marketers. On the one hand, it's easier than ever for brand lovers to find each other and discuss their beloved brand, even from halfway around the world. But on the other hand, the cacophony of online chatter easily drowns out comments, questions, and criticism from would-be brand community members.

Much as brand communities have deteriorated into brand publics, so too have once-strong signals of wealth and status deteriorated into commonplace signals used by everyone. As we've already mentioned, brands are intended to influence our spending habits. In so doing, they also uphold class divisions. Consumers signal their class membership by buying the right brands and avoiding the wrong ones (Holt 1998; Dion and Borraz 2017). For example, wearing a golf shirt with the Ralph Lauren logo says you're middle or upper class. Wearing a logo-free T-shirt may say you're working class—or that you don't care about clothes. Similarly, brands (and the spending habits they influence) can also sharpen divides based on gender and age.

That said, things aren't always so clear-cut anymore. Today, most people in developed countries have access to similar goods and services. In outlet malls, even lower-income earners can afford some high-quality brands. As a result, that Ralph Lauren polo shirt isn't necessarily the sign of wealth it once was. We cannot always distinguish people by what they consume. We have to look, instead, at *how* they consume it. For instance, members of all income groups may be able to eat in a fancy restaurant now and then. But you can tell the wealthy from the poor by the way they use their salad fork (or don't), and the number and type of dishes they order (or don't).

The ways rich people distinguish themselves from the poor will always evolve and change as the poor catch on to their "exclusive" and "secret" consumer choices. Some middle and low-income members will learn how to consume in these same ways, and high-income people will have to create a new way to separate themselves.

The continued blurring and sharpening of boundaries between classes, genders, age groups, and other demographic distinctions means marketers need to know their target audiences well.

They need to give precedence to their most important or primary audience members, telling them what they want to hear, even if it's at the expense of other groups. For example, imagine that marketers have branded a fancy restaurant as a costly dining experience where the most refined food and wine connoisseurs will feel right at home. This may (intentionally) intimidate lower-income, less-experienced diners. The restaurant might lose business (or never acquire it) from these lower-income diners, but attract business from their ritzier target clientele.

Branding Locations

Place branding or **locational branding** is the creation of branded geographic environments where consumers connect with the brand as tourists or visitors (Govers and Go 2016; Boisen et al. 2018; Foroudi et al. 2016). Visitors to Disneyland enjoy Disney entertainments and buy Disney products, but they can also meet "real-life" Disney characters and "feel the magic." Trademarked characters provide exclusive entertainment, living, and dining opportunities. Locational consumers can literally feel the elusive meanings and messages of a brand through the firsthand experience of its branded place.

Similarly, cities, regions, provinces, and even countries have tried to brand themselves by providing a unique, almost trademarked experience. Places like Las Vegas, Venice, and Hawaii readily come to mind as exemplars of this approach. But the number of contenders is rapidly growing as more places vie for business investment and tourism. Each site seeks to brand itself as distinct from the rest, offering unique experiences, attractions, foods, culture, and an overall "vibe."

And just as people come to associate products, companies, or services with their brands, so too do we associate places with specific brands. Place-making elements—the practices, institutions, material things, and representations of a locale—help people form mental associations with that place (Kavaratzis and Kalandides 2015). Those mental associations can change over time as a place's economic, political, social, and other features change—and as branding experts work to shape opinions of that place. But typically, iconic branded places strive to keep old and ancient features alive for naïve visitors.

A longstanding tourism trend is the desire to experience a place's "authenticity"—to see and feel it like locals do, as earlier visitors may have, or even as earlier inhabitants may have done. Many places respond to this challenge. Local residents develop product and service offerings to prop up their place's brand. They project the place's (imagined) identity and culture, catering to tourists' wants.

In this respect, consider the role that *Anne of Green Gables* has played in popularizing Prince Edward Island. PEI is the smallest province in Canada, yet it attracted more than 1½ million tourists in 2019 (CBC News 2019). Attractions include its beaches, bike paths, and beloved fictional character Anne Shirley. The CBC television show *Anne with an E* was based on L.M. Montgomery's books and set on the Island. A columnist for the Charlottetown *Guardian* described the show as the "most significant tourism story by a country mile for Prince Edward Island … in a few decades." Recognizing viewers would be enamoured with the scenic setting, Tourism PEI spent $160,000 to run advertisements targeting visitors during the show (Fraser 2017).

The series created unprecedented interest in PEI. One Tuesday in 2018, a record-breaking four cruise ships pulled into the Charlottetown harbor and disembarked 11,000 people (Bruce 2018). "A day like today, it starts to be an issue. We don't want people waiting in line for half an hour," said the manager of the Green Gables store. The lines were so long that the manager had to find more people to work the cash registers, just to keep things moving.

Place branding isn't limited to the tourism industry. Consider Saint John, New Brunswick. Efforts were made there to brand it "the retirement capital of Canada," so older adults would be more inclined to move there. To do so, the focus was not on tourist attractions or hotel deals, but rather, the city's quaint, scenic, and quiet features.

The long-term impacts of COVID-19 on tourism around the world remain to be seen. Perhaps those in the industry will come to invest even more in place branding as they strive to build back in the wake of the pandemic and show consumers why they should choose their vacation destination over others.

Final Thoughts

In this chapter, we saw that marketers invest heavily in building their brands. Empirical data do not always show a strong causal relationship between, say, exposure to branded content and buying that brand's products or services. Nevertheless, marketers seem to think that consumers who are repeatedly exposed and respond favourably to their branding efforts will gradually develop a liking for their brand.

If branding works the way marketers think, some of it could lead to questionable consumer behaviour. For example, marketers say—and some research suggests—that people are willing to pay more for a product from a brand they trust, like, or want to associate themselves with. If true, that would mean consumers are spending unnecessarily on premium-branded products with the same utility as less expensive second- or third-tier or even unbranded products. They are throwing away hard-earned money on the metaphorical wrapping paper, instead of the gift. In this sense, branding generates higher profits for the manufacturer at the consumer's expense.

What's more, branding may be even more manipulative than advertising. After all, the prevalence of branding skyrocketed once marketers realized that consumers were becoming media literate and resistant to overt advertising. They had to take a more subtle approach. Of course, like branding, advertising also tries to elicit emotional reactions and sell consumers the idea the promoted product will help them shore up their identity. But brands may dive even deeper, suggesting the brand you buy reflects the person you are. Branding helps people display the "type" of person they want to be and associate themselves with people from groups they want to be part of. It may also distance them from people they want to exclude or seem different from.

Branding—and, specifically, the development of brand communities—is especially manipulative when it creates the illusion of consumer control and choice. Today, ordinary people are media producers as well as media consumers, influencing one another's buying decisions through their ratings and reviews. This creates a perhaps misguided sense of trust in the information we receive. Many consumers think they are making decisions based on the unbiased opinions of other consumers just like them. True, these opinions may sound more objective than overt advertising, but that may not really be the case, at least not all the time.

Marketers know that consumers increasingly trust other consumers. So, they develop programs to elicit those positive ratings and reviews. Some brands review their own products and services. Other brands use automated bots to spread fake news and false advertising designed to mislead because it looks like an authentic review, statement, or piece of news. Others still offer incentives for positive ratings and reviews. Consumers don't always work in each other's interests. Often, they work—without pay—*for* brands, sharing, commenting on, and otherwise recommending those brands to their friends and family.

Brand promotion through WOM isn't necessarily a bad thing. If you need a new dishwasher and your mom loves her dishwasher so much you decide to buy the same model, there's no harm done. Brand promotion through WOM only becomes questionable when consumers are misled to think they are getting objective, unbiased product recommendations. This happens when they can't tell if the guidance is coming from someone who is being paid by the manufacturer or receiving the product free in exchange for promoting it. In these cases, branding seems like just another form of advertising—one that's been more cunningly disguised.

By infusing "values" into their products, services, and even their employees, brands can also do social harm. They can perpetuate negative stereotypes, overlook irresponsible behaviour, or project negative images of certain groups. Brands that hinge on exclusivity may subtly mark out the "types" of people who do *not* fit with their image or identity. Some fashion brands typify this trend by targeting slender, stereotypically beautiful women. And, as we saw, "upscale," "elite," "exclusive" brands can contribute to perpetuating class hierarchies. We discuss such class hierarchies next.

Discussion Questions

1. In this chapter we focused on the role of brands in shaping our everyday consumer decisions. Think of the most recent thing that you bought. How did the brand image of the product contribute to your desire for it?

2. Think of a successful 21st-century brand. How did the company use advertising and marketing to create a corporate brand personality? What is the major principle of this brand personality and how does it relate to the actual product?

3. How do political parties use the same principles of branding employed by businesses and major corporations to create powerful self-images?

Quick Quiz

1. Which of the following is an example of a logo?
a. The person who is running the company
b. A piece of commercial artwork for the private market
c. A sign, letter, or symbol that represents a company
d. A company slogan such as "just do it" for Nike
e. A manufactured object put on the marketplace and sold in stores

2. What is loyalty marketing?
a. A marketing technique that uses ideals of the monarch
b. A back-to-the-ages form of marketing
c. A type of marketing used in the Soviet Union
d. A style of advertising that relies on blunt colors
e. A way of retaining customers through incentive schemes

3. E-commerce is:
a. The use of the Internet to buy and sell goods
b. Free delivery of products bought in stores
c. Stores that have self-checkout devices
d. Stores that cater to the tech-savvy youth
e. Stores that are against all forms of technology

4. _____ describes the movement of an innovation from the source outwards or from one culture to another.
a. Fashion
b. Diffusion of innovation
c. Hybridization
d. Brands
e. Socialization

5. What are brand communities?
a. Anyone who buys something for sale is part of a brand community
b. Any conversation that surrounds the idea of buying and selling
c. People who sell things on the public market
d. Flea markets
e. People who are organized around their commitment to certain brands

The answers to the Quick Quiz are provided at the end of the book.

For Further Reading

Origination: The Geographies of Brands and Branding by Andy Pike
Explores how geographical communities create meaning and association through symbolic branding.

Brands: The Logos of the Global Economy by Celia Lury
Lury's book explores the connections between brands and the consumer. *Brands* also looks at the role of branding and marketing in our increasingly globalized world.

Propaganda: The Formation of Men's Attitudes by Jacques Ellul
French philosopher Jacques Ellul takes a sociological approach to the study of propaganda.

Brand Society: How Brands Transform Management and Lifestyle by Martin Kornberger
Kornberger explores the role of branding in business and society. He shows the role of branding in changing business practices and the lives of those who consume those businesses' products.

Dialectic of Enlightenment by Theodor Adorno and Max Horkheimer
Dialectic of Enlightenment uses critical theory to explore the destructive nature of Western culture as a cause of domination in a historical and social context.

Key Terms

Brand
Celebrity
Consumer satisfaction
Customer loyalty
Diffusion of innovation
digital marketing
E-commerce
Fashion
Hybridization
Logo
Loyalty program
Word of mouth

Chapter Eight
Low-Income People and Symbols of Class

Learning Objectives

After reading this chapter, you will be able to:

✓ Understand market segmentation, its shortcomings, and its reliance on big data.

✓ See how basic human necessities are commodified as consumer goods.

✓ Analyze compensatory consumption among low-income earners.

✓ Consider the role of class consciousness in poor people's consumer habits.

In the next eight chapters, we explore how people use consumer goods to signal their membership in a community and, conversely, their separation from other communities.

By breaking consumers down into different demographic groups and looking at their different consumption habits, we've structured these eight chapters by **market segment**. The premise of market segmentation is that different "kinds" of people—for example, wealthy people as opposed to low-income people, or men rather than women—spend their money in different ways. They may also respond to marketing and advertising appeals differently and favour different brands. The underlying assumption is that members of different groups or demographics have varying lifestyles and identities, therefore different wants and needs.

So, to set ourselves up properly for the coming chapters, let's take a closer look at this idea of **market segmentation** and how it has evolved over the past several decades. We'll then go on to discuss other key terms that we'll use in this chapter.

Market Segmentation

One early form of market segmentation involved the development of VALS (Values and Life Style) surveys. The foremost proponent of this type of research, marketing researcher Arnold Mitchell (1983), conceived of nine American lifestyle groups. His typology related buying behaviour to the social, economic, and demographic characteristics of each group. Thus, he distinguished carefully by age, income, and education; he also looked at a variety of attitudes and lifestyle variables.

Consider the group Mitchell calls "experientials." Comprising roughly 11 percent of the adult population in 1983, the experientials were an important chunk of the baby-boom generation. Forty years ago, a majority occupied the middle- or upper-income class and approximately 70 percent had some postsecondary education, compared to 43 percent of the adult population. They were less likely than others to own their home or have a home mortgage, but more likely than any other group to owe over $50,000 in loans. Much of their income (and credit) was consumed by higher-than-average rates of leisure activity. With a love of outdoor recreation, experientials spent their time swimming, playing racquet sports, skiing, and practicing yoga. Motorcycles and racing bikes were also popular in this segment. Experientials generally liked healthy foods and avoided sugary foods and drinks, though they still enjoyed alcoholic beverages like beer and wine.

At home, experientials commonly purchased dishwashers, garbage disposals, video games, and stereos and accessories. You ccould sell experientials eye makeup and shampoo, but forget about aerosol underarm deodorants, feminine-hygiene sprays, aftershave lotions, or room air-fresheners; those were for peasants. And if you invited an experiential home for dinner, hide the margarine, Jell-O, and Planters peanuts. Experientials viewed such snacks as "lower class."

This picture of young urban professionals still holds up pretty well, nearly 40 years later. But as you can guess, there are several problems with this approach to market segmentation, despite its strengths. For one thing, it quickly became obvious to marketers there were more than merely nine groups of consumers. They attempted to solve this problem by building segmentation models around information linked to postal codes and bringing other variables into the mix: the regions of the country consumers lived in, rural-versus-urban-versus-suburban residence, immigrant versus native-born, and so on. But even within these more refined segments, as Camilleri (2018) points out, people do not have all the same preferences, nor does one product completely satisfy everyone.

That is the crux of the problem with market segmentation—one we will return to repeatedly throughout these coming chapters. In real life, low-income people (for example) vary enormously, as do the other demographic groups we consider. A lot more can (and should) be said about each of these groups. Our goal in the next eight chapters is to give the reader a sense of how segmentation works in marketing, and to report some of the things researchers already know about people in these demographic categories. We do not try to paint a comprehensive picture of these groups' consumer habits.

For example, we can hone in on some of the specific industries in which market segmentation has proved especially popular. In respect to vacation travel, for example, marketers continue to distinguish between young and old travelers, those with more and less income, and those who want a more or less active vacation (on this, see for example, Goryushkina et al. 2019). Smaller hotel and resort operators, struggling to compete against larger chains, often narrow their target segment further still, striving to capture a small niche of vacationers like recently-divorced middle-aged women (Naumov 2017).

Such simple methods of segmentation, part theoretical and part intuitive, gave rise to dozens of consumer types, but it was still not fine-grained enough for many marketers. By the early 2000s, marketing was being transformed by computerization, the Internet, and the rise of "big data." A new ability to collect and use huge data sets, much of the information gathered on the internet from social media and other sites, meant that marketers could tailor their advertising to each particular consumer. With large datasets of consumer information, marketers could use algorithms—predictive mathematical formulas—to advise shoppers of things they might like to buy. If they were browsing items in category X, they could be advised that other people with a similar browsing pattern had also browsed or purchased item Y.

However, the buying "suggestions" that emerge from these algorithms are only as good as the quantity and quality of data available in the data base. A small number of observations yields odd and hazardous predictions. What's more, as the old adage goes, "garbage in = garbage out." This means that even where large numbers of observations are available, predictions are risky where the input data are unreliable. Consider, for example, the weird predictions that would result from the (combined) browsing history of an entire household.

In general, both of these problems point to a central weakness of algorithm-based prediction: namely, it is data-driven, not theory-driven. Small or random errors in the data produce "patterns" that we struggle to interpret and use as predictions, but the results may be, in fact, not interpretable. They may be garbage. (For a further discussion of this kind of problem, the more statistically minded reader may want to read *Market Segmentation Analysis: Understanding It, Doing It, and Making it Useful*, by Dolnicar et al. [2018].)

Despite their flaws, marketing today is more focused and precise than a market segmentation strategy merely based on nine lifestyles. However, these data-based strategies also require a great deal of customer browsing and buying data, and a lot of testing; so, in practice, these strategies are only available to Amazon, Google and other very large merchandisers. Smaller marketers continue to rely on more traditional, tried-and-true methods of segmenting the market—splitting up the customer base according to class, gender, age, and so on—then asking the customers a few questions and listening to their answers. With this in mind, we have organized eight chapters of this book according to traditional demographic categories. They continue to be useful, as recent research continues to show.

In this chapter, as noted at the outset, we discuss the first of these market segments: low-income and working-class people. The defining characteristic of this segment is income, which is also one important basis of social class. And social class, as we begin to discuss in this chapter, is a way of separating and ranking people in our capitalist society. Everyone belongs to a social class, whether they recognize and shape their identity in relation to it or not.

Defining Our Terms

For Marx, a **social class** (Grusky 2018) is a set of people who stand in a particular relationship to the means of production, either as owners or wage labourers. However, according to Max Weber, a class is a set of people who share similar **life chances** (Fourcade and Healy 2017; Kim et al. 2018). Weber coined this term to describe the different opportunities different people have to advance their social position (Wodtke 2017).

The concept of social position exists only in socially stratified societies. **Social stratification** refers to the existence of unequal classes in society. These classes are groups of people in the same income or wealth brackets, some higher and some lower. Often, following Weber, social stratification also refers to people with varying degrees of power or status. In our socially stratified society, a significant portion of people live in poverty while a few enjoy extraordinary wealth and comfort (Grusky 2019; Kerbo 2017; Thye and Harrell 2017).

Within each social class, people lead similar lives. They have similar incomes and standards of living, and they share similar values, expectations, goals, and behaviours. On the other hand, there are often vast social differences *between* classes. So, there is usually little movement between classes. Today, **upward mobility** is more limited than it has been for decades. Upward mobility means moving up to a higher social and economic class. Canadian research by Miles Corak (2017) has shown that social mobility is also regionalized, based on local economic growth. People in some regions of Canada have less upward mobility than people in others.

For simplicity, in this chapter, we will parse the population by income percentile. By **low-income** people—people in relative (if not absolute) poverty—we will mean people in the lowest 10 percent to 20 percent of the household income distribution. By **wealthy** people—people of relative (if not absolute) wealth—we mean people in the highest 1 percent or, perhaps 10 percent. We will discuss them in the next chapter. The rest—people in the middle 70 to 80 percent—make up the so-called **middle class**.

However, as this is a book about consumer behaviour, we will focus mainly on families and households, which are the main consumer units in a modern society. According to Statistics Canada, in 2018, the after-tax income of an average economic family in the lowest income decile was

The enormous Packard automobile factory in Detroit, Michigan, which closed in 1958, once employed more than 40,000 people and was the most advanced facility of its type in the world. It has become symbolic of the loss of high-paying working-class jobs in the United States and the consequent increase in economic inequality.

$26,100 and that of an average economic family in the second lowest income decile was $45,000. We would consider these low-income families. By comparison, in 2018, the after-tax income of an average economic family in the highest income decile was $228,800 and that of an average economic family in the second highest income decile was $148,100. By this reckoning, a low-income or poor family spends less than $45,000 per year and perhaps even less than $26,100 per year. A wealthy family spends more than $148,000 and perhaps even (much) more than $228,000 a year. A middle-income family, then, spends between $45,000 and $148,000 a year: clearly, there exists a very wide variation in incomes and lifestyles *between* income classes but also *within* income classes.

Poverty is the condition of not having enough of the things we need for life (Hagenaars 2017; Bourguignon and Chakravarty 2019). **Inequality**, by contrast, is a condition that can occur whether people are living in poverty or not. It simply marks a difference in which one person has more than another person (Goldthorpe 2017; Stehr 2018). Thus, a society can be low-income but equal or low-income but unequal, wealthy but equal or wealthy but unequal. Canadian society is comparatively wealthy but moderately unequal.

That said, unequal societies are likely to have more people than equal societies living in poverty, both in absolute and relative terms. **Absolute poverty** means people do not have the means to meet their basic human needs: food, shelter, water, and health services, among other things. **Relative poverty** is more subjective. It describes a standard of living that is below what is considered acceptable or decent in a given society (Ravallion and Chen 2019; Joyce and Ziliak 2019).

The life experience of low-income people is much harsher in unequal societies than in equal societies. In fact, one could say that it is far worse to be a low-income person in a wealthy, unequal society than to be a low-income person in a low-income, equal society. That's because poor people in a rich society suffer from relative as well as absolute deprivation. And low-income people in Canada today are precisely that: low-income in a relatively wealthy, relatively unequal society.

Today, the favoured method of distinguishing who should be considered low-income is the **market-basket measure (MBM)**. The MBM looks at the cost of a basket of food, clothing, shelter, transport, and other basic needs, considering these costs as necessary for a modest standard of living (Heisz 2019). Based on these, the MBM sets thresholds of poverty. Thresholds vary depending on region and family size. Those with a disposable income below the threshold suitable for their region and family size are considered to live in poverty.

After much consultation, in 2018, the Canadian government set the MBM as "Canada's official poverty line." The *Poverty Reduction Act* requires Statistics Canada to review MBM measures

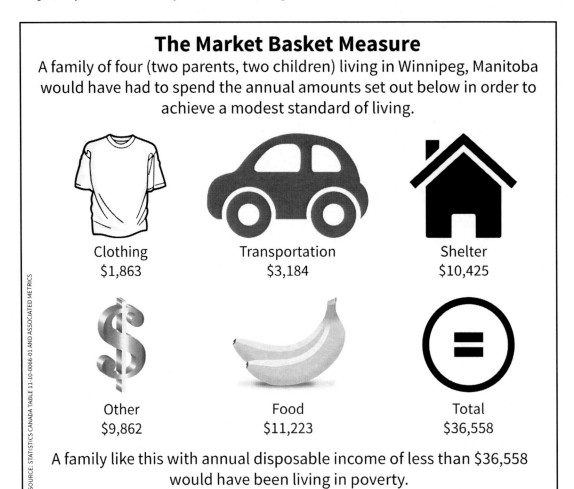

regularly, to ensure they reflect up-to-date costs of living. However, there is little consensus on how often those reviews should take place. The current MBM was last updated in 2008–2010 (Heisz 2019). But a so-called affordability crisis has swept through major cities including Vancouver and Toronto since then. Housing and childcare, as just two examples, cost significantly more today than they did in 2010. And the skyrocketing cost of rental housing has hit low-income Canadians hardest, since they are least likely to own their homes. That means the MBM may not be doing Canadians justice as the official poverty line.

As mentioned above, upward mobility is more limited today. Part of the reason for this is that people from low-income families have less access to higher education than higher-income families. That means they usually stay in the social class in which they were born. More generally, the poorest and wealthiest children in any society are the least mobile. The poorest cannot access the opportunities they need to pull themselves out of poverty, while the wealthiest are usually too well-connected to fail. Chances of upward and downward mobility are about equal in the middle of the income distribution, with people moving up and down the middle-income range.

That said, income mobility is always more common than **wealth mobility**. **Income** refers to money gained through wages and salaries, while **wealth** refers to all household assets, including real estate, savings, and stocks. It's easier for someone to get a raise in income—even a large one—than it is to amass significant wealth in their lifetime. So, even if plenty of people experience upward income mobility, it doesn't mean our society is becoming significantly fairer or more equal. The wealthy are almost certain to retain their wealth, power, and status over decades and generations.

The agents of socialization we discussed earlier—families, schools, and the media in particular—teach us these facts about the class system, though we may not always be aware of them. Wealthy children quickly learn how "classy" people—people with money and power—are supposed to behave. They learn that the most elite children attend private schools with high fees, where they build cultural capital and learn how to consume conspicuously. On the other hand, children who attend public schools in low-income neighborhoods are reminded every day how people live—and expect to live—on the other side of the proverbial tracks.

Living in Poverty: The Commodification of Basic Necessities

In some societies, necessities like housing are seen as basic rights, their provision (and price) regulated by government. But in Canada, housing is a commodity, its price and availability dictated by market forces.

In 2018, Ontario's Conservative government removed rent controls on buildings built after November 15, 2018. Residents in new buildings are now at the mercy of their landlords. Instead of seeing their rent increase incrementally each year with inflation, some tenants may be forced to move out when landlords raise their rent by several hundred dollars per month.

Another example of a basic need that's been commodified to the detriment of low-income people is health care. In Canada, the universal health care system covers about 70 percent of a person's healthcare costs (Mikkonen and Raphael 2010). Vision care, dental care, needles, inhalers,

---

Box 8-1

Housing: A Luxury Good?

High housing costs mean only the wealthiest can afford to live in certain neighbourhoods in Canada. In West Vancouver, for example, the average household net worth is $4.5 million, and the average housing price is $2.8 million (Naraghi 2019). In Westmount, Montreal, the average household net worth is $3.7 million (Naraghi 2019). And the residents in Toronto's Bridle Path community have an average net worth of $22.27 million (Narcity 2016).

Wealthy people dominate the housing market and drive the price for housing upwards. Proper housing is a basic need, but the unreasonable housing prices in Canadian cities have made it a luxury. The cost of housing—even apartments and condominiums, let alone houses—is pushing most Canadians further away from the city and leaving many in debt.

---

mobility aids like crutches, and home-care devices like adapted toilet seats are among the services and products not covered.

As a result, low-income Canadians are unhealthier than wealthy Canadians. They live shorter lives and are more likely to experience chronic illnesses like diabetes or diseases like cancer (Mikkonen and Raphael 2010; Kuhle and Veugelers 2008). Compared with wealthy Canadians, low-income Canadians eat less well, occupy less healthy housing, and also work in jobs with bigger health risks (Vatanparast et al. 2010).

In other words, wealth often equals health in our society. Nutritious food, safe, clean housing, access to green spaces, and opportunities for physical activity and recreation—none of these things are free. What's more, they also require time. It's impossible to prepare fresh meals every day if you're working two eight-hour shifts as a waitress. It's also impossible to fit in an exercise class, the recommended eight hours of sleep, and regular checkups with your doctor. In short, low-income earners may have a harder time finding time to do healthy things than higher earners. So, poverty reduces people's ability to afford the goods and services they need to survive.

Housing, food, and healthcare are among the first things that come to mind when you hear the term "basic necessities." But another, increasingly costly commodity that's become a necessity in recent years is Internet service. Undoubtedly with his own interests in mind, Facebook CEO Mark Zuckerberg writes that access to the Internet is "a basic human right, like access to health care or water" (Goodyear 2016). Yet, for low-income families in Canada, the Internet bill is a heavy burden that causes stress. One Canadian survey reported that to pay for Internet access, 59 percent of households have cut into other budgets: "71 percent went without food, 64 percent cut back on recreation, and 13 percent delayed paying their rent" (Goodyear 2016).

This class-based digital divide distinguishes students from richer and poorer homes. This inequality became glaringly evident in the spring of 2020, when schools closed to slow the spread of COVID-19. As the curriculum eventually moved online, some students struggled to participate because they did not have access to Internet at home and may have formerly relied on free WiFi at libraries to complete their homework (Goldstein 2020).

As mentioned, food—despite being a basic necessity—is also a commodity in our society. In his 1985 book, *All Manners of Food* (see also Pilcher 2017; De Vooght and Scholliers 2016), historical sociologist Stephen Mennell writes that class inequalities may not influence food consumption as much as they have in the past. Even wealthy people order pizza sometimes, for example. And low-income people can eat a wider variety of foods than in centuries past. This is largely thanks to both the mechanization of food production—which has reduced the price of food—and the development of large grocery stores that make more choices easily available (at least in some neighbourhoods). These developments, Mennell suggests, let more low-income earners access more food and healthier options than they would have years ago. (For a merging of these ideas with those of sociologist Pierre Bourdieu, see de Morais Sato et al. 2016).

That said, class differences in eating still exist. At the extreme are homeless people who beg for help outside grocery stores. And think of people who live in **food deserts**, where fresh, high-quality produce and reasonably priced groceries are not readily available (Allcott et al. 2017, 2019; but also, Cooksey-Stowers et al. 2017). Some food deserts are in isolated rural areas, while others are in low-income urban centres. The people who live in these deserts typically belong to different classes than people who can get whatever food they want, whenever they want it (Steven et al. 2018).

In turn, Caspi et al. (2017a, 2017b) note that many low-income people, for these reasons of geography and convenience, do much of their everyday shopping in convenience stores, dollar stores, gas stations, and pharmacies. In addition to being more costly overall, food available in these locations is rarely healthy, fresh, or of high quality, nor do these stores typically try to promote healthy food purchasing.

Box 8-2
The Crisis of Unclean Water on Indigenous Reserves in Canada

Most of us don't think twice about the water we drink, shower in, and wash our hands with. However, those who live on Indigenous reserves are plagued by worries about their water quality every day. One First Nations reserve in Saskatchewan was under a water advisory for more than five years. From 2011 to 2017, the water on the reserve was not deemed clean enough to drink (Graham 2017). Finally, in 2017, the federal government provided the reserve with clean drinking water.

In the Neskantaga First Nations reserve in Ontario, there have been hundreds of evacuations because of the water crisis. Unclean water flows from taps in people's homes, resulting in water-borne illnesses and skin rashes. The reserve had in 2019 been under a boil-water advisory for almost 25 years (Lane and Gagnon 2019). That's common in Indigenous communities: 56 other reserves across Canada must boil their water before using it (Gerster and Hessey 2019).

As discussed in an earlier chapter, people learn their consumption habits in families. As children, we start to learn our eating practices—including what to eat and how to eat it—from our parents. Children mimic their parents' actions, often without being conscious they are doing so (Cruwys et al. 2014). One study—using self-reports, videotaping, and observations—found that children wanted, enjoyed, and were more interested in the foods they had seen their mothers eating (Palfreyman et al. 2015).

Such parental modeling helps explain why people in different social classes learn to eat and enjoy different foods. Higher-income people often grow up consuming more varied and nutritious food—for example, more fresh fruits and vegetables (Drewnowski et al. 2016; Beagan et al. 2016). Lower-income people often grow up eating foods that are nutrient-poor, such as fast food. So, starting in childhood, people in different classes learn to eat well or badly. They learn to buy food from grocery stores rather than take-out places, and to order meals or cook them at home, and they tend to continue these eating behaviours throughout life.

As we saw, primary socialization also transfers class-based values, beliefs, and norms from parents to children. That is, parents teach their kids—either directly or through modeling—to buy foods at certain places and cook them in certain ways. However, they also pass on concerns about convenience and thrift in food shopping and may even pass on the views of health promoters (Steven et al 2018). For example, some may trust nutrition advice offered by doctors—people with recognized credentials whom they see as valid sources of information. Others may find such advice annoying, seeing it as moralistic and judgmental. These views are not always class-based, but they can be.

And, of course, what people eat is not only a matter of social, class-based preferences. As noted, low-income families may not even be able to consistently put food on their tables. In turn, children who grow up chronically hungry, or eating mainly cheap, unhealthy foods, are more likely to report poor health as adults (Schwarzenberg and Georgieff 2018; Alex-Petersen et al. 2017; Wise 2016).

Another significant—and often overlooked—element of good health is stress reduction. People with higher-than-average levels of stress are more susceptible to illness and disease (Mikkonen and Raphael 2010). And it's hard to imagine anything more stressful than being unable to pay your rent or feed your children. As Schilbach et al. (2016: 438) note, being poor is stressful in and of itself, but trying to manage your finances when poor is additionally stressful:

> Being poor means having less money to buy things, but it also means having to spend more of one's bandwidth managing that money. The poor must manage sporadic income, juggle expenses, and make difficult trade-offs. Even when the poor are not actually making financial decisions, these preoccupations can be distracting. Thinking and fretting about money can effectively tax … scarce cognitive resources even further.

In fact, people may even feel the effects of poverty-based stress years after escaping poverty. One study, conducted at Cornell University, linked stress that began with childhood poverty to low-income health in adulthood. "An early history of poverty," the researchers write, "appears to set children on a life-course trajectory of ill health" (Evans and Kim 2007; see also Kim et al. 2019; Shavit et al. 2018; Schenck-Fontaine and Panico 2019). Evans and Kim report that low-income children show higher-than-average blood pressure and stress hormones. Even as adults, they show a decreased ability to regulate those hormones.

Unhealthy ways of coping with this stress make matters worse. Children raised in low-income homes are more likely than average to smoke and drink heavily (Ferraro et al. 2016). Both behaviours can cause life-threatening diseases and poor health. Sometimes, these habits are learned through the socialization practices discussed earlier. For example, heavy social drinking is widely accepted and sometimes even applauded among some groups of working-class men. Children who grow up watching their fathers drink every day may come to think it's normal and expected. In turn, these social norms may influence their alcohol consumption right alongside personal tastes and biological tendencies.

Some people note that low-income earners are more likely than others to harm their health through excessive smoking or vaping (for example, Lahelma et al. 2016; Schroeder 2016) or drinking (Landberg et al. 2020). Part of the problem is that some low-income communities have preserved a smoking culture that's been largely abandoned by high-income earners. Look at the service industry: social smoke breaks are still the norm among many waiters and baristas, while the same are becoming less common among, say, accountants.

So, when low-income earners try to quit, they're surrounded by smokers and constantly tempted. That helps explain why, in 2013, there were twice the number of Canadian smokers in the lowest income level than in the highest (Canadian Institute for Health Information). Similar trends prevail in the United States.

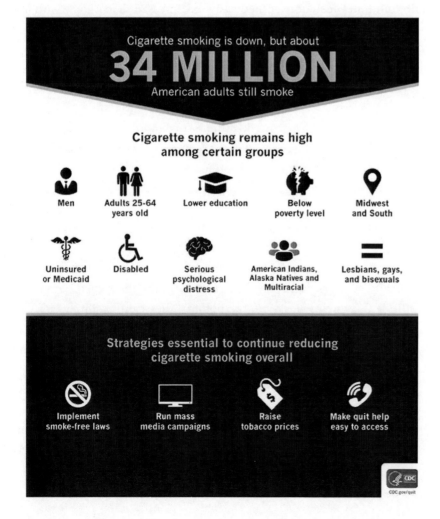

As this infographic from the U.S. Centers for Disease Control and Prevention notes, factors associated with social inequality, including lower levels of education and poverty, are associated with higher rates of smoking. Overall rates of tobacco use have declined dramatically since the mid-1960s, when 42 percent of American adults smoked. Today that figure is around 13 percent. However, 22 percent of American adults living below the poverty line smoked in 2018 according to statistics from the American Lung Association.

Higher-income earners also have easier access to resources that can help them stop smoking. Health insurance covers outlays on some smoking-cessation drugs but may not cover the entire cost. The out-of-pocket expense for these supports can be too much to bear for someone who's already strapped for cash. A vicious cycle emerges, where an expensive cigarette habit worsens already-bad finances, causing significant stress that makes people crave and rely on cigarettes even more.

In sum, even basic necessities are commodities in our capitalist society, bought and sold for competitive market rates. Another by-product of our capitalist society is the idea that time is money.

Spending and Saving, Part I: How Low-Income People Spend Their Time

In North America today, John Robinson and Geoffrey Godbey (1997: 217ff.] argue, "the privileged get the better jobs, rather than more leisure." People with a college or university education work longer hours than people with less formal education. They reportedly sleep less and spend less time on grooming; and they feel more rushed and more stressed than people with less education. When they have leisure time, highly educated people are also more likely to spend it in "worthwhile" activities of a cultural or educational kind, or in fitness activities. There is a self-improvement and future-orientation aspect to these activities which fits with the "concerted cultivation" upbringing we discussed in an earlier chapter. It also fits with the ideas of a **career** as opposed to a **job**.

A job is a paid position, typically with clearly marked-out hours and duties. Almost anyone can get a job of one kind or another, most of the time; often the requirements (and the pay) are not high. By contrast, a career is a paid occupation that needs prolonged training and a formal qualification. Examples include law, medicine, teaching, nursing, architecture, and so on. Included in this category are **professions**, typically overseen by professional associations, which guard entry and regulate the numbers of practicing professionals. Professions are hard to enter and typically pay well.

However, careers do not typically have clearly marked-out hours and duties. People in such jobs are expected, at least ideally, to work until they achieve the results their clients need. Of course, they may charge extra fees for extra work, but the point is, they cannot simply close up shop at 5 p.m. every day and put their clients out of their minds. For that reason, these (usually) high-income workers are always upgrading their qualifications, learning new things, and making new business contacts. And, for that reason, they are often likely to feel stressed and rushed. They are also likely to use their income to buy domestic and other services—that is, time—from others who charge a lower hourly rate than they are earning.

By contrast, lower-income people with "jobs" are, theoretically, able to come home from work, put the job out of their minds, and enjoy more hours of unstructured leisure than their more highly paid counterparts. They may feel less need to continue upgrading their skills or making new work contacts.

In short, jobs and careers are very different, affording different amounts of pay and patterns of time use. The risk of prolonged unemployment also varies between the two kinds of work. People who hold low-level jobs are often at a high risk of losing them, owing to automation or the movement of jobs to other countries where the rates of pay are lower. While there hasn't been much published research in recent years on how low-income workers use their time, more has been done on the time use and life satisfaction of unemployed workers.

One German study (Knabe et al. 2009) found that unemployed people sleep almost one hour longer than employed people and spend almost twice as much time on socializing. They also spend much more time watching TV, doing housework, caring for children, taking private trips, and playing parlor and computer games. Unemployed people who spend time searching for a job—roughly one-quarter of the total—spend about two hours and 11 minutes a day doing so.

These findings reinforce the idea that unemployed people have more free time than employed people and spend at least some of it engaged in leisure activities. However, some studies (Krueger and Mueller 2012; Hoang and Knabe 2019) report that unemployed people enjoy these leisure activities less than employed people. We can't be sure why, but perhaps it has to do with their strained finances. Many leisure activities are costly and unemployed people do not have large discretionary budgets.

What's more, people who have been unemployed in the past are typically frightened they will become unemployed again. So, people report higher levels of sadness and lower levels of life satisfaction when they are unemployed; and *past* unemployment also reduces a person's current life satisfaction, even after that person is re-employed (Knaabe and Ratzel 2008; Krueger and Mueller 2012; Hoang and Knabe 2019). Perhaps that is because people crave "meaningful time use" and a reason for doing what they are doing (Scanlan et al. 2012). Recent research in the U.S. shows that time use during unemployment is highly gendered. Rao (2016) finds that unemployed men and their spouses view unemployment as problematic and in need of immediate correction.

During a man's unemployment, the family organizes home life and marital relations to help men find new jobs. They do not seriously consider alternatives to full-time paid employment. In contrast, demographically similar unemployed women experience a different family response. Like their male counterparts, they spend time job-searching, but they have to fit this into the schedule of their family life—that is, housework and childcare. Their husbands feel it is not imperative for women to find a job immediately; they can take time out to focus on the home and children. As might be expected, this gives rise to gendered tensions between couples about the role of women's paid employment in their marriage and family. Even during unemployment, when gender arrangements at home could change, the behaviors of unemployed women, men, and their spouses remain stuck in traditional notions of gender and work.

Spending and Saving, Part II: How Low-Income People Spend Their Money

It's difficult to find detailed Canadian information on the budgets of poor people: what they earn and what they buy. However, we know from Statistics Canada that, in 2017, families in the bottom income quintile spent an average of $33,764, of which 34.8 percent was spent on shelter, 15.1 percent was spent on transportation, and 14.3 percent was spent on food.

An article in the *New York Times* (Bernard and Russell 2019) examining the budgets of two American families who would not be considered poor but, rather, fall toward the middle of the large "middle class," provides further insight. Even well above the poverty line (which for a family of four is $26,000 per year in the lower forty-eight states), families struggle to pay their bills. The four-member Koch family, with monthly take-home earnings of $4,000 a month, manages to make ends meet, but parents Lauren and Trevor Koch have no health insurance for themselves (their young children are insured through a state program) and little in the way of accumulated savings. The second middle-class family profiled in the article does have health insurance coverage (albeit with a $2,000 deductible) but runs a small shortfall despite monthly take-home income of $5,600. Neither family can be accused of being spendthrifts: groceries and dining out total roughly $800 to $850 a month, or less than $30 a day for four people.

The main takeaway here is that even middle-class families with incomes at or above the national median have little discretionary income after paying for their necessities and regular monthly debts. Clearly, those who earn less fare even worse.

In general, lower-income people spend their money differently than wealthier or more educated people. First, low-income people are more likely to make material rather than experiential purchases (Shavitt et al. 2016). **Material purchases** are purchases of tangible items, such as cars and clothing. **Experiential purchases** are intangible purchases of pleasant life experiences such as vacations, amusement parks, and restaurant dinners (Gilovich and Gallo 2020; Kumar and Gilovich 2016; Bronner and de Hoog, 2018). People of higher socioeconomic status not only make more experiential purchases but report that such purchases increase their happiness more than material purchases.

Spending differences between low- and higher-income people also involve the status-signaling we've discussed throughout this book. Low-income earners are not a homogenous group; different people send different signals through consumption. On the one hand, some crave the luxurious lifestyles of the rich. They might use consumer products to obscure their low-class social position, or to show they aspire to a better life. On the other, some low-income earners begrudge and strive to distance themselves from rich people.

Let's start with the first group of low-income people who aspire to higher social status. These people often display **compensatory consumption** patterns (Shavitt et al. 2016; Landis and Gladstone 2017; Koles et al. 2018), while wealthy people indulge in conspicuous consumption. Said differently, wealthy people more often use consumption to build their reputations and heighten their social identities. Lower-income people more often use consumption to offset feelings of inadequacy, unfairness, or discomfort in their interactions with higher-income people. As Landis and Gladstone (2017: 1518) put it: "People living on [a] low income tend to spend a higher percentage of it on products and services perceived to have high status."

Studies also show that low-income people save less for the future and spend more on expensive brand-name items they cannot easily afford (Moav and Neeman 2010). One reason for this is that poor people are more likely than rich people to be fatalistic and have a weak locus of control

(Kimball and Shumway 2009). That is, poor people are more likely to feel they don't have much control over their own lives, and that all events are predetermined or "fated." If they can't change the future anyway, why bother saving for it?

A second reason for luxury spending among low-income consumers is that they are concerned about their image and want to avoid the stigma of poverty (Grohmann et al 2019). As mentioned in an earlier chapter, some 40 percent of Americans (and an unknown but probably similar fraction of Canadians) are aspirational buyers. That is, they buy luxury items whenever they can, and aspire to buy more. So, rich people are not the only ones who buy luxury

Lower-income people may use compensatory consumption to offset feelings on inadequacy and unfairness and to try to avoid the stigma of poverty.

items. People of other incomes and classes also use these goods to show their status ambitions. For example, they buy luxury cars, party at expensive clubs, or host costly celebrations to appear better off than they really are. They want to impress their community and signal their (false) prosperity to neighbours. In this way, low-income consumers tie their economic status and self-esteem to their purchases (Moav and Neeman 2010; also Ray and Genicot 2019).

Even people in low-income countries indulge in aspects of conspicuous consumption before they have secured enough food, clothing, and shelter (Belk 1988; Johnson et al. 2018; Goor et al. 2018). This suggests that people of all classes consume for social status. However, the specific status symbols used vary by class. High-status people may aspire to own a yacht, an art collection, and have a private chauffeur. Lower-status people may yearn for a car stereo system and cable TV.

By contrast, Moav and Neeman (2010) report that educated, higher-income consumers are likely to save money at a higher rate and do not feel the same need to signal their status with celebrations and luxurious goods. Instead, they flaunt prestigious job titles and professional degrees to mark their socioeconomic status. Low-income consumers' efforts to appear prosperous by buying expensive items may thus backfire. Lavish consumption may perpetuate or worsen their exclusion from the people and groups they want to join (Hamilton 2012). They would do better in the long run saving the money and spending it on education, housing, and health.

Often, this craving for the markers of high status starts in childhood. As discussed in an earlier chapter, children of all social classes come to know the signs of success and prosperity in our society (Roper and La Niece 2009; Holmberg 2018). Poor children, like all children, crave the approval of their peers. And by age 14, they are already choosing products—clothes, binders, computers,

Box 8-3

Victim Blaming and Justifications for Poverty

As mentioned, in North American culture, we have a tendency to "blame the victim"—in this case, to blame poor people for being poor. We reason that, in order to wind up so poor, these people must have spent their money recklessly, gambled it away, chosen to work in a poorly-paying industry, racked up credit card debt, or otherwise mismanaged their finances.

Though often unfounded, these views have deep roots in at least two ways of thinking that are common in our North American consumer culture. First, victim blaming typically goes hand-in-hand with the so-called "just world belief," which holds that people generally get what they deserve in life: poor people deserve to be poor and rich people deserve to be rich. Second, victim blaming stems from a widespread belief in the value of a "meritocracy" where people earn their keep based on their talent and hard work.

In her popular book *On (Not) Getting By In America*, Barbara Ehrenreich offers a few examples to help illustrate why victim blaming is often baseless. She explains that low-income people are limited in their consumer behaviour in many ways that affluent people can ignore and take for granted. For example, affluent people can take refrigeration for granted, but many low-income earners rent rooms without such luxuries that would allow them to buy in bulk at more affordable rates. Affluent people can take secure, lockable space for granted, but without it, you can't preserve and protect your private property. Other things affluent people can take for granted but poor people cannot include fresh water, first aid supplies, shoes and socks, cell phones, a reliable mail service, reliable banking, and access to credit.

So, poor people may sometimes spend their money in ways that seem questionable to wealthier people. But often, they have good (and unavoidable) reasons for doing so. Instead of blaming poor people for spending habits they have little control over, we should be asking what systemic factors backed them into these corners in the first place.

phones, and the like—based on what they know will be popular among their peers. They know their social status will increase if they can own branded rather than generic products. They also know they risk being excluded and bullied if they don't possess the "right" brands. In one study (Elliott and Leonard 2004), low-income children aged eight to 12 said they would rather talk to, and be friends with, someone who wore (expensive) branded running shoes than with someone who wore unbranded ones—whom they said they would be embarrassed to be seen with.

So, low-income children may use expensive and branded items—in this case, running shoes—as status symbols to mask their family's poverty (Elliot and Leonard 2004; see also Schmiedeberg and Schuman 2019; Andersson and Bruck, 2019). If they didn't wear the right running shoes, everyone would know they were poor and judge them harshly for it. This desire for expensive shoes puts pressure on low-income parents who want their children to fit in but cannot easily afford the shoes.

In fact, fashion as a whole puts undue pressure on low-income parents. Since fashion trends have short lifespans and children want what is fashionable to conform with their peers, low-income parents are constantly scrambling to buy their children these items (Isaksen and Roper 2012). To keep up, some reduce spending on needs like food, or on themselves (Elliott and Leonard 2004). For example, they may go without needed clothes so their children can have the latest running shoes. Some low-income households, especially those run by women, have turned to alternative methods, such as bargain-hunting and open communication about the family budget (Hamilton 2012).

Because of peer pressure, consuming the correct possessions at the right time is essential for social acceptance, gaining and keeping friendships, and, in turn, building self-esteem (Isaksen and Roper 2010; 2016). In fact, poverty not only leads to material disappointment; it may also produce materialism. Remember the earlier discussion of social learning theory and compensation theory. We saw that, according to one study, people become materialistic when they have low self-worth (Norberg et al. 2020; Koles et al. 2018). They try to compensate—to make themselves feel better—by buying. Another study by Chaplin, Hill and John (2014) revealed important class differences in materialistic values. Younger children (ages 8–10 years) from low-income families showed roughly the same levels of materialism as their wealthier peers. However, early adolescent (ages 11–13 years) and later adolescent children (ages 16–17 years) from low-income families were more materialistic than higher-income adolescents.

Further analysis showed that this difference was associated with lower self-esteem among the lower-income adolescents. This finding is supported by another large study of urban children. It finds that low-income boys (but not girls) who are surrounded by wealthier neighbours display higher levels of antisocial behaviour than their peers (Odgers et al. 2010; Russell and Odgers 2016). Apparently, growing up alongside wealthier neighbours has a negative effect on low-income boys' behaviour. This effect persisted throughout childhood and remained after controlling the research findings for neighbourhood and demographic measures.

Problems of materialism and low self-esteem may also explain some racial differences in spending. Charles et al. (2007; see also Heffetz 2018), using nationally representative data on consumption, find that in the United States African Americans and Hispanics spend more on visible goods (clothing, jewelry, and cars) than whites with a similar income. This difference is large and fairly constant over time (see also Clingingsmith and Sheremeta, 2018).

Some of the differences are due to status-seeking: youth use conspicuous consumption to suggest they are prosperous and successful. This conspicuous consumption also helps to explain lower spending by racial minorities on relatively invisible items like health and education, as well as their lower rates of savings and wealth accumulation.

Walsek and Brown (2015) propose that worse-off members of unequal societies are likely to devote more of their resources to conspicuous consumption, compared to people in less unequal societies. To test this theory, the researchers used Google Correlate to find search terms that correlated with income inequality, while controlling for income and other socioeconomic factors. They found that, of the 40 search terms used most often by residents of countries with high levels of income inequality, more than 70 percent referred to status goods. These included designer brands, expensive jewelry, and luxury clothing. In contrast, none of the 40 search terms used most often in countries with low levels of income inequality referred to status goods.

Remember, some lower-income people use compensatory consumption to try to make themselves feel better—to compensate for their low self-esteem. But so long as inequality persists, such spending will take these compensatory spenders on a never-ending goose chase. When you climb to the top of one social ladder and step onto the next one, you find yourself on the bottom rung of this new ladder. Winkelmann (2011; see also Huyer-May et al. 2018), for example, notes that people who live in a neighbourhood full of luxury cars are likely to feel less happy or satisfied with their incomes than people who live in less wealthy neighbourhoods, other things being equal. Doubling the number of (say) Ferraris and Porsches in the neighbourhood would have the same negative effect on their happiness as if they had suffered a five percent drop in income. If they lived in a less posh community, with fewer luxury cars, they would be happier with their own cars (and lives).

To summarize, the research shows low-income people spend a significant fraction of their income conspicuously consuming goods that do not relieve their poverty. This conspicuous consumption is intended to make other people think they are wealthier and more economically successful than they really are (Moav and Neeman 2010). Wisman (2008; also, Wisman and Baker 2016) reports this may help explain why U.S. household saving rates are low, compared to rates in other wealthy but more equal countries, and why that rate has declined in recent years.

Low savings rates reflect Americans' belief that vertical mobility is readily possible—the American Dream is alive and well. They think that if they work hard, they may move up the class ladder, and the best way to display this ambition, and their expectation of success, is a high level of visible consumption. Americans feel more compelled to strive for status through conspicuous consumption than do people in other wealthy countries where residents don't feel as uncomfortable about inequality or think they don't have a good chance at upward mobility. The result of believing the future will be better is to save less in the present.

Class Consciousness

So far, we have been focused on the first of two groups of low-income people we mentioned above: those who aspire to become wealthy. But, as mentioned, some low-income earners begrudge and strive to distance themselves from rich people (Yodanis 2006; Loibl and Hira 2016; Thomas 2018).

Sometimes, they do this by finding and expressing value in things other than money. For example, they may underline how loyal they are and how much love they give to their families. Sociologist Carrie Yodanis (2006) saw all of this this play out in her study of low-income women in a small rural fishing community in British Columbia.

These women would talk about how spoiled, lazy, and entitled wealthier community members were, saying that they had never worked hard or struggled to get the things they wanted. Rather than yearning for the lifestyle of the wealthier women, the low-income women in this study poked fun at wealthy women who stayed home all day, volunteered for charities, or had inherited their money. To show how different they were, these working-class women stressed that they worked longer and harder than anyone else. They thought wealth was unfair and undeserved, and prided themselves on the values they associated with their own working-class status: hard work, honesty, and integrity.

Just as there's a clear "pecking order" among high-society women, so too is there a social-status scale in marginalized, low-income communities. There, status is often less about money or cultural capital, and more often about morals and values. In their study of a trailer park called Lakeside, Saatcioglu and Ozanne (2010; see also Saatcioglu and Corus 2016) find five such moral identities on display.

First, the *Nesters* believe people should and do achieve success through hard work and discipline. They see themselves as "good people" with "good-paying jobs" who are leading "good lives."

They look down on neighbours who fail to care for their homes and disrupt the daily park life. A second group, the *Reluctant Emigrants*, are on a downward life trajectory. Forced to downgrade to the more affordable trailer park, they focus on security and protection. Because they fell from relative prosperity, the Emigrants hold on to their childhood goals and strive to return to middle-income life in a traditional home.

The *Community Builders* are sympathetic to other disadvantaged park residents, given their own histories of economic hardship and disability. Like the Nesters and the Reluctant Emigrants, the Community Builders value hard work and discipline, but they are committed to improving the quality of community life in the park, not personal success. The *Homesteaders* value hard work and individual responsibility but face a severe lack of cultural and economic capital. Stoic about challenges they face, the Homesteaders judge neither themselves nor others very harshly. The *Outcasts*, finally, are downwardly mobile and resist a society they consider unfair. They drink, do drugs, and earn money through illegal or disreputable means (for example, strip dancing or dealing drugs).

Box 8-4

Income and Exposure to COVID-19

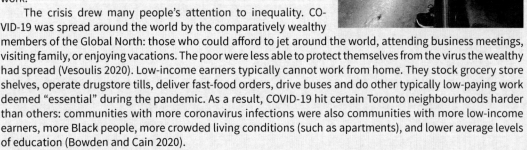

In the spring of 2020, the phrases on everyone's lips were "physical distancing" and "stay home, save lives." Public health authorities advised these were the most important steps people could take to protect themselves and others from COVID-19. But some people were better able to take these steps than others. Large corporations shuttered temporarily while their office staff worked from home. At least some of their employees consisted of well-paid managers whose work is largely done behind a computer. Many small businesses, on the other hand, closed permanently. The people who worked in these local coffee shops, restaurants, retail shops, and other stores were among the millions of Canadians thrown out of work.

The crisis drew many people's attention to inequality. COVID-19 was spread around the world by the comparatively wealthy members of the Global North: those who could afford to jet around the world, attending business meetings, visiting family, or enjoying vacations. The poor were less able to protect themselves from the virus the wealthy had spread (Vesoulis 2020). Low-income earners typically cannot work from home. They stock grocery store shelves, operate drugstore tills, deliver fast-food orders, drive buses and do other typically low-paying work deemed "essential" during the pandemic. As a result, COVID-19 hit certain Toronto neighbourhoods harder than others: communities with more coronavirus infections were also communities with more low-income earners, more Black people, more crowded living conditions (such as apartments), and lower average levels of education (Bowden and Cain 2020).

Canadians also had different abilities to bear the economic burden of physical distancing (*The Economist*, 2020). Low-income earners working the precarious jobs mentioned above cannot protect themselves by taking time off work and staying home. Many live pay cheque to pay cheque. Not working was not an option, since they would be unable to pay their rent or buy groceries. What's more, many of these jobs are not full-time permanent salaried positions. Employers can dismiss workers if they do not show up for a certain number of shifts. Finally, many of these workers do not have health care benefits, paid sick leave, or the freedom to take a leave of absence to care for an ill family member. On the other hand, professionals were able to continue earning their full salaries while working from home. They are also the ones more likely to have savings they could fall back on.

Beyond reinforcing that low-income earners are far from homogenous, these studies suggest that at least some hold strong working-class identities. The notion of class identity implies the Marxist notion of **class consciousness**. Class consciousness is a sense of class solidarity that develops over time, often through conflict with other classes. It includes awareness that you share similar financial circumstances with others.

Class awareness and consciousness seem stronger in many European countries than in Canada and the U.S. In Canada, lower-income people are less likely to describe themselves as working people and more likely to describe themselves as "middle class." They are also less likely to vote according to their objective class interests.

Decades ago, a theory called embourgeoisement emerged to explain these developments. **Embourgeoisement** describes the spread of bourgeois or middle-class values, lifestyles, and aspirations into the working class. It is said to undermine working-class consciousness and, therefore, support for class-based or radical political movements. The term is rooted in Marx's argument that the bourgeoisie ideologically dominates the working class. Orthodox Marxists have since used the concept of embourgeoisement to help explain working-class quiescence under capitalism.

The concept of embourgeoisement gained wider credibility after World War II, when it was taken up by mainly North American liberal scholars such as S. M. Lipset and Clark Kerr. They noted the employment landscape was changing in several ways that hurt working-class people and their solidarity:

- There was a shift away from the traditional industrial economy and especially away from unskilled manufacturing jobs, towards a service and information economy and new knowledge-based occupations.
- Automation gave people who still were manual labourers greater control over their work and reduced their sense of workplace alienation.
- Suburbanization resulted in the break-up of long-established, tightly knit inner-city communities of working-class people, many working in similar occupations.
- There were increasing numbers of full-time jobs with high wages in western countries, as well as a larger role for redistributive social policies and the welfare state.

These shifts brought higher levels of class mobility, and more people moved out of blue-collar into white-collar work. Official statistics from this period showed a relative homogenization of incomes and living standards. Western capitalist societies were literally becoming more middle class. Lifestyles and social values homogenized as well. Rank-and-file workers were now skilled operatives earning higher incomes that allowed them to enjoy the trappings of middle-class life. Even manual labourers—people working in factories on assembly lines, for example—could aspire to own their own cars and homes. They could dress like middle-class people, take part in the same leisure activities as middle-class people, and decorate their homes like middle-class people.

Soon, many adopted the attitudes of middle-class people, too. They started to identify and align themselves with the capitalist enterprise into which they had been integrated and which had served them well. Increasingly, they sent their children to college to get a post-secondary education and even more upward mobility than they had attained.

Many workers took on a middle-class outlook as well: for example, a concern with social status and respectability. They adopted more individualistic, family-minded, and home-centred outlooks. Meanwhile, traditional working-class loyalties to workmates, trade unions, collectivism, and class gradually faded. They faded even more rapidly as many industries moved their factories to other countries, or to states or provinces where unionization could be more easily prevented. Finally, these shifts in lifestyle and thinking translated into voting behaviour. Workers gradually abandoned class-based parties of the left for centrist bourgeois or petit-bourgeois parties.

By the 1970s, theories of worker embourgeoisement had been widely discredited. Commentators from across the political spectrum argued that working-class support for right-wing governments showed workers approved of middle class norms, values, and lifestyles. How else could one explain the rise to power of Ronald Reagan, George W. Bush, and Donald Trump with working-class voter support? Or the rise to power in Canada of Conservatives Mike Harris (in Ontario), Jason Kenney (in Alberta), and Stephen Harper in Canada as a whole?

Some observers tried to explain the seeming disappearance of class identities and loyalties using **mass society theory**. This theory held that, with the disappearance of traditional, "organic," agrarian communities, people experienced isolation and alienation. They hated the political centralization and impersonal bureaucracy associated with modern, large, urban industrial societies. Versions of mass society theory first appeared in the 18th century, in connection with elite fears brought on by the French Revolution.

The French Revolution, marked by such violent events as the storming of the Bastille in 1789, provoked fears among members of the ruling classes of mob rule and the tyranny of the masses.

The ruling classes feared the "tyranny of the majority," disruptive mobs, and demagogic leaders. Although much of this early work was broadly liberal—Alexis de Tocqueville is the principal example—it proved compatible with certain forms of elitism and conservatism.

In the 1930s, similar analyses tried to explain the appeal of fascism and communism. A generation later, David Riesman highlighted the decline of traditional religious and moral attachments and the rise of sophisticated propaganda techniques that could manipulate the masses to achieve consent. In effect, *The Lonely Crowd* was built on a version of mass society theory. It viewed ordinary working people as disconnected and hungry for connection; unbelieving and hungry for belief; and without a political rudder—therefore open to almost any kind of political incitement.

Newer approaches have replaced these monolithic views of mass culture. Cultural studies have carefully explored the segmentation of markets and cultural niches in modern society. They have also pointed out that direct mass manipulation is difficult because people interpret things in different ways. Recent studies of Nazi and Soviet totalitarianism also challenge the model of mass indoctrination. Finally, since the 1960s, we have seen elements of mass culture being leveraged to *resist* authoritarian regimes. This has undermined the idea that mass society and the technologies of mass culture serve mainly to manipulate the masses.

Despite theories like embourgeoisement and the mass society theory that stress class homogenization, we think that class remains an important means of distinguishing between consumption groups or sectors. That is, low-income people are still different from wealthy or even middle-class people in at least two ways.

First, low-income people have **social markers** that clearly distinguish them from middle-class and wealthy people. By a social marker, we mean any feature of a person's speech, appearance, behaviour, or dress seen as reflecting their status in a society. For example, unrefined table manners, in some circumstances, could be a marker of low social status. Social markers of poverty are reflected in cultural capital (and its absence), discussed earlier, which means they also affect a person's life chances. And if low-income people have limited opportunities to improve their lot in life, they will have limited opportunities to take part in our consumer society.

Second, compared with wealthy and middle-income people, lower income people can be marginalized. By **marginalization,** we mean the processes that prevent individuals and groups from fully taking part in society. Marginalized populations can experience barriers to accessing desirable employment, satisfactory housing, good education, clean water, reliable health services, and other social determinants of health. In both senses, low-income people are marginalized in our consumer society. They struggle to access basic needs that have been commodified under capitalism. They also struggle to access consumer goods that serve as markers of success, prestige, and power in our hyperreality.

Final Thoughts

In this chapter, we have drawn generalizations from the research literature on consumer buying. We will do the same in the chapters that follow, in connection with other consumer segments. Our generalizations have not been meant to apply equally to every low-income person in all places at all times. They are no more than an attempt to capture distinctive features of a segment of the population and the way it spends its money today.

In this chapter, we have also seen a strong connection between income, education, status, and social class. This connection is so strong that, often, we cannot say whether a spending difference between (say) low- and higher-income people is due to differences in discretionary income, education, social status, or class culture.

Low-income people sometimes face criticism for spending "foolishly" or "failing" to save adequately. They are told to work harder and indulge themselves less to improve their lot in life. Examples we discussed in this chapter are smoking cigarettes and drinking alcohol. Why, people ask, do low-income people indulge in these expensive habits when they could be spending the money on food, clothes, or saving up for better housing? One explanation we considered is compensatory consumption: low-income people want to make themselves feel better about the cards they've been dealt. They smoke and drink to relieve stress and enjoy themselves.

Other low-income people cultivate an image of hard-working thrift for themselves. One way they do so is by degrading those who do not conform to their notion of what working-class life should look like. When low-income people tell other low-income people to pull themselves up by their bootstraps, they're saying that they themselves typify working-class grit and integrity. By contrast, when middle class people tell low-income people the solution to their problems is "work harder," they're suggesting that they had to sacrifice and work hard to achieve their lot in life, so low-income people should have to too. In short, lower-income and middle-income people are often locked in a conflict over virtue: who deserves blame and who deserves praise, as well as who deserves material comfort and who deserves to suffer. In the next chapter, we take a closer look at wealthy people and their consumer behaviour.

Discussion Questions

1. What evidence in this chapter suggests there is a distinctive low-income spending culture? What evidence suggests that low-income people embrace the same spending culture as everyone else, but cannot afford to fulfill all its requirements?
2. In this chapter, we mentioned that it is worse to be low-income in a wealthy, unequal society than it is to be low-income in a low-income, equal society. Why do you think this is? Do you think that low-income people in wealthy societies face different challenges than low-income people in low-income societies? If so, what kinds of challenges do they face?
3. Families play a major role in socializing children into their social classes. In this chapter, we discussed the impact that social class has on eating behaviour and habits. What are some other class-related habits and behaviours that our families socialize us into?

Quick Quiz

1. Which of the following does NOT characterize a social class?
a. Life chances
b. Standard of living
c. Values
d. Expectations
e. Possession of status goods

2. Seeing high-income people at the top and everyone else striving to join their ranks shows that class structure is a _____.
a. Rigid hierarchy
b. Loose hierarchy
c. Bottom-up hierarchy
d. Fixed hierarchy
e. Stable hierarchy

3. Which of the following statements is true?
a. Low-income children are the most socially mobile
b. The wealthiest children are the most socially mobile
c. There is more downward than upward social mobility in the middle of the income distribution
d. There is more upward than downward social mobility in the middle of the income distribution
e. The wealthiest children in society are the least socially mobile

4. Which of the following statements is NOT true?
a. Low-income people are more likely to make material purchases
b. Low-income people are more likely to use compensatory consumption
c. Low-income people's consumption patterns are intuitive
d. Wealthy people are more likely to engage in experiential purchases
e. Members of unequal societies are likely to devote more of their resources to conspicuous consumption, compared to people in less unequal societies

5. Moav and Neeman (2010) found that _____ consumers were more likely to have higher savings and did not feel the need to signal their status with material goods.
a. Wealthy
b. Higher income
c. Lower income
d. Educated
e. Goal oriented

The answers to the Quick Quiz are provided at the end of the book.

For Further Reading

"A Place in Town: Doing Class in a Coffee Shop" by Carrie Yodanis

In this article, Yodanis explores how socioeconomic differences influence our everyday interactions. She observes that women of various classes "do" class through class-related behaviours and struggles.

Poverty in Canada by Dennis Raphael

In this book, Raphael lays out the causes and consequences of poverty for individuals who live in wealthy, industrialized countries such as Canada. Raphael examines poverty at both the individual and societal level.

Evicted: Poverty and Profit in the American City by Matthew Desmond

In *Evicted*, Desmond looks at poverty and economic exploitation through evictions. He follows eight families who struggle to pay their rent in Milwaukee, Wisconsin.

Key Terms

Agency
Class identity
Consumption sectors
Embourgeoisement
Marginalization
Market segmentation
Mass society theory
Social markers

Chapter Nine
Rich People and Symbols of Taste

Learning Objectives

After reading this chapter, you will be able to:

✓ Evaluate the different types of conspicuous consumption used by different consumers.

✓ Consider how wealthy consumers use cultural capital to distinguish themselves.

✓ Assess why wealthy consumers do more experiential spending than poor consumers.

✓ Identify the ways eating and drinking can display taste and build class identity.

As we began to see in the last chapter, a social hierarchy orders life in our society (Casto and Mehta 2019; Redhead et al. 2019; Kanter 2019). In a hierarchy, people have varying amounts of wealth, status, power and **social distinction.** Social distinction is the process of valuing people differently based on their social status and habits. "Socially distinguished"—that is, wealthy, prominent, or powerful—people behave as though their thoughts, feelings, and actions are more important than those of people lower on the hierarchy (Van den Haak and Wilterdink 2019; Hunting and Hains 2019).

Social distinction is a key ingredient in Bourdieu's theory of culture, which we explore in this chapter. For him, social distinction props up class-based discrimination and exclusion. Powerful people decide who is "distinguished," making those people feel they belong and excluding everyone else. In this sense, as we will see in this chapter, social hierarchies are about rank, control, and dominance. People show their place in the hierarchy through conspicuous consumption, as Veblen told us so long ago. In this chapter, we consider how rich people display their rank and dominance through consumer behaviour.

As we have said throughout this book, consumer behaviour is social behaviour. Often, its goal is to signal a person's social position and social aspirations. Consumer behaviour also aims to identify the group to which one belongs (or aspires to belong), and the groups to which one does not belong (and may even shun). In these senses, all consumption is conspicuous consumption—whether consciously or unconsciously. Not only is communication intended, but that communication also often achieves its goal. Observers of the item that has been purchased can understand its symbolic meaning and value and draw suitable conclusions about the buyer's intent.

All consumer behaviour is also imitative, in this sense. It reveals a social map of the universe in which people prefer some positions to others and, therefore, some goods to others. Indeed, some products may be directly associated with those preferred positions. We consume in hopes of eventually associating ourselves with people whose social status we admire and desire. So, we try to copy the behaviour of these better-placed people and in doing so may end up buying goods and services like the ones they own.

In this sense, poor consumers and rich consumers have some things in common. For one, they both buy these "tickets"—goods that help them gain admission to, or maintain membership in, an institution or social group. People in both groups also crave treats from time to time. The main differences we will see between poor and rich consumers have to do with the *amount* they spend on different types of goods. For example, because they have less money to spend, poor people spend a larger share of their income on basics than rich people do. And because rich people have a lot more money to spend, they spend a larger amount of their income—both absolutely and proportionately—on trophies, through what Veblen called "conspicuous consumption." These differences aside, it is not obvious that either group spends a larger share of its income on treats or tickets.

In these respects, rich people and poor people are very similar; but as we will see in this chapter, there are a few differences between them otherwise. And the class-based acquisition of cultural capital plays a large part in creating these differences.

Defining Our Terms

As discussed in an earlier chapter, **cultural capital** includes a wide variety of symbols and practices—for instance, taste in art, style in dress, and eating habits (DiMaggio 2019; Ollier-Malaterre et al. 2019; Farkas 2017). Members of the ruling class teach their children elegant taste preferences as a way of passing along this class-based cultural capital. In that sense, Bourdieu says cultural capital doesn't just signal class status; it reproduces class domination from one generation to the next.

There are three parts to the full cultural-capital package. The first is called **embodied capital**, which includes human physiology—for example, a healthy and robust appearance (Xie and Min 2019; Mitchell 2019; Cottingham 2016). Employers, business partners, and even friends pay attention to how we look. And people who've been raised, from the moment they're born, to take care of their bodies and present themselves professionally make great first impressions. In heavily class-based societies like the UK, people's social class is often identified by the straightness of their teeth. Children from rich families get orthodontic work, while children from poor families don't.

Second, cultural capital involves **objectification**. This type of capital is shown off through material things—things that are part of our external world and not embodied. This is part of what Bourdieu meant by "taste." Your choice of a refined watercolour over a band poster displays your objectified cultural capital (for example, Sieben and Lechner 2019; Chan 2017; Huang and Liang 2016). Most consumer goods fall into this category and we say more about Bourdieu and taste below.

Finally, some cultural capital reflects the institutions you have associated yourself with; this is **institutional capital**. For example, a degree from the University of Toronto symbolizes more cultural capital than a degree from Erie Community College, and a degree from Oxford University communicates yet more cultural capital. People communicate this capital on their resumes and in job interviews. Depending on the job, some employers choose one applicant over another based on where their qualifications came from (Stilwell 2016; Muyeba 2019; but also, Huang and Cao 2016).

To gain any of these three types of cultural capital, it helps to have **economic capital:** that is, money. For example, to look healthy, you need money to buy orthodontic work or a gym membership. High-class material things—clothing, cars, and jewelry, for example—also need to be bought. Last, university degrees are among some of the costliest consumer products in our society today. That's why people born into lower-income families often stay in lower-income classes their entire lives. To move up the social class hierarchy, they would need money to invest in these three forms of cultural capital.

However, people are also stuck in place, culturally, by their own past investments in non-dominant cultural learning. Just as there is dominant social capital—the kind that Bourdieu discussed—so too is there **non-dominant cultural capital** (Carter 2003; also, Marucci and Elmesky 2016). This is the knowledge and skill that gives a low-income urban black teenager street smarts. In other words, it grants an advantage to that teen within his socially marginalized community that is equal to the advantage dominant cultural capital would grant in an upper-income community. However, that non-dominant cultural capital confers no advantage outside that marginalized community.

Luxury Spending by Wealthy People

In the last chapter, we defined wealthy people as those falling in the highest 10 percent of household income distribution. But even within that narrow slice of the distribution, incomes and wealth vary, and accordingly, so do spending patterns.

As we saw in the last chapter, we get little useful information from survey results provided by Statistics Canada. A survey of spending by households shows that the top income quintile in Canada spent $105,493 in 2017. Of this, 27.4 percent went for shelter, 21.1 percent for transportation, and 12.2 percent for food. Compared to the lowest income quintile, the top income quintile spent a much smaller share of the household budget on housing and a much larger share on transportation. The top quintile households spent somewhat more on food; but as we will see, they differed from poorer households not only in the amounts they spent on food, but also in their styles of spending: what they ate and how they ate it.

Now, let's break down these spending patterns more finely, using available U.S. data. To do so, Emmie Martin (CNBC 2017) uses the imaginary annual budget of a couple living in San Francisco, each person making $100,000 a year. In 2017, when Martin's article was written, that was nearly four times the median annual income in the United States. It puts this imaginary family in the upper class—or at least in the upper income bracket of American society. However, they don't seem that rich at the end of the year, after much of their income has gone to costs that they can't question or control.

As you can see below, taxes and pension savings take a large chunk of this income, as does the mortgage, cost of food, and childcare. Discretionary items such as vacations, children's lessons, and charitable contributions account for $18,000

Box 9-1
How Far Does $200,000 Go?

Gross Income	**$200,000**
Retirement Plan Contributions	($18,000)
Income Taxes (State and Federal)	($56,000)
Net Income	**$127,400**
Childcare (one child)	($24,000)
Food	($12,000)
Mortgage	($36,000)
Home Maintenance	($3,600)
Vacations (two per year)	($8,000)
Car Payment	($6,000)
Gas	($4,800)
Car Insurance	($1,500)
Property Insurance	($1,000)
Life Insurance ($500,000 term policy)	($800)
Property Taxes ($700,000 home)	($8,000)
Clothing	($3,000)
Children's Lessons	($5,000)
Charitable Donations	($2,000)
Consumer Debt	($3,000)
Miscellaneous	($3,000)
Total Expenses	**($121,700)**
Amount Remaining after Expenses	**$5,700**

a year (9 percent of the total), with $5,700—roughly 3 percent of the starting income—left over at the end. Note that the amount spent on food—$12,000 a year, or $1000 a month—is 25 per cent more than lower-middle class families spent on their food. Obviously, the wealthier family enjoys a slightly more expensive diet, but nothing remarkable.

So, rich people: are they different from you and me, or just wealthier? From the budget above, it would seem that rich people have more expenses because they live more expensively than poor people; but otherwise, they are similar. Perhaps that is why some rich people do everything in their power to sharpen the dividing line between themselves and everyone else, and to imply superiority. To draw that dividing line was, as Thorstein Veblen said, the purpose of conspicuous consumption.

As discussed earlier, conspicuous consumption is extravagant spending on goods and services to display income or wealth and social status (Goenka and Thomas 2020; Walters and Carr 2019). To use Veblen's words: "In order to gain and hold the esteem of men, it is not sufficient just to possess wealth or power. The wealth or power must be put in evidence" (Veblen, 1899: 42). To gain high status, you must (1) purchase expensive goods but also (2) make those goods "conspicuous" by flaunting them in plain view.

When he coined the term in *Theory of the Leisure Class* (1899), Veblen was commenting on the United States at the end of the 19th century (for an appreciation of Veblen's work, see Scott 2017). For him, a person's reputation was directly related to the amount of money possessed and displayed. Thus, the basis "of gaining and retaining a good name are leisure and conspicuous consumption" (Veblen 1925: 4). And, in Veblen's view, a "good name" meant honour, prestige, and esteem in the community—all desirable outcomes the wealthy were willing to spend to get. In their efforts to build their "name," Veblen saw that people in the ruling class, through conspicuous consumption, were recreating imagined regal lifestyles from the past that set them apart from the poor, the middle-class, and the just somewhat rich. Horse racing, for example, was a kind of conspicuously wasted time that aristocrats had favored for millennia. So, the new American rich took to it too.

As leisure, sporting, and consumer industries grew over the course of the 20th century, more people from more economic and social classes became better able to join in. Conspicuous consumption, with conspicuous leisure and conspicuous waste, was no longer just for those who didn't have to work at all. Anyone with time and money to spare could also consume conspicuously. This posed a problem for the "original" wealthy—the so-called "old money" families, or "old aristocrats"—who wanted to keep their position on the top rungs of the social hierarchy. In the battle for those limited positions, a distinction emerged between having *money*—specifically, "new money"—and having what is variously described as "class" or "taste." Anyone with money can claim a position in the upper *economic* class. But only those with good taste earn and keep their spot in the upper *social* class.

This distinction has been recognized for centuries. Old aristocrats think their consumption habits are classy and tasteful. Newly wealthy people may consume conspicuously in ways the old aristocrats find tacky. These newly wealthy people thus dilute the symbolism of luxury goods (Kuksov and Xie 2010; Jiang and Guo 2015). Because more people have the same product, it no longer confers prestige. The old aristocrats no longer feel it sets them apart from people with new money. They may seek new, more expensive versions or different products altogether. Why buy designer label clothes if everyone else can afford to do the same?

The ubiquity of luxury marketing makes this "problem" worse. Products of all prices and

---

Box 9-2
Designer Labels for the Masses

Many people want others to see them as high-class. Owning designer goods is an effective way to suggest this status. However, because designer goods come with a high price tag, not everyone can afford them. Many Canadians have found a cheaper alternative to buying their apparel directly from luxury retail stores. Off-price retailers sell apparel from designer brands at discounted prices (Leung, 2015).

Lately, American off-price retailers have been planting their stores on Canadian soil. For instance, Nordstrom Rack is a well-known off-price retailer that has opened in Canada (Patterson, 2018). Experts say the off-price segment is the fastest-growing retail channel for apparel in Canada (Toneguzzi, 2019). Canadian shoppers seemingly welcome the expansion of off-price stores into Canada. Sales of off-price retailers in Canada increased from $2.39 billion in 2015 to $3.24 billion in 2019 (Bedford, 2019).

Off-price stores make luxury more affordable for lower-income buyers. This cheaper alternative allows consumers of different social classes to dress like the rich. In this way, rich people are no longer distinguished by their ability to buy designer clothing. Instead, they rely on suggesting their social status through amassing cultural capital, which is often even more expensive and exclusive than costly material goods.

---

qualities are increasingly labelled "deluxe" or "premium" (Kapferer and Bastien 2009; van Rompay et al. 2019; Perry 2017). Some call this **masstige**, a term for mass-produced products that are nonetheless promoted as prestigious (Kumaret et al., 2019). In this environment, brands traditionally considered "luxuries" need to distinguish themselves. They may do so by highlighting their superior quality. But the sheer volume of self-proclaimed luxury brands often frustrates these efforts.

Some luxury brands instead introduce budget brands. They want to capture consumers beyond the small number of wealthy people who traditionally made up their customer base. In doing so, however, they risk alienating that original customer base. Those wealthy consumers who bought the brand to distance themselves from the masses would now be buying the same brand, if not the same product, as those masses. To avoid losing their most loyal customers, Kapferer et al. (2013) suggest luxury brands must respect three conditions:

1. The prices of these entry lines must reproduce the positioning of the brand vis-à-vis competitors' own entry lines. Chanel fragrances should be priced above Armani or Dior fragrances, for instance.
2. The so-called entry lines must deliver the key brand values and extras.
3. Their price must be far above normal lines, to signify there is no comparison, luxury being another world. With these conditions, the entry lines of famous luxury brands will be perceived as luxury brands themselves.

In the clambering for social status between "old" and "new" money, we see a few types of conspicuous consumption. First is the **bandwagon effect**: a desire to emulate behaviour you admire (or "keep up with the Joneses") (McCormick 1983; see, for example, Gunaruwan 2018). When marketing to people who want to jump on the bandwagon, retailers use big, flashy displays that appeal to the widespread popularity of certain products. One luxury product that has enjoyed astonishing bandwagon-like success across the country is the Canada Goose coat.

Box 9-3

Canada Goose and Social Status

While fashion is not on the list of Canada's top industries, the country's fashion industry is growing, mainly driven by e-commerce and luxury apparel sales (Toneguzzi 2019). Canada Goose is one Canadian brand that has surged in international popularity. Canada Goose jackets cost anywhere from $500 to $1,500 (Cameron 2019). The high-quality materials used to produce the coats allow them to withstand temperatures as low as –30 degrees Celsius. (In the photo to the right, members of an American expedition to the Antarctic are seen wearing their Canada Goose jackets.)

Canada Goose jackets are popular even in countries whose winters are not overly cold. You can find a Canada Goose store in Hong Kong's International Finance Centre (Treleaven 2018). The brand also has a regional office in Shanghai and a massive store in Beijing's Sanlitun. In Asia, families buy these jackets for skiing trips in Japan and for their children who are studying in the West. Canada Goose was the first Canadian company to make it on Deloitte's Global Powers of Luxury Goods list (Treleaven 2018).

Canada Goose jackets aren't highly-demanded luxury goods because they keep you warm; they also communicate social status. The logo on the arm identifies the jacket with the brand and its well-known high price tag. One high school in the UK bans students from wearing the jackets. They do this to avoid an environment where students who cannot afford them are marginalized (Cameron 2019).

Canada Goose is just the start of Canadian luxury fashion. In recent years, magazines have spotted celebrities like Angelina Jolie, Emma Stone, Taylor Swift, and Meghan Markle wearing high-end Canadian brands (Grant 2017). Bojana Sentaler, a Canadian fashion designer says, "Ten years ago when I founded Sentaler, people didn't even know Canada had fashion designers. Now we have some clients who won't wear anything but Canadian" (The Kit 2019).

Second is the **envy premium** (Van De Ven et al. 2010; also, Helien et al. 2018). Consumers are willing to pay more for products that provoke other people's envy. This premium varies depending on who owns the thing you're lusting after. Imagine the owner is someone higher in the class hierarchy than you, whose status, you think, is well-deserved. You're more likely to envy—and pay a premium for—a product that person owns. Now imagine someone higher on the hierarchy than you whose status is, in your eyes, *not* deserved—maybe it is the result of friendship or favouritism. You may envy a product they own, but you're more likely to buy a different version of that product than the one they own.

204 • *Consumer Society*

In the first case, you want to keep up with the high-status person you admire. You try to do so by getting the same things they have, so you can make yourself feel as though you're on their level. In the second case, you want to move away from the high-status person you see as undeserving. It's your effort to stop comparing yourself with people who've outperformed you. Instead, you buy something different that makes you feel like you're "beating" the undeserving individual.

Third is the **snob effect**: a wish to avoid and reject the behaviour of the people you shun (Husic and Cicik 2008; Kiatkawsin and Han 2019). The snob effect is like the envy premium, but in reverse. For example, some wealthy people reject consumer goods that ordinary, lower-income or middle-income people buy. Instead, they want rare, exclusive items that distinguish them from the masses (Amaldoss and Jain 2004; Bastien and Kapferer 2013; Kastanakis and Balabanis 2014).

So, marketers sometimes promote certain luxury products through exclusive, small-circle events. In a bricks-and-mortar retail setting, these products might even be hidden, requiring that customers ask for them. Companies also price their products differently when targeting snob-driven consumers. Usually, as prices rise, people buy less of a given product—but snobs buy *more*. Amaldoss and Jain (2005; also, Butcher et al. 2016) show that in a market that consists of snobs, the demand curve slopes upward: a higher price means more sales. Women's cosmetics is a prime example: among snobs, the demand for these goods grows as the price increases.

In short, different consumers use different types of conspicuous consumption for different ends. They also talk about and judge each other's conspicuous consumption. Conspicuous consumption means both keeping up with one's social superiors and doing markedly better than one's social inferiors (for a critique of Veblen's theories, see Campbell 1995; also, Miller 2018). To do so, wealthy people may denounce certain goods and types of spending as "trashy" or "flashy—for example, they might describe bandwagon goods available to the masses in this way. In their efforts to be seen as truly "high class," many wealthy people want to avoid lavish displays that risk making them seem crude or "tacky" (Galbraith 1984; 2017). They display their status in more sophisticated and subtle ways, with what they like to call "taste."

Sociologist Pierre Bourdieu wrote one of the foundational texts on this notion of taste. He argued that rich people's possession of, and control over, taste was what really separated them from poor- and middle-class people—not just money (see, for example, Boyle and De Keere 2019; Zhang 2020).

In his classic book *Distinction: A Social Critique of the Judgment of Taste,* Bourdieu says "taste" is socially constructed (see Lena, 2019; but see also Mastandrea et al. 2019 on national differences). As a society, we have collectively agreed that, for example, a wall of delicately framed watercolours signals good taste, while a smattering of rock-band posters, or photos of the family, shows poor taste. We've been socialized to see watercolours as markers of "classiness." This notion of taste that wealthy people use to draw a dividing line between themselves and everyone else is arbitrary; wealthy people make it up, and the rest of us (often) go along with it.

As mentioned throughout this book, such cultural socialization happens (partly) at school. Without some training, viewers cannot understand art's significance or its historical meaning. This means that lower-income people, often with less education, usually see art with less insight than more educated, often higher-income people. Some elite private schools even have classes dedicated to art history. There, students learn how to critique and appreciate art. Those skills come in handy when they're later invited to art galleries and other opportunities to mingle with wealthy, influential people. And only the wealthiest families can afford to send their children to private schools where they can gain these advantages.

Typically, people with more education enjoy fine art (Lizardo 2016). And usually people born into families with money and status have access to education. That's why Bourdieu's discussion of art is about much more than art. It is about transferring class position from one generation to the next, through culture and socialization. In another book, *Language and Symbolic Power* (1991), he expands his metaphor. Much like the codes people need to decipher such art, there are also codes that help people unlock other signs of "good taste," including how to speak, how to dress, and where to vacation. Knowing how to display your taste shows your classiness and your class (as examples, see Webster 2019; Das 2019).

Take the example of brand prominence. **Brand prominence** is the conspicu-

Box 9-4
The Luxury of an Expensive Education

Rich parents can increase the chances of their child's academic success by investing money in ways the average Canadian cannot. Many wealthy families send their children to private schools. The class sizes are smaller compared to public schools and the curriculum is rigorous, preparing students for university (Grossberg 2019). Knowing the advantages of private schools, rich families are willing to pay a hefty price for it. Tuition for elite boarding schools in Canada can exceed $60,000 (Kerr 2018)—far more than university tuition for domestic students.

But rich families begin investing in their child's academic success well before elementary school starts. High-end childcare centers hire professionals with degrees in education to teach children pre-literacy and numeracy skills (Bryce et al. 2016). When these children start school, their social, language, and cognitive skills are more advanced and they are more likely to succeed academically compared with other children. But again, the price tag is significant. The richest families in British Columbia spend around $50,000 on childcare before kindergarten starts (Bryce et al. 2016).

ousness of a brand's mark or logo on a product. It is one of the signs of good taste that people with more wealth and cultural capital use to show their status to each other (Berger and Morgan 2010; Bellezza and Berger 2019). When they buy products that are not prominently branded, only elite insiders like themselves can decode these subtle signals.

For example, clear and forthright product branding—like the big Nike "swoosh" on a t-shirt—is recognizable to most people, of every class. However, subtle branding—say, a small, discreet logo—means that only the elite can distinguish "trashy" brands from "classy" ones (Han et al. 2010; Perry et al. 2020). These subtle signals allow higher-income people to feel part of an elite group: one where they're in on a "secret" that lower-income do not know about.

Different types of people use brand prominence differently. Those old aristocrats, for example, feel they do not need to reinforce their status. They are so clearly entrenched in the upper class, they buy subtle, "tasteful" products. Meanwhile, the "new money" people do need to reinforce their status. They want to distinguish themselves from less wealthy people. Their prominently branded purchases therefore scream for attention (Bronsert et al. 2017; Smith Maguire 2019).

Then there are middle-class and poor people. They want to assert their status but cannot afford luxury goods. Instead, they may buy prominently branded fakes or tasteful alternatives. One study focused on women who bought both original and fake luxury fashion products (Perez et al. 2010). The women said they liked buying the forgeries because, doing so, they were being efficient and making the best use of their resources. They also thought it was fun. They were having a bit of an adventure and enjoyed taking the risk. Third, they found pleasure in fooling others. Most importantly, they thought that fake luxury goods helped them build an identity as "savvy" people. Whether wealthy people were duped by the forgeries didn't figure in this equation. These women *thought* they had gamed the system and patted themselves on the back for it.

What's more, forged luxury products may not devalue the original, genuine luxury products (Nia and Zaichkowsky 2000; Kim et al. 2016). Nia and Zaichkowsky (2000) looked at the opinions and attitudes of original luxury brand owners towards fake luxury goods. All respondents found luxury products fun and worth the price they paid for them, whether they were original or fake.

Overall, 70 percent of respondents said the value, satisfaction, and status of original luxury brand names were not decreased by the wide availability of forgeries. Further, most respondents disagreed the availability of counterfeits undermined their efforts to buy genuine luxury brands. However, the nearly 30 percent of respondents who only owned original goods thought counterfeits were inferior products and that ownership of original luxury products was more prestigious.

When it comes to luxury products more broadly, those old aristocrats might dismiss some of them as flashy attempts at grabbing attention (Dubois and Laurent 1994; Schade et al, 2016), electing to display more subtle signs of their wealth. Initially, some speculated this toned-down luxury buying was a moral position. Perhaps spectacularly wealthy people do not want to flaunt luxurious goods in a world where many struggle just to pay their bills. But research suggests otherwise (for example, Davies et al. 2010; Hlee et al. 2019). Consumers take ethics into account to a lesser degree when making luxury purchases than when making utilitarian purchases. Luxury goods are seen as having a smaller social or ethical importance than utilitarian ones. What's more, some think luxury purchases affect the ethical image we portray to our peers and family less than our utilitarian purchases. For all of these reasons, luxury buyers do not typically factor ethical issues into their buying decision.

One factor that does discourage some luxury purchases is price. The snob effect aside, even some wealthy people think certain luxury goods are just too expensive. They do not see enough value in the product to justify its high price (Tynan et al. 2009; Koivisto and Mattila 2018). Luxury brands often try to compensate by focusing on service. As we discussed in an earlier chapter, some consumers want to feel pampered. They seek not just luxury products, but luxury shopping experiences. For instance, they want in-store "extras" like bottled water or champagne while they shop, or luxurious packaging for products ordered online. Luxury brands also rely on the emotional labour of their staff. Salespeople make consumers feel good while they shop, heightening the overall luxury experience.

In sum, high-class taste—or knowing the high-class symbol systems—may set you apart from people born into lower-income families. Such taste can therefore get you further in life. Bourdieu says you need such taste to fit in with wealthy, successful people. Knowledge of middle- and lower-income symbol systems doesn't carry the same advantage. So, what sets rich people apart is their control over the definitions of taste, and their ability to pass on taste down their family line.

That's not to say that material (that is, non-symbolic) aspects of life are unimportant. People need food to survive, and jobs to buy food, so people who control access to jobs—that is, owners of the means of production—hold people's survival in their hands. Marxian sociologists often point out that symbol systems support that power structure. When people don't understand how to dress, talk, and otherwise behave "tastefully," they may be excluded from some elite groups and denied the same wealth and power.

As well, cultural systems often depict wealthy, powerful people in glamorous settings and heroic poses (Berger 2008; Rich 2019; Chang 2019). Often, we see them in the company of other powerful people, doing important things in expensive clothing. So, symbol systems are not,

The Occupy movement held protests in many major cities in 2011 like the one above in Toronto, but did not succeed in forcing significant changes to society's entrenched power structure.

always, all that abstract. They often use material objects to tell a story. And they have real, material results. Often, these symbol systems are gatekeepers, denying working class people access to a higher standard of living.

Powerful groups keep their power partly by encouraging the rest of us to believe in certain ideologies. Ideologies are popular ideas that serve elite, ruling-class interests. To avoid the revolution Marx called for, powerful groups try to hide the ways they benefit from such popular ideologies. They do so by claiming the status quo benefits everyone. Look at the idea of "meritocracy."

We're told we live in a meritocratic society, where people are rewarded for their talent and hard work. Work harder and you'll get rich, they say.

Yet, research shows this is not how our society works. Thanks to taste—and a system of private wealth protected in law—most people stay in the same social class they were born in (Glass and Bilal 2016; Calder 2016). They stay put, no matter how smart or hardworking they may be. Even though it's largely false, the meritocratic ideology justifies the existing unequal distribution of wealth and power in our society. It says rich people *deserve* to be rich because they worked hard to earn what they have. It also says poor people deserve to live in poverty; they must not have worked hard enough to escape it (Day and Fiske 2019; Weber 2020).

These popular beliefs serve the interests of the dominant class (Codd 2017; Kluegel and Smith 2017). When average people think they deserve their station in life, they're uninspired or unwilling to ask for more. That's why wealthy people and powerful groups so often support meritocratic ideas. It's in their best interest to promote the ideologies that uphold their power.

The masses don't always cooperate with this agenda. On many occasions, huge protests have been staged against class inequality. The Occupy movement is only one of many (on the Occupy movement, see Hull 2019; Cloke et al. 2016). But so far, efforts to undermine popular ideologies and overturn the status quo have been unsuccessful. The gap between the rich and the poor continues to grow, and many ordinary people don't even realize they're being fed stories that perpetuate their disadvantage.

Few people connect ideas like meritocratic values with class divides. They buy into beliefs they don't fully understand; they struggle their whole lives to live up to expectations that were designed to keep them in their "place." Ideologies only work when the masses support them. And we're good at agreeing with much of what powerful people tell us.

Experiential Consumption and Self-Actualization

In the last chapter, we noted two key differences between consumers who are poor and those who aren't. First, we noted that lower-income people are more likely to use compensatory consumption (Shavitt et al. 2016; Landis and Gladstone 2017; Koles et al. 2018) to make themselves feel better, while wealthy people use conspicuous consumption to show off their money and status. Second, we noted that low-income people are more likely to make material rather than experiential purchases (Shavitt et al. 2016). In this section, we explore this notion of experiential buying more closely.

Unlike material purchases, which involve owning tangible goods, experiential purchases are intangible and impermanent. Examples include going on vacations, visiting amusement parks, touring art galleries, and dining out in restaurants. Experiential value, in turn, is the value a customer gains from interactions and experiences involving either direct use or distanced appreciation of goods and services (Mathwick, Malhotra, and Rigdon 2001).

Experiential consumption is, for the most part, possible only when people have met their material needs. Political scientist Rob Inglehart says experiential consumption is therefore popular in our **post-materialist** society.

Inglehart's theory of post-materialism holds that, in societies that are stable and sufficiently wealthy, concerns about survival dwindle. People begin to believe that satisfaction and happiness do not come (only) from material plenty, but also from social and cultural experiences (Booth 2018). People who grow up in societies (and time periods) where they can take survival for granted turn their attention elsewhere: for example, towards personal autonomy, self-expression, social justice, and environmentalism. Post-materialism is closely related to psychologist Abraham Maslow's hierarchy of needs. Once basic needs like food and shelter have been met, Maslow says, humans can seek self-actualization: that is, striving towards their full potential.

In keeping with the concepts of post-materialism and self-actualization, wealthier people report that experiential purchases increase their happiness more than material purchases. This is especially the case among those with a long history of economic security—for example, those who come from a long line of wealthy ancestors, as opposed to a newly rich person who was born in the lower or middle class. People who come from "old money," or who have a long history of financial stability, have long enjoyed material plenty and are instead seeking what Holbrook and Hirschman (1982: 132) described as a "steady flow of fantasies, feelings, and fun."

In an earlier chapter, we discussed consumers' wish to be enchanted and the ways marketers strive to fulfill that wish. We crave entertainment, an escape from the monotony of everyday life, and even educational or other experiences that help us find meaning and purpose (Sadachar and Fiore 2017). As mentioned, shopping malls and department stores try to make the experience of shopping itself enjoyable and enchanting. In a world where almost everything available in the mall is also available online, brick and mortar retailers strive to make their in-person environments the enchanting part of the shopping experience.

For example, some marketers use "augmented reality" experiential marketing, using technology that makes reality magical or enchanting (Baharuddin and Rambli 2017.) Consumers seek out such retail environments that offer memorable experiences, since they help them escape their everyday routines (Retief et al. 2018). In such places, they are more likely to make impulsive purchases,

The use of augmented reality to add fanciful or magical elements to shopping and tourism experiences is in its infancy but seems likely to become a more prominent part of everyday life in the years ahead.

especially if the goods for sale are high-priced luxury products.

Experiential marketing for such luxury products plays to people's emotions. It's not enough to emphasize the product's quality or performance (Atwal and Williams 2009). Luxury buyers must see their lifestyle reflected in the product. For example, to sell an expensive automobile, a marketer would not stop at emphasizing the car's top speed or easy handling. They would also call attention to its real leather seats and wooden paneling, invoking images of "the old days," when wealth and automobiles really were rare and unparalleled.

Tourist travel and vacation packaging relies even more on the supply or creation of memories through experiences (Skandalis et al. 2019). Many tourists travel in pursuit of adventure, to fulfill fantasies, and to show off these memories once they return (Kent 2017). Visiting luxury vacation destinations allows wealthy people to maintain their rank—they can participate in cocktail party conversations about refined sites and posh foreign experiences or paint a picture of their worldliness for their social media followers.

Box 9-5

Traveling in Luxury

In 2016, wealthy people in the U.S. spent a total of $45 billion on travel and hospitality (Loudenback 2018). This is more than they spent on apparel, automobiles, and jewelry.

Spending on travel has a long history. A hundred years ago, the ability to go on lavish vacations distinguished rich people from others. Before the rise of air travel, ocean liners were popular among the rich (Cain 2019). An ocean liner was similar to a modern-day cruise ship, though constructed more ruggedly to withstand heavy seas and following a regular schedule from one port to the next; the only ocean liner still in service is the *Queen Mary 2*. Many of these ships were the epitome of luxury; ocean lines hired famous European designers to recreate the environment of grand hotels as they competed for wealthy customers (Khederian 2017). Liners boasted ballrooms, smoking rooms, writing rooms, grand staircases, and veranda cafés.

Eventually, airlines began offering more exclusive, luxurious options for wealthy passengers. The first-class experience in the 1950s included gourmet meals, reclining seats, and cocktail lounges. In 1970, Pan Am introduced the Boeing 747 jumbo jet, complete with a spiral staircase and pianos (Slotnick 2019). Since then, luxury air travel has been constantly upgraded to address the wants of wealthy passengers. In 2014, Emirates Airlines introduced the "Residence First Class Suite": a 125-square-foot private suite that includes a living room, an en suite bathroom with a shower, and a butler. A round trip from New York to Abu Dhabi in the suite costs more than $40,000.

Many rich people opt for a less opulent first-class experience. But even those tickets still cost about 70 percent more than an economy ticket (Hoffower 2018). For most airlines, flying first-class means having priority boarding, extra legroom, larger TV screens, WiFi, free alcohol, and gourmet food. On longer distance flights, first-class may also offer a flat bed, sliding doors for privacy, and showers.

Left: First-class cabins and lounges in early versions of the Boeing 747 rivalled ocean liners in their comfort and opulence. This publicity photo from SAS shows dinner being served aboard the Scandinavian carrier's jumbo jet "Huge Viking" early in the 1970s.

Done right, experiential marketing might even convince some customers to value, want, and enjoy new things. For example, a lecture and wine tasting with a famous sommelier might induce some people to start buying new kinds of wine (Crolic and Janiszewski 2018). This might be especially effective among wine and culinary tourists, who most value informative entertainment, or social-cultural activities that are educational (Schamel 2017). This type of tourist enjoys and seeks out "tourism factories" (Yeh et al. 2019). A tourism factory is a factory that still actively manufactures products, making it a site-seeing destination with an educational component. In Dublin, one of the most popular tourist sites is the Jameson Irish whiskey factory, where people see whiskey being made and get to sample it as well. Such tourism factories are most often visited by well-educated young adults and people traveling with their families.

All of this is related to the snob effect described above. Consumers with a strong need for exclusivity show more favorable attitudes toward luxury experiences (Kim 2016). However, their feelings of power also play a role. Only when feeling powerful do consumers with a strong desire for exclusivity evaluate luxury experiences more favorably.

Eating, Drinking, and Classy Identities

As Bourdieu suggested, the foods we enjoy, the restaurants we frequent, and the ways we consume foods speak to our cultural capital (or lack of it). Research shows that people learn to eat in ways that place them within social groups and signal that they belong. People also show, by their eating, who they want to be and with whom they wish to associate. In these respects, consuming food is like consuming other material objects: it helps to shape a social identity and to place oneself in ranked social order.

Alan Warde's book *Consumption, Food and Taste* (1997; also, Warde 2016, 2017, 2018) looks at the huge range of food choices that help us shape those identities. He describes four "antinomies of taste," or contradictory ideas of what you should eat, then shows their social correlates. They are novelty versus tradition, health versus indulgence, economy versus extravagance, and care versus convenience.

Lower-income people are more likely to believe in the value of economy over extravagance. Meanwhile, higher-income earners may want to show off their healthy diet by bringing gourmet salads to work. In short, people of the same social class typically share the same taste in foods, and it differs from that of other classes (Warde 1997).

Mass media, as discussed earlier, help preserve these beliefs and tastes. Consider the recipe columns in popular women's magazines. Warde found they highlighted each of the contradictory beliefs outlined above, often in the same article or issue. For example, a column might encourage readers to prepare a salad, stressing the idea of health, and then follow up with (unhealthy) dessert recommendations.

Warde also noted many other sources advising people to eat healthily, including magazines, public service announcements, and websites. Today, restaurants and fast-food chains even have to post calorie counts on their menus. But at the same time, many of these sources of advice say junk food can help us feel better when we're having a bad day. Indulgence is seen as a source of comfort.

Some diets even build in "cheat days," reasoning that no one can eat healthy all the time. Consumers thus receive contradictory messages about health and indulgence. Many are self-aware and self-conscious about the healthiness of their eating (Sproesser et al. 2017; Chung et al. 2017.)

New food products also support our beliefs and tastes—especially, the idea that novelty is good (Ji et al. 2016; Gocłowska et al. 2019). Just like other producers of consumer goods, food manufacturers and restauranteurs know that new releases stir up excitement (Warde 1997). People show they are stylish and knowledgeable by being the first to try new things. Product launches and restaurant openings—both of which get covered in the news and on social media—highlight this ideal of novelty.

New products can also be disappointing. You take a risk when you try a new product—when you play into novelty. So, people also have good reasons to stick with what they know. Traditional eating can also bring back good memories. For example, eating turkey and mashed potatoes on Christmas is traditional in many Western families, and replayed without variation year after year. In the magazines Warde studied, recipe columns encouraged readers to keep cooking foods from "the good old days" (Warde 1997). They suggested eating familiar foods is a comforting reminder of simpler times, and many consumers agree (Balogh 2016; Conti et al. 2018; but also, Hanssen and Kuven 2016).

The antinomy of taste most clearly related to class is "economy versus extravagance." Low-income earners are often concerned about the price of food and buy things that are on sale (McKenzie and McKay 2017; Sharaievska et al. 2018). Higher-income people, by contrast, have more money to spend on food and can afford to enjoy more extravagant diets. That may mean lots of fresh produce, or expensive fad cleanses, protein bars, and diet pills. Rich people also distinguish themselves from poorer people through brands. Though people of all classes may buy the same food—say, cheese—at the grocery store, higher-income earners buy more expensive and unusual kinds of cheese.

Less obvious are the ways people of different classes dine out. High-income earners are more likely to spend extravagantly on meals in sit-down restaurants. But low-income earners order in and buy fast-food meals surprisingly often. This is part of the dilemma we explored in the last chapter. Why does someone who is struggling to make ends meet buy a McDonald's burger when they could cook one at home for much less?

As noted in an earlier chapter, author and political activist Barbara Ehrenreich answered this question in her 2001 book *Nickel and Dimed: On (Not) Getting By in America*. She carried out a social experiment, working as a waitress, hotel maid, cleaning woman, nursing-home aide, and Wal-Mart salesclerk to see what it's like to live on minimum wage. Grocery shopping and cooking, she quickly learned, were almost impossible. For one, Ehrenreich found it was impossible to keep a roof—even a trailer roof—over her head with one minimum-wage job, so she wound up working two. On her way to her second shift of the day, she barely had time to visit a drive-thru, much less cook a meal (on this, see Winant 2018; Lemke 2016).

What's more, to cook your own meals, you need a kitchen. Ehrenreich struggled to find a landlord who would rent a place to her, based on her income. She often found herself living in run-down motels or trailer parks. Sometimes this gave her access to a microwave or hot plate, but not a kitchen she could prepare meals in or a freezer to store them. In short, Ehrenreich found that low-income earners often have to play into Warde's antinomies of "indulgence," economy, and convenience. They try their best to be economical but are often forced to splurge on unhealthy junk food for lack of time and cooking equipment.

The next antinomie is care versus convenience. For centuries, women have been told that cooking is a labour of love that shows how much they care for their husbands and children. From this perspective, women who cook from scratch care more for their families, because they're willing to put the time and effort into making them the highest-quality meals. Marketers often play into this account. But they've also discovered that most wives and mothers also have jobs. They don't have time to cook everything from scratch (Okrent and Kumcu 2016; Contini et al. 2018; Hoffman 2016).

Marketers therefore promote products that highlight convenience. For example, they sell pre-made dough so women can still bake pastries after work and in that way show their families they care. Other marketers have made an entire industry out of these competing ideals. Grocery Gateway delivers fresh produce straight to your door so you can spend your "care" time preparing meals instead of wandering grocery store aisles. And Hello Fresh—a company that delivers pre-prepared ingredients and recipes to your home—sells itself as "The Easy Way to Cook Dinner from Scratch."

This idea of "care" is more common in certain households than others. Higher-income women are more likely to have partners who help with the cooking and grocery shopping. Lower-income women more often find themselves on their own. They may not have a proper kitchen or lack the time to use convenient services like Hello Fresh. For them, convenience is more often about fast-food meals that are ready quickly, and locations that are open late to meet the needs of their shift work.

The Social Performance of Eating

So-called "foodies" typify the idea that eating helps shape how others see you. As sociologist Gary Alan Fine says, these consumers of rare and fine foods use their consumption habits to build their identities (Fine et al. 2009).

Foodies eat the way they do to show off their "good" taste: their distinction from those who eat traditional or fast food, for example. They eat in the newest and nicest restaurants, talk about their dining experiences with their friends, and share adventurous dishes on social media. By doing so, foodies show they're part of a refined, classy group (Johnston and Baumann 2010; but see also Johnston, Baumann, and Oleschuk 2019). It's also a way for them to consume conspicuously and draw attention to the lavish meals they can afford (though not all foodie meals are expensive or lavish—just unusual).

There's nothing inherent in a given food that makes it wholesome, fancy, or gross. All foods are socially constructed, in the sense that we assign positive and negative meanings to them. We know this because these meanings change over time and place. In medieval Europe, before industrialization, food was a sign of wealth (Mead 2019; Brears 2016). The wealthy ate well, and the poor ate barely enough to survive. What's more, the food people could afford was a sign of their social class: the poor ate root vegetables and other basics, but rarely meat. Wealthy lords and ladies, on the other hand, were always showing off their status by eating meat, wine, and other rarities. Fat people were envied, not ridiculed. Their ample bodies proved they could afford to eat well when so many were going hungry.

In this sense, eating is a social performance and it changes over the life course as well as from century to century (Bisogni et al. 2002; McKenzie and Watts 2020). We eat certain things, in certain ways, to build our public identities. Often, these even become our private identities—our views of ourselves. When asked, some people describe themselves as "picky eaters" while others say they are "healthy eaters" and others still say they are "food lovers." We choose to eat the foods that will help people see us how we'd like to be seen (Johnston and Baumann 2010).

For example, foodies may opt for the most "exotic" choices to show they have a "refined palette" and that they are cultural as well as gustatory omnivores (Oleschuk 2017). Richard Peterson

Joël Robuchon, a French restaurant located in Las Vegas, has been ranked as one of the five best restaurants in the U.S. As the restaurant's website puts it: "An entrance of checkered black and white marble, a dining room all in beige, purple and black, a garden terrace and its greenery vertical wall make it an extraordinary place, even in Las Vegas." Both the menu and the setting are emblematic of conspicuous consumption on a grand scale.

introduced the term cultural **omnivorousness** in 1992 (but also see Wright 2016). By this term, he meant broad cultural tastes (Johnston et al. 2019; Lin et al. 2019). Studies show that educated middle-class people—people higher in the social hierarchy—are more likely than other people to be cultural omnivores. They are often culturally aware and inclusive, but still selective. They do not want to be associated with low-status or kitschy cultural activities. Some omnivores develop a taste for highbrow styles after becoming upwardly mobile, often through higher education. The economically and culturally advantaged middle classes use omnivorousness to strengthen their identity and distinguish themselves from others.

So, by dining on exotic dishes, foodies build an identity for themselves as "inclusive," or willing to try anything. For example, Canadian foodies will eat at restaurants serving Asian, French, German, and countless other styles of cuisine. This makes foodies seem equitable and open —

even democratic and inclusive, given their wish to consume foreign foods from different cultures (Lucal 2016; Corigliano 2016). And yet, many of these "exotic" foods are expensive—only available to people with plenty of cultural and economic capital (Johnston and Baumann 2010). Foodies thus contribute to inequality because they make it invisible. They indulge in consumer behaviour that is typically open only to higher-income earners, but have managed to attach meanings of inclusivity to this behaviour.

Similarly, Kennedy et al. (2019) find that foodies tend to have high ethical and aesthetic standards. For example, they want to patronize ecologically sustainable, fair-trade companies. Using survey data from food shoppers in Toronto, Kennedy et al. (2019) showed that the highest-status foodies try to balance "culinary sophistication" with "moral considerations." Thus, the researchers suggest high-status foodies possess a "cultural capital 2.0," consuming not just the priciest or most popular goods. Rather, they consume to project their moral values: inclusivity, sustainability, and so on. Again, though, at least some of this is a performance. Foodies may send signals about their inclusivity and sustainability, but their dining experiences are often exclusive and unsustainable.

Similarly, the way people view, choose, and order food is socially constructed and learned (Byrd 2019; de Jong and Varley 2017). Consider just one simple example: how people choose a bottle of wine to pair with their dinner at a restaurant. How do they know what wine to choose? How do they frame and display their wine knowledge? Five academics (Cohen et al. 2008; see also Corsi et al. 2018) set out to answer this question, using comparative data from three countries: France, Australia, and Britain.

Their key finding, sociologically, is there are learned cultural differences in the ways people in different countries choose wine at a restaurant. Of particular note, French people asked for their waiter's advice, while Brits and Aussies didn't. In fact, interaction with the waiter is altogether less common in English-speaking countries. This tells us something important about the social rituals associated with eating out in different countries. Likely, people who eat out often at licensed, good-quality restaurants feel comfortable setting up a respectful relationship with the people serving them. Perhaps the French do better than Brits and Aussies in this regard.

The data also tells us that people have different tastes (on this, see also Lee 2018), and that's why people of different class backgrounds buy differently (Henry 2002). Lower-income people stress the practical value of a good or service, while higher-income people stress its aesthetic or symbolic importance. However, different researchers have different opinions on why this might be the case (Henry 2002).

Some think that lower-income or less educated people have less confidence in themselves and less sense of choice than higher-income people. For them, buying something practical makes them feel stable and secure. Other researchers say this class difference is because low-income people need to be thriftier and more practical. Others, like Bourdieu, think that lower-income, less-educated people get less enjoyment from abstract and aesthetic features of a product. To return to his favorite example, they are less likely to appreciate fine art. Whatever the explanation, people of different classes, with different amounts of money and cultural capital, buy differently.

Class and Selfishness

Just as they reproduce tastes, classes also reproduce values. Examples of values include the individualism we discussed in an earlier chapter, as well as collectivism. Some research shows the rich and powerful may be more individualistic—more selfish—than the poor.

Psychologists Dubois, Rucker, and Galinsky (2015), for example, report that members of higher income groups are more likely than other people to act in unethical ways when it benefits themselves. By contrast, members of lower-income groups are more likely than others to act in unethical ways only when doing so will benefit *others*. Similarly, powerful people and high-income earners are more likely than others to be selfish (Rucker, Dubois, and Galinsky 2010; Rucker et al. 2018). This unethical, self-interested tendency is obvious even when the feeling of power is temporary and induced.

That said, other researchers find little or no evidence to support this claim. For example, Andreoni et al. (2017) agree that many recent studies have shown the rich behaving less morally or ethically—they call it "pro-socially"—than other people. However, they feel the evidence provided so far—largely from American laboratory experiments—prevents us from drawing safe inferences on this topic.

To correct this problem, they examined evidence from a natural field experiment in a Dutch city. Here, envelopes were, on purpose, wrongly delivered to rich and poor households. In every case, a semi-transparent envelope was misdelivered to the mailbox of a chosen household. Equal numbers of envelopes were misdelivered to identifiably rich and poor households. All envelopes contained an easily visible greeting card from "Grandfather," as well as a visible bank transfer card or a banknote that ranged in value from five euros to 20 euros. The address of the intended recipient was clearly written on each misdelivered envelope. Joost, the intended recipient—a real person at a real address—received all the envelopes that were redirected by the original recipient.

The raw data showed the rich recipients behaving more pro-socially than the poor ones: that is, more often re-directing the misdelivered envelope to Joost. So, from that standpoint, and contrary to popular beliefs and recent claims, the rich were more than twice as prosocial, or ethical, as the poor. That is, they were twice as likely as the poor recipients to redirect the envelope to the intended recipient, though they would have suffered no harm by not redirecting it.

Does that prove that poor people are less honest or moral than rich ones? The researchers account for a greater degree of (seemingly) unethical behavior among the poor in two ways, and test for each. First, some poor recipients may have intended to return the envelope but found returning it more difficult as time passed and the stresses of poverty built up. Second, for the poorest recipients, the high marginal utility of money undermined their willingness to return these envelopes. Of this, the researchers write, "When we account for both of these mitigating factors—which themselves are the byproduct of poverty—we find no statistically significant difference in the pro-social tendencies of the rich and poor."

However, the researchers fail to consider at least one other possibility, which is the nationality of the recipients. Many parts of Western Europe, including the Netherlands, teach a strong civic culture of moral behaviour, from primary school onwards (on this, see Veugelers and de Groot 2019; Veugelers and Vedder 2003; Leeman and Pels 2006). It is therefore conceivable that, if one were to run this same experiment in a more individualistic, less civic-minded culture, one might get different results.

Much or most of the social science research on the greed and selfishness of rich people has been conducted in North America, especially the U.S. It remains to be seen whether the results of an American experiment would yield the same results as in the Netherlands.

Final Thoughts

In this chapter, as in the previous one, we have drawn generalizations from the research literature on consumer buying. These generalizations are not meant to apply equally to every high-income person everywhere and at all times. They are no more than an attempt to capture distinctive features of a segment of the population and the way it spends its money today.

Luxury buying is a tool wealthy people use to display their rank and dominance. Consumerism thus reminds people of their place in the social hierarchy. It illustrates wealthy people's spot at the top while encouraging them to continue buying luxurious status symbols to cement that position. Thus, luxury buying showcases the inequality that structures our society. It provides a lavish spectacle of unvarnished and unapologetic privilege.

A high position in the class hierarchy is not just about having money or power. Bourdieu tells us it is also about having more or less taste, and more or less influence over the definition of "good taste." The wealthier, more influential classes define what "good taste" means. They say what's "good" art, food, and fashion. Even though we like to think our taste for certain foods or clothes is a unique element of our personality, it's not. Tastes but reflect underlying social inequalities.

Consumption does not drive the reproduction of these inequalities, but it helps it along. For example, we saw that rich families pass along cultural capital, good "taste," and access to formal education to their children. They do this by teaching them the right foods to eat, the right clothes to wear, the right art to admire, and the right schools to attend. Without wealth or a high income, people's access to these consumer goods is severely limited. And without these resources, chances of upward social mobility are slight.

Finally, we saw in this chapter that some rich people, if not all, consume conspicuously to show their superiority and wealth. They do this to dramatize and sharpen the dividing line between themselves and lower-income people, just as Veblen said. While poor people are largely obliged to focus on thriftiness and "good value" when they buy things, rich people can consume to display their prestige and power.

Some people who grew up in families that had been wealthy for generations may feel bitter towards people who are newly rich. We discussed the "snob effect" and efforts by "old aristocrats" to distinguish themselves from people with this "new money." As Veblen predicted, some of these old aristocrats seek out new luxury goods once earlier luxury items have become too common. Neither the older nor recently wealthy consumers seem bothered by the ethical effects of their buying. They do not worry about flaunting excess while others can barely make ends meet. Consumerism, they might argue, doesn't cause social inequality, poverty, or any observed consequences of inequality and poverty. It just makes the social hierarchy visible.

Discussion Questions

1. Bourdieu argues rich people have different tastes compared to poor people. He states that this is what distinguishes rich people from poor people. He gives the example of rich people appreciating fine art. Do you think that there are significant differences between the tastes of the rich and the poor today?

2. Bourdieu writes that cultural capital not only signals class status, it also reproduces class domination. As a result, people are stuck in their classes for generations. Think about the ways that cultural capital signals class status. How does cultural capital reproduce class domination?

3. In this chapter, we learned that rich people are not the only ones buying luxury goods. "Aspirational buyers" from different classes buy them too. Some people in the middle and lower classes also buy knockoffs. Do you think this devalues luxury goods? Do rich people rely on conspicuous consumption to signal their status, or is it no longer effective?

Quick Quiz

1. According to Bourdieu, people eventually _____ the social hierarchy.
a. Revolt against
b. Internalize
c. Ignore
d. Move along
e. Become aware of

2. Which people tend to be omnivorous consumers?
a. Educated upper-class people
b. Cosmopolitan people
c. Educated middle-class people
d. Uneducated middle-class people
e. Uneducated upper-class people

3. According to Bourdieu, what sets rich people apart?
a. Their distinct taste
b. Their overtly luxurious spending
c. Their Smart cars
d. Their ecologically conscious spending habits
e. Their poor language skills

4. Which ideology justifies the unequal distribution of wealth and power in society?
a. Habitus
b. Bourdieu's ideology
c. Agency
d. Social structure constraints
e. Meritocracy

5. For Bourdieu what are three parts of cultural capital?
a. Embodied, objectified, and institutional
b. Habitus, embodied, and structural
c. Institutional, economic, and habitus
d. Objectified, education, and habitus
e. Embodied, objectified, and social

The answers to the Quick Quiz are provided at the end of the book.

For Further Reading

Consumption, Food and Taste by Alan Warde
Warde evaluates several theories of consumption. He discusses the influence of social class and identity on the foods we choose to eat.

Nickel and Dimed: On (Not) Getting by in America by Barbara Ehrenreich
The author goes undercover to experience life as an unskilled worker in America. UK newspaper *The Guardian* ranked it as one of the 100 most important books of the 20th century.

The Sum of Small Things by Elizabeth Currid-Halkett
The author proposes that a new class dominates American society: the aspirational class. Currid-Halkett discusses classes' consumption habits and how they lead to greater class division.

Key Terms

Authenticity
Conspicuous consumption
Cosmopolitanism
Cultural capital
Cultural omnivorousness
Habitus
Social distinction
Social hierarchy

Chapter Ten
Women and Symbols of Femininity

Learning Objectives

After reading this chapter, you will be able to:

✓ Connect changes in the gendered division of labour with women's consumerism.

✓ See trends in women's buying as results of gender socialization.

✓ Contextualize women's spending on beauty products as part of gendered performances.

✓ Debate whether sexualizing consumer goods empowers or oppresses women.

In this chapter, we move on to the second of our market segments: gender. This chapter is about women consumers and the next is about men consumers. To repeat, the premise of market segmentation is that different "kinds" of people will spend their money in different ways.

Regrettably, though stereotypes abound, there is relatively little research on the differences between men and women consumers. In this chapter, we consider that small body of research.

In the process, we will see that perceptions of women consumers have changed dramatically over the years. Consider the views taken by members of the Frankfurt school three generations ago. These views are captured in this excerpt from a letter that critical theorist Theodor Adorno wrote to psychoanalyst Erich Fromm in 1937. In it, he lays out plans for a possible essay on women:

> One should analyze thoroughly the completely irrational behavior of women in dealing with commodities—shopping, clothes, hairdressing, etc.—and it will probably become obvious that all those moments that seem to serve sex appeal are in reality desexualized. The gesture of the girl who, while giving herself to her lover, is dominated by the anxiety that something will happen to her dress or her hairdo that may ruin dress and haircut appears crucial to me. And I assume that even the sexuality of the woman is largely desexualized, as if her fetish of herself? Her character being a commodity, for example, in the form of the often-occurring sentiment of being-too-good-for-it had constantly interjected itself between the woman and her own sexual activity, even in total promiscuity. Here a social theory of female frigidity could be developed.

Today, many would disagree with this assessment. The idea that women are inherently "irrational" or "anxious" is widely seen as dated and sexist. What's more, Adorno's description frames women in purely sexual terms. "Sex appeal," "sexual activity," and "promiscuity" are described as the ends to which they aspire. Their "irrational" obsession with sexuality and gendered commodities, however, makes them "frigid" and "desexualized"—unsatisfying to the men for whom they supposedly want to be appealing. Finally, Adorno implies women are all the same: concerned with "shopping, clothes, hairdressing, etc." to heighten their "sex appeal."

But it is obvious even to the casual observer—and confirmed by research—that women are not a homogenous group. Women, like men, differ from one another in their motivations, actions, and lived experiences.

All of this reminds us of the importance of intersectionality, which we touch on repeatedly throughout these chapters on market segments. Women consumers are not defined by their sex. Each woman has unique experiences, depending on age, income, ethnicity, education, and so on. Each of these factors and many others influence buying behaviour. But in most of the studies cited below, we lack the detail (or sample size) needed to see these variations among women. We see only the most general differences between men and women.

We therefore run the risk of implying that there is some innate, genetic, or essential difference between men and women that makes them consume differently. We do not believe that to be the case. Likely, there is no biological explanation—no "hardwiring"—that accounts for the different consumption behaviours we see among men and women. Rather, men and women grow up learning—through those agents of socialization discussed earlier—how they are expected to consume (Atari et al. 2016). They try to live up to those expectations by consuming in gendered ways.

Studying both men and women consumers lets us explore two consumer phenomena. First, we consider how people use consumer goods to signal their membership in one gender community, and conversely, their distance from another gender community. Second, we look at how these signals can perpetuate traditional gender norms or make way for new ones.

Defining Our Terms

Women's consumer behaviour reflects not their biological sex, but their gender identity. **Sex** is a category we divide people into based on their reproductive functions. It is determined by biology at birth. **Gender** comprises the set of norms, behaviours, and activities we think fitting for people of a given sex. All the agents of socialization play a part in teaching people their assigned gender (Rosen et al. 2019). These agents accept and love people who conform to the gender rules and exclude and ridicule those who break them. People often break the rules when their gender identity does not align with the gender traditionally associated with their sex. **Gender identity** is an individual's personal sense of their own gender, based on how they feel and act (Rogers and Meltzoff 2017; Martin et al. 2017).

Traditional definitions say there are two sexes—male and female—and two genders: masculine and feminine. By **femininity**, we mean ways of acting and feeling that are prescribed by our culture. Because sex and gender are distinct, men and women alike can present as feminine. However, traditional accounts suggest that women are "naturally" or "intrinsically" feminine. This is part of what is known as biological or gender essentialism. **Gender essentialism** is the belief that gender characteristics are innate and pre-determined based on sex. From this perspective, all men are intrinsically masculine while all women are intrinsically feminine. The related concept of **gender binarism** holds that men and women, masculine and feminine, are distinct and opposite. People can either be one or the other—not both, and not anything else. Both gender essentialism and gender binarism can be captured under the umbrella of the **ideology of gender**. The ideology of gender is the set of widespread social beliefs about "natural" differences between men and women (Somech and Drach-Zahavy 2016).

Feminists question gender essentialism, gender binarism, and the ideology of gender as a whole. They see femininity as an imposed system of rules governing how women *should* act, look, feel, and even think. Simone de Beauvoir was among the first to theorize about how femininity is constructed and imposed on women. Judith Butler later developed the idea of **gender performativity**, which stresses that gender is a performance, a role play, and not an innate or essential quality. It describes the way that people bring gender to life by repeatedly enacting what others expect of them, based on their sex.

What, exactly, are these gendered social expectations? The qualities associated with femininity vary somewhat over time and from one society to another. Some of the most common qualities are passivity, dependence, and weakness. However, the existence of these social and historical variations tells us that femininity is socially constructed (as opposed to biologically determined). If understandings of femininity vary across time and place, changing as societies do, they cannot be genetically or biologically ingrained.

The concept of intersectionality suggests that different forms of discrimination intersect and in doing so produce both unique experiences and varying forms of social oppression.

In the last two decades, researchers and the public alike have started to think beyond gender binarism. Today, we classify a person whose gender identity agrees with their sex as **cisgender**. Under gender binarism, these would be the *only* type of people. But people today identify in a wide range of other ways, including agender, bigender, genderqueer, pangender, gender nonconforming, and gender fluid. Gender binarism does not reflect their lives, experiences, or identities.

Similarly, the traditional definition of femininity is too narrow to apply to all women—even to just cisgender women. There are many types of female experience in our society and, similarly, many types of women consumers. That is why feminists have found particular value in the idea of intersectionality.

Intersectionality, to repeat, is the idea that various forms of discrimination centred on gender, sexuality, race, class, disability, and other elements of identity intersect to produce unique experiences and different types of social oppression. Thus, intersectionality is different from "additive" approaches to identity that suggest disadvantages simply pile up atop one another. Intersectional analyses can focus on identities (e.g. black, woman), on categories of difference, on processes of differentiation, or on systems of domination, such as racism, colonialism, sexism, or patriarchy. Intersectionality is not just about social inequalities but also the dynamics of power that affect and are affected by these inequalities.

From an intersectional perspective, people cannot be reduced to their various "parts." In other words, it is never useful to ask simply, "What is it like to be a woman consumer?" Nonetheless, marketers often ask whether and to what degree gender makes a difference in the ways people spend their money. Companies often develop products to meet what they see as the unique needs and wants of women. And women often use consumerism and consumer goods to perform their gender. But as you read this chapter and the next, remember that gendered consumption is always *also* affected by race, age, class, and a variety of other intersecting variables.

How Women Spend Their Time

Over the last six decades, there has been a revolution in the ways that women in Canada (and other industrial societies) spend their time. Compared to 1960, they are far more likely to hold a full-time or part-time paying job. As they spend more time doing paid work, women have reduced the time they spend on unpaid work (Fisher et al. 2007). Men, for their part, have reduced the amount of time they spend doing paid work, and increased their unpaid work a little. So men's and women's days look increasingly similar over time. Yet women's lives are still different from men's in several ways.

First, women and men still do different amounts of housework (including household purchasing) and child care (Southerton 2006). A **gendered division of labour** persists and continues to influence what men and women buy. In its most traditional formula, the gendered division of labour makes men breadwinners and women homemakers. Women are not paid for the domestic work they do around their homes. Their time and labour is not considered "worth" paying for.

Of course, many families in Canada today do not follow the traditional gendered division of labour (Guppy et al. 2019; Horne et al. 2018). Many men contribute to domestic work, and contribute more hours than men customarily did in the past. Husbands and fathers are spending more time on child care and shopping, though they still do less household cleaning than their wives. That said, even when their husbands pitch in, women still do *more*. Terms like the "double day" or "second shift" still describe the double burden of work for pay and housework that many women face today.

New parents may be especially likely to fall into the traditional division of labour. In one study, expectant fathers said they expected to split chores and child care almost equally, with their female partners doing just a little bit more work. Six months after their child was born, these fathers admitted they did less than they expected. Similarly, women either cut back on paid work to spend more time on housework, or became overwhelmed by trying to do the same amount of paid work while adding on housework (Lockman 2019).

This imbalance persists despite technological advances (made available as consumer products) that lessen the time needed to complete housework today. Washing machines, clothes dryers, dishwashers, vacuum cleaners and home freezers all make domestic chores more efficient. But that doesn't mean laundry, dirty dishes, and meal preparation take care of themselves. Much of the time, women are the ones using these products. In other words, housework may be largely mechanized, but these products do not free women from the longstanding expectation that they are responsible for household chores.

Research also shows that men and women do different types of domestic work (Sullivan 2018; Buchanan et al. 2018). Women do the routine, everyday chores that have to get done, like packing lunches for the kids to take to school every morning. Men are more likely to do tasks they enjoy and that they can opt out of—for example, barbequing on the weekend. Since men and women do different household chores, they often buy different consumer products for their homes. Women will buy cookware, home furnishings, and decorative pieces like picture frames and candles. They also take responsibility for what can sometimes be more burdensome shopping. These include regular trips to the drug store to pick up prescriptions and stops at the grocery store on their way home from work so they can cook dinner.

When it comes to child care, pressures to be a "good mom" have intensified. Parents today are expected to be much more involved in their children's lives than they were in past generations. They are supposed to bond, nurture, and open opportunities for their children in time-intensive and costly ways, such as family vacations or private tutoring. Pressures are mounting for men too, as they are increasingly expected to go beyond breadwinning and play a more active role in their children's upbringing. In turn, many parents are dissatisfied with their "work-life balance" (Hilbrecht 2009).

To make room for their paid work while keeping up with their housework and child care responsibilities, many mothers cut back on their leisure time (Connelly and Kimmel, 2010). In other words, **time poverty** has become a central feature of women's lives. Time poverty refers to a lack of free time, or leftover time after things like sleep, work, and domestic responsibilities have been taken care of.

Sometimes, the housework that people do depends on their income and social status (Buchanan et al. 2018). Wealthy couples can afford cleaning, cooking, and child care services. As discussed in an earlier chapter on poor consumers, wealthy people pay others to do these chores for them so they don't have to. Child care is so expensive that even some middle-income families in Canada today cannot afford it. Some women stay home and care for their children themselves. If they were to work outside the home, they would have to spend their entire pay cheque on day care.

Thus, there are unresolved contradictions around women's work. It's either a complimentary "labour of love"—not worth paying for when you have to do it yourself, for your own home—or a high-end commodity only the rich can afford. And despite the high sums parents pay for childcare, the workers delivering this care are underpaid. In Canada, the average annual salary for an early childhood educator is roughly $35,000.

Given women's continued responsibility for home care and child care, it would make sense that much household spending is done or influenced by women (that is, wives and mothers). Cheryl Russell, former editor of *American Demographics* magazine and now a private business consultant, estimates women influence about 80 percent of North American household spending. But she notes it is difficult to find hard data on this topic. That's because couples have a hard time saying how decisions get made in their own household, and what influence each partner has.

Joint decision-making is especially hard to measure today, as more women work for pay and contribute to the household income. In the past, decision making typically rested more clearly with men: they earned the money and were largely in charge of how it was spent. Even if they have the "final say," though, many men (today and in the past) make decisions *with* their spouses. In particular, many men follow their partners' advice when buying expensive luxury goods (Amirouche et al. 2017). And their wives usually offer such advice about the aesthetics, quality, and price of the product under consideration. While women often deny they have much influence on their partners' spending, men usually say their wives have strong influence, especially when it comes to luxury goods. In short, men's preferences may not prevail, because husbands usually care about what their wives think.

That is a problem for people who study consumer behavior, for two reasons. First, we know all too little about how power and income are shared in couples. Second, the sharing of power and income in couples has changed dramatically in the past generation or two. Men are no longer "heads of households" or the "main breadwinners." They are no longer (solely) in charge of family spending, nor necessarily the major contributors to the family income. So it is hard to tell exactly why men buy what they do, and why women buy exactly what they do. Further, male and female patterns vary by generation and age or life course stage (Funches et al. 2017).

Another complicating factor is whether partners pool their earnings as a family, and whether they exercise equal control over how that common pool is spent (Kenney 2006; also, Eickmeyer et al. 2017). Typically, where young children are present, the wife works fewer hours and/or earns less per hour than the husband, and this affects financial control.

Kenney (2006) notes that in her sample of married and cohabiting women with young children, about 60 percent of the women earn less than 40 percent of their household's income. Only about half of these low-earning women are in couples that use either jointly controlled or woman-controlled pooling systems. For the rest of these low-earning (or non-earning) women, husbands dominate decisions about the use of family funds. Typically, the husbands exercise more financial control because they earn a larger share of the money. The most egalitarian money management is found where wives have incomes roughly equal to that of their partners. This arrangement gives them at least equal control, whether the money is pooled or kept separate. However, women with earnings equal to their husbands make up only 20 percent of the sample.

There is some evidence that this traditional practice—vesting financial and purchasing control in the hands of husbands simply because they earn more—has begun to change. Compared to older married couples, younger couples, childless couples, highly educated couples, and cohabiting couples all tend to enjoy more equal earning power, and more equal participation in spending decisions. Thus, a sample of families containing more childless (married or cohabiting) heterosexual couples or gay and lesbian couples would likely contain a higher proportion of couples practicing financial independence or equal control over pooled resources. Similarly, Vogler et al. (2008; see also Prag et al. 2019) find that high-earning, cohabiting women with partly separate finances are the most able of all women to make autonomous decisions about spending.

Ironically, members of couples that make independent decisions about spending are *less* satisfied with family life, as well as with life in general, than those who make shared decisions. This is reportedly true of both men and women respondents. It suggests that members of couples that (voluntarily) merge their finances and make decisions jointly trust one another more, and feel closer to one another, than other couples.

Perhaps the most important fact to keep in mind here is that this situation is shifting rapidly. Women are spending more years in school, in the paid workforce, and in cohabiting relationships than they were even one generation ago. All of these changes in women's status increase their earnings, savings, and influence within intimate relations. In short, women's influence over family spending is changing rapidly and will likely continue to change dramatically over the next decade.

With this context in mind, let's consider what we can say about women consumers today, as distinct from men consumers who are, often, their husbands, boyfriends, fathers, or sons.

How Women Spend Their Money

First, women tend to have a greater fondness for luxury brands than men do. Spending on luxury goods amounts to as much as $525 billion a year in the United States alone, and women's products account for over half of this spending. When given the choice, women tend to prefer luxury brands over non-luxury brands, to a much higher degree than men. Female consumers say that luxury brands make them feel unique, give their status a bigger boost, and make them feel better than non-luxury brands. One study of female consumers suggests they prefer to consume luxury goods to satisfy their social-status goals (Zhang et al. 2019). What's more, in most markets and product categories, the price for luxury brands that target women is significantly higher than that of luxury brands targeting men (Sauer and Teichman 2011).

Women are also more likely than men to use luxury goods to "guard" their romantic partners. In

Research suggests in our society women both enjoy shopping in traditional retail stores more than men, and also do more shopping online.

one study (Griskevicius and Wang 2013), women were more likely to flaunt luxury products when they were around other women. Such conspicuous consumption, in their mind, deterred other women from chasing their partners. Indeed, the other women who saw these products—including designer outfits and accessories—came to think their wearers had more devoted partners. This belief discouraged them from chasing those partners. They thought their chances were slim, since (these women assumed) the partner was so devoted that he was willing to buy expensive, luxurious goods for his partner.

Combining these elements, women are more likely than men to wear luxury products that, they think, improve their appearance (Hudders 2014). Looking good, in their minds, also deters other women from stealing their mate. It is thought to intimidate those other women, making them feel they cannot compete. So, by warding off romantic rivals, luxurious possessions keep some women feeling confident about their relationships.

Second, women tend to like shopping in brick-and-mortar stores more than men do (Helgesen and Neset 2011). Starting in the 18th century, department stores (and, later, supermarkets) gave women—at least, Western women—a taste of the public domain that many had not enjoyed before (Bowlby 1985, 2000; Nava 1997; for a comparison with Japan, see also Tamari 2018). Stores provided a reason—shopping—for women to leave the domestic space of the home and appear unescorted in public (Wolff 1985; Crossick and Jaumain 2019).

These early department stores provided a wide array of sensory delights to motivate people to buy. These delights grew out of stereotypical understandings of women's likes and wants. By glamorizing them and putting them on display, department stores may have perpetuated those stereotypes. So perhaps department stores were, on balance, neither good nor bad for women. They opened up some new freedoms and granted women a little independence from men, but they also reinforced some stereotypes that persist today, including the idea that shopping itself is feminine. We discuss this view in detail in the next chapter on men consumers, since many men, trying to shore up their masculinity, distance themselves from this "women's activity."

Though women enjoy shopping in brick-and-mortar stores more than men, it is unclear so far whether online shopping is more popular among men or women. Online shopping in general is more common today than ever before, especially as COVID-19 motivates more consumers to browse and buy from the safety of their own homes. However, some say women have been more reluctant than men to embrace online shopping and trust it less (Sajjad and Ayyub 2019). In one study, women were more likely to describe online shopping with unpleasant adjectives and in-person shopping with pleasant ones. The opposite was found to be true of male participants (Dai et al. 2019).

Nevertheless, more women seem to shop online than men. For example, 60 percent of women say they frequently shop on Amazon, compared to 49 percent of men (CNBC 2018). Moreover, women are more likely than men to visit various websites and compare prices for a given product before purchasing. It is possible that these differences have more to do with the sheer amount of shopping women do compared with men. As mentioned above, we think women still do most of the shopping on behalf of their households. That includes shopping for items many people find boring, like toilet paper and other household staples. Maybe women try to minimize the time and effort they spend shopping for these goods by ordering them online. Then they shop for those fun luxury goods mentioned above in brick-and-mortar stores, perhaps treating it as a social outing with friends, or an opportunity for some alone time out of the house.

There are also large differences between *how* men and women shop online. Around 40 percent of women use their phones to shop online, compared to 22 percent of men (CNBC 2018). Part of the reason for this is the sheer number of women's shopping apps. There just aren't as many online shopping apps that target men, so they have fewer reasons and chances to shop on their phones. Men also prefer to see and feel an item before purchasing it, which is of course impossible with online shopping.

Women and men have different ideas around what constitutes a positive online shopping experience (Sohaib et al. 2019). Men tend to focus on value for their money, while women want to be able to trust the site. Men and women also use different criteria to evaluate an online store's trustworthiness. Men want to see assurances that their payments will be processed safely and their personal information will be kept private. Women, on the other hand, use social relations and word of mouth to assess online stores. They consult social media, their friends and family, and online consumer groups to help inform their perceptions of a given store.

Women also find ease of use more important for an online store than do men. Whether they use an online store is influenced by how it easy it is to navigate. At the same time, visual appeal—including colour, imagery, and layout—influences their trust in a site and likelihood of buying a product (Lee and Lee 2019). If they find an online website that is beautifully designed and aesthetically pleasing, women are more likely than men to find shopping there enjoyable (Sohaib et al. 2019).

Third, women are more likely than men to seek out information and ask for help with purchases. For example, among wine buyers, men make limited use of sources of information in buying situations (Barber 2009; Marques and Gaia 2018). If they don't know something, they don't ask. By contrast, women are more apt than men to seek information from a server, sommelier, or store personnel (Atkin and Garcia 2007; Pelet et al. 2017). Women also seek out information by turning to labels and shelf tags and considering whether a product has won any medals or awards.

Fourth, women and men may be equally loyal to brands, but for different reasons. Decades ago, a theory about "relational" versus "collective" loyalty was developed to explain these differences (Baumeister and Sommer 1997). The theory claims that women are more likely to build their identities on close relationships with individuals—say, a particular salesperson. Men, on the other hand, typically lean towards less intimate relationships with a broader group—say, a particular store location and its team of salespeople (Millan and Wright 2017).

In one study (Loureiro et al. 2012), researchers surveyed consumers who bought one of three car brands: Toyota, Ford, and Renault. Every participant said they were satisfied with their purchase. Men and women, however, had different explanations for *why* they were satisfied. Women (more than men) needed to trust the brand to be committed or loyal to it (Sohaib et al. 2019). Often, this trust flowed from personal relationships with particular salespeople. Men, on the other hand, developed attachments to the brand as a whole.

Given their greater attachment to individuals, women are more likely than men to go out of their way to buy a product from a store run by an acquaintance, instead of opting for the store closest to them. It is only when the more distant store is run by a *group* of acquaintances that men show a higher likelihood to buy from that store than women.

In another study, Melynk (2014) asked if consumers were willing to forgo a more attractive alternative in order to stay loyal to a particular organization or employee. Across three experimental studies, the results suggest the answer is "yes" among both female and male consumers, but for different reasons. Once again, the women tended to be loyal to individual employees. Males, on the other hand, felt loyal to the organization. They gave up the alternative to stay loyal to the overall brand.

Fifth, there is some evidence that women are more impulsive buyers than men. One study found they had more "irresistible urges" to buy (Coley and Burgess 2003; Iyer et al. 2019). They also buy things they hadn't planned to more often than do men (Segal and Podoshen 2011). For women, impulse buys tended to be products that heighten social identity—that is, how they appear to others. When men make impulse purchases, these tend to be for instrumental or functional items or products they think will highlight their personal identity—that is, how they see themselves. As we see in the next chapter, for men, buying workshop tools (e.g., wrenches and jigsaws) may fill both functions.

Sixth, women are more likely than men to feel positive emotions when buying (Segal and Podoshen 2011). Seemingly, they experience more of the "retail therapy" effect discussed earlier. That is, they are more likely than men to buy to improve their mood (Faber and Christenson 1996; Haugtvedt et al. 2018). They are not necessarily motivated by the product itself. In fact, many of their "emotional" purchases remain unused (Eccles 2002; Boonchoo and Thoumrungroje 2017).

For women, shopping can be a much more emotional and fulfilling experience than for men. They may feel excited prior to going shopping and move up and down the emotional scale throughout the shopping experience (Saraneva and Saaksjarvi 2008; Fayez and Labib 2016). When they find a bargain, they may feel elated and proud. Later, of course, those feelings of elation may be replaced with guilt and shame for spending. Or, if they do not find the bargain or product they were looking for, they feel disappointed—as though their trip failed.

Finally, compared with men, women consumers buy more goods and services designed to enhance physical appearance. For cultural reasons and through socialization, women tend to be more concerned about their physical appearance than men. The next several sections delve into how and why women spend to change their looks.

Beauty and Beauty Norms

In our society, we usually expect beauty of women, not men. **Bodily (or facial) beauty** is the deeply pleasurable experience someone else's body or face gives us. To some degree, beauty is subjective; some people see beauty where others do not. Marketers have recently leaned into the idea that there are many types of attractiveness. For example, a Dove soap ad campaign featured women of different ages with different facial features and body types (Millard 2009). Many people praised this effort to redefine beauty standards (see also Feng et al. 2020). In particular, consumers approved of the idea that "beauty is as beauty does." They liked the fact that beauty was presented as a performance and not an endowment.

Despite campaigns like Dove's, people continue to view beauty and attractiveness as physical endowments. There is broad agreement in our culture about who is and is not attractive (Langlois et al. 2001; Elmer and Houran 2020). Conventional views of beauty in North America today include sculpted, symmetrical features and slender builds.

Why are women so concerned with beauty? Why do they care enough to spend significantly on goods and services that enhance their appearance? The answers to these questions lie in gender norms that have become entrenched over centuries, and the lifelong processes of socialization we have discussed throughout this book. Our society places tremendous weight on physical appearance—especially women's physical appearance—and women learn this from the moment they are born.

Even in our relatively egalitarian society, women are socialized to see the importance of erotic capital. You'll recall from an earlier chapter Bourdieu's different types of capital: economic, cultural, and social. Yet another type of capital, though not one that Bourdieu discussed, is erotic capital (Catherine Hakim 2010; see also Velasufah and Setiawan 2019; Requena 2017). **Erotic capital** is the value assigned to an individual based on their sexual attractiveness. It has a great importance in wealthy modern societies that are highly sexualized, like ours. Erotic capital has at least six aspects: beauty, sexiness, grace and charm, liveliness and animation, social presentation, and sexual expertise (Hakim 2010).

Erotic capital can be valuable in the labour market. People tend to judge and treat attractive people more positively than unattractive people (Lorenzo et al. 2010). Attractive young women are less likely to be suspended from school and get into trouble with their teachers, and more likely to have higher-than-average grades (Mocan and Tekin 2006; see also Mavisakalyan 2018).

Physically attractive people are even paid more, other things being equal. At least two studies have found evidence of a sizable "beauty premium"—an above-average wage that was given to attractive workers (Mobius and Rosenblat 2011; Scholz and Sicinski 2011). Perhaps as a result of being treated positively throughout their lives, attractive people are more confident and, in turn, come off as more capable.

Women are also overrepresented in jobs that call for "emotional labour": managing customers' feelings, often by suppressing their own (Hochschild 1983; Grandey and Melloy 2017). Salespeople, for example, need to "sell themselves" (Hyman and Price 2016). A friendly, smiling face and pleasant small talk become part of the complete package consumers pay for. This emotional labour is hard and draining, forcing salespeople to use their personality and appearance to close the deal. In effect, they sell themselves just as much as they sell consumer goods.

In sum, women are literally rewarded for beauty. As discussed in earlier chapters, they also learn to prize (and spend in pursuit of) beauty through the media. Both traditional and online media help teach women that they should strive to be beautiful—in particular, that they should strive to

Box 10-1

Shifting Beauty Norms in Canada

Over the past hundred years, the beauty industry has been rocked by countless changes. Consider "flapper girls"—a look that became popular in the 1920s. Bobbed haircuts, slim figures, lots of makeup, smoking, and a flirty personality set these girls apart from the conventional conservative beauty (Elvins 2018). This new look exploded across advertisements and films (Ellison 2016). In particular, many advertisements started promoting weight-loss products, "slimming" clothing, and other goods that claimed to help women achieve the flapper-girl look (Lavertu 2004).

Fast forward a century and beauty ideals have changed. For some, the ideal woman is still slim with symmetrical facial features. For others, the perfect woman looks more like Kim Kardashian, with a much more voluptuous body. Others still consider the "natural" look beautiful. None of these beauty ideals—including the "effortless" natural aesthetic—are easy to live up to. To look "naturally" beautiful, for example, women must use a surprisingly large number of makeup, skincare, and hair products (Kelly 2016). To look like Kim Kardashian, women must undertake a regime of strict diets, intense workouts, and plastic surgery.

There may not be a single definition of what counts as "beautiful" today. But the variety of definitions out there are full of contradictions. Each is difficult to live up to in its own way. Broader perceptions of beauty do not free women from pressure to maintain their physical appearance; they just expand the range of criteria women are expected to meet. Indeed, according to a study done in 2015, one in five Canadian women is not satisfied with her looks (Richard 2015).

be slim. In television shows, characters are twice as likely to comment on a woman's physical appearance as on a man's. Magazines regularly present touched-up pictures of underweight women as attractive and desirable. Magazines that target women typically include articles about weight loss, workouts, and diets. They imply (if they don't proclaim) that these advertised products can help readers look like the impossibly thin women modeling them.

Some media also teach women to focus on their appearance so they can get a romantic partner. Everything from video games to teen magazines teaches young men and women what idealized femininity looks like, and all the consumer products and services women must buy to obtain it. Though some media today are more inclusive, to a considerable degree, traditional representations of women as sex objects meant for men's pleasure still persist (Durham 2008; Meek 2017; Tang-Martínez 2016; Grimes 2003; Rughinis et al. 2016). Some of the themes that researchers have identified as occurring across many types of media include:

- Boys only like girls who look a certain way, so girls must be sure to work hard to look that way.
- It's hard to look sexy, so girls should invest in consumer goods like clothing and makeup to help them achieve that coveted sexiness.
- Sexual violence can be exhilarating and enjoyable.

On that last point, consider the video games teenage boys love to buy. In those games, female leads are often traditionally sexy, with stereotypically beautiful features and body types (Grimes 2003). Yet these female characters take part in stereotypically masculine activities: punching, stabbing, shooting, and killing. In this way, video games sell boys and men an impossible composite: the "perfect blend" of sexy femininity and masculine violence. As consumer products, these video games appeal because they offer men fantasy women they'll rarely, if ever, find in reality. They make women—or, at least, images of and fantasies about women—the products men consume.

Laura Mulvey

Because beauty and sexiness are so treasured, women in our society are often concerned with their body image. **Body image** is the perception a person has of their own physical appearance. It may be completely unrelated to their actual appearance. A slender adolescent girl may genuinely think she is fat. Concerns with body image are increased by what has been called the **male gaze**. Feminist film scholar Laura Mulvey developed this idea in her 1975 text *Visual Pleasure and Narrative Cinema*. It proposed that films are constructed from and for the perspective of a male heterosexual viewer. As a result, women are always displayed as objects for men's gaze rather than independent actors whose value is distinct from how men view them.

Feminists have proposed that the male gaze is prevalent in society as a whole, not just movies. If, as Butler suggested, women are performing their gender, then men are in the audience, watching. From this perspective, the male gaze means treating women's bodies as objects to be surveyed.

Motivated by poor body image and social pressures, many women spend a considerable amount of their time doing **beauty work**, which encompasses activities and practices people use to improve their physical appearance (Samper et al. 2017). These practices include applying cosmetics, tanning, and exercising. Such beauty work makes sense, given the benefits of attractiveness we just discussed. However, under some conditions, women penalize other women who engage too visibly in beauty work. They may view them as cheaters and of poor moral character. Such judgments are especially likely when women see beauty work as transformative (significantly altering appearance), transient (lasting only a short time), and grossly misrepresentative (hiding their true appearance). So, these judgments are often leveled at women who pay for one of the most invasive and costly types of beauty work: cosmetic surgery.

Box 10-2

Going Under the Knife in Pursuit of Beauty

Many factors motivate women to pursue cosmetic surgery. Women who are depressed or have low self-esteem, life satisfaction, and self-rated attractiveness are more likely than other women to seek it out (Furnham and Levitas 2012). Some of these negative feelings could be the result of the continuous pressures women are under to be beautiful and slim.

Some say cosmetic surgery is freeing: that it enables women to achieve the youth and beauty they're striving for. But Morgan (1991; but see also Heyes 2016) suggests that not all women have freely chosen to undergo cosmetic surgery. Brothers, fathers, boyfriends, husbands, and lovers actively encourage women to live up to these standards, or make them feel bad for deviating from them. Male plastic surgeons do the same. They see the female body as a profit-making opportunity, so they play into these impossibly high beauty standards. They offer "free advice" to women whose "deformities"—small breasts, flabby stomachs, concentrations of cellulite—they want to "cure" or "fix." In so doing, plastic surgeons help uphold appearance and eroticism ideals, which, of course, benefit their business.

Compared to men, women see more risk to cosmetic surgery, and yet hold more positive attitudes towards it (Atari et al. 2016). One impetus is social comparison and intra-sex competition. Women want to make themselves as attractive as possible to compete in the dating, mating, and marriage market. Interest in plastic surgery is positively associated with the wish for a mate with high status, education, and attractiveness. These women see cosmetic surgery as the key to achieving this goal.

People—and especially women—also look to cosmetic surgery for help in keeping a mate. In a survey of people in stable marriages, Atari et al. (2017) found that many wives turn to cosmetic surgery, thinking it will improve their physical attractiveness and help them keep a long-term mate. Others are keen to look at least as good as the women they think their partner finds attractive. Plastic surgery, they think, will reduce the risk of partner infidelity and relationship dissolution.

At the same time, women are also more likely to be criticized for failing to do beauty work and to keep up with beauty standards. As technology advances, it's increasingly possible to be "perfect." Plastic surgery allows women to look more like the airbrushed models in magazines. Women who refuse to use these technologies are accused of not caring about their appearance and refusing to be all that they could be. That's why marketers emphasize how their products will make women younger, sexier, and more attractive (Atari et al. 2016). Such advertising is more prevalent in traditional communities, with high rates of marriage and childbearing. It is also prevalent where women marry young, get little education, and do not expect to work outside the home. As these conditions change, advertising (and socialization) become less gendered. However, even in contemporary Canadian society, gendered socialization and advertising persist (Sandlin 2012).

In sum, many women are caught in a double bind. Performing femininity needs significant investments of time, energy, and money. Women must shop for particular kinds of clothes, makeup, hair products, and so on. They must receive certain types of services, like manicures and hair removal. And, to gain the thin ideal, some pour time and money into gym memberships, juice cleanses, and diet pills. Yet, many women are not seen as "truly feminine" unless they hide all of this effort and appear "naturally" beautiful.

Beauty Work: Women's Spending on Makeup and Clothes

The average teenage Canadian girl spends hundreds of dollars on makeup every year (Gentina and Fosse-Gomez 2012). Women's makeup consumption is interesting to sociologists and marketers alike, for at least three reasons. First, such spending reflects our society's ageism. Women are taught that youthfulness is beautiful and sexy. Accordingly, they invest in creams, serums, powders, and more, hoping to preserve a youthful appearance. Marketers both reflect and perpetuate these social norms. They advertise the "wrinkle-erasing" properties of their company's skin-care product, or they feature pretty young models applying the makeup they want to sell. They do this because they know women want to look young—and so marketers reflect this long-established social norm back to us. But in so doing, they also keep it alive, contributing to the ongoing socialization of girls and women in our society.

Second, sociologists and marketers both know that girls have to learn, usually from other girls, the right and wrong way of using such makeup. In the past, that learning may have happened between mother and daughter, or older and younger sisters. Today, YouTube has taken over. Influencers teach girls how to do their makeup through video tutorials. Makeup marketers have hopped on the bandwagon and pay for these tutorials, typically compensating the YouTuber for featuring their items in a how-to video.

Third, for many women, applying makeup is part of a daily ritual. Women apply it systematically (using the same products in the same order) and in the same place (gazing into the bathroom mirror or sitting at a vanity). Often, they apply it at roughly the same point in their day: when they wake up in the morning, or before going to work in a bar at night. Sociologists point out that, like other rituals, including religious ceremonies, the make-up ritual involves repetition, symbolism, codification, and dramatic art.

Marketers understand this and play into make-up rituals to sell their products. They provide simple products to fit the everyday ritual of applying makeup in the morning. These include no-mess applicators, single-step foundations, and other products that go on fast and easy. But they also provide sophisticated products for special ceremonial events. These include false eyelashes and contour palettes meant to create the illusion of the sculpted, symmetrical features our culture defines as beautiful. Beauty brands also provide the in-store female makeup artists who are available to apply these products for customers on special occasions. These employees act as "models," showing the (supposed) effects of their brand's makeup.

Finally, sociologists say makeup is yet another consumer product girls use to send signals about who they are and who they want to be taken for. Sometimes, they use makeup to look appealing to men—perhaps on a date, for example. But girls and women also bond over makeup. They shop for it together, apply it to one another, discuss it and encourage each other to try their favourite "miracle" products, get ready to go out together, and so on. Shopping for, buying, and using makeup lets girls and women show they're part of the group—a group of women that has little (if anything) to do with men.

Marketers also know that teenage girls in particular want to experiment with makeup with their friends. Some cosmetic companies (for example, Mary Kay) appeal to this need by offering "makeup parties" at home. Girls get to try the products together for fun, without the risk of wearing a potentially unflattering product in public. Other companies let customers try products on in their stores. Often, they invest in making these spaces feel glamorous, and set up special, flattering lighting. They also have makeup artists available to answer questions and help customers apply samples. With both at-home and in-store experimentation, girls' makeup-buying experiences become social occasions. These experiences help push girls into buying product after product.

Makeup is just one of the many ways that women (and men) live up to gendered expectations or follow gender scripts. Clothing plays an equally significant role. As children, we learn to dress ourselves through instruction from our parents and hints from our peers. Children and teenagers are quick to let each other know when they don't approve of an outfit.

How we dress becomes even more complicated and consequential when we start to work for pay. Then, workplaces join the chorus of influences, providing rules—sometimes even explicit, written rules—around what attire is appropriate and what is not (Rafaelli and Pratt 1993). These rules differ for men and women. Obeying them can make the difference between landing a job or not, getting promoted or not, and getting a raise or not.

As they grow up, men and women learn to think of workwear differently. Undergraduate men tend to think that professional clothes make people look more intelligent, competent, knowledgeable, honest, and reliable (Peluchette and Karl, 2018; Horgan et al. 2017). Undergraduate women are less likely to think that what they wear affects people's view of their professional abilities. So they often wear clothes *they* like and dress to please themselves.

As the years go by, both men and women refine their ideas about clothes, especially if they are in fields that demand professional dress. In their study of MBA students, Peluchette et al. (2006) found that both men and women used clothes to manage others' views of them. They often thought their clothing could positively improve their treatment at work: get them promotions or raises. MBA students who held management or executive positions were especially likely to dress to impress. Most interestingly, women no longer thought they could get away with dressing just for themselves. They became even more likely than men to do the necessary work on their appearances to shape people's opinions of them.

Women are especially conscious of how costly it can be if people misunderstand their self-presentations. To study this, Kimle and Damhorst (1997; see also Peluchette and Karl 2018) interviewed 24 businesswomen employed in various companies across many professions in an urban centre. Most were in management, and they were all widely experienced. These women felt they could choose different kinds of clothes to express different meanings, including credibility and competence. The ideal businesswoman's image, they said, combined a mix of conservatism, fashion, masculinity, femininity and sexuality, creativity, and conformity.

Obviously, some of these elements—like conservatism and sexuality—are contradictory, causing tensions that need conscious balancing. Balancing wrongly can endanger the woman's credibility. An especially low-cut blouse or short skirt, for example, can suggest a woman hopes to get ahead using her erotic capital, not professional competence. On the other hand, for male professionals, it's a little harder to make such a glaring dress blunder when your only choice is a suit. Of course, there are subtle details of that suit that make a big difference. Maybe there are signs that it is an expensive designer suit—signs that only a fellow senior-level, well-paid executive would recognize. But in general, women have more opportunities to make the "wrong" clothing choices than men and therefore often invest more effort in managing their work image than men (on how this affects presidential elections in the U.S., see Frye 2017). They may also risk sexual harassment if they fail to manage that image effectively.

This need for image management is especially important in organizations and professions that have traditionally been dominated by men. On the one hand, women in these organizations and professions must wear clothes that project the stereotypically "masculine" qualities of leadership and authority. But at the same time, those clothes must also show their "femininity," so as not to be off-putting to tradition-minded colleagues, superiors, and business partners. All of this has clear implications for consumer behaviour: women have to buy more clothing for work and use it more artfully if they hope to enjoy a successful career.

Finally, for their clothing and makeup to matter, girls and women need to show them off. Today, women consumers use social media to display their beauty and sexiness. It gives people a platform to build their own personal brands, as discussed in an earlier chapter. Millennial women, for example, post "thirst traps" on Instagram and Snapchat. These are sexy photos of themselves designed to entice other social media users to publicly say how attractive they are. These selfies are gender performances: displays of erotic capital and femininity using perfectly applied makeup, cute outfits, and the other consumer products we have been discussing. We therefore produce and consume gendered identities online.

At the same time, the Internet helps socialize men and women to consume in gendered ways. Although digital content is gradually diversifying, a good deal of it is still produced for a particular "type" of woman: namely, white middle- to upper-class women (Shade 2009). For example, many mainstream magazines that have always targeted this audience now publish their articles online. That means we see a lot of content about health, beauty, cooking, parenting, and shopping. This gendered content helps teach women how to behave and consume in keeping with gendered conventions. It also reflects our wants as consumers.

Performing and Challenging Traditional Femininity

Even though plenty of people continue to stage traditional gender performances, modern versions of femininity are rewriting the playbook, calling for women to embrace their sexuality. They target women as sexual consumers (Attwood 2005; also, Wood, 2017). We consider both outlooks—traditional and modern—in this section.

First, consider goods we might define as traditionally feminine. These include "foundation garments"—slimmers, shapers, bustiers, and corsets—as well as tight dresses and high-heeled shoes. Such products shape women's bodies into the slender, sexy, traditionally feminine mold, perfecting them for male observation.

These garments are also physically restrictive. They push, pull, and constrain, sometimes even making it difficult to breathe or move freely. High-heeled shoes make it difficult to walk quickly or take long strides. Wearing these garments thus forces women to move in confined, "feminine" ways. They must take delicate little steps, rolling their hips slightly.

So, on the one hand, foundation garments are tools women use to make themselves appealing to men. In this sense, they represent and reinforce women's oppression. They physically trap women into performing traditional femininity. On the other hand, some women buy these products for themselves, not for men. They like and want to look traditionally feminine. Either way, foundation garments perpetuate traditional conceptions of femininity and what women are "supposed" to look like. Whether they use them for men or for themselves, women consumers who buy and wear these garments carry stereotypical appearance norms forward.

There is a similar debate about women's lingerie and sex toys. One side holds that lingerie perpetuates traditional sex roles. It makes women look sexy in the stereotypical ways that men want (or learn to want). In other words, buying and wearing sexy lingerie just helps women conform to traditional standards of sexiness and femininity—standards that men have set (Wood 2016). Thus, lingerie is a consumer good designed to doll women up for erotic observation by men.

The other side of the debate paints a more nuanced picture. Lingerie, from this view, isn't only worn for others (that is, sexual partners). Some women buy lingerie for themselves, to strengthen their own identity and sense of sexual prowess (Jantzen et al. 2006; Sujatha and Sarada 2016). And, like clothing, different types of lingerie reinforce different aspects of identity. Some lingerie can make women feel feminine in the traditional sense: delicate and sexy in the ways that men are thought to like. Other lingerie can make them feel bold and powerful—traditionally male traits. What's more, some men buy and wear women's lingerie. It can help them fulfill feelings of longing, perform their identities, or satisfy sexual urges.

Evidence for both sides of the debate plays out in sex shops. There, women publicly inspect, try on, and buy lingerie. Sometimes, their male partners join them, choosing pieces they like, or paying the bill. Such buying behaviour is one piece of evidence for the traditional argument. If men are choosing and buying the lingerie that they want their partners to wear, the lingerie is "for" them. These men are dressing their partners up in the sexy outfits they like. They are even willing to pay for the pleasure they get from seeing their partners in these outfits. From this view, lingerie plays a role in women's objectification. It's one way that men treat them like dolls, designed for their own sexual pleasure.

On the other side of the debate, men aren't the only ones buying lingerie for their partners. Many women buy it for themselves, as mentioned. And some suggest only confident, independent women venture into sex shops and buy lingerie (Wood 2016). These purchases are public declarations of sexuality that would not have been so acceptable just a few decades ago. As this taboo around women's sexuality gradually fades, some retailers are responding. For example, in the past, sex shops targeted men. They were not widely seen as socially acceptable. In turn, these shops were often pushed out to the margins of big cities. There, men were less likely to be "caught" visiting them. Today, though, sex-shop retailers are leaning into the notion of women's sexual liberation. They uphold the idea that women should be free to explore their sexuality—especially by buying consumer goods like lingerie. In turn, sex shops are increasingly visible, found in central shopping centres (Martin and Crewe 2016). They proudly display products *for* women, such as sex toys designed to heighten women's sexual pleasure. By making shopping for sex toys and lingerie highly visible, these retailers declare women's sexual pleasure fun, glamorous, and even feminine—not shameful, to be hidden away (Attwood 2005).

These views change gradually over time. Marketing for sex products can therefore reflect a mix of traditional and modern values, as we discuss below. We also see this mix in advertisements for products that have little to do with sex. As we saw earlier with alcohol advertisements, marketers have long portrayed women as sex objects, to be enjoyed alongside the advertised product. But today men aren't the only ones with buying power. Marketers must convince women to buy their products, too. Nevertheless, the media continue to show women as homemakers or sex objects, both in advertisements targeting men as well as those targeting women (Vezich et al. 2017). Research suggests that women don't like these images—so why do they persist?

Vezich et al. used brain-imaging technology to answer that question. They found that women *report* liking domestic images more than sexualized images. However, the brain imaging revealed more activity in neural regions associated with reward and arousal when these women viewed sexualized images. Surprisingly, the response to sexualized advertisements is stronger for women who approve of traditional attitudes than for women who report less conventional beliefs. So, even though they *say* they disapprove of sexualized advertisements, some women with traditional values respond positively to them. The researchers propose an explanation. Maybe women raised in more traditional environments, who have had less exposure to sexualized images, find them novel and exciting, causing the heightened brain response.

Another study considered whether the old adage "sex sells" holds true (Dahl et al. 2008; but also, Lee et al. 2017). The researchers conducted four experiments about advertisements with sexual content. They found women were less inclined to dislike the advertisement when it could be interpreted as promoting relationship quality and stability between partners. In other words, they didn't mind ads that portrayed sex as a means to a more traditional end. In contrast, men's attitudes were scarcely affected by these cues about improved relationship quality. They didn't mind whether the content depicted sex for pleasure or sex to heighten a romantic relationship. In sum, sex sells when depicted in certain ways, for certain women with certain values and beliefs.

More recently, the self-care industry began promoting women's sexual health and pleasure. This industry stresses that masturbation is healthy, sophisticated, and a necessary part of every woman's self-care routine. That may be true, but the industry leverages this fact to sell women their products, including sex toys, lingerie, and erotica. Buying these items comes to be seen as another form of pampering, just like buying a manicure.

Websites that sell sex products like lingerie and sex toys to women take a similar approach (Attwood 2005; Lieberman 2016, 2017; Comella 2016). Especially when targeting middle-aged and older women, these websites position their products as feminine and sophisticated, not "dirty" or "slutty." They make less of an effort to justify a product when it's more youthful or funky. Presumably, they think younger women already embrace their sexuality and seek pleasure openly.

Other retailers tap into this celebration of sexuality by organizing "sex parties" for women (Marks and Wosick 2017). They know some women feel comfortable and enjoy openly discussing sex with their friends. They bring their products—again, sex toys, lingerie, and erotica—to parties held in one woman's house. In this setting, women examine and buy sex products in their friends' company. Some may feel more confident with their choices after getting their friends' advice. Others seek reassurance that their wishes for these products are acceptable and healthy. And others still put their own sexual confidence on display, asking questions about and buying the most scandalous products.

Sex product retailers also bring these sex parties to friend groups who do *not* discuss sex as openly. These women may feel anxious about exploring sex products. They may worry that sexy lingerie would undermine their modesty and, in turn, the femininity it is traditionally associated with. For these women, sex products need to be normalized. Retailers therefore mix them in with other products thought to suggest more traditional feminine qualities.

In a sense, these retailers are exploiting a long history around women's sexuality. They have seen more women embracing sexual freedom. And they know those women make up a large part of the consumer population. So these retailers have hopped on the bandwagon. They play into ideas like female liberation by encouraging women to take control of their own sex lives. Sometimes it works. Women report that wearing sexy underwear makes them feel confident, powerful, and in control (Wood 2016). What's more, some products like vibrators allow women to feel sexy and enjoy sexual pleasure without men (Comella 2017; Waskul and Anklan 2019).

That said, whether they're targeting women who are young or old, "traditional" or "liberated," online retailers promise consumers their purchase will be delivered to their home in "discreet packaging." They assume no woman would want her neighbours to know about her sex life, even though their website assures women it's natural and healthy. Overall, these sites may applaud female pleasure, but only as long as it has been sanitized, or depicted in way that makes it socially acceptable.

Final Thoughts

In this chapter, we have seen how age-old elements of gender inequality still linger. Certain products (and their marketing) promise to make women more desirable to men—as though that is the greatest goal to which they can aspire. Different rules also apply to men and women when it comes to physical appearance. A booming consumer market is kept alive by the impossibly high standards our society sets for women. Makeup, shoes, diet pills and more are designed to meet a huge demand for consumer products that will help women live up to these gendered expectations. But our consumer society is also partly responsible for creating that demand. Media that glamorize conventionally beautiful women, and especially effortlessly feminine bodies, teach women to strive for these norms (Atari et al. 2016). In the end, most will fall short. Yet countless companies have profited from women's efforts to achieve the impossible.

In this chapter, we saw once again that consumerism props up inequality. People want material goods because they want to communicate messages to others, whether those messages support their conformity to, resistance against, or indifference to gender norms. People need various types of capital—especially erotic capital—to send these messages.

Economic capital grants them access to these other forms of capital (or keeps them out of reach). Without economic capital, women are at a disadvantage when it comes to performing the femininity that's expected of them. They cannot afford the consumer goods and activities that are seen as contributing to a feminine identity, and their inability to perform the desired femininity reduces their chances of accessing greater economic capital in the future.

These feelings may be especially acute for women, as opposed to men. Traditional expectations persist. Women are expected to live up to strict, narrowly defined appearance norms, perhaps more so than men. Their place in society is defined (in part) by the way they look. Those who cannot look the part stay stuck at the bottom. Consumerism is part of the problem because it is one of the tools women are expected to use to signal their place. But the bigger problem is the hierarchy itself—that people are ranked on their appearance and income.

Discussion Questions

1. This chapter covers the psychological and anthropological approaches to beauty. Briefly summarize each approach and compare them with your own approach.
2. This chapter examines various differences between men and women as consumers. From that list of differences, select three things that *you* do as a consumer (e.g., do you shop in bricks-and-mortar stores?). Compare your selections with those of your peers.
3. How you dress is affected when you start working. How have work and/or school affected how you dress? Reflect on your outfit selections and your work performance when wearing these clothes.

Quick Quiz

1. What is performativity?
a. Changing your customs and mannerisms while being in an unfamiliar situation
b. Judith Butler's notion that gender is a continuing act, rather than a given identity
c. When one person pretends to have feelings for another
d. Adding a lot of makeup to enhance your beauty
e. the concept women's bodies are objects to be looked at

2. What is the male gaze?
a. The notion films are constructed from and for the perspective of a male heterosexual viewer
b. Men hold eye contact longer than females
c. A phenomenon that results in sexual relations only with the opposite sex
d. A gaze that men use to signify their availability
e. A gaze used by men when searching for a partner

3. What type of theory of capital did Hakim (2010) present?
a. Economic
b. Social
c. Cultural
d. Erotic
e. Political

4. Which item below is NOT an element of erotic capital?
a. Beauty
b. Sexual attractiveness
c. Perceived wealth
d. Grace and charm
e. Liveliness and animation

5. What is intersectionality?
a. Feeling as though your brain and biological sex do not match
b. Sexual relations only between people of the opposite sex
c. Another word for bisexual
d. A conflict theory approach that claims men and women encounter conflict daily
e. The idea that various forms of discrimination—gender, sexuality, race, class and disability—can interact to produce particularized forms of social oppression

The answers to the Quick Quiz are provided at the end of the book.

For Further Reading

Gender Trouble: Feminism and the Subversion of Identity by Judith Butler
Butler introduces the idea of gender as a performance. This book analyzes gender, dealing with topics such as heteronormativity and the role of gender in the modern world.

Formations of Class and Gender by Beverley Skeggs
This book analyzes power relations in society. Skeggs explains how women demonstrate their class, femininity, and sexuality.

Erotic Capital: The Power of Attraction in the Boardroom and the Bedroom by Catharine Hakim
Hakim expands on the idea of personal assets—economic, cultural, and social capital. She adds that erotic capital is a fourth type of capital that individuals use to advance in society.

Key Terms

Beauty work
Bodily (or facial) beauty
Body image
Cisgender
Erotic capital
Femininity
Gender
Gender binarism
Gender essentialism
Gender identity
Gender performativity
Gendered division of labour
Ideology of gender
Intersectionality
Male gaze
Sex
Time poverty

Chapter Eleven
Men and Symbols of Masculinity

Learning Objectives

After reading this chapter, you will be able to:

✓ Analyze the relationship between gendered consumption behaviours and inequality.

✓ Interpret advertisements as reflections of marketers' perceptions of men consumers.

✓ Consider men's shopping and conspicuous consumption as gender performances.

✓ Recognize the multiple masculinities men perform through clothing and makeup.

In this chapter, we focus on men consumers, who often learn to shop and consume differently than women. To seem masculine, they distance themselves from consumption practices that people have long judged feminine, including the act of shopping itself. So, to talk about men consumers, we must also continue to talk about women consumers.

As mentioned in the last chapter, these discussions of women and men consumers are focused broadly on two consumer phenomena. First, as we will continue to see in this chapter, consumer goods can send signals about people's gender. Those signals might illustrate conformity to a mainstream gender community, distance from another gender community, or a rejection of gender norms in general. Second, these signals can perpetuate traditional gender norms or make way for new ones.

Just as we saw that women consume in many ways, so too will we see that men consume in many ways. Our goal in this chapter is not to suggest that all men are the same, or that their consumption habits are always different from women's. Indeed, as we observed in the last chapter and will see in this one, men and women are about equally likely to buy treats. Both consumer segments are also likely to buy tickets, though they aim to fit in with and be accepted by different gender groups much of the time. Both also love buying trophies, though, once again, usually towards different ends. As discussed, women tend to buy luxury goods that (they think) elevate their social status and even ward off other women who (they think) might be interested in their partners. Men also use of a variety of trophies for a variety of reasons: some flaunt luxury cars to make themselves feel attractive to women, others sport expensive designer clothing to attract attention in a new way when they lack the sculpted bodies often admired (and flaunted) in gay communities.

So, one of the main differences between women and men consumers is the *reason* they buy tickets and trophies. Both, however, are trying to fit in with different social groups, and to elevate themselves above others. Another key difference is that women are somewhat more likely than men to buy basics for their household—though we can reasonably expect men would buy these basics if their spouses weren't already doing so.

Where there are gender differences, we do not presume they have to do with inherent differences between men and women. Instead, we ask what features of our consumer society lead men and women to shop and buy in these different ways. Namely, we think that socialization teaches women certain consumer behaviours and men, others. And we ask: Do these consumption behaviours prop up inequality?

Defining Our Terms

Masculinity refers to the traits and qualities conventionally (or ideally) associated with boys and men. Like femininity, masculinity is socially constructed. It consists of gender norms and culturally shaped ideas about what it means to be a boy or a man in a given culture (Cornwall and Lindisfarne 2016; Stoller 2020). Conceptions of masculinity change over time, as do conceptions of femity—even within the same culture—and there are many types of masculinity. As we will see, traditional conceptions of masculinity are based on resisting femininity; the less feminine you seem, the more masculine you come across. However, as the study of gender has evolved, researchers have increasingly questioned the idea that masculinity is the opposite of femininity. That idea is at the heart of the gender binaries we introduced in the last chapter. As we saw, many researchers and members of the public now believe there are not just two genders, but many. We explore below this idea of multiple masculinities and how consumerism helps communicate those complex and diverse masculinities.

Hegemonic (or **dominant**) **masculinity** captures at least two ideas related to our cultural views of men and women. First, hegemonic masculinity describes the sociocultural arrangements through which men preserve their dominance over women. In other words, this masculinity protects patriarchy (Connell 2011). **Patriarchy** is a social system in which power and privilege are mainly held by men. Under patriarchy, men dominate as political and business leaders and are "in charge" of their households. So, hegemonic masculinity helps preserve the hierarchies of power and authority between men and women (Messerschmidt and Messner 2018; Messerschmidt 2019).

In North America, traits associated with hegemonic masculinity include assertiveness, strength, and leadership. Although U.S. president Ronald Reagan spent his life as an actor, corporate spokesman, and politician, he was frequently photographed in cowboy garb and while horseback riding on his ranch, images that reinforced voters' perceptions of him as a traditional, straight-shooting leader.

Second, hegemonic masculinity refers to the dominant conception of masculinity in a particular culture. As mentioned, because the notion of masculinity is culturally constructed, there are several understandings of what masculinity means in our society. But at any given time, one form of masculinity rather than others is culturally celebrated. Hegemonic masculinity is the formulation of masculinity currently on top—the most common and accepted version, and the one best positioned to defend patriarchy in a given culture.

For example, in North America, heterosexual masculinity is the hegemonic masculinity. Traits typically associated with this heterosexual hegemonic masculinity include assertiveness, strength, leadership, courage, and sexual dominance over women. Gay men—and the masculinities they are expected to perform—are subordinated. Several practices enforce this subordination, including political and cultural exclusion, cultural abuse, street violence (ranging from intimidation to murder), and economic discrimination. Some heterosexual men and boys are also subordinated for "failing" to perform the traditional masculinity that is expected of them. For example, people may call them names like "wimp," "nerd," "dweeb," "geek," and so on. These words mark these men's divergence from dominant masculinity.

To perform any type of masculinity, including heterosexual hegemonic masculinity, men engage in **manhood acts.** Manhood acts are any acts that involve presenting oneself as a man. The goal of such acts is to secure and keep gendered privilege—that is, to claim membership in the privileged (male) gender group. For example, in an office job, a male manager might display his manhood through his resolve and competitiveness—traits traditionally associated with masculinity. He might show his loyalty to the male hierarchy (the "old boys' club"). And he might remind everyone of his dominance by sexualizing his female coworkers or challenging their authority. These manhood acts remind everyone that the privileged male gender group exists and signal the individual's place within it (Petterson 2016).

Few, if any, men perform hegemonic masculinity perfectly (Connell and Messeschmidt 2005). Such masculinity is an ideal: a fantasy about the types of behaviours and practices that would best underpin patriarchy. Yet, many men benefit from dominant masculinity nevertheless, since they benefit from the advantages that men in general gain from their overall subordination of women. These beneficiaries might enact a **complicit masculinity**, reaping the rewards of patriarchy even though they do not perform the hegemonic masculinity.

Hegemonic masculinity persists today. But in 2009, Anderson developed **inclusive masculinity theory** (IMT) to account for some social shifts. For example, sports and fraternities were (and continue to be) key sites for performances of hegemonic masculinities. As mentioned, one way to assert heterosexual hegemonic masculinity is to condemn and distance oneself from its opposite: gay masculinity. In trying to perform their own heterosexual masculinity, football fans and frat brothers earned a bad reputation for homophobia. But in recent years, plenty of sports fans and fraternity members have been inclusive and welcoming of LGBTQ2S+peoples (Ellis and Cashmore 2012). In this sense, a new kind of masculinity has emerged, consisting of traits like emotional openness, social consciousness, and a celebration (or at least acceptance) of feminism and gay rights.

Inclusive masculinities tend to emerge in inclusive societies. Men are more likely to perform such masculinities in large urban centres, for example, where **homohysteria** can (in some social circles) soften. Homohysteria is the fear of being stripped of your masculinity and assumed to be homosexual. Homohysteria and displays of hegemonic masculinity often go hand in hand. Men who fear that they will be "accused" of being gay try to compensate with hypermasculine displays, womanizing, and homophobia. Homohysteria is alive and well, but perhaps not as rampant as it once was—again, at least not in certain societies. Indeed, many men even view hegemonic masculinity as distasteful (Bridges and Pascoe 2014). They may opt for inclusive masculinities in a conscious effort to distance themselves from hegemonic heterosexual masculinities.

However, when men feel threatened—as though their dominance is in jeopardy—homohysteria and hegemonic masculinity can re-emerge. A brief glance at any social media platform will reveal virulent sexism, homophobia, and homohysteria. Inclusive masculinity theory might overstate the movement towards inclusion—or perhaps the pendulum has swung back slightly, as equal rights movements make some feel as though their position of white male privilege is in jeopardy (Ging 2017; O'Neill 2015). North America's unstable gig economy, the alleged "feminization" of the workplace, and widespread downward mobility, wage stagnation, and underemployment can jar men's sense of masculinity if they have learned to define that masculinity based on their breadwinning role (Kimmel, 2013). Feeling threatened, some men retreat back to performances of hegemonic heterosexual masculinities in their efforts to reaffirm the patriarchy and reclaim their dominant positions within it.

Lastly, there seems to be some degree of awareness among the general public of the notion of **toxic masculinity.** Toxic masculinity calls attention to the elements of traditional masculinities that can be harmful or "toxic." Though the term has been around for decades, it has recently been widely adopted and used in even mainstream explanations for sexism and violence perpetrated by men. Some say the notion of toxic masculinity is an attack on men and manhood—an attempt to vilify and oppress them. Others suggest men themselves (not to mention women) would benefit from a "detoxification" of masculinity, since some of its traits, such as repressing one's emotions, are detrimental to men's well-being.

As we will see, some straight cisgender men today have responded to toxic masculinity with even more extreme versions of inclusive masculinities. They aren't just inclusive—respectful of others' sexuality, rights, and self-presentation. They present *themselves* as openly in defiance of hegemonic heterosexual masculinity—as "softboys." A **softboy** is yet another masculine identity, characterized by a feminine aesthetic and the adoption of some stereotypically feminine attributes as well, such as emotional vulnerability. They are not afraid to order a fruity cocktail instead of a beer at the bar, often sport painted fingernails, join protests for women's rights (and make sure everyone knows they were there). Tiktok eboys often exemplify the softboy aesthetic, donning earrings and pastels—styles seemingly influenced by K-pop boy bands like BTS, famous for their glamorous makeup and carefully coiffed hair.

Perhaps some softboys genuinely denounce toxic masculinity and want to express their "feminine" attributes through these means of self-presentation. But many (women) say the softboy is merely the smarter cousin to the f***boy, who pursues casual sex with multiple women while deceiving them into thinking he has genuine feelings for them. From this view, a man's softboy performance is merely intended to delude women into thinking they are "sweet and sensitive," so that they will sleep with him. In that sense, the softboy could be less of a resistance to toxic masculinity and more of a reformulation of hegemonic heterosexual masculinity.

Multiple Masculinities = Multiple Male Buyers

It is hard to get up-to-date details on the buying patterns of different kinds of men, or the ways marketers try to sell to them. That is mainly because the research from which we would get this information is privately commissioned and privately used. So we must rely on information that is readily available online, likely only a pale reflection of what exists on the hard drives and in the filing cabinets of major marketing agencies. What follows is a review of that limited information from marketers themselves. As you will see, marketers' strategies are straightforward at times, but contradictory at others. The information available to us seems to reveal more about marketers' perceptions of men consumers than the consumption habits of men themselves. And, as you will also see, some of these perceptions are rooted in long histories of sexism and patriarchy.

First, advertisements aimed at men typically appeal to functionality and the product's usefulness (Bhatt and Bhatt 2012). For example, a shampoo ad for women might promise silky, lustrous hair, while one for men might focus on how effectively the shampoo will wash away dirt. Second, marketers believe men want proof—evidence in the form of numbers—so they provide believable numbers wherever possible. How many washes before noticeable results? What proportion of successes per hundred men? Men are more inclined to buy a product that cites clinical proof instead of simply promising an outcome, whereas women are supposedly convinced to buy through the use of graphics, storytelling, and emotional messages. Third, marketers do not think men are browsers, so their advertisements tend to be simple and feature strong colours that catch the eye. Fourth, men allegedly focus on attainable long-term benefits, not immediate (though enchanting) satisfaction.

Baudrillard pointed out these first four assumptions decades ago. In his classic analysis in *The Consumer Society* (1970), he noted that advertisements for men stress their ability to make rational, considered choices. They are clean, simple, and appeal to men logically. Some flatter men by coming right out and saying they are good decision-makers who can be trusted to make the right choice (which, of course, is to buy the advertised product). By contrast, advertisements aimed at women highlight self-indulgence and pleasure. So, it seems marketers haven't changed their approach much in the last 50 years. They continue to believe that, in all their masculine rationality, men are most convinced by utility, evidence, and long-term impact. The implication is that men's less rational, more emotional female counterparts need to have their heartstrings tugged.

We can all think of many men—friends, relatives, co-workers—whose buying habits do not fit this description, just as we all know women who do not consume in the ways we described in the last chapter. To repeat, just because a marketer assumes a given approach will work effectively on a male target audience does not make it true.

Fifth, marketers think men might care more about the value of their time, preferring to buy brands or well-known products if they think they will guarantee results (Bakewell 2006). Sixth, compared to women, who are sometimes more likely to be bargain hunters, men typically pay less attention to cost. They are generally ready to pay any price that seems reasonable, while women look for practicality at a low or, at least, moderate price.

Seventh, marketers can't agree on the amount and type of product information men want. Some say men prefer simple marketing. They just want to know what the product does, and tune out ads that take a lot of effort to digest. Women, on the other hand, allegedly look to social media for lots of detail and description, so they can compare products before they make a buying decision (Keenan 2018). But other marketers are beginning to suggest that men might rely on social media and word of mouth more than originally thought. In one study, 54 percent of men say they use social media to research product information and read reviews (Luth 2016). Similarly, 44 percent of men told their friends about positive experiences they had online around products or brands.

Eighth, marketers disagree on men's interest in the gendering of products. Some say they seem attracted to products and services that are presented as masculine and explicitly for men—preferably with a label stating just that, prominently displayed on the product itself. If you browse the aisles of drug stores, for example, you will usually be able to pick out the "For Men" lines of soaps, hair products, and other grooming items. Their dark, un-patterned bottles—often "masculine" blue or gray—stand out from the stereotypically "feminine" floral patterns and pastel colours of women's products. And in case you happen to miss them, marketers will slap a huge headline on the package proclaiming the item is "For Men." Such marketing creates the impression that men would be embarrassed to be seen buying a basic necessity like soap—as though it is emasculating to groom oneself. To counter such (supposed) embarrassment and ensure men are still willing to purchase these products, marketers are eager to present them in ways that will assure onlookers of the buyer's masculinity.

Box 11-1
Marketing Masculinity

The media help consumers learn how to buy in ways that uphold their gender identity. Marketers often play heavily into stereotypical notions of what it means to be "masculine" and "feminine." Think of pickup truck advertisements, for example. Many feature rugged men doing "manly" things like hauling lumber. They are set to loud "manly" music, with a deep "manly" voiceover. The aim is to make male viewers buy by convincing them that they, too, can be rugged, strong, and manly with the help of a pickup truck. Truck-buying by men is also significant because it represents such a large household purchase. Buying just one truck is equal to a great many small (non-truck) purchases by women.

On the other hand, think of advertisements for women's clothing. Rarely do these advertisements feature "masculine"-looking women—for example, women with facial hair, big muscles, or other features long considered "manly." Most women have been taught to want to look cute, sexy, and feminine, and marketers cater to those wants. So advertising coaxes women to buy a great many pretty things for themselves and the household, while it coaxes men to buy a few, often very expensive items for their own use.

Nevertheless, women seem less concerned about whether the product was made "for" men or women. On the other hand, one study reported that 71 percent of men and 74 percent of women say they prefer gender-neutral messages (Luth 2016). Whatever consumers' true preferences, marketers do seem to let masculinity seep into their messages targeting men. Although some ditch the clichés and one-dimensional stereotypes (such as "the jock" or "the breadwinner"), they also tend to emphasize traits like "bold," "manly," and "confident."

Ninth, marketers develop different kinds of campaigns for different kinds of men. Men of different ages, classes, lifestyles, sexual orientations, and so on are looking for different things, so marketers advertise to them differently (Honigman 2013). For example, when marketing to men in their fifties, marketers may try frightening them about their family's safety and well-being, because these men often feel so responsible for their families. Perhaps they encourage these men to imagine the horrors of getting into a car crash while driving their family around, for example, before offering up the many safety features that come with the pickup truck they are advertising.

Clearly, there is little agreement about how to best market to men. As we saw with the research on women, there is plain disagreement about whether we can generalize about male-versus-female differences. Second, there is seeming disagreement about how much detail men really want before they make a buying decision. Third, there is some disagreement about whether men respond as predictably and forcefully to emotional appeals as women do. There is less disagreement about the importance of Internet advertising, social media, and consumer ratings. These are all important to men, but that fact is so general that it doesn't say much. Internet advertising, social media, and consumer ratings matter in some way to every consumer. The questions marketers must ask are: What *kind* of Internet ads speak to their male target audiences? *How* should they use social media to market to men? *Where* are men turning for consumer ratings they trust?

To repeat, the findings we have discussed in this section seem to reveal more about marketers' perceptions of men consumers than the consumption habits of men themselves. In a Canadian doctoral thesis, Scheibling (2014) brings this view to his study of advertisements for male cosmetic products. He analyzed a sample of 62 grooming product advertisements found in *Esquire* magazine from 2011 to 2013. His purpose was to uncover what and how these texts communicate about men and masculinity.

Scheibling found several themes or types of messages that cropped up throughout many of the ads he studied. The sheer variety of messages marketers try to communicate reinforces the idea of multiple masculinities—that today, there are many different ways to show you're a "real man."

The most prevalent theme, found in 40 percent of the sample, was "body responsibility and control." Advertisements in this category framed control over one's body as a responsibility all "real men" must take. Men who fail to control their bodies, the ads implied, endanger their masculine reputations.

A second theme, found in 23 percent of the sample, was "manning up." In these advertisements, men were urged to assert their dominant, hegemonic masculinity. Assertions of virile power—even hostility—were presented as natural aspects of manhood that need to be upheld, especially as new, "softer" masculinities emerge (like the inclusive masculinities discussed earlier).

A third theme, found in 21 percent of the sample, is "explicit and implicit heterosexuality." Here, good grooming is framed as a normal and important step straight men must take to get women. If you want a girlfriend, the ads say, use deodorant. Besides appealing to heterosexual hegemonic masculinity, these types of ads strive to erase any feminine connotations attached to grooming. They also try to quell the homohysteria mentioned earlier, assuring men that they will not be taken for gay if they take care of themselves; rather, they will gain sexual attention from women.

A fourth theme, also found in 21 percent of the sample, is "work and family." The idea these ads tried to get across was that "real men" are breadwinners and good fathers—yet another expectation placed on men seeking to exhibit hegemonic masculinity. We see similar messaging in ads for cars, especially expensive sports cars such as the Porsche. As signs of wealth, the Porsche confirms its male driver's breadwinning status (Avery 2012). But as a fast, shiny, and sleek sports car, it's also a magnet for attracting women. At the same time, the Porsche SUV—perfect for carting young children around—gets at the "good father" element of hegemonic masculinity. The

Box 11-2

Sexualized Advertising through the Decades

One study examined Italian alcohol advertisements targeting men (Beccaria et al. 2017). Over the decades, women were presented differently in these advertisements. In the 1960s and 1970s, women were portrayed drinking in the company of one or more men. Like the alcoholic drinks themselves, the women in these advertisements were portrayed as rewards to be enjoyed by the successful men.

Advertisements from the 1980s and the 1990s reflected important social changes: especially, higher rates of education and paid work among women. In these decades, housewives and mistresses were still presented in these ads, but so were sportswomen and businesswomen. If the female character in the ad was a successful executive, though, she was always also young and physically attractive. Sex appeal still played a part.

Images of women from the 2000s continued to focus on women's physical appearance. Some women were presented as what the researchers called "status-oriented, pleasure-seeking consumers." These images made women seem obsessed with their appearance, immaculately dressed, made up, and coiffed. Others framed women in the ads as "hypersexual consumers." Drinking was portrayed as an enjoyable social activity for men and a prelude to sex.

In sum, throughout the decades, alcohol advertisements use physically attractive young women to target men. We might say women were seen not so much as consumers in their own right, but props used to motivate men's buying behaviour.

point here is that ads draw upon several different, often contradictory elements of masculinity to sell their products. Marketers "gender bend" brands and products to make sure men see multiple facets of their masculinity reflected.

The last theme in Scheibling's study is "nostalgia," found in 13 percent of the advertisements. Using textual and visual elements that make the advertisement look as though it come from an earlier historical era, the advertisements remind us of simpler times, when gender relations were less "confusing." The author proposes these may appeal to men who strive for a "dapper" appearance today. They may also appear more frequently in cultural moments of homohysteria, or appeal especially to men who feel threatened by women and LGBTQ2S+people's growing rights.

The ads Scheibling studied reflect multiple versions of masculinity, as well as men of various ages, classes, and ethnicities. Many of them depict men being sensitive fathers and husbands. Clearly, marketers wanted to appeal to a wide range of target audiences, so their ads do reflect plural masculinities—that is, they recognize there are many acceptable ways to be a man today. On balance, however, these advertisements relied on longstanding ideals and stereotypes that reinforce hegemonic masculinity. They present clean tidy men, but make sure they are *also* powerful and strong.

To varying degrees, marketing for other types of products tends to follow suit. It is fairly easy, for example, to showcase diverse, inclusive masculinities in ads for clothes, food, or vacation destinations. It is much harder (though still possible) to present varied versions of manhood when marketing traditionally masculine activities: driving trucks, mowing the lawn, or playing contact sports. Indeed, some men turn to certain consumer activities in a concerted effort to reinforce their hegemonic masculinity. Diluting ads for do-it-yourself (DIY) tools, for example, with depictions of inclusive masculinities, might mean missing key market segments.

Box 11-3

DIY Productive Consumption

Consumer goods, if selected properly, can help men perform masculinity effectively. Consider the role of tools and do-it-yourself (DIY) work in the conception and performance of masculinity in our society. Woodworking, log-chopping, and home renovation are all examples of "productive consumption" in our society. Productive consumption describes activities that produce something—say, a new hardwood floor in the living room, for example—and require the consumption of a product or products. Men often use such productive consumption to live up to cultural expectations of masculinity (Moisio et al. 2013). It makes them look like "manly men" and family protectors. As well, productive consumption helps men of different classes shore up their masculinities. Middle-class men in knowledge industries, for example, spend their days sitting in an office. At home, they want to present themselves as craftsmen, capable of "manly" manual labour. Moisio et al. (2013) call this "class tourism." These men take a "vacation" from their professional lives and enjoy the supposedly simpler joys of manual workers. And on the other hand, men who do not earn a lot of money at work—and who therefore do not fit the traditional mold of male breadwinner—can still say they are the head of the house if they are the ones maintaining it.

Consumption Stereotypes and the Ideology of Gender

In our culture, consumers can perform their gender by shopping in certain ways and buying certain products. There is some research to suggest that men and women do indeed shop in different ways and buy different goods, as we discussed in the last chapter. But, as we saw, that research is mixed. In this section, we consider several stereotypes about men and women's consumption that help uphold the ideology of gender. Recall from the last chapter that the ideology of gender is the widespread social beliefs about "natural" differences between men and women that help uphold gender inequality.

Some people use men and women's supposedly different consumption habits as "proof" of these natural differences. Men and women are inherently different, they say, so they naturally shop differently. As mentioned, this idea that men and women are biologically different, and therefore socially different, is very old. We even find it in studies by Theodor Adorno and Max Horkheimer, whose work we examined in earlier chapters. In their classic (1944) essay on consumer behaviour, "The Culture Industry: Mass Culture as Mass Deception," Adorno and Horkheimer say consumerism is tied to gender. For them, everything from consumer products to the act of shopping itself is feminine and therefore "weak." "Real men," they say, are in control of their thinking and actions—not swayed by advertisements and desires for material things. When men do shop or covet consumer products, Adorno and Horkheimer say they become emasculated.

In this analysis, Adorno and Horkheimer have framed the stereotypical traits we associate with masculinity—strength, power, and control—positively. They do so by subordinating the stereotypical traits we associate with femininity: meekness, passivity, and malleability (for an update, see Moore 2019), and by connecting consumer behaviour to women, not men.

We see this same idea—that men who take pleasure in consuming are emasculated—in the works of Karl Marx, George Lukâcs, Wolfgang Fritz Haug, and Gary Cross (Belisle 2003 but for a contrasting view, see Joudrey 2017). Men who embrace this ideology of gender learn to justify their privileged, authoritative role in society. At the same time, women who embrace it learn to tolerate their lesser role in society. The ideology helps us—indeed, pushes us—to perform our physiological differences as though they were destined. From birth onward, we are socialized to perform the gender roles defined by our sex. Whether we are aware of it or not, these roles influence every choice we make, from the jobs we apply for to the shoes we buy for the interview.

Take the example of shopping for Christmas gifts. One study found that people with stronger feminine *identities*—whether men or women—got more involved in Christmas shopping than people with weaker feminine identities (Fischer and Arnold 1994; but see Neale et al. 2018). They also got more enjoyment from it. Men with more egalitarian attitudes, who think men and women should have equal roles, immersed themselves more in Christmas shopping. They spent more time and effort shopping for gifts than men with less equal attitudes. So, gender identities and attitudes towards gender influence consumer behaviour, not biological sex.

Another example is the supposed difference between *how* men and women shop in general. As we touched on in the last chapter, women learn to enjoy the experience of shopping itself (Taylor 2012). They often make an event out of it, planning to go with their friends, taking breaks for lunch, and getting drinks afterwards. Such behaviour is expected and even encouraged among women. Men, on the other hand, typically shop less, enjoy shopping less, shop on their own, and try to finish shopping as quickly as possible (Brakus et al. 2018). Some studies say men see shopping as a task that they need to get done—not a social activity (Bakewell 2006). Instead of considering elements like quality of service, men are said to choose stores based on criteria such as the number of available parking spaces and the length of the checkout line (Bakshi 2012). They think shopping is feminine, so in order to spend the least amount of time and effort on an activity that "emasculates" them, men dash into stores they already know and look only for the products they need.

At least, this has until recently been the generally agreed-upon stereotype of the average male consumer. Today, consumer researchers and marketers are less sure about men's feelings on shopping. On the other, studies such as one by Honigman (2013) find that 43 percent of men think of shopping as a relaxing, enjoyable activity. This directly contradicts the research above, which finds men hate shopping and strive to make the shopping they cannot avoid as efficient as possible.

As discussed in the last chapter, research is also inconsistent when it comes to men's online shopping behaviour. Some studies show that men purchase goods online more than women do (Agudo-Peregrina et al. 2015). Researchers suspect online shopping minimizes the time and effort men need to spend on this "feminine" activity. Whether they are men or women, online shoppers are more goal-oriented; between two-thirds and four-fifths of online shoppers buy items they specifically searched for (Wolfinbarger and Gilly 2001). They do not visit an online store to browse or for the "experience," as they might with in-person shopping. So, if men are indeed more utilitarian consumers than women, it would make sense for them to do more of their shopping online.

However, other research shows that women are slightly *more* likely than men to buy the following things online: food and groceries (a 4 percent difference), clothing and sporting goods (a 6 percent difference), books, magazines and e-learning materials (a 2 percent difference), and medicine (a 2 percent difference). Similarly, data from studies of e-commerce in Europe and the U.S. show only small differences between men and women in purchases of travel, household goods, music and films, and tickets for events. To repeat, then, the jury is still out on if and how men and women differ as online shoppers.

We also see the ideology of gender play out in men's conspicuous consumption. Some research finds that men are more materialistic than women and more likely to consume conspicuously (Segal and Podoshen 2011; Kamineni 2005; Keech et al. 2020; Parisi 2017). Perhaps, some say, that's because men think conspicuous consumption will attract women (Saad and Vongas 2009; Amirouche et al. 2017). For example, buying an expensive car lets men display their worth as a mate—their breadwinning potential, their success, their economic dominance.

In one study, Saad and Vongas (2009) suggest that driving an expensive car is part of a mating ritual. Through an experiment, they show that men's testosterone levels fluctuate alongside fluctuations in their social status. The experiment revealed that men's testosterone levels increased after driving an expensive sports car and decreased after driving an old family sedan. Additionally, the location (and visibility) of the drive (either a busy downtown area or a semi-deserted highway) moderated this response. Lastly, the researchers looked at what happened when, in the presence of a woman onlooker, another man displayed his wealth. In this scenario, the original man's social status was threatened, and their testosterone levels increased. This suggest men respond unconsciously to challenges to their status and competition for women's attention.

Another study confirmed a correlation between testosterone and the desire for luxury items (Healy 2018). In the study, half of the male participants were required to rub testosterone gel on their upper bodies, while the other half rubbed placebo gel over their bodies. The men were then asked whether they preferred a sporty watch or a luxurious, high-status watch. The men with the testosterone gel consistently chose the high-status luxurious watch.

Finally, yet another study suggests women do react to men's conspicuous consumption. Dunn and Searle (2010) experimentally manipulated social status by seating the same models (an equally attractive male and female), expressing identical facial expressions and posture, in one of two cars. One car was a "high-status" car (a Silver Bentley Continental GT), while the other was a "neutral-status" car (a red Ford Fiesta ST). Photographs of the couple in each of the two cars were shown to male and female participants, who were then asked to rate the models' attractiveness. Male participants were not influenced by

Research suggests some men may buy expensive automobiles because doing so lets them display their worth as a potential mate.

the status manipulation; they didn't say the woman model seated in the Bentley was more attractive than the women in the Fiesta. However, female participants rated the male model as significantly more attractive when riding in the Bentley than when riding in the Fiesta. In other words, at least in this instance, wealth does make men more attractive to women.

To repeat, however, this does not mean women are genetically hardwired to prefer Bentleys over Fiestas, or to mate with rich men instead of poor men. Responses to conspicuous consumption are learned, just as we learn how to interpret every other sign and symbol in our consumer society. While many men are still socialized to strive to be breadwinners, many women are still socialized to seek out breadwinning mates—even if they have their own jobs and their own sources of income. Teaching women to rely on men for financial stability is just another way our consumer society upholds the ideology of gender and keeps women subordinated to men.

Indeed, women respond to men's conspicuous consumption differently in different socioeconomic contexts. In one study (Bradshaw et al. 2019), after being primed with recession cues (versus the control group), women rated men who owned luxury-brand items as more attractive. As for men, these recession cues made them want luxury goods more, compared to budget products. To generalize, in times of scarcity, women look for men who display signs of wealth. Men

Consuming meat—as well as cooking it outside over an open flame—carries with it masculine associations in Western society.

know this, and in times of scarcity, they strive to buy the luxury goods they know will make them appeal to eligible women.

One final example of consumer patterns and stereotypes that underpin the ideology of gender is meat eating. Many people in our society, both men and women, love to consume meat. But such consumption has, historically, been linked to heterosexual hegemonic masculinity in Western cultures (Rozin et al. 2012; for discussions of the cultural meanings of meat, see Tyler 2019; Oleschuk et al. 2019; Deutsch 2017). Many people view meat as masculine because in tribal societies, men (not women) were hunters. Meat therefore came to be associated with strength and power: two qualities typically considered "masculine." Consuming meat, in turn, signals that masculinity. What's more, in some cultures, meat is offered only to boys and men. In others, the preferred cuts of meat (muscle as opposed to viscera) are reserved for men. Finally, meat is often seen as nutritious and necessary for strength and muscle. Men are therefore often encouraged to eat meat so they can grow strong—another quality stereotypically associated with masculinity.

In short, meat eating is symbolically loaded. Some men and women choose their foods accordingly, to display their gender identities. Men, for example, might order a hamburger on a date, while women order a salad. In one study (Rozin et al. 2012), women said they didn't like meat as much, compared with men. The researchers suggest this helps them seem "feminine," because they are not associating themselves with the masculine qualities of strength and power. Instead, they are displaying a tiny, ladylike appetite.

Overall, then, some research finds differences in the ways men and women consume, while other studies present contradictory evidence. Perhaps gender norms in our society are shifting, and men and women are striving to perform new, more inclusive femininities and masculinities. Nevertheless, stereotypes and assumptions abound. There may not be hard data to prove that men and women shop differently or buy different consumer goods, but people believe in those differences regardless. In our consumer society, we hold these supposed differences up as evidence that men and women are inherently different. This ideology of gender quietly justifies our unequal status quo, validating men's continued dominance.

Clothing, Cosmetics, and Manhood Acts

In the last chapter, we discussed that women are often more concerned with physical appearance than men. Well, most men sit somewhere on a continuum from not caring very much at all about their looks to caring very much—or at least, their self-presentation is intended to tell others that they do or do not care what they look like.

One part of this puzzle is the homohysteria defined earlier. Many gay men use clothing and cosmetics as forms of self-expression. Just like any other consumer, they use bodily adornments and grooming to visibly display who they are and the social groups they belong to. Makeup and clothes can clearly and quickly distinguish these gay men from straight men (Visconti 2008). Nowhere is this display more explicit than Pride celebrations, where LGBTQ2S+peoples and allies sport glitter, feather boas, all the colours of the rainbow, and the loudest outfits they can imagine to celebrate progress towards inclusion and push for even greater equality (Kates and Belk 2002).

Straight men, for their part, are socialized to believe that "real men" do not care what they look like. They are strong, rugged, and too focused on their manly responsibilities to be bothered with the "feminine" concerns of physical appearance. (These are precisely the types of widely held views that Scheibling saw marketers trying to combat in their ads for male grooming products.) To remind everyone that they embody heterosexual hegemonic masculinity, some straight men try to look disheveled and grungy. They avoid outfits that seem too "put together"—and certainly do not wear any makeup—to distance themselves from the gay men who invest so much in their appearance.

Of course, this is a black-and-white account; it reflects experiences at the extremes of the continuum. We have already seen that men in our society perform multiple masculinities, and that homohysteria ebbs and flows. What's more, fashion styles considered "gay" and "straight" are fluid and constantly changing (Visconti 2008). Many gay men do not dress or adorn themselves in ways that signal their membership in the gay community. Some, still sensing the stigma around non-heterosexuality, strive to hide their sexuality by dressing according to dominant standards. Others, whether they are "out" or not, just prefer presenting in ways that project heterosexual hegemonic masculinity. And, as the metrosexual movement reminds us, many straight men are very interested in fashion, spend a great deal of time and money on clothing, and are often mis-recognized as gay men. Similarly, some TikTok "eboys" and K-pop boy bands present themselves in what some consider feminine ways. They wear carefully applied makeup and earrings, choose pastel and floral-patterned clothing, dye their hair, and otherwise go to great lengths to perfect their distinctive look. Many of these so-called "softboys" identify as cisgender straight men. Their self-presentation suggests a rejection of hegemonic heterosexual masculinities and remind us that the consumer goods with which men adorn themselves are not always intended to express their sexuality.

With these many and varied forms of masculinity in mind, let's consider gay men's consumption more closely.

First, as noted, loud outfits and daring makeup are markers of membership in only some gay social circles. Other forms of gay self-presentation, though fashionable, are more restrained (Pereira and Ayrosa, 2012). For example, gay professionals who are open about their sexuality tend to pay close attention to colour and fit when choosing work wear (Chen et al. 2004). Many say they prefer stretchy, fitted items that do signal their gayness, albeit more subtly than they might if they were marching in the Pride Parade, for example. Outside of work, these gay men wear "provocative" outfits they thought would help them attract other gay men.

Physical fitness plays a big part in such sexual provocation in many gay communities (Kates and Belk 2002). Unlike the heterosexual hegemonic masculinity, gay masculinities stress high standards of physical fitness. These standards are learned directly from friends within the gay community and reinforced when visiting "gay-oriented consumer places," such as a gay nightclub where scantily-clad men show off their sculpted physiques (Pereira and Ayrosa 2012; Gomillion and Giuliano 2011). In turn, these ideals influence the clothes that physically fit gay men buy. Tight, fitted clothing, for example, allows them to flaunt their bodies (Reilly, Rudd and Hillery 2008).

Box 11-4

"Feminine" Clothes Become "Manly" Clothes

Sports attire for men is changing. One item of apparel gaining in popularity is compression tights for men. Compression tights pressurize blood vessels and show off muscle definition (Campbell 2016). Though they were previously frowned upon for looking too feminine, plenty of men today are starting to wear them. One student from Western University, Dominique Duncan, says he still feels "manly" when wearing compression tights because they put his muscles on display—without having to remove the leg hair he worries conceals his definition.

Ben Barry, a professor at Ryerson University, suggests such shifts in popular clothing reflect changing gender norms (Campbell 2016). In this case, some men have no shame in wearing a garment once seen as feminine and appropriate only for women. Companies like Lululemon that sell compression tights help create and sustain these views. By expanding their men's line, Lululemon hoped to double their revenue by 2023 (Sagan 2019). Achieving that ambitious goal requires rebranding themselves from a feminine retailer focused on yoga wear to a male-inclusive store with workout wear suitable for "manly men." Seemingly more malleable gender norms make this rebrand a little easier; if people think garments like compression tights are "manly," Lululemon might be able to successfully sell a wide range of workout gear to men.

At the same time, though, not every man is entirely accepting of compression tights (or malleable gender norms). Most men still wear loose basketball shorts over their compression tights (Campbell 2016). So, gender norms and the styles of clothing that are seen as "masculine" and "feminine" do not change overnight. These perceptions shift gradually. As more big-name brands like Lululemon market garments like compression tights as "masculine," more consumers will presumably start seeing them as such.

However, not all gay men have toned, muscular bodies they can accentuate through clothing. This has at least two consequences related to consumerism. First, those who are wealthier and more confident might turn to internationally recognized luxury-brand clothing lines such as Calvin Klein or DKNY (Kates 2002). Luxury clothing, for gay men, often signals power, status, and success (Altaf et al. 2012). Many use it to raise their self-image and compensate for the poor body image they might develop due to the high standards for physical fitness in the gay community. Like heterosexual men seeking "trophy wives," these gay men may try to draw in potential mates by displaying their material wealth—in this case, through designer clothes.

Second, much as we discussed with women in the last chapter, the pressure to achieve this impossibly high standard of physical fitness can become overwhelming. The media alone—never mind friends, gay reference groups, family, and others—play a big role in teaching gay men this standard and showing them how consumption can help achieve it. Men's magazines like *GQ* and *Men's Health* increasingly objectify the male body through eroticized male models (Rohlinger 2002; Blanchin, Chareyron and Levert 2007). And, recognizing our culture's gradual shift towards inclusiveness and support for gay rights, companies commodify sexual liberation for economic profit. Whereas gay men used to be erased from mainstream media, now, they are proudly displayed as advertising tools to help companies sell "forward-thinking" or "liberal" products.

As more sexualized images of men (and women) circulate in the media, human bodies increasingly

Box 11-5
Gendered Stereotyping in Advertisements

For years, advertisements have used stereotypes to convince consumers to buy products. Consumers are used to seeing the sexy model in the cologne commercial, or the macho man in the razor commercial. Today, though, more consumers seem displeased with these stereotypes.

According to a survey conducted by Gandalf Group, less than half of Canadians feel that advertisements are less sexist now than they were in past decades (Krashinsky 2016). In other words, they don't think much has changed. What's more, participants in this survey think advertisements are sexist towards both men and women. They depict men in stereotypical ways: for example, "dumb but hot," or "uncaring workaholic father."

The point here is not to debate whether women or men are portrayed less favourably in the media, or who suffers most from stereotypical representations in advertisements. Rather, stereotypes are harmful for both men *and* women. They perpetuate outdated gender norms, prop up unrealistic expectations, and contribute to body image issues for people of all sexes. We've made some strides towards more diverse, inclusive representations of men and women in the media, but as Gandalf Group's survey showed, Canadians think we still have a long way to go.

become commodified objects. They represent ideals, and, in trying to emulate those ideals, people develop a poor body image, even harbouring hatred for their own bodies. As discussed in the last chapter, people turn to consumption to combat these feelings of low self-esteem, buying goods and services to help change their bodies such as diet pills, gym memberships, and plastic surgery (Gladden 2006).

This is not to say that consumers are brainwashed victims of the media. We all have agency and we can choose to believe in, question, reject, or model our lives (or not) after what we see in the media. Consumers also have pre-existing beliefs that influence the media they choose to consume. For example, one study found that men with more traditional beliefs about a man's role watched more sports and action movies, and read more men's magazines, than other men (Giaccardi et al. 2016). We do not blindly do as the media tells us; often, we seek out media that reinforce existing beliefs.

Makeup is yet another consumer good that gay men (and some straight men) use to enhance their physical appearance (Rinallo 2007). Makeup used to be considered acceptable for women only; it was a tool to enhance and showcase femininity. Today, men buy and wear makeup—especially makeup specifically designed and marketed for them.

Research suggests these new ways of marketing and selling makeup are helping gay men feel more comfortable buying and using it. First, gay men may be especially inclined to buy makeup when it is explicitly designed for and marketed towards men (McNeill and Douglas 2011). Second, some cosmetics companies have created designated counters for men in their brick-and-mortar stores (Shimpi and Sinha, 2010). These designated safe spaces allow men to try and ask questions about the products, without worrying that sales associates or other shoppers will judge them for looking at "women's goods." Third, as more gay men wear makeup in the media, others feel safer following suit. They might feel more comfortable turning to fashion and makeup blogs—even those targeting women—to learn which products to buy and how to apply them (Kates and Belk 2001).

To sum up, gay men's consumption habits reinforce a theme we have discussed throughout this book: namely, that people use consumer goods to signal their belonging in a given social group, and their distance from another group. Gay men use clothing and makeup to show they belong to the gay community, and straight men use clothing and a lack of makeup to show they belong to the straight community.

However, as we saw in this section, the boundaries between these communities are fluid. Metrosexual clothing and grooming choices among straight men throw their heterosexuality into question (Rinallo 2007). And traditionally "manly" presentations among gay men conceal their homosexuality. As mentioned, perhaps we live in a time and in a society with minimal homohysteria. Perhaps (at least some) men no longer feel the need to distinguish between these two groups so explicitly.

Media Messages about Gender

In this and many other chapters, we have asked if media and advertising contribute to social problems. In this chapter about men and masculinity, we ask: do media and advertising, through all the explicit and implicit messages they send about gender, contribute to gender inequality?

As we learned, the idea that "sex sells" persists in some industries and advertising campaigns. Though we have seen some progress and there are now many positive depictions of women in media, some still display women as homemakers or sex objects. We see these representations both in advertisements targeting men as well as those targeting women. We also see the growing sexualization and commodification of men in advertisements. As an agent of socialization, these media depictions can help teach and uphold gender norms.

Media in general as well as marketing for gendered products reflect this confused mix of "old" and "new" views. On the one hand, some media spread harmful myths about women's sexuality. Some video games are consumer goods designed mainly with men in mind. They depict women through the male gaze, as sex objects for men's viewing pleasure. Some lingerie purchases play the same role: men select the pieces they like, pay for them, and adorn their sexual partners with them. By dressing their partners up in the ways that they consider sexy, they objectify the women, turning them into idealized sex objects.

On the other hand, some stores and websites celebrate women's sexuality. They offer a new slant on sex, depicting it as fun, sophisticated, and healthy. Gender-inclusive, sex-positive products and marketing are signs of progress. But it's important to recognize retailers' motives. Their objective is profit. They create products they think will sell and market those products in ways they think will appeal to buyers. Today, some are leaning into the currently trendy notions of sex positivity and women's power. But they only support these values in the specific, limited ways they know will appeal to mainstream consumers. They may try to convince their customers that women's sexual pleasure is nothing to be ashamed of, yet they promise to deliver sex toys and lingerie in "discreet packaging." The implication is that these goods are indeed shameful, and women need to hide them.

Retailers comfortably mix these contradictory views because their goal is to sell things, not promote a feminist agenda. This is not to say that retailers and marketers should take responsibility for making our society embrace women's sexuality. Rather, it's to highlight that they will only take their efforts so far. Retailers will always omit messages and shy away from products that consumers could see as "radical," but could perhaps help socialize those consumers in more sex-positive ways. If they think their audience would respond well to a more sanitized depiction of sex, they will opt for it over depictions that could help normalize women's bodies and sexual pleasure. And retailers will change their current approach altogether if other, less inclusive attitudes become the new norm.

The same goes for corporate celebrations of gay rights. As we saw in this chapter, companies are co-opting human rights movements for their own capitalist gain. We are slowly starting to see greater (albeit stereotypical) representation of gay men in the media. Marketers are reflecting the greater inclusivity they believe their target markets want to see. Similarly, TikTok has become an advertising giant when it comes to reaching youth, with whom the social media platform is hugely popular. As they consume content on TikTok, these youth are increasingly exposed to, and even create their own content in the image of, influencers who perform their masculinity in less stereotypical, more progressive ways. No longer do they see only aggressive, rugged male models in the media; part of youth male socialization today includes observing and possibly imitating such "softboy" influencers.

But what will happen if homohysteria suddenly swells? Or if homophobia intensifies as more men seek to hold on to the dominance they fear losing as we move towards greater equality? Both consumer goods themselves, as well as advertising for those goods, could take a turn back toward the heterosexual hegemonic masculinity we examined in this chapter.

Final Thoughts

In this chapter, as in the last, we saw some evidence for different consumption habits among men and women. We also discussed a good deal of contradictory research that makes it hard to know just how different men and women's consumption behaviours really are. What we *do* know is that any consumption differences between men and women are socially constructed. One reason we know this is because the consumer goods considered masculine and feminine change over time.

When we say the consumption differences between men and women are socially constructed, we mean two things. First, when men and women enact different styles of consumption, or buy different types of goods, those behaviours are influenced by socially constructed gender norms, not by genetic differences between men and women. As we saw in this chapter, in our society, shopping has historically been considered a feminine activity. In their efforts to uphold gender norms, many women shop a lot and many men avoid it. We are socialized to believe in and conform to these norms.

Second, sometimes, these consumption differences seem almost fabricated, or at least, a holdover from decades past. We saw in this chapter that there aren't many conclusive answers when it comes to the specific ways men and women shop; some studies say one thing, while others say the opposite. Despite this absence of hard data, popular belief holds that men and women *are* different types of consumers. We hold on to gendered stereotypes like "women are shopaholics" and "men hate going to the mall." These stereotypes hang around because they help uphold the ideology of gender. By reminding people that men and women are (supposedly) different types of beings, gendered consumption stereotypes support gender inequality.

We also saw in this chapter and the last that men and women rely on consumer goods to help them perform gender roles. Men and women are socialized to uphold different appearance norms and take part in a gendered division of labour. To live up to those expectations, they focus on products and services that enhance their appearance and signal their role as breadwinner, homemaker, mother, or father.

In short, gender performances are important to many people for many reasons. Some want to conform to traditional norms and consumer goods are one way they can do so. Others, however, want to challenge those norms; consumer goods can also help achieve that goal. As we have seen, these goods are one tool people can use to show they belong to one (or several) gender communities, and to distance themselves from others.

In this chapter, we also asked if these consumption patterns are problematic. Do they cause social problems like gender inequality? We saw that certain consumption habits among men and women can help prop up the ideology of gender. Consumer goods enable performances of gender that perpetuate dominant masculinities and traditional gender roles.

For example, when bought by certain consumers in certain contexts, sexy lingerie may objectify women. And household goods like dishwashers make the double shift possible. Meanwhile, expectations for women to do certain kinds of shopping—like grocery shopping—make that double shift even longer. As discussed in earlier chapters, consumption does not necessarily *cause* these social problems. It does not cause female objectification or an unequal division of household labour. Consumption is, however, one variable that helps ensure these problematic features of our consumer society persist.

Gender inequality also means men and women often take part in the economy in different ways. They typically do different types of paid work, for different wages. That gives them different amounts of capital with which to take part in our consumer society. So-called "women's work" is also valued differently than men's work. Women continue to do more domestic labour: especially, more household chores and childcare. This work is devalued and therefore unpaid. Yet it helps preserve our capitalist economy by caring for the current workforce and raising the next generation of capitalist profit-makers.

Discussion Questions

1. Hegemonic masculinity is specific to each individual culture. Compare what it means to be masculine in two different cultures you are familiar with.

2. Sometimes women and men buy different consumer goods to help them perform their gender. Think about your mindset while shopping. Do you think about whether a member of another gender will like what you bought or not? Reflect.

3. Some families fall into traditional family patterns. This means there is a gendered division of labour at home and in the paid workplace. Think of how parenting was divided during your upbringing. When you have a family of your own, will you do the same, or something different?

Quick Quiz

1. What is gender identity?
   a. Your gender as determined by birth
   b. The degree to which an individual identifies with masculine and feminine personality traits
   c. Whether a woman wears makeup or not
   d. Believing that gender does not exist
   e. A way to distinguish one individual from another

2. What is hegemonic (or dominant) masculinity?
   a. When men act subordinate to women
   b. Men who empower women and make them feel respected in the workplace
   c. The sociocultural arrangements through which men preserve their dominance over women
   d. The dominant conception of masculinity in a particular culture
   e. Both (c) and (d)

3. What is one flaw in Adorno and Horkheimer's study of consumerism?
   a. They emphasized positive male stereotypes and negative female stereotypes
   b. They did not collect enough data
   c. They only looked at female consumers
   d. They emphasized that men and women are biologically different
   e. They did not use proper citations

4. Gender roles tend to be stricter in societies that _____.
   a. Have large populations
   b. Have small populations
   c. Have equal pay
   d. Have high rates of childbearing
   e. Have low rates of childbearing

5. What is the double ghetto?

a. Gendered division of labour both at home and in the paid workplace

b. A place of poverty and crime

c. A negative way to describe an individual

d. Two ghetto areas placed next to each other

e. The perpetuation of a ghetto society

The answers to the Quick Quiz are provided at the end of the book.

For Further Reading

The Consumer Society by Jean Baudrilliard

In this classic text, Baudrillard presents a comprehensive overview of the sociology of consumption. In the process he provides a thorough theory of social consumption.

The Culture Industry: Enlightenment as Mass Deception by Theodor Adorno and Max Horkheimer

In *The Culture Industry*, Adorno and Horkheimer explore the notion of a "culture industry." They view the culture industry as a product of late capitalism, where the purpose of every product is to satisfy mass capitalistic consumers.

The Lolita Effect by Gigi Durham

Durham analyzes how media messages promote early maturation and sexualization of pre-adolescent girls. Durham uses examples from pop culture and provides counseling for parents and caregivers on how to raise sexually healthy young women.

Key Terms

Hegemonic (or dominant) masculinity

Homohysteria

Manhood acts

Masculinity

Masculinity theory

Patriarchy

Softboy

Toxic masculinity

Chapter Twelve
The Global South and Symbols of Modernity

Learning Objectives

After reading this chapter, you will be able to:

✓ Link colonialism with consumer relations between the Global North and South.

✓ Explore why industrialization produces varying degrees of modernity and prosperity.

✓ Understand the dynamics of selling consumer products across cultural divides.

✓ See how nations' positions in the global economic order evolve.

In this chapter, we focus on consumer behaviour in, and commerce with, the so-called **Global South**. The Global South consists of low- and middle-income countries in Asia, Africa, Central and South America, the Middle East, and the Caribbean. On the other hand, the **Global North** consists of high-income nations in Europe, North America, Asia, and the southwestern Pacific Ocean. Income aside, various social, political, and cultural features differentiate the Global North and South. Namely, countries in the Global North are (generally speaking) democratic, technologically advanced, politically stable, and dominant in world trade and politics. Countries in the Global South typically are younger democracies, making them less politically stable. As globalization continues, companies in the Global North tend to expand into the Global South. As we will see, when it comes to consumerism and beyond, the Global North typically dominates and even exploits the Global South.

Just as we have discussed poor consumers and rich consumers, men consumers and women consumers, in this chapter we look at consumers in the Global South and ask: How do they spend their time and money? What signals do they send with their buying? Which groups do they strive to show membership in, and which do they aim to distance themselves from?

Defining Our Terms

Globalization is the increase in the volume, scale, and velocity of social (and environmental) interactions across the world. It describes how people, governments, economies, and organizations around the globe interact and integrate.

Globalization is not quite as simple and obvious as it may have seemed a decade ago. In the past four or five years, the tendency of the world's politics, economics, and culture has been toward protectionism, isolationism, and xenophobia, respectively. COVID-19 has only exacerbated counter-globalization (ironically, given it is a global pandemic). These countertrends affect consumer patterns as well as other social and economic patterns. We can't predict what the next five, ten, or twenty years will bring, but it seems unlikely that the world will swing back to the kind of guarded isolationism that characterized much of the world in the mid-twentieth century. Technological and economic forces are just too strong.

When we look specifically at the relationship between consumerism and globalization, we find that globalization involves international trade and the exchange of consumer goods across borders, and encompasses the ways that companies build an international presence. And it has to do with the ways some parts of the world establish economic, political, and cultural dominance over others.

Globalization became a popular topic for sociologists in the 1990s. One of their key insights is that globalization consists of two contradictory processes: **homogenization** and **differentiation**. The former refers to the spread of economic, political, cultural, and consumption patterns across the world, creating a feeling of sameness everywhere you go. People can eat McDonald's hamburgers in Moscow as well as Manchester and pay for them using a Mastercard linked to a bank account in Madras. Differentiation, on the other hand, refers to the regional and national differences that persist. Because our world is highly interconnected, these differences stand out.

Box 12-1

COVID-19 Shines a Light on Global Inequality

The rapid and uncontrolled spread of COVID-19 around the planet illustrates just how interconnected our world is today. Air travel was just one of the most highly scrutinized means by which the virus was carried from country to country. In an effort to "flatten the curve," borders were closed; international businesses and supply chains had to rethink their operations; and long-distance travel ground to a halt.

The virus impacted the Global North and Global South very differently. Both wealthy and poorer nations alike suffered great human, social, and economic losses. But generally the Global North was better equipped to weather the storm. These wealthier countries had comparatively strong economies and health care systems. They were able to quickly mobilize funds to purchase more personal protective equipment for health care workers, build new hospitals or expand existing ones, and turn automobile and other manufacturers into ventilator producers.

Countries in the Global South, on the other hand, did not have such resources to draw on. As Chema Vera, interim executive director of Oxfam International, put it: Madrid has "a doctor for every 250 people. Now consider a country like Zambia—which has one doctor for 10,000 people. In Mali, there are three ventilators per million people. Coronavirus, yes, threatens us all—and it preys through the colossal cracks that divide our world" (World Economic Forum 2020).

We can see that life in the Canadian province of Ontario is different from life in the American state of Alabama. You may be able to visit McDonald's in many places around the world, but the chain's product localization efforts let tourists have a great laugh noting the little ways McDonald's adjusts its offerings depending on the city and country it's operating in (Panwar et al. 2017). Other signs of differentiation include the different experiences you would have trying to find a job or housing in each place. Women, racialized people, and LGBTQ2S+ people would also have different experiences living in each of these places.

There are different views on why and how globalization happens. The **strong globalization thesis** holds that, today, global economic forces are more influential than national political ones. Said differently, global market forces, not states or voters, dictate national economic policymaking. That is because globalization has undermined the ability of democratic governments to solve internal problems—for example, to reduce economic inequality. By contrast, the **weak globalization hypothesis** holds that states are still important and national economic policies, even those aimed at egalitarianism, are still possible.

Today's world differs from a past world system where economies were organized independently, state by state (Amin 2004; Phelps 2017). Defined by geographical place, each national economy was regulated by the state. In contrast, globalization is a reconfigured world system where every national economy relates to the global one. On this international stage, some economies and states are more powerful than others. So, rather than a mosaic of independently operating national economies, our globalized world brings those national economies into relation and competition with one another. The result is a hierarchy of economic and political power.

Some scholars question the strong globalization thesis. They say globalization doesn't happen in the same way in every place around the world, over and over again throughout history; often, this is referred to as the hybridization thesis. In this view, globalization impinges differently on different places; a global economy thrives because it leverages the strengths of unique countries, regions, and cities. Countries do not fend for themselves. Rather, they contribute their strengths— say, natural resources or capital. They expend less effort doing things they're not good at, instead relying on others around the world for these products and services. Under this system, nations benefit most when they have access to privileged resources and assets. They grow prosperous when they can offer what is in demand and highly valued. So, for some nations, globalization is a story of cooperation and progress. For others, it is a story of dependence and exploitation.

Anti-globalization protests like this one in Edinburgh, Scotland, have occurred frequently over the last two decades.

Thus, globalization has sparked many **anti-globalization movements**. Anti-globalization movements are backed by a worldwide network of social protestors, non-governmental organizations, and civil society groups who oppose policies that permit unrestricted trade and investment. Their work is closely related to and, indeed, almost synonymous with the anti-capitalism movement. Unlike traditional political movements, the anti-globalization movement does not have an appointed leader, a headquarters, or a fee-paying membership. It is known as "a movement of movements" because it is constantly evolving and growing to include ever-more organizations people may choose to affiliate with.

Generally, the anti-globalization movement aims to bring to the attention of the leaders and citizens of the Global North what it says are the serious, negative consequences of globalization. These include displacing peasants and Indigenous farmers, the crowding-out of local businesses by transnational corporations, and the "race to the bottom" in labour and environmental standards. In particular, they worry about human rights, citizenship, and accountability (Falk in Dunning 2003; Sorenson 2017). Some Western companies hire workers from nations with lax labour laws. They are legally free to exploit these workers, paying them poorly, or asking them to work long hours in unsafe conditions. In this case, globalization means pursuing profit at the expense of human lives.

One consequence of globalization has been a shift in the world's wealth. To be sure, the world is still very unequal, economically, and inequalities of income and wealth still persist, both within countries and between countries. However, one important shift in the last fifty years has been a movement of jobs, incomes, and wealth from the (high-wage) Global North to the (low-wage) Global South. With dramatic rises in the GDP per capita in China, India, and some other large Global South countries, the world's middle class has expanded dramatically. This expansion of the middle class in formerly poor countries has coincided with, and taken place largely in response to, the hollowing out of the middle class in rich Global North countries. They include the United States, United Kingdom, Canada, and other countries that have lost large numbers of unionized manufacturing jobs to countries in the Global South.

The result of this massive shift has been a noticeable reduction in the inequality of incomes and wealth throughout the world. Today, income inequality in the world is lower than it was in 1970. In that sense, globalization has started to homogenize economic and social conditions around the world. Chief influences have been the expansion of world trade, the global spread of industrial technology, and the growth of major cities around the world. However, continued inequality has continued to motivate vast and increasing numbers of people to migrate from the Global South to the Global North. We will discuss the consequences of this massive immigration in the next chapter.

Globalization has also started to homogenize cultural conditions around the world, in a process often called **Westernization**. There are many definitions of what can be considered a "Western" country. Generally, the West includes Europe, North America, and Australia. Westernization means learning about and even adopting the social practices of these Western nations. It is a process of assimilation. As Western nations extend their economic and political influence around the world, other local identities and cultures may be lost. Some argue that Westernization is the 21st-century form of cultural **imperialism**. By imperialism, we mean the policy of extending a country's influence over less powerful states. Imperialism has always existed. Greece, Rome, Ottoman Turkey, Spain, Britain and many other countries have extended their domains by imperial rule.

The Industrial Revolution introduced a new form of imperialism. Capitalist industrialization would eventually reach its limit in high-income nations. In turn, these nations wanted to expand commercially. Doing so meant taking over other pre-capitalist societies that had yet to industrialize. High-income European nations would therefore compete throughout the world for raw materials, markets, low-wage labour, and high-return investments. They would colonize "primitive" nations, import capitalism and industrialism, and reap the profits.

Some mistake this Westernization process for simple modernization. They see it as a way for low-income nations to join the capitalist market and, eventually, enjoy its rewards. Imperialist globalization may benefit low-income nations. But it also brings negative consequences. Generally, imperial powers assumed they were racially, intellectually, and spiritually superior to the peoples they dominated. The effects of imperialism often included breaking down traditional forms of life, disrupting indigenous civilizations, and imposing new religious beliefs and social values. In response, anti-globalization movements strive to protect local practices, enshrining their differences. These protests may help with the processes of differentiation described above.

Others do not equate the cultural changes ushered in by globalization with Westernization. Instead, they see a new global cultural system. They suggest that globalization is intermingling cultures across the world and in this way, creating a new worldwide culture (Craig and Douglas 2005; Cleveland et al. 2016). At least in some contexts, people see the world as a single place. It is a continuously constructed environment, not one divvied up by geographical borders. From this view, globalization is not only about the constraints of geography on social and cultural arrangements receding. It is also about people becoming *aware* that they are receding.

Many social and cultural developments help support the global cultural system:

- *Cultural interpenetration.* Increased immigration around the world has led to the diffusion of cultural goods. For example, as sizeable immigrant communities emerge, nearby retail shops and restaurants start offering products and services from their home country.
- *De-territorialization.* Modern communications technology helps cultures from around the world influence each other. Cultures are therefore no longer confined to defined geographic locations.
- *Cultural contamination.* Mass media spread products, ideas, and images around the globe, blurring cultural boundaries. The process is helped along by increased consumer travel and more exposure to culturally diverse media.
- *Cultural pluralism.* Consumers can have multiple identities. For example, female Catholic Korean immigrants in California are members of the California culture, the Korean culture, the immigrant culture, and the Catholic culture. And, as we have discussed throughout this book, consumers buy differently to perform these different identities.
- *Hybridization.* Cultural and ethnic mixing create new cultural forms and practices. A good example is intermarriage, where people bring different cultural values together into one family.

Far from least important today are *worldwide information systems and digital communication technologies.* These developments help people see themselves as members of a culture that crosses borders around the world. It will be interesting to see if COVID-19 promotes a one-world sensibility—as seen in many people's rallying cries, "we're in this together"—or will roll back much of globalization, as nations try to fend for themselves and secure crucial goods and services like vaccines and PPE.

Some explain globalization in terms of **neoliberalism**. Broadly, neoliberalism describes political policies that favour reducing the state's role in economics. For example, neoliberal policies typically support strong private property rights, free markets, and free trade. Proponents think these approaches benefit everyone because they give entrepreneurs and businesses more opportunities to generate wealth. Marxist economists like David Harvey (2006; 2018) point out that neoliberalism leaves no room for the welfare state. Pricing for all goods and services, including vital services such as health, is left to the discretion of the market—no matter if inequality results, or people are left without access to those goods and services. As neoliberalism rose in the mid-1970s, the welfare state declined as a political model.

Many of neoliberalism's key trends—especially deregulation, privatization, and the withdrawal of the state—were in play in the early 1980s. The term itself, however, did not gain currency until the early 2000s. Today, it is a catch-all term for any political program or platform that prioritizes financial markets over basic human needs. In this sense, neoliberalism is not only an economic model, but also a social order and a configuration of power.

Box 12-2

The Supply Chain for Personal Protective Equipment (PPE)

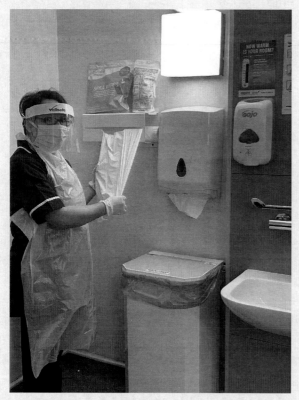

Amidst the COVID-19 pandemic, consumers around the world suddenly became deeply concerned with goods they may previously have taken for granted: health care supplies such as masks, ventilators, and disposable gloves.

As cases surged, health care professionals working in hospitals, long-term care facilities, retirement residences, and other essential institutions were putting their own health at risk by treating and caring for those who had fallen ill. Supplies of personal protective equipment (PPE) quickly dwindled. PPE includes medical gear used as a last line of defense against hazards, such as masks, face shields, goggles, or gloves. Manufacturers around the world struggled to increase their production of such equipment enough to meet the skyrocketing demand. And political leaders desperate to protect their citizens began bidding against each other to secure their own supply. Manufacturers that entertained or even encouraged such bidding were accused of price gouging and "pandemic profiteering" (Connolly 2020).

One such example unfolded in early April 2020. American President Donald Trump ordered supplier 3M, which Canada relied on for its medical masks, to stop exporting to Canada (and Latin America) (Connolly 2020). A shipment of masks was even stopped at the border, prompting panic that Canadian health care workers would exhaust their supply. Eventually, an agreement was reached and the masks were released into Canada, but not before Ontario premier Doug Ford declared in a news conference that he would be urging Canada to reconsider its reliance on the U.S. for such critical supplies.

How People Spend Their Time in the Global South

Anywhere in the world, people spend time to make money. For people who earn hourly wages, time spent at work means an income they can rely on to meet their needs and (if they can work long and hard enough) their wants. Time spent working can also mean a boost to the local economy and your nation's position in the world order.

In this sense, time, like money, is a basic economic resource that can be used to create well-being and wealth (Williams et al. 2015). Sociologists have been studying time use for over a century. In the last 20 years, many have used "time-budget" methods to study the time-use patterns of women in lower-income countries (see Budlender 2007, for a review and critique of such studies). A time budget is a log or diary of the activities a person engaged in over a specified period—typically, over a 24-hour day. Usually, the subjects themselves keep the diaries, entering information continually over the day—often, every 15 minutes—and noting the sequence and duration of each activity.

As mentioned in an earlier chapter, many women around the world today are "time poor" because they are trying to add paid work outside the home to their already full days of housework and childcare. **Time poverty** means a person is short of discretionary time (Kalenkoski and Hamrick 2014). That is, they do not have enough time after engaging their paid and unpaid work, and necessary activities like sleeping, to build their social and human capital.

We see evidence of women's time poverty in several studies across different nations. Here is just a handful of examples:

- One study conducted in urban China found that workers are more likely to be time poor if they are women, married, living with children or older adults, low-paid, and in societies with high rates of overtime work and low minimum wage standards (Qi and Dong 2018).
- Another study found that roughly 18 percent of all individuals across various sub-Saharan African countries are time poor (Blackden and Woden 2006). Women were much more likely to be time poor than men (24.2 percent versus 9.5 percent, respectively), and people living in rural areas were more likely to be time poor than those living in urban areas (18.8 percent versus 15.1 percent, respectively). Married women were also more likely to be time poor than single women.
- A final study revealed that women living in rural areas in Guinea are more likely to be time poor if they live with people with disabilities (Bardasi and Wodon 2006). That suggests that women continue to hold chief caregiving responsibilities in Guinea, especially for aged and infirm relatives.

Time poverty can have negative individual and societal consequences. On the individual level, one study (Urakawa et al. 2020) from Japan found that, just like financial poverty, time poverty can produce harmful health consequences, such as a higher likelihood of illnesses. And, by definition, time-poor people are missing out on opportunities to build their social and human capital. They have diminished family time, leisure time, and time for recreational activities. With limited social capital, time-poor people might struggle to get ahead.

On the broader societal level, time poverty constrains economic development (Blackden and Woden 2006). It can hold countries in the Global South back. For example, in some low-income countries in the Global South, women spend large amounts of time doing work that infrastructure, automation, or consumer goods help with in high-income nations in the Global North. If they lack access to running water or electricity, for example, women in the Global South spend many more hours washing their clothing than women in the Global North who have washing machines and dryers. That means they have less time to put towards paid work outside the home that can help develop their local economies. So, women in the Global North have some supports to help ease their time poverty.

There are two other key differences between time-poor women in the Global North and South. First, in the Global South, children are less burdensome than they are in the Global North. Perhaps less "concerted cultivation" is expected from parents in the Global South. Maybe children in the Global South even help with household chores or contribute to the family income. Second, in the Global South, with some variation, additional adults—even male adults—reduce the time poverty of other adults. This varies from one culture to another, depending on that culture's notions of masculinity and women's domestic responsibilities. In the Global North, as we saw in an earlier chapter, men do not typically help ease women's burden of childcare or housework very much.

In short, time poverty is a pressing problem throughout the world, especially for women. In the Global South, time poverty for women impedes modernization and economic development.

How People Spend Their Money in the Global South

Thanks to international trade, air travel, and the other underpinnings of globalization, geographic distance is no longer a barrier for companies looking to expand.

The challenge is that people in different parts of the world have different histories, wants, needs, values and concerns from the "average" North American. For example, many consumers do not value secularism, individualism, or self-expression as much as North Americans do. So they view the same products differently from North Americans.

Another problem is that, as discussed above, much of the Global South has a history of colonial exploitation by the Global North. Thus, people who live in the Global South may have mixed feelings about goods and services from the Global North. On the one hand, they may view at least some of the goods as glamorous and desirable. On the other hand, they may view the promotion of these goods as a form of intrusion: a new attempt at exploitation and cultural domination. These people may be hostile towards, or at least wary of, American or European imperialism in its new, consumerist guise. So, they may try to prevent or at least moderate the adoption of these new, foreign goods and ideas.

Centuries of cartographic convention lead us to expect to see pictures of the Earth positioned with the North Pole at the top. But in this striking photograph taken by the astronauts of Apollo 17 in 1972, Antarctica appears at the top, with the continent of Africa in the centre of the globe—an unusual perspective in which for once the Global South dominates the globe and the "developed" nations of the Global North are relegated to the periphery or completely invisible.

To sell and market to the Global South, companies must overcome a legacy of **othering**. Othering means seeing a group of people as intrinsically different from oneself. Othering occurs when people in the Global North see people in the Global South as foreign and alien. It is about constructing lower-income countries, cultures, and people as underdeveloped, inferior, irrational, threatening, and exotic. In the past, the idea that the West (or Global North) was superior—politically, intellectually, and morally—was used to justify colonial occupations.

On the other hand, some companies try to better understand the culture, wants, and needs of their target consumers around the world. However, using local culture for marketing can constitute cultural appropriation. **Cultural appropriation** happens when one cultural group takes over the creative or artistic forms, themes, or practices of another group. Generally, it describes Western appropriations of non-Western or non-white forms and often carries connotations of exploitation and dominance.

With this background in mind, let's consider some spending trends in the Global South. As with all of our other market segments, we find that the research on this segment is mixed. You'll also see that studies are most often focused on a particular country, a particular type of consumer good, or a particular segment. It wouldn't be accurate to apply these findings to the Global South as a whole. In this section, we review the studies that are available, identify some broad themes, and note where more research must be conducted.

First, we can confidently say that, compared to past decades, global trade has exploded. It has made many products newly available in low-income countries. These new goods vary in terms of brand, price, and quality. Consumers in the Global South now face an excess of choices. For example, one study of women in Malaysia found that large markets are disorienting and often lead to poor purchasing decisions (Mokhils 2016).

Second, just like consumers in high-income countries, some of those in low-income countries prefer brand name products. They too believe that branded products are higher quality than no-name products.

Third, however, unlike some North American consumers, those in the Global South sometimes prefer non-local brands. The media play a role. Much of the media content viewed in the Global South is from (or heavily influenced by) the West. It makes some people want to mimic Western lifestyles through their purchases (Alden et al. 2000; but see also Cleveland and Bartsch 2018). Also, consumers in these counties may desire foreign goods because they want to be included in the global market. They want to feel part of something big and exciting.

In India especially, people tend to welcome and even prefer foreign goods. India has always been a classist society, thanks to its ancient caste system (Alden et al. 2000). Since imported goods are still relatively rare and expensive in India, only members of the upper class can afford them. In addition, because of India's history of colonialism, many Indian people were socialized to feel that local goods are inferior to western ones. We see similar patterns in other low-income nations. For example, in Kinshasa, the capital of the Democratic Republic of the Congo, buying imported goods is a symbol of high social standing (Trapido 2011).

Fourth, one consumer product that has spread like wildfire around the world is the Internet. More than half of the global population is online. The Internet is thus a key tool for **global**

marketing. As its name suggests, global marketing aims to address the world market as a whole. It integrates promotional activities, rather than differentiating them across countries or other divisions. Some products and marketing initiatives lend themselves to global marketing better than others. For example, a global brand, corporate reputation management, investor communications, corporate social responsibility, environmental and ethical marketing, and global client management may leverage global marketing efforts.

Box 12-3
Shopping Malls: A Relic of the Past in the Global North?

As millions of Canadians make purchases online, brick-and-mortar sales are declining (Fernholz, 2019). However, there are some disadvantages to e-commerce. First, the Canadian economy is negatively affected because of tax revenue lost on international purchases. Additionally, by avoiding taxes, international retailers can lower their prices and edge out Canadian retailers (Westfield 2018). According to *Retail Insider*, earnings for many companies have declined by at least 25 percent due to the shift to e-commerce. This raises the question for many retailers of whether brick-and-mortar operations will remain viable.

There are also logistical challenges to e-commerce in Canada. Given the country's sparse population density, the cost of delivery is expensive. The hybrid purchase model is a growing trend that could help. Consumers order a product online but pick it up at the store. For consumers, the hybrid model combines the convenience of online shopping with the satisfaction of leaving a store with a bag of new goods (Export. gov). For retailers, the hybrid model saves them those costly delivery fees. In some cases, as with clothing purchases, the hybrid model might also reduce returns, since consumers can try the clothes on before taking them home (Westfield 2018).

The Internet also supports international purchases. Goods from around the world can easily be purchased in low-income countries via the Internet. In India, just as in North American countries, online shopping for clothing has become popular, especially among women. About half spent more than 2000 rupees (about $37) a month on online clothing shopping (Chaudhary and Gowda). The majority use their mobile phones to make these purchases.

Fifth, in addition to the changing global market, low-income nations are also seeing changes in their own economies. For example, more people in low-income countries are going to supermarkets rather than small food shops, changing the nature of food shopping completely (Berdegué et al. 2005; Berdegue and Readon 2016). These larger food stores obtain their products from a variety of sources, so they can offer their customers more choices.

Sixth, many low-income countries are experiencing increased gender equality. More women around the world are going to school, working, and sharing household responsibilities more evenly than they have in the past. These changes impact the economy and, in turn, consumer behaviour by giving more people earning and spending power. What's more, a study conducted in Southeast Asia found that education, labour force participation, and household decision-making made women feel more powerful (Phan 2016). Perhaps they are also beginning to feel as though they have more say in household purchases.

In short, people in the Global South have many new opportunities to join the consumer world of the Global North. However, a great many people in the Global South are still without the money they need to fully participate in this new world. In general, the Global South remains much poorer than the Global North. This global wealth inequality is, in part, the result of five centuries of colonialism. It is only in the last few decades that large, prosperous middle classes have emerged in China, India, Brazil, and other countries in the Global South. Leaving aside Brazil and South Africa, such middle classes have yet to emerge in large numbers in Africa and South America. So, our discussion of international consumption would be incomplete without a discussion of international inequality: what caused it, and how it is changing.

The International Dimension: Specialization and Industrialization

Today, unequal information flows, innovation, capital, and brute force all ensure that some nations continue to dominate others. Such domination impacts consumer behaviour among citizens of the dominating and dominated countries.

More specifically, colonialism impacts nations' ability to specialize and trade. We've long known these things are important for economic growth. Adam Smith drew attention to specialization and trade in his 1776 book *The Wealth of Nations*, as did Émile Durkheim (1892) in his classic work *The Division of Labor in Society*.

Specialization is not unique to industrial societies, but it is a hallmark of industrialism. For example, before industrialization, a single skilled artisan, or small group of them, would build an entire vehicle. But in the early 20th century, Henry Ford used labour specialization on assembly lines to mass produce cars for the lowest possible cost. On an assembly line, car production was divided into small, repetitive tasks completed by different workers. Because of this division of labour, Ford dramatically increased productivity, reducing car manufacturing costs from $575 to $99 in less than two years.

There are many benefits of specialization. Industrial factories, with their elaborate division of labour, can produce more accurate copies of a product per hour at a lower cost than a single craftsperson. That lowers the price of goods, and in turn, sales go up, producing profits, prosperity, and wealth.

Bearing that in mind, why don't all nations modernize and profit equally? That is, why do some countries specialize and industrialize later than others? And why does global industrialization produce less modernity and prosperity in some nations than others?

In answering that question, social researchers have considered various arguments.

One unconvincing approach says prejudice stunts modernization and prosperity. People in the Global North often discriminate against products from the Global South. Depending on their country of origin (CO), some brands are in higher demand than others. These views are largely based on stereotypes, however. And those stereotypes help maintain the dominance of the Global North over the Global South. Consider, for example, how consumers may prefer a German-designed car to one of Mexican or Indian origin. But today some German-designed cars are made in Mexico (e.g., Volkswagen) and an Indian company owns Jaguar! As well, cars from Japan were once regarded as tin cans but now are seen as premium products. South Korean cars have made a similar move up the value/prestige ladder.

Martin et al. (2010; 2019) suggest that marketers can change these negative stereotypes by casting the CO in a favourable light. When people see images that remind them of a given CO, the authors hypothesize they automatically think of the stereotypes. But if they see images that counter those stereotypes, they won't be as quick to judge. So, they suggest, advertisers can use counter-stereotypical imagery to make consumers view products more favourably and, in turn, make them more likely to buy.

This conclusion is based on the presumption that stereotypes can be broken or changed. But prejudices against a CO may reflect deep cultural beliefs and continuing historical processes. Consider the bias in some Islamic countries against products from the Global North. These prejudices are rooted in Western colonization and interventionism in the Middle East. In one study, fundamentalists were turning low-income Turkish consumers against Western brands (Izberk-Bilgin 2012). They did this by labeling the brands "infidels."

According to Islamist stereotypes, consumers who buy infidel brands draw attention to themselves and their prestige. This shames less well-off people. Fundamentalists suggest infidel brands thus promote indecency and inequality. Second, these brands are said to violate Islamic traditions and morals because they promote Western customs and lifestyles. The result is a moral disorder (*halal-haram*). Third, fundamentalists say infidel brands are instruments of tyranny (*zulm*) that oppress Muslim identity and victimize Muslim consumers. In this context, importation is not a gateway to prosperity. Conceivably, there can be a market society that is compatible with Islam, but it may need to develop locally, rather than through the global market.

So, there are prejudices against goods from both the Global South and Global North. However, these prejudices alone cannot explain the extent and duration of global inequality—especially the continued subordination of the Global South. If we were to believe this theory, we would blame poorer countries for their own poverty. The implication is that, by refusing to buy from the Global North, poorer countries doom themselves to continued have-not status. We do not think this is true. Instead, Immanuel Wallerstein proposes a more convincing approach.

Trading in the World Order

Wallerstein (1974; for a commentary, see Coccia 2018), in a classic work on the world system of inequality, says global inequality began a long time ago. Poorer nations are therefore not responsible for their poverty. Instead, the problem lies in what Wallerstein calls the "world system." Over hundreds of years, he says, capitalists built an exploitative international division of labour and unequal trade relations. It was this growth of the capitalist world economy that created deep global inequalities.

According to Wallerstein, the present capitalist world economy began in the late 15th century, around the time of Christopher Columbus's voyage to the New World. In the wake of the Black Death in the mid-14th century and the subsequent decline of European agricultural production, a growing merchant class sought wealth through long-distance trade. During this era, members of the capitalist world waged wars against less powerful countries. As they won those wars, they gradually absorbed smaller countries and competing economies.

Through military conquest and colonization, European states imposed an unequal international division of labour. These European states shared capitalist labour with outlying regions—but unevenly, and with different shares in the profits. Wallerstein labels the four different categories of nations that emerged as core, semi-periphery, periphery, and external countries. We will discuss each of these in turn.

Immanuel Wallerstein (1930–2019) was an American sociologist and economic historian.

From 1500 to 1700, northwestern Europe (including England, France, and Holland) developed into the first, most stable core region. These European states had strong central governments, vast (by the standards of the time) bureaucracies, and huge mercenary armies. These institutions helped local capitalists gain control over international commerce and extract profits from their trade.

Core states promoted (and still support) capital build-up in the world economy. They had (and still have) the political, economic, and military power necessary to enforce different rates of exchange between the core and the periphery. As well, different types of states had (and still have) different patterns of consumption. These play an essential part in creating an unequal balance of power. This power allows core states to dump dangerous goods in peripheral nations and pay lower prices for raw materials than would be possible in a free market. It also allows them to exploit the periphery for cheap labour and pollute the periphery's environment. Often, they erect trade barriers and quotas that favour the most powerful nations (for example, the USMCA, the revised version of the North American Free Trade Agreement).

Nowhere have these patterns been clearer than in Central and South America. The American government carved out a sphere of influence in that region. Citing the so-called Monroe Doctrine, they claimed to have a right and need to do so. The Monroe Doctrine, first stated in 1823, claimed to free the newly independent colonies of Latin America from European intervention. In practice, however, it justified almost continuous intrusion on the domestic affairs of Central and South American countries by the American armed forces, espionage agencies (e.g., the CIA), and industrial interests.

Naturally, U.S. multinationals were glad to have government assistance in their efforts to own land and control policymaking in these countries. The United Fruit Company, for example, welcomed the U.S. government's assistance, which ensured cheap land and low-cost labour in the countries where United Fruit harvested bananas for sale in the United States. As well, the Mafia welcomed American efforts to overthrow Fidel Castro in Cuba.

Thanks to this unequal balance of power, peripheral nations lack strong central governments or are controlled by other states and economically are typically relegated to exporting raw—not manufactured—materials to core nations. Core nations rely on coercive labour practices (at one extreme, slavery) to do this most efficiently. With help from their armies, banks, and large corporations, core regions plunder peripheral areas for their cheap labour, raw materials, and agricultural production. Through unequal trade relations, core nations can seize much of the surplus capital produced by periphery nations.

Anne McClintock's book *Imperial Leather* connects this imperial colonization of racialized people to the domestic colonization of women (on this, see also Chrisman 2018). McClintock argues that home life in England was "colonized." Each home was "ruled" by its patriarch and women did unpaid work under his reign. These domestic arrangements reaffirmed the reproductive, economic, and political measures used to colonize countries overseas by making it seem as though such dominance and subordination were natural and inevitable. Both foreign and domestic colonization projects assumed some people are superior and others inferior. They also assumed some labour deserved to be paid and other types did not. And, both types of colonization subordinated people against their will. All of this was justified using pseudo-scientific notions of "natural" inequality: it was claimed that men and women were naturally unequal, as were white and non-white people.

Racist (and sexist) ideologies helped to justify the imperialism that benefited Great Britain, France, and other European countries economically. The colonial exchange between the core and the periphery resulted in the formation of a new class of powerful European landlords who became aristocratic farmers in the colonies. These local landlords subjugated local indigenous populations and imported African slaves so they could extract raw materials to export to Europe. As noted above, they relied on the strength of the central core region to enforce local control and grow wealthy by servicing that core.

Semi-peripheral nations, now as then, lie between the two extremes of core and periphery. These areas are either core regions in decline or peripheral countries trying to improve their position in the world economic order. Some declining cores that became semi-peripheries during the early period (1500–1700) include Portugal, Spain, Italy, southern Germany, and southern France. Some think Canada today is semi-peripheral, trying to climb into the core.

Wallerstein identified a few key milestones in the changing world order. First, rulers increasingly used state power to collect taxes, borrow money, and expand the state bureaucracy. Second, core countries established an absolutist state rule. The idea of "absolutism" freed the monarch from older feudal laws. It also removed aristocratic competitors for the crown. Increasingly, the national military expanded to support the monarchy and protect the state from invasions (and civil unrest). To fuel the growth of local capitalist groups, many core states also expelled minorities. These expulsions eliminated ethnic competition in the merchant class.

A third step was the rise of a dominant merchant class. After 1500, a small group of elite merchants made enormous profits through long-distance trade with the Americas and the East. They used some of their new wealth and power to strengthen their hold over European agriculture and industry. This dominant merchant class provided the capital necessary for industrializing European core states. Finally, after 1750, industrialism dramatically boosted capitalist profits.

In the 17th and 18th centuries, European states searched for new exploitable markets. Independent Latin American countries became peripheral zones in the world economy. So did previously isolated areas on the American continent. In the 19th century, even Asia and Africa entered

Jasper, Alberta, in 1942. As Canada's population grew with the influx of European settlers, a new market was created for manufactured goods from so-called "core" nations like Britain and the United States. In turn, Canada, arguably a semi-peripheral nation in the world system, exported agricultural goods and natural resources to those core countries, while at the same time developing its own industries, many of them closely linked to agriculture and resource extraction.

the order as new peripheral zones. Exploiting these new peripheral zones gave birth to new core nations such as the U.S. and Germany. Also in the 19th century, core regions shifted their interests from agriculture *and* industry to purely industry. Then, in the 20th century, core areas even encouraged the rise of certain industries in peripheral and semi-peripheral zones. They wanted to sell machine tools and more advanced industrial products to these regions.

Wallerstein's theory explains why modernization had different effects in different parts of the world. The inequalities between core, peripheral, and semi-peripheral nations—first established 500 years ago—remain to this day, although in different forms. As the capitalist economy expanded, it altered the politics and working conditions of the places it penetrated. Rather than providing prosperity for all, capitalism increased economic and social inequalities between different parts of the world.

Nation-states have a reduced role in combating internal inequality today. States do help regulate and control activities within their borders. For example, countries can promote certain kinds of innovation, through taxation and redistributing national revenues. They can also regulate working conditions and uphold a social welfare system. However, much of this work is influenced by economic interests. Today, the main actors in global capitalism are multinational corporations that influence state governments through bribes and election spending. Policies on taxation and working conditions are therefore not necessarily reflective of the majority's wants. Instead, they often reflect the interests of wealthy, powerful capitalists who can afford to sway politicians.

As strong as Wallerstein's theory is, it's missing at least one thing: he ignores the role of ideas in our globalizing world. Ideas—especially ideas about consumption—spread like wildfire across the globe today, thanks to travel and mass communications. For example, claims-makers can use ideas to "manufacture consent" for foreign influence. That is, groups with money can use various forms of media to persuade people to tacitly consent to their actions. They can even influence people to think their dependence on the core nation is good or natural.

We see such manipulation among wealthy people and their racialized, underpaid, and often exploited "help." Some employers remind their cleaning ladies and nannies that they "enjoy" tidying up, or that their culture raises them to be good caregivers. Others say they are doing their employees a "favour" by paying them the lowest wages possible, because those are still higher than the wages they could earn back home. By spreading these ideas, wealthy people try to justify their domination of others. They sustain the postcolonial agenda by ensuring the labour of people from the periphery remains devalued and underpaid.

Further, capitalism diffuses culture outward from the Global North. It spreads advertising and propaganda that promote the Western way of life. In particular, as capitalism reaches new nations, it brings materialist consumer values with it. Citizens of these nations develop a "need" for luxury material goods. As a result, Western materialist values are penetrating new regions across the world.

In early research on this topic, Ger and Belk (1996; see also Belk 2017, 2019) explored the rise of materialism among students in 12 countries. Results varied widely from country to country, reflecting their dramatic differences in consumerism.

In Romania, Ukraine, Germany, and Turkey, people were moving away from traditional, negative views of consuming and towards materialism. The U.S., New Zealand, Thailand, and Israel saw similar, though less dramatic, changes. Meanwhile, India and other nations in Europe (except reunified Germany) remained traditional. Sweden showed the lowest culture of materialism and maintained its tradition of social democracy and income equality.

In countries where materialism was on the rise, people showed a growing desire for consumer products that would increase their prestige. Prosperity began to grow, as did jealousy and insecurity. Not everyone benefited equally from that new prosperity. Some felt relative deprivation. Even though life was essentially the same or perhaps even better, they felt it was getting worse because those around them were suddenly doing better. Rapid social change also increases social comparisons of several kinds. People started comparing the present with the past and comparing themselves with wealthier people and consumers in wealthier nations.

The results of this study suggest that materialism is not unique to the West. It is also not directly related to wealth, contrary to prior studies of consumer culture. Many people in low-income nations are *more* materialistic than consumers in the West. This study found that countries experiencing rapid and dramatic social and economic growth experience the highest levels of materialism. Part of the problem is that these changes cause normative confusion. In their new world, people don't know what to value anymore. They lose their sense of what's normal and expected. Amid this confusion, globalization swoops in with Western values and lifestyles. Materialism takes hold as the new norm.

Despite these two key omissions—an inattentiveness to the spread of ideas and the spread of Western culture—Wallerstein's theory is convincing. For him, global inequality is the result of a capitalist world economy. By consolidating their political, economic, and military power, European nations exploited international labour and trade. At present, core nations continue to amass surplus capital at the expense of peripheral countries, which are denied their share in the profits.

Although they do not benefit equally from capitalism, members of both core and periphery states occasionally do their fair share of consuming, as Sidney Mintz has shown in his classic work, *Sweetness and Power: The Place of Sugar in Modern History* (1986; but see also Ventura 2017; Halloran 2016). Like Wallerstein, Mintz views Europe as the centre of consumption and its colonies the centre of production. But, Mintz proposes, we overlook some of the forces at play when we see peripheral countries *exclusively* as centres of production, and core countries *exclusively* as centres of consumption. Instead, he proposes there is a "triangle of trade."

When it comes to sugar in the 17th century, the triangle looked like this: British goods were sold to African colonies, making the empire a centre of production, and Africa one of consumption. African slaves were then imported to the American colonies—they were "false commodities," traded as though they were consumer products. That trade relationship made the African colonies a centre of production, and the American ones, consumption. But then, American sugar was sold to European centres by British merchants. Each country was both a producer and a consumer.

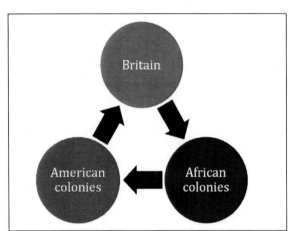

That does not mean, however, that each country enjoyed equal power or profit in this trade triangle. Notice that the American and African colonies are on the bottom of the triangle, propping up Britain. That's because the home country benefited the most from this relationship. It had colonized the regions that would come to be known as the "sugar islands." In the 17th century, the British created a plantation system to grow sugar cane in Jamaica and Barbados. They realized they could exclusively supply sugar produced on these plantations to the rest of Europe, for enormous profit.

First, they had to build a global market for sugar. Previously, sugar had been a rare commodity consumed by the upper classes to mark their social status. But after the establishment of the plantation system and the subsequent mass production of sugar, prices came down, making sugar available for just about everyone. European sugar companies started familiarizing people who had never even heard of sugar with its taste and uses.

Mintz says this process made sugar consumption a national custom and household staple in Britain and throughout much of the British Empire. With a new mass market ready to be dominated, the British poured labour and capital into sugar production in their colonies. As production increased, they expanded the market further, continuing to drive up international demand for their product. For Mintz, sugar is thus a colonial product that helped spread capitalism around the world.

Newer studies following in Mintz's footsteps include *Sugar and Civilization: American Empire and the Cultural Politics of Sweetness* by April Merleaux and Erika Rappoport's *A Thirst for Empire: How Tea Shaped the Modern World*.

China Catches Up to the Core

During the last century, some peripheral or "external" nations industrialized and started catching up to the core nations. These nations included ones that had formerly been cut off from the capitalist world economy—hence outside of or "external" to it. Two key examples are China and Russia. Between 1500 and 1900, neither participated heavily in the growing global capitalist system. They focused on internal commerce more than trade with other countries.

But China has recently become a global economic power and full-fledged participant in the world economy. Once considered a Western outlier, East Asia is now deeply materialistic. Overspending, overconsumption, and Western-style luxury buying is becoming increasingly common. More people are buying goods on credit, running up household debt, and watching their savings decline (or failing to amass any to begin with).

At first, this seems surprising, given that traditional Chinese culture values thrift, restraint, and good manners—all of which deter materialism and consumerism. These traditional values are explicitly taught in Chinese elementary schools. Children learn that frugality is good, while waste is "sinful" (Chan 2006; see also Gbadamosi 2019). What's more, consumer choice was highly restricted under Maoism. So, what happened?

A few key forces pushed China into the capitalist world economy. First came industrialization. As China grew wealthier, money took on new symbolic value (Durvasula and Lyonski 2010). As in the United States, money came to mean power, especially for Chinese young people. More people wanted to accumulate material goods and assets so they could amass social status and influence.

At the same time, cultural values shifted. Traditional collectivism persisted while individualism grew (Sun et al. 2016). In the past, there were five traditional Chinese ideologies that influenced consumer behaviour: Confucianism, Taoism, *Guanxi*, collectivism, and *Mianzi*. People who follow the first two—Confucianism and Taoism—may be less materialistic. That's because Confucianism focuses on how we treat other people (Lua 2009). It values "filial piety," which is respect for parents and ancestors. Taoism emphasizes the natural flow of things, unity, and balance. These two philosophies prioritize families. People who believe in them tend to spend in ways they think will benefit their families. For example, a Confucian or Taoist may spend extra money on their children's education (Lua 2009).

On the other hand, *Guanxi,* collectivism, and *Mianzi* contribute more directly to materialism. *Guanxi* culture focuses on maintaining relationships, which you can do by purchasing gifts for others. Collectivism tells people to put the needs of the group above their own. It also leads towards a "group mentality" and a need to "fit in."

Today, that can push people towards materialism. As we have seen in earlier chapters, those who want to fit in often compare themselves to others (Chan and Prendergast 2008; Prendergast et al. 2019). They see the products their friends, neighbours, or colleagues have, and reason they need them too, if they want to be part of the group (Lua 2009). One study found that social Chinese youth are more materialistic than their less-social peers (Chan et al. 2006). For some of these youth, material possessions themselves are associated with friendship (Chan 2005, 2019; Rustagi and Shrum 2017). So, for collectivists, spending is a means to social acceptance.

Beijing, the capital of the People's Republic of China, has increased in population more than tenfold over the past seven decades, but even more remarkable has been the economic growth of the city and of China as a whole. The city's total economic output in 2016 was no less than 90 times what it had been in 1978.

Before we examine the fifth and final traditional Chinese value, it's important to note the rise of a non-traditional one: individualism. Common in the West, it's the belief that people should prioritize themselves over their communities—the exact opposite of collectivism. In cultures with a strong sense of individualism, materialism also tends to be strong (Sun et al. 2016). That's because individualistic people come to think they can express themselves—their individuality—through consumption. For example, they can buy clothes they think reflect their personalities, or tell others something about their identity.

Research suggests individualism is growing in China. One study, for example, found that Chinese university students are more individualistic than people in their parents' generation (Wang and Xu 2009; Qi and Wang 2017). That helps to explain part of their materialism, since they are increasingly interested in self-expressive spending. Interestingly, though, these same university students also maintained collectivist attitudes. So, Chinese youth are also still interested in spending that helps them fit in. Again, traditional collectivism and the new individualism seem to have combined to make the perfect storm. Both push people to consume for different reasons (Sun et al. 2016).

The fifth and final traditional Chinese value, *Mianzi*, amplifies the effect. Mianzi emphasizes reputation. Believers want to purchase products that elevate people's perception of them (Lua 2009). Often, this means buying luxury goods that display their high social status (Zhang and He 2011). For example, in China, women who wear designer clothes are understood to be in faithful relationships (Griskevicius and Wang 2013). These expensive clothes are therefore not just a way of showing off their money. Rather, they help women signal their reputation to other women, letting them know they are loyal and committed.

Mianzi has also helped build up a market of counterfeited luxury goods (Wilcox et al. 2008). When buying something to boost your reputation, brand name means everything (Audrin et al. 2017). It's better to show off your new purse with a (fake) Chanel logo on it than to buy a generic purse. Mianzi has therefore led many Chinese consumers to value brand names over quality. In turn, counterfeiting has become common (Wan et al. 2009; Priporas et al. 2020). Pirated CDs are another example. *Mianzi* leads people to think the reputational boost of having the latest music outweighs the moral implications of stealing (Wan et al. 2009). Others see pirated and counterfeit products as trial runs. They may want to invest in the real thing to authentically boost their reputation but are wary of the cost. Using the fake version lets them see what the product is like before they invest significantly (Gentry et al. 2001; Bhatia 2018).

Finally, *Mianzi* has also inspired worldwide shopping among Chinese consumers. Luxury goods are needed to build your reputation, but not all such goods are available at home. Some people therefore take their search abroad. In fact, some people choose a vacation destination based on the availability of luxury goods there (Rovai 2016). When abroad, people from China tend to visit famous retailers to purchase luxury goods and brands that will boost their status back home. Retailers have taken notice. Around the world, many try to weave aspects of Chinese culture into their offerings to attract these eager vacationing consumers.

In sum, changing cultural values were among the factors that led to the spread of materialism. Another was the end of the Maoist era. Under Deng Xiaoping and his successors, China deliberately followed a new policy of opening up the economy and pursuing economic growth while maintaining the rule of the communist party. While many aspects of Western consumerism are now evident in China, they have been adapted to Chinese culture (and to the regime's political agenda). If anything, the encouragement of greater consumption by the Chinese themselves reflects the government's realization that the basis of China's economic expansion needs to be broadened beyond an over-reliance on exports to other countries.

Following Mao's death, Western influences infiltrated China more easily. Western movies, advertisements, and goods started circulating and influencing Chinese culture. These Western products and mass communications sent different messages from what children were learning in school (Chan 2006). Their curriculum may have stressed frugality. But as we saw in our discussion of the media, advertisements try to sell the pleasure of consumption itself. People started to get the impression that they could pursue happiness by buying things.

Western media and goods also shaped Chinese consumption in specific markets. For example, they have shaped new appearance norms and notions of beauty. As you'll recall from an earlier chapter, these norms encourage people to spend throughout their lives on makeup, clothes, weight-loss products and services, and even cosmetic surgery. These Western aspects of consumer culture also taught people to rethink their gender identities. They had been used to wearing sexless uniforms during the Maoist period. Now they had more choice. They could buy dresses like the ones they saw in American movies, and hats like the ones they saw in American ads. Clothing consumption became a new way for people to express themselves.

These economic, cultural, and social changes have led to more intense and widespread materialism and consumption. In fact, one study shows Chinese youth may even surpass American youth on these fronts. Podoshen, Li, and Zhang (2011; see also Xiao and Tessema 2019) asked university students in both countries several questions about consumption. They used a materialism scale that included items like, "I admire people who own expensive cars, homes, and clothes" and "I'd be happier if I could afford to buy more things." Their results showed that Chinese young adults are significantly more materialistic than American young adults.

This newfound materialism may threaten traditional aspects of Chinese culture. For example, children used to put money aside so they could eventually care for their elders. However, Podoshen, Li, and Zhang (2009) say some young Chinese people may be indulging in short-term consumption that risks their future economic stability, including the ability to support aging parents.

China furnishes just one example of these processes. As new countries (and classes) enter the world economy, they quickly adopt Western materialistic values. But that doesn't mean every society becomes a replica of (say) the United States. Different products are advertised differently in different places, to appeal to audiences who consume for different reasons. Consider the depiction of beauty in different cultures.

Frith et al. (2005; see also El Jurdi and Smith 2018) looked at advertisements in women's fashion and beauty magazines in Singapore, Taiwan, and the U.S. A significant fraction of Asian advertisements displayed cosmetics and facial beauty products, while clothing dominated U.S. advertisements. These findings suggest that Americans base beauty more on a woman's body, while in Singapore and Taiwan, people base beauty more on her face.

Across cultures, most of these advertisements used Caucasian models. Caucasian female models comprised 91 percent of women in the U.S. ads, 65 percent in Singaporean ads, and 47 percent in Taiwanese ads. Some say this is a form of cultural imperialism. Foreign advertisers try to push Western notions of beauty on Asian consumers by using white models to spread appearance norms.

The "types" of beauty displayed in advertisements vary across the three countries. Models made up to look sexy were more common in U.S. advertisements (32 percent) than in advertisements in Singapore (19 percent) and Taiwan (22 percent). On the other hand, Taiwanese ads more commonly showed models who looked cute, like the "girl next door" (27 percent). But the most popular type in all three countries was "classic."

Advertisers cast models of different races to play these roles. Caucasian models were more likely to be in the sexy ads (27 percent) than Chinese models (11 percent). But Chinese models were more likely to play the "girl next door" (25 percent) than Caucasians (16 percent). However, both Caucasian and Chinese models filled the "classic" role in roughly equal numbers. That suggests certain aspects of beauty are seen as universal, shared by Eastern and Western cultures.

Final Thoughts

In this chapter, we focused, as we have in previous chapters, on poverty and income inequality. However, unlike other chapters, however, we considered these issues on a global scale.

On one hand, we considered neoliberal views that imply every nation has opportunities to become prosperous, should they choose to seize them. Social thinkers who followed Adam Smith and Emile Durkheim proposed that societies evolve and prosper through specialization and industrialization. At the centre of this are so-called "market forces." By this reckoning, all societies modernize in more or less the same ways. As a result, all nations and cultures eventually develop a single, uniform set of beliefs and activities, helped by a common set of technologies.

Such theorists see the free market as a key to modernization, industrialization, and prosperity. This view fits well with the neoliberal ideology. Neoliberalism calls for a freeing up of global markets, mainly by reducing the right of states to intervene in the economy. Champions of neoliberalism assume that such free markets provide the greatest good for the largest number of people. When people (supposedly) have the maximum freedom to chase their individual goals, they (seemingly) also create maximum prosperity for everyone.

The pro-business governments of American president Ronald Reagan (1981 to 1989) and British prime minister Margaret Thatcher (1979 to 1990) started this trend. They deregulated markets about 40 years ago. For Canada, neoliberalism gained ground after the negotiation of the first free trade agreement between Canada and the U.S. in 1987. This initiative was supposed to help goods and capital more easily flow both ways between the countries. In fact, free trade opened Canada to U.S. capital far more effectively than it opened American markets to Canadian manufacturers. (For recent discussions of the trade relations between Canada, the U.S., and Mexico, see Bakas et al. 2019; Marki and Russo 2019; and Villareal and Fergusson 2017.)

In theory, the world system is meant to help everyone, in every country, share in the profits of a global capitalist economy. It is supposed to help the poorest, peripheral countries industrialize, prosper, and "catch up" to the core nations that have been benefiting from capitalism for years. But in practice, the capitalist world system perpetuates the status quo. Nations that have long been powerful continue to enjoy massive profits, often at the expense of disempowered ones.

Some continue to view capitalist development, industrialization, and material goods as signs of progress. In the sense that they can lift people's standards of living, they are. However, the related developments of inequality, exploitation, and materialism suggest we are not *only* making progress. We are also continuing a 500-year-long history of colonial exploitation and imperialism, as Wallerstein pointed out. And we are introducing new problems related to materialism to more people around the world. So, as much as we must spread the benefits of capitalism and consumerism across the globe, we must also consider the issues that can come along with them.

Discussion Questions

1. In what ways does globalization foster growth in various countries? Think about the role of your own country in the context of a globalized world.
2. How has Westernization historically impacted the way nations developed? How has it created cultural, economic, and political differences among nations?
3. What are factors that inhibit market penetration and global marketing? What are some companies that have been affected by these factors, and how?
4. How has the internet influenced globalization? Does it affect certain countries more so than others? If so, how?

Quick Quiz

1. Which of the following is NOT one of the five ways globalization causes intermingling between cultures in the global marketplace?
a. Deterritorialization
b. Socioeconomic integration
c. Cultural pluralism
d. Cultural interpenetration
e. Hybridization

2. _____ describes political policies that favour reducing the state's role in economics.
a. Classical liberalism
b. Globalization
c. Economic freedom
d. Neoliberalism
e. Conservatism

3. What is an example of a marketing initiative that can leverage global marketing?
a. Product placement in a story
b. Environmental and ethical marketing
c. Small non-targeted social media campaign
d. Not using a business plan
e. Worker-owned businesses

4. What is the term for seeing a group of people as intrinsically different from oneself?
a. Discrimination
b. Racism
c. Labelling
d. Othering
e. Localizing

5. Which of the following is attributed to Immanuel Wallerstein?
a. World systems theory
b. Market regulation theory
c. Downsizing theory
d. Company/employee satisfaction theory
e. Baby boomer modelling system

The answers to the Quick Quiz are provided at the end of the book.

For Further Reading

Imperial Leather by Anne McClintock
This book looks at British imperialism, analyzing the socioeconomic climate of Britain. It also offers a commentary on the dangers of colonialism.

The Wealth of Nations by Adam Smith
The Wealth of Nations is a classic text on what builds wealth and prosperity in nations. The book is a fundamental piece of writing within economic studies. Smith emphasizes the development of the free market.

The Economic Consequences of the Peace by John Maynard Keynes
In *The Economic Consequences of the Peace*, Keynes argues the Treaty of Versailles needed a more far reaching plan for peace for the sake of healing the world economy.

Key Terms

Antiglobalization
Cultural appropriation
Global culture
Global marketing
Globalization
Imperialism
Market access
Market penetration
Neoliberalism
Orientalism

Chapter Thirteen
Immigrants and Symbols of Acculturation

Learning Objectives

After reading this chapter, you will be able to:

✓ Evaluate immigrants' consumption as a reflection of their acculturation.

✓ Recognize the different agents of consumer socialization for immigrants.

✓ Consider how institutionally complete ethnic enclaves reflect and influence immigrant consumer preferences and habits.

✓ Note the complexities of international marketing in a globalized world.

In this chapter, we focus on two main aspects of immigrants' consumer behaviour. First, we consider how members of different ethnic communities use consumption to show they belong to those communities. Conversely, we examine how they use consumerism to show they are *not* members of other communities, including, sometimes, their new host culture.

It should be said, at the outset, that an immigrant's buying is a decisive indication of whether and how hard they are trying to acculturate. Acculturation for immigrants is, largely, if not entirely, about buying "tickets": items that display their determination to be accepted as average, normal members of the host society. Not all immigrants have enough money to do this, at least in the beginning. Not all immigrants know what to buy to fit in with the host society, at least in the beginning. And as we will see, some immigrants actively resist doing this. They are sometimes even more resistant to adopting Western fashions and styles than people who have remained at home, where the immigrants originated. But given a chance and an opportunity, the most characteristic feature of immigrants and their families is that they do buy the tickets they need to belong, and sometimes even overdo the effort.

These concerns are heightened today for many immigrants to Canada, especially Asian immigrants, because of COVID-19. The virus's spread worsened existing racism; Asian students faced bullying in schools, and ethnic restaurants suffered losses even before the lockdown in spring 2020 because patrons began associating their food with COVID-19. It is too soon to tell what long-term impact the pandemic will have on discrimination, racial and ethnic identity, and the ways consumers use goods to signal or hide those identities. For example, will Chinese brand-name clothing be desirable or reviled? Will tourism to Asia decline?

What we *do* know is that acculturation is a key part of any immigrant's experience, whether one strives to acculturate, actively resists it, or stumbles into it. However, acculturation is neither simple nor linear; rather, it depends on several key variables. And increased acculturation does not guarantee increasingly mainstream consumption. As we will see, different immigrants consume in different ways to show their acculturation (or lack thereof).

Defining Our Terms

Immigrants are people who come to live in a country other than their place of birth. Global migrations produce **ethnic groups** and **ethnicity**. **Ethnic groups** are groups of people living outside of their ancestral home (Harff 2018; Platt and Parsons 2018). Usually, members share a common culture, heritage, background, and language. **Ethnicity** is often defined as a shared sense of belonging to an ethnic group. The term also refers to the features of an ethnic group that distinguish it from other ethnic groups (Tonkin et al. 2016; Bauböck and Rundell 2018; Fishman 2017).

For millennia, global migration—especially migration by people escaping oppression—has been referred to as a **diaspora**, from the Greek word meaning a scattering or dispersion. Today, we use the term to mean the voluntary or involuntary scattering of people from a geographic homeland who then create a distinctive community and identity based on that history. **Diasporic** (or **transnational**) **networks** emerge in turn. These consist of people in the homeland and immigrants in other countries (Griffin-El and Olabisi 2019).

This chapter is about the ways immigrants show their membership in communities—and there are many different communities immigrants can feel a part of. Every migrant group can be viewed simultaneously as:

1. An **enclave**: a group within a host society;

2. A **national group** with a distant homeland; and

3. A **transnational community** with branches around the world.

Thus, immigrants today are participants in three connected social structures. We discuss each in turn.

First, an ethnic enclave is a geographic region where people of a given ethnicity concentrate to preserve their culture and lifestyles. They live, work, shop, and go to school there. (Ojo and Shizha 2018; Danzer et al. 2018).

Second, national groups may preserve ties with their homeland. Kinship and other social networks help people and resources flow between the origin (old home) and destination (new home) (Minahan 2016; Joshanloo et al. 2016). One practical connection is remittances: money sent as payment or as a gift. Remittances are one way members of the diaspora preserve financial and other ties with their homelands. Through investments, donations, support for political parties, financial contributions to social causes, or paying taxes, members of the diaspora can preserve a wide variety of different financial contacts with their homelands.

Box 13-1
Remittances

Many immigrants leave family members behind when they come to Canada. Through remittances, these immigrants send money back home to their loved ones. The money is intended to help with different expenses, depending on the socioeconomic conditions of the home country. For example, among those sending money to lower-income countries, 73 percent sent the funds to cover their family's living expenses (Statistics Canada 2019). Of those sending money to higher-income countries, only 40 percent of the money sent was to pay for living expenses.

Remittances are important for the economies of low-income countries. The World Bank reports that total remittances to low- and middle-income countries are almost three times larger than foreign aid to these countries (Todd 2014). Remittances therefore make up a big portion of these countries' GDP. The Philippines is the number one beneficiary of remittances from Canada. In 2017, Canadians sent $1.2 billion back to the Philippines (Dunham 2019).

Remittances themselves have become consumer services: immigrants must pay companies or banks to send them. Fintech firms such as TransferWise offer lower fees (Reynolds 2019). Legacy money-transfer companies such as Western Union charge more but their services are more widely available. (A Western Union office in Angeles City in the Philippines is shown above.) Bank transfers are the most reliable but have the steepest rates.

Third, diasporas everywhere create global linkages within ethnic groups and transnational groupings based on ancestry (De Lazzari 2019; Morgan 2016; Arjmand 2018). Political events in the home country often have effects on the migrants and their politics in the new homeland. Often, these distant events unify the immigrants and strengthen their ethnic identity and loyalty to the original home country. They may politicize the group and mobilize support for local (ethnic) institutions. They may also change relationships between the immigrant group and the host society, or between two immigrant groups.

When immigrants arrive in a new country—and for years after that—they may face a new culture. In the broadest terms, they **assimilate**. Assimilation is the process through which immigrants join the social mix, by adopting the language, values, beliefs, and behaviours of the dominant group (Crul 2016; Kivisto 2017; Jiménez 2018). As a result, immigrants may lose their original culture, religion, and ethnic identity. Integration, on the other hand, describes bringing those original aspects of an immigrant's culture into their new society. They may adopt aspects of their new culture but keep aspects of their original culture. For example, they may come to speak the dominant language, but keep their original religion.

In Canada, ethnic enclaves and diasporic networks easily fit into the multicultural framework. **Multiculturalism** is a belief that all citizens of all ethnicities are equal. If they wish, they should be encouraged to preserve their cultural heritage, ethnic identities, and ways of life (Prato 2016; Kymlicka 2020; Meer 2016). Multiculturalism is an official policy in Canada. First adopted in 1971 by the federal government, the policy is intended to promote tolerance and acceptance by encouraging "racial and ethnic harmony and cross-cultural understanding" (Citizenship and Immigration Canada 2008c). However, perhaps unintentionally, it also preserves ethnic segregation.

Using Consumerism as Proof of or Resistance to Acculturation

Acculturation, as studied by sociologists, is about learning how to declare cultural distinctiveness, defy anti-immigrant or anti-group sentiment, and shape positive public views of the group. However, acculturation is also about learning how to take part fruitfully in the daily life of the host culture. Immigrants typically adopt one of four acculturation strategies (or some combination of them) when they arrive in a new country (Berry 2005). First, some keep a positive orientation towards their own group. They wish to preserve their heritage, culture, and identity. Second, others do not uphold that positive orientation. Third, some adopt a positive orientation toward the host society and wish to take part in this larger society. Fourth, others do not (Berry 1980; for a recent application, see Xing et al. 2020; Seginer and Mahajma 2018).

Immigrants who follow the **integration** strategy prefer contact and participation in the larger society. They do so even at the expense of their participation in their own cultural heritage. On the other hand, immigrants who follow the **marginalization** strategy lessen their contact with and participation in *both* the larger society and their own heritage cultural community. This isolates them from other people in both groups.

First-generation immigrants may be less inclined towards the integration strategy. Sometimes, they continue to identify with their traditional culture. In turn, they seek products with

Box 13-2

Assimilation and Non-Immigrants: Indigenous Peoples

Though not immigrants, Canada's indigenous peoples have nonetheless been the target of vigorous efforts to assimilate them into settler society. The Indian Act (1876) forbade Indigenous people from expressing their culture and identity—a form of cultural genocide (Henderson 2006). To enforce their assimilation, the Act made residential schools compulsory. The first residential school, the Mohawk Institute, was estab-

lished in what is now Brantford, Ontario (Miller 2012). Run by Christian churches, the schools' goal was to assimilate Indigenous youth into Euro-Canadian society. This meant taking them from their families, wiping them of what they knew, and creating new identities for them. On arrival, the administration cut the youths' hair, washed their bodies, and stripped them of their traditional clothes. Their days were heavily regimented by harsh staff (Miller 2012).

Many Indigenous youth suffered malnutrition, health problems, and mental difficulties. Disease was prevalent due to overcrowding and lack of care. Many students were abused mentally, physically, and sexually. Instead of preparing youth for civilization, they were left without a sense of identity and emotional wounds. The last residential school officially closed in 1997 (*Canadian Geographic* 2018). Later, in 2006, litigation was settled with the Indian Residential Schools Settlement Agreement. The settlement brought healing and compensation, as well as the Truth and Reconciliation Commission. In 2008, Stephen Harper formally apologized to students of the residential school system (Miller 2012).

symbolic ethnic meanings. Some feel nostalgic for their country of origin and material goods help remind them of home (Mehta and Belk 1991; for an update, see Buschgens et al, 2018). One study compared the favourite possessions of Indians living in India with those of Indians who immigrated to the United States. They found that immigrants gain a sense of security from possessions brought with them from India. They come to treasure Indian artifacts, movies, and songs more than Indians living in India. For some, these possessions bring back memories of their youth. Others keep gifts and photographs that remind them of the people they left behind. Others still rely on religious objects to perform rituals that give them a sense of comforting familiarity and continuity.

However, many second- and third-generation immigrants launch themselves fully into cultural integration, at least when they are buying things (King 2008). Those who want to blend in quickly will often adopt a pattern of buying that helps others recognize them as (aspiring) members of the host society. They make similar purchases, in similar ways, to the mainstream consumer population. For example, they will buy homes in culturally mixed neighbourhoods and wear fashions that are common in the host society.

Immigrants following the integration strategy usually experience less stress and adjust more successfully to the host country than immigrants following a marginalization strategy. Immigrants who take intermediate (assimilation and separation) approaches experience intermediate levels of stress.

This is an important discovery. For a long time, researchers only considered one side of acculturation. They assumed that non-dominant groups would either move from a "traditional" way of living to one resembling that of the dominant society—or they wouldn't. This assimilationist or "melting pot" view of acculturation has now been replaced by the multidimensional view presented above, which suggests there are many possible choices, not just two.

This change in thinking occurred for several reasons. First, observation shows that full assimilation is not the only form of acculturation. It has not always taken place and it is rarely the goal of acculturating groups. We know that because cultural groups throughout the world have not disappeared after immigration. Cultural homogeneity has not always resulted from intercultural contact. On the contrary, resistance to assimilation (that is, separation) and the formation of new cultures after contact are common. Second, it is now clear that acculturation is two-dimensional. It means choosing what to do about one's old group *and* what to do about the new group.

Acculturation is also two-dimensional in another sense (Jun et al. 1993; Kizgin et al. 2018). It involves cultural identification, which has to do with attitude change. It also involves behavioural changes that are only slightly related.

Cultural identification, for example, is influenced by an immigrant's preference for residency. If they like and prefer to live in, say, Canada, they may identify culturally as Canadian. Level of acculturation, on the other hand, has more to do with where a person grew up in their home culture. It has to do with whether they grew up in an urban or rural region, for example. And it also has to do with the direct contact they have with their new culture.

Since it is multi-dimensional, the rate and degree of acculturation varies depending on how it is measured. For example, one study examined the acculturation rate of Hispanic-American immigrants (Jun et al. 1994; for an update, see Suarez-Orozco et al. 2018). When researchers used language to measure assimilation, Hispanic-American immigrants appeared to assimilate rapidly over time, since they began using English more. On the other hand, when cultural self-identification was used to measure acculturation, the results were not as strong or as linear.

This has practical implications for consumer behaviour and marketing. Marketers play an essential role in cultural integration (Penaloza and Gilly 1999; Bundy 2017). They can alter immigrants' consumption patterns, encouraging them to leave behind the consumer habits of their cultures of origin and adopt instead the practices of their new culture. If they have immigrated to North America, that new culture is materialistic—perhaps even more so than the culture they left behind.

On the other hand, many retailers and marketers cater to immigrants' wants and needs. In their endless search for profit, retailers and marketers try to tap into immigrants' wish to preserve their original culture, or fit in with their new culture, or balance the two. Other retailers and marketers *are* immigrants and they cater to clientele within their ethnic community. These businesses and marketers help preserve consumer patterns from their culture of origin (Penaloza 1993; see also Sevim and Hall 2016).

Immigrants can also impact businesses' and marketers' success (Penaloza and Gilly 1999; see also Bundy 2017). To gain their business, marketers must "acculturate" to immigrants' needs. They must learn, translate, and adjust. Gaining immigrants as customers can, in turn, mean changes to local economies and markets. Marketers' ability to adjust to immigrants' wants and needs can affect their own business, and, through their impact on the local economy, non-immigrant consumers as well.

There is no rigorous way of detecting how much immigrants impact businesses and marketers, or vice versa. All researchers can reliably see is that these impacts occur. For example, one study asked if Asian-Indian consumers' interest in ethnic apparel varied based on their acculturation (Rajagopalan and Heitmeier 2005; Pires and Stanton 2019). Unsurprisingly, they found that those with low levels of acculturation were more likely to buy Indian ethnic clothing. As they gradually acculturated to western culture, they became less likely to buy Indian ethnic clothing. However, once they became fully acculturated, they became (once again) more likely to buy Indian ethnic clothing.

At first blush, these results seem counterintuitive. Shouldn't immigrants consume in increasingly mainstream ways the more acculturated they become? The researchers suggest consumption is not a reflection of acculturation alone. It also reflects how immigrants would like to be seen by the mainstream population. For example, an immigrant may not be acculturated at all. However, they may want to prove to others that they fit in and have successfully adjusted to life in their new home. Conspicuously consuming mainstream goods can help them send those signals.

In this particular study, Asian-Indians who are new to the U.S. and gradually acculturating tried to visually show they identified with their new western culture. For them, that meant shying away from Indian ethnic apparel. However, as these consumers became more comfortable in their new environment, they wanted to re-connect with their original culture. They were more acculturated at this point, and felt confident enough to start buying Indian ethnic apparel again.

Other studies confirm acculturation is not always a linear process. For example, one examined consumption among Quebeckers who identified to varying degrees as English and French (Kim et al. 1990; see also El Banna et al. 2018). They found evidence of consumption differences between strongly francophone and strongly anglophone respondents. However, there was no evidence that, across all products, consumers preferred a francophone product more strongly if they felt strongly French-Canadian.

Similar findings emerged from a study of Australian-Chinese consumers (Quester and Chong 2001; see also Weber et al. 2016). This one focused on three types of products: toothpaste, stereos, and cars. The researchers wanted to see how acculturation influenced Australian-Chinese consumers' information search, product evaluation, buying behavior, and post-buying evaluation. As with the Quebec study, they found that acculturation affected consumer behaviour in minor ways. But they found little evidence that effect was linear or mapped onto a steady progression of acculturation.

A final study looked at brand preferences among Indian consumers in the UK (Vijaygopal 2012). Assimilated immigrants were mainly familiar with brands popular in the UK. Integrated people, who were strongly attached to both Indian and UK culture, were familiar with both ethnic and host brands. Separated people, who mainly preserved their traditional culture, preferred mainly ethnic brands to host brands.

Consumer Purchases Signal Acculturation

Again, these nuances arise in part because immigrants may try to signal their acculturation (or their resistance to such acculturation). They also arise because the mainstream societies into which immigrants acculturate are culturally diverse (Horencyk 1997; Slot et al. 2018). Many societies—especially multicultural ones like those we have in Canada—mix many cultures. There are various aspects of a given culture immigrants may acculturate to, or not. Immigrants may also choose to acculturate more in some spheres—say, in adopting particular cultural values—and less in others—say, changing their religion.

For example, Lee and Um (1992; see also Min 2017) surveyed Korean immigrants and native-born Americans. The two groups evaluated the quality of certain products differently: cars, stereos, laundry detergent, and coffee. In part, this was because of their different cultural values. The native-born Americans were much more individualistic than the Korean immigrants, who valued family more. When evaluating products, Korean immigrants therefore took their families into consideration. This was true even for those participants who were considered acculturated, and who had become more individualistic. So, even when these immigrants partially adopted one American value, they still consumed differently.

The CBC sitcom *Kim's Convenience*, based on the stage play of the same name, portrays the lives of a Korean-Canadian family. Much of the show's humour is grounded in the differing attitudes of the parents, both born in Korea, and their Canadian-born children, now young adults.

Similarly, even the most acculturated immigrants may view certain products in ways native-born people never would. For example, one study pointed out that many Koreans are hostile towards Japanese people. In turn, they refuse to buy Japanese goods and services. These attitudes and buying decisions even held true, the researchers found, among Koreans who had immigrated to the U.S. and acculturated (Song and Shin 2004; 2019). Those who had lived in the U.S. for over 20 years were less likely to buy a Japanese car than recent immigrants. They had had the most time to acculturate, but they had also lived in Korea when anti-Japanese sentiment was still strong. More recent immigrants grew up in Korea hearing about an improved Korean-Japanese relationship. Thus, aspects of the culture of origin continue to influence attitudes and consumer behaviour for decades after immigration and acculturation.

Complicating matters further are family members. As discussed in an earlier chapter, children often sway their parents' consumer behaviour. Their influence is especially interesting when it comes to immigrant families because members of different generations have often acculturated to different degrees. For example, one study looked at Chinese immigrant families with teenage children (Laroche et al. 2007; see also Kizgin et al. 2020). Parents who had acculturated were often more swayed by their children's consumption wishes. Those with strong ethnic identities, on the other hand, were less influenced by their children.

Various factors influence the ways and degrees to which immigrants assimilate. For their own reasons, they may want to keep strong ties with their cultural origins. But they are also perceptive of and responsive to the attitudes of people in their new host culture (Kizgin et al. 2018). Some native residents also feel threatened by immigrants (Rohmann et al. 2006; Leudicke 2015). They think immigrants can and should assimilate. Other native residents do not think this way. Yet, immigrants may *sense* (accurately or inaccurately) that native residents want them to assimilate, or do not want them in "their" country at all.

So, for example, immigrants to Israel from the former Soviet Union may think native Israelis expect them to assimilate. They may feel these expectations are much stronger than their own willingness to assimilate. In turn, some become anxious about signaling their acculturation. They want to ensure native Israelis see that they are adjusting to fit in. Other immigrants become hostile. They may not want to acculturate and perceived pressure from native Israelis to do so can make them feel unwelcome. It doesn't matter whether native Israelis do, in fact, expect immigrants to assimilate or not. This expectation pushes immigrants to acculturate or resist acculturation.

Other immigrants eventually rethink their culture of origin. Once they start to acculturate, they may start believing their new and old cultures are similar. Again, it doesn't matter whether the two cultures are, in fact, similar or not. Immigrants may come to think norms and behaviours from their new culture were also present in their culture of origin. This makes acculturation and loyalty to the host society much easier.

It's harder to see these likenesses when the host culture excludes or has negative attitudes towards immigrants (Luedicke 2011). Again, the host culture may exclude and dislike immigrants, or the immigrants may think so (Florack et al. 2003; Eberl et al. 2018). Either way, these circumstances often push immigrants towards separation or marginalization (Piontkowski et al. 2000; Van Oudenhoven et al. 2016). Immigrants who separate think of themselves as typical members of their ethnic group or country of origin. They take pride in their membership in these groups, and want to set themselves apart from mainstream groups and signal their ethnicity. They may do so by buying the ethnic clothing mentioned above or patronizing ethnic stores. In contrast, people who become marginalized feel indifferent towards their ethnic group or country of origin. They make no special efforts to reinforce or display their membership. In turn, they stay on the fringes of both their original and new cultures.

Together, these processes of acculturation, native residents' attitudes towards immigrants, immigrants' views of those attitudes, and immigrants' wish to fit in or stand out, all influence consumption. They help shape views of what counts as "normal" consumer behaviour. They also define which groups can access opportunities for consumer behaviour. For example, if immigrants are seen as threats, they may have difficulty securing a job and, in turn, consuming (Kizgin et al. 2018). They may also be excluded from consumption sites like nightclubs if a bouncer decides they don't meet the "dress code." They may be kept out of community and recreation facilities if staff decide they aren't following unspoken social rules. And they may be excluded from restaurants and coffee shops if native residents are inclined to stare, whisper, or make blatant comments.

These practices and attitudes vary from one country to the next. They also vary within countries. For example, large cities are generally more welcoming of immigrants than rural communities. These variations help explain at least three kinds of immigrant behaviour. First, they help explain why immigrants comfortably integrate in some settings, while in other settings, they set up institutionally complete enclaves at a safe distance from the surrounding society. We discuss institutional completeness more below.

Second, such variations also help explain different spending and saving patterns among different immigrant groups (Fontes 2011). Consider retirement savings. European and Asian immigrants who have lived in the U.S. for longer periods of time and are more acculturated are more likely to have retirement savings. In fact, they are just as likely to have these savings as native-born Americans. Latin American immigrants, on the other hand, are less likely than native-born Americans to have retirement savings.

That's because European immigrants are typically older, so they have worked longer and had more time to save than their younger counterparts. But, to repeat, they have also typically lived in the U.S. longer than Latin American immigrants. That means they have had more time to acculturate. Indeed, European immigrants are more likely to speak English at home, suggesting greater acculturation. And they are more likely to own a home. Of course, owning a home is costly and therefore out of reach for many immigrants who face barriers to employment. But home ownership can also be a sign that an immigrant feels "settled" in their new culture—as though they are literally at "home."

Finally, unlike other immigrants, European immigrants less often have strong ethnic identities. They acculturate more smoothly, and face less resistance from native-born people, because they do not cling to their cultures of origin.

Another study suggests acculturation may be even more important than employment opportunities when it comes to savings. It measured acculturation by asking how much time participants had spent in the U.S. and whether they planned to remain temporarily or permanently. It also asked whether they spoke Spanish at home and what their citizenship status was (Perry 2008; Weisfeld-Spolter et al. 2018). The results showed that more acculturated Hispanic consumers were more likely to have a bank account, regardless of income or education. Opening a bank account wasn't only about having a good job that produced enough income to warrant doing so. Many Hispanic immigrants felt that setting up a U.S. bank account tied them to their new country: it was a sign of settling in.

These two examples remind us that immigrants are not a homogenous group. Most countries do not exclude, hate, or feel threatened by *all* immigrants. More often, they welcome or at least tolerate some, and reject others. In turn, some immigrants come to feel at home in their new countries. They buy things that reflect those feelings of ease and settlement, including purchasing a home and saving for retirement. Others feel excluded. Sometimes, they *are* excluded from the employment market altogether. That makes it impossible for them to buy homes or build up savings, whether they feel at home in their new countries or not.

Third and finally, variations in acculturation and attitudes towards immigrants help explain participation in popular religious holidays. Christmas is perhaps the best example. One study of Muslims living in Britain points out that immigrants experience tension around Christmastime (Khan 2018). They ask themselves whether they should take part in Christmas celebrations—purchasing gifts, decorations, greeting cards, and the other consumer trappings of the holiday—because they feel part of British society, or whether they should we avoid them because of the conflict with their Islamic faith.

Box 13-3
Adapting to Religious Practices in the Host Society

As new Canadians, Harmeet Singh and Manpreet Kaur were surprised to see so many people out buying Christmas decor and decorations. Christmas is celebrated in India, but religious ceremonies such as Diwali are far more significant (Bowden 2019). During their first Christmas in Canada, they exchanged gifts with their colleagues and friends. They learned that people put a personal touch on their gift giving by adding cards. They decided to adopt this practice during their second Christmas. Kaur also enjoys baking, and Christmas allowed her to get out her mixing bowls. In all, the couple enjoyed the energy around the holiday, which was similar to the excitement back home for Diwali, and settled into their own celebrations fairly easily.

Puneeta Varma hasn't transitioned so smoothly. When she came to Canada, she recognized that holidays are celebrated differently here. They were much shorter and less extravagant than what she was used to back home. Wondering how she could maintain her own traditions within this new culture, Varma eventually compromised. She altered the scheduling of the holidays to suit her work schedule and the school schedule of her two daughters, shifting most of the celebrating to the weekend (Abedi 2019). Although efficient, it was not ideal. Holidays like Diwali include prayers on a specific day, so the meaning is not exactly the same by shifting the practices to the weekend (Abedi 2019). Varma worries if the holidays she celebrated as a child are not practiced with diligence, they will not remain a significant part of her daughters' lives.

Even those moving within Canada struggle to adapt to different holiday practices in their own country. Jennifer Fox grew up in Thornhill, Ontario. With the large Jewish population around her, Jennifer's Jewish practices received accommodation. She could take days off for Jewish holidays or ask for extensions to celebrate Shabbat (Abedi 2019). Things changed when Fox moved to Halifax. With a smaller Jewish community, professors at her university were not willing to make room for her Jewish practices, and she had to make compromises to fit in with the broader culture.

These questions typify what Khan terms an "acculturation trade-off." Immigrants are constantly asked to weigh the costs and benefits of acculturating. Situations like Christmas celebrations force them to make such a trade-off. On the one hand, they might integrate themselves within their new cultures and, in turn, feel like they are more "at home," though that may come at the cost of piety and loyalty to their faith. On the other hand, they might stay strictly loyal to their faith, making them feel good about their commitment to their culture of origin. But that may come at the cost of inclusion and integration in their new culture.

Khan's study revealed that many opt for a degree of compromise. For example, all the Muslim participants rejected Christmas Day as being the birthday of Jesus Christ or Prophet Isa. More religiously conservative participants recognized and reflected on the Prophet Isa on Christmas Day. Liberally religious participants celebrated Christmas Day in a way aligned with British culture. However, they justified those celebrations by pointing to Islamic beliefs in the importance of family.

The public nature of certain Christmas celebrations also has an effect. In the privacy of their own homes, Muslims can choose whether they do or do not want to celebrate Christmas, and how, with few (if any) social consequences. But outside of their homes, some would gain social approval by, for example, attending celebrations like their office Christmas party. These visible ways of celebrating can put pressure on Muslims to participate.

Consumer Socialization among Immigrants

As you will recall from earlier chapters, agents of socialization play a key role in teaching people what to buy. At least three different agents influence immigrants as consumers (Kamano 1999; Flynn et al. 2013). First, they are influenced by the culture in which they grew up. Second, immigrants are influenced by the culture into which they have arrived. From their moment of arrival, media and other sources direct them to live and buy in new ways. Third, they are influenced by income. Often, immigrants earn less than native-born Canadians with similar levels of education and experience. We discuss each of these three influences in turn.

First, childhood socialization experiences vary from one ethnic group to another. Consider, as just one example, the differences in consumer behaviour between Caucasian-Canadian families and Chinese-Canadian families (Kim et al. 2009; Yang et al. 2014). Chinese-Canadian parents are more alert to social comparison than Caucasian-Canadian parents, and their children know it. Chinese-Canadian children also exercise more influence over family buying than Caucasian-Canadian children. And Chinese-Canadian children tend to make more practical, less impulsive consumer decisions than Caucasian children. This suggests that people in family- and community-oriented cultures (like the Chinese) learn to control their impulsive tendencies better than people raised in individualistic cultures like Canada. But this is subject to change. The longer Chinese Canadian children live in Canada, the more impulsive they may become.

Second, school also plays a part in immigrant children's cultural integration. They learn from their parents, the mass media, and their peers how "people like them" are "supposed" to behave, dress, eat, and otherwise consume. That is, they learn what is expected of immigrants in general

(Bondy et al. 2019; Lash 2018; Peguero et al. 2017). Some of these children receive additional cultural training in minority private or parochial schools (Brinkerhoff 2016; Lung-Amam and Gade 2019). Most of these parochial schools are organized around a religious denomination: Catholic, Jewish, and Evangelical Protestant, for example. However, the students who attend these schools typically belong to only a few ethnic communities. Thus, the schools provide training in ethnicity as well as religion. That is, these schools teach aspects of the immigrants' home culture as well as aspects of the new culture in which they currently live.

But attendance at these schools depends on the third socialization factor: family income. Tuition fees may apply, and students must also be able to afford to live nearby. That makes people's culture a commodity, something immigrant parents are willing to pay to pass along to the next generation.

Finally, all three variables are influenced by racialization. Since 1980, more and more immigrants to Canada have been racialized people from Asia, the Caribbean, and South and Central America. Racial prejudice—both real and imagined—may affect their consumption patterns. As mentioned, some immigrants respond to discrimination by building institutionally complete ethnic enclaves.

Ethnic Enclaves and Institutional Completeness

Clearly, settling in a new country has its challenges. These include exclusion from mainstream society and, as immigrants acculturate, the risk of losing their traditional language, culture, and values. Some immigrants, fearing these challenges, settle in institutionally complete ethnic enclaves.

Canadian sociologist Raymond Breton (1964; for a recent application, see Light and Isralowitz 2019) defined institutional completeness as "a set of institutions (for example, stores, schools, churches, and newspapers) that help people preserve their traditional culture, social connections, language, and religious beliefs." Institutional completeness allows immigrant consumers to continue buying goods and services they may have bought in their countries of origin (Sandeep 2015). It is also interesting because, to have institutional completeness, you need local immigrant entrepreneurship.

Researchers (Liu 2014; Schuch and Wang 2015; Zhou and Cho 2010; Sandeep 2015) point out that such entrepreneurship has many benefits, including:
- Supporting local economic interests and community cohesion;
- Meeting the unmet market needs of ethnic communities;
- Creating job opportunities, especially for immigrants;
- Supporting individual economic success and upward mobility for immigrants;
- Revitalizing and fueling the commercial development of abandoned communities; and
- Preserving immigrants' cultures of origin.

Given the opportunity, many immigrants prefer to shop in local stores that offer ethnic goods and services. First-generation Chinese-Canadian consumers, for instance, usually prefer to shop at Chinese-run businesses and stores and consume ethnic goods (Wang 2004; Wang and Hernandez 2018). In turn, they teach their children to do the same. Parents with a strong sense of cultural identification influence their child's consumption habits towards ethnic goods and services. Similarly, peers of the same cultural and ethnic background have a direct effect on a person's consumption of ethnic goods and services. Such consumer behaviour signals belonging in the Chinese-Canadian community.

Consider ethnic food consumption as an example. One study (Adenkunle et al. 2013) examined the buying patterns of Chinese immigrants in the Greater Toronto Area (GTA). In this population, women do most of the shopping for their households. They spend most of their total monthly income on ethnic vegetables—native Chinese vegetables such as bok choy, Chinese greens, Chinese broccoli, and lettuce, for example. Collectively, Chinese immigrant women in the GTA spend an average of $21 million on these vegetables each year. These vegetables are expensive, but women buy them to preserve and display their ethnic identity. Of course, they likely also purchase them because they prefer their taste and anticipate that they and their families will enjoy eating them. But as well as these practical buying considerations, seeking out and buying ethnic vegetables is one way that Chinese immigrant women showcase their ethnic identities.

Some immigrants choose to settle in institutionally complete ethnic enclaves in their new homelands. Such enclaves often remain cultural loci even after the immigrant population has become more widely distributed in the broader community. For instance, so-called "Little Italies" are found in many large North American cities. Pictured above are celebrations in a Little Italy located in the Bronx, New York.

One reason we know this is that, for many ethnic groups, *where* you buy goods is just as important as the goods themselves. Ethnic vegetables have become increasingly available at North American grocery store chains. However, many Chinese immigrants continue to buy vegetables from Chinese-owned groceries stores in ethnic enclaves like Toronto's Chinatown. Again, this conscious choice helps Chinese immigrants preserve their cultural identity. It also supports Chinese business owners, helping them to continue the community's institutional completeness.

As another example, many Haitian mothers buy and serve their children beef, yams, beans, and rice, as these are staples in Haitian culture (Laura 2000; Deitz 2018). These dishes are often shared with friends and family members during celebratory events and gatherings. By continuing to eat Haitian foods after emigrating, Haitian immigrants preserve secure connections to their culture, and build cultural identities in their children.

Similarly, in one study carried out on the American east coast, Asian immigrants spent considerable amounts of money on ethnic produce each month (Govindasamy et al. 2007, 2017). Respondents also included Hispanic and Mexican immigrants. A majority (59 percent or more) in each subgroup were "more willing" to buy ethnic produce from ethnic outlets. Most of them lived within 10 or 20 miles of an ethnic grocery store, suggesting a degree of ethnic segregation. Their priorities for selecting produce were freshness, quality, store availability, and price. Besides these considerations, however, half or more of respondents from each subgroup were willing to a premium for ethnic produce, compared to American substitutes.

For many, such ethnic food choices are signals of identity and group membership. Holidays, family celebrations, and special occasions offer opportunities to pass on cultural values through the foods that are served. People are especially likely to use food to preserve their heritage if they have extended family living nearby. When ethnic foods are different from mainstream foods, people are often motivated to protect their traditions. They do so by buying specific ingredients, serving traditional treats, or cooking treasured family recipes. And these practices are nothing new. They have likely accompanied all immigrants and all immigration throughout history.

For example, Hamlett et al. (2008) examined some of the food shopping strategies adopted by early immigrants on their arrival in Britain between 1947 and 1975. (See Noble and Ang, 2018 for a comparable Australian study.) They found that South Asian immigrants to Britain in the 1950s and 1960s, like all other consumers, both changed and preserved cultural traditions through food consumption and shopping. The stores and supplies available constrained their opportunities for cultural expression through food shopping and use. Nevertheless, households organized themselves to provide the necessary labour to carry out South Asian cooking practices, and ingredients were sought in shops of other ethnic groups. Religion played a role here too. Muslim consumers often avoided butcher's shops in their search for halal meat.

During the 1960s, hubs of South Asian shops emerged across Britain, making it far easier for South Asian groups to get cultural foodstuffs. However, South Asians living outside these districts developed strategies to get any culturally specific goods they needed. Dual shopping was a common practice. This involved buying essential products at local stores and traveling further afield for South Asian spices and special ingredients.

The gradual arrival of the supermarket changed the British retail landscape. Early British supermarkets had little to offer South Asian consumers in specialty ethnic foods. When large supermarkets finally began to offer ethnic goods, some South Asian consumers remained reluctant to use them. They stayed loyal to the retail outlets they'd relied on for years.

Class, age, gender, and economic status also shaped the food practices of the South Asian population in Britain. If women worked outside the home, they were more likely to invest in convenience foods, increasingly available in supermarkets and self-service stores. In households that prized labour and thrift above convenience, convenience foods and freezable products reportedly had little appeal. In some homes, religious and cultural preference, plus the practical difficulties of shopping, meant that men were responsible for buying the food. Older women or those with language difficulties often found shopping a daunting experience and preferred to rely on other members of their family to shop for food.

Today as in the past, commitment to ethnic tradition is often generational. Many immigrant parents feel a responsibility to preserve their cultural traditions through food. Sometimes their children may prefer Westernized food. By buying a Happy Meal at McDonald's, for example, immigrant teens get a chance to socialize with their peers and share experiences with them. Cultural integration often means developing twin loyalties. For example, consider second-generation Korean migrants in Australia (Sutton-Brady and Jung 2010; see also Seger-Guttman et al. 2017). First-generation Korean immigrants to Australia often retain a strong preference for traditional Korean foods and practices, but children of these immigrants tend to move smoothly between their old and new cultures. They may buy Korean videos but enjoy watching English-language cooking shows popular among native-born Australians. They share Korean dinners with their parents and then eat Australian foods at breakfast and lunch with their friends. These Australian-Koreans quickly move back and forth between two different consumer cultures.

The term ethnic enclave still carries negative connotations. In the past, people used the phrase almost synonymously with "ghetto" to describe marginalized neighbourhoods for poor,

Vancouver's Chinatown is the largest such enclave in Canada. The neighbourhood has been designated a national historic site by the Canadian government.

unassimilated immigrants. Today, however, many incoming ethnic groups arrive with higher-than-average education and economic resources. They are not pushed into ethnic enclaves on the fringes. Rather, they have the *means* to create their own ethnic economy and freely choose to do so (Zhou and Lin 2005; Zhou et al. 2019).

Consider the Chinatowns in Toronto and Vancouver today. Broadly speaking, these two modern Chinese enclaves share certain characteristics with historic Chinatowns. For example, like old Chinatowns, these new ones serve the needs of immigrants that remain unmet by mainstream society. They also provide opportunities for jobs and entrepreneurship. But unlike old Chinatowns, they are better connected to the outside world in economic, social, and political terms. And, with middle- and upper-income residents and shoppers, they can no longer be stigmatized as ghettos.

To fight these stereotypes, some immigrants turn to conspicuous consumption. Many high-income immigrants use non-ethnic luxury brands from Europe or North America to signal their status and prestige (Kwak and Sojka 2010; Byun et al. 2020). Younger immigrants report an even greater inclination to buy high-priced prestige brands than older immigrants. This buying inclination bears little connection to time spent in the host country, education, and ethnic origin.

Young Korean immigrants in particular may be especially likely to follow these patterns. Many retain the collectivist values of their culture of origin. These values push them to follow the crowd, buy in to ever-changing trends, and play the game of jostling for social status (Choi et al. 2005; Lee 2010). What's more, young Korean immigrants are less thrifty and more materialistic than their ancestors (Sung 2017).

This combination of values from their original and new cultures leads young Korean immigrants to buy luxury goods as status markers (Hwang et al. 2013). They value luxury clothing in particular because it's a sign of prestige (Jin, Sternquist, and Koh 2003; Kim and Jin 2020). The high prices of fashionable goods do not seem to deter consumption; in fact, they may increase it because recognizable expensive brands send the strongest signals.

Of course, not all Korean immigrants can afford to buy luxury brands. Lower-income earners often buy forgeries instead (Wilcox et al. 2009; Bian et al. 2016). Korea has one of the largest counterfeit markets in the world, alongside China and Taiwan (Riston 2007; Rojek 2017). The collectivist drive to fit in and the materialist yearning for social status lead to purchases of counterfeit goods. Owning a fake version of a desirable product is considered better than not owning the product at all (Lee and Workman 2011; Wilcox, Kim, and Sen 2009).

Materialism and the need to fit in are also strong among Chinese immigrant youth. One study found that many Chinese youth prefer to buy products that are popular and heavily marketed in their ethnic community. For example, after famous Chinese Olympian athlete Liu Xiang endorsed Nike shoes and Coke, Nike and Coke sales spiked among Chinese youth (Chan 2007, 2019).

These values are so strong that they trump ethical considerations. They also trump interest in buying from local ethnic shops. So, while many ethnic enclaves are thriving economically and home to successful immigrant entrepreneurs, others continue to struggle. In the U.S., immigrant entrepreneurs focus on low-profit retail and sales (Bates and Robb 2014). Only the least desirable market niches are accessible to them. Indeed, businesses located in minority neighbourhoods that mainly serve local clienteles typically post low profits and are unlikely to survive. When they start struggling financially, ethnic minority entrepreneurs are especially vulnerable because they are less likely to secure loans (Bewaji et al. 2012).

Acculturation as Hybridization

At the same time, entrepreneurs in ethnic enclaves enjoy unique opportunities. Some immigrants negotiate complex identity changes, such as a sense of conflict between their ethnic origins and the values, wishes, and behaviours to which they have acculturated in their new culture (Cleveland and Xu 2019; Dercourt et al. 2014). Making matters worse, when shopping in mainstream stores, immigrants may feel their identities are questioned. They may not feel their right to be living in their new home country is fully recognized, or that their culture of origin is appreciated. Immigrant-owned stores in ethnic enclaves can try to strike a balance. Carefully designed displays, sales teams, retail environments, and goods all help customers perform this "hybrid" of identities.

As an example, Fowler et al. (2006; see also Azab and Clark 2017) studied Hispanic Americans' shopping experiences and preferences. Of all the influences considered—which included price, stock, general layout, design, and more—the quality of customer relations was most important to these consumers. For Hispanic immigrants, language misunderstandings are significant. They are often willing to overlook other failings if they feel they are being treated well by sales associates. Immigrant Hispanics will view a store especially favourably if a sales associate communicates with them in Spanish, which they consider a sympathetic approach.

Whatever a customer's origin, a friendly salesperson sells products and enhances the store's image, while an aloof or condescending one can quickly lose a customer. However, Hispanic consumers are especially sensitive on this score. Given their experiences at home and in the host society, Hispanic consumers fear rejection, ridicule, or intimidation. Limited English language skills may increase their fears. A friendly associate who smiles and tries to help, even while speaking English, is setting a good tone. However, the ideal is to have bilingual sales associates in the store. When salespeople cannot answer questions or do not try to help, Hispanic consumers (and many others) will often choose to leave the shop.

Other studies of hybridization look at Turkish students in Denmark (Ger and Ostergaard 1998; Bebek 2017). Women Turkish immigrants in particular must negotiate contradictory cultures. They are caught between different interpretations of femininity: the stricter and more traditional version from home, and the more liberal version in their new host country. Many Turko-Danish youth thus build new, multi-dimensional identities that they express through their clothing (Ger and Ostergaard 1998; Bebek 2017). Some try to hide their Turkishness so they can fit in. But even when they dress like native-born Danes, native-borns can tell they are not Danish. These young people constantly try to mix different styles of clothing depending on the situation and the people around them.

Hispanic Americans and Turko-Danes are just two examples. Many immigrants struggle to anchor a sense of real identity amid unfamiliar experiences that can provoke anxiety. They can no longer take their affiliations for granted, as they could at home. Often, they develop competing ideologies about what distinguishes the two cultures: how the values of their home and new cultures are similar and different. Some immigrants view their new consumer culture as an intrusion that threatens to dissolve their cultural authenticity. Others see consumer culture as a neutral ground, as though they've been given a blank slate and an abundance of consumer opportunities to paint it in whatever way they'd like.

Building and Displaying Ethnic Identity through Consumption

In a multicultural society like Canada, cultural integration is common. It is rarely *complete*, however. As mentioned, immigrants' consumer choices are influenced both by their new culture and the one they left behind. Often, as we have said, they buy goods to preserve a part of their cultural and religious identity (Salley-Toler 2014). Some do this because they fear losing these identities to the Western culture and the customs that now surround them. We see this happen in many different ethnic groups.

For example, Muslim immigrants to the West sometimes use their clothes to show off their ethnic identity (Ajala 2018). Such clothing may include T-shirts and hoodies with faith-related slogans such as "I love my Prophet" or "I am Muslim every day." Other favourite products pay homage to political events such as the Palestinian and Syrian conflicts. For Muslim immigrants living in the West, these clothes help foster a sense of belonging and community. They help unify Muslims behind their shared religious beliefs and ethnic identity.

What's more, Muslim clothing can help fight the negative opinions and stereotypes that many Westerners hold. For example, the hijab has been hotly debated in Canada, with some Canadians (especially in Quebec) saying it undermines women's rights. Some favorite Muslim products have slogans that directly address these views. By buying and wearing these clothes, Muslims push back against stigma and show their pride in their community.

Indeed, Muslim-made products have become increasingly popular in the North American market. Islamic soft drinks such as Mecca Cola are just one example (Boubekeur 2018). To compete with this, some North American brands have recently started to offer products aimed at Muslim consumers. A famous example is Nike's "Pro-Hijab," a hijab designed for women to wear while exercising. With these products, Western companies are tapping into new markets. The women who buy them preserve their religious identity while showing they are part of their new North American community.

Similarly, young Iranians in the UK use consumer goods to build and affirm a sense of self, and to resist the dominant order (Jafari and Goulding 2016). However, while doing so, some may experience a clash between the traditional attitudes of their parents or grandparents and the liberalizing forces of Western consumption. These contradictions can lead to a "torn" self. For example, while living in Iran, some of these young people may have craved more freedom. In the UK, perhaps they have become more independent. However, few can ignore their religion outright in their new homes.

These paradoxes are surfacing in Iran, too. On the one hand, developing a market economy in Iran has promoted individualism, while on the other, restrictive religious, political, and institutional forces continue to limit individual freedom. The Iranian state continues to demand that its citizens comply with the prescribed Islamic social order and avoid a full-scale adoption of secular Western values.

Like Iranian immigrants to the West, Caribbean immigrants to the UK and North America buy in ways that signal their cultural identity (Laura 2000). Many Haitian immigrants buy Haitian cuisine and equip their homes with Haitian decor. Some Caribbean immigrants even take a stand against consumer conformity. They see North American staples like fast food as unnecessary and wasteful, so they refuse to buy them. Some go a step further, critiquing African Americans for consuming many American-made products, saying it's "so mainstream" (Laura, 2000; also, Brown et al. 2020).

The Situational Factor: Cues and Primes

In sum, many immigrants choose to consume in ways that reflect their culture of origin *and* in new ways associated with their new home culture. In what situations will they prefer one type of product over the other?

In early research on this topic, Russell Belk (1974) pointed out that situational factors influence consumer behaviour, even in immigrants (for a recent application of this, see Calvo-Porral and Levy-Mangin 2019). So, for example, an immigrant from Ireland is more likely than usual to talk about being Irish on St Patrick's Day, in the company of other Irish people. And these situational tendencies increase if the group in question faces danger or exclusion in the place it lives.

For most of the year, Irish immigrants may neither think about their ethnic status nor consume in distinctly ethnic ways, but, rather, behave and consume in much the same way as other Canadians. That's what we mean by situational ethnicity: it is ethnicity whose performance is evoked by particular situational cues. Otherwise, it lies hidden within a person's private identity.

Stayman and Deshpande (1989) explored the impact of two situational elements—social surroundings and antecedent conditions—on ethnic food choices (for an application, see Olsen 2016). They saw that Chinese, Mexican, and Anglo subjects all have particular ideas about the "right" food to consume when they are out with business associates. They consume different foods when they are out with parents. The researchers also found that situational cues increase "felt ethnicity." So, for example, priming Chinese and Mexican subjects with ethnic cues—like calling attention to their birthplace or native culture—increases the strength of their ethnic identification. Thus, ethnicity is not just who one is, but also how one feels about it. Mexicans who feel (or are made to feel) "very Mexican" will behave in more "Mexican" ways as consumers.

Forehand and Deshpande (2001; see also Lord et al. 2019) examined ethnic primes: verbal or visual cues that draw attention to ethnicity. These primes, they found, increase consumers' awareness of their ethnicity. As we have seen, such awareness can affect a person's response to targeted advertising and their buying plans. For example, when Asian participants were ethnically primed, they responded more favourably to advertisements targeting Asians and to those with Asian spokespeople. By contrast, exposure to Asian ethnic primes did not affect Caucasian participants.

These studies point to two potentially fruitful avenues for future research. First, they show it is necessary for researchers (and marketers) to understand why and when ethnicity is focal in consumer situations. People in a multiethnic society have many ethnic and other identities that are important to them—say, their gender identity. As well, different ethnic groups bring different sensitivities to store visits. For example, they may be more or less alert to signals of prejudice, exclusion, and discrimination. As a result, we may expect differences in the effect of situational factors on members of different ethnic groups.

Bear in mind that ethnicity is a part of a person's identity, and identity has many sides. As consumers, we perform our identity using particular consumer items, and any identity performance responds to many cues from the outside world. Reed et al. (2012) provide a set of propositions about identity performance that helps us think about how and when immigrant consumers are likely to perform their ethnicity (or not). They specify the following five basic principles that can help researchers model identity performance.

First, they note that identity performance (Shang et al. 2020; Yousafzai 2019) increases when the identity is an active part of the self. This occurs when someone already assigns great importance to being Black or an immigrant, for example. Second, many people unconsciously associate their identity with certain stimuli, and this association increases the person's response to the stimuli. Third, the evaluation of identity-linked stimuli depends on how central the identity is to the relevant domain. A shop in which all the signs are in an immigrant's native language will be likely to call forward the ethnic identity.

Fourth, however, these reactions to situational cues are not automatic. People oversee their own behaviours to manage and reinforce their identities. They choose to express their ethnic identity or not, given the cues in the situation. Fifth and finally, all identity-linked behaviours help consumers manage the prominence (and contradiction) of multiple identities. People decide how prominent to make their ethnic identity, given others in the environment, for example. People who want to build a relationship with a customer will not call attention to historically critical ethnic differences: for instance, between Israelis and Palestinians, Armenians and Turks, or Hindus and Sikhs.

Marketing to a Globalized World

Massive migration, tourism, and media consumption have all helped to spread a global consumer culture, and nowhere is this new global consumer culture more obvious than in Asia. Some brand managers create regional brands that underline the shared experience of globalization in that region of the world. In doing so, they try to create a multicultural experience, filling their advertisements with diverse cultural referents. These regional brands contribute to reimaging Asia as urban, modern, and multicultural (Cayla and Eckhardt 2008; Alden and Nariswari 2017).

Since opening its first store in Seattle in 1971, Starbucks has extended its brand globally. It now operates 30,000 locations in 70 countries, including the outlet pictured above in Seoul.

Globalization is arguably the most critical issue facing international marketing managers today (Cleveland and Laroche 2006; Moro et al. 2018). Capitalism, advertising, and cosmopolitanism are dissolving the boundaries between national cultures. Some think these changes are speeding up the rise of global consumer culture. If so, the conventional method of using countries as cultural units of analysis is increasingly irrelevant. Most of the world's countries are already multicultural and growing ever more so. Even within homogeneous nations, people vary in the extent to which they identify with and adhere to the dominant cultural norms. Many researchers think that this increased globalization is reducing the homogeneity of consumer behaviours *within* countries and increasing the likenesses *across* countries.

With the globalization of consumer patterns, cosmopolitan, pan-cultural lifestyles are emerging. Cosmopolitanism ideals include mobility and flexibility. Expatriate professionals may be seen as living cosmopolitan lifestyles (Thompson and Tambyah 1999; Kjeldgaard 2018). In theory, cosmopolitanism ideally suits our rapidly globalizing world. Being able to follow opportunities, new markets, and exciting trends around the world can set professionals up for success. However, research suggests cosmopolitanism also creates tensions that people negotiate through their consumption and leisure practices.

Expatriates, for example, often say they miss their homes, long for a sense of community, and seek out familiar consumer goods to soothe their sentimentality. What's more, some feel they have blurred the boundaries between tourism and regular, everyday life. In so doing, expatriates experience a normlessness and rootlessness that many find hard to endure. That is perhaps why so many people struggle to preserve a vestige of their traditional identity.

We see similar patterns in every modern multicultural society. For example, Haitian immigrants to the United States use consumer goods to show switches between their culture of origin and the host culture (Oswald 1999; Kreuzer et al. 2017). For immigrants as for others, consumer goods are signs that communicate a person's sense of self and a person's preferred group membership at any given moment. When people of different ethnicities live together, the consumer market fragments to meet their various preferences and needs. After all, ethnic minorities may shop in different ways. Anglo-Americans are often loyal to local stores and rely on friends' suggestions. African Americans are much more responsive to attractive and fashionable displays. Hispanic Americans and Korean Americans like television and radio advertising in their own language. Chinese Americans are thrifty shoppers and look for bargains. They also follow the advice of family members when buying consumer goods. Japanese Americans are eager credit-card users and look for a wide selection of products in the shopping mall.

These observations oversimplify group differences. However, they suggest that different groups have been socialized to spend in different ways. As we have seen, sellers often adjust to meet these buying preferences.

Even in societies that aren't as multicultural, people buy into the traditional culture to varying degrees. Japan, for example, upholds a robust traditional identity *and* takes part in the capitalist world. People with strong Japanese identities continue to eat traditional Japanese food (Cleveland et al. 2015). Meanwhile, people with weaker Japanese identities become less loyal to local goods and cuisine. This is true especially of those who are invested in the global market. They readily eat pizza, hamburgers, and soft drinks. Other Japanese people fall in the middle. They identify with both Japanese and Western consumer culture, so they consume traditional goods like tea and sushi. They also use global products like email and social media (Cleveland et al. 2015).

Consumer behaviour doesn't depend on ethnicity alone. It depends on *how much* a person identifies with their traditional culture. We see the truth of this among people of various ethnicities. For example, Hispanic Americans with strong Hispanic identities buy differently than those who are more deeply rooted in their Anglo host culture. Those with strong Hispanic ethnic identities are more brand conscious, buy the same products habitually, and become overwhelmed when there's too much variety (Segev 2014).

All of these examples have one thing in common. No matter their background, people who want to preserve their ethnic identity use consumer products to help them do it. They buy products that show they're different from the people in their host country. At home, ethnic culture may not have been as noticeable or tangible. However, once there's a chance it could fade away, some people express their ethnic identities in material terms. They remake their culture of origin as consumer goods—costumes, food, music and more—to anchor their traditional identity in this new market.

Final Thoughts

Many immigrants bring their lifestyles, customs, religions, and more to Canada, and preserve them for a while. However, many immigrants and their descendants eventually blend into broader Canadian society in specific ways. For many immigrants, the products they consume, and where they buy those products, also changes. As we have seen, consumption is a unique part of cultural integration. Even a family that has lived in Canada for generations may preserve consumption practices that remind them of their ethnic heritage. Traditional foods and clothing are notable examples. Families who have otherwise blended in culturally will often buy these items to celebrate special occasions.

Among immigrants and ethnic groups, consumption can play a crucial role in identity formation. In previous chapters, we saw how wealthy people use conspicuous consumption to project power and high social status and how men and women use consumption to craft their gender identities. Consumption serves the same purpose when it comes to race and ethnicity. Namely, it is one means through which ethnic inequality is perpetuated in our society.

Many immigrants consume in ways that preserve their ethnic identity or aspects of their culture of origin. They may do so for sentimental reasons, or to preserve ties with their family members back home. Or they may do so to highlight their difference from native-born people and declare their own cultural distinctiveness. Many immigrants consume for a combination of these reasons. But all of these motivations often are bound up with countering stereotypes and discrimination, whether real or imagined.

Another way that immigrants respond to discrimination is by forming ethnic enclaves. These tightly organized communities rely on shared ritual, religion, and language to keep people together. They also use consumption to signal their cultural identities. For example, immigrants in these communities buy traditional foods from ethnic grocery stores. Here again, we see that consumption is used as a tool to highlight difference—in this case, the difference from white, native-born Canadians.

Ethnic enclaves can open employment and entrepreneurial opportunities to immigrants. We saw that institutionally complete ethnic enclaves help also preserve cultural traditions. Sometimes, these ethnic enclaves are set up in response to exclusion, hatred, or forced assimilation. But once established, native-born people may see them as evidence that immigrants have rejected their new host culture. People who feel threatened by immigrants, believing these newcomers endanger their home culture, may bristle to see a greater ethnic presence. They feel irritated by stores opening, more advertisements targeting ethnic communities, and more immigrants buying goods that signal their "loyalty" to their cultures of origin.

Ethnic consumer goods are tangible reminders of difference. They give material shape to cultural, social, economic, racial, and sometimes religious differences between immigrants and native-born people. These differences in and of themselves are neither bad nor good. Rather, we, as a society, build meaning around these differences. Namely, we base our social hierarchies on them. By buying and displaying ethnic goods, immigrants may—in some people's eyes—draw attention to and perpetuate their Otherness.

Discussion Questions

1. How do immigrants adapt to the local culture? Explain two strategies we have discussed. Why do different immigrants use different strategies? How do outcomes vary when different strategies are used?
2. What does "acculturation trade-off" mean? Give three kinds of immigration behaviours that explain variations in acculturation.
3. Why are young immigrants showing a trend of conspicuous consumption? What positive and negative effects does that have on local ethnic businesses?
4. How do different processes of socialization influence the consumption pattern of immigrants?
5. From shopper experience to food consumption, what roles do ethnic identification play in consumerism? Compare the universal and cultural-specific elements.

Quick Quiz

1. What is true about multiculturalism?
a. It is a regional policy in Canada
b. It encourages assimilation of immigrants
c. It promotes cross-cultural understanding
d. It eliminates ethnic segregation
e. It breaks down diasporic networks and institutional completeness

2. Why was the assimilation view of acculturation replaced by the multidimensional view?
a. Full assimilation is always the goal of acculturating groups
b. Cultural groups tend to disappear after immigration
c. Cultural homogeneity resulted in intercultural contact
d. Resistance to new forms of culture was common after contact
e. The assimilation view was never replaced

3. What is the difference between cultural identification and level of acculturation?
a. Cultural identification is about behaviour
b. Cultural identification depends on the home culture
c. Acculturation depends on immigrants' preferences
d. Acculturation depends on contact with the new culture
e. Cultural identity is a process of complete identity re-formation

4. What shapes the definition of "normal" consumer behaviour among immigrants?
a. Process of acculturation
b. Native residents' attitudes towards immigrants
c. Immigrants' views towards natives' attitudes
d. Immigrants' wishes to fit in or stand out
e. All of the above

5. How do spending habits build identity through consumption?
a. Chinese women purchase ethnic vegetables because they are cheap
b. Chinese women purchase from ethnic stores to support institutional completeness
c. Chinese youths reject materialism to fit in with local peers
d. Muslim immigrants refuse to buy faith-related slogan T-shirts to fight stereotypes
e. Young Iranians in the UK conform to traditional attitudes and avoid adoption of secular Western values

6. How does cosmopolitanism influence expatriates?
a. It provides them with more opportunities and new markets
b. It creates tension between consumption and leisure practice
c. It strengthens their sense of community and soothes homesickness
d. It draws a clear boundary between tourism and regular life
e. It diminishes their motivation to preserve a traditional identity

The answers to the Quick Quiz are provided at the end of the book.

For Further Reading

Immigration and Acculturation: Mourning, Adaptation, and the Next Generation by Salman Akhtar
The author examines the psychological trauma of immigrants and the impact of immigration on their daily lives, as well as the change in postmigration identity and how unresolved conflicts in first-generation immigrants affect the next generation.

The Cambridge Handbook of Acculturation Psychology by David L. Sam and John W. Berry
The book discusses theories and current research in acculturation psychology from the perspective of cross-cultural psychology, looking at individuals in the process of acculturation.

People's Movements in the 21st Century: Risks, Challenges and Benefits by Ingrid Muenstermann
People's Movements in the 21st Century captures the most recent challenges of immigrants, using a wide variety of case studies from countries including Canada, Germany, Norway, and Brazil.

"Consumer cultural identity: Local and global cultural identities and measurement implications" by Yuliya Strizhakova and Robin Coulter
This paper offers a framework for the interaction between local and global identities. It considers how these identities affect the conceptualization of consumption practices, and argues that consumer engagement with global-local discourses shapes a person's identity.

Key Terms

Acculturation

Colorism

Diaspora

Ethnicity

Ethnoscape

Institutional completeness

Global flows

Global nomadism

Glocalization

Stereotype

Chapter Fourteen
Young People and Symbols of Subversion and Conformity

Learning Objectives

After reading this chapter, you will be able to:

✓ Interpret youth consumption as a means of socially constructing age.

✓ Link changing social roles with changes in spending across the life course.

✓ Identify the consequences of technology, digital advertising, and social media on youth.

✓ Draw connections between youth identity formation and consumption.

This chapter is about young people—specifically, teenagers aged 13 to 19—and their consumer behaviour. As we have already discussed in earlier chapters, it's during childhood that we learn many of the values, behaviours, and patterns that will shape the rest of our lives. Namely, the foundations for materialism are laid. Shopping, spending, and saving habits are taught. Product and brand preferences start to develop. These things influence household spending—i.e., through the products children push their parents to buy for them. But they also shape the consumers that children will grow up to become.

Learning about consumerism continues in adolescence. Today's youth are growing up in a different world than did their parents. Instagram influencers are filling their feeds alongside their "real" friends, exposing them to new products, brands, methods of self-presentation, and more. Unlike past generations, today's youth can buy with the click of a button. Generation Z's spending habits have thus been revolutionized by technology.

Despite these developments, some old influences persist. Peers of similar ages help shape each other's buying behaviour. They don't just impact whether their friends buy "cool" or "uncool" things; peers perpetuate the idea that one's identity is reflected in what you purchase. For youth, consumer products and shopping decisions therefore carry enormous weight: their friends' acceptance, their own self-esteem, and a sense of self that hinges on buying the "right" things. As a result, and paradoxically, young people are both agents of subversion and conformity in our society. On the one hand, they often make efforts to subvert—undermine and mock—grown-up middle-class society. On the other hand, they also make considerable efforts to conform to the norms and expectations of their peers. And though consumer behaviour at all ages is about achieving and signalling membership in a desired group, nowhere is this motive as powerfully obvious as it is among adolescents.

Defining Our Terms

Young consumers, especially **teenagers**, increasingly wield spending power in our society (see, for example, Duffett 2017; Berg 2018; Biraglia et al. 2017). Technically, teenagers are 13 to 19 years old. But in popular use, the age range is less precisely defined. Often, "teenager" is understood to mean an adolescent between puberty and adult; that is, someone who has not yet attained full maturity.

The first generation of teenagers with increased spending power came of age during the economic boom that followed World War II. They grew a new market for consumer goods specifically targeting teens. Producers of music, fashion, and cosmetics were more than ready to fulfill their desires. Teenage culture became a cornerstone of Western consumerism. As the "first" teenagers grew up, many of the generation's features (e.g. a foregrounding of rock and pop over other types of music) came to be incorporated into mainstream culture.

This chapter is also about the culture created by and for teenagers, often called **youth culture** (Nayak 2016; Roudometof 2019; Woodman and Bennett 2016). Strictly speaking, this is a subculture, though that is often debated, especially among functionalist writers and their critics. Youth cultures are explained either by the experience of adolescence, or by the manipulation of young people's spending and leisure through advertising and other mass media. The functional separation of home, school, and work supposedly makes teenagers increasingly distinct from adults. Teenagers may also be more self-conscious than adults, and more subject to peer-group (rather than parental and other adult) influences. Finally, to repeat, teenagers' relative affluence after the Second World War also created a large and profitable market for goods and services specifically directed at young consumers. Within that market, distinctive youth fashions and styles in clothes, music, and leisure emerged. These preferences are also markers of youth culture.

Box 14-1
Youth Subculture in the 1920s

Spanning the period from July 28, 1914, to November 11, 1918, the First World War was long and hard-fought. When it ended and Canadian soldiers returned home, there was economic prosperity and a loosening of moral norms, especially among single people in their teens and twenties. The period is now known as the Roaring Twenties.

Partly as a response to all of this "immorality," in March 1918 the federal government imposed prohibition, making it illegal to make "intoxicating" drinks. The enormous underground demand for alcohol led to the emergence of bootleggers, who illegally trafficked liquor.

Equally dramatic was the emergence of flappers—young women known for their energetic freedom and preference for a lifestyle that many adults viewed as outrageous, immoral, and dangerous. These young women helped push the barriers in economic, political, and sexual freedom for all women. Consumer goods such as flapper dresses and makeup helped them display their bold new identities.

As we have seen in our discussion of various market segments, people cannot be defined exclusively by one demographic trait, such as age. Over the decades, research on youth culture has evolved to reflect the various intersections that lead different youth to experience it differently.

First, class helps shape different youth cultures (see, for example, Grubb 2016; Cox et al. 2019; Lyons et al. 2019). Early research distinguished between the so-called college cultures of (mainly) middle-class youth and the "rough" or "corner" cultures of their working-class counterparts. College cultures, this research suggested, helped youth manage the gap between conformist attitudes to achievement and the otherness of adolescent school life. Corner cultures, in contrast, were viewed as a response to working-class academic failure. They centred around the neighbourhood gang rather than the school. And they were thought to reflect working class teens' search for alternative—even deviant—status, identity, or rewards. A moral panic arose around this working-class youth culture's style and aggressiveness. Neo-Marxist studies saw the culture as a symbolic protest against the dissolution of the traditional working-class neighbourhood community and mainly working-class forms of leisure (such as soccer).

Second, throughout the 1980s, feminists pointed to the invisibility of girls in the mainstream literature on youth. Since then, more research on gender variations in youth culture has been conducted. Third, ethnic youth have also received more attention. Fourth, and above all, since the mid-1970s the notion of the independent teenage consumer and rebel has crumbled. Researchers have turned their focus instead to the youth labour market, and the dependence of young people on the household. They recognize that, today, youth culture is increasingly shaped by unemployment and/or precarious employment.

In response, many young people have turned to social media as a way of sharing ideas and grievances. In the process, they often form **subcultures**. Typically, a subculture is seen as a self-defined group that holds different values, norms, beliefs, and lifestyles from the majority. They consciously define themselves as different or apart from mainstream culture. Postmodernists suggest that social fragmentation and diversity have made subcultures even more culturally significant than the supposedly dominant culture.

Subcultures that react against mainstream culture are sometimes termed countercultures (see, for example, Whiteleyn and Sklower 2016; Lingel 2017; Coates 2016). A counterculture is a social group or movement whose values and way of life oppose the mainstream. Sometimes, they reject mainstream culture outright. The term is often used specifically to refer to "hippie" culture: the mix of alternative lifestyles and practices that spread through the U.S. and other Western countries in the 1960s. These countercultures embraced peace and civil rights. They also experimented with drugs, mystical practices, and communal living, animated by the decade's popular music.

Some suggest youth cultures or subcultures give the highest priority to hedonic needs and hedonistic consumption. **Hedonic needs** demand short-term, affective happiness, rather than a sense of pleasant contentment (see, for example, Yu and Bastin 2017; Budruk and Lee 2016). **Hedonistic consumption** is the opposite of the so-called Protestant ethic: it demands pleasure in the moment, not self-discipline in the interest of long-term goals. As mentioned, Weber suggested the Protestant ethic, with its acceptance of work and accumulation as a duty, rejection of hedonistic pleasures, and strong individualism (especially in the matter of salvation or self-worth), influenced the growth of capitalism in early modern Europe.

Some young people are oblivious to, or contemptuous of, the ideals of the Protestant ethic. Or at least, this is the way they are stereotyped. They want to live in the moment (Hamilton 2019) and, in that way, find meaning in their lives. Some prioritize experiences over possessions (Caprariello and Reis 2018). They tend to value **self-expression** above all—that is, the expression of one's feelings, thoughts, or ideas, especially in writing, art, music, or dance.

Young people are also often intent on gaining social approval from their peers by following current styles and trends. By **style**, we mean the particular way people represent themselves, as distinct from their actual thoughts and feelings. Thus, youth may develop a subcultural style: a shared pattern of codes that represent cultural identity and membership in the group. This stylization is a simplification, exaggeration, or idealization of one's self-presentation, not a true or natural presentation of oneself.

For that reason, many youth (and people of other ages) are concerned with **authenticity**. That is, they want to be seen as authentic or "real." They want people to think that the style they project matches up with their true inner self. Someone who buys trendy clothes will not necessarily gain social approval from their peers. In fact, they may be scorned and rejected, accused of being a "poser." Youth therefore try to balance conformity with authenticity. Adding to the complexity, they often want to develop and display their *own* personal style to meet their need for self-expression (Vannini and Williams 2016; Wang 2017).

The rise of social media has provided almost unlimited opportunities for self-expression (Shane-Simpson et al. 2018). Here, teens can publicly identify as members of a youth subculture, using consumer goods to signal their belonging. They can also create and preserve **virtual identities**: identities forged online that can be different from an individual's "true," authentic identity (Spracklen and Spracklen 2018; Mitra 2016). Platforms like Instagram, Facebook, and Twitter allow people to build virtual identities. They may share only the most glamorous moments of their lives, curated to project a certain image. Filters and Photoshop help users make everything in their photo or video—including themselves—picture-perfect. What their followers see on their social media channels may therefore not resemble what an individual actually looks, dresses, or talks like.

Social media allow youth to project these identities much further than they can through in-person interactions. Through social media, they can reach people around the world, as opposed to only in their neighbourhood mall or schoolyard.

Of course, people of all ages are active on social media. Middle-aged and older adults even outnumber teens on certain apps, such as Facebook. Social media marketers therefore focus their efforts on specific channels, depending on who they are targeting. Platforms where teens *are* especially active—such as Snapchat and TikTok—allow these marketers to build brand awareness among, if not advertise directly to, youth.

Socially Constructing Age by Consuming

Age is a social construction, made up and preserved by us as a society. Of course, there are signs of age: wrinkles and greying hair, for example. But there is often no physiological reason for people to behave in the ways they have been socialized to see as "age appropriate." For example, there is no reason that young women should buy revealing clothes, and older women should not. Yet young women are praised for wearing such clothing, and older women scorned. In short, what is and is not "age appropriate" is up for debate (Nind and Hewett 2018; Lazar and Litvak Hirsch 2018).

Still, as a society, we have decided that people of different ages should act, talk, and consume in certain ways. And people of different ages usually conform to these unspoken rules. They use material goods to signal the way they have been taught people of their age are supposed to act, look, dress, or eat. As mentioned, we know age is socially constructed because its meanings change over time. In fact, the idea of "childhood" didn't exist until the late medieval period, as we learn from French historian Philippe Ariès. In his classic work *Centuries of Childhood: A Social History of Family Life* (1963), Ariès showed that childhood was invented to meet social needs. As those needs changed, so too did expectations for children's behaviour (see also Collins 2019).

The social invention of childhood was closely tied to the development of primary education (Edelstein 2017; Gunn 2019). Before the invention of childhood, poor families who could not afford to send their children to vocational schools had them work instead. They learned how to earn a living by serving as apprentices. These "children" lived in an adult world with adult concerns—that is, making money with which to support their families.

In the sixteenth century, schooling became more widespread and child labour and protection laws were introduced. Young people (say, under age 10) were no longer viewed as proto-adults with adult-like tasks to perform in the home and workplace. Instead, people came to view them as different kinds of beings, with pre-adult developmental needs to fulfill before they were allowed to enter adult life.

In the nineteenth century, public education became compulsory in many countries. All families were forced to give up their children to this developmental, educational task, for at least some part of their youth. Since then, as the paid workforce has required ever-more educated workers, formal education has continued to increase in length and complexity. In effect, this growth of education has extended "cultural childhood"—a life stage of non-adulthood characterized by social marginality, irresponsibility, and economic dependence.

As historian Joseph Kett (1971) has shown, it was only in the late 19th and early 20th century that the idea of "adolescence" emerged (also, Woodside 2016). Gradually, more young people got more and more education and remained economically dependent on their parents for a longer time.

If we count going to school as "free time," adolescents have the most free time in our society (Robinson and Godbey 1999). If we count school as a work, the free time adolescents enjoy is roughly equal to that of seniors and young people 18 to 24 years old. However, adolescents largely escape doing housework, childcare, and shopping, compared with their older siblings and parents. That means they get more sleep, watch more television, play more sports, have more hobbies, and spend more time at social, cultural, and religious events than any other part of the population.

Of course, there are gender differences in these patterns. Teenage girls reportedly do more home care and childcare than teenage boys; also, more grooming and personal hygiene. However, even so, the domestic work teenage girls do typically has little effect on the responsibilities of mothers and older siblings.

Only gradually are these teenagers transitioning into adult life. Zuzanek (2005) reports that Canadian, U.S., and Dutch teens carry heavier loads of paid work than students in other industrialized countries. Nonetheless, in 2001–03 Canadian high school students aged 15 to 19 reported 40 minutes of paid work on school days and 80 minutes on weekends.

Sometimes, adolescents' time use and lifestyle relates to emotional and health problems. Rising levels of time pressure, going late to bed, skipping meals at home, and too much of time spent with mass media all contribute to teens' developmental and emotional vulnerability. "Over-" and "under-" structured patterns of daily life and leisure may contribute to stress and emotional imbalance.

Compounding these lifestyle factors are the emotional "wiring" and social maturation that largely occur during adolescence (Zuzanek 2005). Starting in the late 19th or early 20th century, psychologists "discovered" the emotional turbulence and rebelliousness that that adolescents are known (or stereotyped) for today (Linders 2017). Throughout history, rebellion has often been associated with youth, and young people have often signaled their rebelliousness in symbolic ways. Some of them have behaved rebelliously—for example, smoking, drinking, or having sex—against the wishes of their parents and older generations more generally (Ganiron et al. 2017; Harris and Harris 2016; Weinstein 2017).

Israeli sociologist S. N. Eisenstadt (1956; 2002) reviewed decades of data on youth rebelliousness and intergenerational conflict. He observed that, today and in the past, such rebelliousness and conflict tended to arise in societies that do not organize work around family and kinship relations. Said another way, young people are more likely to act independently of their families' wishes when their family no longer controls their occupational, economic, or marital future. All of the social changes noted above—the rise of compulsory

Changes in the organization and nature of work have allowed young people more freedom in modern societies.

schooling, the decline of the family as a unit of production, and industrialization—slowly loosened families' control over youth. Young people no longer grew up to work on the family farm; they got a job outside of the home and worked under a boss who was not their father. This reorganization of work meant youth had more freedom to behave as they wished, regardless of what their parents thought about it.

Today, most youth are preparing for work lives that have little (if anything) to do with their families. So the possibility of rebellion is great, compared with a century ago. They do not only behave rebelliously; they rebel symbolically, using consumer goods to draw attention to their rebelliousness (see, for example, Purkiss 2016; Holdsworth et al. 2017; Alexandrowicz 2020). In our consumer society, consumer goods can signal this rebelliousness.

In part, that is because people are becoming active consumers at an ever-younger age. Today, children own products earlier generations never even dreamed of, like iPads and electric bicycles. They also buy or at least choose their own clothes at earlier ages. Many have a hefty allowance or money to spend from gifts and after-school jobs. Clearly it means something different to be an adolescent or young adult today compared to three decades ago, or three centuries ago.

This fact tells us something we have already learned about other social categories in this book. Namely, such categories are social constructions. We collectively make up categories like women, men, racialized people, young people, and old people. True, people in these groups share things in common. But we, as a culture, make those things significant. We draw attention to those shared features and minimize differences that blur the boundaries between these categories.

Again, we see that age is socially constructed, not dependent on the number of years a person has been alive. Today, certain kinds of consumption are widely thought to signal full-fledged adulthood. Buying a house and a car, paying for a wedding, being financially stable enough to afford the many trappings babies need—these consumer goods and behaviours are markers of "grown-ups." People who have not been able to get these things, whatever their age, may not be seen as "adults" by those with traditional views on age. That's why it's so common to hear baby boomers—born roughly between 1946 and 1964—telling millennials to "grow up" and "act their age."

In sum, Ariès and Kett show that these socially constructed age groups organize our lives and carry assumptions about the "right" and "wrong" ages at which to do certain things. These social expectations help control what we buy and how we spend our money. They change over time, as Aries explained, but they also change from one society to another, as we learn from the **life course perspective** on aging (Veldman et al. 2017; Hirschi and Gottfredson 2017). This means that consumer behaviour by age will also vary from one society to another.

Spending Across the Life Course

Sociologist Glen Elder (1999; also, Elder and George 2016) proposed that people experience age differently, depending on their personal history and cultural context. Elder put forward several principles that link his theory to consumerism. First, he said historical context influences our consumer behaviour. For instance, people who live in times of war travel less, relax less, and buy fewer luxury goods than people who live in times of peace, no matter what age they are. That's because dangers are greater and luxury goods are scarcer in times of war.

Second, Elder said social transitions have different effects depending on when these transitions happen. For example, it matters if a mother bears her first child at the age of 14, 27, or 40. She and her baby will live in different material conditions, with different opportunities for advancement, depending on how much school and work experience she acquired before giving birth. Third, Elder noted that our experience of age depends, in large part, on the experiences and actions of others to whom we are closely connected. For example, as we saw in an earlier chapter, parents can raise their children in ways that foster materialism.

But the critical point of the life course perspective is to explain how and why lives are similar, despite individual variations. This likeness exists because of our culture and our society, which influence consumer behaviour. Wherever we live, age has an effect on how we spend our money and what goods we spend it on. As we grow older, our priorities and needs change, and our consumer behaviour changes with them. As well, our age-based opportunities and constraints change too. For example, most 40-year-olds have more spending power than most four-year-olds. But most 40-year-olds also have priorities and constraints that keep them from spending foolishly. For instance, they may have partners and children they must support.

Some opportunities and constraints are less material. For example, marketing plays a big role in teaching consumers of different ages how to spend. On the one hand, marketing is supposed to appeal to people's wants. Market researchers explore what people of different ages want, then give it to them. But marketing also shapes those wishes. It helps "produce" different kinds of consumers by telling children they should want candy, teenagers that they should want video games, adults that they should want lawnmowers (Coulter 2012a). Repeatedly viewing these advertisements makes people think they *do* need and want such products, and that these are natural, unavoidable wishes for people their age.

It also helps shape their views of other age groups. For example, advertisements promoting fidget spinners to millennials may reinforce older adults' views of them as lazy, with too much time on their hands. Meanwhile, advertisements for assisted living homes can confirm youth's views of older adults as infirm.

So-called "tweens" represent a new market for consumer goods companies—a market many social researchers would argue was created by the companies themselves in order to increase sales and profits.

Finally, companies and marketers invent new target audiences by creating new age groups. Just as childhood was made up to meet new social needs (according to Ariès), capitalists invent new age categories so they can promote new products.

"Tween girls" are just one example (Coulter 2010; 2018). Product-makers and marketers say these girls are more mature than children, but not adolescents yet, either. That means they need all sorts of unique products and services—like the special line of tween girls' clothing sold by the Nordstrom department store chain. And they need to be marketed to in unique ways, to help them realize these products and services are just what they've been looking for.

We have no certain way of knowing how much of this trend of inventing new age segments is the result of actual consumer demand as opposed to marketing. Indeed, some of these goods are likely developed to meet genuine needs. Some tweens may outgrow their clothes (both physically and emotionally), but their parents don't want them wearing outfits designed for older girls that they see as "inappropriate." But at the same time, it's in capitalists' best interests to convince consumers that people of ever-narrower age groups "need" different clothes. Do you think a nine-year-old girl is wholly different from an 11-year-old girl? If you do, you're going to spend a lot of money refreshing her wardrobe every few years to make sure people think you're a good parent who dresses her daughter properly. Capitalists profit when consumers think their clothing must change every few years.

Market research is grounded in the reality that age affects consumer behaviour. Studies show that people spend their money differently, depending on how old they are. In broad terms, older adults resist change. They are therefore less likely than younger people to change their shopping preferences (Bird et al. 2011) and their opinions about a product (Ivan and Penev 2011). In turn, older adults are often more loyal to their brands of choice, compared with younger people (Lambert-Pandraud et al. 2010). For example, when buying new cars, they are more likely to buy the same brand as their old car.

By contrast, young people generally like novelty. They aren't as loyal to brands as their older counterparts (Lambert-Pandraud et al. 2010; 2017). If a different brand appeals to them more, they are at least willing to try it. This is especially the case for materialistic youth, who are most likely to try new products (Bamossy et al. 2003; Sirgy et al. 2019). At the same time, however, youth may care more about what others think. By the age of eight, they buy products they think will help them fit in (Cantor 2001; Hughes 2017). When buying things, young people are more concerned with what others will think than older adults.

One feature that older and younger people have in common is their love of shopping malls. Many older adults spend their leisure time here. For them, a mall is not just a place to buy products. It is also a place to reduce loneliness, provide entertainment, and help stay active (Kang et al. 2005; Can et al. 2016). These benefits are especially appealing for people who are retired and/or live alone. They get to meet with friends, walk around, and people-watch. Young people also go to malls for sociability and excitement. Teenagers who are too young to go to bars and nightclubs meet their friends at the mall on weekends. Even those without much spending power can usually afford to make an outing out of visiting the food court.

The Impact of Materialism and Advertising on Youth

Members of generation Z have never known a world without digital technology. Born roughly between 1995 and 2015, this age group has also been referred to as iGeneration, gen tech, and digital natives. These names highlight how much digital technology has affected them. These youth are always "plugged in" and "online." Brands do their best to exploit their tech-orientation in many ways (Spero and Stone 2004; Sethna et al. 2016).

First, the tech industry itself has exploded. New laptops, headphones, telephones, tablets, speakers, televisions, and more are constantly being released. Youth have been conditioned to want the newest model, or the version with the latest upgrade. And they're willing to spend large amounts to get it.

Second, the Internet has provided brands with unprecedented advertising power, as noted in earlier chapters. A generation of youth who spend most of their waking hours staring into a screen means brands can promote themselves literally 24/7. As just one example, many brands have social media accounts that they use to push their products. As noted, social media has also opened up a new world of brand ambassadors and influencers. Even average people use these platforms to share deals, products, and services with their friends. Linking to the restaurant you want to try or sharing the coupon code for a sale is much easier when you can send it instantly through a direct message on Instagram. In this sense, the digital age has made third-party endorsements all the more popular, benefiting companies along the way.

Social media bring many benefits for youth, enabling self-expression, helping them feel a sense of ownership over their self-presentation, forging new friendships between people who would have never met in "real life," and sometimes even giving youth access to information they wouldn't have wanted to ask their parents about.

But there are drawbacks—and some say youth may be especially affected. Canadian youth spend significant fractions of their lives on their devices. Teenagers between 15 and 19 spend, on average, a minimum of three hours each day looking at their favourite social networks; 18 percent of these users admitted that they cannot resist the urge to constantly check their social media accounts (Drug Facts 2019). With so much time being spent on the Internet, many parents struggle to oversee and censor the content their children are consuming (Linn and Novosat 2008; Austin et al. 2020). What's more, as mentioned, many youth have not fully developed their sense of self. Still malleable, children might be more easily swayed to change their behaviours, beliefs, and values to meet social expectations.

That could make them especially vulnerable to advertisements. The fast-food and soft-drink industries have both come under fire for targeting young people, who may not be media literate, with morally questionable advertisements. Children often don't know much about nutrition and healthy choices. So, when they see an advertisement for fast food, there may not be anything holding them back from begging their moms to buy them some. In this way, advertising can induce children to make unhealthy choices.

Even food advertisements that aren't aimed directly at young children still affect them (Roberto et al. 2010; Bragg et al. 2018). An estimated 60 percent of the fast-food advertisements children see weren't actually meant for them (Brownell et al., n.d). And when children see a food advertisement, they are likely to develop positive feelings towards it (French and Story 2004; Marlatt et al. 2016). Also troubling is the fact that fast-food chains, like all companies, strive to build their brand to keep loyal customers for life.

Some say that advertising to children isn't an issue because a parent should be able to say "no" to unhealthy requests. But it's impossible for parents to control their kids' food consumption. For one, fast food is popular because it's *fast* and easy. Busy, tired, stressed parents just have to hand over their credit cards, and dinner for the whole family will be on the table in minutes. What's more, many pre-teens and teenagers have access to their own spending money. Their parents aren't with them every second of the day, keeping them from buying unhealthy meals; they can buy fast-food on their own.

On the other hand, there are those who say we should ban all unhealthy advertisements that are directed at children. But this isn't realistic, either (Beales 2004; Rowthorn 2019). As mentioned, most fast-food advertisements kids see weren't even meant for them. Instead, some have proposed that industries should be required to regulate, to the best of their ability, what they show children. And children should be encouraged, both by their parents and through the media, to make healthy choices (Salinsky 2006; Brownson and Eyler 2016).

The soft-drink industry has resisted efforts to regulate advertisements targeting children as well as other taxes and regulations intended to to cut consumption of such beverages.

The food and beverage industry has done everything possible to prevent and resist regulation (Asquith 2009; Peterson 2018). Their profits depend on selling large volumes of sugar- and calorie-packed products. So, food and drink advertisers who target children have developed many strategies to sidestep accusations that their products cause poor health. First, they offer to set up self-imposed rules and policies, such as cuts in sugar and calories in their food and drinks. These amount to public-relations stunts, designed to convince consumers that the "low-cal" or "sugar-free" products are healthier. In fact, the changes are often small or offset by the addition of other ingredients to preserve taste.

At other times, the food and drink industry has tried to stir up doubt about their role in contributing to obesity and poor health. For example, they deprecate research findings and public health warnings as "pseudo-science," claiming they have no basis in fact, and that consumers of all ages can safely enjoy their products (Herrick 2016). Yet others say consumers (that is, parents) should defend their right to make their own buying decisions. They should take responsibility for regulating their children's consumption of fast food and sugary drinks. All of these strategies help the industry fight off intervention and control in the form of policies that might hurt profitability.

Turning Children into Consumers

From the time we are born until we die, people see us as members of age groups. The significant age groups in our society include infancy, childhood, pre-teenage (or tween-age), adolescence, early adulthood, middle age, and old age. As we transition from one age bracket to the next, we take on new social rights and responsibilities. What this means for consumer behaviour is that, as people enter new age groups, they (usually) get and spend differing amounts of money on new and different things.

As people transition from children to tweens, tweens to adolescents, adolescents to college students, and so on, they gain access to more money and learn how to spend that money "properly," given their new opportunities and responsibilities (Chopik et al. 2018; Symonds et al. 2019). This means that aging, as a factor in consumption, is a continuous process of learning to adjust to new buying opportunities and constraints. We need to learn how to spend money as good students, as good parents, or as good grandparents.

In large part, we learn these spending practices from our parents, family, and friends or peer groups, which are made up mostly of people of our own age. They suggest what to buy, where to buy

---

Box 14-2

Vegetarianism and Veganism among Canadian Youth

While some youth love fast food, others take the opposite route. They follow a vegan or vegetarian diet—and they make sure everyone knows it.

According to a 2018 poll, more than half of the Canadians who identify as vegetarians and vegans are under the age of 35. This demographic was three times more likely to consider themselves vegetarians or vegans than people 49 or older (*The Globe and Mail* 2019). These changes may be the result of increased health consciousness and more dietary restrictions. But they also may be the result of youth wanting to give off the impression they are health-oriented, trendy, and hip.

As we saw in earlier chapters, eating is a social performance. It helps us tell others the kind of people we are. Some young vegans and vegetarians rely heavily on their diet to send these signals about their identity. They are widely stereotyped as die-hards who are willing to tell anyone who will listen all about veganism or vegetarianism, and even pressure others to change their own diets. Young people are also known (or stereotyped) for frequenting the trendiest restaurants and letting the world know they are eating there by posting all about it on social media. For vegans and vegetarians, eating "healthy" foods at cool restaurants helps them show off their healthy, cool identity.

---

it, how much to spend on it, and how to justify the expense. And, as the research literature shows, this begins in childhood. We start learning how to be competent consumers as children, and we never stop learning.

The process by which a child becomes a consumer involves at least four transitions (Valkenburg and Cantor 2001; Hong et al. 2017). First, a consumer feels wants and preferences. Second, they search to fulfill them. Third, the consumer chooses and purchases a product, and, finally, they evaluate the product and its alternatives. This consumer behaviour develops in distinct phases, so each of these tendencies emerges one at a time.Even when children are as young as five, peers influence this process and shape each other's consumer attitudes and values (Hota 2006; Hota and Bartsch 2019). But between the ages of eight and 12, the opinions of peers come to play an increasingly important role. In this period, children develop a better ability to evaluate and compare products. They begin to look more closely at the many characteristics of a toy, for example. They also become more critical of entertainment that is repetitive or poorly produced. As they come to see and understand distinctions between toys, many of them develop a taste for collecting cards, dolls, cars and trucks, or other sets of small objects.

In the later years of elementary school, children also develop an ability to recognize and interpret other people's emotions. So, for example, by age four or five, children can explain why their friends are happy, angry, or sad. In time, they extend this ability to interpreting television programs and other fictional accounts of behaviour. Increasingly, they come to understand their friends' motives and interact with more awareness (Pons and Harris 2019).

Seeing their friends' reactions to their own behaviour and that of others, they come to better understand the "rules" of social life (Furth 2017). Gradually, they develop a strong commitment to the norms of their peer group and to the opinions of other children about what is cool and what is not. In this way, they learn how to behave in public. Most especially, they learn how to avoid being ridiculed by their peers. This concern with ridicule extends to evaluating what they wear, what they eat, how they talk, and even what they watch on television.

By the age of nine or 10, children start to lose interest in toys and gravitate toward products that allow them to play with others, including sports equipment and musical instruments with a social function. Increasingly, they want to be members of teams, bands, and gangs. Their sensitivity to peer opinions and attitudes is intense. Among other things, this sensitivity alerts them to peer opinions about the media, advertising, and parental advice. In turn, peers' views influence the ways children view advertisements, and, therefore, those ads' effectiveness. Talking with peers about advertising helps them develop their defenses against it and makes them want to explore a broader range of information about consumer products before buying.

It's also at this age that children begin visiting stores and even buying things on their own with some regularity. They begin to develop and perfect brand preferences, once again with the help of their peers. Thanks to a growing loyalty to brand names and because of marketing that targets children, children come to have a lot of influence on household purchases.

Box 14-3
Canadian Brands Geared towards Youth

Young people have considerable amounts of purchasing power, especially when it comes to influencing their parents' buying decisions. A 2008 study evaluated the attitudes and spending habits of 3.3 million Canadian youth aged seven to 14. As well as influencing food and entertainment decisions, kids choose the clothing their parents purchase for them 95 percent of the time (Mediaincanada.com 2019).

Canada's Centre for Digital and Media Literacy attributes this increased influence to changes in family structure. Smaller family sizes, dual incomes, and postponing children until later in life means more parents have more disposable income than they did in past generations. Guilt also plays a role. Time-strapped parents buy their kids things to try to make up for not spending enough time with them (MediaSmarts 2019).

For their part, more companies have started working with psychologists to craft sophisticated marketing strategies to reach children (MediaSmarts 2019). Many think these practices are unethical, since companies are profiting from the emotions and insecurities of minors. Through manipulative advertising, companies place increasing importance on conformity. This leads children to be more materialistic and self-conscious about what they don't have. In the end, they compare their materialistic belongings to their peers. This behaviour leads to depression, loneliness, and isolation, all of which are harmful.

By age 12, children have developed some skill in all forms of consumer behaviour. They can gather information, decode advertising, and deal with store clerks. They have learned how to identify their own preferences and how to search for ways to fulfill these preferences. From the early years of elementary school onward, they have learned how to choose and make purchases. Beginning in the later years of elementary school, they have learned how to compare products. What's more, they have learned both social and economic reasons for buying things.

Social reasons have a lot to do with conspicuous consumption and gaining the approval of peers (Poorthuis et al. 2019). For example, children want to have the clothes, computers, and phones that their classmates have approved. Economic reasons, on the other hand, stress practical and cost-related features. When buying for these reasons, people look at price, bargains, and value for money. Economic reasons are often seen as better socialization outcomes. That is, we'd rather our children bought things because they were high quality, useful, and reasonably priced, not because they want to impress another child in their class.

Social motives for consumption are learned through family and peer communication, media, and advertisements. These same factors also influence economic motives for consumption, but in the opposite direction. Certain types of family communication, media, and advertisements weaken those economic motives. On the other hand, increasing age, maturity, and personal deliberation, improved by family advice and by conversation, strengthen such motivations.

When they reach adolescence, children usually have more money to spend and more information about available consumer items. They also receive more advice from their friends about the right and wrong ways to spend that money. Research in neuroscience, psychology, and marketing shows that adolescents are more impulsive than adults (Pechmann et al. 2005; Melbye et al. 2016). They experience more intense urges and are less able to resist acting on them. Often they experience emotions that overwhelm them. When it comes to consuming, these extreme emotions and impulsiveness can mean more impulsive buying.

Building Identity through Consumption

Adolescents also tend to be more anxious and self-conscious than adults (Pila et al. 2020; Muris et al. 2018). Many embarrass easily and fear looking ridiculous in social encounters. Part of this anxiety is caused by the unique transitional phase in which youth find themselves. They are not children anymore, but they're not adults yet, either. Many young people are trying to figure out who they are and shape their identities. On the one hand, they want to be independent—free from their parents—and unique. But young people also develop their sense of self by considering how their peers will view their actions and choices (Maguire and Stanway 2008; Theoridis and Miles 2019). This struggle between wanting to develop a unique image but also be socially accepted creates feelings of anxiety (Russel et al. 2018). We experience similar feelings at every age, but they are extreme during our teenage years. That's because, again, emotions in general can be especially strong in this phase of development, and many youth have yet to figure out "who they are."

Building your identity is closely linked to consumption. As mentioned, teens have already developed an understanding of symbolic consumption. They see the social meanings of consumer objects. They use this understanding to build their identities and label others. As we have noted, youth use consumer goods to project an image of themselves they want others to see. When repeated over and over, this self-presentation becomes their "style."

While in this transitional period, however, many teens go through different phases with their style. They may wear only jeans and hoodies for a while, then decide they prefer dresses and sandals. Then they may decide they don't care much about clothes at all and focus instead on the food they eat, building their identities as vegans, for example. In this sense, consuming goods to create a style is performative. Not everyone has an inner sense of self that urges them to buy the particular goods that reflect it. Instead, youth (and adults) experiment with different looks and goods, trying to send messages about the "self" they'd like to be to those around them.

Take a well-known example: wearing a baseball cap turned around. The baseball cap, especially when it is worn back to front, is an emblem of the social underclass and people who want to be taken as sympathetic to the underclass. In Britain, this type of youth is known as the Chav. In the media and elsewhere, Chavs are typically identifiable as unemployed (or precariously employed) youth who are never far from alcohol, drugs, cigarettes, junk food, sex, and violence. They tend to wear baseball caps, track suits and trainers, and gaudy gold and diamond jewelry (that is, "bling"). They are coarse, wasteful, and go to extremes in everything. Parents and other adults may disapprove of them, but they seem attractive to many teenagers (for more, see Pointer 2018; Adiseshiah 2016; Back 2016; Scerri 2017).

For many young people, Chavism is a walk on the wild side, however fake and short-lived. To consume Chav commodities is to remove oneself, if only briefly, from the not-Chav life of one's parents, workmates, and classmates, and to feel superior or hip as a result. Consider this take on the term in the online *Urban Dictionary*:

> Chav stands for Council House Affiliated Vermin. [The usual Chav] is a person that stands outsides McDonald's all the time but doesn't actually have enough money to actually go in.… Most chavs listen to "ganstazz" music from people that are usually girls that show as much as flesh possible or men that talk fast about drugs, guns, booze and shooting people, which is all that stimulates a chav's mind. They all like to pretend that they are black but are also extremely racist as well.

Other sources provide a different take on the term's origins. A Wikipedia entry notes:

> By 2005 the term had become widespread in its use as to refer to a type of anti-social, uncultured youth, who wear a lot of flashy jewellery, white trainers, baseball caps, and sham designer clothes; the girls expose a lot of midriff. In his 2011 book, *Chavs: The Demonization of the Working Class*, Owen Jones surmised that the word is an attack on the poor. In the 2010 book *Stab Proof Scarecrows* by Lance Manley, it was surmised that "chav" was an abbreviation for "council housed and violent." This is widely regarded as a backronym, a constructed acronym created to fit an existing word.

Whatever the origin of the term, Chav is a widely understood persona, with generally understood tendencies. Whether as a working-class dropout, drug dealer, or petty thief, the Chav has turned his back on mainstream, middle-class society.

Many young people today are attracted to the possibility of easy pleasure and popularity. Chavism seems to offer that easy pleasure and popularity without any hassle. Why struggle with getting high grades and pleasing teachers if you can get pleasure and popularity without the trouble? Or, even better, why struggle with getting pleasure and popularity if you can give the impression of being a Chav by dressing, acting, and talking like one? Just buy the clothes, learn the lingo, and hang out! From this standpoint, Chavism is a type of consumerism as much as it is a state of mind.

Chavism is likely to have a short shelf life as a form of consumerism, however, as do many other forms of countercultural consumerism. It is also likely to change meaning and possibly even become a term of ridicule, as we saw in the *Urban Dictionary* description above. Consider the fate of the related terms hepcat, hippy, and hipster. This set of terms originated in the 1940s. It was, through its various incarnations, associated with rejection of mainstream, middle-class life and acceptance of the underclass. Hip or hep people had their own special language. They dressed in outlandish clothes. They commonly used recreational drugs that were associated with underclass or marginalized populations. Middle-class North Americans hated them.

Yet today, if you look up "hipster" in the *Urban Dictionary*, you find the following: "hipster is often used as a pejorative to describe someone who is pretentious or overly trendy." Captured here is the sense of moral superiority that often characterizes rebellions of young people against their elders. What is missing is any sense of the social rebellion that motivated these earlier versions of "hipness." Maly and Varis (2016: 14) capture some sense of the rebellious or subversive side of present-day hipsterism in the following summary:

> The recognisable [hipster] style comes with a discourse of authenticity and realness. The style can be bought but buying it does not make one a "real hipster." It is the authenticity discourse that functions as an instrument of distinction; the distinctions are being made between the mainstream and hipsters, but also between "real" hipsters and "fake" ones.

Businesses and marketers strive to discover new trends in rebelliousness and then help to invent (or refine) consumer products that symbolize them. They aim to create products that will stylistically express the outrage or discontent young people are feeling. Some forms of outrage do not lend themselves to much consumer elaboration. For example, **straight edge** was a (male) subculture that originated from hardcore punk (Sim and Baker 2016). Its adherents stopped using alcohol, tobacco, and other recreational drugs, and avoided casual sex. Like grunge, straightedge was a severe subculture, compared with the hippies or the Chavs, so it did not allow much material elaboration (in the form of clothing or jewelry). Perhaps therefore, it did not command much commercial attention.

In sum, young people—like Chavs, hipsters, and other rebels—use consumer goods to show their rebelliousness. Clothing is often a key means of subversion for them: they cultivate a personal style to show they reject the status quo. When young people use consumer products to show their rejection of the status quo, we call it **stylistic subversion**.

Often, stylistic subversion is paradoxical. Many, though not all, types of youth counterculture result in consumer goods that suggest (and materialize) their stylistic subversion. Yet many, if not all, of these youth countercultures include statements of contempt at the materialism and trendiness of mainstream society. As the markers of symbolic subversion become materialized in clothing and jewelry in mainstream shopping malls, consumerism kills the movement that fed it. Old rebellious clothing—the zootsuits, bongs, hippy beads, Chav baseball caps, and Gangsta bracelets—move to the back of mom and dad's closet. Their children (or grandchildren) come home with new "attitudes" and new consumer items of symbolic subversion (Rubinstein 2018; McColl et al. 2018).

Of course, some youth focus on trying to send other, less-subversive stylistic messages to adults. They want to look mature and fit in with those older than they are (see, for example, Henry 2017). Looking grown-up is especially important at work, as young people recognize that some adults dismiss them as naïve or inexperienced. One way that young women try to appear more mature is through wearing makeup. Even if a 16-year-old looks her age, many people figure she must at least be old enough to buy and wear makeup if she's doing just that. So, some young women use consumption to signal to adults that they belong.

Peer Role Models—in "Real Life" and Online

Adolescents often identify peers as their most important role models—not adults. They look to their friends, classmates, and others their age to help them separate themselves from their parents' influence and form their own individual identities. As a result, susceptibility to peer influence peaks in early adolescence, then slowly declines throughout high school.

Adolescents spend more unsupervised time with peers and less time with parents or other adults. This greater social engagement with peers compounds the self-consciousness mentioned earlier. In turn, self-consciousness and social anxiety make adolescents more receptive to high-status, heavily advertised brands. Again, that's because they're going through a role transition: moving from one role (dependent child) to another (independent adult). During these transitions, teens feel uncertain about their ability to live up to expectations and fill their new roles successfully. This doubt can cause them to rely more on symbols of good consumer behaviour, by following the example of celebrities and sports heroes (Yasin 2019). Especially during transition periods, people embrace these celebrated role models to signal that they too will reach their desired goals.

Besides high-status role models, adolescents are also attracted to image advertising: advertising that shows the value of a particular brand as a status symbol. Such advertising suggests that the featured brand makes a person look better, impress friends, and attract the interest of sexual partners.

This is obvious in image advertising for tobacco. Studies in various countries have shown that adolescents are more likely than adults to smoke the most heavily advertised cigarette brands

The incidence of smoking and vaping among young people remains a major public health concern. Although the percentage of young people who smoke cigarettes has dropped dramatically over the past several decades, the U.S. Centers for Disease Control and Prevention reported that in 2020 about 20 percent of high school students had vaped—that is, used an e-cigarette—in the past 30 days.

(for example, Pierce et al. 1991; for an update dealing with e-cigarette advertising, see Margolis et al. 2018). What's more, adolescents who smoke (or plan to smoke) develop self-images that are similar to the advertised images of cigarette smokers. In other words, smokers and likely smokers try to make themselves appear like the smokers being advertised to them: they aim to project the same idealized image. On the other hand, antismoking advertisements can reduce youth's plans to smoke (Andrews et al. 2004; Berry et al. 2020; Netemeyer et al. 2016). But these campaigns interact with peer influence. For instance, having many peers who smoke may be more influential to a teen than seeing many antismoking advertisements.

Advertisements—both for and against certain behaviours—are especially effective among adolescents who are self-conscious and doubt themselves. Those with low self-esteem are especially trusting of advertised messages, likely because they are desperate to know what they should buy, and don't trust themselves to make such judgments. Brand consciousness also increases in adolescence, and teens increasingly rely on popular brands to project their image and bolster feelings of self-worth.

That's why celebrities can play a significant role in convincing adolescents to buy certain goods. Trend-conscious adolescents look to the media and advertising to find the latest products, services, and fashions. Often, they see famous athletes they look up to modeling or approving products and brands. These become the products and brands adolescents see as cool, and they buy them so they too can be on trend.

As we have seen in previous chapters, social media play a key role in driving such consumer behaviour, especially among young people (Chae et al. 2015). Traditional advertisements from brands are pushed out through these channels constantly. And because platforms like Twitter, Instagram, and Facebook are often used on smartphones, these advertisements reach consumers all day, every day. But, as noted, social media have also supported the rise of influencers. These accounts display lives of luxury, travel, unique fashion, or other attractive qualities that followers want for themselves. Followers develop a sense of personal connection to the influencers, viewing them as trustworthy, likable, and similar to themselves (Djafavora and Rushworth 2017).

In turn, Instagram has become a niche for advertising products to young people. The platform stands out from other social media apps because it is uniquely visual: it (mainly) shares photos, rather than text (Casalo et al. 2018). These photos tell users a story by portraying a life that they themselves want to gain. As a result, they impact buying more than the simple text reviews some other websites allow.

Another reason for Instagram's success as an advertising platform is that brands take advantage of the sensed trustworthiness and expertise of Instagram influencers. People (mistakenly) see influencers as regular consumers who have tried a brand's products and approve of them—not a paid advertiser. Consumers therefore see influencer ads as more organic and trustworthy than celebrity approvals in what are clearly paid advertisements, such as those on TV (Djafavora and Rushworth 2017).

The big question that marketers and consumers alike are asking is: Do Instagram influencers really drive buying? Despite their more "organic," "trustworthy" appearance, research shows that youth know influencers are paid for their supports (Djafavora et al. 2017). Youth are also largely aware that Instagram is a positive platform: people do not typically share negative reviews or aspects of their life.

Nevertheless, youth still say they generally trust influencers' reviews: they think influencers will only support products they believe in, based on their own experience with them. This trust falters a little when consumers don't think the product being reviewed fits the influencer's personality or aesthetic. In other words, youth can sense the inauthenticity described above. It weakens too when the influencer doesn't have real experience using it (Chae et al. 2015). For example, youth in Djafavora's (2017) study said they would doubt an influencer's opinion on a weight-loss program they were promoting if that influencer had always been thin.

Trust also depends on how "normal" consumers think influencers are (Audrezet et al. 2018). When consumers think influencers are like them and have similar personality traits, they see the influencers as more trustworthy. Influencers are also more likely to be believed if they come across as a regular person who just happened to get famous because they have an attractive Instagram page. Instead of seeing them as a traditional, full-fledged celebrity, consumers think these average influencers are more "real" and personally connected with them. In turn, consumers are more likely to think these influencers "understand" them and would not encourage them to spend their money on a product they did not genuinely like.

It's easy to understand why celebrities and influencers matter to adolescents. Even the latter, who are supposed to be "normal" people consumers can relate to, clearly have beautiful homes, bodies, faces, products, or whatever helped them amass their thousands of followers. People want to be just like these picture-perfect influencers, which is why we follow them and take their buying advice. But why are adolescent consumers so ready to follow the advice and suggestions of their peers? After all, they're probably just as lost, confused, anxious, and self-conscious.

Part of the answer is ridicule (Wooten 2006; Abedinfard 2016). Children learn a lot from teasing and ostracism (or exclusion). Targets (and observers) of ostracism learn which products to avoid and which to embrace. They receive clear and uncomfortable reminders of the social costs of nonconformity. The result is a feeling of inadequacy and concern about belonging. So, whenever possible, most adolescents try to obey group norms. However, parental rules, budgetary limits, and changing fashions may complicate their efforts. When targets cannot easily replace unfashionable possessions, they endure the results of having them.

Consumerism to Deflect Ridicule

Adolescents often identify middle school—grades six to nine—as the time they experienced the greatest ridicule about their possessions. Ridicule is especially effective in enforcing conformity among this age group because, as mentioned, their identities are still fragile. The way they see themselves is easily influenced by the appraisals of others, so they especially fear public ridicule. In turn, they become concerned with which brands are most popular and what clothing is most fashionable. These concerns are especially marked among youth from low-income neighbourhoods. Often, they chase expensive goods their families cannot afford.

Identity formation happens against this backdrop of ridicule, whether teens experience it firsthand or fear it. They rely on well-known brands to communicate their sense of self, linking those brands and their own identities (Chaplin and John 2005; John and Chaplin 2019). Between the ages of eight and 18, they create more sophisticated connections between themselves and these brands. Peers play an increasingly important role, as children move from childhood into adolescence.

Not surprisingly, materialism also increases (Chaplin and John 2007; Chaplin et al. 2019). However, children with high self-esteem show little change in their level of materialism as they age. As mentioned above, that's because youth with low self-esteem often rely on advertisements to tell them how to act and what to buy. Those who are self-assured, by contrast, are less likely to lean on consumer goods to define their identities.

The good news is that not all peers ridicule and tear down each other's confidence. Peers (and parents) can also build self-esteem by providing support and acceptance. In so doing, peers can reduce other youth's need to compensate for poor self-esteem by buying material goods, and materialistic tendencies decrease.

Parents can also temper peer influence—both positive and negative. If teens have weak relationships with their parents, they may be more susceptible to bad behaviour. For example, peers can influence each other to drink alcohol. They do this by modeling heavy drinking, pushing their friends to drink more, and bringing their friends into contact with other adolescents who drink a lot. These influences become especially forceful when teens' relationships with their parents are weak, negative, or non-existent (Hayes et al. 2004; Gentina et al. 2018).

Peer influence works through social comparison: by making adolescents want to be more like their cool friends (Wheeler and Suls 2019). They want to earn the company and approval of these friends, and they think copying them will achieve these goals (Mangleburg et al. 2006; Gentina et al. 2016; Mishra et al. 2018). Where shopping is concerned, friends exert two kinds of influence: informational and normative. Informational influence has to do with teens' desire to be right—to buy the "right" pair of shoes or the "right" camera in order to show they have good taste. Normative influence has to do with teens' wish to be liked by their friends.

Some adolescents want to shop with peers who seem more knowledgeable about brands and products, so they can reduce the risk of buying the wrong thing. These knowledgeable friends exert informational influence, by providing information and steering others clear of bad buys. Group shopping excursions can be desirable for teens because they feel more confident that they'll end up with the best product and best brand.

On the other hand, adolescents also risk social disapproval and embarrassment by their friends on these group trips. That's why adolescents who are more susceptible to influence by friends may shop less often with them. They want to avoid the potential normative reactions their friends may offer during shopping.

Final Thoughts

In this chapter, we saw that, like people of all ages, young people rely on consumer goods to build their identities. However, because they are in the midst of "finding themselves," youth cling to trendy goods even more. Everything from their self-esteem to their personal sense of identity to their friendships is based on their ability to buy the "right" goods and services. With so much at stake, it's no wonder youth become preoccupied with consumer goods—perhaps dangerously so.

What's more, today's youth grew up in the digital age. They can, and are often expected to, craft online identities. Frequently these are personas that differ (at least slightly) from the identity youth project in "real" life. They have a good deal of control over the ways they represent themselves. Many choose to paint glamorized pictures of their lives. They showcase only their most stylish outfits and post only the most carefully made up selfies. Youth also have permanent windows into their peers' lives online. Any time of day (or night), from any location with cell service, they can see what their classmates and friends are doing, buying, and wearing.

As a result, they are constantly engaged in social comparisons. They are continuously reminded to think about how they measure up, or don't. This constant preoccupation with image—both their own and others'—can feel stressful. Constantly comparing yourself to others impacts your mental health. It also uses up time and energy that could be directed to other concerns, such as genuine friendships, or homework. So, as we have seen for people of all ages, some youth in our society may indeed have a dangerous preoccupation with consumer goods.

Like other consumers, youth use material goods to shape and signal their identities. They also lean on these goods to show they belong to some desirable groups, and to distance themselves from other, less desirable groups. Finally, youth also consume to subvert. They buy, use, and wear consumer goods that symbolize their rejection of mainstream culture. For example, in this chapter, we saw that Chavs buy and wear baseball caps, tracksuits, and trainers to signpost their difference from, say, their parents. They don't want to look like an average working person. They think dressing differently reflects how cool or rebellious or morally superior they are. Consumption can provide an outlet for rebelliousness or, at least, deviance from the norm. It is one way some youth express their dislike for and difference from the mainstream.

Discussion Questions

1. This chapter discussed the influence advertising has on youth during the decision-making process. Why might marketers focus their attention on young individuals during transitional phases? Is this ethical?

2. Effective marketing not only appeals to people's wishes, it also shapes what they desire. Have you been persuaded to purchase anything after routine exposure to advertisements? What? Why might these goods benefit more from repetitive advertisements?

3. Erving Goffman coined the term "impression management." He defined it as the conscious or subconscious process by which people attempt to influence how others perceive them. Why might youth be more prone to take part in impression management? When are times that you have tried to influence how others perceive you?

Quick Quiz

1. What is subversion?
a. Rebellion against authority and conventional society
b. Legitimizing and respecting conventional society
c. Accepting or yielding to authority or the established system
d. Misbehavior to interrupt, embarrass, or confuse conventional society
e. The routine condescension that youth face

2. What is hedonistic consumption?
a. The consumption of goods necessary for survival
b. Items that bring similar levels of pleasure to all consumers
c. Items that have varying degrees of pleasure depending on how they are consumed
d. Items consumed for short-term pleasure
e. Items consumed for long-term pleasure

3. "Chav" refers to a stereotyped group in which region?
a. Romania
b. Venezuela
c. Britain
d. North America
e. Central America

4. Why do children with high self-esteem show little change in levels of materialism as they age?
a. They help enforce conventional norms by ostracizing others
b. They have easier access to high-end brands
c. They have constant access to consumer goods at every age
d. They are less likely to lean on consumer goods to define their identity
e. Their identities are more likely to fluctuate as they age

5. Why is ridicule especially effective in enforcing conformity in middle-school students?
a. Youth in this age group have large numbers of friends compared to older individuals
b. Youh in this age group are concerned about their parents' opinions
c. Youth of this age are not materialistic
d. The identities of youth of this age are still fragile
e. Sarcasm is lost on youth in this age group

The answers to the Quick Quiz are provided at the end of the book.

For Further Reading

Youth Subcultures and Subversive Identities by Nikola Božilović
Božilović explores the crafted identities among youth subculture groups in relation to their subversion and symbolic representation within mainstream culture.

Youth and Sexualities: Pleasure, Subversion, and Insubordination in and out of Schools by Mary Louise Rasmussen, Eric Rofes, and Susan Talburt
Youth and Sexualities questions the knowledge that educators and youth workers have in respect to identity and community among queer youth. The book also explores how queer youth subvert their experiences with homophobia into pleasure, power, and confidence.

"The effects of television advertising on materialism, parent-child conflict, and unhappiness: A review of research" by Moniek Buizjen and Patti M. Valkenburg
This article analyzes the hypothesized unintended effects of advertising on materialism, parent-child conflict, and unhappiness.

Key Terms

Bricolage
Counterculture
DIY culture
Hedonic needs
Hedonistic consumption
Self-expression
Social media,
Style
Stylization
Subculture
Teenagers
Virtual identities
Youth culture

Chapter Fifteen
Seniors and Rituals of Contentment

Learning Objectives

After reading this chapter, you will be able to:

✓ Explain marketers' recent interest in and targeting of older consumers.

✓ Recognize age-related stereotypes and how business and marketers perpetuate them.

✓ Consider the role of social interaction in seniors' shopping habits.

✓ Assess common theories aiming to explain brand loyalty among seniors.

This chapter is about elderly or senior Canadians (those aged 65 and over) and their buying habits. As we have seen with every other market segment discussed so far, there are many "types" of seniors who consume in different ways for different reasons. We first discuss seniors seeking consumer goods and services to help simplify their lives. These seniors experience physical and mental health problems and, to increase their comfort and reduce their anxiety, they look for consumer products or services that are easy to use and make them feel good.

However, not *all* seniors experience such health problems or consume to alleviate them. In our culture, views of seniors are clouded by stereotypes and assumptions. One is that seniors are all infirm. Contrary to this stereotype, many seniors live vibrant, active lives. When it comes to consumerism, some want to show off the wealth they've amassed over a lifetime of hard work and sacrifice, so they buy what we have called trophies. Their purchases may increase their comfort, but they also send messages about their identity and show they are successful members of society. So, second, we also explore seniors as a contented segment of the population who consume in ways that enhance and communicate that contentment.

As with every other market segment, we see seniors consuming to send signals about who they are and what social groups they belong to. However, seniors are often different from the young people we discussed in the last chapter. Many young people are desperate to fit in with their peers, so they buy so-called tickets whenever they can. These are items that show they conform to prevailing teenage notions of fashion, coolness, hipness, and rebellion. By contrast, seniors rarely buy tickets: they don't care much whether and how they fit in to someone else's fashion agenda. They may buy treats and even trophies, and of course, they buy basics; but tickets—comparatively speaking—are not on their agenda.

In fact, that may be one of the most distinctive features of the life cycle: as people get older, they start to disengage from the concerns, habits, and fashions of their earlier lives. Perhaps there are exceptions to this rule, as when seniors remarry or move into new communities. (For a discussion of the so-called "disengagement theory," see Francese and Rurka, 2016; DeLiema and Bengtson, 2017). But in many cases, they spend on new types of "basics"—mobility devices, for example, versus basics they bought in their earlier years, like baby food and diapers for their kids. And they indulge in treats like vacations.

Defining Our Terms

In this chapter, when we say **senior**, we mean a person over the age of 65. But seniors are being increasingly segmented as a consumer market (Halaschek-Wiener et al. 2018). People aged 65 to 74 are often very different—with different consumer wants and needs—from (say) people aged 80 to 89.

Most research uses **chronological age** to predict (or explain) buying behaviour (Zniva and Weitzel 2016). Chronological age measures how old a person is in years. It's the number we say when asked how old we are. Yet, how people feel, and how they perceive their own age, is also very important in determining what and how they consume. A healthy, young-feeling 75-year-old may be interested in an adventure vacation and not interested in a retirement community, while a less-healthy, older-feeling 75-year-old may feel otherwise. Unfortunately, there is little agreement yet on how to measure these aspects of non-chronological (e.g., psychological) age.

One loose approach is known as **subjective age**. Subjective age is an individual's psychological construct of how old he or she feels or is perceived to be. Research suggests higher subjective age is positively related to **technological anxiety** and negatively related to **global consumer innovativeness** (Cheron and Kohbacher 2018). Technological anxiety measures reluctance to buy and use high-tech products. Global consumer innovativeness is a constructed scale that measures features such as openness to, enthusiasm for, and reluctance toward innovativeness.

Whether they are 65 or 95, seniors have lived a long time. They have passed through many roles and statuses, entered and left many relationships, faced and survived many difficulties. With this long personal history behind them, many seniors are especially interested in rites of passage, because rites of passage celebrate and glorify survival (Shaw 2017; Richards 2019).

A **rite of passage** is a ritual associated with a change of status (Van Gennep (2019). Such a change of status could be from youth to adulthood, or from unmarried to married. Usually, these rites of passage are celebrated and marked with rituals. For Émile Durkheim, **rituals** are the stylized expression of social solidarity. They make people feel connected or bound together. Later research on rituals by British anthropologists from Bronislaw Malinowski to A. R. Radcliffe-Brown and Meyer Fortes suggested that rituals make the social order visible.

Although often associated with religion, rituals exist in all societies. Rituals that are especially relevant to seniors have to do with retirement, memorialization, care, widowhood, death, and mourning (see, for example, Aulino 2019; Bäckström 2018; Koskinen-Koivisto 2019). Increasingly, senior rituals have included remarriage.

Rituals are important for many seniors because they tend to be creatures of habit. Their behaviour is ritualized not because they are incapable of imagining change, but because they can't see much point in it. What's more, unlike young people, they gain comfort and contentment from ritualized behaviour. For example, research on the psychological impacts of rituals suggest some use ritual as a means of making sense of their world and keeping a coherent worldview. As we will see, seniors' love of ritual can impact their shopping behaviour, brand loyalty, product preferences, travel, and more.

How Seniors Spend Time and Money

Seniors are rapidly becoming a major part of the consumer market, especially in the prosperous Global North. That is mainly because, with declining birthrates, young people account for a smaller fraction of the total population with seniors making up a larger fraction. Seniors are also living longer and in relative prosperity, compared to past generations.

Seniors are different in many ways from the young people we discussed in the last chapter. Some of those youth use consumption to subvert society. Few seniors want to subvert society or even seem to subvert society. Seniors are also different in many ways from people aged 25 to 65. This "middle-aged" population is mainly focused on their jobs and families. They work hard to earn more money they can use to support their loved ones. They also want to gain and show suc-

---

Box 15-1

The Numbers on Seniors' Contentment

In recent years, research has increasingly sought to explore and refine the finding that seniors are more contented with their lives than people of other ages (see for example, Netburn 2016; Li 2016; Devi 2018; Leone 2019). In one study, Uppal and Barayandema (2018), working for Statistics Canada, used the 2016 General Social Survey on Canadians at Work and Home to assess the life satisfaction of seniors in Canada.

They had available information on overall life satisfaction, as well as information on nine major domains of life that typically affect people's life satisfaction. These included the standard of living; health; life achievements; personal relationships; feeling part of the community; time available to do things one likes doing; quality of local environment; personal appearance; and feeling safe. Their findings were congruent with the findings of other similar studies at other times and places.

First and most important, the data confirmed that seniors are more satisfied with their lives than those in younger age groups. Men and women in their sixties, seventies, and eighties had higher average life satisfaction scores than men and women aged 20 to 59. In fact, the evidence showed that life satisfaction levels increase with age past age 20. That said, senior women had higher levels of life satisfaction than senior men.

What makes seniors happy? Of the nine domains of life examined in this study, seniors were most satisfied with their safety, their local environment, and their personal relationships. Though still satisfied for the most part, seniors were least satisfied with their own health. It could be expected that, as they passed into and through their eighties, and their health declined significantly, their satisfaction would similarly decline. Conversely, family income had little influence on their life satisfaction, so long as it was sufficient to meet their needs. Thus, except at the very bottom of the income distribution, family income was not significantly associated with life satisfaction among seniors. This aligns with cross-national findings that show income has little influence on happiness or satisfaction, once people have an income that affords them a threshold of material comfort.

As in many other studies of life satisfaction and happiness, social integration played an important part. More than eight in 10 seniors report that they "always" or "often" have someone they can depend on to help when they really needed it. Those who reported this had higher than average levels of life satisfaction. Personal characteristics such as age, marital status, and location of residence also matter, along with other factors like stress levels, satisfaction with the amount of time spent with family, and the importance of religious and spiritual beliefs. Immigrant seniors also reported higher levels of satisfaction than Canadian-born seniors.

---

cess, which, as we have discussed, they do by buying and displaying consumer goods. Seniors are less interested in gaining and displaying success. Their careers have now leveled off or even ended. In short, they are less likely than ever before to feel that they have to prove anything to anyone, or even to keep everyone aware of their goals, interests, and day-to-day activities.

Perhaps this has to do with survey findings showing that seniors (on average) are far more contented and happier with their lives than people at any other age. This is especially when compared with adolescents and young adults, who experience more self-doubt and career uncertainty and, as discussed earlier, buy tickets in their clamour for acceptance and inclusion. By contrast, seniors spend their time and money enjoying their lives and symbolizing that contentment. For example, seniors are likely to travel more, join more clubs and groups, and spend more leisure time in the company of others. Some go back to school. Others do volunteer work. Some develop new hobbies and some surf the Internet. Others still revive skills (such as playing a musical instrument) that they enjoyed when younger.

Seniors get to spend their time and money on all of these things because, as John P. Robinson and Geoffrey Godbey note in *Time for Life,* they have an enormous amount of leisure time to fill:

Longer lifespans, better health, ample leisure time and greater prosperity have made seniors in North America a lucrative market for a wide array of businesses, including those in the travel and tourism industry.

an estimated 53 hours a week for men and 48 hours for women. The five-hour difference reflects the persisting traditional male-female domestic inequalities we discussed earlier; they narrow as people age, but never disappear. Much of this leisure time goes into television viewing, Robinson and Godbey report.

That said, Robinson and Godbey's book reports on trends between 1965 and 1985. Since 1985, compulsory retirement has been abolished in most occupations and jurisdictions. As a result, many seniors have continued working. At the same time, seniors today are healthier and more prosperous than seniors in 1985, let alone 1965. Today's seniors are increasingly baby boom children, who managed to amass and inherit a lot of money as working adults. This allows them to help out their younger family members financially, when needed. At the same time, these converging trends—better health, more money, and discretionary participation in the workforce—have made seniors a new source of spending power in our society. In particular, many seniors can fill their abundant leisure time with travel and other rewarding (but costly) activities.

These trends have also given marketers new opportunities to create and sell new products aimed at seniors. As mentioned, people are living longer than ever before. That means we're seeing new age groups—for example, people who are 100 years old and over. People in these new age groups are demanding new products, and capitalists are inventing new things to sell them (see, for example, Duque et al. 2019; Glende et al. 2016). At the same time, large numbers of adults are reaching retirement age, including the baby boomers, who were born roughly between 1946 and 1964. As this large slice of the population leaves or prepares to leave the workforce, our economy and consumer markets shift.

Within this larger group, we're seeing two subgroups emerge, with different spending power. On the one hand, as mentioned, some retirees worked good jobs and are now living comfortably on pensions and savings. They are spending their money on new hobbies, traveling, vacation homes, and other forms of leisure. But others do not have that luxury. Though they may be roughly 65—traditionally, the age of retirement—they may not be able to afford to stop working. Or they may not want to.

Box 15-2
Aging in Historical Perspective

Over the past few decades, the senior population in Canada has increased. In 2019, seniors made up 17.5 percent of the Canadian population. Seniors constitute a greater portion of the population than do children under age 14 (Statistics Canada 2019). As a result, health care and other supports for seniors are becoming increasingly important.

A century ago, the care given to seniors was different than it is today. Issues that come with old age, such as lack of mobility, often went unsolved and neglected. For example, lightweight, collapsible wheelchairs were not invented until 1933 (Anderson 2015). What's more, seniors who did not have a family ended up living in "workhouses" or "poorhouses." These were institutions that housed society's most vulnerable populations. Rather than being a haven for seniors, the living conditions were poor. Residents were separated by sex, obliged to wear uniforms, and even referred to as "inmates" (Anderson 2015). It was an experience comparable to a well-organized prison.

One such facility was the Wellington County House of Industry and Refuge, which opened in Fergus, Ontario in 1877. Though originally meant for indigent persons of any age, its population of seniors swelled to the point that it was repurposed as the Wellington County Home for the Aged in 1947. The facility closed in 1971 and is now a museum and national historic site (Tyler 2009).

Today's seniors are better cared for than a century ago. Technological advances have played a big role in improving their standard of living and quality of life. For example, smartphone applications can oversee medication, heart rate, blood pressure, and detect falls (Medical Alert Advice). Tracking this information helps families and caregivers understand and monitor seniors' changing medical needs. It also makes it easier for doctors to assess how their patient is doing between check-ups (Aging.com) and adjust prescriptions accordingly. One senior commented, "The monitoring system makes you feel supported and like you have a team behind you. You don't feel abandoned. They help you with your condition and monitor you on a daily basis" (Telus 2018). Yet despite such improvements, there remains room for further advances.

Marketing to Address Aging

Marketers tune in to these population changes to sell their products. To do their jobs well, they need to know our society's age distribution—that is, the size of different age groups in our society—and how it is going to change. For example, they find it useful to know that the Canadian population is aging and will likely continue to do so. They also need to know why that is happening, so they can tap into consumers' changing wants and needs.

One important consideration is that the population isn't aging *only* because of improvements in public health, nutrition, and medical care that help people live longer. Even more important is fertility. Young adults today are having fewer children than they were generations ago. The average age of a population rises rapidly when fewer babies are born. Given current childbearing patterns, our society will have an increasing proportion of consumers who are seniors, because there will be fewer children and adolescent consumers. That doesn't mean every business abandons goods and services for children and youth. But it can mean that businesses begin developing new products and services, that existing goods are made-over to serve seniors, and that new seniors-focused businesses emerge (Rousseau 2018; Ma and Cheng 2018).

Marketers also pay attention to geographic variations in the age distribution. For example, many young people are leaving places with poor job prospects and moving to places where they think they have a better chance of finding work. As a result, the average age is rising in small towns and rural areas. We see this in the Maritimes: of the provinces and territories, New Brunswick has the highest proportion of residents over the age of 65.

Even the senior population itself is aging overall. For example, the number of centenarians continues to increase. In 2016, about 8,000 Canadians were 100 years old or more, nearly double the number in 2006 (Statistics Canada 2016).

Since seniors are such a large and growing part of the population, businesses increasingly cater to their consumer needs. This was not always the case. Unlike their younger counterparts, some seniors did not take up technology like social media right away. That made them hard to reach and influence. Even if businesses could market to them, seniors also tend to resist change and remain loyal to their brands of choice. These consumer habits made them unattractive to many brands.

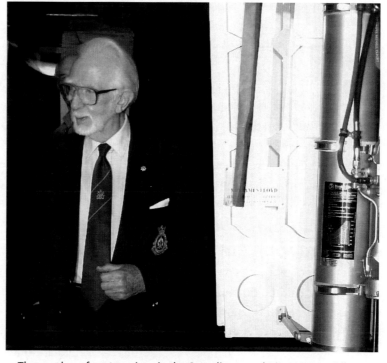

The number of centenarians in the Canadian population grew rapidly in the first decades of the 21st century. Pictured above is James C. Floyd, who was still alive at age 106 at the time of writing of this book. Floyd was the chief designer for the Canadian-built Avro Canada C102 Jetliner, the prototype of which first flew in 1949. Although the C102 Jetliner never went into production, Floyd supervised a number of other cutting-edge projects after being named Avro's chief engineer in 1952, including the highly advanced but ultimately ill-fated Avro Arrow jet fighter plane. Here he is seen standing next to a replica of the Avro Arrow at the Canadian Air and Space Museum in 2006. Floyd was inducted into Canada's Aviation Hall of Fame in 1993.

But as they make up more of our population, seniors are becoming harder for brands and marketers to ignore. First, as noted, many of them have money to spend. Sometimes they create demand for niche products and services—a demand that businesses are becoming more eager to meet. Examples include assisted living services (e.g., in-home nurses) and health-care products (like walkers), as well as niche eating and tourism practices, as we will see (for instance, Balderas-Cejudo et al. 2019).

Second, our aging population will impact businesses by influencing their marketing. Many seniors don't like to be advertised to as though they are "old" (Ivan and Penev 2011). This is especially true if the target customer is in, say, their fifties, as opposed to their nineties (Carrigan and Szmigin 2001; Dunan and Domenico 2019). But no matter their age, people don't like to see themselves as infirm, incapable, or weak. Seniors, like other age groups, don't appreciate being negatively stereotyped.

On the other hand, some people think seniors deserve special treatment. For example, they want discounts and special offers designed specifically for seniors. They say they have worked hard and contributed for decades; now, it's their turn to be taken care of and appreciated. Most marketers are still trying to navigate these murky waters. The effect or merit of such "identity discounts" continues to be debated (McCullough 2018).

Third, businesses are already being affected by the aging workforce. That wave of Baby Boomers approaching retirement age has implications for employee benefits, job training, job discrimination protocols, eldercare programs, and pension design. Building a healthy, encouraging workplace is key for keeping employees happy and, in turn, productive. But those healthy supports are also expensive. Businesses therefore do not only see a "new" target market of seniors with deep pockets to buy their products. Some also see seniors as a drag on their bottom lines. Fourth and finally, the aging population affects younger workers, who may have to take time off work to care for older family members.

Segmentation and Stereotypes

As mentioned, marketers are still trying to figure out how to talk to different types or "segments" of people, including different segments of seniors (Koubaa et al. 2017; Eusébio et al. 2017; Baş 2016). The problem is, knowing only a person's chronological age doesn't help much. People grow old biologically, psychologically, and socially. And that aging happens in different ways, at different rates, for different people. As a result, marketers are often forced to rely on stereotypes. Common stereotypes make seniors out to seem sick, lonely, and uninterested in romance and adventure (Machado and Sousa 2019; Ramírez and Palacios-Espinosa 2016; Petery et al. 2019). Some seniors are indeed in poor health. And we know social isolation is a real problem for many (Kim and Kang 2005; Lee et al. 2018). But we also know plenty of seniors do not fit this description. Many, who are in good health, are avid travelers, volunteers, and employees. Marketers who try to lump all seniors together risk offending consumers rather than attracting them.

Instead, many marketers use segmentation. They divvy up the senior market into different categories: say, 50-to-60-year-olds who live active lifestyles, or 60-to-70-year-olds who enjoy dining out. There's still generalization and stereotyping involved. But this approach helps consumers see themselves reflected in marketing campaigns. It ensures, as much as possible, that the marketing efforts will show how their unique needs and preferences are met by the product being marketed.

Consider one example of age-based segmentation. Weijters (2002; see also Guido et al. 2018) looked at the features, interests, and consumer habits of four segments: socially active employees, socially inactive employees, socially active retirees, and socially inactive retirees.

First, compared to people who work, retirees are less extroverted. They attach more importance to being respected and having accomplished something in life. They have much more leisure time and spend more hours a day watching television and listening to the radio, though they go to the movies less often. Retirees consider visiting family, going out shopping, gardening, and going on excursions more important than working people do. Finally, a key insight for marketers is that they prefer to hear about promotions by phone as opposed to, say, email.

Second, compared to socially inactive people, socially active people are more agreeable, attach more importance to a sense of belonging, have lower cognitive ages, and indicate greater brand

Box 15-3

Discounts for Seniors

Many stores provide seniors' discounts. For example, Rona and Reno-Depot give 15 percent off to customers aged fifty years and older once a month. M&M Meat Shops offer up to 10 percent off every Tuesday. McDonald's gives seniors free small coffees. Travel agencies, transportation companies, hotels, and banks all follow suit with discounts of their own (Marowits 2019).

However, not all seniors take full advantage of these discounts. Recognizing this, TD Canada Trust decided to make sure their senior customers received the reduced monthly account fees they were entitled to. TD automatically applied this discount to eligible customers, even if they didn't claim it (Carrick 2018). By automating this process, 450,000 senior customers across Canada received the repayment. It is likely that had this process remained unautomated, the majority would have lost out on the financial perk (Carrick 2018).

Although businesses like TD are working to ensure lower prices for seniors, not all Canadians are on board. In the past, senior discounts were meant to address the constraints that pensioners on fixed incomes faced. In the mid-1970s, the Canadian government reported that 30 percent of seniors in Canada were poor. That put them among the poorest populations in our country. But much has changed. Social policies have helped Canada advance in addressing seniors' financial restraints. Today, baby boomers are "the richest, most comfortable and longest-living folks this country has ever produced" (Taylor 2013). This is not to say that all seniors are well-off. However, some are much better off than in previous generations. It can even be argued that some seniors today are more financially stable than their younger counterparts.

One senior living in Toronto said he sees grabbing discounts like a "game." He admits that he doesn't need the discounts but collecting them "becomes part of the fun" (Marowits 2019). Some Canadians have been frustrated by this mindset and question if senior discounts are necessary or deserved. They argue that circumstances have changed and that seniors are no longer the most in need of discounts. Perhaps younger generations, who have children to care for, would be better served by these discounts. Or maybe age shouldn't play a role at all. Discounts could be given to people who earn less than a pre-determined amount.

loyalty. They watch less television, have higher discretionary incomes, and are more satisfied with their financial position. Relative to inactive seniors, they also consider visiting friends, attending courses, practicing sports, and going to the theatre and concerts as more important. As for the marketing angle, socially active people are less interested in price and promotions when shopping.

These profiles are invaluable to businesses and marketers. Businesses use them to develop products and services they know different types of people will want and buy. And marketers use them to tailor their efforts to consumers' preferences. For example, perhaps one business would communicate a special sale happening at the mall by phone to retirees. But another might pitch a night out at the theatre with friends to the socially active group who don't care as much about promotions.

Others still would use this knowledge to decide whether they even wanted to bother with some segments at all. For example, they may opt to ignore socially inactive retirees, and focus on their socially active counterparts, who are less sensitive to price and have a higher (discretionary) income.

Once they've landed on their segments, marketers start thinking about how they should **position** their products and services. Positioning refers to the image or impression of a company and its products that marketers want their customers to have. For example, a glassware company may position itself as classy, and its products as ideal for those with refined taste who love to entertain. This positioning reflects what marketers think their segments value. It also lets companies carve out a niche, by showing consumers how they're different from the competition.

Positioning may not have as big of an impact on seniors as it does on people of other ages. They are often more concerned with product features. Segmentation, for seniors, can therefore mean different things. It may mean developing special products, for example. Sometimes, it means creating special promotions, like the seniors' discounts noted above. Or, it could even mean coming up with a creative way of delivering a product or service. For example, perhaps some seniors prefer to have their products delivered to their homes, instead of shopping for them in stores. Though they can be effective, these tactics are also costly. Businesses must weigh the benefits of capturing senior consumers against the costs.

Segmenting the Tourism Market: An Example

As mentioned, many seniors like to spend their spare time travelling. Of course, some seniors come up against barriers that keep them from traveling (Chen and Wu 2009; Kim et al. 2019). Travel can be difficult for those experiencing age-related mobility and health issues (Fleischer and Pizam 2002; Hung and Lu 2016). Others do not have large incomes, and they cannot afford to travel. Others still whose spouses have passed away may not want to vacation alone.

However, despite these impediments, many retired seniors travel a lot more than seniors did in the past. As a result, seniors have become prime targets for the tourism and recreation industries (Śniadek 2006; Otoo and Kim 2020). After all, as mentioned, they are a quickly growing and fairly affluent market. As retirees, they also have more free time and flexibility than middle-aged working people, who only have a few weeks off each year (Kazeminia et al. 2013). Many are relatively free from the family obligations of younger adults with small children. They've outgrown the days of being expected to put their children's needs above their own. Now, they are seeing personal development, self-education, fun, and entertainment as the prizes they deserve for their busier days full of sacrifices for work and family (Aging in Place 2019).

Compared to earlier generations of retirees, today's seniors are in good health, and many are willing to pay to maintain it. Others feel their lives are coming to an end and want to see the world while they're in good enough health to do so (Wen et al. 2020; Jacobsen et al. 2018). For these and other reasons, one survey found that over 80 percent of baby boomers had travel at the top of their bucket list (Aging in Place 2019).

Gambling is one of the most popular leisure activities among retirees. A casino in Laughlin, Nevada, reports that at least three-quarters of their consumers are retired (Loroz 2004; Ciofi 2019). What is it about casinos that so attracts retired adults? For one, gambling requires little physical activity or, in many instances, skill. Even those with mobility challenges can use slot machines. And while their abilities may be declining in other areas, seniors can feel successful when they win big at the casino (Elton-Marshall et al. 2018).

Second, bright colours, flashing lights, and attractive prizes give retirees a sense of excitement that disrupts the monotony of their daily lives. Third, retirees who may live alone or see their friends and family less often than they used to can interact with casino employees, easing the social isolation they may otherwise face. In sum, gambling can reduce isolation and increase pleasure and excitement (Thang 2006; Thang et al. 2019). But, of course, gambling is not always the healthiest form of consumption. It can be addictive and even overturn people's relationships and financial stability. For those retirees living on a fixed income, gambling can tear through the savings that were supposed to let them live comfortably for the rest of their lives.

It's hard to say whether seniors created a demand for certain types of travel and recreation, or these industries created certain types of trips and activities to tap into this profitable market segment. Either way, we see seniors using their vacation time in distinct ways, compared to younger adults. For example, seniors account for a large fraction of cruise ship passengers (see Box 15-4).

Seniors represent a significant market for out-of-season holidays, with benefits for both the travel industry and seniors themselves. By being able to travel off-season, they pay less for plane tickets and accommodation. As opposed to the tropical party destinations popular with younger adults, seniors usually prefer quiet places with mild climates. Finally, they look for high quality, comfort, and safety, but also fast and inexpensive means of transport, and, occasionally, assistance for people traveling alone.

These are all broad generalizations. But the tourism industry, like many others, has segmented the senior market. For example, researchers have studied the range of senior travelers in Australia, broken down by the kind of holiday they prefer, as well as by their age, education, and income (Horneman et al. 2002; but see also Lewis and D'Alessandro 2019).

They label their first "type" of senior traveler as *conservatives*. Accounting for nearly half of the market, this segment looks for reliable holiday packages. They want to visit big cities and look for quality services at the right price. This group of seniors does a lot of research to decide on the destination and type of holiday they want to take to reduce their risk of disappointment. They en-

Box 15-4

Cruise Ship Vacations

Noticing their appetite for vacations, the travel industry has taken measures to meet seniors' needs. Airports offer cart rides for seniors with disabilities or mobility issues. Seniors also enjoy priority boarding and can get special help throughout their journey on the plane (Aging in Place 2019). However, once they get off the plane, seniors are often left on their own. That's why cruises are a favourite of many seniors, especially those with mobility issues. Once aboard the ship, everything is taken care of for passengers. Elevators and wheelchair-accessible staterooms make mobility less of a challenge than in other travel options (Aging in Place 2019). A variety of restaurants, shops, and activities cater to many different tastes and interests. On-board health professionals are prepared with the equipment and medications necessary should any medical issues arise (Dunhill Travel Deals).

Many cruise lines report that people who are 50 years and older make up the largest number of passengers (Aging in Place 2019). Some seniors even live full-time on cruise ships. Living on a cruise ship is often cheaper than living in an assisted living home as most cruise ships offer all-you-can-eat meals, entertainment, and other comforts (Bieber 2017). For those who don't want to commit to living on a ship fulltime, many cruise lines offer long-term alternatives. For example, Oceania offers cruise trips that last as long as 200 days (Oceania Cruises 2019).

joy family-type fun, and though they will splurge occasionally on fine food and luxury items, they rarely overindulge. Most importantly, they avoid surprises and threats to their personal security.

Pioneers, the second segment, represent about one-quarter of the market. They may be the most poorly targeted segment when it comes to the experiences and services available to meet their needs. Pioneers are younger, more educated seniors who are still active and seeking new experiences. They seek adventure, though with safety and security in mind. Many are attracted to outdoor, historic, and cultural experiences. With an independent mindset, they prefer self-learning and exploration rather than guided activities. This makes them especially averse to travel agents, the mass media, and clubs as sources of travel information.

Aussies, the third segment, represent about 15 percent of the senior demographic in this Australian sample group. They usually have less formal education and lower incomes. Aussies treasure family time during their holidays, are less interested in the arts, historical events, or cultural attractions, and are more attracted to quiet cities and the countryside. In cities, they can enjoy relatively cheap entertainment, like the movies, and the countryside is the perfect setting for picnicking and other family-friendly activities. Aussies often make their own fun, but comfort, security, and familiarity with a holiday destination are essential. They seek information about potential destinations through word-of-mouth recommendations and rarely rely on other sources.

A fourth group, the *big spenders,* make up a small fraction of the senior market (about 10 percent). They are wealthy enough to pay for luxury. Big spenders are usually older and are looking for nightlife, entertainment, and shopping in the city. They want to experience new places, and demand quality facilities, services, and entertainment while doing so. They also enjoy exclusive retreats that guarantee a high standard of service where they can indulge in fine food. Big spenders use travel agents to help them plan their holiday vacations.

Indulgers are another minor market segment, accounting for less than 10 percent of the total. Like big spenders, they seek exclusive retreats with fine food and wine and will pay to get the best. They are often highly educated. Their preferred holiday settings are diverse; their main concerns are that their standards of quality and luxury can be met. Indulgers are looking for a break from their daily routine and want to splurge on themselves through nightlife and entertainment. They often base their travel plans on destinations available through rewards programs.

Enthusiasts, finally, are the smallest segment (less than 5 percent). They love to party and enjoy meeting new people. They want to have a good time on vacation, filled with nightlife and shopping. Security, safety, and quality facilities and services are important to them. Enthusiasts typically gain their travel information through organized groups or travel clubs, and often travel in such groups. They are willing to pay to get the right experience.

The types and proportions of senior tourists and travelers do, of course, change over time, and other studies find even more motivations. The key point is that not all seniors travel for the same reasons. Some travel out of feelings of nostalgia—a desire to return to the ancestral homeland or rediscover places that meant a lot at an earlier age (Phau et al. 2016). Some seniors travel to live in a different culture, sightsee, or meet and talk to new people (Lee and Tideswell 2005; Shaw et al. 2016). The social aspect of traveling can be especially important, since many seniors report feeling lonely and isolated, especially after they retire (Kim and Kang 2005). Others look for rest and relaxation, learning opportunities, or an escape from their day-to-day lives at home (Chen and Wu 2009).

Just as businesses benefited from the invention of the "tween" life stage, so too have they benefitted from the segmentation of seniors. Now, countless products, experiences, destinations, holiday packages, attractions, accessories and other consumer goods can be sold to address the unique needs of different "types" of older travelers.

Another win for the industry is seniors' increasing use of the Internet (Schimmele and Davidson 2019; Seifert and Schelling 2018; Anderson and Perrin 2017). Like other Internet users, many seniors also rely on word-of-mouth recommendations to clarify and confirm the information they get online. To feel more assured before they make their purchase, they will turn to friends, relatives, or even other Internet users in chat rooms and travel message boards. However, many feel that travel agencies and other industry experts whom they connect with online give them all the information they need to feel confident in their purchases. In turn, growing numbers of seniors are buying vacations, flights, and activities online.

Seniors, Technology, and Socializing

More seniors today are computer-savvy, and they like to spend their spare time surfing the Internet. When it comes to consumption, technology is important in two ways. First, technologies themselves are consumer products. Smartphones, laptops, tablets, Apple watches, headphones, video-game consoles—all of these and more are pricey products marketed to consumers. Second, many technologies, once purchased, enable further consumption. For example, computers make it easier for people to buy other products through online shopping. And as people shop or otherwise use the Internet, marketers can send them more advertisements for more products. Technology thus becomes a conduit for marketing—one that is available any time of day or night, from the comfort of seniors' own homes.

Researchers have been studying seniors' technology use for decades and continue to do so (for example, Karanasios et al. 2020; Jacobson et al. 2017; Quan-Haase et al. 2016). On average, seniors are still less eager to buy and use new technology than younger consumers (Putten and Glende 2016; Kim et al. 2016). Some aren't confident in their own technical and digital skills. Others say they are wary of online shopping specifically because they are concerned about security, loss of privacy, and the true value of what is on offer (concerns shared by consumers of other ages as well) (Poole 2001; Kim et al. 2016). Others still worry their eyesight may not be good enough to stare at small smartphone screens and digital monitors.

However, all of this is changing. Seniors today are not entirely opposed to trying new technology. Rather, they may need to be persuaded to use these technologies in different ways than young and middle-aged consumers. To this end, Putten and Glende (2016) present 10 ways to improve **technology acceptance** by seniors. Technology acceptance refers to a person's plan to use technology and whether she starts and keeps using it. This acceptance is influenced by many factors, including whether use is voluntary, prior experience with technology, and buying power. A few of their suggestions to improve technology acceptance include:

- Make the technology useful and easy to use.
- Ensure seniors know it exists and show the benefits to them.
- Do not stigmatize people with limited technical skills; instead, help them develop and preserve the skills they need to use a given piece of technology.
- Many seniors may want some support from real humans; make sure it's available.
- Assure seniors that their privacy and data will be secured, at low cost and low risk.
- Offer seniors training and support.
- Market technology to family and caregivers of the senior, so they can encourage its adoption.

These and other strategies appear to be working. McMurtrey et al. (2010; see also Jacobson et al. 2016) find evidence the "digital divide" between young and old may be dwindling. Between 55 percent and 70 percent of seniors in this study own at least one computer, either a desktop or laptop (or perhaps both). Of those who do not own a computer, two-thirds report that they have access to one. The main reason these seniors use computers is to access the Internet. Though most participants did not shop online, a significant number did, and those who buy online do so repeatedly. What this group likes most about e-commerce is the convenience: they can browse products from the comfort of their home, and have purchases delivered. A larger percentage use the Internet to research products they're interested in buying, including medicine; the travel destinations, vacation packages, and activities mentioned above; and clothing. Most of these technology accepters are wealthy, since they are the ones who can afford new technology such as smartphones and laptops. Researchers expect the divide to continue shrinking since, over time, more and more seniors will have used technology in their younger days.

In addition, more seniors are discovering that online shopping meets many of their needs in ways in-person shopping cannot. For example, an online store doesn't care if you take a little more time to make a purchase decision, or have trouble reading a price tag. By contrast, a busy salesperson in a store might get impatient. The Internet can also provide information from many different sources at once. Comparing prices, for example, is easier online than if you need to hike from store to store. And buyers do not have to contend with long queues or unsympathetic sales staff. Instead, seniors have more control over the pace of their transactions online.

At the same time, by making the transition to online shopping many seniors would lose what they see as one of the key pleasures of live commerce—socializing and interacting with others.

Many seniors find themselves spending more time alone, and less time with family and friends than they did in their earlier years (Kim and Kang 2005; Hwang et al. 2016). According to a survey, 81 percent of Canadian seniors reported feeling lonely and isolated (Brown 2019). For some, shopping in brick-and-mortar stores is one of the main opportunities they have to get out of the house and socialize (King et al. 2016). Several studies find that seniors say they visit shopping malls not only to buy things, but to curb loneliness and find people to talk to (Kim and Kang 2005; Calvo-Porral and Lévy-Mangin 2019).

In response, mall owners and retailers have started designing these spaces to provide relaxing and comfortable environments where seniors can spend time socializing. They have also realized that most seniors buy *something*, even if they come to the mall for purely social reasons. For example, they may join their friends for a coffee in the food court or buy something they see in a store window while walking with their family. That means it's in the best interests of mall owners and retailers to attract seniors who want to socialize.

Similarly, mall owners have discovered that special events like fashion shows and gymnastic exhibitions give seniors something to do. The more they come to expect these social forms of entertainment, the more likely they are to return to the mall for future visits, where they are likely to continue buying. Malls are also playing into seniors' wish for conveniently co-located services. For example, they are adding banks, medical, dental or vision offices, health-screening services, and post office branches.

Retailers, for their part, tap into older shoppers' yearning for social connections by hiring older salespeople. Isolated, lonely consumers may reach out to these salespeople for company and conversation under the guise of getting their recommendations or help. But once they have connected, these salespeople can help convince the older customer to buy.

One industry that has excelled at catering to older adults' need for social contact is the food industry. Seniors spend more money at grocery stores than their younger counterparts (Bellenger et al. 2004; see also Lesakova 2016). For that reason, plenty of research has been done on their food-shopping habits. Pettigrew et al. (2005; 2017) found that older shoppers valued friendly employees, easy-to-use trolleys and baskets, convenient placement of products on supermarket shelves, and short, fast-moving checkout lines. Similarly, Moschis et al. (2004; Moschis, 2017) found that nine in 10 seniors said they patronized stores because it was easy to locate the foods and products they were looking for. Large majorities also chose locations near their home, those with familiar brands and items, and those with price cuts and seniors' discounts. Finally, seniors tend to focus on the availability of products that meet their health needs; how easy it is to return products and get refunds; assistance provided by store personnel; and the recommendation of same-age peers.

These are all factors that consumers of any age might consider. What sets seniors apart is the fact that they choose grocery stores that give them an opportunity to socialize (King et al. 2016). More than half said they patronize a grocery store because they find it a comfortable place to chat with other shoppers or staff.

As retailers have realized the importance of customer service to older consumers, many are training staff to memorize regulars' needs and product preferences. This happens not just in grocery stores, but also in restaurants. Some stores are trying to improve customer loyalty by going the extra mile of bringing seniors' groceries to their cars for them. Or they may pack purchases in such a way as to make it easier for seniors to walk or take public transport home. Recognizing that older consumers may have mobility and other health needs, retailers design stores to make it easy for seniors to find what they are looking for, and to socialize. Big, easy-to-read signs help them navigate, while liberal return policies meet seniors' demands. Finally, some retailers are even bundling their services, offering pharmacies, drug stores, and cleaners all under one roof.

For seniors who live alone, social interactions with retail workers, bank tellers, grocery-store staff, and others are particularly enjoyable. But other seniors with mobility challenges may find it difficult to make these trips as often as they'd like. Perhaps they shop just once a week and spend the other six days at home alone.

Some say the Internet—specifically, social media—is the perfect solution to combat such loneliness (Trocchia and Janda 2000; Mazur et al. 2019). It allows seniors to connect with family, friends, and acquaintances from the comfort of the home. They can also use social media to make plans to meet with others outside their home (Comfort Keepers 2016).

Indeed, seniors are the fastest-growing group of Internet users. Many have begun to use social media (Get Cyber Safe 2018). Some say they particularly enjoy communicating with others and sharing their photos on social media. It helps them feel connected to the world around them (Davison 2013). For instance, one study canvassed residents at Forest Hill Retirement Living in Toronto. "I want to check up on my grandchildren," one resident declared. "I want to see what they're doing, their girlfriends, their boyfriends, what nonsense they're up to" (Davison 2013).

Even online shopping can offer seniors a sense of connection. They don't just make financial transactions; they may also chat with retail workers and support staff. Or perhaps they visit forums where they can ask questions about products that they're interested in buying and strike up conversations with other consumers.

To find out more about this, Nimrod (2009; also, Okun and Nimrod 2019) looked at online communities among seniors. He examined a full year of data from 14 of these communities, which included 686,283 messages. Results showed a constant increase in seniors' daily activity throughout the year. They talked mainly about these 13 subjects: "fun online," retirement, family, health, "work and study," recreation, finance, religion and spirituality, technology, aging, "civic and social," shopping, and travel. Overall, these communications were more positive than negative, leading Nimrod to conclude that online communities provide social support, contribute to self-preservation, and give seniors opportunities for self discovery and growth. They help seniors make new friends and keep in touch with old ones, despite mobility and transportation limitations. By offering them both a leisure activity and an expanded social network, these communities contrib-

Studies show that older adults are now the fastest-growing segment of Internet users. Not only are many seniors using social media and other online applications for recreational purposes, but many seniors who continue to be employed on at least a part-time basis have had to master such technologies at work as well.

ute to seniors' well-being. Perhaps as a result, they are gaining popularity.

It's important to remember, however, our earlier discussions of these online communities. Every day, social networking sites become more about advertising and less about genuine connections and conversations. Once-popular chat rooms, designed only to facilitate discussion among people interested in the same topics, aren't as widespread as they once were. And it's next to impossible to find an online community that has not been monetized. Most are peppered with advertisements along the sidebars and in pop-up windows that try to take you away from the social interactions you came to the site to enjoy.

It may be better for some isolated seniors to have any social interaction at all, regardless of whether advertising is involved. This is true whether it's chatting with a fellow retiree about gardening or with a salesperson about their next vacation package. But it's worth noting the fundamental difference between these two types of interactions—and between interactions that happen in person and those that happen online (on this, see Ringer and Anestis 2018; Zhang et al. 2018).

A virtual salesperson won't be there to comfort you after a bad day or celebrate your latest success; they only offer social interaction when you're planning to buy something. And a computer screen or smartphone can't give you a much-needed hug. Technology can help relieve isolation and loneliness, especially for seniors who may not be able to leave their homes as often as they'd like. But that doesn't mean it can replace genuine face-to-face human contact.

Brand Loyalty and Habitual Consumption

Brand loyalty is one of the most distinctive features of senior consumers. It sets them apart from younger consumers—for example, millennials—who can be less loyal.

Seniors are often slow to change their patterns and routines. This has both positive and negative implications for businesses. On one hand, seniors are often more reluctant to try new products and experiences than their younger counterparts. Businesses may therefore struggle to gain new customers from this age group. But because seniors are often predictable and loyal customers, businesses have an easier time retaining them than they do younger, flightier consumers.

Of course, these patterns don't always hold. At all ages, some consumers change their preferred brand frequently, whereas others remain attached to it for long periods. But the *proportion* of consumers engaging in these buying behaviors varies across age ranges. As well, long-established products often attract new consumers—one of the advantages to having a longstanding, strong brand reputation. Meanwhile, the success of a new brand may be fleeting.

Research from several industries confirms these trends. Lambert-Pandraud and Laurent (2010) examine the French perfume market (see also Phua et al. 2020). There, some market leaders are decades old, while hundreds of new competitors launch each year. Results show that younger consumers change their preferred brand often, benefiting relatively recent entrants into the market. By comparison, seniors usually remain attached for longer periods to the same preferred brand. A classic study by Pandraud et al. (2005; Lambert-Pandraud et al. 2017) explores automobile purchases (but see also Dehdashti et al. 2018). They found that seniors often buy the same brand when they buy a new car. They consider fewer brands, fewer dealers, and fewer models, and choose long-established brands more often.

Pandraud et al. discuss four theories that could help explain this buying behaviour: involvement, expertise, national preference, and gender. First, older buyers may not be interested in cars, and therefore have less involvement in the buying process. This lack of interest causes them to consider fewer brands, and opt for the brand they're already used to, since they aren't interested enough to shop around for something new. If they do switch brands, this lack of interest draws them to long-established brands they've heard of and trust, rather than newer brands they would have to research and learn about. However, in their data, the researchers find no support for this theory; seniors are no less interested in cars than younger consumers.

Second, some propose that seniors have more amassed expertise, since they have longer histories of buying and driving cars. That lengthy experience contributes to a routinized decision-making process: they've bought so many cars over the years, the process becomes monotonous, and they just end up buying the same thing over and over. However, this theory does not hold up either. Generally, people with expertise seek out *more* information, consider *more* brands, and take *more* test drives than people with less expertise. Expertise tends to increase searches for information, but age significantly decreases those searches.

Third, some think national preference may play a part: for example, older French buyers may only want to buy a French-made car, leading them to consider only a few national brands and ignore other possibilities. Indeed, in Pandraud et al.'s (2005) data, national preference had a significant, positive impact on buying behavior. People who preferred products from certain countries were more likely to buy cars made by those countries. However, this preference is not correlated with age: seniors are no more likely to have strong preferences for cars made in certain countries than consumers of other ages. So this isn't the factor that explains seniors' brand loyalty either.

Research suggests older car buyers tend to buy the same brand that they have purchased previously. Data gathered by car makers also shows that long-established "legacy" brands like Cadillac and Lincoln attract older purchasers than brands that were introduced into the market more recently. For these and other reasons, car manufacturers often continue to market the same nameplates for many decades. The first generation of the Ford Thunderbird was introduced in 1955, with the eleventh (and so far final) generation of the car ceasing production six decades later in 2005. The Chevrolet Suburban, an SUV manufactured by General Motors, holds the record as the automotive nameplate that has been in continuous production for the longest duration. The first generation (then a station wagon) debuted as a 1935 model, with the twelfth generation coming to market in 2021.

Finally, some say women make up a greater fraction of older car buyers and are more cautious consumers. This caution makes them choose the same brands repeatedly. However, in Pandraud et al.'s (2005) sample and in the overall population, the percentage of female car buyers is smaller among older groups than among younger groups. The researchers therefore discard this theory, too. Instead, they put forward four other explanations, based on research in gerontology and psychology: biological aging, cognitive decline, socio-emotional selectivity, and decision (risk) aversion.

Pandraud et al. (2005) suggest, first, that older consumers usually stick with known car brands because their physical capacities start declining. Of people aged 80 and older, more than half say they have problems walking, and shop only "occasionally" or "never." They are more restricted in when they leave the house, and where they go. Thus, age-related physical weakness may reduce the number of dealers that older consumers can visit. Again, however, segmentation is important. Many consumers in their sixties and seventies don't have such significant mobility limitations, and could explore more dealers and test-drive more brands, if they wanted to. So, biological aging can only partially explain the results.

A second factor may be memory. Some older consumers' memories may limit the set of vehicles they are considering to previously owned or already-known brands. Others are no longer able to evaluate several complex choices in detail. Recent studies have used neuroimaging techniques to show the age-related decline of working memory. Working memory helps us encode information in our long-term memory and recover recent events. With their lessened working memory, seniors may avoid certain complicated cognitive efforts, such as a comparison of alternative choices. Choosing the same brand that they already know is just easier.

Third, there's socio-emotional selectivity theory. It suggests some seniors view their time horizon as limited. These consumers highlight feelings and emotions, and their interest in new information declines. For example, they give top priority to close, well-known, emotional contacts over new, informative ones. They therefore interact with fewer people—mainly, those they already know well. So, some seniors may want to interact with familiar car dealers they have developed a rapport with over the years.

What's more, older consumers are more likely than younger ones to insist they made a good buy. They assign positive features to the goods they choose, and negative features to the ones they reject. For example, they are usually satisfied with their previous car, which *they* chose to buy. This tendency may also extend to car dealers themselves: older consumers may think most highly of the dealer they ultimately selected and think those they didn't choose are inferior.

However, in a later study of 88,000 purchases of 60 grocery brands from six categories, Phua et al. (2020) show clearly that older consumers do not buy older brands more often than newer brands. Older consumers also do not principally buy older brands. Rather, brands of all ages compete for consumers of all ages. For older brands, despite the advantage of long-term exposure to older consumers, such advantage will fade if these brands fail to maintain a competitive presence in the market, as older consumers try and become loyal to newer brands.

To some degree, then, but only to some degree, seniors may pick brands in different ways than younger adults (Cole et al. 2008; Hettich et al. 2018). First, aging can make it hard for people to deliberate and weigh choices efficiently. That makes some older consumers make poorer-quality decisions as they age. On the other hand, some skills may improve with age. For example, in some circumstances, seniors may make higher-quality decisions than younger adults because they organize the decisions they're going to make, focus on emotional goals, and have more experience.

Sometimes, it's better to have experience than it is to collect and analyze a lot of new information about different competitors and products. For example, it can be good to have years of experience consuming a certain brand of tea and knowing confidently that you enjoy it and your body processes it well. This is better than just reading through dozens of product reviews of different teas and still not knowing what they taste like.

To make good decisions, consumers must have accurate, timely information; but they also have to be able to understand that information and its implications for them. They need to be able to distinguish important differences between their brand and product choices and weigh factors to match their needs and values. Finally, they must be able to make trade-offs and, in the end, a choice. Aging-related changes in information processing suggest that older and younger adults may differ in the abilities that help support sound decision-making.

In sum, seniors often use information differently than younger consumers. That said, most consumer decision-making is driven by habit, whatever the age of the buyer. As purchases are repeated over time, they become habitual. Buying certain products and brands becomes routine, and thus unconscious. Habituation reduces the deliberate thought needed to act. Having built up these buying habits over longer periods of time, seniors are more likely to continue them.

These habits make the idea of cognitive decline muddier. Perhaps age-related cognitive deficits lead some older consumers to rely on automatic, habit-driven behavior. However, field studies show the real-world performance of seniors is usually on par with that of younger adults. Maybe it's not that seniors have decreased cognitive abilities and are therefore less able to gather and analyze as much information as their younger counterparts. Maybe older consumers just *spend* fewer cognitive resources because they feel they can rely on the habits they've developed over the years.

Some of these habits may have been developed decades earlier. As we have seen, several studies show a tendency for seniors to prefer long-established choices. The *nostalgia mechanism* suggests consumers develop these preferences during a "critical period" between ages 15 and 30 and keep them for life. An alternative theory proposes that consumers can develop, over the years, an attachment to a movie star, a music style, or a brand. This can happen even if their first meeting with it occurs at a later age, much beyond the "critical period."

Final Thoughts

Compared to children, young adults, and middle-aged people, seniors are typically less avid consumers. They are less inclined to use consumer goods to show off their status, declare their group membership, or show their social ambitions. They are also relatively indifferent to the communicative properties of consumer goods—except, perhaps, when they use consumer goods to symbolize their contentment. We have also seen that, across many different industries, seniors are more loyal to their preferred brands, place greater emphasis on product features and quality, and seek out deals and price cuts.

This can be interpreted in at least two ways. Some psychologists say this departure from average consumption habits is a result of senescence or cognitive impairment, risk aversion, or a blind loyalty to tried and true ways. On the other hand, a sociologist might conclude that seniors' buying habits reflect self-confidence and self-knowledge. Perhaps they know who they are and what they want. They are reluctant to spend their time, money, and energy trying to communicate a youthful adaptability and hipness to others.

That said, we also identified ways in which older and younger consumers are similar. Both groups, for example, are increasingly being segmented into smaller sub-categories. Just as we see tweens, pre-teens, and young adults on one end of the age spectrum, so too do we see "young-old," "middle-old," and "old-old" adults at the other. Businesses develop different products to sell to each of these subcategories, and marketers promote these products in different ways.

We also saw that, just like younger adults, seniors may consume in antisocial, risky, and otherwise problematic ways. One example of such problematic behaviour we explored in this chapter is gambling. Casinos are major attractions for many seniors. Some find casinos attractive because they are among the few social spaces that are physically and socially accessible for seniors. They satisfy a craving for excitement, social interaction, and a sense of accomplishment. However, gambling can be financially devastating. It can exhaust the savings retirees are counting on to support them.

Gambling can also strain relationships. Friends and family members may disapprove of a loved one's gambling, especially if it is becoming a problem financially. If they overspend, they risk being unable to support themselves, causing some family members to worry they will need to assume that responsibility. These fears can be overwhelming for members of the so-called sandwich generation: middle-aged adults caught between trying to care for their young children and aging parents. Already stretched thin, these middle-aged adults may fret over their parents' gambling habit, or the many cruises they treat themselves to. They know they wouldn't be able to manage additional expenses, should their parents suddenly find themselves in need.

Gambling, although an enjoyable recreational activity for many seniors, can also have negative social consequences.

Other people complain about the spending habits of seniors in general. Seniors' discounts, for example, have attracted some negative attention. Today, teenagers, young adults, and middle-aged adults work in a precarious labour market (if they can find work at all). Many earn low wages, do not receive benefits, and lack job security. Those with children live on a tight budget. Meanwhile, seniors today are well-off, compared with the seniors from a few generations ago for whom the discounts and deals were originally created. As more of them buy luxury vacations, second homes, and other non-essentials, younger people question their need for special treatment.

Discussion Questions

1. In this chapter, we learned that many seniors are not interested in gaining and signifying their success. Why might this be? How might this shape their consumer behaviour? In what ways might seniors spend their money instead?

2. More seniors are starting to use technology. The digital divide between the young and old is diminishing. How might technology improve or worsen the everyday lives of seniors? Do you think that social communication through the Internet should be encouraged? Or is it more important for seniors to have face-to-face interactions?

3. We learn from this chapter that seniors have distinct consumer habits. What are some examples of these habits and why might they appeal to a business?

Quick Quiz

1. A transition from youth to adulthood is an example of a _____.
a. Process of segregation
b. Process of integration
c. Rite of passage
d. Ritual
e. Symbolic demarcation

2. What is segmentation?
a. Dividing up a market into different categories based on consumer characteristics
b. Dividing up a market based on the type of product being sold
c. A change of status
d. The distinct and differentiated life stages
e. Segmenting consumers in a market based on socioeconomic status

3. What is positioning?
a. Marketers making efforts to target a certain consumer group
b. The image of a company and its products that marketers want their customers to have
c. Marketing a product in a strategic location to attract the targeted consumer group
d. The way that customers interpret and perceive a company and its products
e. The unintended messages that a company conveys through marketing

4. Which type of senior traveler makes up the smallest segment of the tourism industry?
a. Indulgers
b. Enthusiasts
c. Pioneers
d. Aussies
e. Big Spenders

5. Who are the "ailing outgoers"?
a. Infirm but unsociable seniors
b. Seniors who often overindulge and splurge on luxuries
c. Seniors who are willing to pay a high price for a good travel experience
d. Seniors who are active and enjoy adventures
e. Infirm but sociable seniors

The answers to the Quick Quiz are provided at the end of the book.

For Further Reading

Engaging Older Adults with Modern Technology: Internet Use and Information Access Needs by Robert Zheng, Robert Hill, and Michael Gardner
This book explores how seniors can use the Internet and technology to facilitate life-long learning.

Marketing to Seniors by Michael Walker
Marketing to Seniors reveals distinct characteristics of the senior market. The book explores how people, such as friends and family, influence senior purchasing decisions.

The Mature Market: A Gold Mine of Ideas for Tapping the 50+ Market by Robert Menchin
This book helps marketers understand how to strategically reach and appeal to the senior market.

Key Terms

Rites of passage
Rituals
Market segment
Senior

Chapter Sixteen
Bending and Breaking the Rules

Learning Objectives

After reading this chapter, you will be able to:

✓ Question just how "deviant" impulsive buying is in our consumer society.

✓ Note the motivations behind compulsive spending.

✓ Identify consumers' use of rationalization and neutralization to justify their deviance.

✓ Understand how marketers can enable rule-bending and -breaking.

For most people in the West, consuming comes as naturally as breathing. We buy, sell, and use consumer goods hundreds of times every day. It's how we're raised.

So, unless you think critically about it, as we have done in this book, consumerism can feel impulsive and lawless. But you know, from reading this book, that there *are* rules to consumerism. You need to buy the right things, at the right time, with the right people for consumption to be meaningful. Most of the time, you need to buy these things with money—not, say, fur pelts. And to get that money, you need to participate in our capitalist economy by getting and keeping a job. So every time you consume, you're following the social rules that underpin our consumer-capitalist society.

As discussed, we spend our whole lives learning these rules. That does not, however, mean they are always clear or easy to follow. Even people who are trying hard to follow the rules often end up breaking them (Kahane and Savulescu 2012). More surprisingly, our society prizes certain kinds of abnormality and extreme behaviour (see, for example, Goldman and Hogg 2016; Abrams et al. 2018). Most people would love to be abnormally rich, abnormally beautiful, and abnormally popular. Conversely, we abhor other kinds of abnormality. No one wants to be abnormally poor, abnormally plain, or abnormally isolated. Some people break social rules to achieve desired kinds of abnormality or to avoid other, feared kinds. That is because good kinds of abnormality are thought to bring greater happiness and well-being—the very things we think we can obtain through consumption.

As we will learn in this chapter, people who break the rules of consumer society are sometimes simple lawbreakers: they acquire goods without paying for them. Others who break the rules of consumer society are people who do not consume enough or consume in the "right ways." They may also be reclusive, rebellious, or antisocial in other ways. From this standpoint, the prototypical rule-breaker of consumer society is Charles Dickens' fictional character Ebenezer Scrooge, the central figure in his classic work *A Christmas Carol.*

The story starts with a character sketch of Ebenezer Scrooge—an aged, solitary, and rich but unhappy man. If you had to describe Scrooge in a few words, you might choose greedy, selfish, ungenerous, and unloved. Most of all, Scrooge is unsociable and antisocial. He doesn't spend his money on anyone (even himself) and he doesn't spend time with anyone. He is not a member of consumer society in any sense whatever, socially or materially.

Over the course of three nights, Scrooge is visited by the ghost of Jacob Marley, his former business partner, and three spirits: the Spirits of Christmas Past, Christmas Present, and Christmases Yet-to-Come. So frightened is Scrooge by the last spirit, who foretells Scrooge's impending and unlamented death, that he changes his life. In short order, Scrooge buys a gift for someone (a Christmas turkey) and goes to visit his long-ignored relatives. Said another way, Scrooge becomes a consumer, a sociable member of society—and is immediately accepted and beloved by others. Scrooge is saved, spiritually and socially, by pledging to become a paid-up member of consumer society.

Some researchers have read this story as a fable about the transformative power of fears about death (Jonas et al. 2002). We see another moral to the story. Namely, in a consumer society, social isolation is equivalent to death, and social isolation is a correlate (or consequence) of failure to spend time and money on others. This, we would argue, is the true "Scrooge effect." And if that is true, then rule-bending and rule-breaking in our consumer society is tied up with proper and sufficient spending behaviour.

Behaving like Scrooge is the worst kind of rule-breaking in a consumer society, and as Dickens shows, it results in contempt, exclusion, and isolation. But as we will see in this chapter, there are many kinds of deviant consumer behaviour. As always, deviant behaviour reveals the hidden boundaries, rules, and expectations of our society.

Defining Our Terms

Deviance means violating social norms. Some forms of deviance involve breaking formal, institutionalized rules, such as laws. Other forms of deviance involve breaking informal, social rules, like your friends' or parents' expectations.

When it comes to consumer behaviour, there are many forms of deviance. In a classic analysis entitled "Deviant Consumer Behavior," Moschis and Cox (1989) map consumer deviance. An adapted and expanded version of their "map" is presented in Box 16-1.

Box 16-1

Consumer Behaviour: A Typology as Viewed from the Perspective of Society

		Demands that Society Places upon its Members	
		Behaviour that is NOT Regulated	*Behaviour that is Regulated*
Desirability of Behaviour	**Normative Behaviours**	RATIONAL BEHAVIOUR Examples include: • Following directions on how to use products safely and correctly • Following energy conservation guidelines • Following recycling and waste disposal guidelines	MANDATORY BEHAVIOUR Examples include: • Proper and honest use of payment processing systems • Following government requirements for obtaining a driver's license • Following traffic and parking regulations
	Deviant Behaviours	NEGLIGENT BEHAVIOUR Examples include: • Compulsive shopping (e.g., "shopaholic" behaviours) • Buying goods on impulse • Using products incorrectly, inappropriately, or in an unsafe fashion	FRAUDULENT OR CIMINAL BEHAVIOUR Examples include: • Stealing (e.g., shoplifting) • Fraudulent use of credit cards, counterfeit money, or other payment instruments • Driving while under the influence of drugs or alcohol

Source: Adapted from Moschis and Cox (1989).

Moschis and Cox (1989) suggest that for a consumer behaviour to be considered deviant, it must be non-normative or undesirable in the eyes of most members of society. To repeat, some consumer behaviour is deviant because it's criminal: there are laws (or regulations) that prohibit it. Shoplifting and credit card fraud are examples of criminal consumer behaviours. Some consumer behaviour is unregulated and therefore non-criminal deviant behaviour. Examples include product misuse, compulsive buying, and impulse buying.

As we have discussed throughout this book, social norms are socially constructed. Because deviance is any violation of a social norm, it is also socially constructed. We know this because deviant and criminal behaviours are viewed differently in different cultures. Certain kinds of deviance, such as murder, are abhorred almost universally. But when it comes to minor crimes and non-criminal deviance, perceptions vary widely.

One cross-cultural study of consumer deviance by Babakus et al. (2004) looked at attitudes toward deviant consumer behaviour in Austria, Brunei, France, Hong Kong, the UK, and the U.S. (Babakus et al. 2004; for another application see also Cova et al. 2018). Respondents were asked to rate their response to these behaviours on a five-point scale, with 1 being the most off-putting and 5, the most tolerable. The results are shown in Box 16-2.

Box 16-2
Views of Deviant Consumer Behaviours, Selected Countries

Type of deviant consumer behaviour	Overall	Rank	US	UK	France	Austria	Brunei	Hong Kong
Drink a can of pop in a store but don't buy it	1.8	1	1.3	2.2	1.7	2.9	1.2	1.4
Make use of a long-distance calling code that isn't your property	1.8	2	1.2	2.2	1.6	3.0	1.5	1.3
Tell insurance company something was stolen so you can collect the money, when in fact you lost it	2.3	4	1.3	2.5	2.1	3.9	1.7	2.0
Change the price on an item in a retail store	1.9	3	1.3	2.1	1.8	3.4	1.3	1.5
Use the phone at work for a personal call	2.4	7	1.8	3.2	2.5	2.2	1.9	2.6
Don't tell your restaurant server the bill was wrongly calculated to benefit you	2.3	6	1.8	3.2	2.5	2.2	1.6	2.4
Don't say anything if given too much change at store	2.7	8	2.2	3.2	2.5	2.5	2.4	3.4
Take towels from hotel or blanket from airplane as a souvenir of trip	3.1	11	3.0	3.6	3.0	2.3	3.2	3.6
Book a hotel room intended for two people (two double beds) and have more than two people stay in the room	2.3	6	2.0	3.1	2.2	1.8	2.2	2.5
Take advantage of a "free trial" offer	3.0	9	3.2	3.6	3.6	1.6	3.0	3.4
Jump the queue when there's a long line-up	3.1	10	3.4	3.7	3.8	1.5	3.3	2.8

Note 1: Overall rankings (second column) range from 1 (most offensive) to 5 (most tolerable).
Note 2: US: *n* = 192. UK: *n* = 220. France: *n* = 166. Austria: *n* = 208. Brunei: *n* = 176. Hong Kong: *n* = 188.
Source: Table adapted from E. Babakus et al. (2004), Reactions to unethical consumer behavior across six countries in *Journal of Consumer Marketing* 21(4): 257.

This research shows that people in different counties hold different views of what is right and wrong or, more precisely, how right or wrong a behaviour may be. Age and religious affiliation are also significant, consistent predictors of consumer ethical views. Specifically, Eastern religions are more ethical. That is, they are usually less tolerant of these questionable behaviours. Young Christian women were also likely to respond negatively to all of these questionable behaviours.

This means the rules of consumption are fluid, depending on who's following or breaking them, and who's judging the following or breaking. What seems normal to some consumers is deviant to others.

As mentioned, the rules are more rigid when it comes to criminal consumer behaviours (Moschis and Cox 1989). First, **shoplifting** is the theft of merchandise from retail establishments (Ling and Cramer 2017). The most frequently stolen types of goods are cosmetics, which are small in size but often expensive (Smith 2014). Electronics, toys, and games also have high theft rates. Most shoplifters are not experienced criminals and they do not steal because they are unable to afford goods; they shoplift for the thrill and excitement of getting away with breaking the rules (Ling and Cramer 2017). People who feel socially excluded are more likely to shoplift in search of exhilaration and something to boost their mood.

Shoplifting is thus quite common: 60 percent of consumers admit to having shoplifted at some point in their lives. It is a major problem for retailers, who lose an estimated $50 billion to shoplifting per year (Korgaonkar et al. 2019). Recent technological changes to the checkout process at many stores may make matters worse (Aloysius et al. 2019). Self-serve checkouts may cut retailers' labour costs, but they make it easier for customers to walk off with products they haven't paid for.

A second form of criminal consumer behaviour is **product misuse**: when a consumer uses a product in a way its manufacturer did not intend and could not have expected. Some forms of product misuse can result in injury or even death. One example is the use of pharmaceutical drugs such as opioid painkillers without a prescription (Swank et al. 2016; Bourin and Chagraoui 2017).

Third, **credit card fraud** is fraud committed using a payment card, such as a credit card or debit card. Credit card fraud cost an estimated $416 billion in 2017 (Ryman-Tubb et al. 2018). Consumers may commit credit card fraud in order to purchase goods or services directly, or they may transfer their target's money into their own account.

In this chapter, we will consider a variety of extreme, unethical, or antisocial consumer behaviours, though our discussion is far from exhaustive and could easily be extended. We begin with a behaviour that is perhaps the least deviant of many we will discuss, because it is the most common, least extreme, and least antisocial.

Impulsive Consumption

By **impulsive consumers**, we mean people who spend money on a whim, without any forethought. On the one hand, impulsive buying is deviant because it breaks the presumed "rule" of consumer behaviour that one evaluates one's options carefully before buying. But everyone has impulses, and everyone acts on them from time to time (Fenton-O'Creevy et al. 2018; Badgaiyan et al. 2017).

In fact, merchants depend on impulsive buyers for an important share of their revenue. That's why they display certain goods at the front of the store, near the cash registers. They know that many people, when paying, will decide at the last minute to add a few pleasant, inexpensive items to their bill: a magazine or a chocolate bar, for instance. So, in a sense, impulsive buying is not deviant, even if it is largely irrational. It is so common that it is predictable—the norm. In chapter 1, we used the figure of Donald—the trophy buyer—to represent impulsive buyers, although not all of Donald's boastful purchases are impulsive. However, impulsive purchases do tend to be unusual or eye-catching: often, they provide a dash of enchantment to an otherwise humdrum day.

Depending on what we consider "normal," we can see impulsive buying as both normal *and* deviant. More accurately, impulsive buying is normal in certain contexts and deviant in others. Namely, impulsive buying is common in places where people engage in special or non-routine activities. One example is Las Vegas. Impulsive shopping is part of the city's sex, gambling, and drinking culture. This may be because sex, gambling, and drinking tend to attract and promote impulsive spending. Sudden windfalls (like gambling wins) may motivate some to spend impulsively. Conversely, remorse over misbehaviour or gambling losses may also motivate such spending, as consumers strive to make themselves feel better.

Another example is the airport. Here too, as in casinos, people are wrested away from their routine activities. Impulsive buying may be motivated by misbehaviour while away from home, or just by the wish to bring something home for oneself, a spouse, or one's children, as a memento of the trip.

Even big-ticket impulsive buying is a regular feature of our culture, then. To ease the discomfort we may feel about such deviance, our culture provides excuses and rationalizations. This is the point of the slogan, "What happens in Vegas, stays in Vegas." Actions that would be judged as deviant or improper in any other place are excusable in Las Vegas (see, for example, Van Laer et al. 2019; Cosgrave 2016). They are not to be publicized elsewhere, where they may elicit shame or embarrassment.

In other words, Las Vegas has become a "deviance service centre"—a place where misbehaviour (including impulsive buying) is normal and forgivable, as part of the "Vegas experience." Here, even though not at home, one can take part in heavy drinking, high-stakes gambling, the purchase of sex services from strangers, and big-ticket impulse buying without feeling guilty! It's all part of a brief "fantasy life" that doesn't say anything about who you really are, only about where you are visiting.

That said, large-scale impulsive buying outside these islands of forgivable deviance—like Vegas and airports—is just an extreme version of normal materialist behaviour. It could be the ultimate result of a culture that values money and material goods over all else. Research suggests this may be the case. Impulsive consumer behaviour is predictable, but not according to socio-demographic variables such as gender, age, ethnicity, or income (Amos et al. 2013). These factors are relatively unimportant for impulse buying. Rather, almost anyone can be led to buy impulsively, given the right combination of dispositional and situational factors.

Dispositional factors are lifestyle and personality traits, which can include general impulsiveness. **Situational factors** include time pressure, such as having a salesperson bearing down,

The iconic sign proclaiming "Welcome to Fabulous Las Vegas" was erected in 1959. Fifty years later it was added to the U.S. National Register of Historic Places. The vast increase in the size of the gambling, tourism, and entertainment industries led to a tenfold increase in the city's population over that five-decade period.

waiting for you to make a decision. They also include retail environment, such as product assortment, store layout, and store size, as we saw above with the example of products placed near the cash registers. Finally, situational factors include social influences that encourage buying behaviour, such as shopping with friends you want to impress.

Unlike the other socio-demographic factors mentioned, age does influence impulsive spending. Young consumers—especially adolescents—are more impulsive than older ones (Lin and Chen 2012). But social circumstances make all the difference. If they are deeply influenced by their peers, and fear negative judgment from those peers, teens will likely buy impulsively.

Social and material circumstances can also impact dispositional ones. Take self-control, which many see as a personality trait. People buy impulsively when their self-control fails, for various reasons (Baumeister 2002; Vohs et al. 2018). First, conflicting goals reduce self-control. For example, if one of your goals is to feel refreshed and energized, you may impulsively buy a six-dollar latte. That goal—and the purchasing decision you took to actualize it—directly undermines your other goal of saving money.

Second, self-control is a resource just like energy or patience. It depletes gradually as you use it, making it less effective. Tired consumers are more likely to buy impulsively than well-rested ones. Confused or harried consumers are more likely to buy impulsively than people with time to spare. Any environment that produces anxious and distracted dispositions—for example, crowded, noisy, and brightly lit casinos or shopping malls—will increase the risk of impulse buying.

Often, people buy impulsively to escape negative emotions and low self-esteem (Verplanken and Sato 2011). Impulse buys make them feel better instantly. But as we discussed in earlier chapters, the pleasure of consumption is short-lived. Soon, the feelings of low self-esteem return, and another impulse buy is made to temper them. Impulse buying therefore tends to be cyclical and repetitive. So, impulse buying may be relatively common and, in that sense, "normal." That does not mean, however, that it is healthy or good. Just the opposite: it seems to be one of the costs we pay for materialism.

Compulsive Buying and Shopping Addiction

Compulsive consumers are different from impulsive consumers. Compulsive buying—with shopping addiction at its extreme—is pathological by definition. It's included in the DSM-V—the *Diagnostic and Statistical Manual of Mental Disorders*, which health professionals use to assess and diagnose mental disorders—alongside a variety of other compulsive behaviours, as a type of treatable mental illness. In chapter 1, we used "Anton" to represent compulsive buyers: people who buy (and often hoard) in a fruitless effort to deal with persistent negative feelings, from depression to anxiety.

Compulsive buying combines an irresistible urge and a loss of control (Hollander, Baker, Kahn and Stein 2006; on compulsive young people, see also Peris and Schneider 2016). Compulsive consumers know they shouldn't spend the money or buy the desired object, but do so anyway. As well, such compulsive buying brings regular and predictable harm. In these respects—the irresistible urge, the loss of control, the predictable harm—compulsive buying is like every other addiction (e.g., to alcohol, drugs, or gambling).

The medical definition of addiction has seven criteria, based on those used by the American Psychiatric Association in the DSM-V and by the World Health Organization (International Statistical Classification of Diseases and Related Health Problems, 10th revision). To determine whether a person has a shopping addiction, medical professionals ask patients questions in seven categories, including whether the amount they shop has increased over time, whether they've tried to shop less, whether they suffer withdrawal symptoms when not shopping, if they have difficulties controlling how much they shop or continue to shop despite negative consequences, whether other activities are put off or neglected because of shopping, and if they spend significant time and energy thinking about shopping or trying to avoid it.

Estimates of the lifetime prevalence of shopping addiction in North America vary, but the most widely agreed figure is roughly 6 percent of the population. This means that, in the course of their lifetime, roughly one in every seventeen Canadians will succumb to a spell of shopping addiction, when they cannot control their spending on consumer items. The length of this spell will vary from one person to another, just like spells of alcohol, drug, or gambling addiction. As well, the social and financial consequences of the spell will also vary.

From a social standpoint, addictions have many harmful consequences, including negative health consequences for addicts and their loved ones. As with gambling addiction, compulsive shopping or shopping addiction can run a family into deep financial trouble over a course of years, depending on what the addict buys. Yet, in Canada and elsewhere, we have not yet taken significant action to help compulsive shoppers. Largely, that is because there hasn't been a high degree of concern about this addiction. Perhaps, although it can be harmful to individuals and families, compulsive shopping is compatible with consumerism and materialistic values and for that reason, we allow it to continue as a "normal" part of our culture.

Like impulsive buying, compulsive shopping can be considered normal or deviant, depending on context. In one sense, compulsive buying is a deviant form of consumerism, which goes against the norms of materialistic behaviour. First, it ignores at least some external concerns, like appearances and prestige. Compulsive buyers aren't buying to impress others or show off their status. Thus, compulsive buying is not communicative buying: not intended to signal status or membership in a group. In fact, shopaholic purchases often result in social *disapproval*, especially from significant others like family members. Second, it is inner-directed: the result of an irresistible urge with roots in one's personal history. Compulsive buying

Box 16-3
Compulsive Consumers in the Media

In the film *Confessions of a Shopaholic*, our protagonist is a compulsive shopper named Rebecca Bloomwood. Her character is first introduced when her credit card gets declined as she's trying to buy a scarf. She meets her love interest when he lends her the money after she lies about wanting to get it for her sick aunt.

In the movie, Rebecca isn't punished for these reckless—even unethical—choices. She never changes her ways. She's constantly lying, avoiding her debt collector, and covering up her irresponsible spending. Eventually, Rebecca's credit cards are maxed out, her relationships are destroyed, and she even loses her job. Her "rock bottom" moment is short lived, though. She makes up with her best friend and love interest, and "solves" her debt problem in an afternoon by selling all of her clothes (including the scarf).

This rather rosy depiction of compulsive consumption wasn't received well. It was released during an economic depression in Canada. Many people were in such financial trouble that they were losing their homes. Seeing Rebecca spend frivolously, then miraculously become debt-free, seemed to suggest that shopping addictions aren't that bad. Even if you lose everything, the movie implied you can still have a happy ending. Many Canadians knew first-hand that's not always true.

is anxious, and fraught with urgency. It is intended to satisfy the consumer's own wants and needs.

But on the other hand, some say compulsive buying is closely related to materialism (Reith 2017). Both compulsion/addiction and materialism are responses to capitalism, which demands extreme productivity and consumption. People are expected to spend half their time working as efficiently as possible, and consuming and playing the rest of the time. People spend compulsively because our capitalist, consumerist society teaches and encourages them to.

Evidence suggests that more materialistic people are more likely to be compulsive buyers (Dittmar 2005; Jung 2017). For example, younger people are more likely to be compulsive buyers than older people. This is in large part because younger people are typically more materialistic.

So, compulsive buying is indeed pathological: a response to an irresistible urge. But it seems that urge is amplified by materialism. Materialistic people think consumer goods will make them feel happy and satisfied. This belief, coupled with the pathological need to buy, may lead to compulsive consumption. Compulsive buying is especially problematic for people who lack financial management skills. These skills include budgeting, making payments on time, saving money, managing credit card debt, and having an idea of your net worth (Pham et al. 2012). Compulsive buyers do not do these things. Sometimes, they are not even aware of them.

Consumers who in fact follow such practices fall into a few different categories. First, there are "value seekers." They use financial management practices to improve their material well-being. They may spend big, but again, they manage that spending for their own benefit. Then there are "highly conscientious" consumers (Donnelly et al. 2012). They plan for the future very well. In turn, they manage their money better, have more savings, and acquire less debt. On the other hand, people who think possessions will make them happy tend to manage their money poorly.

Financial management practices are at odds with our consumer society, especially for materialists. Materialism discourages prudence and encourages compulsive and impulsive buying. In turn, materialistic people often have more financial worries (Gardarsdottir and Dittmar 2012; Zhang et al. 2017). Sometimes, counterproductively, they even rely on buying to raise their sagging spirits (Irwin 2018; Burke 2018).

Box 16-4
Retail Therapy

Popular songs tell people that they need to buy to be happy. In Ariana Grande's song "7 Rings," she sings about retail therapy. In the wake of a tragic concert bombing, an ex-boyfriend's death, and a recent breakup, she shops to try to manage her trauma.

Although most consumers can't afford to spend as lavishly as Grande, many do shop to reduce stress and improve their mood (Forbes). Over 80 percent of youth say they shop to help them disconnect from social media (Kearney 2019, in CNBC). Gen Z say they shop for health and wellness products to relax and make themselves feel better. Marketers lean into the idea, encouraging consumers to "treat themselves."

Having said that, recent studies suggest consumers also see retail therapy as wasteful and pointless (*Psychology Today*, 2013). This is especially true when people go beyond retail therapy and stray into compulsive buying. They risk falling into debt, and retail therapy exacerbates their financial struggles.

Compulsive spenders typically have poor financial management skills. Funnily enough, merchandisers have even developed products to meet this need—more goods to acquire in your efforts to stop acquiring more goods. For example, apps can help consumers track their spending and set budgets.

Materialism and Fetishism

To repeat, **materialism** means prioritizing material possessions over other concerns (see, for example, Flynn et al. 2016; Jaspers and Pieters 2016; Kasser 2016). It can be seen as a form of social deviance in that, when it gets out of hand and consumers lose control of their buying, it can be harmful or dangerous. It can also be seen as a form of psychopathology that hinders people's ability to form and maintain close personal relationships.

Fetishism or **commodity fetishism** robs material goods of their human origin (Hope 2019; Lavalette and Ferguson 2018; Andrews 2018). The result in both cases—materialism and commodity fetishism—is a fascination with material items that lacks human meaning or connection.

Fetishism is a psychological process in which an apparently non-sexual thing (animate or inanimate) is given the value of a sexual object. For example, the proverbial shoe fetishist finds the mere sight of shoes arousing. Freud argued that, at first, fetishists want to look at sexual body parts (e.g. breasts and genitals). Out of fear and shame, they look away. However, the alternate thing they repeatedly look away at—such as another person's feet—comes to remind them of the thing they wanted to see. Eventually, the alternate object—the mere shoe, separated from its owner's foot—becomes the actual object of desire.

Some see commodity fetishism as a typical characteristic of capitalist, consumerist societies. Here, the consumer object—almost any consumer object—becomes a fetish, in that it is a substitute for the social relations that it supplants. Others, following Marx, take a different view. They see commodity fetishism as a tendency to value consumer goods in monetary terms, instead of in terms of the human labour that went into creating them.

From this Marxist perspective, commodity fetishists view goods as having intrinsic value in and of themselves. This value is created by the human labour that goes into making the commodity. This value is not the same as market value, which is a function of relative scarcity. To use Adam Smith's famous example from *The Wealth of Nations* (1776), we value diamonds over fresh water. Even though diamonds are useless, because

Box 16-5

Commodity Fetishism

Diamonds and Marriage

Today, diamonds are one of the most precious gems sold worldwide, especially as engagement rings. But their rise to fame has been a recent development. De Beers, now the world's leading diamond company, began a marketing campaign in 1947 with the slogan "A Diamond is Forever" (American Gem Society). They framed diamonds as symbolizing eternity and permanence. The bigger (and therefore more expensive) the diamond, the more it showed how much a man loved his wife-to-be. On the other hand, small, cheap-looking rings attract judgment. The recipient may feel unappreciated—as though she's unworthy of a big, expensive ring. Some of this has to do with judgment from others. Friends and family could assume that the man does not love her enough to purchase a large diamond, or that he is too poor to afford one.

That being said, some people are shifting their views on diamonds. In the early 2000s, controversy erupted around "conflict" or "blood" diamonds that were being used to fund wars in Africa (*The Canadian Encyclopedia*). Many did not want to buy conflict diamonds. Today, lab-grown or synthetic diamonds are becoming more fashionable as alternatives. They are cheaper and hard to tell apart from mined diamonds. Men can spend less money on a symbol of their love, but still have a dazzling token that their wives can show off. That our views on diamonds evolve with time confirms that their value is socially constructed. They epitomize commodity fetishism.

they are scarce, we pay more for them than the water we need to survive. We arbitrarily attach meaning and value to goods that don't necessarily reflect their value for survival, nor how much time and effort it took to create them.

Most theorists agree that commodity fetishism is common in capitalist societies. However, we can view it as deviant in the sense that it obscures people's true reasons for buying and valuing consumer goods. It is driven by unconscious motives and false beliefs, not by reason and practical concerns. In that sense, it is pathological, even if common.

Rationalizations that Help Us Break the Rules

Possibly, North Americans consume the way they do—that is, in (often) excessive and dangerous ways—thanks to socialization. As we have already seen, certain brands (like Las Vegas) encourage people to break the rules with impunity. Even if parents provide the perfect foundation for financial responsibility, the media and peers can derail it.

Or perhaps excessive consumerism is inevitable in our capitalist society. Our culture teaches that non-conformity is admirable and even heroic. So, people consume in strange, extreme ways because they think it is admirable and better-than-normal. If this is true, it pays for advertisers to appeal to this heroic streak in North American consumers.

This is the idea at the heart of *The Hero and the Outlaw* (2001), a widely discussed book by Margaret Mark and Carol S. Pearson (for a slightly modified take on this, see Pearson 2017). In it, they look at marketing techniques and archetypes brands use to create meaning among consumers.

As we discussed in an earlier chapter, popular brands can become iconic. To have such a successful brand, marketers must understand the needs and wants of their customers. They have to know what motivates a consumer to buy a product. One way that marketers try to gain this understanding is through **motivation theory**, which proposes that consumers are always being pulled in different directions. Specifically, they are pulled toward stability and mastery (on the one hand) and independence and belonging (on the other).

No one understood these factors of motivation better than psychoanalyst Carl Jung (Jung 1990). He suggested that archetypes are stories and characters that resonate deep within our unconscious psyche. We see them in mythology, fiction, and, arguably, brands. According to motivational theory, brands need to motivate consumers to buy something through appeals to the human psyche. Archetypes do this, which is why they can be powerful branding tools for businesses to bridge the gap between a product and the consumer's motivation to buy the product (for commentary on Jung and his archetypes, see Lawson 2018; Silva et al. 2019.)

Mark and Pearson dive into 12 of these archetypes, which they group into four themes, the most important of which (for our purposes) is rule-breaking. Under this rubric of "rule-breaking," we find three archetypes: the hero, the outlaw, and the magician. These archetypes glorify and glamorize rule-bending and rule-breaking. They take risks to see a change in the world. The hero triumphs over evil—sometimes by bending the rules. The outlaw only follows his or her *own* rules, ignoring those laid down by society. And the magician applies sacred and personal knowledge to make things work better. These archetypes satisfy the mastery element of consumer motivation theory. Brands like Nike and FedEx use the hero archetype. The outlaw has been adopted by MTV, Jack Daniels, and Harley Davidson. Lastly, Mastercard and AT&T rely on the magician.

Sociologist Robert Merton famously called criminals "innovators" because they creatively adapt to anomie. In a similar way, Mark and Pearson call rule-benders and rule-breakers cultural icons, to be honoured or at least respected.

The Hero and The Outlaw argues that to maximize meaning, brands must maximize their use of these archetypes. They are so powerful that they can do the work *for* marketers (for recent discussions of this, see Gupta 2017; Farcas and Muresan 2018; Bushueva 2019). Archetypes reach into people's unconscious psyche and resonate with deeper personal needs and wants than the product can alone. In other words, Mark and Pearson think products don't sell themselves. Cool features that meet practical needs are not enough. That's because there's always a competing product that can fulfill consumers' practical needs just as well, if not better.

When brands leverage rule-breaking archetypes like the hero, outlaw, and magician to sell their products, they might encourage people to break rules more generally. That is, they present rule-breaking as a good, admirable, and attractive thing to do. But sometimes, people need more than encouragement to break the rules: they need ways of justifying and explaining their bad behaviour to others, so others do not punish them. And there are many types of punishment to fear as a result of rule breaking, since people use various techniques to control and punish other people.

Techniques of Control

Communities have ways of preventing and controlling rule-breaking behaviour, however they define it. These techniques include guilt and gossip. **Embarrassment** is also a powerful deterrent (Hershcovis et al. 2017; Krishna et al. 2019). For example, young people are often embarrassed when buying condoms. Though sex outside of marriage is common enough, many young people have been told not to do it. A rule has been set, and by buying condoms, they are publicly admitting that they plan to break that rule. The unpleasant feeling of embarrassment is supposed to stop them from buying condoms and, in turn, having sex.

To avoid unpleasant feelings like embarrassment and guilt, people often devise elaborate strategies to hide their behaviours (Arndt and Turedi 2017). For example, they'll go to a self-checkout instead of facing a cashier. Or they'll buy other products like magazines to "mask" the condoms they are buying. This suggests that, to mask embarrassment, people will buy things they don't need and spend more money than they had intended. One creative study confirmed this hunch. Nichols, Raska, and Flint (2015) asked one group of undergraduate students to imagine buying an embarrassing product (hemorrhoid treatment or vaginal itch cream) and another to imagine buying a non-embarrassing product (bandages). The students were told they could buy other, non-embarrassing products too: candy or gum, personal care products, magazines, snacks, and drinks. Finally, the researchers asked participants to rate the degree of embarrassment they would feel if they had to buy that item on a real shopping trip.

Those asked to imagine buying hemorrhoid cream or vaginal itch cream spent significantly more money than people asked to imagine buying bandages. People who said they were embarrassed easily were especially likely to spend more. This suggests people do indeed buy extra products to try to cover up embarrassing ones. However, this strategy of piling up extra goods does not always work. You would need other attention-grabbing items to draw attention away from the embarrassing item (Blair and Roese 2013). Otherwise, the volume of added items just draws attention to the embarrassing one.

The effects of consumer embarrassment extend beyond products such as condoms and laxatives. In fact, the risk of embarrassment affects a host of industries, such as online dating, the weight-loss industry, and the plus-size clothing industry. Considering the widespread impact of consumer embarrassment, marketers need to understand its causes—and develop ways to mitigate it.

Sometimes, purchasing *other* consumer products can help alleviate feelings of embarrassment caused by purchasing an embarrassing product. As Dong, Wang, and Wyer (2013) note, people who feel embarrassed are often motivated to avoid social contact—that is, to hide their faces. At the same time, they are motivated to restore the positive image of themselves that has been tarnished by the embarrassing product (or, in other words, to restore the face they lost). These consumers might buy commercial products that literally mask their face (i.e., hide it, as sunglasses or a big hat can do) or repair it (e.g., restorative cosmetics). However, research shows these two coping strategies have different consequences. Symbolically repairing one's face with cosmetics reportedly reduces feelings of embarrassment and restores a person's willingness to engage in social activities. However, symbolically hiding one's face with sunglasses or a big hat apparently has little impact.

Though people may buy extra products to hide embarrassing ones (like the condoms and hemorrhoid cream mentioned above), they sometimes avoid buying embarrassing products altogether. So, it is in the interest of marketers to find ways of reducing the embarrassment associated with buying certain products that, unlike condoms and itch creams, may be discretionary items, not necessities. Accordingly, researchers have done work on this topic, to find out ways to reduce or eliminate embarrassment that stands in the way of a potential purchase.

As Puntoni, de Hooge and Verbeke (2017) show, social context counts for a lot. In general, people do not want to do embarrassing things in front of other people who might ridicule them. So, for example, a man who is concerned about hair loss is less likely to order a hair stimulation product (like Rogaine) if he views the ad or product in the presence of another person with a full head of hair. Likely, this embarrassment effect is even heightened when people view advertisements or products in the presence of others whose good opinion they consider necessary. For example, men are especially unlikely to respond well to an advertisement for Viagra or penis enlargement in the presence of a woman they are dating.

Marketers can help consumers avoid or minimize public embarrassment in various ways. One such technique is to change product packaging, using colour and design to make the product look discreet and sophisticated, and definitely not weird or ridiculous. Or, marketers could offer alternative purchase methods such as vending machines or online sales and mail delivery of sensitive products (such as condoms) to minimize the threat of public observation. Other marketers try to change social conventions and stigmas around sensitive products (Krishna, Herd, and Aydinoglu, 2018).

Social mishaps in service settings are especially likely to produce feelings of embarrassment in the consumer. One obvious cause is a vague service script: failing to give the employee a clear idea of what to say to a customer under various circumstances—for example, if their credit card isn't working properly (Wu 2010). Another cause of embarrassment is attributing the mishap to the consumer, rather than to the server or a glitch in the technology, for example. Problems like these are especially likely to spiral out of control if there are other customers present, and especially if these other customers are acquaintances of the consumer.

Lunardo and Mouangue (2019) note that, though many people enjoy shopping for luxury goods, some people feel embarrassed doing so, especially in luxuriously appointed stores. To solve this problem, they propose an alternative sales space with less cachet: pop-up stores. This refers to a temporary itinerant retail space intentionally opened for only a short time period. Thanks to their somewhat ad hoc design, customers view them as less luxurious than traditional luxury stores. As a result, they produce less embarrassment and more buying among customers. Consumers who do not value exclusivity when shopping exhibit the lowest degree of anticipated embarrassment, so they are most likely to be motivated to buy in a pop-up retail store.

Some rule-breakers avoid embarrassment or social stigma through what social researchers Sykes and Matza (1964; see also Maruna and Copes 2017) call **techniques of neutralization**. Neutralization is a defense mechanism that consumers use to downplay the consequences of their behaviour (McGregor 2009). For example, rule-breakers might point out that their rule-breaking doesn't harm others, or that everyone is doing it. Marijuana smokers, for example, have used this rationalization for decades. Indeed, there are rationalizations (justifications or neutralizing strategies) to fit almost every occasion. One can deny responsibility ("It's not my fault"), deny the legitimacy of laws or regulations ("Speeding tickets are just money grabs"), or justify one's bad actions by comparing them to what other people have done ("What I did is nothing compared to what *she* did"). Sometimes appeals are made to higher authorities or moral principles ("I had to do it to protect my family") or to necessity ("I had no other choice").

It stands to reason, then, that marketers who can help (potential) consumers neutralize feelings of guilt (or potential guilt) about an activity or purchase will make more sales. Researchers have done some work to figure out how such techniques of guilt neutralization might work, with interesting results. Antonetti and Macklan (2014) find that when a purchase decision includes an ethical dilemma, consumers express guilt or pride even when the purchase is not intentional—that is, when the purchase was forced by circumstances. Even when they explicitly recognize that the purchase is unintentional, participants still report emotional reactions because they feel responsible for the outcomes. Moreover, these emotional responses may have a positive influence on their future purchase of sustainable alternatives.

Guilt has both personal and social dimensions, these authors show. The activation of personal norms plays a mediating role in the experience of guilt and pride. This means that people with principles of which they are aware (or become aware) are likely to feel guilty, while less-principled (or less aware) people are less likely to feel guilty and need techniques of neutralization. Equally important are the perceptions of social visibility: people generally don't like to be seen doing something bad or unpopular. And consumers who believe in altruistic values are more likely than others to perceive ethical behaviour—e.g., fair trade buying—as a personal obligation. Violating these altruistic values in turn, contributes to experiences of guilt.

However, as Gruber and Schlegelmilch (2013) point out, consumers often find ways around the positive norms and values they normally endorse in relation to sustainability. In fact, they scarcely seem to take environmental sustainability into account when buying goods and services. Using survey data, these authors show how neutralization strategies are used to legitimize inconsistencies between norm-conforming attitudes and norm-ignoring (actual) behaviour. So, for example, a highly principled proponent of environmental sustainability may jet from one part of the world to another many times a year to promote sustainability education abroad. In doing so, however, he is enlarging his own ecological footprint and setting an example for doing so. In this way, the continued use of neutralization produces behaviour that is uncertain, unpredictable, and often unprincipled.

Therefore, as Antonetti and Macklan (2013) point out, marketers should appeal to a combination of guilt and pride. This combination will allegedly reduce consumers' ability to neutralize their sense of personal responsibility. It will tell them, "Yes, you can make a difference to the climate crisis, and the destruction of humanity is your fault if you fail to take action." The resulting inability to rationalize away their personal responsibility persuades consumers that they affect sustainability outcomes through their purchasing decisions.

It is not only the rule-breaker who looks for ways to neutralize their wrongdoing. Even the state is occasionally complicit. Canadian sociologist James Cosgrave (2010) points to gambling as a case in point. Research shows gambling is an addiction that can destroy lives and tear families apart. Casinos and racetracks are therefore morally questionable, deviant spaces because they encourage dangerous spending. But governments profit from these spaces. To secure those profits, the state must neutralize the harm done by (and to) problem gamblers. They excuse and cover up this form of deviance in the interest of making money. For example, they say gambling is a personal choice and, therefore, problem gambling is a personal responsibility—not an addiction that governments have actively encouraged and profited from.

On the other hand, some marketers use guilt to promote their products. However, researchers contest the effectiveness of guilt appeals. Antonetti and Baines (2014: 14) review the literature on this topic and suggest that "[t]he use of reactive guilt reminds consumers of their past failures. This … could engender a negative reaction from consumers, leading to derogation of the source of the message, especially if consumers perceive a manipulative intent." Instead, to be effective, appeals should present issues as having a clear and personal relevance to their lives (Antonetti and Baines 2014). They should frame the individual consumer as responsible for other people's suffering or benefit, stressing that their personal consumer choices can hurt or help others. They should refer to potential advantages the individual buyer could obtain from a specified choice and neutralize resistance to buying that is based on guilt. Appeals that are moderately intense but highly credible (and not perceived as manipulative) are most likely to achieve the intended results.

So, for example, late afternoon and early evening television advertisements on cable news networks like CNN or CTV News Channel target senior viewers with some post-secondary education and discretionary income. Some ads are repeated every day, and many times each day. They feature advice about reverse mortgages ("you don't have to feel guilty you're not leaving any money to your children"); information about save-the-animals organizations and children's hospitals ("for less than a dollar a day, you don't have to feel guilty about suffering, helpless creatures"); and medications that can increase your energy level and sociability ("you don't have to feel guilty about ignoring your friends and grandchildren anymore").

In sum, consumerism can evoke an array of emotions. Many marketers play into these emotions, especially guilt and pride, to convince consumers to buy their products—even if it means breaking some rules in the process.

Deviant Products and Services

So far, we have mainly discussed how consumers break the rules of consumption in general. For example, consumers can spend impulsively or compulsively on anything; the product or service itself isn't necessarily the deviant part of the equation. But there are also products and services that are considered deviant in and of themselves. In this section, we examine three such goods: pirated goods, substances, and reviled goods that inspire fear of "product contagion."

Digital piracy—copying and then selling music or movies—is a crime and poses a massive problem for the entertainment industry. Preventive tactics have been largely unsuccessful. One study (Cockrill and Goode 2012) found three kinds of DVD users: serious pirates or "Devils," opportunists or "Chancers," and non-pirates or "Angels." Devils pirate DVDs at least twice a month. They actively seek out opportunities to pirate. They are typically students between 18 and 25 years old. Chancers are low-level pirates. If the chance to pirate comes along, they take it, but they do not go out of their way to create these opportunities. Finally, Angels and Receivers do not pirate DVDs and express no intent to do so.

The neutralization tactics introduced above influence whether consumers pirate or not. For example, they might say their actions don't hurt anyone, so they are permissible. When it comes to pirating, Devils and Chancers don't think their behaviour causes harm. They don't see it as an ethical issue, so they pirate with a clear conscience and no expectation of punishment. Angels, on the other hand, say they think pirating is unethical. That's why they don't do it.

Harris and Dumas (2009) note that misbehaviour is increasingly common in these kinds of peer-to-peer activities, including copying (i.e., pirating) music, movies, software or video games. Such behaviour affects the entertainment sector as a whole and costs the industry billions of dollars each year. Research shows that peer-to-peer file-sharers employ (often multiple) techniques of neutralization in order to pre-justify or post-event rationalize their activities, including: denial of victim; denial of injury; denial of responsibility; claim of normality; claim of relative acceptability; justification by comparison; and appeal to higher loyalties.

Views about pirating goods vary from one culture to another, however (Monroe 2016; Gergely et al. 2017; Sahni and Gupta 2019). For example, in North America, piracy is illegal and

This cartoon was published on the Pirate Bay file-sharing website, which facilitates access to copyright-protected material, including popular movies and books. The site's operators and other advocates of a more lenient approach to copyright enforcement argue that copyright laws are designed to protect wealthy Western companies at the expense of easy access to information for ordinary people. Peter Sunde, Fredrik Neij, and Gottfrid Svartholm, who founded the site, were charged with copyright infringement and found guilty by a Swedish court. Sentenced to a year in prison, they were released after serving reduced sentences. The site continues to operate.

many people think it is unacceptable and immoral. But in China, piracy is so widespread, it's hard *not* to take part (Stephens and Schwartz 2013). There are plenty of convenient retailers with broad selections of the latest, uncensored Western music and movies for extremely low prices. These goods are almost irresistible when compared with the small selection of legally imported CDs and DVDs consumers must travel to a distant store to shop for.

Yet another type of rule-breaking involves consuming controversial substances. Marijuana is a good example. Only recently legalized, some still question whether it's safe or ethical. Plenty of people buy and smoke it. But, as mentioned, they often use neutralization tactics to justify their behaviour. They can sense it breaks at least some people's unspoken rules.

What's more, some rules are more clearly stated than others. Laws are clearly codified rules that everyone is supposed to know. Breaking them is supposed to result in punishment. But depending on the law being broken, punishment doesn't always happen. For example, enforcement of laws against drunk and disorderly behaviour varies over time, and from place to place.

One reason for that may be the lavish spending alcohol (and drugs) often bring about. As we have discussed, people are likely to spend impulsively in fast-paced environments, where their better judgment is blurred by substances. Dance clubs, for example, play loud music, encourage wild dancing, push visitors to socialize with strangers, and facilitate drinking, creating an atmosphere that feels entirely different from everyday life (Goulding et al. 2010; Peter and Williams 2019). The usual rules don't apply in these spaces—including the usual rules against drunkenness, and the usual rules of spending. That makes them hot spots for businesses to turn a profit and marketers to push their brands. Business leaders turn a blind eye to and even encourage this particular kind of rule breaking.

That is, they encourage organized, controlled partying—such as that in nightclubs—because this partying supports capitalist growth. On the other hand, most major cities—at one point in their history or another—tend to publicly crackdown on drinking in public, prostitution, and illegal drug deals. After all, business leaders and politicians do not benefit financially from these illicit activities, in the same ways they benefit from the spending that happens in sanctioned party spaces. And these same illicit activities taint communities in the eyes of the bourgeoisie, making them less likely to want to live, work, party, and spend money there.

Motivations for Breaking the Rules

We have noted throughout this chapter that rule-breaking is widespread and, at least in that sense, normal and natural. We have also noted that there are many factors that motivate, explain, and justify rule-breaking—to oneself and to others.

It should not surprise us that people put their own interests ahead of all else, much of the time. People ultimately consume to satisfy their own desires. As we will see in the next chapter, they may *wish* companies were socially responsible, but at the same time be unwilling to take on a greater price burden, or turn away quality goods, in support of such responsibility. The majority of consumers will only be willing to pay more for ethical products if the product's functional and symbolic attributes are preserved. Similarly, many will not adopt ethical behaviours that require extra effort on their part, such as recycling, going to special stores, and so on.

Consumers sometimes justify their own unethical behaviour by pointing to unethical practices in the so-called "developing world." There, low wages and the risk of environmental damage are seen as the "price" to pay for the reward of economic growth. This rationale is more common in individualist and capitalist societies like the U.S. and Australia (Eckhardt et al. 2006). In more collectively-oriented societies like Germany and Sweden, unethical consumption is often justified by placing responsibility on the government. That is, in these societies, consumers think: if the government hasn't done anything about it, it cannot be worth our concern.

A group of Quebec researchers (D'Astous and Lengendre 2008; also, Hay and Bree 2017 on ethical socialization) considered the question of why most consumers aren't ethically responsible, most of the time. By implication, they were asking what, if anything, could be done to increase ethically responsible consumption.

They noted that consumers showed varying degrees of agreement with three main arguments against SRC (socially responsible consumption) behaviours. First, there was the **economic rationalist** argument: namely, the cost of the behaviour is greater than its benefit. Second, there was the **economic development reality** argument: namely, ethical and moral idealism is less important than economic growth. To achieve a desired standard of life, it is necessary to put aside certain ethical considerations. Third, there was the **government dependency** argument: the government doesn't do anything to stop unethical consumption, so it must not be that bad.

D'Astous and Lengendre's (2008) study was conducted in Canada, a capitalist country characterized by a high degree of individualism. Their findings reflect this. The most popular Canadian responses fell into the economic rationalist category, followed by economic development and government dependency. The researchers expected and found that consumers who agreed with justifications for unethical consumption were less likely to adopt ethical consumption practices.

At the other extreme, consumers who knew more about ethical consumption also had greater concerns about it. They sought to inform themselves more about the issue and developed expertise about it. These well-informed consumers, with a higher degree of knowledge about ethical consumption, were less likely to invoke any of the justifications on the questionnaire. They were also less likely to justify unethical choices if they thought their personal choices, as consumers, could have an impact.

So, in the end, rule-breaking—or any other kind of unethical or antisocial behaviour—reveals a sense that bad behaviour doesn't make a difference, because good behaviour doesn't make a difference either. What makes a verifiable difference is whether a particular action improves a person's own well-being or standing in the eyes of others. In the next chapter, we will consider what people do if they think their good behaviour *can* make a difference.

Too Many Possible Explanations

We have seen in this chapter that explanations of consumer deviance are "over-determined." Over-determination is a common problem in social science explanations. It occurs when many—indeed, too many—factors contribute to explaining a given event or behaviour.

More troubling is the fact that explanatory variables in an over-determined explanation are often highly correlated with one another. That means it may be impossible to assign a causal priority to any one of them; that is, to say X is the most important factor, twice as important as Y. Consider how this over-determination has contributed to our present problem.

We noted in an earlier chapter that "materialism" is a thorny concept and different theoretical approaches explain it in different ways. As noted, some see materialism (as illustrated by Anton) as a psychopathology that requires individual therapy. Some see it as a developmental disorder that produces compensatory behaviour (as illustrated by Donald). If such compensatory behaviour hasn't disappeared with the passage out of adolescence, it too may require psychotherapy. Some see materialism as a social and cultural disorder—a result of the alienation and cultural degradation caused by capitalism. Such materialistic behaviour, as illustrated by Tamara, cannot be fixed by psychotherapy—only by social criticism and reform. (Marx felt it could only be fixed by the revolutionary overthrow of the capitalist order.)

As we noted earlier, these three explanations are compatible with each other. To a degree, they merely focus on different points in the causal chain and, accordingly, prescribe different remedies. As C. Wright Mills told us, personal troubles (e.g., psychopathologies) are merely private versions of public issues—problems of the society as a whole. And it may be easier to adjust a person's psychic state—i.e., to make him or her more "normal"—than to change a society in which "normality" is a form of psychological or spiritual sickness. Obviously, these are difficult questions better left for another time. However, it would be wrong to leave the discussion of rule-bending and rule-breaking without raising these issues, since they are always present. For in the end, rule-breakers are made, not born.

Final Thoughts

In this chapter, we returned to one of our key questions: Does consumerism cause problems we should worry about? Namely, if it causes materialism or shopping addictions, are those bad things we should make an effort to address? We've discussed, in other chapters, why we think materialism and shopping addictions are indeed bad. In this chapter, we saw why they may be especially troubling. Namely, they are some of the most normal, expected attitudes and behaviours in a consumer society.

For instance, we saw that impulse buying is so common and predictable, we can't even consider it deviant. What could be more normal than buying the flat-screen TV all your friends and co-workers have, and that dozens of advertisements keep pushing you to get? From this view, people who reliably control their impulses to buy are the outliers in our consumer society. Especially in certain contexts—such as Las Vegas—large-scale impulse buying is expected. It is the norm.

Such excessive consumption may be a result of materialism: that is, prioritizing material possessions over all else. For many, in our consumerist society, spending is more important than saving. Overspending and impulse buying go hand in hand with materialism. These behaviours stem from a widespread belief that money and material goods matter most in life. Even compulsive buying—a pathology some see as dangerously far from normal—may be considered an unavoidable response to the belief that consumer goods make you feel happy and fulfilled.

In this sense, consumerism and materialism feed each other. Our culture teaches us to crave material goods, and that consumption is the key to satisfying that craving. This cycle, to answer our key question, can indeed be problematic. It can cause devastation as extensive as lost homes and drained retirement funds.

That helps answer another key question we posed in this chapter: Do people in our society have a dangerous or unhealthy preoccupation with consumer goods? Why might some people consider this preoccupation unhealthy? We learned that, in our culture, this kind of preoccupation with consumer goods is made to seem normal. The "rules" of consumer behaviour in our society promote behaviours that would, in other contexts, seem bizarre, deviant, or pathological.

An example is impulsive buying. Merchants want and promote impulsive buying. They depend on impulsive buyers to provide an important share of their revenue. Similarly, our consumer society is comfortable with compulsive (or addictive) buying by consumers who know they shouldn't spend the money or buy the desired object but do so anyway.

Certainly, compulsive behaviour—giving in to the irresistible urge, the loss of control, the predictable harm—is like alcohol or gambling addiction. Yet compulsive buying fits with the belief that buying is therapeutic and helps a person achieve happiness. That search for happiness through consumption is one reason people buy fake or counterfeit goods: they help the consumer belong, or appear to belong, to a higher status group. And belonging makes people feel good.

Whatever consumer behaviour you were raised to see as "normal," several techniques of social control ensure you adhere to it. These include shame, embarrassment, guilt, and gossip. People fear these things, and generally strive to avoid them. That means they generally follow the rules, as defined by the people they admire and seek approval from. This is true even if your norm is *breaking* the rules. As we saw, some brands say it's noble and heroic to go against the grain and forge your own path. If your circle of friends think deviance from the mainstream is cool, you're more likely to conform to that norm.

Finally, we learned that even laws—the strictest of rules—are often bent, broken, and inconsistently enforced. People of different ages, in different countries, with different religious beliefs and values think differently about buying fake or pirated goods, for example. And some illegal behaviours are even encouraged, if they lead to profits for powerful people, corporations, and governments. So, when it comes to consumerism, the rules aren't usually designed to protect the greater good; often, the rules are there to ensure ever-more spending, materialism, and capitalist growth. Although it may not be good for people, unhealthy spending is good for capitalism.

Discussion Questions

1. Impulse control is a major factor in compulsive spending, but there are other factors involved. What biological, mental, or socioeconomic factors do you think might also play a contributing role?

2. Parents are typically involved in shaping the consumption habits of their children. Can you think of ways that your parents have shaped yours? Do you think your parents made you more aware of the way you spend money and your beliefs about it?

3. Alcohol is considered to be a ritualized part of consumer life. Sometimes, people's senses are inhibited, and they are "not themselves." How do you think this affects their personal lives and relationships? How could it be seen as positive? Negative?

Quick Quiz

1. What is materialism?
a. Excessive concern with material possessions
b. Constantly shopping for expensive things
c. A psychological process in which a non-sexual thing is given the value of a sexual object
d. Devaluing and discrediting people whose social identity deviates from society's normative expectations
e. Being predisposed to rapid, unplanned reactions to stimuli without regard for the negative consequences of these reactions

2. What is NOT considered deviant behaviour in a capitalist society?
a. Ignoring concerns like appearances and prestige
b. Refusing to conform to popular consumption habits
c. Altruistic consumption
d. Never being satisfied with what they have
e. Socially confident buying

3. Who was the main influence on Mark and Pearson's idea of brand archetypes?
a. George Herbert Mead
b. Karl Marx
c. Carl Jung
d. Erving Goffman
e. Jean Baudrillard

4. What happens when well-socialized people break the rules of society?
a. They feel the need to break more rules
b. They feel guilty or ashamed
c. They are indifferent
d. They want to buy lots of expensive items
e. They want to be heroic rule-breakers

5. How do disgusting products best transfer their off-putting qualities?
a. They are placed near other products
b. They are in a transparent package, and the "aura" affects other products around them
c. They are in physical contact with other products
d. They are hidden in opaque packaging
e. They are placed on a different shelf on their own

The answers to the Quick Quiz are provided at the end of the book.

For Further Reading

Influence: The Psychology of Persuasion by Robert B. Cialdini
Cialdini describes six universal principles that are used as "weapons of influence." He also discusses how to defend oneself against these forms of influence.

The Hero and The Outlaw by Margaret Mark and Carol S. Pearson
Authors Mark and Pearson elaborate further on Carl Jung's "archetypes" in the context of today's consumer society. The authors do this by looking at marketing techniques used to create meaning amongst consumers.

Techniques of Neutralization: A Theory of Delinquency by Gresham M. Sykes and David Matza
Sykes and Matza discuss five methods of neutralization used in juvenile delinquency and how they can also apply throughout society.

Key Terms

Commodity fetishism
Credit card fraud
Deviance
Digital piracy
Dispositional factors
Economic development reality
Economic rationalist
Embarrassment
Fetishism
Government dependency
Impulsive consumers
Materialism
Motivation theory
Product misuse
Shoplifting
Situational factors
Techniques of neutralization

Chapter Seventeen
Buying as a Means of Protest and Social Change

Learning Objectives

After reading this chapter, you will be able to:

✓ Explain the shortcomings of common criticisms of consumerism.

✓ Assess whether consumer societies are natural and inevitable.

✓ Consider the factors that make some consumer movements attract strong followings.

✓ Evaluate the effectiveness of ethical consumerism, boycotts, and buycotts.

This chapter is about consuming as a way to protest. That means we will cover topics including "voting with your money," boycotts and "buycotts," and consumer responsibility. These topics are part of a bigger debate about consumerism and the consumer society. This debate hinges on a puzzle political philosopher Bernard Mandeville pointed out centuries ago: the private vice of greed leads to the public virtue of economic growth (Mandeville 2019; Wei 2018; Jechoutek 2018). Today, many economists, politicians, researchers, and members of the general public continue to say consumerism should be encouraged—not protested against—because it stimulates our economy. In turn, more people around the world can enjoy a higher standard of living. From this view, the consumer society is *every* society's inevitable future. It emerges from the fundamentally human desire to live a better, more comfortable life. And who would protest a poor person's desire for better living conditions?

But as we will see in this chapter, the debate is not that black and white. Some people do indeed protest consumerism and the consumer society. They do not believe it is natural, nor desirable. Instead, they point to what they see as the downsides, including the climate crisis, inequality, and exploitation. From this view, our consumer society is harmful, and we should work to reduce these harms.

Many attempts have been made to that end. We've seen some seek greater consumer power and protection. Others question the idea of buying for status instead of buying only what we need. Others still challenge the idea of a consumer society as a whole. Their approaches and goals may be different, but people who question, resist, or protest in our consumer society have one thing in common: they are all still consumers. They can use their buying and spending power to protest; they can use consumer goods and services to show their identities as protestors; and they can (perhaps unintentionally) undercut those identities by failing to consume in ways that support their agenda.

So, in this chapter, we look at consumption as a political, public phenomenon—not only an individual, private one. In so doing, we will see that the consumer society itself is political. It's molded to suit people's needs at a given moment. It does not naturally emerge from people's innate wish to raise their standard of living. And it is not magically unfolding along its own predetermined course. If consumerism was an unavoidable product of human nature, we wouldn't see such diverse efforts to shape, co-opt, and even dismantle it.

Criticisms of Consumerism Considered

A **protest** is any form of expression that aims to bring about change. To protest, there must be something—a person, cause, company, incident, etc.—you are protesting *against*. The very idea of a protest therefore implies you believe there is something wrong with whatever it is you are protesting. After all, you want that thing to change. Protests against the consumer society therefore imply there is a problem (or many problems) with consumerism. To start this chapter, then, we must ask what those might be.

In his aptly-titled article, "What is Wrong with Consumerism?" Colin Campbell (2010; see also Lambert 2019; Martinez 2016) lays out five of the most common criticisms of consumerism.

These are the need criticism, the materialism criticism, the addiction criticism, the selfishness criticism, and the irrationality criticism. Before we explain each of these criticisms, note that Campbell thinks they're all misguided. They wrongly blame individual consumers, he says, instead of looking at consumption as a whole.

First, the **need criticism** assumes that consumerism is about buying more than you need. Those who take this view think that if people only bought what they needed, we wouldn't be in the midst of a climate crisis and we could also improve the distribution of resources for society's most vulnerable members.

The main weakness of this criticism is that it fails to define what humans need. Consider food. All humans need food to survive. However, food also fulfills social, psychological, and cultural needs we have discussed in earlier chapters. So, "need" is a subjective idea, based on the life goals of people and their culture.

Second, the **materialism criticism** assumes that consumerism is inherently materialistic. It makes people value material objects *too much*—more than nonmaterial goods like personal relations, love, and their community (for reflections on this issue from various spiritual viewpoints, see Choudhury 2019; Lee and Ahn 2016; Belhadj and Merdaoui 2017).

Campbell identifies a few problems with this perspective. The first is that people are buying services as much as they are buying material goods. In recent years, we've seen massive growth in personal services (like gyms and spas) and entertainment (like concerts, cinema, and theatre). This contradicts the idea that people are placing too much value on material goods. Second, this critique is only applied to specific products and consumers and not others. For example, people who spend money on art or wait hours in line to see the Mona Lisa are rarely accused of materialism. In this sense, accusations of materialism are often criticisms of low cultural capital and/or popular culture. This criticism favours certain types of consumption over others.

Next, the **addiction criticism** assumes that consumerism is a form of addiction. From this perspective, people consume excessively to feed their addiction. "Fast fashion" is typically held up as an example to show how quickly styles and commodities change. People need to keep buying and re-buying new versions of the same articles to stay "in fashion." (See also Reith 2018 and Hsu 2017.)

As we have seen, some people *are* addictive consumers, such as shopaholics. However, Campbell says they make up only a small fraction of all consumers. He also suggests that consumers are addicted to novelty, which one can only experience with new buys. Consider moviegoers, who see several films every year. They do not continually revisit the cinema because earlier movies could not satisfy their addiction. Instead, they go back because they want to see a *new* film. This repetitive consumption is driven by novelty, not by an obsession that cannot be satisfied.

Fourth, the **selfishness criticism** argues that people consume because they are selfish (see also Wilson 2017; Hyland 2017; and Azevedo 2020). From this standpoint, consumerism is evidence of an empty soul and a hunger for meaning in life.

Campbell points out that, technically, all consumption is done to satisfy wishes, making consumption "selfish" by definition. Critiquing it is therefore meaningless because so long as consumption exists, its selfishness will too.

Finally, the **irrationality criticism** argues that people consume because they mistakenly think that buying and owning more goods will make them happy. Indeed, research reveals that, at a certain point, happiness plateaus even as income and consumption increase. And how can consumer behaviour be rational when we see so many cases of "buyer's remorse"? (For recent research on the irrationality of consumer behavior, see Doláková and Krajíček 2016; Opatrny 2018; Trevisan 2016).

Nevertheless, Campbell notes that happiness is elusive and it's impossible to know if people are trying to gain happiness (or another irrational goal) when they consume. As well, some acts of consumption seem more geared to finding brief pleasure or satisfaction than long-lasting happiness.

Campbell does not think that consumerism is beyond criticism. Instead, he thinks academics and others who stand behind these perspectives need to criticize more carefully. They need to take the bigger picture into account, instead of chalking consumerism up to misguided decisions made by individuals. For example, they need to look at our broader capitalist economy, consumption as a social norm, and the cumulative effect of consumer behaviour. In the following pages, we take this more macro view. We begin by looking, in very general terms, at how consumerism spread around the world following the Second World War.

Consumerism as the Carrot

One of the grand narratives we examine in this chapter is the idea that consumerism will naturally take hold in all societies. All humans want to live comfortably, this story suggests, and capitalist consumerism helps them raise their standard of living. However, consumerism is political. It is a tool used throughout history to advance various political agendas.

Because we live in North America, let's start with the agendas North Americans have used consumerism to push. These include democracy, capitalism, and Westernization. After World War II, mass consumption was a powerful ideological weapon used in the Cold War. In America, consumption became equated with democracy. The government encouraged returning service members and their families to consume their way to prosperity. Their nuclear families, living in suburbia, became a propaganda tool. Champions of the American capitalist model of economic growth pointed to these families as icons of success. They held them up as models of the Western consumerist way of life. And they contrasted them with the production-oriented, central-planning bias of Soviet Communism.

The American model of consumerism (Bergman 2018; Logan 2017; Wells 2018) was exported to the rest of the world. It was pushed especially hard in the reconstruction programs of war-ravaged Europe. Administrators and marketing professionals promised people prosperity and satisfaction under democracy. And they promised global governance and peacekeeping under consumerism. For example, they pointed to the United Nations' Universal Declaration of Human Rights. The Declaration emphasizes the need to protect individuals' fundamental rights, something which aligned with the notion of the consumer as a seeker of greater choice. At the time, people were also especially tired of poverty and suffering. Totalitarianism had brought enough hardship.

They were therefore promised a new way of doing things that would bring prosperity. The "new way" consisted of the economic system encapsulated within the Bretton Woods institutions (the World Bank, International Monetary Fund, and the General Agreement on Trade and Tariffs).

The consumer society therefore rose in the second half of the twentieth century. Developing nations started moving through the stages of modernization that Western states had already experienced. In the broadest terms, rapid economic development and globalization followed (Steenkamp 2019; but also Ger et al. 2018).

In sum, one of the reasons consumerism took off at this time was because Westerners, in the midst of the Cold War, wanted to

The so-called "Kitchen Debate" between Soviet first secretary Nikita Khrushchev and Richard Nixon, then U.S. vice president, occurred at the American National Exhibition in Moscow on July 24, 1959. The exhibition featured a model home filled with labour-saving appliances and other consumer goods intended to display the high standard of living enjoyed by average Americans in the post-war years. Khrushchev dismissed U.S. economic accomplishments, claiming that "in another seven years, we'll be at the level of America, and after that we'll go farther." As matters turned out, the Soviet economy's stagnation during the three decades following the Kitchen Debate helped precipitate the collapse of the USSR in December 1991. Khrushchev himself had been forced from power in 1964. In 1968, Nixon was elected U.S. president but later resigned in disgrace because of the Watergate scandal. In an interesting footnote to history, Khrushchev's son moved to the United States after the dissolution of the Soviet Union and became a naturalized U.S. citizen.

bring capitalism and the ways of the West to other parts of the world. Consumerism—all the nice things people could buy to make themselves comfortable—was just the carrot. Material comfort (via consumerism) was touted as the reward for adopting capitalism and the Western way of life.

Consumerism has also been used to further all sorts of other political ends (Van Dam and Jonker 2017; Wirt 2017; Aveyard et al. 2018). To name just a few examples:

- In the Boston Tea Party of 1773, American colonists protested against Great Britain's imposition of "taxation without representation." No less than 342 chests of tea, imported by the British East India Company, were dumped into the harbour. This protest wasn't intended to challenge democracy, capitalism, or consumerism; rather, Americans were demanding what they saw as their fair share of the benefits of those systems.
- Governments have used tax incentives or propaganda campaigns to encourage consumption of domestic (instead of foreign) products. Consider, for example, the British Empire Marketing Board's promotion of imperial goods in the late 1920s and early 1930s.

- Boycotts have served many liberal causes, including campaigns against the marketing of breast milk substitutes or the apartheid regime in South Africa. But they have also served devastating agendas, such as the Nazi-orchestrated boycott of Jewish stores.

In short, consumerism does not magically arise. More often, it is foisted on societies by powerful groups who stand to benefit. What's more, consumerism is not just a means to greater material comfort. Rather, it can be a powerful way of speaking up for your rights, for resisting government, for showing your loyalties, and for supporting causes you believe in. The way consumers spend (or don't) gives them a certain amount of power.

Box 17-1
Boycotts in Canada, Then and Now

In Canada, World War I caused a backlash against goods and people of German descent. The war led nationalist Canadians to label and seek out "untrustworthy" people. The government imprisoned over 9,000 German Canadians in isolated camps across the country (Cook 2018). In Ontario, the city of Berlin (seen here in a postcard from 1910) was renamed Kitchener. Riots in Victoria, Winnipeg, and Montreal targeted German-owned businesses (D'Amato 2014).

A century later, in March 2018, U.S. President Donald Trump imposed tariffs against certain Canadian goods. In response, Canadian consumers undertook a boycott of their own. Some criticized U.S. goods and brands including Starbucks, Walmart, and McDonald's. Boycotters used the hashtag "BoycottUSProducts" on Twitter in protest (Dangerfield 2018). A few Canadian restaurants promoted their "Trump-free" dishes, made without any ingredients imported from the U.S. The boycott even extended to the tourism industry, with indications that at least some Canadians chose to vacation at home rather than travel to the U.S. (Reints 2018).

One commentator noted that "the U.S. and Canada share $25 billion in food trade, which means the impact of a boycott wouldn't be insignificant" (Bosse 2018). However, according to Dalhousie University professor Sylvain Charlebois, food production is too complicated for a Canadian boycott of U.S. products to be effective. Fresh produce is straightforward enough. A country-of-origin sticker tells consumers where produce was grown. But processed foods pose a challenge. Our globalized food system is highly integrated. A maple leaf on food packaging is a sign the product is Canadian, but that may only reflect the final stage of processing (Bosse 2018). Boycotters may think they're buying Canadian when they are not.

Consumers have recognized such political motivations for years, and have organized to protect themselves. Consumer cooperatives, for example, achieved impressive growth in Europe in the late 19th and early 20th centuries (Talonen et al. 2016; Sadowski 2017; Gonzalez 2017). Consumer cooperatives are consumer-owned enterprises that are managed democratically with the aim of providing better service, as opposed to making profits. In a sense, they undercut the power of the capitalist owners of the means of production, and put some of that power back into the hands of consumers. By the end of World War I, over 20 percent of the German population belonged to a cooperative. In Russia, so distrustful were the Bolsheviks of the decentralized cooperative movement that they tried to place them under centralized control.

Since World War II, many national cooperative movements have declined. However, they still have a significant presence in Scandinavia, while roughly 19 million Japanese belong to a thriving cooperative sector. The cooperatives have not just provided an alternative model for economic ownership. Through organizations such as the International Co-operative Alliance, they have been important supporters of a more just and equitable marketplace.

For example, allied with the cooperative movement, early labour activists boycotted slave-grown sugar. Following their efforts, other consumer activists organized to defend the rights and conditions of the workers who made the products sold in department stores. The anti-sweating movement inspired Clementina Black, honourary secretary of the Women's Trade Union Asso-ciation, to call for creation of a "con-sumers' league" in Britain in 1887. Though the organization did not en-dure, it led to the National Consum-ers League and this, in turn, inspired consumer leagues in other European countries. Those leagues became closely associated with "white label" campaigns, which identified manu-facturers thought to uphold good working conditions for their em-ployees.

These examples show—as we have seen throughout this book—that capitalist consumerism can make life very comfortable for those at the top, and very uncomfortable for everyone else. Cooperatives, la-bour activism, and white label cam-paigns are just a few examples of the ways consumers have tried to stand up for themselves and make con-sumerism work for them, too.

A second wave of consumer ac-tivism began in America in the sec-ond quarter of the twentieth century and has continued since (Lightfoot 2019; Weaver 2019; Minocher 2019). In 1929, the Consumers Research or-ganization was created and, in 1936, Consumers Union (best known for its magazine *Consumer Reports*).

Box 17-2
No Jobs, No Labour Laws, No Share in the Profits

In her celebrated book *No Logo* (2009; see also Jordan and Klein 2020), Canadian author and activist Naomi Klein looks at the ways large cor-porations increase profits. Namely, they focus on creating and upholding their brand. Manufacturing becomes less critical, as does labour-man-agement relations. North American and European companies send their production work to factories in other, usually poorer, parts of the world. Often, they do this indirectly, through a broker overseas. The broker provides them with information on the cheapest labour force available, builds the factory, and staffs it with workers. These individual factories lower produc-tion prices even further and subcontract to other factories in other low-income places.

Often, the result is unregulated working conditions, where workers suffer (U.S. Department of Labor 2017). Most are young women and children, working long hours far away from their families. They are managed military style, with supervisors who watch their every move. Many factory buildings are poorly built, posing severe risks to worker safety. These factories turn out products for next to no wages, and then the large corpo-rations sell them in the Global North at dozens of times the manufacturing cost.

These organizations began to test branded products and compare them with one another. They proved popular with newly well-off shoppers negotiating their way around a more complex and technological marketplace where the traditional skills of the housewife-shopper were no longer as useful. Comparative testing also took hold in Europe after World War II when reconstruction policies brought wealth to growing numbers of consumers.

Consumer associations emerged all across Europe in the 1950s. In 1960, several of these, with the U.S. Consumers Union, came together to form the International Organization of Consumers Unions (IOCU) (Hilton 2017). The IOCU has gone on to expand into the developing world. Today, there are around 250 organizations affiliated to IOCU from well over 100 countries. As it has expanded beyond the wealthy West, the international consumer movement has started working to ensure access to basic consumer needs, rather than appraising the relative value of different branded goods. The work of these organizations, as with the work of the cooperative movement before them, thus serves as a powerful reminder. Namely, a consumer society can be about fairness and trying to ensure everybody has a chance to take part—not only about enabling those people who can afford it to consume even more.

From its beginning, the consumer movement challenged the powers of businesses over consumers. Most fundamentally, protesters said, businesses threaten consumers' physical safety through dangerous goods. They also threaten consumers' economic well-being. Such activism led to many legislative measures designed to heighten consumer protection. They culminated in 1985, with the United Nations Guidelines on Consumer Protection. These guidelines drew on the best practices of measures introduced over the previous two decades. Again, such consumer protections complicate the idea that consumer society expands naturally and inevitably. What *does* seem natural and inevitable about a consumer society is that it exploits workers and breeds inequality. Consumers have had to work hard to put structures in place that minimize their risk.

Consumer Movements and the Search for Ethical Products, Brands, and Business Models

Clearly, consumer societies have rich histories of protests of all sorts. But what makes a protest take off? What galvanizes people to join the cause? In this section, we examine consumer movements and the factors that drive them.

A **consumer movement** is a form of activism (Forno 2013). It can be supported by individual consumers, organizations, and social groups. Some consumer movements aim to empower individual consumers, helping consumers to get the most value for their money and to make our consumer society safer and fairer. Other consumer movements challenge the fabric of consumer society itself. They want to see more systemic change.

All social movements, whatever their goal, draw on a repertoire of collective action that has built up over centuries. They use older tactics like sit-ins, petitions, hunger strikes, and civil disobedience, but also use new tactics like hacktivism, whistle-blowing, and public (online) shaming. Increasingly, social movements rely on protest tactics that control consumer behaviours, like boycotts and "buycotts," which we discuss in greater detail in the next section.

Researchers often use **resource mobilization theory** to explain why some social movements attract a strong, sustained following, and others fall flat (John and Mayer 2017). Resource mobilization theory sees social movements as the capacity of disgruntled people to organize. Without discontent, there would be no social movements (according to this theory). Yet dissatisfaction is a constant of human life. Without resources, though, discontent can never show itself as a social force. A social organization needs effective leadership, public support, money, legal aid, ties with influential officials and public personalities, and access to the mass media. Occasionally, organizing also means getting and learning to use weapons.

Without access to critical resources, discontented people cannot change society or resist the powerful. Successful social movements indicate greater access to resources, not necessarily less contentment. Similarly, an absence of protest movements does not mean that people are content. More often, it shows a lack of resources among the dissatisfied, as well as state effectiveness at suppressing protest.

Resource mobilization theory helps explain why movements vary in size and militancy, and why some are more successful than others. This theory focuses on both tangible assets (such as money) and intangible assets (such as leadership), as well as links to existing cultural beliefs and goals and social connections to vital social institutions.

But not all wealthy, well-connected people join social movements. The most critical predictor of participation in protests is whether one is asked to join (Schussman and Soule 2005; Earl et al. 2017). Politically liberal and politically involved people are more likely to join a social movement. They are also more likely to have the "civic skills" necessary for social activism. For example, they are likely to have the ability to organize events and to communicate with movement members, the public, and mass media.

People are also more likely to join a social movement when they feel they are joining a community and that their protest is likely to succeed. Also, people want to do what is socially approved. They are more likely to support popular, widespread movements than deviant ones. Finally, people are more likely to join movements that give them a sense of belonging and (occasionally) a feeling of emotional arousal.

"Protest camps" (Brown and Feigenbaum 2017) fulfill many of these criteria. These are camps set up by activists to provide a meeting place for protesters, or to block activities they oppose. One well-known example is the camps set up by Indigenous protesters in Houston, B.C. to prevent work on a natural-gas pipeline. Some members of the Indigenous community supported the pipeline and eagerly accepted the contract work that was awarded to Indigenous businesses. However, others took part in the protest camp as a means of "reclaiming" the lands they felt they had been displaced from. Entire buildings were erected over several years to block the pipeline and protest practices including over-logging, grazing on their hunting lands, over-hunting, and gas and oil pipelines in general.

Ethical consumer movements also fulfill the participation criteria noted above. Everyone in our consumer society consumes. Ethical consumption is popular, widespread, trendy, socially approved, makes people feel like they're doing good—and "all" they have to do to be part of this movement is buy an ethical version of a product or service they were going to buy anyway.

Ethical consumerism means buying goods and services that are "ethical"—whether that means they are ethically sourced, manufactured, distributed, marketed, or all of the above. The ethical consumer movement is based on the belief that consumers can vote with their money. By buying ethical goods and services, protestors believe they can encourage businesses to implement ethical practices.

Box 17-3

Ethical Eating

Canadian sociologist Josee Johnston (2004; Huddert Kennedy et al. 2019) explored ethical consumerism as it relates to food. For example, companies like Whole Foods Market (now owned by Amazon) offer organic foods that align with consumers' values of sustainability.

Johnston points out that when companies move from offering conventional goods to sustainable or ethical ones, we often think they are responding to public, government, and media pressure for reform. But often, they are also responding to business opportunities: organizations see consumer demand, so they build new markets, restructure their manufacturing, or increase efficiencies to meet it. They benefit in the form of higher profits when more customers buy from them, instead of their "unethical" competitors.

However, not all consumers *can* buy from these sustainable companies. Ethical consumption is mostly available to wealthy elites. Whole Foods and many other organic, sustainable food markets, food delivery services, and farmers' markets aren't affordable for many. That makes ethical eating undemocratic, by definition (for more about the Whole Foods marketing strategy, see Luangrath et al. 2017; Schor and Fitzmaurice 2017; and Conaway et al. 2018).

Indeed, Johnston finds that consumers who are economically and culturally privileged—that is, high-income earners with a Euro-Canadian background—are more likely to eat ethically. People who do not enjoy these same privileges do not engage in the same degree of ethical eating. But these less privileged consumers still have to contend with the moral issues surrounding their food choices. Ethical consumer activism has shifted many consumers' views of food, no matter their financial and cultural background. In turn, many consumers *want* to adopt sustainable and ethical food practices. But the prices of sustainably grown foods make ethical consumption accessible only to the privileged few.

Though they may mean well, some of these "ethical consumers" are not doing as much good as they think. That's because of the difference between ethical practices focused on consumption and those focused on consumerism (Littler 2011). Being anti-consumption just means using less. On the other hand, being anti-consumerism means opposing the production methods, worker treatment, and advertising practices companies use today. Many "ethical consumers" would struggle to pinpoint which of these things they are aiming to do. And, if they think they are anti-consumerism, they may be deluding themselves. For example, ethical consumers may opt not to buy products from brands known to use sweatshops. They do so because they think it's unfair for corporations to exploit people for their own financial gain (Aßländer 2019; Powell 2018; Sarpong 2018).

But where do these consumers draw the line? Labourers who work in better conditions than sweatshops are being exploited too: the companies they work for earn huge profits while they probably don't even earn a living wage. Some ethical consumers push their protest even further, buying raw materials so they can make their own products at home. But what about the people harvesting or assembling these materials? They too are exploited for their labour.

From this vantage point, "ethical consumerism" may be impossible. Free-market capitalism wants a divide between rich and poor. No capitalist transactions can be "ethical" if you're concerned about socio-economic equality, labour relations, or exploitation. They may even make things worse. Look at the support for "fair trade" products (Ladhari and Tchetgna 2017; Zerbini et al. 2019). These products are allegedly developed in ways that are fair to workers and less harmful to the environment. The most visible fair trade products in Canada include coffee, cocoa, tea, and bananas. Consumers reason they are willing to pay a little more for their daily cup of coffee so that bean farmers in developing countries can earn fair wages.

But these farmers are still being exploited. Even under fair trade agreements, they earn mere cents for producing bags of coffee beans, while massive corporations like Starbucks charge several dollars for every cup of coffee they sell. All the while, fair trade coffee consumers think they're doing the right thing. This complacency can blur our view of reality, making us think we've done our part to bring justice to the world. In this way, ethical consumption may stunt progress by making people feel like they have already helped when they haven't.

As the example of fair trade coffee shows, ethical consumption is often part of a marketing ploy. Companies know their customers are genuinely concerned about social inequality, environmental instability, and social justice. They tap into those concerns when building their brand and advertising campaigns to ensure customers feel they are doing the right thing by buying their products. Indeed, seeing the official Fairtrade logo on a product can be enough to convince Canadian consumers to buy (Globescan Consumer Study, 2017). In one study, 85 percent of Canadians said they would have a positive impression of a brand if it was licensed to carry the mark (Fairtrade Canada 2017).

Some companies and marketers have reasonable goals and genuinely think their efforts have a positive impact. Others purposefully mislead consumers for their own gain. **Greenwashing** is a typical example. It's the process of making untested or misleading statements about the environmental benefits of a product, service, technology, or company practice (Rouse 2019). Greenwashing is essentially false advertising used by companies to imply they follow environmentally sustainable practices or provide green products and services when they do not. The term emerged in the 1980s. It was then that hotels started encouraging guests to reuse their towels, instead of having them washed and replaced each day (Gössling et al. 2019; Han and Hyun 2018). Hoteliers launched the initiative because they wanted to save money on laundry costs and increase profits. But you'll notice the cards on your hotel towels today still say you're helping the environment by holding onto the same set until your stay is over. Such greenwashing helps hotels brand their profit-making as green.

Consumers, businesses, and marketers alike often react against this line of reasoning by asking what difference it makes. If less laundry gets done, and less water is wasted, who cares what the hotel's goals were? The planet still benefits, they say. This is a fair point. What consumers should be asking, though, is if these initiatives inspire complacency. Even if every single hotel guest went through just one set of towels per stay, the hotel is still doing an astronomical amount of laundry.

Then there is the water they use to wash dishes, clean the floors, wash the bathrooms, and allow each guest to have as many long showers and hot baths as they wish. Recycling towels makes a difference, but not a huge one in the grand scheme of things.

And again, it may even hurt more than it helps. Through greenwashing, hotels make you think you're doing the environmentally responsible thing by staying with them—even though hotels are some of the most wasteful places around. Saving your towels makes you feel like you're saving the planet. In turn, you feel a little less guilty about all the other ways you're hurting it.

> ## Box 17-4
> # Greenwashing
>
> The fashion industry is notorious for greenwashing. One example is the way clothing companies tout bamboo as an environmentally-friendly material. Marketers will claim that little or no pesticides are needed to produce bamboo, since it has antimicrobial and biodegradable properties. But this is misleading. Bamboo cannot just be used in its natural form to make clothes. Its hard fibers must be turned soft—a process that requires countless chemicals and ends up creating rayon or viscose. These products are not environmentally friendly at all. In fact, they contain no trace of the original bamboo plant or its antimicrobial properties (Desjardins 2019). Troublingly, studies show that these false claims of "greenness" work; they do influence buying patterns.

On the other hand, some consumers are very aware of greenwashing. For them, it has become so ordinary and commonplace, it can have the opposite of its intended effect. These jaded consumers have seen so much greenwashing, they now report cynicism about green initiatives. When introduced to products being marketed as environmentally friendly, they are skeptical. They think companies are just packaging their cost-saving efforts as green. Many also suspected that these companies were exploiting the allure of greener products by charging higher prices.

Amid all of this, we must ask: Whose responsibility is it? The perspectives we've reviewed so far blame the consumer. The idea that consumers should have to define exploitative labour, or resort to making their own products, or beware of deceptive marketing ploys like greenwashing puts the onus on them. It shifts ethical responsibility from businesses to buyers. But as we've seen, it's impossible for people to consume in truly ethical ways; consumerism is, in many ways, inherently exploitative and narcissistic (Murray 2020).

Making people responsible for ethical consumption is just setting them up to fail. Real change would need to happen from the top down. Businesses themselves would need to start producing and selling in truly ethical ways, so consumers would have truly ethical products to choose from.

Enchanting Consumers through Ethical Consumption and Moral Communities

As mentioned, one factor pushing consumers towards ethical consumption movements is a desire to feel like part of a community. For some, globalization has diluted local cultures, communities, and grassroots groups. Some consumers resist this sense of global homogenization by intentionally buying local. An interesting example is community supported agriculture (CSA). CSA programs allow consumers to buy shares in or work at farms in exchange for produce. People who opt into these programs receive weekly boxes of local, organically grown produce for a set number of months. Farmers encourage members to visit their farms and host periodic gatherings to build a sense of belonging and community. In their study of CSA, Thompson and Coskuner-Balli (2007; also, Coskuner-Balli 2020) find that proponents romanticize these programs. CSA members are enchanted by their consumption—enamoured with the idea of connecting with the land and the people who grow their food. What's more, the consumers in this study saw their participation in CSA programs as a critique of global capitalism. CSA consumers condemn globalized agriculture for producing bland and uninteresting foods. CSA re-enchants them by providing stimulating variety and emotional connections. In a way, these consumers (feel like they) are protesting against McDonaldization by enjoying local and diverse food.

CSA stresses the social and spiritual qualities of food. Farmers report experiences of enchantment when inspecting their produce and detailing their characteristics. Consumer participants, for their part, praise CSA social events for creating a sense of community with potlucks, tasting events, and farm tours. They also say CSA reverses feelings of emotional detachment brought on by separating food production and consumption. Thus, one reason people take part in social movements (and social experiments) is to experience enchanting new communities, as opposed to impersonal everyday routine.

Other commercial enterprises are not always so successful at producing a sense of enchantment and **moral community** among consumers. A moral community is a social group bought together based on friendship, trust, and lofty goals (Robinson 2018). For example, the company Zipcar positions its brand as "young, innovative, and green." Zipcar markets themes of environmentalism, sustainability, and the spirit of community to help cultivate brand affinity. However, research by Bardhi and Eckhardt (2012) suggests

Car-sharing company Zipcar was founded in 2000, with the goal of providing more flexible car rental options to consumers. It was later acquired by legacy car rental giant Avis Budget Group.

that Zipcar's effort to form and mobilize a moral community has mostly failed. Zipcar encourages its users to take "ownership" of their cars—for example, to name and care for the cars they use, and to use the car provider in their own neighbourhood. But survey data reveal that because the car is used by many, users often feel that it is not their responsibility to care for. Some even feel disgusted when made aware that someone else has used the car.

Zipcar wants people to see car sharing as a more cost-effective, convenient, and environmentally responsible way of traveling. However, Zipcar users just want to reduce expenses and increase convenience. They hold Zipcar accountable for keeping the cars in good working condition; they do not feel a duty to keep the car in good repair.

Contrary to Zipcar's hopes, a moral community has failed to form. Not even a strong "brand community" (Wang et al. 2020; Ewer et al. 2016) is in evidence, virtually or otherwise. There is no clear sense of sharing among Zipcar users. They may be like-minded people, but they see Zipcar as a service provider, not a community-builder. Their failure to build a community around a lifestyle idea highlights a universal problem experienced by all social movements: How can one create a large, active community on demand?

As mentioned, one of the factors that drives such community formation is social norms. People want to do what is "normal" and socially approved, which means they are more likely to join popular, widely approved social movements. Researchers and marketers alike lean into this fact, taking what is known as the **social norms approach (SNA)** to achieve both good and (sometimes) bad ends. SNA is a strategy intended to motivate people to take a given action or behave in a given way (Burchell et al. 2013).

Traditional SNA emerged in the late 1980s and aimed at reducing the use of cigarettes, alcohol, and drugs among university and college students. Since people often overestimate or underestimate the habits of their peers, SNA tries to help people overcome mistaken views of these norms. For example, if college and university students understand that their friends don't drink as much or as often as they think, that understanding may help temper their own drinking because they aren't trying to keep up with their friends. In this sense, SNA exploits people's wish to conform to what they understand to be the norm.

Box 17-5

Is Ethical Tourism the New Norm?

Some consumer behaviour can harm tourist destinations and perpetuate the global inequalities we discussed earlier in this book. Ethical tourism is tourism that does not abuse the destination—for example, by damaging the local environment (Goodwin and Francis 2003; Ganglmair-Woollscroft and Woollscroft 2016). Responsible tourism is taking responsibility for issues in the destination and not worsening them. For example, when visiting developing nations, responsible tourists would patronize local businesses instead of international chains.

Ethical tourism has taken off in recent years, though not necessarily because consumers themselves are more ethical. Many people today say they don't travel across the world to sit on a Westernized resort; they want an "authentic" experience with "the locals." When weighing similarly priced vacations, some consumers opt for ethical choices (Goodwin and Francis 2003; Fang 2020).

That said, plenty of consumers still prefer those Westernized resorts precisely because they do not have to interact with locals who may be different from themselves. Language and cultural barriers can also make it hard for them to leave these resorts and find local attractions on their own. And, much of the time, ethical or responsible vacations are more expensive. Extra money must be spent to guarantee good wages for local workers or to use eco-friendly facilities.

Against this backdrop, and in the wake of COVID-19, it will be interesting to see how Canada's new strategy for attracting tourists to its shores, announced in May 2019, will play out. The goal of this new strategy was to raise Canada's standing as a tourist destination from 18th in the world to the Top 10. (For recent international discussions of this problem of attracting tourists, see Marumo et al. 2018; Keyvanfar et al. 2018; Sharbatian and Bagheri 2019). To do so, Canada planned to invest in specific kinds of tourist destinations within our nation. These include the LGBTQ2S+ community, mainly found in our largest cities; Indigenous regions; Northern regions; and rural regions. Large cities aside, these are regions of Canada that need the most help with economic development.

In the consumer world, an example of SNA is how stores display their "best-seller" items. By showing what the majority chose, the store tempts the customer to conform to the same choice. Companies and marketers might also try to leverage SNA for good, manipulating social norms (or the perception of social norms) to mobilize people for social change. But it's not always as effective as we might hope, as the failure of many green campaigns has shown. Rettie et al. (2014) found that consumers cared less about whether a product or service was "green" if they thought it was normal. Some unsustainable behaviours go unchallenged because consumers think everyone does them. Similarly, green activities that have not been normalized are less likely to be adopted.

Reactive Branding and Reputation Management

As social movements pick up steam, companies react, trying to defend their reputation and, in turn, their profits. But do they actually *change* their behaviour and address the problems protestors call them out on? Or do they just sweep the issue under the rug with a re-brand akin to greenwashing? And what if a movement doesn't muster enough support to hit companies where it hurts—that is, their bottom line?

One strategy protestors increasingly use to voice their concerns is the **boycott**: when consumers withdraw from commercial relations with an organization, to punish or protest against them. To cite a classic example, Wang, Lee, and Polonsky (2013) studied the boycott of BP (the former British Petroleum) products after their ecologically devastating oil spill in the Gulf of Mexico. They found the three U.S. states bordering the Gulf (Texas, Mississippi, and Louisiana) were most

After an explosion on an offshore drilling rig resulted in the ongoing discharge of large amounts of petroleum into the Gulf of Mexico in 2010, controlled burns were conducted to try to prevent further spread of the oil. Almost five million barrels of oil poured into the Gulf before the damaged well was successfully capped.

engaged in the boycotting. Those who lived further from the oil spill were less affected by it, and as a result, were also less likely to join the boycott. As well, the people who took part viewed the oil spill as shockingly bad—not just a minor ethical infraction. Boycotts associated with "shameful" offenses are more successful at forcing the offending organizations to make concessions than those associated with lesser crimes.

Protest groups may need to focus their attention on the most egregious offences to exert the highest impact. A boycott-triggering event may also set off other actions beyond the boycott itself, like expensive lawsuits and even criminal prosecution. However, boycott-induced drops in sales are often short-lived, as was the case with the BP boycott. It died out quickly once the leaking oil well was capped, suggesting that merely symbolic, firm-specific boycotts do not last long.

Other research confirms this. Consider the boycott of a European-based food multinational that closed two of its factories, resulting in large job losses (Klein, Smith and John 2004; but also, Wiedmann et al. 2017). Consumers began to boycott the company's products almost immediately after the factory closings were announced. At first, the company lost 11 percent in market share, but its revenues recovered to pre-boycott levels after only five months. Most people surveyed did not take part in the boycott. Participants needed to think the boycott was both a fitting "punishment" for the "crime" of closing the factories, and likely to succeed. Participation also depended on whether consumers were pressured to take part—for example, pushed into it by their friends or family. Many gained social rewards from involvement, including a boost in self-esteem. Finally, they needed to deal with giving up a preferred brand. People who were under no such social pressure, or who were fond of the company's products, did not engage in the boycott.

Conflicting loyalties may also limit people's willingness to take part in boycotts, as we learn from animal rights campaigns. Some animal rights-related boycotts are successful, but others are not. Often, success depends on the meaning of the activity under protest (Einwohner 1999; see also Hahn and Albert 2017; Andersch et al. 2018). For example, many people living in rural areas see hunting as something both natural and central to their identities, and therefore refuse to boycott it. Though it is not central to people's identities, animal experimentation is important in the hugely profitable pharmaceutical and cosmetics industries. So many people do not boycott companies that rely on animal testing either. Alternately, circuses and fur coats are less essential and central to people's identities and are thus more likely to produce a boycott.

In recent years, many people have been active in movements where consumers start buying a product thought morally or socially better than another product. Boycotts punish bad behaviour, while such **buycotts** raise the bar by focusing attention on (and rewarding) best practices (Schmelzer 2010; Lightfoot 2019; Hershkovitz 2017). Unlike boycotts, buycotts are often small in scale, since taking part means buying goods that are usually more expensive than the alternatives. Also unlike boycotts, buycotts do not need collective mobilization. Buycotts may become habitual patterns of everyday life, but boycotts are temporary. Finally, buycotts are less confrontational than boycotts, being more concerned with "consuming morally" than educating or influencing other consumers.

So, boycotts and buycotts are effective to varying degrees, depending on many factors, including the specific context in which the protest is being waged. On the other hand, negative attention from mass media seems to successfully pressure misbehaving companies to take some sort of action. In one study, Islam and Deegan (2010; also, Islam, Deegan, and Haque 2020) examine the effects of negative media attention towards two large global clothing and sports retail companies (H&M and Nike) on their labour practices. The media shamed these companies for their poor working conditions and the use of child labour in developing countries. The researchers look at how the negative media attention affected the corporations' social disclosure in their annual reports over 19 years. They saw these organizations rush to clear their names of bad behaviour. The more extreme the media shaming, the more elaborate the disclosure to clear their public image. So, at the least, media shaming makes companies strive to improve their reputation. That doesn't necessarily mean it makes them change their unethical practices.

Take another example: Abercrombie and Fitch was forced to rebrand itself after it was boycotted. The brand was known not only for sexualizing outfits for teens, but also for favouring white and "pretty" customers and workers over those of other races. After firing its former CEO and rebranding itself, the brand's sales significantly increased. Again, this example shows the effect of customers who practice "ethical" consumption. Indeed, in their efforts to regain consumers' respect and business, many other companies have also re-branded themselves as "ethical" retailers—such as Eliza Faulkner and Free Label clothing stores, for example (Zhu 2019).

It can be argued that companies' adoption of ethics-conscious branding, although it makes consumers feel they are supporting a good cause, merely distracts customers from pursuing government policy changes and other initiatives that might help shape more ethical practices. Given that, are ethical consumption practices worth the trouble? Should consumers spend extra money buying clothes from sustainable brands or continue to buy fast fashion? In the end, consumers have choices to make, and their choices often have consequences. So, in deciding to shop ethically or not, consumers need to find out whether their efforts are having an effect. Perhaps they need to double down with a firmer type of protest.

Corporate Responsibility Campaigns

Besides branding, another tactic that corporations often use to keep consumer complaints (and increased state control) at bay is the adoption of corporate social responsibility (CSR) campaigns (Ali et al. 2017; Edinger-Schons et al. 2019; Rahman et al. 2017). CSR initiatives are designed to showcase the ways a corporation is giving back and supporting good in its local community or the world. For major corporations, doing these good deeds can improve their reputation and, in turn, their profitability. And such acts of social goodwill can improve consumers' views of the company's products (Chernev and Blair 2015). They create a "halo" for the company that extends' to people's views of their offerings. But this usually happens when the consumers are mostly ignorant of the products themselves. They just see the CSR campaign, not the unethical practices that go into making the product itself, or the disastrous results the product leaves in its wake.

This halo effect is stronger when consumers see socially responsible behaviour from the company—for example, when they see the company's employees volunteering to support a charity. It's also stronger when those actions align with the consumer's own moral values—for example, if the charity is one the consumer also supports. Finally, the halo effect can be strengthened when consumers hear about a company's CSR campaign by word of mouth as opposed to the company's own advertisements. People know companies use such advertisements to showcase how great they are. That makes them less believable. On the other hand, the halo effect becomes weaker when consumers think a company's actions are driven by self-interest—i.e., profits—rather than by altruism.

Ethical Capital and the Reputation Economy

Boycotts, buycotts, public shaming, and consumer movements in general are all predicated on the idea that consumers can "vote with their dollar." From this view, the consumer society is a democracy and money is the ballot consumers use to tell companies what they want.

In more academic terms, our consumer society endorses the idea of consumer sovereignty. **Consumer sovereignty** is the notion that, in a free market economy like ours, consumers should get the goods and products they want at competitive prices (see Tadajewski 2018; Mann et al. 2019; Chirat 2020). It is also the proposition that consumers are the best judges of their own interests. Consumer sovereignty assumes consumers have access to a profusion of (up-to-date) knowledge to make their "rational" decisions. On this basis, consumption patterns can be safely decided by the market. Consumers face fixed prices of goods and services, which reflect the costs of production. They are left to maximize their own well-being by choosing whatever combinations of goods and services suit them best.

In other words, our consumer society expresses its democratic values through consumption. In turn, some have expressed concern about an important aspect of our democracy: the **public sphere** (see, for example, Verhoest 2019; Fenton 2018). This term refers first to the open discussion among community members about their common concerns, and second to state activities that are central to defining that community. On the other hand, we have the private sphere—everything that lies outside the scope of the state. It also refers to personal ends, distinct from the public good and matters of public concern.

From the 18th century onward, liberal political theory has assigned democratic governance to the public sphere. This has included the business of framing opinion, discussing the meaning of politics, and compelling the state to justify its actions. Jürgen Habermas is perhaps the leading modern theorist of these political roles. He studied how the public sphere has been transformed since the 18th century. This examination has been central to all later debates ([1962] 1989). (For commentary on this work, see Burkart 2018; Rountree 2018; Benhabib 2019).

Top: Jürgen Habermas in 2014. Bottom: Hannah Arendt in 1933.

Habermas said the public sphere should promote conversation about the proper goals of society. It was created largely to address the sorts of public issues on which state policy might bear, and is based on a notion of the public good as distinct from private interest and the social institutions, like private property, that help people take part independently in the public sphere. However, it is also concerned with forms of private life, notably the family, that prepare people to act as autonomous, rational-critical subjects in the public sphere.

Another influential modern theorist of the public sphere was Hannah Arendt. She studied how action in public could shape the world (*The Human Condition*, 1958; for a commentary on this, see Nixon 2020; Young-Bruehl and Kohn 2018). Like Arendt, many modern scholars highlight the recent emergence of modern forms of governance. They point out that a liberal, national, and representative model of the public sphere only emerged in the 19th century. Both the left and right deplore the decline of a public sphere in which large numbers of people take part. They associate it with the rise of private interests at the expense of concern for the general good, and also with the decline of rational public debate about public affairs.

People are concerned about this perceived decline of the public sphere because social inequality is growing in most societies in the Global North, including Canada. Though inequality of wealth and income has grown, the values associated with egalitarianism have remained popular, if only through lip service. **Egalitarianism** is a social doctrine with the goal of equality among all members of a society—or all humanity (see, for example, Oppenheim 2018; Reynolds 2019; Gold 2019). The idea underlies many efforts to redistribute wealth or reduce social inequality. Two versions of equality are usually identified: equality of opportunity and equality of condition. The former is more closely associated with liberalism, the latter with socialism and communism, although there are many combinations.

Liberal supporters of egalitarianism generally want to equalize the competition among people in society. This leveling of the playing field may require the intervention of the state in matters of social welfare. However, many liberal egalitarians also consider inequality of outcome to be a positive good that provides incentives for talent and effort. It encourages people to try their hardest to succeed. Most modern liberal democratic societies prefer a mix of the two. They aim to moderate social inequality to assure greater equality of opportunity. Welfare policies, public education, and progressive taxation are among the most common forms of support for such goals.

Canadian author and activist Naomi Klein also discusses the decline of the public sphere in her book *No Logo* (2009; see also Jordan and Klein 2020), mentioned earlier. In it, she considers the shift in consumer focus from manufacturing to marketing and branding. On the one hand, she points out that branding has infiltrated public life, undermining democracy in the true sense of the word. Even political ideas are branded, Klein notes. There are fewer and fewer places where people can come together as citizens, rather than as consumers. One example is the mall, which is designed to look like a town square. But unlike real town squares, where community members gather to connect and socialize, malls are privately owned and obstruct the freedoms of the town square.

On the other hand, Klein also says consumers can launch social movements to protest unethical consumer behaviour. She points out the many efforts that protestors have made to reclaim public attention, such as "culture jamming," which means altering the message of or spoofing advertisements. Shopping alone won't be enough to change the world, Klein posits. It's not as simple as casting your (money) ballot in favour of one brand of makeup over another. Instead, Klein says we need a global movement that champions ethical trade.

Such a movement is a key part of Adam Arvidsson and Nicolai Pietersen's argument in their book *The Ethical Economy* (2013). Arvidsson and Pietersen agree with the line of reasoning we've been discussing in this chapter. Namely, they say ethical consumption is not enough; it mostly just benefits wealthy business owners. Instead, these authors take Campbell's earlier point to heart and propose we shouldn't be putting the onus on consumers to buy responsibly. Instead, we need to transform our economy, so it rewards ethical behaviour. We need, therefore, to strive for ethical capitalists as well as ethical consumers (Betta 2016; McEachern 2016). And to change the behaviour of businesses, Arvidsson and Pietersen say we need to change the values our economy rewards.

But here's where their argument may go astray. These authors suggest that we must shift our focus to **ethical capital.** Ethical capital is gained by adhering to the public's values. In other words, companies earn ethical wealth when others affirm their actions. And they lose ethical capital when others disapprove of their actions. In turn, ethical and economic values coincide to create a new way of organizing wealth that relies on reputation—a reputation economy.

According to Arvidsson and Pietersen, reputation economies are growing in importance. Companies are striving for ethical behaviour because they know it will improve their reputation and, in turn, their profits. For example, having ethical capital (that is, a reputation for moral behaviour) is valuable for an organization trying to build an attractive brand.

The reputation economy (Gandini 2016) would finally democratize our economy, these authors claim. It would give consumers the power to influence the ways values are set, putting value creation into the hands of the public. That means the economy and its actors would be guided by the interests of the people, not just the interests of the wealthy elite.

Here are just a few of the problems we see with this theory. First, Arvidsson and Pietersen seem at first to agree with Campbell, and say we need to transform the capitalist economy itself. However, they end up putting the burden on consumers to do so. Consumers are the ones responsible for praising ethical behaviour and therefore building up actors' ethical capital. Without their influence, businesses would continue acting unethically, purely for profit.

Second, we already see the dangers of leaving ethics in the hands of consumers. Look at the behaviour social media users reward. Billions of likes, positive comments, and shares build up the reputations of reality-TV stars and YouTubers. In turn, they are being paid to sell everything from weight-loss teas to sunglasses. Sure, plenty of consumers also use social media to speak for ethical behaviour and businesses and to tear down the reputations of those who behave unethically. But we disagree with Arvidsson and Pietersen's suggestion the "democratization" of the economy would make businesses perform more ethically. It would only make them perform in ways the public applauds. And, as we know from studies of representation in general, not everyone's voice gets heard or listened to—not even in a democracy.

Final Thoughts

In this chapter, we discussed the fact that the consumer society we live in is often presented as the unavoidable result of human nature. People, this argument goes, naturally crave material comfort. They will always want more, and they will always want more than they need. Consumer societies, from this perspective, arise naturally to meet natural human demand.

But, in fact, consumer societies are deeply political. Sometimes, their expansion is driven by governments trying to encourage other nations to adopt their values, as was the case during the

Cold War. Sometimes, they are driven by neo-colonialism, as was the case when Western nations began trading with developing ones to advance their own capitalist agendas. Sometimes, they are driven by industrialization and globalization, as today when people use consumer goods to stand out and assert their unique identities in an increasingly homogenized, anonymous world. Often, they are caused by a complex mix of all of these factors and more.

The continued existence of today's consumer society has come to seem inevitable to many observers, particularly after the collapse of the USSR, whose communist economic system represented the clearest alternative to Western capitalism for most of the 20th century. There are, however, many alternative ways of organizing economies and societies, and it would be historically naive to think that the present situation represents some sort of "final state" or "end of history." And even within the various capitalist countries there are widely divergent views and policies on such matters as income inequality, social welfare programs, environmental protection, and the like.

So, we do not think consumerism is part of human nature. Nor do we think it is always acceptable or unavoidable. People could choose to live differently—to organize themselves in ways other than a consumer society. And they would not need to give up material comfort or a high standard of living to do so. Industrialization, globalization, and even materialism and consumerism are not bad in and of themselves. They become problematic when, under capitalism, their benefits are shared unevenly, and when people have uneven opportunities to take part in them. For example, is it socially or economically necessary for a CEO to be paid 300 times what their average employee earns?

Is consumerism a problem that we should worry about? Or can we leverage it for good? We have seen throughout this book that consumerism has some good effects, such as boosting standards of living. We have also seen that not everyone shares in those good effects equally. And, we have seen that consumerism is associated with some bad effects, such as shopping addictions. Finally, we have seen that consumerism is deceptive: a mask for exploitative capitalism and a distraction from problems like inequality or even just the monotony of everyday life. In this chapter, we looked at how people behave when they think consumerism is bad—how they try to do something about it. And we looked at how, often, their efforts to "do something" involve consuming.

Bearing in mind that consumerism brings some good, we think the bad also warrants attention. And protesters have been drawing that attention for decades. Boycotts and buycotts, for example, are two ways consumers can express dissatisfaction and pressure companies to change their ways. Even if they do not take part in formally organized protests, consumers may still "vote with their dollar." They can choose to buy products that align with their morals. In this sense, consumerism can, sometimes, be leveraged for good. "Good" (that is, ethical) consumerism can be a means of challenging "bad" (i.e., unethical) consumerism.

That said, we identified at least two problems with this view. For one, there's no such thing as "good" (that is, ethical) consuming. If every capitalist product is the result of exploited labour, is it ethical to buy anything? If every capitalist product harms the environment, is it green to buy anything? Is it enough to choose the less exploitative, less environmentally damaging alternative?

What's more, due to their high cost, some "ethical" products are accessible only to wealthier people. As a result, these goods symbolize and help prop up inequality. Because they can only afford cheaper goods, lower-income earners bear the moral brunt of unethical production practices like sweatshop labour. And when we rally against exploitative production by boycotting manufacturers of low-cost products, we may be hurting lower-income consumers. In targeting and criticizing dollar stores and the like, these consumers are prevented from exercising their only possible buying power. So, ethical consumption can reinforce class divides while ignoring the history of disadvantaged groups and their access to consumer products.

The second problem is that consumers shouldn't be the ones bearing this burden to begin with. As Campbell suggested at the start of this chapter, it isn't their responsibility to enforce ethical behaviour among businesses. Rather, businesses shouldn't be sacrificing ethics for the sake of wider profit margins. So, a key takeaway from this chapter is that, despite protestors' good intentions, buying is not the most effective way to protest consumerism. Perhaps more focus is needed on our capitalist consumer society as a whole, rather than on the individual consumption choices we each make.

Discussion Questions

1. In this chapter, we talked about how it is difficult for a boycott to be effective. Why is this? What are some examples of social or economic delays, expenses, and inconveniences that indirectly influence the efficiency of a boycott?

2. Think of contemporary consumers who are interested in pursuing large-scale actions, significant changes to social norms, or shifts in the capitalist economy. Why might they want to do this? What are some examples of such deviance?

3. Adam Arvidsson and Nicolai Pietersen write that ethical consumption is insufficient. Why isn't responsible consumption enough to build an ethical consumer society? What are some ways to transform the economy in order to reward ethical behaviours?

Quick Quiz

1. What is symbolic violence?
a. Small-group interactions that use symbols when they consume
b. Consumption patterns of members from different ethnic communities who use consumer goods to show they belong to those communities
c. The illegal consumer choices and misdeeds of the middle-class members of the business world
d. Imposition on subordinated groups by the dominant class an ideology that legitimates and naturalizes the status quo
e. The salience of ethnicity and ethnic cues for consumer behaviour

2. Which statement is false about post-Fordism?
a. It is linked to a shift from blue-collar manual work to white-collar work
b. It is more likely to involve teamwork and seek input and participation from employee's decision making
c. It is a system of mass production
d. It places more emphasis on social and technical skills
e. It tends to deskill the workforce

3. As discussed above, what is a factor that contributed to the globalization of consumer culture?
a. Improvements in technology and communication
b. People's increased desire to purchase local goods
c. Increased use of consumer ethical goods
d. People's growth in economic status
e. Adoption of social capital among citizens

4. What is ethical capital?
a. The resources available to an individual on the basis of honor, prestige or recognition
b. A reputation for moral behaviour
c. The social factors that promote the social mobility of an individual
d. The collection of knowledge behaviours, and skills used to display high social status and competence
e. The evaluation of other cultures according to preconceptions originating in the standards and customs of one's own culture

5. What is the social norm approach (SNA)?
a. The tendency of people to conform to rules because they fear punishments that come with deviance
b. The act of consumers using moral decoupling rather than normal justification in making a decision
c. The understanding that mechanical production of cultural products makes oppressive regimes of consumption seem normal

d. The exploitation of people's wish to follow the rules
e. Regulation of people's consumer choices is made a personal responsibility and a requirement for being viewed as "normal"

The answers to the Quick Quiz are provided at the end of the book.

For Further Reading

No Logo: No Space, No Choice, No Jobs by Naomi Klein
The book focuses on issues such as culture jamming, corporate censorship, and sweatshops in the West and the East. Klein explores branding and makes connections with the alter-globalization movement.

The Earthscan Reader on Sustainable Consumption by Tim Jackson
Tim Jackson examines the challenges associated with more sustainable consumption. Through psychological, economic, and sociological dimensions, the book discusses the present environmental alternatives to a world dominated by consumerism.

The Rebel Sell: How the Counterculture Became Consumer Culture by Andrew Potter and Joseph Heath
In the book Potter and Heath explore the various ways that counterculture movements have fuelled capitalism and money-making devices.

Key Terms

Boycott
Greenwashing
Post-Fordism
Symbolic violence
Virtual community

Chapter Eighteen
The Future of Consumerism

Learning Objectives

After reading this chapter, you will be able to:

- ✓ Understand the environmental and health consequences of capitalism and consumerism.
- ✓ Consider the gigantism of capitalism and a future of production on size-appropriate scales.
- ✓ Recognize the implications of surveillance and personalization in marketing.
- ✓ Picture the costs of self-perpetuating capitalist consumerism for future generations.

In this final chapter, we look forward into the future of consumerism and predict what it might hold. This task would be ambitious even under normal circumstances. Now, as COVID-19 wreaks havoc on our global economy and upends the ways we shop and the goods we buy, the future of consumerism has become even more difficult to predict.

On the other hand, we have several decades' worth of data and predictions of what's to come in terms of our planet. We will also consider the possible impacts of the climate crisis on consumption, and vice versa.

Let's start with a parable about the human condition that may be relevant to predicting the future: the famous legend of King Midas.

Two Parables about Humanity

The wealthy ruler of Phrygia in Asia Minor, Midas wanted even more wealth, thinking that gold yielded the greatest happiness. One day, Dionysus, the god of wine and revelry offered to grant any wish Midas might make. After thinking awhile, Midas said, "I hope that everything I touch becomes gold." The next day, Midas woke up to find his wish had come true. Everything he touched immediately turned into gold. When Midas hugged his beloved daughter, even she turned into a golden statue! Despairing, Midas prayed to Dionysus to take back this accursed wish. The god, feeling sorry for him, told Midas to go to the river and wash his hands. Midas did so and when he got back home, everything he had touched had returned to its original form. After that, Midas was a wiser person, in his wishes and his actions. His people led prosperous lives and when Midas died, they all mourned the passing of their beloved king. The End.

Now, let's compare that story with another parable about the human condition.

As the world's population approached four billion people in the early 1970s, the Club of Rome, a global think tank, commissioned distinguished researchers at MIT to find the limits to economic and population growth. To do so, the authors created the so-called World3 model. This was a computerized method for studying the future of the world by simulating interlinked changes likely to occur over the next 100 years (i.e., by 2070).

Their model explored five major trends of global concern: worldwide industrialization, rapid population growth, widespread hunger, a polluted environment, and the depletion of non-renewable resources. Their book-length report, *The Limits to Growth* (Meadows et al. 1972), showed that the world's natural resources would be either exhausted or prohibitively expensive within 100 years. This would almost certainly occur unless humanity began immediately to reduce its economic and demographic growth. By the 2070s, humanity would start to die off, through pollution, hunger, lack of needed materials, or otherwise (For commentary on this study, see Meadows 2019; Heath et al. 2019; Ansell and Cayzer 2018).

This was one of the report's two main conclusions. The second was that humanity could still survive. Slowing and, ultimately, stopping growth would help to achieve global equilibrium, so all human material needs could be fulfilled, and every person could reach his or her human potential. The authors proposed that the sooner people began to strive for global equilibrium, the sooner it could be achieved; and achieving such balance would reduce the dire risks of global collapse.

Despite the sensation this book created, its conclusions were widely criticized and, in the end, ignored. However, persuaded of the importance of their findings, the authors revised and republished their classic work under the title *Limits to Growth: The 30-Year Update* (2004). Here the authors stressed that humanity was still in desperate straits. The gap between the rich and poor had grown rapidly. Essential non-renewable resources were becoming harder and more expensive to obtain. Worst of all, the natural environment was showing signs of severe strain. Under these conditions, humanity now had to limit the damage to earth and its human population (Meadows, Meadows and Randers 2004). (For a commentary on this study, see Jackson and Webster 2017; Moon 2016; Estes 2017). The time for sustainable development had passed. However, as before, their conclusions were widely criticized and then ignored. The End.

Well, not quite the end. On August 8, 2019, the international IPCC (Intergovernmental Panel on Climate Change) released a new report intended to influence upcoming negotiations about the worsening global climate crisis. More than 100 experts compiled the report, around half of them from low-income countries. These experts reported that, without drastic changes in global land use, agriculture, and human diets, efforts to curb greenhouse gas emissions and the impacts of climate change will fail.

Researchers also noted the danger to tropical rain forests, because of hastening rates of de-forestation. Unstopped, deforestation could turn much of the remaining Amazon forests into desert, possibly releasing over 50 billion tonnes of carbon into the atmosphere. Such deforestation, like other important climatic changes (for example, the melting of the polar ice caps), would make many parts of the world uninhabitable. It would also reduce agricultural production and force hundreds of millions of starving refugees out of their home countries. Countries

In September 2020, sea-ice coverage in the Arctic Ocean reached its second-smallest extent during the past four decades, almost 2.5 million square kilometres less than average. Arctic temperatures in the summer of 2020 averaged 8 to 10 degrees Celsius higher than usual. Such shifts are making themselves felt in weather patterns worldwide, and are likely to intensify over the course of the 21st century.

of the Global North are already seeing surges of immigrants, refugees, and asylum seekers from the Global South, and these numbers will increase dramatically.

The point of our comparison between the Midas parable and the limits-to-growth parable is to remind the reader that humanity makes dangerous decisions. Like Midas, humans have enriched themselves beyond limit, at great cost to the planet. Like Midas, humanity is just beginning to see and fear the costs of this choice. Unlike Dionysus in the Greek myth, Mother Nature may not give humanity a second chance.

Defining Our Terms

Environmentalism is the belief that our environment—the earth on which we live—is critical for human survival. It also describes concern for the environment and, sometimes, efforts to protect it (Woodhouse 2018; McKanan 2017; Zelko 2020).

Today, being an "environmentalist" also means being a conservationist—a person who wants to preserve the environment as it is. "Environmental studies" can mean geography, biology, chemistry, law, history, politics, and many other disciplines. And the concerns of environmentalism can range from architecture to the stratosphere, from the water supply to the diversity of species on the planet.

Beginning in the 1970s, some ecologists and philosophers have been suspicious of **mere environmentalism** (Sutton 2019), which they define as practices and policies that take into account only human interests. Some of these critics seek to orient our entire approach to include concern about the biosphere as a whole, while others have expressed concern about the welfare of deprived groups of people (especially in developing countries) and have called for a focus on equity and justice, as well as efforts to leave a worthwhile environmental heritage for future generations.

A related concept is **sustainability** (Heinrichs et al. 2016; Caniglia et al. 2017; Berkes and Ross 2016). Sustainability is the property of a system—in this case, the natural system of planet earth—that allows for both its use and long-term regeneration. In fisheries, the term "maximum sustained yield" refers to the largest amount of fish that can be caught without permanently endangering the fish supply. In forestry, it refers to the largest number of trees that can be cut down without compromising the ability of the woodland to renew itself over time.

Sustainable development refers to development that meets people's needs today but doesn't compromise future generations' ability to meet their needs. Common principles in sustainable development include dealing transparently and systematically with risk, doubt, and irreversibility. Sustainability also means ensuring an appreciation and restoration of nature, and integrating concerns about nature into social, human, and economic goals. There can be no sustainability without good governance, community participation, intergenerational equity, and commitment to best practices. Failure to act sustainably is understood to carry great costs to humanity as well as the natural ecosystem.

Another strain of environmentalism is **ecofeminism**. Ecofeminism is a marriage of ecology and feminism. It is the study of women's connections to nature and how they inspire particular forms of environmental activism, stewardship, and spiritual attachments to earth. Ecofeminism proposes there is a connection between the domination of women in patriarchal societies, and the domination and degradation of nature by industrial capitalism. The term was coined by French feminist and science fiction writer Françoise d'Eubonne in *Le Féminisme ou la Mort* (*Feminism or Death*) (1974). She envisioned a future in which feminist attitudes prevailed, thus saving the planet from its seemingly inexorable course towards eco-death. (For an expansion of her views, see MacGregor 2017.)

How Consumerism Affects the Environment

Recall our four prototypical consumers from the first pages of this book. First, Anna is a consumer mainly of basics. She budgets and plans her buying carefully. She does not buy more than her family needs. Yet even Anna is contributing to environmental destruction, because with global population growth, there are simply more "Annas" every year than there were the year before. Most demographers think this growth will continue, though at a slowing rate, until around 2100, when the world's population will have reached about 11 billion (an increase of 3.3 billion from its current level). It may then start to decline.

Next, Anton is mainly a consumer of treats, and if anything, he is more bent on destroying himself than on destroying the environment. That is the nature of all addictions—whether they are addictions to alcohol, drugs, gambling, or (in this case) shopping. Still, Anton's single-minded preoccupation with buying and hoarding things, and the pain he feels when he is unable to do this, also promotes the continued production, distribution, and sale of consumer items. The Antons of the world are far less numerous than the Annas, but they do damage to the environment nonetheless.

Tamara is mainly a consumer of tickets: items that communicate her membership in a particular group, or her aspiration to belong to that group. As Riesman and his colleagues said in *The Lonely Crowd,* such behaviour contributes mainly to the destruction of informed political debate, not the direct destruction of the environment. However, the destruction of informed political debate is, itself, an impediment to solving the problem of environmental destruction. When people are preoccupied with shopping for new cars and household items, they don't have much time to think about the climate crisis and what they might do to stem it. Beyond that, the continued growth of a global middle class means that hundreds of millions of new Tamaras are joining the world's ticket-buying class every year. That translates into a lot of new demand for cars, household items, and other middle-class acquisitions, and an intensified race by all to "keep up with the Joneses."

Of our four "typical buyers," Donald is perhaps the most directly and powerfully implicated in destroying the global environment. His pursuit of global trophies at any cost is promoting the destruction of animal species and natural habitats—Donald and his children love to hunt wild game—while condoning and profiting from the reckless extraction of natural resources in previously protected locales. His livelihood may even come from the construction of ever-more grandiose, spectacular, and unnecessary business enterprises, like those we described in Las Vegas. As Veblen warned us, the trophy-seeker revels in conspicuous waste: the waste of time, money, and (of course) natural resources. Waste—the systematic and competitive creation of garbage—is no friend to the natural environment.

So, each of our consumer types contributes to environmental destruction, directly or indirectly, and this problem will continue or even increase in the coming years. Perhaps it would be fairer to say that each of our consumer motives contributes to environmental destruction, since each of our four characters is an "ideal type," not a real person. Every real consumer has a mix of buying motives. Our biggest danger, then, is that the world's population is growing in size and is transitioning from basic buying motives to increased treat-buying, ticket-buying, and trophy-buying. That transition pattern is largely why the environment is being destroyed, and consumerism is a large part of the ideological base for this destruction.

As time passes, this gradual trend to environmental destruction is modified in various ways, sometimes speeded up and sometimes slowed down. Moderating factors include changes of government, wars, trade deals, and most recently, the global impact of the COVID-19 virus.

The Impacts of COVID-19 on Consumerism

As COVID-19 first swept Canada in the spring of 2020, businesses—big and small, in-person and online, product suppliers and service deliverers—simply tried to stay afloat through the crisis itself. Some were better equipped to weather the storm than others. Many small local businesses folded quite quickly under lockdown conditions. The average cost of the pandemic on small businesses in Canada was estimated at $214,915 (CFIB 2020); 22 percent of small business owners said their sales declined 100 percent, and 19 percent said their sales declined to one-quarter of pre-pandemic levels or less.

But amid the chaos, those businesses that survived also tried to prepare to operate in whatever "new normal" might emerge on the other side. Even today, no one has a clear view of what those long-term circumstances might look like. The future of consumerism depends on questions we cannot yet answer. These include how many people the virus will infect, how many lives it will claim, and how long it will spread before a vaccine and cure are available. The answers to these questions control how much the economy will decline and over what period of time.

The future of consumerism also depends on many other variables we cannot even foresee at all right now, such as how international relations might evolve. All of this is to say that the predictions we can make about the future are, at the moment, based on shaky assumptions. We simply do not have enough information on which to make educated guesses. So, in this chapter, we will stick to some very general forecasting, all while bearing in mind the many unexpected loops this pandemic has thrown us for.

First, in looking ahead to the future, many businesses are wondering whether they will have a motivated consumer base whenever the pandemic recedes. In March 2020, over 3.1 million Canadians had lost their jobs, or their work hours had been reduced, due to COVID-19 (Statistics Canada 2020). People between the ages of 25 and 54 suffered the largest decrease in employment. Women were more likely to lose their jobs than men.

The Canadian government responded to the issues of job loss and reduced income in many ways. It extended the due date for paying income tax, increased the Canada Child Benefit, provided increased financial aid to Indigenous peoples, and implemented the Canada Emergency Response Benefit (CERB), which provided qualifying individuals $500 a week for up to 16 weeks. There were also initiatives created to help businesses. The Canada Emergency Wage Subsidy (CEWS) was designed to help businesses keep running and avoid layoffs, while the Canadian Emergency Business Account (CEBA) provided interest-free loans of up to $40,000 for struggling small businesses and non-profit organizations (Service Canada 2020). Nevertheless, many businesses (38 percent of respondents) said these programs could not keep them afloat.

Job insecurity also affected the temporary foreign workers that Canada's agriculture industry heavily relies on. Coming from several countries, including Mexico, Guatemala, and Jamaica, these workers typically fill 20 percent of all the jobs in Canada's agriculture sector (Shadid et al. 2020). As long as we need travel and border restrictions to slow the spread of COVID-19, these workers face challenges getting into the country. It remains to be seen what impact this will have on Canada's agricultural production in the longer-term future.

The long-term effects of the COVID-19 pandemic on patterns of spending and consumption remain unclear.

We can reasonably anticipate that, whatever the cause, unemployment and job insecurity will depress consumer spending. Initial precautions to slow the spread of the virus in the second quarter of 2020 resulted in a decline in economic activity larger than any seen since World War II (Buck et al. 2020). Discretionary spending fell significantly, partly because people had less money to spend on non-necessities, partly because of lack of places to spend it. In an uncertain economy, where so many people have lost their jobs and do not yet know what their financial future holds, consumers also become more cautious spenders. In an interesting twist, the pandemic also resulted in Canadians saving at a higher rate than had previously been the case.

In their article "How consumer-goods companies can prepare for the next normal," McKinsey & Company authors Buck et al. (2020) rely on observations made in Asia (where the virus hit first). They also rely on what was learned in the last recession (2008–09) to predict what our future could hold. They suggest that five trends that emerged during the crisis will persist during the period of economic recovery from COVID-19 and beyond:

Increased price sensitivity. Consumers say they intend to spend less because they are unsure how much and how long the pandemic will impact the economy. Following the 2008 recession, some ways consumers responded to this uncertainty included reducing spending outside of the home (e.g., eating out at restaurants less often), as well as on luxury goods and cosmetics. Some looked for deals and discounts more attentively, started shopping at value retailers, or opted for cheaper brands.

Businesses are trying to make calculated guesses based on some of these consumer trends. For example, some middle and high-income consumers—including those who have been able to work from home throughout the pandemic and may even be *saving* money because they've eliminated their commuting costs—are now taking advantage of discounts and deals to do more shopping now than they usually do. In response, big-name brands like Nike, Macy's, and Sephora are offering big discounts to drive up sales. Some stores are even offering free shipping and services that are usually exclusive to their loyalty members.

Higher digital engagement. E-commerce and online media flourished while everyone was stuck at home. For retailers with brick-and-mortar stores, online sales may have been their only source of revenue. If customers enjoyed their new digital shopping experience, perhaps they will continue to patronize these brands online in the future. What's more, store closures have forced people who otherwise would have avoided e-commerce to give it a try. Older adults, for example, might become more comfortable shopping online. Finally, we do not yet know how cautious and fearful consumers will be, even after lockdowns and physical distancing measures have been lifted. They may try to avoid crowded gathering places, including brick-and-mortar stores.

Greater attention to wellness and hygiene. Many people have aimed to stay healthy while in lockdown. They purchased at-home exercise equipment, rented it from savvy local gyms, and joined virtual workout classes. This attention to wellness isn't necessarily new; plenty of consumers were already paying outrageous monthly fees for boutique fitness club memberships pre-pandemic. However, the new twist is a preoccupation with hygiene. All of the handwashing and sanitizing people are doing to avoid contracting the coronavirus could stick. Marketers may start emphasizing cleanliness in their advertisements and lean into single-use packaging.

"Nesting" at home. Some people may have found a new pleasure in staying in. Many have spent their time at home renovating, gardening, re-organizing their closets, and purging their garages. They may have also discovered new at-home activities they enjoy, as reflected in skyrocketing sales of breadmakers. Perhaps they will continue to opt to spend more time at home, even if the risks of going out are reduced. Or, we could see the exact opposite among some groups. After spending so much time stuck inside, at least some people will be desperate to be out and about again.

Corporate social responsibility. Research from the Edelman Trust Barometer showed that, as of early April 2020, a majority of consumers thought brands should be playing a role in helping to solve challenges related to COVID-19 (Dallaire 2020). In the midst of the crisis, many brands jumped at the opportunity to show how they were making a difference.

However, consumers seem intent to respond only to those brands that are genuinely contributing—not those merely seeking to position themselves in a positive light. For example, of those Canadians polled, 65 percent said a company's response to COVID-19 would have "a huge impact" on their likelihood of patronizing that brand in the future, but 71 percent indicated that brands would "lose my trust forever" if they put profits before people while their community was in crisis. Early data suggest Canadians are willing to vote with their money: 26 percent say they have already started using a new brand that has been compassionate or innovative in its response to the virus. The ways brands communicate during the crisis will impact how consumers see them long after. In the future, brands may invest more significantly in corporate social responsibility efforts, especially if challenges related to COVID-19 persist.

The only thing we can be sure of at this point is that COVID-19 and iniatives like #metoo and Black Lives Matter will impact our consumer society in the future. Whether that impact will be big or small, long or short-lived, remains to be seen. We have already seen the Black Lives Matter movement reorienting consumer behaviour. Through the movement, social responsibility efforts associated with a brand became even more prioritized. People were made more aware of diversity and representation in their shopping choices, with many of the consumers trying to support more Black-owned businesses.

Dealing with the Climate Crisis in Modest Ways

Advertisers, marketers, and consumers are finally becoming more aware of and more responsive to the global climate crisis—at least, more so than they were in 1972 and 2004, when the two "limits to growth" books were published. As a result, we hear more discussion about "green" and "eco-friendly" manufacturing, marketing, and buying today than ever before (Barbarossa and De Pelsmacker 2016; Reczek, Trudel and White 2018). The current consumer response, and the response of marketers to this consumer response, may be far too little, far too late, but it is (at last) a response.

We cannot give the climate crisis as much space as it deserves. What follows is therefore only a brief discussion of research on the link between consumerism and climate change, as well as consumer and marketer responses to environmental issues.

One such response has been vegetarian and vegan eating. Vegans do not eat or buy any products that are made from or exploit animals. This means not eating meat and cheese, but also not buying shampoo or conditioners that were tested on animals, or clothing made from animal products. According to Statista, there are approximately 1.2 million vegetarians in Canada. Of those, 850,000 are vegans (Bedford 2019). Most of these self-identified vegans are based in British Columbia, where there is a growing trend of millennials adopting ethically conscientious shopping habits. Indeed, most vegetarians and vegans in Canada are under the age of 35. As these folks get older, and start having kids, they will likely raise their families vegan, which means we might see greater numbers of vegans in future years (Flanagan 2018). Even those who are not vegetarian or vegan are making the effort to eat less meat. In Canada, beef and pork consumption are in a long-term decline (Bedford 2019).

The restaurant and packaged goods industries are picking up on these animal-friendly trends. As one journalist wrote, this "plant-based renaissance" in the Canadian restaurant scene is catering to those who are joining the vegan movement (Bresge 2018) with the opening of many plant-based restaurants and cafes.

Consumers are also increasingly interested in recycling and re-use. Others still have developed a taste for fair trade products, as mentioned (Strong 1996; Chatzidakis et al. 2016). The increasingly well-informed consumer is also challenging manufacturers and retailers to guarantee the ethical claims they are making about their products.

These consumer responses bring us back to a question we posed earlier: Can individual consumption decisions make a difference? And should consumers bear that responsibility? As discussed in the last chapter, the answer appears to be "no." A much-discussed example is plastic straws. Eliminating them from your consumption habits does make a difference to a certain degree, but given the urgency of the climate crisis, using metal straws isn't enough to lower carbon emissions. So, environmental sustainability is not a personal lifestyle project. It is a huge responsibility our entire world must bear. It demands change on an international scale, underpinned by policies that go beyond influencing individual consumer behaviour (Moisander 2007; Ferguson et al. 2017). The onus for stopping climate change cannot rest with individual consumers alone. It is (also) the responsibility of manufacturers, retailers, governments, corporations and others who are doing large-scale irreparable damage, and who wield power an individual consumer could never overcome.

Changes in consumption patterns by individuals, such as the use of metal rather than plastic straws, however laudable, are unlikely in themselves to address the environmental crisis in the absence of sufficient efforts by businesses and governments.

So, what are these institutions doing about climate change? The short answer is, not nearly enough. According to the Canadian Environment and Climate Change Department (CNN 2019), Canada has been warming at a faster rate than the rest of the world. The Canadian government enacted legislation to meet the Paris Climate Agreement goal of limiting global warming by reducing the emission of greenhouse gases. But are these efforts enough?

The largest Canadian contributors to greenhouse gas emissions are the oil and gas (27 percent) and transport (24 percent) sectors. To target emissions caused by transport, the Canadian government is investing more in public transport. It is providing $182 million in funding for electric and alternative-fuel transport and investing in the development of cleaner fuels for cars. Canada is aiming to reduce oil and gas methane emissions by 40 percent by 2025. The government is also introducing a clean fuel standard that aims to achieve 30 million tonnes of annual cuts in greenhouse gas emissions by 2030.

Few nations are on track to meet their Paris Accord promises to limit carbon emissions. Large low- and middle-income countries like Brazil, Russia, India, and China continue to produce CO_2 emissions at a high and growing rate, as they compete for wealth and power with wealthier industrial countries. Most egregiously, the U.S. has renounced its earlier commitment to the Paris Accord.

The United States (and to some degree Canada) also lag behind European countries in adopting ecological modernization (EM) policies and practices. EM in the EU stresses industrial efficiency and technological development (Schlosberg and Rinfret 2008; Peterson 2017; Certoma 2016). Its goal is to move beyond the perceived conflict between economic development and environmental quality. Such initiatives have made little progress in North America.

That world leaders—not to mention manufacturers, conglomerates, and others spurring consumerism along—are doing so little to address the climate crisis is disconcerting. Clearly, we cannot rely on government alone. Indeed, as with many large-scale problems, solutions to the climate crisis will likely be international, interdisciplinary, and inter-institutional. The best ideas from a wide range of thinkers in many different fields need to come together. Such interdisciplinary thinking has yet to yield a satisfying solution to the climate crisis. So, of course, much more research, policy making, organizing, and protesting remains to be done. However, one analysis—drawing on sociology, philosophy, history, and religion—yielded some interesting starting points.

Capitalist Gigantism and a Call for Size-Appropriate Scales

In his book *Small is Beautiful* (1973), German-British statistician and economist E.F. Schumacher conducted an interdisciplinary examination of society's means of production and consumption (for recent commentaries, see Corbett 2018; Eriksen 2018). One of his central points is that our consumer society is obsessed with gigantism. Capitalism itself is a gigantic, fast-paced form of production that places such production over human relations. Those means of production are also huge and rely too heavily on modern technology, transport, and globalization. And they serve a market that is huge: desperate to spread the same goods across the planet through mass production.

In the end, Schumacher says, capitalism creates a supreme dilemma of man-as-producer versus man-as-consumer. Man-as-producer is seen as wasting money when, for example, he travels first class or buys luxury products. Meanwhile, when man-as-consumer does the same, he is seen as meeting a natural human desire to increase his standard of living. We are all of us caught in this dilemma of consumption versus production, and we cannot hope to solve the sustainability problem until we sort it out.

On the one hand, the modern economy is driven by what Schumacher calls a "frenzy of greed" and an "orgy of envy." It causes frustration and insecurity. The need to build a monster economy grows out of greed that can finally lead to violent conflict. On the other hand, Schumacher suggests, religion may help temper these destructive forces. He draws on the writings of Gandhi, who said: "Earth provides enough to satisfy every man's need, but not every man's greed." (For commentary on these views, see Ossewaarde-Lowtoo 2020; Shivdas and Chandrasekhar 2016; Hill 2018.)

With all of this in mind, Schumacher does not suggest decreasing the quantity of goods produced. Rather, he says production needs to be conducted on "size appropriate scales." Goods can be produced in ratio to the population size of a city, for example, rather than on a mass scale. In turn, negative environmental effects are limited.

Box 18-1

Downshifting

Downshifting is the voluntary decision to lessen one's income and/or consumption (Kemp-Benedict and Ghosh 2018; Peyer et al. 2017). Typically, downshifters are seeking more balance in their lives. Many want to devote more time to their families, health, or hobbies.

By consuming less (and making sure others know they are consuming less), downshifters use consumption to shape their identities as minimalists. Ironically though, for some, efforts to downshift prompt even more consumption, whether that is buying metal straws and reusable travel mugs, or constructing a brand new "tiny house" in which they can live out their new minimalist lifestyle.

Some have even built their personal brands around minimalism. Marie Kondo, for example, is a tidying specialist, best-selling author, and star of a hit Netflix show that broadcasts her "KonMari" minimalist approach. Even though minimalism undercuts capitalism and materialism in theory, Kondo shows it can be the very thing that supports capitalism and materialism.

That said, Schumacher could not have predicted developments over the last half-century. For example, he could not have predicted the Internet, or how much more our world would globalize. He might not have predicted that people would still be doubting whether climate change is even real in 2020. So, we are not suggesting that Schumacher has solved the climate crisis. Still, Schumacher's analysis may provide a model for future considerations. For one, as mentioned, it's interdisciplinary. For another, it proposes systemic action. He doesn't suggest consumers can change the world by buying fair trade coffee, for example. Rather, he explores how we might reorganize our modes of production, so they are more sustainable.

Indeed, some of the most promising policy choices for reducing environmental damage focus on producers and distributors. They aim to encourage the development and use of environmentally harmless technologies in mining, manufacturing, transport, and commerce. These strategies, which indirectly lower the environmental impact of delivering consumer goods and services, may have far greater effect than direct efforts to change consumer behavior.

But perhaps the most interesting thing about Schumacher's work *is* that it was published almost 50 years ago. Even then, people could see that capitalism and mass consumerism would lead to ruin. Even then, people could see the dangers of ranking profit over human lives. Even then, people could see capitalism and consumerism are driven by reckless greed and envy. But almost half a century later, we have yet to make significant progress towards addressing these issues. In fact, we have steadily made them worse. Clearly, the problem of environmental sustainability is far from solved, and its solution will face many difficulties (Baland et al. 2018; Howes et al. 2017).

So, the climate crisis will be at the heart of the future of consumerism. In earlier chapters, we saw how people are already leveraging consumerism to take a stand on issues like the climate crisis. Probably, the future will be marked by further ethical consumerist movements. We can expect to see much more activity by animal rights or environmental protection movements, for instance.

The Share Economy

In the last 20 years, largely in response to this climate crisis (as well as the rise of the gig economy, a concern with economic inequality, and a wish to de-commodify the market for consumer goods), we have seen the rise of a so-called "share economy" (Frenken and Schor 2017).

Now, humans have always shared. When we talk about this supposedly new "share economy" today, it's often lauded for being so progressive, innovative, and technologically disruptive. But low-income urban groups relied on reciprocity and interdependence for their survival decades ago (Stack 1974). To say the sharing economy is "new" is to ignore the sharing that the working classes and people of colour have historically practiced.

What *is* new about today's sharing economy is that it is grounded in "stranger sharing" (Schor 2014a). In past decades, sharing was limited to family, friends, and neighbours. Today, using new technology, it is possible to share among people who do not know each other and lack friends or connections in common. One reason for this change is that it is easier today, using new technology, to document, predict, and therefore control deviant behaviour.

Many of the new sharing platforms throw strangers together in intimate situations, such as sharing one's home or car, for example. Technology makes such sharing less risky, since consumers are required to provide their personal information and are often publicly "reviewed" (Schor 2014b). For example, Uber drivers can rate their passengers, letting other drivers know about potentially rowdy or otherwise unpleasant customers. And Airbnb lets visitors review their hosts' homes, so future vacationers have a sense of what they're getting into.

As we saw in the last chapter, some consumers believe—and some marketers encourage the belief—that the sharing economy offers opportunities for ethical consumption. For example, an Uber that transports three strangers theoretically takes three separate cars, and all their emissions, off the road. And an Airbnb stay offers income to a "small business owner" instead of a hotel conglomerate. On these and many other sharing platforms, production is conducted, as Schumacher said, on local, "size appropriate" scales.

Indeed, most participants—whether as members of for-profit or not-for-profit organizations—see the sharing economy as an opportunity to build new kinds of markets, from the bottom up. They think the sharing sector can promote personalized exchanges that are ethically sound and based on ideals of community. In addition, these participants believe the share economy can help its workers achieve financial autonomy—to get out from under the exploitative capitalist owners of the means of production. If true, the share economy could humanize our neoliberal market.

Or so we are told. Though it is widely praised for being ethical on a number of fronts, the sharing economy draws consumers for different reasons. For example, younger and low-income groups are more economically motivated to use and provide shared assets (Bocker and Meelen 2016). That is, they participate in this economy because it helps them save money, or at least spend less money than they would if they didn't share.

Today, there are even clothing rental services. As we have noted, the fashion industry constantly expects consumers to have and display something new. Luxury clothing rental services have given lower and middle-income individuals a chance to display personal style, without having to buy fake designer items or spend too much on them. Concern for the environment, or for responsible modes of production, are not motivating their spending.

What's more, sharing companies themselves may struggle to find the balance between upholding a socially or environmentally responsible mandate while simultaneously growing their business. Schor et al. (2016) found that, on the one hand, a time bank and a food swap did not get much business, but they preserved their commitments to equality and access. On the other hand, Craftworks and Wintrepreneur both enjoyed robust participation. However, they adhered less well to the sharing ethos. Reportedly, each favored white males with high cultural capital and many participants complained about excessively competitive and exclusionary practices.

So, platforms in the share economy vary in their effects and their success in realizing stated ethical goals (Schor and Atwood-Charles 2017). Some parts of the share economy, like Airbnb, are becoming more like conventional commerce: room and home rentals in the traditional sense. Airbnb commodifies previously intimate, private realms of life, making it a mere extension of conventional neoliberalism.

Some platforms satisfy their workers' financial needs, but there is also mounting evidence of income inequality in many. And there is evidence that some promote discrimination by race, gender, or class. That is, they are advantaging people who already have human capital or other advantages, though they claim to provide widespread opportunity to less privileged people. At the end of the day, they are businesses trying to compete in a capitalist society. They wouldn't be able to thrive if they didn't catch onto its capitalist ways. In these respects, they continue the worst, most exploitive aspects of the "gig economy." This means that consumers who *do* patronize sharing companies with the hopes of consuming more ethically are sometimes deluding themselves (Fitzmaurice et al. 2020).

At present, it seems the share economy is here to stay, even if it is not living up to (or even trying to live up to) the ethical aspirations of some of its consumers. It remains to be seen how these share platforms will evolve; whether governments will provide strong rules to achieve better results; and whether workers will unite to improve their situations. And it remains to be seen if changes to this economy really can bring about a humanized market, where production happens on "size appropriate" scales.

Problems of Surveillance and Control

As noted, in our digital world, technologies increasingly mediate our experiences of consumption (McGuigan and Manzerolle 2014). We shop online and return unwanted products by mail to companies in different countries. In this "omnipresent marketplace," of "ubiquitous commerce" or "u-commerce," markets are no longer constrained; exchange happens easily across borders, between people of different cultures.

The same forces that make commerce widespread make surveillance (and therefore control) widespread too (Manzerolle and Smeltser 2011). Information-communication technologies are routinely used to watch consumers. For example, customer relationship management (CRM) systems gather and store consumer information including age, address, contact information, length of relationship with the business, and recent transactions. This new attentiveness can be used for good purposes, since these systems "listen" and respond to consumer wants and needs. For instance, they send you marketing emails at the exact moment they know you're most likely to want whatever product they're selling. This thinking reflects what Ballantyne and Varey (2007; also, LeMeunier-Fitzhugh et al. 2016) call service-dominant (SD) logic.

Ballantyne and Varey propose that seller-buyer relations in the future will be organized by SD logic. In SD logic, the connection between a buyer and seller isn't restricted to the point of sale, where money is exchanged for a good. Rather, that relationship extends both ways, pre- and post-sale. For example, consumers interact with brands starting at a young age, but may not buy anything from that brand until they are adults. After their purchase, they continue engaging with that brand, whether through customer service experiences in the traditional sense, or through exposure to marketing campaigns.

However, many observers worry that this surveillance can also be used for malign purposes, and no nation has taken this malign surveillance role as far as China. There, the "social credit" system has already punished over 12 million people with domestic travel bans. Under this scheme, citizens are rated on their compliance with social norms and rules. Behaviour that can earn you a ban varies from obstructing footpaths with electric bikes, to smoking in non-smoking areas, to riding a train without a correct ticket. So, often, the social credit system watches people's consumption and punishes deviant behaviour by restricting their future consumption.

In the West, many consumers don't mind giving out their information. In fact, some like the content, news stories, and advertisements that algorithms can curate on their behalf by tapping into this information. So, in the future, we may see increasingly sophisticated technology being used by increasing numbers of businesses to gather increasingly fine-tuned consumer information.

That possibility is startling given that, in 2018, political consulting firm Cambridge Analytica gathered and then sold data from millions of Facebook users without their consent (Cadwalladr and Graham-Harrison 2018; Berghel 2018). Because the data revealed personal details about the Facebook users, taken from their profiles, it could be used to enable "behavioural

Canadian Christopher Wylie (right), a former Cambridge Analytica employee, helped to reveal the company's covert "scraping" of data gathered from people's Facebook accounts and the sale of that data to organizations attempting to influence electoral outcomes.

microtargeting." That is, it helped predict what types of messages, stories, and imagery people would respond to best. In this instance, the data was used to inform political advertisements. Potential voters were divided into 32 "personality styles," and political messages were adapted to appeal to each. This approach has reportedly influenced the 2016 U.S. presidential election, the Brexit referendum in the UK, and perhaps other elections as well. Perhaps no other advertising tactic to date has been so secret, dangerous, or influential as this one.

It took this degree of manipulation, surveillance, and undermining of democracy to elicit public outcry. Before the Cambridge Analytica scandal, many consumers were apathetic towards data protection. Back in 2014, former CIA contractor Edward Snowden made news headlines as he was charged with espionage. He had leaked classified details around the surveillance of digital and telephone communications by American intelligence. But the public was more interested in why Snowden would suffer exile to expose what they didn't all see as a bad thing. According to the CIA, the data were being gathered to help them identify terrorist threats early on (Laterza 2018; Sharaf 2017). How could that be a bad thing? If it was being used for good, consumers thought, why put up a fight to protect their private information? Just four years later, the effects of data protection were clarified. Increasingly, we have become aware that such data are being collected to monitor, control, and sell products (and ideas) to a public that is unaware of being watched.

With neoliberalism, the world's economies have become interlocked through international finance, tax havens, and free trade agreements. Multinational corporations and international humanitarian organizations have hastened this globalization, as has the global recognition of refugee, drug, debt, environmental, and terrorist problems. These processes of globalization have also resulted in the spread of Western materialist values and neoliberal capitalism. The main beneficiaries have been the leaders of multinational corporations and the owners of businesses who outsource their labour (Erixon 2018; Elson 2019).

In some smaller ways, it also benefits consumers—at least, those in the Global North. Thanks to globalization, we have access to a wider variety of products at lower prices. We can even buy products from across the world and have them arrive at our front door in days. With all of these benefits coming to comparatively wealthy Westerners, it seems likely that globalization will continue in its present form. That is, it will continue unless those who do not enjoy these benefits successfully resist it.

The Future of Marketing

In the 1990s, some predicted "the death of advertising." In hindsight, it's clear that advertising has not died. It has, however, evolved and expanded (Dahlen 2016).

In the past, people talked about advertisements as though they were channels: print, radio, and television, for example. But today, advertising is about much more than the platform it's deployed through. Indeed, advertisers today often launch their own media: websites, apps, "advergames" and other owned opportunities, rather than paying for the right to broadcast their message on someone else's platform. So Dahlen (2016) defines advertising today as "brand-initiated communication intent on impacting people." Consumers receive, engage with, shape, respond to or ignore, and seek out or avoid advertisements; they are no longer passive audience members.

In years to come, the marketplace for *all* goods and services will continue to respond to changes in our society, whether technological, demographic, or otherwise. For example, as we saw earlier, businesses will have to meet the needs of our aging population. They will also need to offer products and services that support immigrants. Marketing will also need to evolve to ensure these (and other) demographic groups know about and understand the value of the offerings being tailored to them (Dietrich et al. 2017; Kahle et al. 2017). Many consumers will still yearn to be assured that they are buying things of value—things they *need*. So marketers will still have to educate consumers about why they need their products and services. And they will need to be increasingly sophisticated in these efforts, as they begin targeting new groups based on the demographic trends mentioned above.

As noted, producers of these goods and services will continue to buy and sell in a global—not local or even national—marketplace. For that reason, marketing will happen increasingly through the Internet and perhaps through other, equally wide-reaching means we have yet to invent. So far though, the Internet has a much more extended reach than any traditional marketing method (Dahlen 2016). It can transcend borders that other forms of marketing get stuck behind (Kumar and Gupta 2016).

Despite all the information we have about online consumption, there are still gaps. That's because people use the Internet in different ways (Harris and Rae 2009; see also Awad 2019) and, in turn, respond differently to digital marketing. For instance, social media platform use can be predicted based on demographics, with teens clustering around Snapchat, young adults on Instagram, and middle-aged and older adults on Facebook. Different "types" of people engage with content in different ways. Those Li (2007) describes as "critics" are likely to leave comments. "Spectators" will consume content, but won't leave traces, such as likes or shares. And "inactive" people may not even see online content at all. As much data as marketers already collect, they will need to gather and analyze even more to tap into their customers' digital preferences.

We will also likely see advances in the use of technology to support customer service. Already, many businesses are using artificial intelligence (AI) to provide instant, 24/7 customer support online. Automated chats, for example, allow consumers to get instant answers to common questions while online shopping, often from a bot. At the same time, companies are also using technologies to scan the web and identify poor customer reviews on Yelp, trolling on Twitter, and other signs of negativity. Companies must try to mitigate these critiques, so the millions of others who can see them online don't start thinking less of their brand. Here, too, automated attendants are proving useful. As AI and related technologies advance, these customer support and engagement practices will likely only become more sophisticated.

The integration of technology into customer service benefits businesses: consumers will feel their needs being effectively and efficiently met (Kumar and Gupta 2016). But what are the dangers? For one, job loss. Customer service has long been cited as one of the few jobs that can't be done by a machine. But today, it seems likely that auto-attendants will eventually replace call centres. (Not to mention the high-tech coffee machines that will replace baristas and self-serve check-outs that will replace cashiers.) Automated customer service may not be good for people currently working in such industries.

It may not be good for consumers, either. We have seen, throughout this book, that people may be growing increasingly materialistic. Automated customer service further enables constant shopping and spending (Jayarathna et al. 2019; Stelzer et al. 2016). Gone are the days when you could only price match, complain, order, return, inquire, sign up, and cancel during regular business hours. In the future, it seems everyone will have a bot at their beck and call any time, day or night. That would make it harder for already-struggling consumers to scale back. It could also push more consumers to shop and spend more problematically.

Technology will also enable even more personalized, targeted forms of marketing (Kumar and Gupta 2016). Marketers have long known they can't convince customers to buy by relying only on shiny objects, cool packaging, and catchy slogans (Ballantyne and Varey 2008). At least, they cannot convince many of them, and not for long. First, marketing is about showing consumers how a product or service will meet their needs and help them achieve their goals. To do that, marketers must first know what their consumers want and need. We can expect that they will only gather more and more details on these topics. That is, they will be able to know, with increasing accuracy, what segments they should target. Then, marketers need to tailor their content to reflect the unique wants and needs of each of those segments. Evolving technology will help them do this with greater degrees of sophistication.

Today it would be challenging (though not impossible) to target all of these segments simultaneously. Already, we have tools that let us personalize online marketing. Cookies, for example, keep track of your browsing history. Marketers can set up their websites to show you custom content, based on what you've already looked at online.

We can reasonably expect these practices to continue and advance (Dahlen 2016). If technology continues to advance at the rate it has, marketers will soon be able to create custom advertisements for every one of their segments. In the future, each of us may have our own, personalized experience, tailored to our unique wants and needs. There are big incentives for businesses to become increasingly manipulative. They stand to profit from it. More rules, and their consistent enforcement, could moderate this trajectory. But the powerful multinational corporations we have discussed have so far have proven largely successful in keeping these rules at bay. One exception is Canada's Anti-Spam Legislation, discussed in Box 18-2.

Box 18-2

Permission Marketing and Anti-Spam Legislation

In countries like the U.S., permission marketing means getting consent from the consumer before sending them advertising material. This approach can help build trust in a brand. It also usually yields greater consumer engagement. After all, the consumer has clearly opted in and shown interest in the product.

In Canada, permission marketing is the law when it comes to many digital tactics. The Canadian Radio-television and Telecommunications Commission oversees Canada's Anti-Spam Legislation (CASL). As its name suggests, this law was designed to protect Canadians from spam and other abuses of digital technology. It requires businesses to get express consent from consumers before sending them promotional messages. If a business doesn't get that consent, and sends consumers advertising messages anyway, they may be fined (Shaykevich 2018; Kablan 2018).

It may sound like a win for the consumer. And it's true, CASL may reduce the unwanted digital advertisements consumers receive—the data isn't yet in on this relatively new law. But the thing is, CASL can also help businesses, as mentioned above. It forces businesses to make themselves look trustworthy and honest—something we know the careful consumers of today are looking for. So, in a sense, CASL is helping companies stay competitive in an increasingly tough market.

Marketing may be getting more sophisticated, but so are consumers (Kumar and Gupta 2016). Just as it has opened new possibilities for advertisements, so too has the Internet given consumers easier access to information. They can now compare products and prices quickly and easily. They can also get WOM recommendations from just about anyone—not only their "real-life" friends and family. Many consumers today are better informed about the products, services, and brands they are patronizing. That can make it harder for marketers to convince them to buy *their* offering.

Trust in advertisements has also dwindled (Clemons et al 2007; 2016). At first, digital marketing was a good way to approach consumers who were tired of TV and magazine commercials. Now that digital marketing has become ubiquitous, as traditional commercials once were, more consumers are aware of its functions and mystifications. More consumers today see advertisements, from every source, for what they are: blatant asks for money. They are even becoming adept at identifying tactics like #SponCon, which is purposely designed to look like regular, everyday content from their friends and family. Tired of being bombarded by sales pitches, more and more consumers are going "back" to traditional WOM as their trusted source of product and brand recommendations. In this way, technological innovation doesn't always change the marketing game—at least, not for the long term. In fact, we may expect to see push back against some of the more intrusive marketing tactics that have emerged in recent years.

Final Thoughts

Here is what we can safely say about the future of consumer behaviour, following Schultz (2016).

We can assume a free-market economy and consumers with discretionary resources will continue to exist, at least for now. Consumers will continue to have more and more knowledge about available products, and more and more products will be available. Therefore, sellers will have to focus their efforts on understanding buyer wants and needs instead of trying to create those needs and wants. This will force marketers to build and preserve individual customer relationships and focus on one-to-one communication with the help of data and analytics, leading to the decline and perhaps even death of traditional mass advertising and communication.

Research in advertising will shift dramatically with the increasing availability of large data sets (see, for example, Lusk 2017; Vanhala et al. 2020). Traditional research methods such as focus groups and research panels may then be replaced by more detailed analyses of large-scale, longitudinal data sets. Besides, the developments in neuroscience will allow academics and professionals to learn more about how the human brain gets, internalizes, and is influenced by marketing communications.

Current economic and psychological theory will be replaced by behavioural economics, a science that explains the behaviors of consumers in the marketplace. The availability of data, neuroscience and tools such as data science will allow marketers to measure the impact and effect of advertising strategies they employ. This will promote more precise advertising spending.

Most dangerously, as suggested earlier, more consumers may transition from buyers of basic items to buyers of treats, tickets, and trophies. We know very little, at this point, about the factors that cause buyers to make these transitions: to become more like Anton, more like Tamara, or more like Donald. Each of these transitions is dangerous and costly to the environment, to society, and to the buyers themselves.

So, perhaps the most important question to ask is: what do we *want* the future of consumerism to look like? What we have learned is that consumerism in and of itself is not necessarily bad. In our consumer society, much consumption is unavoidable. We must consume to survive. But some elements of our consumer society are excessive. As well, some are political. Namely, by propping up capitalism, our consumer society perpetuates an unequal, exploitative status quo that benefits the few at the top at the expense of the many on the bottom.

The "real" problem, we have seen, is our capitalist economic system. It breeds inequality, despair, envy, and a tendency toward excess. Much of the time, it also prioritizes profit over environmental sustainability. This is true even when consumers and mass media shame companies for their unethical practices. Often, companies simply greenwash and rebrand in order to win back customers and drive sales. Again, that's because capitalism values profit above all else. Human rights, human lives, and the environment factor in only when companies are targeting so-called ethical consumers who might wage a boycott that threatens sales.

Amidst all of this, consumerism serves as a mask. The promise of material plenty entices consumers to, at best, turn a blind eye to the unfair, exploitative capitalist regime, and at worst, value and champion it. Consumer societies meet so many of our basic human wants and needs. They enchant us, promising to glamorize the day-to-day drudgery of our work and home lives. They offer instant gratification at all hours of the day or night, from anywhere with an Internet connection. They help us belong to social groups and showcase our belonging. They help us express, stay connected with, and reimagine our ethnicities and cultural traditions.

Caught up in the rat race—and even enjoying rewards like belonging and inclusion—people in consumer societies come to feel content with the status quo. Consumerism encourages them to approve of (or at least quietly tolerate) capitalism because it seems to be the key to material comfort and social admiration. We become less likely to resist, revolt, or rebel. And when we do protest, it is often through consumption: the very thing that keeps us bound to the capitalist system we should be questioning.

Capitalist consumerism is thus self-perpetuating, meaning its future—at a fundamental level—could reasonably hold much of the same. After all, the acquiescence we see today can be traced at least as far back as the 1950s. At that time, as Riesman et al said in *The Lonely Crowd*, North American societies became increasingly other-directed. People's increased wish for cooperation and prosperity was good. But the bad side of this change was a loss of political interest and political goals.

Other-directed people, today as 70 years ago, have little autonomy or understanding of themselves and their motives. They are, as political theorist Benjamin Barber said in his book *Consumed* (2007), infantilized. These "child" consumers are without deep principles or political insights. They know little about the society they live in. They are without independent, well-considered goals, or ideas about what a "good society" might be. They do not have the capacity to participate in democracy, behave morally, or fulfill their duties as citizens. A nation of other-directed people is likely to lack coherence and leadership because the goals in such a society are personal. In this other-directed nation, people will focus on goals like marriage, a healthy family, a secure job, and a family home. All they see is "the pursuit of happiness," through consumption.

So, here we are, 70 years after the publication of *The Lonely Crowd*, living in markedly unequal societies. As Baudrillard warned, every day, we drown in "alternate facts." We are scared silly by lies about violent crime and dangerous immigrants. Politicians promise us impossible tax cuts that can come only by cutting the cost of government at the expense of the poor.

Lacking deep principles or political insights, but willing to cast a ballot, some citizens will think almost anything and vote for nearly anyone. They hope that, by doing this, they can reduce their confusion, return the world to "normal," and enjoy insulated, quiet family life. Consumer society gives them the material signs of well-being they need to feel fulfilled, valued, and happy. It gives them a sense of purpose and helps them to fit in. So long as they can ignore people who are deprived, excluded, or disadvantaged by this consumer capitalist society, they can feel just fine.

Others have been so disappointed and discouraged, they have abandoned the political system altogether. They do not bother voting, thinking it won't make a difference. The consumer society distracts them from their dissatisfaction and fills the apathetic void in their lives, whether through a retail-therapy-induced high or the (sometimes misguided) feeling that they can make a difference by joining consumer movements and protests.

We have built such a house for our consumer society. To rebuild this house—to live in other, more principled and more aware ways—we will have to lessen our fascination with consumer goods and turn our attention elsewhere. We will have to care less about fitting in and appearing successful to others and think more about what a good society might be. We will have to look at the capitalist system currently at the foundation of that society. It's likely that at least some of us are not ready for that task.

Discussion Questions

1. This chapter examined Jürgen Habermas' perception of the public sphere. According to him, what should the public sphere promote in society? What are its principles based on?

2. In this chapter, we discussed the limited efficacy of modest changes in individual behaviour (e.g., using metal rather than plastic straws) in addressing the environmental crisis. What changes, if any, have you made in your consumption choices because of concern over the environment? Do you think they have made a difference to the wider world?

3. Think about what it means to be a part of a network society. How are you increasingly connected to consumers around you?

Quick Quiz

1. What is a network society?
a. A society where groups of individuals with common interests are united
b. A society where the service sector generates more wealth than the manufacturing sector of the economy
c. A society where social relationships that are no longer geographically bounded are enabled through new communication technology
d. A society that adheres to strict gender norms
e. A society that prioritizes taxation and redistribution of wealth

2.   What political and moral philosophy supports egalitarianism?
a.   Liberalism
b.   Conservatism
c.   Socialism
d.   Communism
e.   Capitalism

3.   What is true about ecofeminism?
a.   It calls for a radical reordering of society in which male supremacy is eliminated in all social and economic contexts
b.   It focuses on women's ability to use nature as a source of power for their equality and equity
c.   It posits that the "female nature" or "female essence" attempts to revalue and redefine characteristics ascribed to femaleness
d.   It asserts that the domination of women in patriarchal societies and the degradation of nature by industrial capitalism are related
e.   It states that women are exploited through capitalism and the individual ownership of private property

4.   What is NOT a common principle in sustainable development?
a.   Controlling the community's consumption habits
b.   Dealing transparently and systematically with risk, uncertainty, and irreversibility
c.   Ensuring appropriate valuation, appreciation, and restoration of nature
d.   Integrating environmental, social, human, and economic goals in policies and activities
e.   Community participation

5.   What is downshifting?
a.   The action of increasing one's income but decreasing one's consumption tendencies
b.   Increasing profits that allow for greater spending
c.   Forced action of having to spend less on consumer goods
d.   Lowered level of consumption due to instant decrease of income level
e.   Voluntary decision to lessen one's income and consumption

The answers to the Quick Quiz are provided at the end of the book.

For Further Reading

Consumer Society: Critical Issues and Environmental Consequences by Barry Smart
Barry Smart argues that the consumer society contributes to the systemic creation of consumption as a social activity. Smart analyzes the globalization of consumption, political and environmental consequences, and issues brought by modern consumer culture.

Consumerism Reconsidered: Buying and Power by Mica Nava
Nava critically considers the ability of consumerism to create new forms of economic, political, personal, and creative participation. The book suggests that a kind of "utopian collectivism" lies within the consumerist project. Nava illustrates the political complexities that are implied by the ability to consume.

The McDonaldization of Society: An Investigation into the Changing Character of Contemporary Social Life by George Ritzer
Ritzer is concerned with the way rationalization is played out in the context of consumer culture. This occurs through the processes of efficiency, calculability, predictability, and control. Ritzer uses McDonald's as a metaphor for a world that makes us consume in particular ways.

Key Terms
Consumer sovereignty
Ecofeminism
Egalitarianism
Environmentalism
Greenwashing
Network society
Public sphere
Sustainability

Acknowledgements

This book has been three or four years in preparation, with lots of thinking and rethinking, organizing and reorganizing, writing and rewriting. We think we have finally gotten it right, thanks to many people who helped us and advised us.

Foremost among them was our publisher, David Stover. Since the beginning, David has encouraged us, reviewed us, and patiently put us back to work in sometimes startlingly new directions. In short, he has been a sponsor, mentor, and editor, as well as publisher. For all of this, we are hugely indebted to David and hope he likes the result of all our hard work.

In the shadows of this process there have been anonymous reviewers, and we don't know who they were or how many there may have been. However, these reviewers were also helpful in keeping us on track, or sometimes getting us on a new track. Every suggestion was extremely helpful and moved us along with all that rethinking, reorganizing, and rewriting.

We were assisted by a large number of undergraduate students at the University of Toronto over the last few years, both as paid work-study students and unpaid volunteer interns. Several of these students stood out and we are grateful to them for their insight and hard work: (alphabetically) Zara Ahmad, Justine Beaule, Victoria Chi, Nabi Dressler, Megan Hill, Rui Liu, Sarah Mercer, William (Buzz) Lanthier Rogers, Zoe Sebastien, Dhuvaraha Srikrishnara, Maddy de Welles, Julia Wong, and Xingyu (Juanita) Xiong. Working with these students has been one of the greatest pleasures in writing this book. Their energy and enthusiasm reminded us, again and again, how lucky we are at the University of Toronto, and in Canada, to have such a variety of talented young people from all over the world.

Finally, we—Nikki and Lorne—were happy to work together again on this, our fourth or fifth project together. Despite the many uncertainties and false starts in writing this book, we got from A to Z once again and probably couldn't have done so without each other's help. So, thanks partner! It's been a pleasure.

As for you, dear reader, we hope you like this book, find it interesting, and glean some fresh perspectives from it.

Lorne Tepperman
Nicole Meredith
Toronto, 2021

Answers to Quick Quizzes

Chapter 1. 1e. 2b. 3d. 4b. 5c. Chapter 2. 1b. 2e. 3a. 4c. 5e. Chapter 3. 1c. 2c. 3a. 4e. 5a. Chapter 4. 1a. 2c. 3d. 4e. 5a. Chapter 5. 1d. 2e. 3d. 4b. 5e. Chapter 6. 1c. 2c. 3a. 4c. 5c. Chapter 7. 1c. 2e. 3a. 4b. 5e. Chapter 8. 1e. 2a. 3e. 4c. 5d. Chapter 9. 1b. 2c. 3a. 4e. 5a. Chapter 10. 1c. 2a. 3d. 4c. 5e. Chapter 11. 1b. 2e. 3a. 4d. 5a. Chapter 12. 1b. 2d. 3b. 4d. 5a. Chapter 13. 1c. 2d. 3d. 4e. 5b. 6a. Chapter 14. 1d. 2d. 3c. 4d. 5d. Chapter 15. 1c. 2a. 3b. 4b. 5e. Chapter 16. 1a. 2d. 3c. 4b. 5c. Chapter 17. 1d. 2b. 3a. 4b. 5d. Chapter 18. 1c. 2a. 3d. 4a. 5e.

References

Aakhus, M., et al. (2017). Putting consumers to work: 'Co-creation'and new marketing govern-mentality. In *The Work of Communication: Relational Perspectives on Working and Organizing in Contemporary Capitalism*, pp. 1-28. Chicago: University of Chicago Press.

Abdallah, S. (2018). An intelligent system for identifying influential words in real-estate classifieds. *Journal of Intelligent Systems*, 27(2), 183-194.

Abedinifard, M. (2016). Ridicule, gender hegemony, and the disciplinary function of mainstream gender humour. *Social semiotics*, 26(3), 234-249.

Abrams, D., et al. (2018). Deviance credit: Tolerance of deviant ingroup leaders is mediated by their accrual of prototypicality and conferral of their right to be supported. *Journal of Social Issues*, 74(1), 36-55.

Acemoglu, D., et al. (2011). The consequences of radical reform: The French Revolution. *American Economic Review*, 101(7), 3286-3307.

Acemoglu, D., et al. (2019). Democracy does cause growth. *Journal of Political Economy*, 127(1), 47-100.

Adam, H., et al. (2018). The shortest path to oneself leads around the world: Living abroad increases self-concept clarity. *Organizational Behavior and Human Decision Processes*, 145, 16-29.

Adenkunle, B., Filson, G. and Sethuratnam, S. Immigration and Chinese food preferences in the Greater Toronto Area. *International Journal of Consumer Studies* 37: 658-665.

Adiseshiah, S. (2016). 'Chavs','Gyppos' and 'Scum'? Class in Twenty-First-Century Drama. In *Twenty-First Century Drama*, pp. 149-171. London: Palgrave Macmillan.

Adorno, T.W. and Horkheimer, M. (1997 [1944]). "The Culture Industry." In Adorno, T. W., & Horkheimer, M. (1997), *Dialectic of Enlightenment* (Vol. 15). London: Verso.

Aghara, V. N., et al. (2018). Sales promotion as a leverage strategy for improving sales and profitability in alcohol beverage industry. *International Research Journal of Management, IT and Social Sciences*, 5(4), 18-25.

Agnew, S., Maras, P., & Moon, A. (2018). Gender differences in financial socialization in the home—An exploratory study. *International Journal of Consumer Studies*, 42(3), 275-282.

Agrawal, S., & Sangapala, P. (2020). Does community size matter in the settlement process? The experience of Syrian refugees in Lethbridge in Alberta, Canada. *Journal of International Migration and Integration*, 1-20.

Ahamat, A., et al. (2017). Factors influencing the adoption of social media in small and medium enterprises (SMEs). *International E-Journal of Advances in Social Sciences*, 3(8), 338-348.

Ainsworth, M. D. S. (1969). Object relations, dependency, and attachment: A theoretical review of the infant-mother relationship. *Child Development*, 969-1025.

Ainsworth, M. D. S. (1978). The Bowlby-Ainsworth attachment theory. *Behavioral and Brain Sciences*, 1(3), 436-438.

Ajala, Imène. (2018). Muslim youth and consumerism: A study of Islamic street wear. *Contemporary Islam* 12(1):57–71.

Akers, R. L., & Jennings, W. G. (2016). Social learning theory. *Wiley Handbooks in Criminology and Criminal Justice*, 230-240.

Aknin, L., et al. (2020). Does Spending Money on Others Promote Happiness? A Registered Replication Report. *Journal of Personality and Social Psychology* 119 (10): 1037/pspa0000191.

Albo, G., & Panitch, L. (Eds.). (2019). *Beyond Market Dystopia: New Ways of Living: Socialist Register 2020*. Monthly Review Press.

Alden, D. L., & Nariswari, A. (2017). Brand Positioning Strategies during Global Expansion: Managerial Perspectives from Emerging Market Firms. In *The Customer is NOT Always Right? Marketing Orientationsin a Dynamic Business World*, pp. 527-530. Springer, Cham.

Alden, D. L., et al. (1999). Brand positioning through advertising in Asia, North America, and Europe: The role of global consumer culture. *The Journal of Marketing* 63 (1): 75-87.

Alden, Dana L., et al. (2000). Effects of brand local and nonlocal origin on consumer attitudes in developing countries." *Journal of Consumer Psychology*, 9(2), 83-95

Alex-Petersen, J., et al. (2017). Long-term effects of childhood nutrition: evidence from a school lunch reform. IZA Discussion Paper Series. Bonn: IZA Institute of Labor Economics.

Alexander, J. (2020, March 28). Liquor sales up 40% in B.C. during COVID-19 scare. Retrieved from https://bc.ctvnews.ca/liquor-sales-up-40-in-b-c-during-covid-19-scare-1.4870580.

Alexander, V. D. (2018). Public institutions of "high" culture. In *Routledge Handbook of Cultural Sociology*, pp. 369-377. Routledge.

Alexandrowicz, C. (2020). *Acting Queer: Gender Dissidence and the Subversion of Realism*. Springer Nature.

Ali, W., Frynas, J. G., & Mahmood, Z. (2017). Determinants of corporate social responsibility (CSR) disclosure in developed and developing countries: A literature review. *Corporate Social Responsibility and Environmental Management*, 24(4), 273-294.

Alkon, A., & Guthman, J. (Eds.). (2017). *The new food activism: Opposition, cooperation, and collective action*. Univ. of California Press.

Allcott, H., Diamond, R., & Dubé, J. P. (2017). *The geography of poverty and nutrition: Food deserts and food choices across the United States*. National Bureau of Economic Research.

Allcott, H., et al. (2019). Food deserts and the causes of nutritional inequality. *The Quarterly Journal of Economics*, 134(4), 1793-1844.

Allen, J., & Farber, S. (2019). Sizing up transport poverty: A national scale accounting of low-income households suffering from inaccessibility in Canada, and what to do about it. *Transport Policy*, 74, 214-223.

Allison, T. H., et al. (2017). Persuasion in crowdfunding: An elaboration likelihood model of crowdfunding performance. *Journal of Business Venturing*, 32(6), 707-725.

Aloysius, J. A., et al. (2019). Shoplifting in mobile checkout settings: Cybercrime in retail stores. *Information Technology & People* 32(5):1234-1261

Altaf, Joyce Gonçalves, Irene Raguenet Troccoli, Christiane Bara Paschoalino, and Maria Angélica Luqueze. 2012. Luxury clothing: A mirror of gay consumers' sexual options? *Revista Eletrônica de Ciência Administrativa* 11(1):162-177.

Altundemir, M. E. (2012). The impact of the financial crisis on American public universities. *International Journal of Business and Social Science*, 3(8).

Amagir, A., et al. (2019). SaveWise: The design of a financial education program in the Netherlands. *Citizenship, Social and Economics Education*, 18(2), 100-120.

Amaldoss, W., & Jain, S. (2005). Pricing of conspicuous goods: A competitive analysis of social effects. *Journal of Marketing Research*, 42(1), 30-42.

Amaturo, E., Costagliola, S., & Ragone, G. (1987). Furnishing and status attributes: A sociological study of the living room. *Environment and Behavior*, 19(2), 228-249.

Amin, A. (2004). Regulating economic globalization. *Transactions of the Institute of British Geographers*, 29(2), 217-233.

Amirouche, Marion et al. (2017). Luxury toys for men: When will women will let us decide and buy on our own? *Procedia Computer Science*, 122:548–55.

Amos, C., Holmes, G. R., & Keneson, W. C. (2014). A meta-analysis of consumer impulse buying. *Journal of Retailing and Consumer Services*, 21(2), 86-97.

Amos, C., Holmes, G., & Strutton, D. (2008). Exploring the relationship between celebrity endorser effects and advertising effectiveness: A quantitative synthesis of effect size. *International Journal of Advertising*, 27(2), 209-234.

An, J., Kwak, H., Jung, S. G., Salminen, J., & Jansen, B. J. (2018). Customer segmentation using online platforms: isolating behavioral and demographic segments for persona creation via aggregated user data. *Social Network Analysis and Mining*, 8(1), 54.

Andersch, H., Lindenmeier, J., Liberatore, F., & Tscheulin, D. K. (2018). Resistance against corporate misconduct: an analysis of ethical ideologies' direct and moderating effects on different forms of active rebellion. *Journal of Business Economics*, 88(6), 695-730.

Anderson, Eric. (2010). *Inclusive masculinity: The changing nature of masculinities*. Routledge.

Anderson, M. & Perrin, A. (2017). *Technology use among seniors*. Washington, DC: Pew Research Center for Internet & Technology.

Andersson Bruck, K. (2019). Child poverty in rich contexts: The example of Sweden. *Global Studies of Childhood*, 2043610619849501.

Andreoni, J., Nikiforakis, N., & Stoop, J. (2017). *Are the rich more selfish than the poor, or do they just have more money? A natural field experiment* (No. w23229). National Bureau of Economic Research.

Andrews, D. (2018). Error or absurdity? A non-cognitive approach to commodity fetishism. *The European Journal of the History of Economic Thought*, 25(5), 738-755.

Ansell, T., & Cayzer, S. (2018). Limits to growth redux: A system dynamics model for assessing energy and climate change constraints to global growth. *Energy Policy*, 120, 514-525.

Antonetti, P., & Baines, P. (2015). Guilt in marketing research: an elicitation–consumption perspective and research agenda. *International Journal of Management Reviews*, 17(3), 333-355.

Antonetti, P., & Maklan, S. (2013). Feelings that make a difference: How guilt and pride convince consumers of the effectiveness of sustainable consumption choices. *Journal of Business Ethics*, 124(1), 117-134

Antonetti, P., & Maklan, S. (2014). Exploring postconsumption guilt and pride in the context of sustainability. *Psychology & Marketing*, 31(9), 717-735.

Arendt, H. (2013). *The Human Condition*. University of Chicago Press.

Ariès, P. (1962). *Centuries of Childhood*. Harmondsworth, UK: Penguin.

Arjmand, R. (2018). *Migration, Diaspora, Muslim Transnational Communities and Education*.

Armstrong, G. M., et al. (2018). *Marketing: An Introduction*. London: Pearson.

Arndt, A. D., & Ekebas-Turedi, C. (2017). Do men and women use different tactics to cope with the embarrassment of buying condoms? *Journal of Consumer Behaviour*, 16(6), 499-510.

Arthur, C. (2012). Financial literacy education for citizens: What kind of responsibility, equality and engagement? *Citizenship, Social and Economics Education*, 11(3), 163-176.

Arvidsson, A. (2005). Brands: A critical perspective. *Journal of Consumer Culture*, 5(2), 235-258.

Arvidsson, A. (2006). 'Quality singles': internet dating and the work of fantasy. *New Media & Society*, 8(4), 671-690.

Arvidsson, A. (2009). *The Rise of Brands* by Liz Moor. *The Sociological Review*, 57(1), 207-210.

Arvidsson, A., & Caliandro, A. (2015). Brand public. *Journal of Consumer Research*, 42(5), 727-748.

Arvidsson, Adam, and Nicolai Peitersen. (2013). *The ethical economy: Rebuilding value after the crisis*. Columbia University Press.

Arvidsson, Adam. (2006). *Brands: Meaning and value in media culture*. Routledge.

Aßländer, M. S. (2019). Sweated labor as a social phenomenon: Lessons from the 19th century sweatshop discussion. *Journal of Business Ethics*, 1-16.

Asquith, K. (2009). A critical analysis of the children's food and beverage advertising self-regulatory initiatives. *Democratic Communiqué*, 23(2), 41

Atari, Mohammad, et al. (2017). Consideration of cosmetic surgery as part of women's benefit-provisioning mate retention strategy. *Frontiers in Psychology* 8:1389.

Atari, Mohammad, et al. (2016). Women who are interested in cosmetic surgery want it all: The association between considering cosmetic surgery and women's mate preferences. *Adaptive Human Behavior and Physiology* 3(1):61–70

Atkin, T., Nowak, L., & Garcia, R. (2007). Women wine consumers: information search and retailing implications. *International Journal of Wine Business Research*.

Attwood, Feona. 2005. Fashion and Passion: Marketing Sex to Women. *Sexualities* 8(4), 392–406.

Atwal, G., & Williams, A. (2017). Luxury brand marketing: The experience is everything! In *Advances in Luxury Brand Management*, pp. 43-57. Palgrave Macmillan, Cham.

Audrezet, A., et al. (2018). Authenticity under threat: When social media influencers need to go beyond self-presentation. *Journal of Business Research*.

Audrin, Catherine et al. (2017). When symbolism overtakes quality: Materialists consumers disregard product quality when faced with luxury brands. *Journal of Economic Psychology*, 61:115-123

Aulino, F. (2019). *Rituals of Care: Karmic Politics in an Aging Thailand*. Cornell University Press.

Austin, E. W., et al. (2020). Effects of family-centered media literacy training on family nutrition outcomes. *Prevention Science*, 21(3): 308-318.

Aveyard, S., Corthorn, P., & O'Connell, S. (2018). *The Politics of Consumer Credit in the UK, 1938-1992*. Oxford University Press.

Awad, N. A. (2019). Examining the impact of e-Shopping on customer loyalty. *International Journal of Online Marketing*, 9(3), 82-94.

Ayeh, J. K. (2019). User segmentation based on perceived richness of consumer-generated media.

Azab, C., & Clark, T. (2017). Speak my language or look like me? Language and ethnicity in bilingual customer service recovery. *Journal of Business Research*, 72, 57-68.

Azevedo, A. (2020). Recognizing consumerism as an "illness of an empty soul": A Catholic morality perspective. *Psychology & Marketing*, 37(2), 250-259.

Babakus, E., et al. (2004). Reactions to unethical consumer behaviour across six countries. *Journal of Consumer Marketing*, 21(4), 254-263.

Back, L. (2016). Inscriptions of love. In D. Nonini (ed.), *Sensing the City: A Companion to Urban Anthropology*. Hoboken, NJ: Wiley-Blackwell.

Bäckström, B. M. (2018). Death, mourning and post-death rituals of elderly migrants. *Mortality*, 1-12.

Badgaiyan, A. J., Dixit, S., & Verma, A. (2017). If brands are people, then people are impulsive: Assessing the connection between brand personality and impulsive buying behaviour. *Journal of Brand Management*, 24(6), 622-638.

Baía, J. P. (2019). Adolescent's perception of his influence on family vacations purchase decisions: A consumer socialization perspective. *International Journal of Marketing, Communication and New Media*.

Bakas, D., Jackson, K., & Magkonis, G. (2019). Trade (dis) integration: The sudden death of NAFTA. *Open Economies Review*, 1-13.

Bakewell, Cathy and Vincent-Wayne Mitchell. 2003. Generation Y female consumer decision-making styles. *International Journal of Retail & Distribution Management* 31(2):95–106.

Bakshi, S. (2012). Impact of gender on consumer purchase behaviour. *Journal of Research in Commerce and Management*, 1(9), 1-8.

Balaji, M. S., et al. (2016). Determinants of negative word-of-mouth communication using social networking sites. *Information & Management*, 53(4), 528-540.

Baland, J. M., Bardhan, P., & Bowles, S. (Eds.). (2018). *Inequality, cooperation, and environmental sustainability*. Princeton University Press.

Balderas-Cejudo, A., Patterson, I., & Leeson, G. W. (2019). Senior Foodies: A developing niche market in gastronomic tourism. *International Journal of Gastronomy and Food Science*, 16, 100-152.

Ball, S. J. (2018). Commericalising education: profiting from reform! *Journal of Education Policy*, 33 (5): 587-589.

Ballantyne, D., & Varey, R. J. (2008). The service-dominant logic and the future of marketing. *Journal of the Academy of Marketing Science*, 36(1):11-14.

Balogh, P., et al. (2016). Consumer willingness to pay for traditional food products. *Food Policy*, 61: 176-184.

Bamossy, Gary, et al. (2003). Understanding materialism among youth. *Journal of Consumer Psychology* 13(3): 278-288

Bandura, A. (2019). Applying theory for human betterment. *Perspectives on Psychological Science*, 14(1), 12-15.

Bandura, A., & Walters, R. H. (1977). *Social Learning Theory* (Vol. 1). Englewood Cliffs, NJ: Prentice-Hall.

Bang, H., et al. (2019). How the level of personalization affects the effectiveness of personalized ad messages: the moderating role of narcissism. *International Journal of Advertising*, 38(8), 1116-1138.

Bang, Y., et al. (2019). Did you just assume my reality? Baudrillard's hyperreality in the progression of food photography. Presentation. Southern California Conferences for Undergraduate Research, Fall 2019.

Barbarossa, C., & De Pelsmacker, P. (2016). Positive and negative antecedents of purchasing eco-friendly products: A comparison between green and non-green consumers. *Journal of Business Ethics*, 134(2), 229-247.

Barber, Benjamin R. *Consumed: How Markets Corrupt Children, Infantilize Adults, and Swallow Citizens Whole*. W.W. Norton and Company, 2007.

Bardasi, E., & Wodon, Q. (2006). Measuring time poverty and analyzing its determinants: concepts and application to Guinea. *Gender, Time Use, and Poverty in Sub-Saharan Africa*, 73, 75-95.

Bardhi, F. and Eckhardt, G. M. (2012). Access-based consumption: The case of car sharing. *Journal of Consumer Research*, 39(4), 881-898.

Barnaud, C., et al. (2018). Ecosystem services, social interdependencies, and collective action. *Ecology and Society*, 23(1).

Baş, M. (2016, May). Common constraints of tourism market segments: Examples of senior tourism and disabled tourism. In *International Conference on Tourism Dynamics and Trends*, pp. 54-72.

Bass, F. M., et al. (2007). Wearout effects of different advertising themes: A dynamic Bayesian model of the advertising-sales relationship. *Marketing Science*, 26(2), 179-195.

Bastien, V., & Kapferer, J. N. (2013). More on luxury anti-laws of marketing. In *Luxury Marketing*, pp. 19-34. Gabler Verlag, Wiesbaden.

Bastos, W., & Levy, S. J. (2012). A history of the concept of branding: practice and theory. *Journal of Historical Research in Marketing*.

Batat, W. (2009). Building Consumption Skills Through Teenage Empowerment: A Powerful and Invisible Determinant of Customer Relationships. *ACR North American Advances*.

Batat, W. (2019). *Experiential Marketing: Consumer Behavior, Customer Experience and The 7Es*. Routledge.

Bates, T., & Robb, A. (2014). Small-business viability in America's urban minority communities. *Urban Studies*, 51(13), 2844-2862.

Batinga, G. L., de Rezende Pinto, M., & Resende, S. P. (2017). Christmas, consumption and materialism: discourse analysis of children's Christmas letters. *Revista Brasileira de Gestão de Negócios-RBGN*, 19(66), 557-573.

Battle, K., & Torjman, S. (2013). *Poverty and Prosperity in Nunavut*, p. 14. Ottawa: Caledon Institute of Social Policy.

Baubock, R., & Rundell, J. (Eds.). (2018). *Blurred Boundaries: Migration, Ethnicity, Citizenship*. Routledge.

Baubock, Rainer, and Thomas Faist. *Diaspora and Transnationalism: Concepts, Theories and Methods*. Amsterdam: Amsterdam U Press, 2010.

Baudrillard, J. (2016). *The consumer society: Myths and structures*. Sage.

Baudrillard, J. (2018). On consumer society. In *Rethinking the Subject* (pp. 193-203). Routledge.

Bauman, Z. (2007). Collateral casualties of consumerism. *Journal of Consumer Culture*, 7(1), 25-56.

Bauman, Zygmunt (2007). *Consuming life*. Cambridge: Polity.

Baumann, C., & Krskova, H. (2016). School discipline, school uniforms and academic performance. *International Journal of Educational Management*.

Baumeister, R. F. (2002). Yielding to temptation: Self-control failure, impulsive purchasing, and consumer behavior. *Journal of Consumer Research*, 28(4), 670-676.

Baumeister, R. F., & Sommer, K. L. (1997). What do men want? Gender differences and two spheres of belongingness: Comment on Cross and Madson (1997).

Baumrind, D. (1966). Effects of authoritative parental control on child behavior. *Child Development*, 887-907.

Baumrind, D. (1967). Child care practices anteceding three patterns of preschool behavior. *Genetic Psychology Monographs*.

BBC News. (2020, 21 April). Coronavirus lockdown protest: What's behind the US demonstrations? Retrieved from: https://www.bbc.com/news/world-us-canada-52359100.

Beagan, B., Chapman, G. E., & Power, E. M. (2016). Cultural and Symbolic Capital with and Without Economic Constraint: Food shopping in low-income and high-income Canadian families. *Food, Culture & Society*, 19(1), 45-70.

Beales, J. Howard (2004). Advertising to Kids and the FTC: A Regulatory Retrospective That Advises the Present. Federal Trade Commission. https://www.ftc.gov/public-statements/2004/03/advertising-kids-and-ftc-regulatory-retrospective-advises-present.

Bebek, G. (2017). *Turkish Consumers' Response to Westernised Ethical Consumption Culture: An Acculturation Theory Approach*. The Association for Consumer Research.

Beccaria, F., et al. (2017). From housekeeper to status-oriented consumer and hypersexual imagery: Images of alcohol targeted to Italian women from the 1960s to the 2000s. *Feminist Media Studies*.

Belhadj, T., & Merdaoui, A. (2017). Islamic values and materialistic consumption culture: An exploratory study. *International Journal of Islamic Marketing and Branding*, 2(1), 1-14.

Belisle, D. (2003). Toward a Canadian Consumer History. *Labour*, 52, 181-206.

Belisle, D. (2006). A labour force for the consumer century: Commodification in Canada's largest department stores, 1890 to 1940. *Labour/Le Travail*, 107-144.

Belisle, D. (2011a). *Retail nation: Department stores and the making of modern Canada*. Vancouver: UBC Press.

Belisle, D. (2011b). Virtue and Vice: Consumer Culture in English Canadian Fiction Before 1940. *International Journal of Canadian Studies* (43), 165-186.

Belk, R. (2017). Consumer culture theory. In *Routledge Handbook on Consumption* (pp. 13-24). Routledge.

Belk, R. (2019). The future of globalization: A comment. *International Marketing Review* 36(4).

Belk, R. W. (1974). An exploratory assessment of situational effects in buyer behavior. *Journal of marketing research*, 11(2), 156-163.

Belk, R. W. (1988). Possessions and the extended self. *Journal of consumer research*, 15(2), 139-168.

Belk, R. W., & Pollay, R. W. (1985). Images of ourselves: The good life in twentieth century advertising. *Journal of Consumer Research*, 11(4), 887-897.

Bell, D. (1980). *The winding passage: Essays and sociological journeys, 1960-1980.* Cambridge, MA: Abt Books.

Bellenger, Dan; Curasi, Carolyn; & Moschis, George. (2004). Patronage Motives of Mature Consumers in the Selection of Food and Grocery Stores. *Journal of Consumer Marketing* 21(2), 123-133.

Bellezza, S., & Berger, J. (2019). Trickle-Round Signals: When Low Status Is Mixed with High. *Journal of Consumer Research.*

Benhabib, S. (2019). For Jürgen Habermas on his 90th birthday. *International Journal of Constitutional Law*, 17(4), 1047-1049.

Benjamin, W. (1999). *The arcades project.* Cambridge, MA: Harvard University Press.

Benkler, Y., Faris, R., & Roberts, H. (2018). *Network propaganda: Manipulation, disinformation, and radicalization in American politics.* Oxford University Press.

Benson, M. (2016). *Lifestyle migration: Expectations, aspirations and experiences.* Routledge.

Berdegué, J. A., & Reardon, T. (2016). Impacts of the supermarket revolution and the policy and strategic responses. In *Creating Food Futures* (pp. 149-161). Routledge.

Berdegué, Julio, et al. (2005). Supermarketization of the 'Emerging Markets' of the Pacific Rim: Development and Trade Implications. *Journal of Food Distribution Research* 36(1).

Berezan, O., et al. (2017). Style before substance? Building loyalty through marketing communication congruity. *European Journal of Marketing* 51 (7/8).

Berg-Sorensen, A. (2016). *Contesting secularism: Comparative perspectives.* Routledge.

Berg, L. (2018). Young consumers in the digital era: The selfie effect. *International journal of consumer studies*, 42(4), 379-388.

Berger, B. M. (2018 [1977]). Review of *Popular Culture and High Culture: An Analysis and Evaluation of Taste. Contemporary Sociology* 47 (6): 672-675

Berger, C., et al. (2018). *Communication theory.* Toronto: eCampus Ontario.

Berger, J. (2008). *Ways of seeing.* Penguin.

Berger, J., & Ward, M. (2010). Subtle signals of inconspicuous consumption. *Journal of Consumer Research*, 37(4), 555-569.

Berghel, H. (2018). Malice domestic: The Cambridge analytica dystopia. *Computer*, (5), 84-89.

Bergman, T. (2018). American television: manufacturing consumerism. *The Propaganda Model Today: Filtering Perception and Awareness.* London: University of Westminster Press.

Berkes, F., & Ross, H. (2016). Panarchy and community resilience: Sustainability science and policy implications. *Environmental Science & Policy*, 61, 185-193.

Bernard, Tara Siegel and Karl Russell (2019, 3 October). The Middle-Class Crunch: A Look at 4 Family Budgets. *New York Times.*

Bernardini, J. (2019). The postmodern infantilization of the media. *Fast Capitalism*, 11(1).

Berry, C., et al. (2020). A Longitudinal Assessment of Corrective Advertising Mandated in United States v. Philip Morris USA, Inc. *Journal of Business Ethics*, 1-14.

Berry, J. W. (1980). Acculturation as varieties of adaptation. *Acculturation: Theory, models and some new findings.* Boulder: Westview Press.

Berry, J. W. (2005). Acculturation: Living successfully in two cultures. *International journal of intercultural relations*, 29(6), 697-712.

Bershady, H. J. (2017). *Ideology and social knowledge.* Routledge.

Betta, M. (2016). Ethical Capital. In *Ethicmentality: Ethics in Capitalist Economy, Business, and Society* (pp. 123-137). Springer, Dordrecht.

Bhat, S. A., & Darzi, M. A. (2016). Customer relationship management. *International Journal of Bank Marketing.*

Bhatia, V. (2018). Examining consumers' attitude towards purchase of counterfeit fashion products. *Journal of Indian Business Research.*

Bhatt, D., & Bhatt, K. (2012). A Study of Buying Behaviour Among Male Shoppers Regarding Branded Apparels. *Quest-Journal of Management and Research*, 2(2), 13-25

Bhattacharjee, A. et al. (2014). Tip of the Hat, Wag of the Finger: How Moral Decoupling Enables Consumers to Admire and Admonish. *Journal of Consumer Research*, 39: 1167-1184.

Bhattacharjee, A., & Mogilner, C. (2013). Happiness from ordinary and extraordinary experiences. *Journal of Consumer Research*, 41(1): 1-17.

Bian, X., Wang, K. Y., Smith, A., & Yannopoulou, N. (2016). New insights into unethical counterfeit consumption. *Journal of Business Research*, 69(10), 4249-4258.

Bienen, H. S. (2012). The financial future of research universities. *Social Research: An International Quarterly*, 79(3), 631-634.

Bijmolt, T. H., & Verhoef, P. C. (2017). Loyalty programs: Current insights, research challenges, and emerging trends. In *Handbook of marketing decision models* (pp. 143-165). Springer, Cham.

Biraglia, A., Metastasio, R., & Carroll, A. (2017). Self-categorization theory and perception of coolness. An explorative study among British teenagers. *Rassegna di Psicologia* 34(2): 47-57

Birch, L., Savage, J. S., & Ventura, A. (2007). Influences on the development of children's eating behaviours: from infancy to adolescence. *Canadian journal of dietetic practice and research* 68(1), s1.

Bird, S. et al. (2011). Fear and fire: Ethical social marketing strategies for home fire safety for older people. In: *World Social Marketing Conference*, Dublin, Ireland, 11-12 April, 2011.

Bisogni, C. A., Connors, M., Devine, C. M., & Sobal, J. (2002). Who we are and how we eat: A qualitative study of identities in food choice. *Journal of Nutrition Education and Behavior*, 34(3), 128-139.

Biswas-Diener, R., & Wiese, C. W. (2018). Optimal levels of happiness. *Handbook of well-being.* Salt Lake City, UT: DEF Publishers.

Black, I., & Veloutsou, C. (2017). Working consumers: Co-creation of brand identity, consumer identity and brand community identity. *Journal of Business Research*, 70, 416-429.

Blackden, C. M. & Wodon Q. (Eds.). (2006). *Gender, Time Use, and Poverty in Sub-Saharan Africa.* World Bank Working Paper 73. World Bank.

Blair, S., & Roese, N. J. (2013). Balancing the basket: The role of shopping basket composition in embarrassment. *Journal of Consumer Research*, 40, 676–691.

Blanchin, A., Chareyron, C., & Levert, Q. (2007). *The customer behaviour in men's cosmetics market.* School of Business and Engineering, University of Halmstad.

Boccella, N., & Salerno, I. (2016). Creative economy, cultural industries and local development. *Procedia-Social and Behavioral Sciences*, 223, 291-296.

Böcker, L., & Meelen, T. (2017). Sharing for people, planet or profit? Analysing motivations for intended sharing economy participation. *Environmental Innovation and Societal Transitions*, 23, 28-39.

Bodine, A. (2003). School uniforms, academic achievement, and uses of research. The *Journal of Educational Research*, 97(2), 67-71.

Bodine, Ann. (2003). School uniforms and discourses on childhood. *Childhood* 10(1), 43-63.

Bodinger-deUriarte, C. (2019). *Interfacing Ourselves: Living in the Digital Age.* Routledge.

Boghani, R.R., et al. (2016). Children's Influence on a Mother's Purchase Decision: Shaped by TV Advertisements and Preferred Product Categories. *Children*, 8(31).

Boisen, M., et al. (2018). Reframing place promotion, place marketing, and place branding-moving beyond conceptual confusion. *Cities*, 80, 4-11.

Bolino, M., Long, D., & Turnley, W. (2016). Impression management in organizations: Critical questions, answers, and areas for future research. *Annual Review of Organizational Psychology and Organizational Behavior*, 3, 377-406.

Bondy, J. M., Peguero, A. A., & Johnson, B. E. (2019). The children of immigrants' bonding to school: Examining the roles of assimilation, gender, race, ethnicity, and social bonds. *Urban Education*, 54(4), 592-622.

Boonchoo, P., & Thoumrungroje, A. (2017). A cross-cultural examination of the impact of transformation expectations on impulse buying and conspicuous consumption. *Journal of International Consumer Marketing*, 29(3), 194-205.

Booth, D. E. (2019). Post-Materialism's Social-Class Divide: Experiences and Life-Satisfaction. *Journal of Human Values.* Published online October 15, 2020.

Borden, L. M., Lee, S. A., Serido, J., & Collins, D. (2008). Changing college students' financial knowledge, attitudes, and behavior through seminar participation. *Journal of Family and Economic Issues*, 29(1), 23-40.

Borgatti, S. P., Everett, M. G., & Johnson, J. C. (2018). *Analyzing social networks.* Sage.

Bosse, D. A., & Phillips, R. A. (2016). Agency theory and bounded self-interest. *Academy of Management Review*, 41(2), 276-297.

Boubekeur, A. (2005). Cool and Competitve Muslim Culture in the West. *isim Review*, 16, 2.

Bourdieu, P. (1979). Symbolic power. *Critique of anthropology*, 4(13-14), 77-85.

Bourdieu, P. (1983). The field of cultural production, or: The economic world reversed. *Poetics*, 12(4-5), 311-356.

Bourdieu, P. (1987). What makes a social class? On the theoretical and practical existence of groups. *Berkeley Journal of Sociology*, 32, 1-17.

Bourdieu, P. (1990). Artistic taste and cultural capital. *Culture and society: Contemporary debates*, 205-215.

Bourdieu, P. (1998). *The state nobility: Elite schools in the field of power.* Stanford University Press.

Bourdieu, P. (2011). The forms of capital. *Cultural theory: An anthology*, 1, 81-93.

Bourdieu, P. (2013). *Distinction: A social critique of the judgement of taste.* Routledge.

Bourdieu, P., & Nice, R. (1980). The aristocracy of culture. *Media, Culture & Society*, 2(3), 225-254.

Bourdieu, P., Calhoun, C., LiPuma, E., & Postone, M. (Eds.). (1993). *Bourdieu: Critical perspectives.* University of Chicago Press.

Bourguignon, F., & Chakravarty, S. R. (2019). The measurement of multidimensional poverty. In *Poverty, Social Exclusion and Stochastic Dominance* (pp. 83-107). Springer, Singapore.

Bourin, M., & Chagraoui, A. (2017). Use, Abuse and Misuse. In *Consumer Perception of Product Risks and Benefits* (pp. 429-457). Springer, Cham.

Boutelle, M. (2008). Uniforms: Are They a Good Fit?. *The Education Digest*, 73(6), 34.

Bowlby, J. (1960). Separation anxiety: A critical review of the literature. *Journal of Child Psychology and Psychiatry*, 1(4), 251-269.

Bowlby, J. (1973). *Attachment and Loss: Volume II: Separation, Anxiety and Anger.* London: The Hogarth Press and the Institute of Psycho-analysis.

Bowles, S., & Gintis, H. (2002). Schooling in capitalist America revisited. *Sociology of Education*, 1-18.

Boyle, B., & De Keere, K. (2019). Aesthetic labour, class and taste: Mobility aspirations of middle-class women working in luxury-retail. *The Sociological Review*, 67(3), 706-722.

Bradley, G. (2017). *The good ICT society: From theory to actions* (Vol. 20). Taylor & Francis.

Bradshaw, H.K., et al. (2020/online 2019). Scarcity, sex, and spending: Recession cues increase women's desire for men owning luxury products and men's desire to buy them. *Journal of Business Research* 120: 561-568.

Bragg, M. A., et al. (2018). Marketing food and beverages to youth through sports. *Journal of Adolescent Health*, 62(1), 5-13.

Braider, Jessica. (March 30 2019). Family Dinner Statistics, at https://www.thescramble.com/family-dinner/family-dinner-statistics/.

Brakus, D., et al. (2018). A cross-national study of evolutionary origins of gender shopping styles: she gatherer, he hunter?. *Journal of International Marketing*, 26(4), 38-53.

Brasel, S. A., & Hagtvedt, H. (2016). Living brands: consumer responses to animated brand logos. *Journal of the Academy of Marketing Science*, 44(5), 639-653.

Brashear-Alejandro, T., et al. (2016). Leveraging loyalty programs to build customer–company identification. *Journal of Business Research*, 69(3), 1190-1198.

Bratu, S. (2019). Can Social Media Influencers Shape Corporate Brand Reputation? Online Followers' Trust, Value Creation, and Purchase Intentions. *Review of Contemporary Philosophy*, (18), 157-163.

Braun, S. S., & Bierman, K. L. (2019). Emotion Socialization in Schools. *The Encyclopedia of Child and Adolescent Development*, 1-12.

Brears, P. (2016). Food, Eating and Identity in Early Medieval England. *Medium Aevum*, 85(2), 352.

Bresciani, S., & Del Ponte, P. (2017). New brand logo design: customers' preference for brand name and icon. *Journal of Brand Management*, 24(5), 375-390.

Breton, R. (1964). Institutional completeness of ethnic communities and the personal relations of immigrants. *American journal of Sociology*, 70(2), 193-205.

Bridge, G. (2007). A global gentrifier class?. *Environment and Planning A*, 39(1), 32-46.

Bridges, T., & Pascoe, C. J. (2014). Hybrid masculinities: New directions in the sociology of men and masculinities. *Sociology Compass*, 8(3), 246-258.

Brinkerhoff, J. M. (2016). Assimilation and heritage identity: lessons from the Coptic diaspora. *Journal of International Migration and Integration*, 17(2), 467-485.

Brito, F. W. C., & de Freitas, A. A. F. (2019). In search of "likes": the influence of social media on consumer behavior in travel consumption. *PASOS: Revista de Turismo y Patrimonio Cultural*, 17(1), 113-128.

Brodie, R. J., et al. (2013). Consumer engagement in a virtual brand community: An exploratory analysis. *Journal of business research*, 66(1), 105-114.

Bronnenberg, B. J., Dubé, J. P., & Moorthy, S. (2018). The economics of brands and branding. Available at SSRN: https://ssrn.com/abstract=3244180 or http://dx.doi.org/10.2139/ssrn.3244180.

Bronner, F., & de Hoog, R. (2018). Conspicuous consumption and the rising importance of experiential purchases. *International journal of market research*, 60(1), 88-103.

Bronsert, A. K., Glazer, A., & Konrad, K. A. (2017). Old money, the nouveaux riches and Brunhilde's marriage strategy. *Journal of Population Economics*, 30(1), 163-186.

Brown, A. D. (2017). Identity work and organizational identification. *International Journal of Management Reviews*, 19(3), 296-317.

Brown, G., & Feigenbaum, A. (Eds.). (2017). *Protest camps in international context: Spaces, infrastructures and media of resistance*. Policy Press.

Brown, N., McIlwraith, T., & de González, L. T. (2020). Globalization. *Perspectives: An Open Introduction to Cultural Anthropology, 2nd Edition*.

Brown, S. (2016). *Brands and branding*. Sage.

Brown, S., & Wijland, R. (2018). Figuratively speaking: of metaphor, simile and metonymy in marketing thought. *European Journal of Marketing*.

Brownell, Kelly D., Jennifer L. Harris & Marlene B. Schwartz. (n.d.). *Evaluating Fast Food Nutrition and Marketing to Youth. Fast Food f.a.c.t.s: Food Advertising to Children and Teens Score*. Yale Rudd Centre for Food Policy and Obesity.

Brownson, R. C., & Eyler, A. A. (2016). Future Directions for Improving Public Health through Policy. In Amy A. Eyler et al. (eds.), *Prevention, Policy, and Public Health*, pp. 349ff. Oxford: Oxford University Press.

Brubaker, R. (2017). Revisiting The 'diaspora' diaspora. *Ethnic and Racial Studies*, 40(9), 1556-1561.

Bruce, N. I., Foutz, N. Z., & Kolsarici, C. (2012). Dynamic effectiveness of advertising and word of mouth in sequential distribution of new products. *Journal of Marketing Research*, 49(4), 469-486.

Brunsma, D. L., & Rockquemore, K. A. (1998). Effects of student uniforms on attendance, behavior problems, substance use, and academic achievement. *The Journal of Educational Research*, 92(1), 53-62.

Buchanan, T., McFarlane, A., & Das, A. (2018). Educational attainment and the gender gap in Childcare in Canada: A decomposition analysis. *Margin: The Journal of Applied Economic Research*, 12(4), 458-476.

Buck, R., Francis, T., Little, E., Moulton, J., and Phillips, S. (2020, April). How consumer goods companies can prepare for the new normal. McKinsey. https://www.mckinsey.com/industries/consumer-packaged-goods/our-insights/how-consumer-goods-companies-can-prepare-for-the-next-normal.

Budlender, D. (2007). A critical review of selected time use surveys.

Budruk, M., & Lee, W. (2016). Importance of managing for personal benefits, hedonic and utilitarian motivations, and place attachment at an urban natural setting. *Environmental management*, 58(3), 504-517.

Bugge, A. B., & Almås, R. (2006). Domestic dinner: Representations and practices of a proper meal among young suburban mothers. *Journal of Consumer Culture*, 6(2), 203-228.

Buhr, H., Arora-Jonsson, S., & Pallas, J. (2017). Scrutinizers: Media. In *Corporate Governance in Action* (pp. 139-162). Routledge.

Buijzen, M., & Valkenburg, P. M. (2008). Observing purchase-related parent–child communication in retail environments: A developmental and socialization perspective. *Human Communication Research*, 34(1), 50-69.

Bundy, L. (2017). Expatriates go shopping: food and shopping acculturation. *International Journal of Retail & Distribution Management*.

Burchell, K. & Rettie, R. & Patel, K. (2013). Marketing social norms: Social marketing and the 'social norm approach.' *Journal of Consumer Behaviour*, 12: 1-9.

Burkart, R. (2018). On Habermas: Communication and Understanding: Key Concepts for Public Relations. In *Public Relations and Social Theory* (pp. 272-292). Routledge.

Burke, Kellie. (2018). The Neuroscience Behind Retail Therapy. All Regis University Theses. 864. https://epublications.regis.edu/theses/864.

Burns, M. J. (2019). Behavioral Addictions. In Michael D. Reiter (ed.), *Substance Abuse and the Family*, 2nd ed., pp. 164-178. New York: Routledge.

Buschgens, M., et al. (2018). How Regional Diasporic Consumer Experiences Produce Transnational Imaginary. *Advances in Consumer Research*, 46.

Bushueva, A. (2019). Creativity as a Professional Skill of the Manager in the Era of Globalization. *Ad Alta: Journal of Interdisciplinary Research* 10 (2): 154–157.

Butcher, L., Phau, I., & Teah, M. (2016). Brand prominence in luxury consumption: Will emotional value adjudicate our longing for status? *Journal of Brand Management*, 23(6), 701-715.

Butler, J. (1987). Variations on Sex and Gender, Beauvoir, Wittig and Foucault. *Feminism as a Critique*. University of Minnesota Press.

Butler, J. (1999). Subjects of Sex/Gender/Desire. Gender trouble: Feminism and the subversion of identity (2-43). Taylor & Francis.

Byker, C. J., et al. (2014). Food waste in a school nutrition program after implementation of new lunch program guidelines. *Journal of nutrition education and behavior*, 46(5), 406-411.

Byrd, K. M. (2019). *Real Southern Barbecue: Constructing Authenticity in Southern Food Culture*. Rowman & Littlefield.

Byun, S. E., Long, S., & Mann, M. (2020). Drivers and dynamics of brand prominence preferences among the Chinese little emperors residing in the US. *Journal of Fashion Marketing and Management: An International Journal*.

Cadwalladr, C., & Graham-Harrison, E. (2018, 17 March). Revealed: 50 million Facebook profiles harvested for Cambridge Analytica in major data breach. *The Guardian*, 17, 22.

Cai, Z., & Heathcote, J. (2018). College tuition and income inequality. Staff Report 569, Federal Reserve Bank of Minneapolis.

Calder, G. (2016). *How inequality runs in families: Unfair advantage and the limits of social mobility*. Policy Press.

Calder, L. (2012). Saving and Spending. In Frank Trentmann (ed.), *The Oxford Handbook of the History of Consumption*. Oxford: Oxford University Press.

Calderon, J., Ayala, G. X., Elder, J. P., Belch, G. E., Castro, I. A., Weibel, N., & Pickrel, J. (2017). What happens when parents and children go grocery shopping? An observational study of Latino dyads in Southern California, USA. *Health Education & Behavior*, 44(1), 5-12.

Calma, A., & Dickson-Deane, C. (2020). The student as customer and quality in higher education. *International Journal of Educational Management*.

Calvo-Porral, C., & Lévy-Mangin, J. P. (2019a). Profiling shopping mall customers during hard times. *Journal of Retailing and Consumer Services*, 48, 238-246.

Calvo-Porral, C., & Levy-Mangin, J. P. (2019b). Situational factors in alcoholic beverage consumption. *British Food Journal*.

Camilleri, M. A. (2018). Market segmentation, targeting and positioning. In *Travel marketing, tourism economics and the airline product* (pp. 69-83). Springer, Cham.

Campbell, C. (1987). *The romantic ethic and the spirit of modern consumerism*. Oxford: Blackwell.

Campbell, C. (2005). The craft consumer: Culture, craft and consumption in a postmodern society. *Journal of consumer culture*, 5(1), 23-42.

Campbell, C. (2006). Considering others and satisfying the self: The moral and ethical dimension of modern consumption. In C. Henning (ed.), *The Moralization of the Markets*. New York: Routledge.

Campbell, C. (2010). What is wrong with consumerism? An assessment of some common criticisms. *Anuário filosófico*, 43(2), 279.

Campbell, C. (2018). The Romantic Ethic. In *The Romantic Ethic and the Spirit of Modern Consumerism* (pp. 259-299). Palgrave Macmillan, Cham.

Campbell, C. (1997). *Romanticism, introspection and consumption: A response to Professor Holbrook*. Consumption, Markets and Culture 1(2): 165-173.

Campbell, N., & Kean, A. (2016). *American cultural studies: An introduction to American culture*. Routledge.

Campos, P. F. (2015, 4 April). The real reason college tuition costs so much. *The New York Times*, 4.

Caniglia, G., et al. (2017). Experiments and evidence in sustainability science: A typology. *Journal of Cleaner Production*, 169, 39-47.

Canning, J. (2019). The UK Teaching Excellence Framework (TEF) as an illustration of Baudrillard's hyperreality. *Discourse: Studies in the Cultural Politics of Education*, 40(3), 319-330.

Canova, L., Rattazzi, A. M. M., & Webley, P. (2005). The hierarchical structure of saving motives. *Journal of Economic Psychology*, 26(1), 21-34.

Cantone, L., Cová, B., & Testa, P. (2017). Loss of Brand Iconicity: The Alfa Romeo Case. In *Marketing at the Confluence between Entertainment and Analytics* (pp. 469-473). Springer, Cham.

Cantor, Joanne & Patti M. Valkenburg, "The development of a child into a consumer"(2001) *Applied Developmental Psychology* 22, 61-74

Cantwell, B. (2019). Are international students cash cows? Examining the relationship between new international undergraduate enrollments and institutional revenue at public colleges and universities in the US. *Journal of International Students*, 512, 512-525.

Cappellini, B., Marshall, D., & Parsons, E. (Eds.). (2016). *The practice of the meal: Food, families and the marketplace*. Routledge.

Caprariello, P. A., & Reis, H. T. (2018). Attitudes and social cognition: To do, to have, or to share? Valuing experiences over material possessions depends on the involvement of others. In *Relationships, Well-Being and Behaviour* (pp. 76-112). Routledge.

Capuzzi, D., Stauffer, M. D., & O'Neil, T. (2016). Theories of Human Development. In

D. Capuzzi & M.D. Stauffer (eds.), *Human Growth and Development across the Lifespan: Applications for Counselors*, pp. 25-54. Hoboken, NJ: Wiley.

Carah, N., and Brodmerkel, S. (2020). Critical perspectives on brand culture in the era of participatory and algorithmic media. *Sociology Compass*: 2-12

Carey, L., et al. (2018). Vintage Fashion: A Cross-Cultural Perspective. In *Vintage Luxury Fashion* (pp. 69-94). Palgrave Macmillan, Cham.

Carfagna, L.B., et al. (2014). An emerging eco-habitus: The reconfiguration of high cultural capital practices among ethical consumers. *Journal of Consumer Culture*, 14(2), 158-178.

Carlson, B. (2019). *Concerted Cultivation, Academic Achievement, and the Mediating Role of Non-Cognitive Factors*. (Doctoral dissertation, Portland State University).

Carlson, L., & Grossbart, S. (1988). Parental style and consumer socialization of children. *Journal of Consumer Research*, 15(1), 77-94.

Carrigan, Marylyn & Szmigin, Isabelle. (2001a). Learning to Love the Old Consumer. *Journal of Consumer Behaviour* 1(1), 22-34

Carrigan, Marylyn & Szmigin, Isabelle. (2001b). Time, consumption and the older consumer: An interpretive study of the cognitively young. *Psychology and Marketing* 18(10): 1091-1116

Carrillo, M., Gonzalez-Sparks, A., & Salcedo, N. U. (2018). Social power of preadolescent children on influence in their mothers' purchasing behavior. *Journal of Economics, Finance and Administrative Science* 23(45): 150-166.

Carter, D. S. (2020). Neoliberalism in Higher Education and Its Effects on Marginalized Students. In *Feminist Responses to the Neoliberalization of the University: From Surviving to Thriving*, p. 19. Lexington Books.

Carter, Prudence L. (2003). Black Cultural Capital, Status Positioning, and Schooling Conflicts for Low-Income African American Youth. *Social Problems* 50(1):136–55.

Caruso, M. L., & Cullen, K. W. (2015). Quality and cost of student lunches brought from home. *JAMA Pediatrics*, 169(1), 86-90.

Casaló, Luis V., et al. (2018, July). "Influencers on Instagram: Antecedents and Consequences of Opinion Leadership." *Journal of Business Research*.

Caspi, C.E., et al. (2017). Association between store food environment and customer purchases in small grocery stores, gas-marts, pharmacies and dollar stores. *International Journal of Behavioral Nutrition and Physical Activity*, 14(1), 76.

Caspi, C.E., et al. Food and beverage purchases in corner stores, gas-marts, pharmacies and dollar stores. *Public Health Nutrition*, 20(14), 2587-2597.

Casto, K. V., & Mehta, P. H. (2019). Competition, dominance, and social hierarchy. In *The Oxford Handbook of Evolutionary Psychology and Behavioral Endocrinology* (pp. 295-315). Oxford: Oxford University Press.

Cayla, J., & Eckhardt, G. M. (2008). Asian brands and the shaping of a transnational imagined community. *Journal of Consumer Research*, 35(2), 216-230.

Certomà, C. (2016). Postenvironmentalism beyond Post-environmentalism. In *Postenvironmentalism* (pp. 69-94). New York: Palgrave Pivot.

Chacko, M. A. (2019). Freedoms in the khaki: gendering a 'gender-neutral'uniform. *Gender and Education*, 1-17.

Chae, I., Bruno, H. A., & Feinberg, F. M. (2019). Wearout or Weariness? Measuring Potential Negative Consequences of Online Ad Volume and Placement on Website Visits. *Journal of Marketing Research*, 56(1), 57-75.

Chae, I., Stephen, A. T., Bart, Y., & Yao, D. (2017). Spillover effects in seeded word-of-mouth marketing campaigns. *Marketing Science*, 36(1), 89-104.

Chae, I., Andrew Stephen, Yakov Bart, and Dai Yao. 2015. "Spillover effects in seeded word-of-mouth marketing campaigns." Said Business School.

Chan, K. (2019). Perception of Material Possessions and Personality Traits Among Adolescents. *Humanities and Social Sciences Review*, 9(1), 115.

Chan, K. (2004). Material World: Attitudes towards Toys in China. *Young Consumers* 6(1):54-65.

Chan, Kara & Prendergast, Gerard. (2008). Social comparison, imitation of celebrity models and materialism among Chinese youth. *International Journal of Advertising*, 27(5), 799-826

Chan, Kara & Wei Fang (2007). Use of the internet and traditional media among young people. *Young Consumers*, 8(4) 244-256

Chan, Kara and Cong Zhang. (2007). Living in a Celebrity-Mediated Social World: the Chinese Experience. *Young Consumers* 8(2):139–52.

Chan, Kara and Gerard P. Prendergast. (2008). Social Comparison, Imitation of Celebrity Models and Materialism among Chinese Youth. *International Journal of Advertising* 27(5):799–826.

Chan, Kara (2005). Material World: Attitudes towards toys in China. *Young Consumers*, 1 (6), 54-65.

Chan, Kara. (2004). Store visits and information sources among urban Chinese children. *Journal of Consumer Marketing*, 4 (22), 178-188

Chan, Kara, Hongxia Zhang and Iris Wang. (2006). Materialism among Adolescents in Urban China. *Young Consumers* 7(2):64.

Chan, Kara, Yu Leung Ng, and Edwin K. Luk. (2013). Impact of Celebrity Endorsement in Advertising on Brand Image among Chinese Adolescents. *Young Consumers* 14(2):167–79.

Chan, Kara; Zhang, Hongxia and Wang, Iris. (2006). Materialism among adolescents in urban China. *Young Consumers*, 7 (2) 64-77

Chan, Kara. (2006) Consumer Socialization of Chinese Children in Schools: Analysis of Consumption Values in Textbooks. *Journal of Consumer Marketing* 23(3):125-132.

Chan, R. S. K. (2017). Global habitus: Multilingual identity differences expressed through cultural capital. *Educate~*, 16(1), 25-34.

Chandler, D. (2017). *Semiotics: the basics*. Taylor & Francis.

Chang, A. (2019). *Painting in the People's Republic of China: the Politics of Style*. Routledge.

Chapin, F. S. (1928). A quantitative scale for rating the home and social environment of middle class families in an urban community: A first approximation to the measurement of socio-economic status. *Journal of Educational Psychology*, 19(2), 99.

Chaplin, L. N., & John, D. R. (2007). Growing up in a material world: Age differences in materialism in children and adolescents. *Journal of Consumer Research*, 34(4), 480-493.

Chaplin, L. N., & John, D. R. (2010). Interpersonal influences on adolescent materialism: A new look at the role of parents and peers. *Journal of Consumer Psychology*, 20(2), 176-184

Chaplin, L. N., Hill, R. P., & John, D. R. (2014). Poverty and materialism: A look at impoverished versus affluent children. *Journal of Public Policy & Marketing*, 33(1), 78-92.

Chaplin, L. N., Shrum, L. J., & Lowrey, T. M. (2019). Children's materialism and identity development. In *Handbook of Research on Identity Theory in Marketing*. Edward Elgar Publishing.

Chaplin, L., & Lowrey, T. (2009). The Development of Consumer-Based Consumption Constellations in Children. *Journal of Consumer Research, 36*, pp. 757-777.

Chaplin, L., et al. (2016). How Do Children Derive Happiness from Past Experiences? Developmental, Experimental, and Longitudinal Evidence. *ACR North American Advances*.

Charles, Christopher A. D. and Shua-Kym Mclean. (2017). Body Image Disturbance and SkinBleaching. *British Journal of Psychology* 108(4):783–96.

Charles, Kerwin Kofi, Erik Hurst, and Nikolai Roussanov. (2009). Conspicuous Consumption and Race.*The Quarterly Journal of Economics* 124.

Chatterji, M., Welner, K. G., Blanco-Ramírez, G., & Berger, J. B. (2014). Rankings, accreditation, and the international quest for quality. *Quality Assurance in Education*.

Chatzidakis, A., Kastanakis, M., & Stathopoulou, A. (2016). Socio-cognitive determinants of consumers' support for the fair trade movement. *Journal of Business Ethics*, 133(1), 95-109.

Chaudhary, Karishma and Gowda, Kavitha (2018). Analysis of Online Buying Pattern of Women Consumers with Reference to Apparels in India. *Academy of Marketing Studies Journal* 22(2).

Chen, C., & Wu, C. (2009). How motivations, constraints, and demographic factors predict seniors´ overseas travel propensity. *Asia Pacific Management Review*, 14, 301–312.

Chen, F. P., & Leu, J. D. (2011). Product involvement in the link between skepticism toward advertising and its effects. *Social Behavior and Personality* 39(2), 153-159.

Chen, H., & Volpe, R. P. (1998). An analysis of personal financial literacy among college students. *Financial Services Review*, 7(2), 107-128.

Chen, J., Tang, T. L. P., & Tang, N. (2014). Temptation, monetary intelligence (love of money), and environmental context on unethical intentions and cheating. *Journal of Business Ethics*, 123(2), 197-219.

Chen, J., Yang, X., & Smith, R. E. (2016). The effects of creativity on advertising wear-in and wear-out. *Journal of the Academy of Marketing Science*, 44(3), 334-349.

Chen, Joseph, May Aung, James Liang, and Tina Sha. 2004. The Dream Market: An Exploratory Study of Gay Professional Consumers' Homosexual Identities and Their Fashion Involvement And Buying Behavior. Acrwebsite.org.

Chernev, A., & Blair, S. (2015). Doing Well by Doing Good: The Benevolent Halo of Corporate Social Responsibility. *Journal of Consumer Research, 41*, 1412-1425.

Chéron, E., & Kohlbacher, F. (2018). Older Consumers' Adoption of Innovation in Japan: The Mediating Role of Cognitive Age. *Journal of International Consumer Marketing*, 30(4), 244-259.

Cheung, M. L., Pires, G. D., & Rosenberger III, P. J. (2019). Developing a conceptual model for examining social media marketing effects on brand awareness and brand image. *International Journal of Economics and Business Research*, 17(3), 243-261.

Chirat, A. (2020). A reappraisal of Galbraith's challenge to consumer sovereignty: Preferences, welfare and the non-neutrality thesis. *The European Journal of the History of Economic Thought*, 1-28.

Choi, J., Kim, Y., Sung, J., & Yu, H. (2017). Are self-endorsed advertisements for unhealthy food more effective than friend-endorsed advertisements? *Social Behavior and Personality*, 45(7), 1069-1084.

Choi, K. W. (2017). Habitus, affordances, and family leisure: Cultural reproduction through children's leisure activities. *Ethnography*, 18(4), 427-449.

Chopik, W. J., Bremner, R. H., Johnson, D. J., & Giasson, H. L. (2018). Age differences in age perceptions and developmental transitions. *Frontiers in psychology*, 9, 67.

Choudhury, K. (2019). Materialism, consumerism, and religion: A Buddhist vision for nonprofit marketing. *International Journal of Nonprofit and Voluntary Sector Marketing*, 24(3), e1634.

Chrisman, L. (2018). Gendering imperialism: Anne McClintock and H. Rider Haggard. In *Postcolonial contraventions*. Manchester University Press.

Chung, C. F., et al. (2017, May). When personal tracking becomes social: Examining the use of Instagram for healthy eating. In *Proceedings of the 2017 CHI Conference on Human Factors in Computing Systems* (pp. 1674-1687).

Ciofi, J. (2019). Aging and Identity in the Landscape of the Mega-Casino. *Aging, 4*, 17-2019.

Clarke, P. (2008). Parental communication patterns and children's Christmas requests. *Journal of Consumer Marketing*, 25(6), 350-360.

Clemons, E. K., Wilson, J., Matt, C., Hess, T., Ren, F., & Jin, F. (2016, January). Online Trust: An International Study of Subjects' Willingness to Shop at Online Merchants, Including the Effects of Promises and of Third Party Guarantees. In *2016 49th Hawaii International Conference on System Sciences (HICSS)* (pp. 5220-5229).

Cleveland, M., & Bartsch, F. (2019). Global consumer culture: epistemology and ontology. *International Marketing Review*.

Cleveland, M., & Laroche, M. (2007). Acculturaton to the global consumer culture: Scale development and research paradigm. *Journal of Business Research*, 60(3), 249-259.

Cleveland, M., & Xu, C. (2019). Multifaceted acculturation in multiethnic settings. *Journal of Business Research*, 103, 250-260.

Cleveland, M., Laroche, M., & Takahashi, I. (2015). The intersection of global consumer culture and national identity and the effect on Japanese consumer behavior. *Journal of International Consumer Marketing*, 27(5), 364-387.

Cleveland, M., Laroche, M., Pons, F., & Kastoun, R. (2009). Acculturation and consumption: Textures of cultural adaptation. *International Journal of Intercultural Relations*, 33(3), 196-212.

Cleveland, M., et al. (2016). Identity, culture, dispositions and behavior: A cross-national examination of globalization and culture change. *Journal of Business Research*, 69(3), 1090-1102.

Clingingsmith, D., & Sheremeta, R. M. (2018). Status and the demand for visible goods: Experimental evidence on conspicuous consumption. *Experimental Economics*, 21(4), 877-904.

Cloke, P., Sutherland, C., & Williams, A. (2016). Postsecularity, political resistance, and protest in the occupy movement. *Antipode*, 48(3), 497-523.

Clow, K. E. (2016). *Integrated advertising, promotion, and marketing communications.* Pearson Education India.

Coates, C. M. (2016). *Canadian Countercultures and the Environment.* University of Calgary Press.

Coccia, M. (2018). World-System Theory: A sociopolitical approach to explain World economic development in a capitalistic economy. *Journal of Economics and Political Economy*, 5(4), 459-465.

Cockrill, A., & Goode, M. M. (2012). DVD pirating intentions: Angels, devils, chancers and receivers. *Journal of Consumer Behaviour*, 11(1), 1-10.

Codd, J. A. (2017). Neo-liberal education policy and the ideology of choice. In *Contesting Governing Ideologies* (pp. 19-35). Routledge.

Coelho, P.S., et al. (2018). On the relationship between consumer-brand identification, brand community, and brand loyalty. *Journal of Retailing and Consumer Services*, 43, 101-110.

Cohen, A. C., & Dromi, S. M. (2018). Advertising morality: Maintaining moral worth in a stigmatized profession. *Theory and Society*, 47(2), 175-206.

Cohen, E., et al. (2009). A cross-cultural comparison of choice criteria for wine in restaurants. *International Journal of Wine Business Research*, 21(1), 50-63.

Cohen, N. S., & Shade, L. R. (2008). Gendering Facebook: Privacy and commodification. *Feminist Media Studies*, 8(2), 210-214.

Cole et al (2008), Decision making and Brand Choice by Older Consumers. *Market Lett*, 19:355-365

Cole, S. J. (2018). Use Value as a Cultural Strategy against Over-Commodification: A Durkheimian Analysis of Craft Consumption within Virtual Communities. *Sociology*, 52(5), 1052-1068.

Coley, A., & Burgess, B. (2003). Gender differences in cognitive and affective impulse buying. *Journal of Fashion Marketing and Management: An International Journal.*

Collins, R. (2019). *The credential society: An historical sociology of education and stratification.* Columbia University Press.

Comella, L. (2016). Repackaging sex: Class, crass, and the good vibrations model of sexual retail. In *New sociologies of sex work* (pp. 225-238). Routledge.

Comella, L. (2017). *Vibrator nation: How feminist sex-toy stores changed the business of pleasure.* Duke University Press.

Compen, B., De Witte, K., & Schelfhout, W. (2019). The role of teacher professional development in financial literacy education: A systematic literature review. *Educational Research Review*, 26, 16-31.

Conaway, R. N., et al. (2018). Amazon Whole Foods: When E-Commerce Met Brick-and-Mortar and Saved the Brand of Conscientious Capitalism. *Journal of Marketing Development and Competitiveness*, 12(3).

Connell, P. M., Brucks, M., & Nielsen, J. H. (2014). How childhood advertising exposure can create biased product evaluations that persist into adulthood. *Journal of Consumer Research*, 41(1), 119-134.

Connell, R. W., & Messerschmidt, J. W. (2005). Hegemonic masculinity: Rethinking the concept. *Gender & Society*, 19(6), 829-859.

Connelly, R., & Kimmel, J. (2010). *The time use of mothers in the United States at the beginning of the 21st century.* WE Upjohn Institute.

Contandriopoulos, D., Larouche, C., Breton, M., & Brousselle, A. (2018). A sociogram is worth a thousand words: proposing a method for the visual analysis of narrative data. *Qualitative Research*, 18(1), 70-87.

Conti, C., et al. (2018). Survey on food preferences of university students: from tradition to new food customs? *Agriculture*, 8(10), 155.

Contini, C., et al. (2018). Investigating the role of personal and context-related factors in convenience foods consumption. *Appetite*, 126, 26-35.

Cook, D. T. (2009). Knowing the child consumer: historical and conceptual insights on qualitative children's consumer research. *Young Consumers*, 10(4), 269-282.

Cooksey-Stowers, K., Schwartz, M. B., & Brownell, K. D. (2017). Food swamps predict obesity rates better than food deserts in the United States. *International Journal of Environmental Research and Public Health*, 14(11), 1366.

Corak, M. (2017). *Divided landscapes of economic opportunity: The Canadian geography of intergenerational income mobility.* Research Group on Human Capital-Université du Québec à Montréal.

Corbett, J. (2018). Democratic innovations and the challenges of parliamentary oversight in a small state: is small really beautiful?.

Corciolani, M., Grayson, K., & Humphreys, A. (2020). Do more experienced critics review differently? *European Journal of Marketing.*

Corigliano, M. A. (2016). Wine routes and territorial events as enhancers of tourism experiences. In *Wine and tourism* (pp. 41-56). Springer, Cham.

Cormack, P. (2004). *Sociology and mass culture: Durkheim, Mills, and Baudrillard.* University of Toronto Press.

Cormack, P. (2008). True Stories of Canada: Tim Hortons and the Branding of National Identity. *Cultural Sociology*, 2(3), 369-384.

Cormack, P., & Cosgrave, J. F. (2013). *Desiring Canada: CBC Contests, Hockey Violence and Other Stately Pleasures.* University of Toronto Press.

Cormack, P., & Cosgrave, J. F. (2014). Theorising the state celebrity: a case study of the Canadian Broadcasting Corporation. *Celebrity Studies*, 5(3), 321-339.

Cornwall, A., & Lindisfarne, N. (Eds.). (2016). *Dislocating masculinity: Comparative ethnographies.* Taylor & Francis.

Corradetti, C. (2017). Frankfurt school and critical theory.

Corsi, A. M., Cohen, J., & Lockshin, L. (2017). How consumptions occasions shape consumer preferences: a discrete choice experiment approach. In *10Th international conference of the academy of wine business research, Sonoma State University, Rohnert Park.*

Cosgrave, J. (2016). Doubling Down on Goffman: A Commentary on Dmitri Shalin's 'Erving Goffman, Fateful Action, and the Las Vegas Gambling Scene'. *UNLV Gaming Research & Review Journal*, 20(1), 7.

Cosgrave, J. F. (2010). Embedded addiction: The social production of gambling knowledge and the development of gambling markets. *Canadian Journal of Sociology (Online)*, 35(1), 113.

Coskuner-Balli, G. (2020). Citizen-Consumers Wanted: Revitalizing the American Dream in the Face of Economic Recessions, 1981-2012. *Journal of Consumer Research.*

Costa, R. P., Infante, P., Afonso, A., & Jacinto, G. (2019). Making Sense of The Lonely Crowd, Today: Youth, Emotions and Loneliness in a Networked Society. In *Emotions and Loneliness in a Networked Society* (pp. 155-178). Palgrave Macmillan, Cham.

Cottingham, M. D. (2016). Theorizing emotional capital. *Theory and Society*, 45(5), 451-470.

Coulter, N. (2010). Looking for savvy girls in the post-girl-power era. *Jeunesse: Young People, Texts, Cultures*, 2(1), 177-187.

Coulter, N. (2012). From toddlers to teens: The colonization of childhood the Disney way. *Jeunesse: Young People, Texts, Cultures*, 4(1), 146-158.

Coulter, N. (2016). "Missed Opportunity": The Oversight of Canadian Children's Media. *Canadian Journal of Communication*, 41(1).

Coulter, N. (2018). "Frappés, friends, and fun": Affective labor and the cultural industry of girlhood. *Journal of Consumer Culture*, 1469540518806954.

Coulter, N. H. (2009). *Tweening the girl: the crystallization of the tween market 1980-1996* (Doctoral dissertation, School of Communication-Simon Fraser University).

Coulter, R. H., & Pinto, M. B. (1995). Guilt appeals in advertising: what are their effects? *Journal of applied psychology*, 80(6), 697.

Cox, K. C., Stewart, S. A., Lortie, J., & Barreto, T. S. (2019). Different strokes for different folks: Generational differences, social salience, and social performance. *The International Journal of Entrepreneurship and Innovation*, 20(3), 170-18

Craig, C., & Douglas, S. (2005). Beyond national culture: implications of cultural dynamics for consumer research. *International Marketing Review*, 23(3), pp. 322-342.

Creusen, M. E. (2010). The importance of product aspects in choice: the influence of demographic characteristics. *Journal of Consumer Marketing.*

Crocker, R. (2018). From 'Spaceship Earth' to the Circular Economy: The Problem of Consumption. In *Unmaking Waste in Production and Consumption: Towards the Circular Economy.* Emerald Publishing Limited.

Cross, S. N., et al. (Eds.). (2018). Hyperreality and globalization, culture in the age of Ronald McDonald. *Journal of International Consumer Marketing*, 8(3-4), 1-15.

Crossick, G., & Jaumain, S. (Eds.). (2019). *Cathedrals of Consumption: European Department Stores, 1850-1939.* Routledge.

Crul, M. (2016). Super-diversity vs. assimilation: how complex diversity in majority-minority cities challenges the assumptions of assimilation. *Journal of Ethnic and Migration Studies*, 42(1), 54-68.

Cruwys, T., Bevelander, K. E., & Hermans, R. C. J. (2015). Social modeling of eating: A review of when and why social influence affects food intake and choice. *Appetite*, 86, 3-18.

Cucchiara, M. (2008). Re-branding urban schools: urban revitalization, social status, and marketing public schools to the upper middle class. *Journal of Education Policy*, 23(2), 165-179.

Cucchiara, M. B., & Horvat, E. M. (2017). Perils and Promises. *Schools and Society: A Sociological Approach to Education*, 213.

d'Eaubonne, F. (1974). *Le féminisme ou la mort.* FeniXX.

D'Enbeau, S. (2011). Sex, feminism, and advertising: The politics of advertising feminism in a competitive marketplace. *Journal of communication inquiry*, 35(1), 53-69.

d'Astous, A., & Legendre, A. (2009). Understanding consumers' ethical justifications: A scale for appraising consumers' reasons for not behaving ethically. *Journal of business ethics*, 87(2), 255-268.

Dahl, Darren W., et al. (2009). Sex in Advertising: Gender Differences and the Role of Relationship Commitment. *Journal of Consumer Research.*

Dahlen, M., & Rosengren, S. (2016). If advertising won't die, what will it be? Toward a working definition of advertising. *Journal of Advertising*, 45(3), 334-345.

Dai, W., et al. (2019). Like or want? Gender differences in attitudes toward online shopping in China. *Psychology & Marketing*, 36(4), 354-362.

Dallaire, J. (April 2020). Driving trust (and purchase) during a pandemic. *Strategy.* Retrieved from: https://strategyonline.ca/2020/04/07/driving-trust-and-purchase-during-covid-19/

Danaher, P. J. (2017). Advertising effectiveness and media exposure. In *Handbook of Marketing Decision Models* (pp. 463-481). Springer, Cham.

Dandaneau, S. P. (2019). The Power Elite at 50: C. Wrights Mills' Political Sociology in Midlife Crisis. *Fast Capitalism*, 2(1).

Danes, S. M., Huddleston-Casas, C., & Boyce, L. (1999). Financial planning curriculum for teens: Impact evaluation. *Journal of Financial Counseling and Planning*, *10*(1), 26.

Danes, S., & Haberman, H. (2007). Teen financial knowledge, self-efficacy, and behavior: A gendered view.

Daniels, T., & Spencer, J. (2019, March). Developing Polo Tourism as a Niche Market in the Western Cape Province, South Africa. In *2nd International Conference on Tourism Research* (p. 54).

Das, M. (2019). Postcolonial Macau: Race, Morality, Taste, and Power. *Gastronomica: The Journal of Critical Food Studies*, *19*(1), 113-114.

Davies, G., Rojas-Méndez, J. I., Whelan, S., Mete, M., & Loo, T. (2018). Brand personality: theory and dimensionality. *Journal of Product & Brand Management*.

Davies, I. A., Lee, Z., & Ahonkhai, I. (2012). Do consumers care about ethical-luxury? *Journal of Business Ethics*, *106*(1), 37-51.

Davies, S., & Guppy, N. (1997). Fields of study, college selectivity, and student inequalities in higher education. *Social Forces*, *75*(4), 1417-1438.

Davies, S., & Hammack, F. M. (2005). The channelling of student competition in higher education: Comparing Canada and the US. *The Journal of Higher Education*, *76*(1), 89-106.

Davies, S., Maldonado, V., & Zarifa, D. (2014). Effectively Maintaining Inequality in Toronto: Predicting Student Destinations in Ontario Universities. *Canadian Review Of Sociology/Revue Canadienne De Sociologie*, *51*(1), 22-53.

Davis, D. (2013). *A history of shopping* (Vol. 11). Routledge.

Day, M. V., & Fiske, S. T. (2019). Understanding the Nature and Consequences of Social Mobility Beliefs. In *The Social Psychology of Inequality* (pp. 365-380). Springer, Cham.

De Groot, J. (2016). *Consuming history: Historians and heritage in contemporary popular culture*. Routledge.

De Jong, A., & Varley, P. (2017). Food tourism policy: Deconstructing boundaries of taste and class. *Tourism Management*, *60*, 212-222.

De Lazzari, C. (2019). *Transnational Politics, Citizenship and Elections: The Political Engagement of Transnational Communities in National Elections*. Routledge.

De Mooij, M. (2018). *Global marketing and advertising: Understanding cultural paradoxes*. SAGE Publications Limited.

De Mooij, M. (2019). *Consumer behavior and culture: Consequences for global marketing and advertising*. Sage.

De Veirman, M., Cauberghe, V., & Hudders, L. (2017). Marketing through Instagram influencers: the impact of number of followers and product divergence on brand attitude. *International Journal of Advertising*, *36*(5), 798-828.

De Vooght, D., & Scholliers, P. (2016). Introduction. Food and Power: Studying Food at (Modern) Courts. In *Royal Taste* (pp. 15-26). Routledge.

Deb, R., & Lodh, S. (2016). Perception about credit cards. *Journal of Commerce & Accounting Research*, *5*(4), 18-36.

Debord, G. (1992). *The society of the spectacle*. 1967. Paris: Les Éditions Gallimard.

Deenanath, V., Danes, S. M., & Jang, J. (2019). Purposive and Unintentional Family Financial Socialization, Subjective Financial Knowledge, and Financial Behavior of High School Students. *Journal of Financial Counseling and Planning*, *30*(1), 83-96.

Dehdashti, Y., Ratchford, B. T., & Namin, A. (2018). Who searches where? A new car buyer study. *Journal of Marketing Analytics*, *6*(2), 44-52.

Deitz, S. E. (2018). *The Food And Culture Of Haiti*. All Student-Created Educational Resources. 10. https://dune.une.edu/an_studedres/10

DeLiema, M., & Bengtson, V. L. (2017). Activity theory, disengagement theory, and successful aging. *Encyclopedia of geropsychology*. Springer Singapore, 15-20.

Denis, D., MCQUAIL, W., & SVEN, D. (2016). *Communication models for the study of mass communications*. Routledge.

Deutsch, C. (2017). Meathooked: The History and Science of Our 2.5-Million-Year Obsession with Meat. *Agricultural History*, *91*(1), 128.

Devi, M. S. (2018). *Are Older People Happier than Younger People? A Psychological Inquiry* (Doctoral dissertation).

Devinney, T., Eckhardt, G., & Belk, R. (2006). Why don't consumers behave ethically? The social construction of consumption. *Obtenido enero*, *9*(2009), 171.

Dharmesti, M., et al. (2019, 19 December). Understanding online shopping behaviours and purchase intentions amongst millennials. *Young Consumers*. Online ahead-of-print.

Diener, E. D., Emmons, R. A., Larsen, R. J., & Griffin, S. (1985a). The satisfaction with life scale. *Journal of Personality Assessment*, *49*(1), 71-75.

Diener, E., Horwitz, J., & Emmons, R. A. (1985b). Happiness of the very wealthy. *Social Indicators Research*, *16*(3), 263-274.

Dietrich, T., et al. (2017). *Segmentation in social marketing*. Springer Singapore.

Dikčius, V., et al. (2019). Who convinces whom? Parent and child perceptions of children's engagement in parental purchase decisions. *Journal of Promotion Management*, *25*(2), 252-269.

DiMaggio, P. (2019). Social structure, institutions, and cultural goods: The case of the United States. In *Social theory for a changing society* (pp. 133-166). Routledge.

Dittmar, H. (2005). Compulsive buying–a growing concern? An examination of gender, age, and endorsement of materialistic values as predictors. *British Journal of Psychology*, *96*(4), 467-491.

Dixon, H., et al. (2006). Pester power: snackfoods displayed at supermarket checkouts in Melbourne, Australia. *Health Promotion Journal of Australia*, *17*(2), 124-127.

Djafarova, Elmira and Chloe Rushworth. (2017). Exploring the credibility of online celebrities' Instagram profiles in influencing the purchase decisions of young female users. *Computers in Human Behavior*. 68:1-7.

Doláková, B., & Krajíček, J. (2016). Influences on Consumer Rationality. *European Financial Systems 2016*, 119.

Dolnicar, S., & Leisch, F. (2014). Using graphical statistics to better understand market segmentation solutions. *International Journal of Market Research*, *56*(2), 207-230.

Dolnicar, S., Grün, B., & Leisch, F. (2018). *Market segmentation analysis: Understanding it, doing it, and making it useful* (p. 324). Springer Nature.

Dong, P., Huang, X., & Wyer Jr, R. S. (2013). The illusion of saving face: How people symbolically cope with embarrassment. *Psychological Science*, *24*(10), 2005-2012.

Dong, X., Chang, Y., Liang, S., & Fan, X. (2018). How online media synergy influences consumers' purchase intention. *Internet Research*.

Donnelly, G., Iyer, R., & Howell, R. T. (2012). The Big Five personality traits, material values, and financial well-being of self-described money managers. *Journal of Economic Psychology*, *33*(6), 1129-1142.

Donohue, K. G. (1999). What Gender is the Consumer?: The Role of Gender Connotations in Defining the Political. *Journal of American Studies*, *33*(1), 19-43.

Dorotic, M. (2019). Keeping Loyalty Programs Fit for the Digital Age. *NIM Marketing Intelligence Review*, *11*(1), 24-29.

Douglas, Mary and Douglas Isherwood (1996). *The World of Goods: Towards an Anthropology of Consumption*, rev. ed. (London: Routledge, 1996).

Doyle, Bertram Wilbur (1937) *The Etiquette of Race Relations in the South: A Study in Social Control*.

Draganska, M., Hartmann, W. R., & Stanglein, G. (2013, June). Internet vs. TV advertising: a brand-building comparison. In *th Conference on the Economics of Advertising and Marketing* (pp. 26-27).

Drenten, J., Okleshen Peters, C., & Boyd Thomas, J. (2008). An exploratory investigation of the dramatic play of preschool children within a grocery store shopping context. *International Journal of Retail & Distribution Management*, *36*(10), 831-855.

Drew, C., Gottschall, K., Wardman, N., & Saltmarsh, S. (2016). The joy of privilege: Elite private school online promotions and the promise of happiness. In *Elite Schools* (pp. 99-112). Routledge.

Drewnowski, A., et al. (2016). Geographic disparities in healthy eating index scores (HEI–2005 and 2010) by residential property values: findings from Seattle obesity study (SOS). *Preventive Medicine*, *83*, 46-55.

Dubois, B., & Laurent, G. (1994). Attitudes towards the concept of luxury: An exploratory analysis. *ACR Asia-Pacific Advances*.

Dubois, B., & Laurent, G. (1996). The functions of luxury: A situational approach to excursionism. *ACR North American Advances*.

Dubois, D., Rucker, D. D., & Galinsky, A. D. (2015). Social class, power, and selfishness: When and why upper and lower class individuals behave unethically. *Journal of Personality and Social Psychology*, *108*(3), 436.

Dubos, R. (2017). *Social capital: Theory and research*. Routledge.

Duffett, R. G. (2017). Influence of social media marketing communications on young consumers' attitudes. *Young Consumers*.

Duffy, B. E., & Pooley, J. D. (2017). "Facebook for academics": The convergence of self-branding and social media logic on Academia.edu. *Social media+ society*, *3*(1), 2056305117696523.

Dunn, E. W., Aknin, L. B., & Norton, M. I. (2008). Spending money on others promotes happiness. *Science*, *319*(5870), 1687-1688.

Dunn, M. J., & Searle, R. (2010). Effect of manipulated prestige-car ownership on both sex attractiveness ratings. *British Journal of Psychology*, *101*(1), 69-80.

Dupont, S. (2018). The family life cycle: An essential concept for looking at contemporary families. *Thérapie Familiale*, *39*(2), 169-181.

Duque, E., et al. (2019, October). A systematic literature review on user centered design and participatory design with older people. In *Proceedings of the 18th Brazilian Symposium on Human Factors in Computing Systems* (pp. 1-11).

Durante, K. M., & Laran, J. (2016). The effect of stress on consumer saving and spending. *Journal of Marketing Research*, *53*(5), 814-828.

Durham, M. G. (2009). *The Lolita effect: The media sexualization of young girls and what we can do about it*. Abrams.

Durkheim, É. (2013). *Durkheim: The division of labour in society*. Macmillan International Higher Education.

Durvasula, Srinivas and Steven Lysonski. 2010. "Money, Money, Money – How Do Attitudes toward Money Impact Vanity and Materialism? – the Case of Young Chinese Consumers." *Journal of Consumer Marketing* 27(2):169–79.

Dussel, I. (2005). When appearances are not deceptive: A comparative history of school uniforms in Argentina and the United States (nineteenth–twentieth centuries). *Paedagogica Historica*, *41*(1-2), 179-195.

Eberl, J. M., et al. (2018). The European media discourse on immigration and its effects: A literature review. *Annals of the International Communication Association*, *42*(3), 207-223.

Eccles, S. (2002). The lived experiences of women as addictive consumers. *Journal of Research for Consumers*, *4*, 1-17.

Eckhardt, G. M., Belk, R., & Devinney, T. M. (2010). Why don't consumers consume ethically?. *Journal of Consumer Behaviour*, *9*(6), 426-436.

Edelstein, S. (2017). Reading Children: Literacy, Property, and the Dilemmas of Childhood in Nineteenth-Century America by Patricia Crain. *The Journal of the History of Childhood and Youth*, *10*(3), 453-455.

Edinger-Schons, L. M., Lengler-Graiff, L., Scheidler, S., & Wieseke, J. (2019). Frontline employees as corporate social responsibility (CSR) ambassadors: A quasi-field experiment. *Journal of Business Ethics*, *157*(2), 359-373.

Edwards, C. (2017). *Turning houses into homes: a history of the retailing and consumption of domestic furnishings*. Routledge.

Edwards, T. K., & Marshall, C. (2018). Undressing policy: a critical analysis of North Carolina (USA) public school dress codes. *Gender and Education*, 1-19.

Ehrenreich, B. (2010). *Nickel and dimed: On (not) getting by in America*. Metropolitan Books.

Eickmeyer, K., Manning, W. D., & Brown, S. L. (2017, April). What's Mine is Ours? Income Pooling in Complex Families. In *PAA 2017 Annual Meeting*. PAA.

Einwohner, R. L. (1999). Practices, opportunity, and protest effectiveness: Illustrations from four animal rights campaigns. *Social Problems, 46*(2), 169-186.

Eisenstadt, S. N. (1971). *From generation to generation: Age groups and social structure.* Transaction Publishers.

El Banna, A., et al. (2018). Ethnic identity, consumer ethnocentrism, and purchase intentions among bi-cultural ethnic consumers: "Divided loyalties" or "dual allegiance"? *Journal of Business Research, 82,* 310-319.

El Jurdi, H., & Smith, S. (2018). Mirror, mirror: national identity and the pursuit of beauty. *Journal of Consumer Marketing.*

Elberse, A., & Anand, B. (2007). The effectiveness of pre-release advertising for motion pictures: An empirical investigation using a simulated market. *Information Economics and Policy, 19*(3-4), 319-343.

Elder, G. H. (2018). *Children of the great depression.* Routledge.

Elder, G. H., & George, L. K. (2016). Age, cohorts, and the life course. In *Handbook of the life course* (pp. 59-85). Springer, Cham.

Ellen, P. S., Wiener, J. L., & Fitzgerald, M. P. (2012). Encouraging people to save for their future: Augmenting current efforts with positive visions of the future. *Journal of Public Policy & Marketing, 31*(1), 58-72.

Elliot, E. A. (2016). Craft consumption and consumer transformation in a transmodern era. *Journal of Business Research, 69*(1), 18-24.

Elliott, R., & Leonard, C. (2004). Peer pressure and poverty: Exploring fashion brands and consumption symbolism among children of the 'British poor'. *Journal of Consumer Behaviour, 3*(4), 347-359.

Ellis, W., et al. (2018). Peer groups as a context for school misconduct: the moderating role of group interactional style. *Child Development, 89*(1), 248-263.

Ellul, J., & Kellen, K. (1973). *Propaganda: The formation of men's attitudes* (pp. 116-120). New York: Vintage Books.

Elmer, E. M., & Houran, J. (2020). Physical attractiveness in the workplace: Customers do judge books by their covers. *Beauty in Business, 14.*

Elson, A. (2019). The Benefits and Perils of Globalization. In *The United States in the World Economy* (pp. 1-17). Palgrave Macmillan, Cham.

Elton-Marshall, T., et al. (2018). Marital status and problem gambling among older adults: An examination of social context and social motivations. *Canadian Journal on Aging/La Revue canadienne du vieillissement, 37*(3), 318-332.

Engbers, T. A., Thompson, M. F., & Slaper, T. F. (2017). Theory and measurement in social capital research. *Social Indicators Research, 132*(2), 537-558.

Eriksen, T. H. (2018). Small is beautiful, but is it viable?. In T.H. Eriksen & Ramola Ramtohul (eds.). *The Mauritian Paradox: Fifty Years of Development, Diversity and Democracy,* p. 123. Reduit, Mauritius : University of Mauritius Press.

Erixon, F. (2018). The Economic Benefits of Globalization for Business and Consumers. *European Centre for International Political Economy.*

Estermann, T., & Claeys-Kulik, A. L. (2013). Financially sustainable universities. *European Universities.*

Estes, R. J. (2017). Donella H. "Dana" Meadows: a Designer of Systems for Advancing Quality of Life (1941–2001). *Applied Research in Quality of Life, 12*(1), 233-235.

Estevez, A., et al. (2017). Attachment and emotion regulation in substance addictions and behavioral addictions. *Journal of Behavioral Addictions, 6*(4), 534-544.

Eusébio, C., et al. (2017). Social tourism programmes for the senior market: a benefit segmentation analysis. *Journal of Tourism and Cultural Change, 15*(1), 59-79.

Evans, A. E., Wilson, D. K., Buck, J., Torbett, H., & Williams, J. (2006). Outcome expectations, barriers, and strategies for healthful eating: a perspective from adolescents from low-income families. *Family & Community Health, 29*(1), 17-27.

Evans, G. W., & Kim, P. (2007). Childhood poverty and health: Cumulative risk exposure and stress dysregulation. *Psychological Science, 18*(11), 953-957.

Evans, J., & Hesmondhalgh, D. (Eds.). (2005). *Understanding media: inside celebrity.* Open University Press.

Evergreen, S., & Sabarre, N. (2019). Branding for the Independent Consultant: Basic to Advanced. *New Directions for Evaluation, 2019*(164), 101-113.

Ewen, S. (2008). *Captains of consciousness advertising and the social roots of the consumer culture.* Basic Books.

Ewer, M., Veale, R., & Quester, P. (2016). Virtual world, real engagement: building brand attachment via hosted brand community online events. In *Looking Forward, Looking Back: Drawing on the past to Shape the Future of Marketing* (pp. 845-848). Springer, Cham.

Faber, R. J., & Christenson, G. A. (1996). In the mood to buy: Differences in the mood states experienced by compulsive buyers and other consumers. *Psychology & Marketing, 13*(8), 803-819.

Faerber, A. E., & Kreling, D. H. (2014). Content analysis of false and misleading claims in television advertising for prescription and nonprescription drugs. *Journal of General Internal Medicine, 29*(1), 110-118.

Falk, P., & Campbell, C. (Eds.). (1997). *The shopping experience* (Vol. 52). Sage.

Fang, W. T. (2020). Responsible Tourism. In *Tourism in Emerging Economies* (pp. 131-151). Springer, Singapore.

Fang, W. T. (2020). Rural Tourism. In *Tourism in Emerging Economies* (pp. 103-129). Springer, Singapore.

Fărcaş, P. A., & Mureşan, C. M. (2018). The Importance of the Archetypal Features on Millennials in the Context of Brand Differentiaton: A Qualitative Approach. *Acta Technica Napocensis-Series: Applied Mathematics, Mechanics, And Engineering, 61*(3_Spe).

Farkas, G. (2017). *Human capital or cultural capital? Ethnicity and poverty groups in an urban school district.* Routledge.

Farrugia, D. (2018). Youthfulness and immaterial labour in the new economy. *The Sociological Review, 66*(3), 511-526.

Fay, B., & Larkin, R. (2017). Why Online Word-of-Mouth Measures Cannot Predict Brand Outcomes Offline: Volume, Sentiment, Sharing, and Influence Metrics Yield Scant Online–Offline WOM Correlations. *Journal of Advertising Research, 57*(2), 132-143.

Fay, B., Keller, E., & Larkin, R. (2019). How measuring consumer conversations can reveal advertising performance. *Journal of Advertising Research, 59*(4), 433-439.

Fayez, M., & Labib, A. (2016). Investigating the effect of the" big five" personality dimensions on compulsive buying behavior of Egyptian consumers. *Journal of Business and Retail Management Research, 10*(3).

Featherstone, M. (1982). The body in consumer culture. *Theory, Culture & Society, 1*(2), 18-33.

Featherstone, M. (1987). Lifestyle and consumer culture. *Theory, Culture & Society, 4*(1), 55-70.

Featherstone, M. (1988). In pursuit of the postmodern: An introduction. *Theory, Culture & Society, 5*(2-3), 195-215.

Featherstone, M. (1990). Global culture: An introduction. *Theory, Culture & Society, 7*(2-3), 1-14.

Featherstone, M. (1990). Perspectives on consumer culture. *Sociology, 24*(1), 5-22.

Featherstone, M. (1998). The flâneur, the city and virtual public life. *Urban Studies, 35*(5-6), 909-925.

Featherstone, M. (2007). *Consumer culture and postmodernism.* Sage.

Featherstone, M. (2010). Body, image and affect in consumer culture. *Body & Society, 16*(1), 193-221.

Featherstone, M. (2017). Public life, information technology, and the global city: New possibilities for citizenship and identity formation. In *Identity and social change* (pp. 51-76). Routledge.

Featherstone, M. (2018). Consumer Culture and Its Futures: Dreams and Consequences. In *Approaching Consumer Culture* (pp. 1-46). Springer, Cham.

Featherstone, M., & Turner, B. S. (1995). Body & Society: an introduction. *Body & Society, 1*(1), 1-12.

Featherstone, M., et al. (Eds.). (1995). *Global modernities* (Vol. 36). Sage.

Featherstone, Mike. "Automobilities: an introduction." (2004): 1-24.

Federici, S. (2019). Social reproduction theory. *Radical Philosophy, 2*(4), 55-57.

Feller, Y. (2019). Oy Tannenbaum, Oy Tannenbaum! The Role of a Christmas Tree in a Jewish Museum. *The Public Work of Christmas: Difference and Belonging in Multicultural Societies, 7,* 142.

Feng, Y., Chen, H., & He, L. (2019). Consumer Responses to Femvertising: A Data-Mining Approach of Dove's "Campaign for Real Beauty" on YouTube. *Journal of Advertising, 48*(3), 292-301.

Fenton-O'Creevy, M., & Furnham, A. (2019). Money attitudes, personality and chronic impulse buying. *Applied Psychology.*

Fenton-O'Creevy, M., Dibb, S., & Furnham, A. (2018). Antecedents and consequences of chronic impulsive buying: Can impulsive buying be understood as dysfunctional self-regulation? *Psychology & Marketing, 35*(3), 175-188.

Fenton, N. (2018). Fake democracy: The limits of public sphere theory. *Javnost-The Public, 25*(1-2), 28-34.

Ferguson, K. E., et al. (2017). Consumer perceptions of sustainability: an exploratory study. *International Journal of Business, Marketing, and Decision Sciences, 10*(1), 1-21.

Ferlic, Kyle, 2018 Going Frictionless: Retailers Must Focus on Shopping, Not Buying quotes Pamela Danziger 2018 http://www.logile.com/articles/frictionless-retail-puts-focus-on-shopping-not-buying/.

Fernandes, D., Lynch Jr, J. G., & Netemeyer, R. G. (2014). Financial literacy, financial education, and downstream financial behaviors. *Management Science, 60*(8), 1861-1883

Fernandes, S. F., & Panda, R. (2018). Social reference group influence on women buying behaviour: A review. *Journal of Commerce and Management Thought, 9*(2), 273-291.

Fernandez, K. and Lastovicka, J. (2011). Making Magic: Fetishes in Contemporary Consumption. *Journal of Consumer Research, 38,* pp. 278-299.

Ferraro, K. F., Schafer, M. H., & Wilkinson, L. R. (2016). Childhood disadvantage and health problems in middle and later life: Early imprints on physical health? *American Sociological Review, 81*(1), 107-133.

Ferreira, F. A., & Castro, C. (2020). Medical tourism in Portugal: A potential niche market. In *Advances in Tourism, Technology and Smart Systems* (pp. 615-625). Springer, Singapore.

Fiese, B. H., Foley, K. P., & Spagnola, M. (2006). Routine and ritual elements in family mealtimes: Contexts for child well-being and family identity. *New Directions for Child and Adolescent Development, 2006*(111), 67-89.

Fine, A., DeSoucey, M., & Demetry, D. (2009). Comment on Josée Johnston and Shyon Baumann/2. The foodie's dilemma: Snobbery no more: Sociologica.

Fine, Gary Alan. *Thorstein Veblen's Theory of The Leisure Class as Contested Text.* Taylor and Francis Group, Aug. 1994.

Firmin, M., et al. (2006). School uniforms: A qualitative analysis of aims and accomplishments at two Christian schools. *Journal of Research on Christian Education, 15*(2), 143-168.

Fischer, E., & Arnold, S. J. (1994). Sex, gender identity, gender role attitudes, and consumer behavior. *Psychology & Marketing, 11*(2), 163-182.

Fisher, B. W., Curran, F. C., Pearman II, F. A., & Gardella, J. H. (2018). Do School Policies and Programs Improve Outcomes by Reducing Gang Presence in Schools? *The Wiley Handbook on Violence in Education: Forms, Factors, and Preventions,* 227.

Fishman, J. A. (2017). Language and ethnicity: The view from within. *The handbook of sociolinguistics,* 327-343.

Fitzpatrick, S. (2019). *The Ethical Imagination: Exploring Fantasy and Desire in Analytical Psychology.* Routledge.

Flatters, P., & Willmott, M. (2009). Understanding the post-recession consumer. *Harvard Business Review, 87*(7/8), 106-112

Fleischer, A., & Pizam, A. (2002). Tourism constraints among Israeli seniors. *Annals of Tourism Research*, 29(1), 106-123.

Fletcher, C. (2017). The school of tomorrow: promoting electronic multimedia education in the 1960s. *History and Technology*, 33(4), 428-440.

Florack, A., et al. (2003). Perceived intergroup threat and attitudes of host community members toward immigrant acculturation. *The Journal of Social Psychology*, 143(5), 633-648.

Flurry, L. A., & Burns, A. C. (2005). Children's influence in purchase decisions: a social power theory approach. *Journal of Business Research*, 58(5), 593-601.

Flynn, L. R., Goldsmith, R. E., & Kim, W. M. (2013). A cross-cultural study of materialism and brand engagement. *Journal of Multidisciplinary Research*, 5(3), 49-69.

Flynn, L. R., Goldsmith, R. E., & Pollitte, W. (2016). Materialism, status consumption, and market involved consumers. *Psychology & Marketing*, 33(9), 761-776.

Fontes, A. (2011). Differences in the likelihood of ownership of retirement saving assets by the foreign and native-born. *Journal of Family and Economic Issues*, 32(4), 612-624.

Forehand, M. & Deshpande, R. (2001). What We See Makes Us Who We Are: Priming Ethnic Self-Awareness and Advertising Response. *Journal of Marketing Research*, 38(3), 336-348.

Forno, F. (2013). Consumer movements. *The Wiley Blackwell Encyclopedia of Social and Political Movements*.

Foroudi, P., et al. (2016). A framework of place branding, place image, and place reputation. *Qualitative Market Research: An International Journal*.

Fourcade, M., & Healy, K. (2017). Classification situations: Life-chances in the neoliberal era. *Historical Social Research/Historische Sozialforschung*, 23-51.

Fowler, D. C., Wesley, S. C., & Vazquez, M. E. (2007). Simpatico in store retailing: How immigrant Hispanic emic interpret US store atmospherics and interactions with sales associates. *Journal of Business Research*, 60(1), 50-59.

Fracassi, C. (2017). Corporate finance policies and social networks. *Management Science*, 63(8), 2420-2438.

Franzese, A. T., & Rurka, M. M. (2016). Theories of Aging. *Encyclopedia of Family Studies*, 1-9.

French, S. & M. Story. (2004). Food Advertising and Marketing Directed at Children and Adolescents in the US. *International Journal of Behavioral Nutrition and Physical Activity* 1:3

Frenken, K., & Schor, J. (2019). Putting the sharing economy into perspective. In *A Research Agenda for Sustainable Consumption Governance*. Edward Elgar Publishing.

Fresco, E. (2015). Impassioned Objects And Seething Absences: The Olympics In Canada, National Identity and Consumer Culture. Unpublished dissertation.

Frisby, D., & M. Featherstone (eds.). (1997). *Simmel on culture: selected writings*. Sage.

Frith, K., Shaw, P. & Cheng, H. (2005). The Construction of Beauty: A Cross-Cultural Analysis of Women's Magazine Advertising. *Journal of Communication*, pp. 1-17.

Fritz, K., Schoenmueller, V., & Bruhn, M. (2017). Authenticity in branding—exploring antecedents and consequences of brand authenticity. *European Journal of Marketing*.

Frizzell, Sara (2019, August 2). Trudeau rehashes old federal funding in housing announcement for Nunavut. CBC News at https://www.cbc.ca/news/canada/north/trudeau-housing-nunavut-iqaluit-1.5234413.

Fromm, Erich. (2013 [1976]). *To Have or To Be?* London: Bloomsbury Academic.

Frønes, I. (2016). Socialization in Sociological Perspectives. In *The Autonomous Child* (pp. 11-35). Springer, Cham.

Frye, L. (2017). *Defining a Presidential Look: An Analysis of Hillary Rodham Clinton's Presidential Campaign Dress*. Indiana University Press.

Funches, V., Yarber-Allen, A., & Johnson, K. (2017). Generational and family structural differences in male attitudes and orientations towards shopping. *Journal of Retailing and Consumer Services*, 37, 101-108.

Fung, W. K., & Cheng, R. W. Y. (2017). Effect of school pretend play on preschoolers' social competence in peer interactions: gender as a potential moderator. *Early Childhood Education Journal*, 45(1), 35-42.

Furnham, A. (1999). The saving and spending habits of young people. *Journal of Economic Psychology*, 20(6), 677-697.

Furnham, A., & Goletto-Tankel, M. P. (2002). Understanding savings, pensions and life assurance in 16-21-year-olds. *Human Relations*, 55(5), 603-628.

Furnham, Adrian and James Levitas. 2012. Factors That Motivate People to Undergo Cosmetic Surgery. *Plastic Surgery* 20(04):47–50.

Furth, H. G. (2017). Young children's understanding of society. In *Issues in Childhood Social Development* (pp. 228-256). Routledge.

Gajanova, L., Nadanyiova, M., & Moravcikova, D. (2019). The Use of Demographic and Psychographic Segmentation to Creating Marketing Strategy of Brand Loyalty. *Scientific Annals of Economics and Business*, 66(1), 65-84.

Galán, A. A., et al. (2019). Large-scale analysis of user exposure to online advertising on Facebook. *IEEE Access*, 7, 11959-11971.

Galbraith, J. K. (2017). *The culture of contentment*. Princeton University Press.

Gallego, I., García, I. M., & Rodríguez, L. (2009). Universities' websites: Disclosure practices and the revelation of financial information. *The International Journal of Digital Accounting Research*, 9(15), 153-192.

Gandini, A. (2016). Digital work: Self-branding and social capital in the freelance knowledge economy. *Marketing Theory*, 16(1), 123-141.

Gandini, A. (2016a). Digital work: Self-branding and social capital in the freelance knowledge economy. *Marketing Theory*, 16(1), 123-141.

Gandini, A. (2016b). *The reputation economy: Understanding knowledge work in digital society*. Springer.

Gane, M. (2017). Baudrillard. *A Companion to Continental Philosophy*, 581-587.

Ganglmair-Wooliscroft, A., & Wooliscroft, B. (2016a). Diffusion of innovation: The case of ethical tourism behavior. *Journal of Business Research*, 69(8), 2711-2720.

Ganglmair-Wooliscroft, A., & Wooliscroft, B. (2016b). Ethical holiday behavior, well-being and orientations to happiness. *Applied Research in Quality of Life*, 11(1), 83-103.

Ganiron, T. S., Fajardo, P., Baniago, P. A., & Barcelona, M. (2017). Evaluating the factors affecting high school student rebellion. *World Scientific News*, 80, 158-176.

Gans, H. J. (2017a). Racialization and racialization research. *Ethnic and Racial Studies*, 40(3), 341-352.

Gans, H. J. (2017b). The politics of culture in America. In *Social Policy and Public Policy* (pp. 353-361). Routledge.

Gao, H. (2018). Nonmaterial Culture. *ICCC International Digital Design Invitation Exhibition*, 23-23.

Garcia-Alexander, G., Woo, H., & Carlson, M. J. (2017). Social interaction, socialization, and group influence. In *Social Foundations of Behavior for the Health Sciences* (pp. 59-79). Springer, Cham.

Garcia, E. (2016). The need to address non-cognitive skills in the education policy agenda. In *Non-cognitive skills and factors in educational attainment* (pp. 31-64). Brill Sense.

Garðarsdóttir, R. B., & Dittmar, H. (2012). The relationship of materialism to debt and financial well-being: The case of Iceland's perceived prosperity. *Journal of Economic Psychology*, 33(3), 471-481

Gavish, Y., Shoham, A., & Ruvio, A. (2010). A qualitative study of mother-adolescent daughter-vicarious role model consumption interactions. *Journal of Consumer Marketing*, 27(1), 43-56.

Gavriel-Fried, B., & Shilo, G. (2016). Defining the family: The role of personal values and personal acquaintance. *Journal of Family Studies*, 22(1), 43-62.

Gbadamosi, A. (Ed.). (2019). *Exploring the Dynamics of Consumerism in Developing Nations*. IGI Global.

Genoese, A. N. (2016). Millennials as Consumers: Can Businesses Survive As Is? Undergraduate honors thesis, University of San Diego.

Gentina, E., Hogg, M. K., & Sakashita, M. (2017). Identity (Re) construction through sharing: A study of mother and teenage daughter dyads in France and Japan. *Journal of Retailing and Consumer Services*, 37, 67-77.

Gentina, E., Huarng, K. H., & Sakashita, M. (2018). A social comparison theory approach to mothers' and daughters' clothing co-consumption behaviors: A cross-cultural study in France and Japan. *Journal of Business Research*, 89, 361-370.

Gentina, E., Rose, G. M., & Vitell, S. J. (2016). Ethics during adolescence: A social networks perspective. *Journal of Business Ethics*, 138(1), 185-197.

Gentina, E., Shrum, L. J., & Lowrey, T. M. (2018). Coping with loneliness through materialism: Strategies matter for adolescent development of unethical behaviors. *Journal of Business Ethics*, 152(1), 103-122.

Gentina, E., Shrum, L. J., Lowrey, T. M., Vitell, S. J., & Rose, G. M. (2018). An integrative model of the influence of parental and peer support on consumer ethical beliefs: The mediating role of self-esteem, power, and materialism. *Journal of Business Ethics*, 150(4), 1173-1186.

Gentina, Elodie and Jean-Louis Chandon. (2014). "The Role of Gender on the Frequency of Shopping with Friends during Adolescence: Between the Need for Individuation and the Need for Assimilation." *Recherche Et Applications En Marketing* (English Edition) 29(4):32–59.

Gentina, Elodie, et al. (2014). How National Culture Impacts Teenage Shopping Behavior: Comparing French and American Consumers. *Journal of Business Research* 67(4): 464-70.

Gentry, James W., Sanjay Putrevu, Clifford J. II. Shultz, and Siraj Connuri. (2001). How About Ralph Lauren? The Separation of Brand and Product in Counterfeit Culture." In *Advances in Consumer Research 28*, pp. 49-59, Mary C. Gilly and Joan Meyers-Levy (eds.). Valdosta, GA: Association for Consumer Research.

George, J. M. (2016). Religious and Fictional Narratives: An Ontological Comparison with Reference to Max Weber's 'Disenchantment of the World'. *International Journal of Philosophy and Social Sciences*, 1(1), 53-62.

Ger, G. & Belk, R. (1996). Cross-cultural differences in materialism. *Journal of Economic Psychology*, 17, pp. 55-77.

Ger, G., et al. (2018). Debunking the myths of global consumer culture literature. *The SAGE Handbook of Consumer Culture*, 79-101.

Ger, G. & Per Østergaard. (1998). Constructing Immigrant Identities in Consumption: Appearance among Turko-Danes. In *Advances in Consumer Research*, Vol. 25, ed. Joseph W. Alba and J. Wesley Hutchinson.

Gerber, E. M., Hui, J. S., & Kuo, P. Y. (2012, February). Crowdfunding: Why people are motivated to post and fund projects on crowdfunding platforms. In *Proceedings of the International Workshop on Design, Influence, and Social Technologies: Techniques, Impacts and Ethics* 2(11).

Gergely, M., Rao, V. S., & Al Khaili, N. E. (2017). A Cross-National Experimental Examination of Software Piracy Behavior.

Gerhard, P., Gladstone, J. J., & Hoffmann, A. O. (2018). Psychological characteristics and household savings behavior: The importance of accounting for latent heterogeneity. *Journal of Economic Behavior & Organization*, 148, 66-82.

Ghanem, S. M. E. S., Nadia, E. A., & Yacout, O. M. (2017). Consumption-Related Coping Strategies of Low-Income Consumers: A Literature Review. In *Marketing at the Confluence between Entertainment and Analytics* (pp. 147-160). Springer, Cham.

Giaccardi, Soraya, L. Monique Ward, Rita C. Seabrook, Adriana Manago, and Julia Lippman. 2016. "Media and Modern Manhood: Testing Associations Between Media Consumption and Young Men's Acceptance of Traditional Gender Ideologies." *Sex Roles* 75(3-4), 151–63.

Gilbert, J. (2008). *Anticapitalism and Culture* (p. 224). Berg Publishers.

Gilbert, J. (2013). What kind of thing 'is' neoliberalism?. *New Formations*, 80(80), 7-22.

Gilovich, T., & Gallo, I. (2020). Consumers' pursuit of material and experiential purchases: A review. *Consumer Psychology Review*, 3(1), 20-33.

Gimenez, M. E. (2019). *Marx, Women, and Capitalist Social Reproduction: Marxist-Feminist Essays*. Brill.

Ging, D. (2019). Alphas, betas, and incels: Theorizing the masculinities of the manosphere. *Men and Masculinities*, 22(4), 638-657.

Gittins, C. B., & Hunt, C. (2019). Parental behavioural control in adolescence: How does it affect self-esteem and self-criticism? *Journal of Adolescence*, 73, 26-35.

Glass, T. A., & Bilal, U. (2016). Are neighborhoods causal? Complications arising from the 'stickiness' of ZNA. *Social Science & Medicine*, 166, 244-253.

Gledhill, J. (2018). Neoliberalism. *The International Encyclopedia of Anthropology*, 1-11.

Glende, S., Conrad, I., Krezdorn, L., Klemcke, S., & Krätzel, C. (2016). Increasing the acceptance of assistive robots for older people through marketing strategies based on stakeholder needs. *International Journal of Social Robotics*, 8(3), 355-369.

Gocłowska, M. A., Ritter, S. M., Elliot, A. J., & Baas, M. (2019). Novelty seeking is linked to openness and extraversion, and can lead to greater creative performance. *Journal of Personality*, 87(2), 252-266.

Goenka, S., & Thomas, M. (2020). The malleable morality of conspicuous consumption. *Journal of Personality and Social Psychology*, 118(3), 562.

Goffman, E. (1949). Presentation of self in everyday life. *American Journal of Sociology*, 55, 6-7.

Goffman, E. (1986). *Stigma: Notes on the management of spoiled identity*. Prentice Hall.

Goh, K. Y., Heng, C. S., & Lin, Z. (2013). Social media brand community and consumer behavior: Quantifying the relative impact of user-and marketer-generated content. *Information Systems Research*, 24(1), 88-107.

Gold, M. (2019). The Swiss Paradox: Egalitarianism and Hierarchy in a Model Democracy. *Social Analysis*, 63(1), 22-43.

Goldin, C. D. (2016). Human capital. In *Handbook of Cliometrics*. Heidelberg, Germany: Springer Verlag.

Goldman, L., & Hogg, M. A. (2016). Going to extremes for one's group: The role of prototypicality and group acceptance. *Journal of Applied Social Psychology*, 46(9), 544-553.

Goldman, R. (2005). *Reading ads socially*. Routledge.

Goldman, R., & Miller, A. (2019). Searching for Value in the Discourses of Commodity Fetishism. *Fast Capitalism*, 10(1).

Goldman, R., & Papson, S. (1994). Advertising in the age of hypersignification. *Theory, Culture & Society*, 11(3), 23-53.

Goldthorpe, J. H. (2017). Social inequality and social integration. In *Social Policy and Public Policy* (pp. 32-40). Routledge.

Gomes, L., & Murphy, J. (2003). An exploratory study of marketing international education online. *International Journal of Educational Management*, 17(3), 116-125.

Gomillion, Sarah C., and Traci A. Giuliano. (2011). The Influence Of Media Role Models On Gay, Lesbian, And Bisexual Identity. *Journal of Homosexuality* 58(3):330-354.

Gonzalez, R. A. (2017). Going back to go forwards? From multi-stakeholder cooperatives to Open Cooperatives in food and farming. *Journal of Rural Studies*, 53, 278-290.

Goodin, R. E. (2018). Emulation and the Transformation of Social Norms. *Social Research: An International Quarterly*, 85(1), 53-72.

Goodrich, K., & Mangleburg, T. F. (2010). Adolescent perceptions of parent and peer influences on teen purchase: an application of social power theory. *Journal of Business Research*, 63(12), 1328-1335.

Goodwin, H., & Francis, J. (2003). Ethical and responsible tourism: Consumer trends in the UK. *Journal of Vacation Marketing*, 9(3), 271-284.

Goor, D., Ordabayeva, N., Keinan, A., & Crener, S. (2020). The impostor syndrome from luxury consumption. *Journal of Consumer Research*, 46(6), 1031-1051.

Gopinath, S., Thomas, J. S., & Krishnamurthi, L. (2014). Investigating the relationship between the content of online word of mouth, advertising, and brand performance. *Marketing Science*, 33(2), 241-258.

Gordon, B. R., Zettelmeyer, F., Bhargava, N., & Chapsky, D. (2019). A comparison of approaches to advertising measurement: Evidence from big field experiments at Facebook. *Marketing Science*, 38(2), 193-225.

Gorman-Murray, A. (2018). Thrown-togetherness: Queering the interior in visual perspectives. In *Queering the interior*, pp. 15-25.

Górnik-Durose, M. E., & Boroń, K. (2018). Not materialistic, just neurotic. The mediating effect of neuroticism on the relationship between attitudes to material assets and well-being. *Personality and Individual Differences*, 123, 27-33.

Goryushkina, N.E., et al. (2019). Basic principles of tourist services market segmentation. *International Journal of Economics and Business Administration* 7(2): 139-150.

Gössling, S., Araña, J. E., & Aguiar-Quintana, J. T. (2019). Towel reuse in hotels: Importance of normative appeal designs. *Tourism Management*, 70, 273-283.

Goulart Sztejnberg, R., & Giovanardi, M. (2017). The ambiguity of place branding consultancy: Working with stakeholders in Rio de Janeiro. *Journal of Marketing Management*, 33(5-6), 421-445.

Gould, K. A., Pellow, D. N., & Schnaiberg, A. (2015). *Treadmill of production: Injustice and unsustainability in the global economy*. Routledge.

Goulding, C., Shankar, A., & Canniford, R. (2013). Learning to be tribal: facilitating the formation of consumer tribes. *European Journal of Marketing*, 47(5/6), pp. 813-832.

Govers, R., & Go, F. (2016). *Place branding: Glocal, virtual and physical identities, constructed, imagined and experienced*. Springer.

Govindasamy, R., Kelley, K., & Simon, J. E. (2017). Ethnic Greens and Herbs. *Journal of ASFMRA*, 43-55.

Govindasamy, R., et al. (2007). Demographics and the Marketing of Asian and Hispanic Produce in the Eastern Coastal U.S.A. The State University of New Jersey, Rutgers, New Brunswick. Report No. P-02903-2-07.

Gram-Hanssen, K., & Darby, S. J. (2016, April). Are 'home' and 'smart' contradictory concepts or fluid positions that will converge. In *Proceedings of the DEMAND Centre International Conference* (pp. 1-9).

Gram-Hanssen, K., & Bech-Danielsen, C. (2004). House, home and identity from a consumption perspective. *Housing, Theory and Society*, 21(1), 17-26.

Gram, M. (2011). The Death of' Pester Power': Intergenerational Food Shopping. *ACR European Advances*.

Grandey, A. A., & Melloy, R. C. (2017). The state of the heart: Emotional labor as emotion regulation reviewed and revised. *Journal of Occupational Health Psychology*, 22(3), 407.

Granovetter, M. (2018). *Getting a job: A study of contacts and careers*. University of Chicago Press.

Granovetter, Mark. *The sociology of economic life*. Routledge, 2018.

Grewal, L., Stephen, A. T., & Coleman, N. V. (2019). When posting about products on social media backfires: The negative effects of consumer identity signaling on product interest. *Journal of Marketing Research*, 56(2), 197-210.

Griffin-El, E. W., & Olabisi, J. (2019). Diasporic synergies: Conceptualizing African entrepreneurship based upon trans-local networks. *Journal of African Business*, 20(1), 55-71.

Griffin, E. (2017). The Industrial Revolution: Social costs and social change. In *Routledge Handbook of the History of Sustainability* (pp. 106-119). Routledge.

Grimes, S. M. (2003, November). " You Shoot Like A Girl!": The Female Protagonist in Action-Adventure Video Games. In *DiGRA Conference* (pp. 1-15).

Grimes, S. M. (2006). Online multiplayer games: a virtual space for intellectual property debates? *New Media & Society*, 8(6), 969-990.

Grimes, S. M., & Feenberg, A. (2009). Rationalizing play: A critical theory of digital gaming. *The information society*, 25(2), 105-118.

Grimes, S. M., & Fields, D. A. (2012). Kids online. In *A new research agenda for understanding social networking forums*. The Joan Ganz Cooney Center at Sesame Workshop. Cisco Systems. MacArthur-UCHRI Digital Media and Learning Research Hub, Kalifornian yliopisto, Irvine (pp. 1-69).

Grimmer, M., & Grube, D. C. (2019). Political branding: A consumer perspective on Australian political parties. *Party Politics*, 25(2), 268-281.

Grodach, C., et al. (2017). Manufacturing and cultural production: Towards a progressive policy agenda for the cultural economy. *City, culture and society*, 10, 17-25.

Gross, S. M., et al. (2019). Role of the elementary school cafeteria environment in fruit, vegetable, and whole-grain consumption by 6-to 8-year-old students. *Journal of Nutrition Education and Behavior*, 51(1), 41-47.

Grubb, V. M. (2016). *Clash of the generations: Managing the new workplace reality*. John Wiley & Sons.

Gruber, V., & Schlegelmilch, B. B. (2014). How techniques of neutralization legitimize norm-and attitude-inconsistent consumer behavior. *Journal of Business Ethics*, 121(1), 29-45.

Grusky, D. (2019). *Social Stratification, Class, Race, and Gender in Sociological Perspective*. Routledge.

Grusky, D. B. (2018). Marxian Theories of Class: 14: Karl Marx: Alienation and Social Classes. In *Social Stratification* (pp. 149-164). Routledge.

Guarneri, J. (2017). Popular Culture. *A Companion to the Gilded Age and Progressive Era*, 190.

Guerreiro, J., Rita, P., & Trigueiros, D. (2016). A text mining-based review of cause-related marketing literature. *Journal of Business Ethics*, 139(1), 111-128.

Guido, G., Pichierri, M., Pino, G., & Conoci, R. (2018). The segmentation of elderly consumers: A literature review. *Journal of Customer Behaviour*, 17(4), 257-278.

Gulbrandsen, I. T., & Just, S. N. (2016). *Strategizing communication: Theory and practice*. Samfundslitteratur.

Gunaruwan, T. L. (2018). Decorative consumption and socio-demographic antecedents: Revelations from a study on wristwatches and houses among Colombo office workers. *Economic Research*, 5, 2.

Gunn, A. C. (2019). Foucauldian discourse analysis in early childhood education. *Oxford Research Encyclopaedias*.

Guppy, N., Sakumoto, L., & Wilkes, R. (2019). Social Change and the Gendered Division of Household Labor in Canada. *Canadian Review of Sociology/Revue canadienne de sociologie*, 56(2), 178-203.

Gupta, V. (2017). Celebrity Endorsement-An Analysis of Brand Image and Celebrity Image. *International Journal of Applied Marketing and Management*, 2(2).

Ha, L. (2019). Advertising Effects and Advertising Effectiveness. In M.B. Oliver et al. (eds.), *Media Effects: Advances in Theory and Research*, 4th ed. New York: Routledge.

Habermas, J. (1989 [1962]). *The Structural Transformation of the Public Sphere* (Thomas Burger & Frederick Lawrence, Trans.). Cambridge: Massachusetts Institute of Technology Press.

Habib, M. M. (2018). Culture and Consumerism in Jean Baudrillard: A Postmodern Perspective. *Asian Social Science*, 14(9).

Habib, S., & Patwardhan, P. (2019). Training to Lead in an Era of Change: Insights from Ad Agency Leaders. *Journal of Advertising Education*, 1098048219840783.

Hackley, C., & Hackley, R. A. (2017). *Advertising and promotion*. Sage.

Hackley, C., Hackley, R. A., & Bassiouni, D. H. (2019). Imaginary futures: Liminoid advertising and consumer identity. *Journal of Marketing Communications*, 1-15.

Hadad, S. (2017). Knowledge economy: Characteristics and dimensions. *Management Dynamics in the Knowledge Economy*, 5(2), 203-225.

Hagenaars, A. J. (2017). The definition and measurement of poverty. In *Economic inequality and poverty: International perspectives* (pp. 148-170). Routledge.

Hahn, T., & Albert, N. (2017). Strong reciprocity in consumer boycotts. *Journal of Business Ethics*, 145(3), 509-524.

Hakim, Catherine. 2010. Erotic Capital. *European Sociological Review* 26(5): 499-518.

Halaschek-Wiener, J., et al. (2018). The Super-Seniors Study: Phenotypic characterization of a healthy 85+ population. *PloS one, 13*(5).

Hallem, Y., Arfi, W. B., & Guizani, H. (2018, June). How do Emotions Influence Brand Attachment? The Mediation Role of Brand Authenticity: An Abstract. In *Academy of Marketing Science World Marketing Congress* (pp. 801-801). Springer, Cham.

Hamilton, K. (2012). Low-income Families and Coping through Brands: Inclusion or Stigma? *Sociology, 46*(1), 74–90.

Hamilton, K., & Catterall, M. (2006). Consuming love in poor families: children's influence on consumption decisions. *Journal of Marketing Management, 22*(9-10), 1031-1052.

Hamilton, Kathy. 2011. "Low-Income Families and Coping through Brands: Inclusion or Stigma?" *Sociology* 46(1):74–90.

Hamlett, J., et al. (2008). Ethnicity and consumption: South asian food shopping patterns in Britain, 1947—75 1. *Journal of Consumer Culture, 8*(1), 91-116.

Han, H., & Hyun, S. S. (2018). Eliciting customer green decisions related to water saving at hotels: impact of customer characteristics. *Journal of Sustainable Tourism, 26*(8), 1437-1452.

Han, Y. J., Nunes, J. C., & Drèze, X. (2010). Signaling status with luxury goods: The role of brand prominence. *Journal of Marketing, 74*(4), 15-30.

Hand, M. et al. (2007a) 'Home Extensions: space, time and practice', *Environment and Planning D: Society & Space*, 25(4).

Hand, M., & Shove, E. (2007b). Condensing practices: Ways of living with a freezer. *Journal of Consumer Culture, 7*(1), 79-104.

Handler, M. (1929). False and misleading advertising. *Yale LJ, 39*, 22.

Hanssen, I., & Kuven, B. M. (2016). Moments of joy and delight: The meaning of traditional food in dementia care. *Journal of Clinical Nursing, 25*(5-6), 866-874.

Hardy, J. (2018). Branded content: Media and marketing integration. In *The Advertising Handbook* (pp. 102-117). Routledge.

Harff, B. (2018). *Ethnic conflict in world politics*. Routledge.

Harris, A., & Harris, B. (2016). *Do hard things: A teenage rebellion against low expectations*. Multnomah Books.

Harris, J. L. (2008). *Priming obesity: Direct effects of television food advertising on eating behavior and food preferences*. Dissertation, Yale University.

Harris, L. C., & Dumas, A. (2009). Online consumer misbehaviour: an application of neutralization theory. *Marketing Theory, 9*(4), 379-402.

Harris, L., & Rae, A. (2009). Social networks: the future of marketing for small business. *Journal of Business Strategy, 30*(5), 24-31.

Harris, M. N., & Teasdale, B. (2017). The indirect effects of social network characteristics and normative beliefs in the association between adolescent depressive symptomatology and binge drinking. *Deviant Behavior, 38*(9), 1074-1088

Harris, R. (2004). *Creeping conformity: How Canada became suburban, 1900-1960* (Vol. 7). University of Toronto Press.

Hartley, J. (2019). *Communication, cultural and media studies: The key concepts*. Routledge.

Harvey, D. (2007). *A brief history of neoliberalism*. Oxford University Press, USA.

Harvey, D. (2018). *The limits to capital*. Verso books.

Harvey, J. A. (1996). Marketing schools and consumer choice. *International Journal of Educational Management, 10*(4), 26-32.

Harvey, M., McMeekin, A., & Warde, A. (2010). *Qualities of food*. Manchester University Press.

Hassan, M. et al. (2016). Facebook, self-disclosure, and brand-mediated intimacy: Identifying value-creating behaviours. *Journal of Consumer Behaviour, 15*, pp. 439-502.

Hastings, G., & Stead, M. (2017). *Social marketing*. Taylor & Francis.

Hastings, J. S., Madrian, B. C., & Skimmyhorn, W. L. (2013). Financial literacy, financial education, and economic outcomes. *Annu. Rev. Econ., 5*(1), 347-373.

Hastings, O. P. (2016). Not a lonely crowd? Social connectedness, religious service attendance, and the spiritual but not religious. *Social Science Research, 57*, 63-79.

Hattke, F., Vogel, R., & Woiwode, H. (2016). When professional and organizational logics collide: Balancing invisible and visible colleges in institutional complexity. In *Multi-level governance in universities* (pp. 235-256). Springer, Cham.

Haugtvedt, C. P., Herr, P. M., & Kardes, F. R. (2018). Compulsive Buying: Review and Reflection: Ronald J. Faber and Thomas C. O'Guinn. In *Handbook of Consumer Psychology* (pp. 1027-1044). Routledge.

Hay, C., & Brée, J. (2017). "I think about it and then I forget": Socially responsible consumption: an exploratory study on the new perspectives of socialization from childhood (No. hal-02022277).

Hayakawa, H., & Venieris, Y. (2016). Consumer interdependence via reference groups. In *Behavioral Interactions, Markets, and Economic Dynamics* (pp. 81-99). Springer, Tokyo.

Hayes, T. (2007). Delphi study of the future of marketing of higher education. *Journal of Business Research, 60*(9), 927-931.

Hayward, K., & Smith, O. (2017). Crime and consumer culture. *The Oxford handbook of criminology*, 306-328.

Heath, A. W., Stappenbelt, B., & Ros, M. (2019). Uncertainty analysis of the Limits to Growth model: sensitivity is high, but trends are stable. *GAIA-Ecological Perspectives for Science and Society, 28*(3), 275-283.

Heffetz, O. (2018). *Expenditure Visibility and Consumer Behavior: New Evidence* (No. w25161). National Bureau of Economic Research.

Hegarty, N. (2014). Where we are now: The presence and importance of international students to universities in the United States. *Journal of International Students, 4*, 223-235.

Heinrichs, H., Martens, P., Michelsen, G., & Wiek, A. (2016). *Sustainability Science*. Springer Netherlands.

Heisz, A. (2019, July 28). An update on the Market Basket Measure comprehensive review. Government of Canada, Statistics Canada.

Hellén, K., Sääksjärvi, M., & Kauppinen-Räisänen, H. (2018). ENVY: Narcissistic consumer traits predicting benign and malicious envy. In *Seven Deadly Sins in Consumption*. Edward Elgar Publishing.

Henry, K. J. (2017). *Living in a Grown-up World: An Exploration of the Realities of Young People Providing Care and Implications for a Canadian Context* (Doctoral dissertation, City University of Seattle).

Henry, P. (2002). Systematic variation in purchase orientations across social classes. *Journal of Consumer Marketing*.

Hepworth, M. (2002). Privacy, security and respectability: The ideal Victorian home. In *Ideal Homes?* (pp. 25-37). Routledge.

Hershcovis, M. S., et al. (2017). Targeted workplace incivility: The roles of belongingness, embarrassment, and power. *Journal of Organizational Behavior, 38*(7), 1057-1075.

Hershkovitz, S. (2017). "Not Buying Cottage Cheese": Motivations for Consumer Protest-the Case of the 2011 Protest in Israel. *Journal of Consumer Policy, 40*(4), 473-484.

Herzfeld, M. (2018). Cultural intimacy and the politics of civility. In *Handbook of Political Anthropology*. Edward Elgar Publishing.

Hettich, D., Hattula, S., & Bornemann, T. (2018). Consumer decision-making of older people: a 45-year review. *The Gerontologist, 58*(6), e349-e368.

Heydon, J. (2017). Finding McLuhan: The mind/the man/the message. *Canadian Journal of Communication, 42*(3).

Heyes, C. J. (2016). Revisiting Feminist Debates on Cosmetic Surgery: Some Reflections on Suffering, Agency, and Embodied Difference. In *Cosmetic Surgery* (pp. 51-64). Routledge.

Highmore, B. (2019). Home Truths: Identity and Materiality in the Postwar Interior. *A Companion to Contemporary Design since 1945*, 173-188.

Hilbrecht, M. J. (2009). Parents, employment, gender and well-being: A time use study.

Hill, S. (2018). Building the Harmony of Humanity. In *The Kyoto Manifesto for Global Economics* (pp. 375-393). Springer, Singapore.

Hill, S., & Kristina M. Durante. (2011). Courtship, Competition, and the Pursuit of Attractiveness: Mating Goals Facilitate Health-Related Risk Taking and Strategic Risk Suppression in Women." *Personality and Social Psychology Bulletin* 37(3):383–94.

Hilton, M. (2017). The organised consumer movement since 1945. In *The Expert Consumer* (pp. 187-203). Routledge.

Himelboim, I., & Golan, G. (2018). A network approach to viral advertising: The role of traditional influencers, new influencers and low-influencers. In *American Academy of Advertising. Conference. Proceedings (Online)* (pp. 9-9). American Academy of Advertising.

Hirschi, T., & Gottfredson, M. R. (2017). Control theory and the life-course perspective. In *The Craft of Criminology* (pp. 241-254). Routledge.

Hirschman, E. & LaBarbera, P. (1989). The meaning of Christmas. *ACR Special Vols.*

Hlee, S., Lee, J., Yang, S. B., & Koo, C. (2019). The moderating effect of restaurant type on hedonic versus utilitarian review evaluations. *International Journal of Hospitality Management, 77*, 195-206.

Hoang, T. T. A., & Knabe, A. (2019). Time use, unemployment, and well-being: an empirical analysis using British time-use data.

Hochschild, A. R. (2012 [1983]). *The managed heart: Commercialization of human feeling*. Univ. of California Press.

Hoffman, R. (2016). Convenience foods and health in the elderly. *Maturitas, 86*, 1-2.

Hogan, B., et al. (2019). Assessing the stability of egocentric networks over time using the digital participant-aided sociogram tool Network Canvas. *Network Science*, 1-19.

Hogan, J. E., Lemon, K. N., & Libai, B. (2004). Quantifying the ripple: Word-of-mouth and advertising effectiveness. *Journal of Advertising Research, 44*(3), 271-280.

Holbrook, M. B., & Hirschman, E. C. (1982). The experiential aspects of consumption: Consumer fantasies, feelings, and fun. *Journal of Consumer Research, 9*(2), 132-140.

Holbrook, M. B., & Hirschman, E. C. (2015). Experiential consumption. *The Wiley Blackwell Encyclopedia of Consumption and Consumer Studies*, 1-3.

Holdsworth, C., Laverty, L., & Robinson, J. (2017). Gender differences in teenage alcohol consumption and spatial practices. *Children's geographies, 15*(6), 741-753.

Holiday, S., et al. (2018). Television advertising's influence on parents' gift-giving perceptions. *Journal of Consumer Marketing*.

Hollander, E., Baker, B. R., Kahn, J., & Stein, D. J. (2006). Conceptualizing and Assessing Impulse-Control Disorders.

Hollebeek, L. D., Juric, B., & Tang, W. (2017). Virtual brand community engagement practices: a refined typology and model. *Journal of Services Marketing*.

Holmberg, C. (2018). Adolescents' food communication in social media. In *Encyclopedia of Information Science and Technology, Fourth Edition* (pp. 6940-6949). IGI Global.

Holmes, M. (2011). Emotional reflexivity in contemporary friendships: Understanding it using Elias and Facebook etiquette. *Sociological Research Online, 16*(1).

Holt, D. (2016). Branding in the age of social media. *Harvard Business Review, 94*(3), 40-50.

Holt, D. B. (1998). Does cultural capital structure American consumption? *Journal of Consumer Research, 25*(1), 1-25.

Holt, D. B. (2002). Why do brands cause trouble? A dialectical theory of consumer culture and branding. *Journal of Consumer Research, 29*(1), 70-90.

Holt, D. B. (2003). *Brands and branding*. Boston, MA: Harvard Business School.

Holt, D. B. (2005). How societies desire brands: Using cultural theory to explain brand symbolism. *Inside Consumption*, 273-91

Holt, D. B. (2006). Jack Daniel's America: Iconic brands as ideological parasites and proselytizers. *Journal of Consumer Culture, 6*(3), 355-377.

Holt, D. B. (2012). Cultural brand strategy. *Handbook of marketing strategy*, 306

Holt, D. B. (2018). Whiskey: marketplace icon. *Consumption Markets & Culture*, 21(1), 76-81.

Holt, D. B., & Holt, D. B. (2004). *How brands become icons: The principles of cultural branding*. Harvard Business Press.

Holt, D. B., & Thompson, C. J. (2004). Man-of-action heroes: The pursuit of heroic masculinity in everyday consumption. *Journal of Consumer Research*, 31(2), 425-440.

Holt, D. B., Quelch, J. A., & Taylor, E. L. (2004). How global brands compete. *Harvard Business Review*, 82(9), 68-75.

Holt, D., & Cameron, D. (2010). *Cultural strategy: Using innovative ideologies to build breakthrough brands*. Oxford University Press

Hong, Y., Tran, A. N., & Yang, H. P. S. (2017). Services and relationship marketing: Perspectives on young consumers. In *Young Consumer Behaviour* (pp. 208-229). Routledge.

Honigman, B. (2013). How Millennials Are Shopping: 20 Interesting Statistics & Figures, S.L.: S.N.

Hope, S. J., Muñiz Jr, A. M., & Arnould, E. J. (2009). How Brand Communities Create Value. *Journal of Marketing*, 73(5), 30-51.

Hope, W. (2019). 15 Time, Globality and Commodity Fetishism. *Political Economy of Media Industries: Global Transformations and Challenges*, 59.

Horgan, T. G., et al. (2017). Gender and appearance accuracy: Women's advantage over men is restricted to dress items. *The Journal of Social Psychology*, 157(6), 680-691.

Horkheimer, Max, & Theodor W. Adorno. (2002 [1944/1947]). *Dialectic of enlightenment: Philosophical Fragments*. Ed. G.S. Noerr. Trans. E. Jephcott. Stanford, CA: Stanford University Press.

Horne, R. M., et al. (2018). Time, money, or gender? Predictors of the division of household labour across life stages. *Sex Roles*, 78(11-12), 731-743.

Horneman, Louise et al. (2002). Profiling the Senior Traveler: An Australian Perspective. *Journal of Travel Research* 41, 23-37

Hota, M., & Bartsch, F. (2019). Consumer socialization in childhood and adolescence: Impact of psychological development and family structure. *Journal of Business Research*, 105, 11-20.

Hota, M., & McGuiggan, R. (2005). The relative influence of consumer socialization agents on children and adolescents–examining the past and modeling the future. *ACR European Advances*.

How, A. (2017). *Critical theory*. Macmillan International Higher Education.

Howes, M., et al. (2017). Environmental sustainability: a case of policy implementation failure? *Sustainability*, 9(2), 165.

Howie, K. M., et al. (2018). Consumer participation in cause-related marketing: An examination of effort demands and defensive denial. *Journal of Business Ethics*, 147(3), 679-692.

Hsu, C. (2017). Unconsciousness by Design: Addictive Technologies and the Escape from Freedom.

Huang, G., & Li, H. (2016). Understanding media synergy. In *Advertising in new formats and media. Current research and implications for marketers*, 97-114.

Huang, H., & Liang, G. (2016). Parental cultural capital and student school performance in mathematics and science across nations. *The Journal of Educational Research*, 109(3), 286-295.

Huang, J. Y., et al. (2017). Catching (up with) magical contagion: A review of contagion effects in consumer contexts. *Journal of the Association for Consumer Research*, 2(4), 430-443.

Huang, M., & Cao, L. (2016). The Relationship between Institutional Capital and Competitive Advantage: Literature Review and Future Research. *Open Journal of Business and Management*, 4(01), 94.

Huang, W. J., et al. (2016). Bundling attractions for rural tourism development. *Journal of Sustainable Tourism*, 24(10), 1387-1402.

Huang, X. (2019). Understanding Bourdieu-Cultural Capital and Habitus. *Rev. Eur. Stud.*, 11, 45.

Huang, Y., Oppewal, H., & Mavondo, F. (2013). The influence of ethnic attributes on ethnic consumer choice of service outlet. *European Journal of Marketing*.

Huddart Kennedy, E., Baumann, S., & Johnston, J. (2019). Eating for Taste and Eating for Change: Ethical Consumption as a High-Status Practice. *Social Forces*, 98(1), 381-402.

Hudders, L., et al. (2013). Consumer meaning making: The meaning of luxury brands in a democratised luxury world. *International Journal of Market Research*, 55(3), 391-412.

Hudders, Liselot et al. 2014. The Rival Wears Prada: Luxury Consumption as a Female Competition Strategy. *Female Luxury Consumption* 12(3): 570-587.

Hughes, A. (2017). Brand, branding and brand culture among young consumers. In *Young Consumer Behaviour* (pp. 119-137). Routledge.

Hull, R. W. (2019). Finding Marx in the Occupy Wall Street Movement. *Social Forces*.

Hung, K., & Lu, J. (2016). Active living in later life: An overview of aging studies in hospitality and tourism journals. *International Journal of Hospitality Management*, 53, 133-144.

Hunting, K., & Hains, R. C. (2019). Discriminating taste: maintaining gendered social hierarchy in a cross-demographic fandom. *Feminist Media Studies*, 19(4), 542-557.

Hurlbert, J. S., Beggs, J. J., & Haines, V. A. (2017). Social networks and social capital in extreme environments. In *Social Capital* (pp. 209-231). Routledge.

Husic, M., & Cicic, M. (2009). Luxury consumption factors. *Journal of Fashion Marketing and Management*, 13(2), 231-245.

Hutchinson, Andrew. (2019, 18 Dec.). New Report Looks at the Growth of Influencer Marketing on Instagram. *Social Media Today*, www.socialmediatoday.com/news/new-report-looks-at-the-growth-of-influencer-marketing-on-instagram-1/569277/.

Huyer-May, B., Schmiedeberg, C., & Schumann, N. (2018). Neighborhood Effects on Children's Subjective Deprivation: Are Poor Children's Perceptions of the Economic Situation in their Home Influenced by their Neighborhood? *Child Indicators Research*, 11(1), 291-305.

Hwang, J., et al. (2016b). Tackling social isolation and loneliness through community exercise programs for seniors. *The University of British Columbia Medical Journal*, 8(1), 40-41.

Hwang, W. Y., et al. (2016a). Evaluating listening and speaking skills in a mobile game-based learning environment with situational contexts. *Computer Assisted Language Learning*, 29(4), 639-657.

Hyland, T. (2017). McDonaldizing spirituality: Mindfulness, education, and consumerism. *Journal of Transformative Education*, 15(4), 334-356.

Hyman, L. (2012). *Debtor nation: The history of America in red ink* (Vol. 72). Princeton University Press.

Hyman, R., & Price, R. (Eds.). (2016). *The New Working Class?: White-Collar Workers and their Organizations: A Reader*. Springer.

Ifrach B, Maglaras C, Scarsini M (2013) Bayesian social learning from consumer reviews. Technical Report 2293158. SSRN

Ikonen, P., Luoma-aho, V., & Bowen, S. A. (2017). Transparency for sponsored content: Analysing codes of ethics in public relations, marketing, advertising and journalism. *International Journal of Strategic Communication*, 11(2), 165-178.

Inglehart, R. (2018). *Culture shift in advanced industrial society*. Princeton University Press.

Irwin, C. (2018). Emotional Outlet Malls: Exploring Retail Therapy. *BU Well*, 3(1), 8.

Isaksen, K., & Roper, S. (2016). Brand Ownership as a Central Component of Adolescent Self-esteem: The Development of a New Self-esteem Scale. *Psychology & Marketing*, 33(8), 646-663.

Isaksen, Katja Jezkova and Stuart Roper. 2012. "The Commodification of Self-Esteem: Branding and British Teenagers." *Psychology & Marketing* 29(3), 117–35.

Isin, F. B., & Alkibay, S. (2011). Influence of children on purchasing decisions of well-to-do families. *Young Consumers: Insight and Ideas for Responsible Marketers*, 12(1), 39-52.

Islam, M. A., & Deegan, C. (2010). Media pressures and corporate disclosure of social responsibility performance information: a study of two global clothing and sports retail companies. *Accounting and Business Research*, 40(2), 131-148.

Islam, M. A., et al. (2020). Corporate human rights performance and moral power: A study of retail MNCs' supply chains in Bangladesh. *Critical Perspectives on Accounting*, 102163.

Ivan, Catalin & Penev, Alexander (2011), Chinese Consumer Attitudes towards the Electric Vehicle. Thesis, Master of Science in Business Administration, Linkoping University

Iyer, G. R., et al. (2019). Impulse buying: a meta-analytic review. *Journal of the Academy of Marketing Science*, 1-21.

Jack, T. (2018). Representations: A critical look at media's role in cleanliness conventions and inconspicuous consumption. *Journal of Consumer Culture*, 1469540518806958.

Jackson, T., & Webster, R. (2017). Limits to Growth revisited. In C. Deeming & P. Smyth (eds.). *Reframing global social policy: Social investment for sustainable and inclusive growth*, p. 295ff. Bristol, UK: Policy Press.

Jacobsen, J. K. S., et al. (2018). Exploring length of stay: International tourism in south-western Norway. *Journal of Hospitality and Tourism Management*, 35, 29-35.

Jacobsen, M. H., & Poder, P. (Eds.). (2016). *The sociology of Zygmunt Bauman: Challenges and critique*. Routledge.

Jacobson, J. (2013). Authentic: The Politics of Ambivalence in a Brand Culture. *Canadian Journal of Communication*, 38(4).

Jacobson, J. L. (2010). Moustachioed men and marathon moms: The marketing of cancer philanthropy.

Jacobson, J., & Mascaro, C. (2016). Movember: Twitter conversations of a hairy social movement. *Social Media+ Society*, 2(2), 2056305116637103.

Jacobson, J., Lin, C. Z., & McEwen, R. (2017). Aging with technology: Seniors and mobile connections. *Canadian Journal of Communication*, 42(2).

Jantzen, Christian, Per Østergaard, and Carla M. Sucena Vieira. 2006. "Becoming a 'Woman to the Backbone.'" *Journal of Consumer Culture* 6(2):177–202.

Jarvis, H., Pratt, A. C., & Wu, P. C. C. (2016). *The secret life of cities: Social reproduction of everyday life*. Routledge.

Jaspers, E. D. T. (2018). *Opening up on consumer materialism*. CentER, Tilburg University.

Jaspers, E. D., & Pieters, R. G. (2016). Materialism across the life span: An age-period-cohort analysis. *Journal of Personality and Social Psychology*, 111(3), 451.

Jayarathna, H. M. et al. (2019). Automated Collection of Customer Feedback Using Facial Expression and Machine Learning Techniques.

Jechoutek, K. G. (2018). Vices and Virtues Revisited. In *Religious Ethics in the Market Economy* (pp. 31-40). Palgrave Macmillan, Cham.

Jeffries, S. (2016). *Grand hotel abyss: The lives of the Frankfurt School*. Verso Books.

Jeřábek, H. (2017). *Paul Lazarsfeld and the origins of communications research*. Taylor & Francis.

Jessen, S. B., & DiMartino, C. (2016). *Perceptions of prestige: A comparative analysis of school online media marketing* (No. 230). Working Paper.

Jhally, S. (2014). *The codes of advertising: Fetishism and the political economy of meaning in the consumer society*. Routledge.

Ji, M., et al. (2016). Food-related personality traits and the moderating role of novelty-seeking in food satisfaction and travel outcomes. *Tourism Management*, 57, 387-396.

Jiang, Y., & Guo, H. (2015). Design of consumer review systems and product pricing. *Information Systems Research*, 26(4), 714-730.

Jiménez, T. R. (2018). Pushing the conversation about assimilation forward. *Ethnic and Racial Studies*, 41(13), 2285-2291.

Jin, B., Sternquist, B., & Koh, A. (2003). Price as hedonic shopping. *Family and Consumer Sciences Research Journal*, 31(4), 378-402.

John, D. (1999). Consumer Socialization of Children: A Retrospective Look at Twenty-Five Years of Research. *Journal of Consumer Research*, 26, pp. 183-213.

John, D. M., & Mayer, N. Z. (2017). Resource mobilization and social movements: A partial theory. In *Social movements in an organizational society* (pp. 15-42). Routledge.

John, D. R., & Chaplin, L. N. (2019). Children's Understanding of the Instrumental Value of Products and Brands. *Journal of Consumer Psychology*, 29(2), 328-335.

Johnsen, C. G., & Sørensen, B. M. (2017). Traversing the fantasy of the heroic entrepreneur. *International Journal of Entrepreneurial Behavior & Research*.

Johnson, C. M., et al. (2018). From Gucci to green bags: Conspicuous consumption as a signal for pro-social behavior. *Journal of Marketing Theory and Practice*, 26(4), 339-356.

Johnson, E. and M. Sherraden. (2007). From financial literacy to financial capability among youth. *Journal of Sociology & Social Welfare* 34(3), 119-146

Johnson, S. E., et al. (2019). Poverty, Parental Mental Health and Child/Adolescent Mental Disorders: Findings from a National Australian Survey. *Child Indicators Research*, 12(3), 963-988.

Johnston, J. (2002). Consuming global justice: Fair trade shopping and alternative development. In *Protest and Globalisation*. Sydney: Pluto.

Johnston, J. (2008). Counter-hegemony or bourgeois piggery? Food politics and the case of FoodShare. In *The fight over food: producers, consumers, and activists challenge the global food system*, pp. 93-120. University Park: Pennsylvania State University Press.

Johnston, J. (2008). The citizen-consumer hybrid: ideological tensions and the case of Whole Foods Market. *Theory and Society*, 37(3), 229-270.

Johnston, J., & Baker, L. (2005). Eating outside the box: FoodShare's good food box and the challenge of scale. *Agriculture and Human Values*, 22(3), 313-325.

Johnston, J., & Baumann, S. (2014). *Foodies: Democracy and distinction in the gourmet foodscape*. Routledge.

Johnston, J., & Laxer, G. (2003). Solidarity in the age of globalization: Lessons from the anti-MAI and Zapatista struggles. *Theory and Society*, 32(1), 39-91.

Johnston, J., & Taylor, J. (2008). Feminist consumerism and fat activists: A comparative study of grassroots activism and the Dove real beauty campaign. *Signs: Journal of Women in Culture and Society*, 33(4), 941-966.

Johnston, J., Baumann, S., & Oleschuk, M. (2019). Omnivorousness, Distinction, or Both? In *The Oxford Handbook of Consumption*, 361.

Johnston, J., Szabo, M., & Rodney, A. (2011). Good food, good people: Understanding the cultural repertoire of ethical eating. *Journal of Consumer Culture*, 11(3), 293-318.

Johnston, L. (2018). Homes and familial places: Transitional spaces. In *Transforming Gender, Sex, and Place* (pp. 38-58). Routledge

Jones, A. B. (2018 [2020 print]). Perceptions of School Uniforms in Relation to Socioeconomic Statuses. *Research in Middle Level Education* 43 (6): 1-13.

Jones, C. W. (2019, December). Personal branding: 'Encoding a personal brand through semiotics: a case study'. In *3rd International Conference and Exhibition on Semiotics and Visual Communication*. Cambridge Scholars Publishing.

Jones, Glen A. (2014). An introduction to higher education in Canada. In K. M. Joshi and Saeed Paivandi (eds.), *Higher education across nations* (vol. 1, pp. 1-38). Delhi: B. R. Publishing.

Jones, J. (2006). College students' knowledge and use of credit. *Journal of Financial Counseling and Planning*, 16(2).

Jones, O. (2012). *Chavs: The demonization of the working class*. Verso.

Jones, Pamela Blyth. (1990). Knowledge of Consumer Rights and Unfair and Deceptive Practices: A Comparison of Older and Younger Consumers. Thesis, Masters of Science. Virginia Polytechnic Institute and State University.

Jones, T. Y. (2017). *School Uniform Policy and Academic, Attendance, and Safety: A Study on the Influence of School Uniform Policy on Student Achievement*. Doctoral dissertation, University of St. Francis.

Jordan, A., & Klein, N. (2020). Branding, privacy, and identity: growing up in surveillance capitalism. *Journal of Children and Media*, 1-8.

Josephson-Storm, J. A. (2017). *The myth of disenchantment: Magic, modernity, and the birth of the human sciences*. University of Chicago Press.

Joshanloo, M., et al. (2016). Conceptions of happiness and life satisfaction: An exploratory study in 14 national groups. *Personality and Individual Differences*, 102, 145-148.

Joudrey, S. L. (2016). What a man: Portrayals of masculinity and race in Calgary stampede ephemera. *Cultural Studies? Critical Methodologies*, 16(1), 28-39.

Jowett, G. S., & O'donnell, V. (2018). *Propaganda & persuasion*. Sage Publications.

Joyce, R., & Ziliak, J. P. (2019). Relative poverty in Great Britain and the United States, 1979-2017.

Jun, S., Ball, A. D., & Gentry, J. W. (1993). Modes of consumer acculturation. *ACR North American Advances*.

Jun, S., Gentry, J. W., Ball, A. D., & Gonzalez-Molina, G. (1994). Hispanic acculturation processes: Evidence against assimilation. *ACR Asia-Pacific Advances*.

Jung Choo, H., Moon, H., Kim, H., & Yoon, N. (2012). Luxury customer value. *Journal of Fashion Marketing and Management: An International Journal*, 16(1), 81-101.

Jung, C. G. (1990). *The Archetypes and the Collective Unconscious*. 1959. Trans. RFC Hull. New York: Princeton UP.

Jung, J. (2017). Impact of motives on impulsivity and compulsivity in compulsive buying behavior. *Social Behavior and Personality: an international journal*, 45(5), 705-718.

Jyoti, D. F., et al. (2005). Food insecurity affects school children's academic performance, weight gain, and social skills. *The Journal of Nutrition*, 135(12), 2831-2839.

Kablan, S. (2016). Fighting Spam. How Stringent is the Canadian Legal Arsenal. An Analysis in the Light of the U.S. CAN-SPAM Act. *CJLT* 16:2, 339.

Kahle, L. R., et al. (2017). Aviary Segmentation: Theory and Method. In *The Customer is NOT Always Right? Marketing Orientationsin a Dynamic Business World* (pp. 657-657). Springer, Cham.

Kahn, P. E. (2014). Theorising student engagement in higher education. *British Educational Research Journal*, 40(6), 1005-1018.

Kail, R. V., & Cavanaugh, J. C. (2018). *Human development: A life-span view*. Cengage Learning.

Kaizer, A. J., et al. (2016, March). Behind Box-Office Sales: Understanding the Mechanics of Automation Spam in Classifieds. In *International Conference on Passive and Active Network Measurement* (pp. 248-260). Springer, Cham.

Kalenkoski Charlene, M., & Hamrick, K. S. (2014). Time Poverty Thresholds in the USA. In *Encyclopedia of Quality of Life and Well-Being*, Michalos, Alex C., ed.. New York: Springer.

Kamano, S. (1999). Comparing individual attitudes in seven countries. *Social Science Research*, 28(1), 1-35.

Kamineni, R. (2005). Influence of materialism, gender and nationality on consumer brand perceptions. *Journal of Targeting, Measurement and Analysis for Marketing*, 14(1), 25-32.

Kan, M. Y., & Laurie, H. (2018). Who is doing the housework in multicultural Britain?. *Sociology*, 52(1), 55-74.

Kang, Jukyeong & Kim, Youn-Kyung (1998). Ethnicity and Acculturation: Influences on Asian American Consumers' Purchase Decision Making for Social Clothes. *Family and Consumer Sciences Research Journal*, 27 (1), 91-117

Kanter, R. M. (2019). The future of bureaucracy and hierarchy in organizational theory: a report from the field. In *Social theory for a changing society* (pp. 63-93). Routledge.

Kapferer, J. N. (2012). Abundant rarity: The key to luxury growth. *Business Horizons*, 55(5), 453-462.

Kapferer, J. N., & Bastien, V. (2017). The Specificity of Luxury Management: Turning Marketing Upside Down. In *Advances in Luxury Brand Management* (pp. 65-84). Palgrave Macmillan, Cham.

Kapferer, J. N., Klippert, C., & Leproux, L. (2014). Does luxury have a minimum price? An exploratory study into consumers' psychology of luxury prices. *Journal of Revenue and Pricing Management*, 13(1), 2-11.

Kapferer, Jean-noël, and Vincent Bastien. (2009). The Specificity of Luxury Management: Turning Marketing Upside Down. *Journal of Brand Management* 16(5-6):311-322.

Kaplan, David H., and Wei Li. *Landscapes of the ethnic economy*. Lanham: Rowman & Littlefield, 2006.

Kaplan, M. (2020). The Self-consuming Commodity: Audiences, Users, and the Riddle of Digital Labor. *Television & New Media*, 21(3), 240-259.

Karanasios, S., Cooper, V., Adrot, A., & Mercieca, B. (2020, January). Gatekeepers Rather than Helpless: An Exploratory Investigation of Seniors' Use of Information and Communication Technology in Critical Settings. In *Proceedings of the 53rd Hawaii International Conference on System Sciences*.

Karray, S., & Debernitz, L. (2017). The effectiveness of movie trailer advertising. *International Journal of Advertising*, 36(2), 368-392.

Kastanakis, M. N., & Balabanis, G. (2014). Explaining variation in conspicuous luxury consumption: An individual differences' perspective. *Journal of Business Research*, 67(10), 2147-2154.

Kates, S. M. (2002). The protean quality of subcultural consumption: An ethnographic account of gay consumers. *Journal of Consumer Research*, 29(3), 383-399.

Kates, S. M., & Belk, R. W. (2001). The meanings of lesbian and gay pride day: Resistance through consumption and resistance to consumption. *Journal of Contemporary Ethnography*, 30(4), 392-429.

Katz, E., & Lazarsfeld, P. F. (1966). *Personal Influence, The part played by people in the flow of mass communications*. Transaction Publishers.

Katz, S. (2019). *Cultural aging: Life course, lifestyle, and senior worlds*. University of Toronto Press.

Kavaratzis, M., & Kalandides, A. (2015). Rethinking the place brand: the interactive formation of place brands and the role of participatory place branding. *Environment and Planning A*, 47(6), 1368-1382.

Keech, J., Papakroni, J., & Podoshen, J. S. (2020). Gender and differences in materialism, power, risk aversion, self-consciousness, and social comparison. *Journal of International Consumer Marketing*, 32(2), 83-93.

Keil, R. (2017). Global suburbanization. In *The Globalizing Cities Reader* (pp. 463-470). Routledge.

Keller, K. L. (2020). Consumer Research Insights on Brands and Branding: A JCR Curation. *Journal of Consumer Research*, 46(5), 995-1001.

Keller, M., & Ruus, R. (2014). Pre-schoolers, parents and supermarkets: co-shopping as a social practice. *International Journal of Consumer Studies*, 38(1), 119-126

Kellner, D. (2017). The Elvis Spectacle and the Culture Industry. In *Sonic Synergies: Music, Technology, Community, Identity* (pp. 51-61). Routledge.

Kellner, D. (2019). Media Culture and the Triumph of the Spectacle. *Fast Capitalism*, 1(1).

Kellner, D. (2020). Critical Perspectives on Television from the Frankfurt School to the Politics of Representation. In *A Companion to Television*, 15-37.

Kelly, J. G. (2017). Exploratory behavior, socialization, and the high school environment. In *Adolescent Boys in High School* (pp. 245-256). Routledge.

Kelly, Kathryn. (2009). Consumed: How Markets Corrupt Children, Infantilize Adults, and Swallow Citizens Whole (review). *Rhetoric and Public Affairs* 12 (1).

Keltie, E. (2017). *The culture industry and participatory audiences.* Springer.

Kemp-Benedict, E., & Ghosh, E. (2018). Downshifting in the fast lane: A post-Keynesian model of a consumer-led transition. *Economies, 6*(1), 3.

Kendall, N. (2015). *What is a 21st Century Brand?: New Thinking from the Next Generation of Agency Leaders.* Kogan Page Publishers.

Kennedy, J. R. (2015, April 29). Canadians urged to watch homegrown movies on National Canadian Film Day. Global News.

Kenney, C.T. (2006). The power of the purse: Allocative systems and inequality in couple households. *Gender & Society* 20, 354–381.

Kenrick, D. T., et al. (1996). Power, harassment, and trophy mates: The feminist advantages of an evolutionary perspective. In *Sex, power, conflict: Evolutionary and feminist perspectives,* 29-53

Kent, S. (2017). "Hold on, I have to post this on Instagram": Trends, Talk, and Transactions of the Experiential Consumer.

Kerbo, H. (2017). Social stratification. In *The Wiley-Blackwell Encyclopedia of Social Theory,* 1-4.

Kerrane, B., & Hogg, M. (2011). How best to get their own way?: children's influence strategies within families. *ACR North American Advances.*

Kett, Joseph F. K. (1971). Adolescence and Youth in Nineteenth-Century America. *The Journal of Interdisciplinary History* 2, 283–98

Keyvanfar, A., et al. (2018). A Sustainable historic waterfront revitalization decision support tool for attracting tourists. *Sustainability, 10*(2), 215.

Khamis, S., Ang, L., & Welling, R. (2017). Self-branding, 'micro-celebrity' and the rise of Social Media Influencers. *Celebrity Studies, 8*(2), 191-208.

Khan, H., et al. (2018). The use of branding and market segmentation in hotel marketing: A conceptual review. *Journal of Tourism Intelligence and Smartness, 1*(2), 12-23.

Kiatkawsin, K., & Han, H. (2019). What drives customers' willingness to pay price premiums for luxury gastronomic experiences at michelin-starred restaurants? *International Journal of Hospitality Management, 82,* 209-219.

Kiełczewski, D., Bylok, F., Dąbrowska, A., Janoś-Kresło, M., & Ozimek, I. (2017). Consumers' Competences as a Stimulant of Sustainable Consumption. *Folia Oeconomica Stetinensia, 17*(2), 97-114.

Kil, H., Noels, K. A., Lascano, D. I. V., & Schweickart, O. (2019). English Canadians' cultural stereotypes of ethnic minority groups: Implications of stereotype content for acculturation ideologies and immigration attitudes. *International Journal of Intercultural Relations, 70,* 104-118.

Kilbourne, W., et al. (2017). Sustainable Consumption, Consumer Culture and the Politics of a Megatrend. In *The SAGE Handbook of Consumer Culture,* 478.

Kim, C., et al. (2018). The sources of life chances: does education, class category, occupation, or short-term earnings predict 20-year long-term earnings?. *Sociological Science, 5,* 206-233.

Kim, C., Yang, Z., & Lee, H. (2009). Cultural differences in consumer socialization: A comparison of Chinese–Canadian and Caucasian–Canadian children. *Journal of Business Research, 62*(10), 955-962.

Kim, H. L., et al. (2019). Seniors: Quality of Life and Travel/Tourism. In *Best Practices in Hospitality and Tourism Marketing and Management* (pp. 241-253). Springer, Cham.

Kim, H., et al. (2017). Social comparison, personal relative deprivation, and materialism. *British Journal of Social Psychology, 56*(2), 373-392.

Kim, J. E., et al. (2016). Narrative-transportation storylines in luxury brand advertising: Motivating consumer engagement. *Journal of Business Research, 69*(1), 304-313.

Kim, J. H. (2020). Luxury brands in the digital age: perceived quality and gender difference. *The International Review of Retail, Distribution and Consumer Research, 30*(1), 68-85.

Kim, Jung-Hwan et al. (2012). U.S. Luxury Fashion Consumption:Factors Affecting Attitude and Purchase Intent. *Journal of Retailing and Consumer Services.*

Kim, N., Chun, E., & Ko, E. (2017). Country of origin effects on brand image, brand evaluation, and purchase intention. *International Marketing Review.*

Kim, P., Vaidyanathan, R., Chang, H., & Stoel, L. (2018). Using brand alliances with artists to expand retail brand personality. *Journal of Business Research, 85,* 424-433.

Kim, S., Gajos, K. Z., Muller, M., & Grosz, B. J. (2016, September). Acceptance of mobile technology by older adults: a preliminary study. In *Proceedings of the 18th International Conference on Human-Computer Interaction with Mobile Devices and Services* (pp. 147-157).

Kim, Y. (2016). Cultural orientation affects consumer responses to charity advertising. *Social Behavior and Personality: An International Journal, 44*(7), 1081-1088.

Kim, Y. K., Kang, J., & Kim, M. (2005). The relationships among family and social interaction, loneliness, mall shopping motivation, and mall spending of older consumers. *Psychology & Marketing, 22*(12), 995-1015.

Kim, Y., Lee, S., Jung, H., Jaime, J., & Cubbin, C. (2019). Is neighborhood poverty harmful to every child? Neighborhood poverty, family poverty, and behavioral problems among young children. *Journal of Community Psychology, 47*(3), 594-610.

Kimball, M., & Shumway, T. (2009). *Fatalism, Locus of Control and Retirement Saving.* University of Michigan, mimeo.

Kimle, P. A., & Damhorst, M. L. (1997). A grounded theory model of the ideal business image for women. *Symbolic Interaction, 20*(1), 45-68.

Kimmel, M. S. (2013a). Introduction: America, the angry. In *Angry white men: American masculinity at the end of an era* (1-30). Nation Books.

Kimmel, M. S. (2013b). Targeting women. In *Angry white men: American masculinity at the end of an era* (169-198). Nation Books.

Kimmel, M. S. (2013c). White men as victims: the men's rights movement. In *Angry white men: American masculinity at the end of an era* (99-134). Nation Books.

King, D. K., et al. (2016). Safe, affordable, convenient: environmental features of malls and other public spaces used by older adults for walking. *Journal of Physical Activity and Health, 13*(3), 289-295.

King, J. D., & McConnell, J. B. (2003). The effect of negative campaign advertising on vote choice: The mediating influence of gender. *Social Science Quarterly, 84*(4), 843-857.

Kingsnorth, S. (2019). *Digital marketing strategy: an integrated approach to online marketing.* Kogan Page Publishers.

Kirkman, E. (2019). Free riding or discounted riding? How the framing of a bike share offer impacts offer-redemption. *Journal of Behavioral Public Administration, 2*(2).

Kiseleva, E. M., et al. (2016). The theory and practice of customer loyalty management and customer focus in the enterprise activity. *International Review of Management and Marketing, 6*(6S), 95-103.

Kivisto, P. (2017). The origins of "new assimilation theory". *Ethnic and Racial Studies, 40*(9), 1418-1429.

Kizgin, H., et al. (2020). The impact of social media on consumer acculturation: Current challenges, opportunities, and an agenda for research and practice. *International Journal of Information Management, 51,* 102026.

Kizgin, H., et al. (2018). Consumption of products from heritage and host cultures: The role of acculturation attitudes and behaviors. *Journal of Business Research, 82,* 320-329.

Kjeldgaard, D. (2018). Will Consumer Cosmopolitanism Save the World? Should It? In *Cosmopolitanism, Markets, and Consumption* (pp. 267-275). Palgrave Macmillan, Cham.

Kjeldgaard, D. & Askegaard, S. (2006). The Glocalization of Youth Culture: The Global Youth Segment as Structures of Common Difference. *Journal of Consumer Research, 33,* 231-247.

Klein, J. G., Smith, N. C., & John, A. (2004). Why we boycott: Consumer motivations for boycott participation. *Journal of Marketing, 68*(3), 92-109.

Klein, N. (2000). *No Logo: No Space, No Choice, No Jobs.* Vintage Books Canada.

Kluegel, J. R., & Smith, E. R. (2017). *Beliefs about inequality: Americans' views of what is and what ought to be.* Routledge

Knabe, A., & Rätzel, S. (2010). Better an insecure job than no job at all? Unemployment, job insecurity and subjective wellbeing. *Economics Bulletin, 30*(3), 2486-2494.

Knabe, A., et al. (2010). Dissatisfied with life but having a good day: time-use and wellbeing of the unemployed. *The Economic Journal, 120*(547), 867-889.

Knoll, J., & Matthes, J. (2017). The effectiveness of celebrity endorsements: a meta-analysis. *Journal of the Academy of Marketing Science, 45*(1), 55-75.

Köcher, S., et al. (2019). New hidden persuaders: An investigation of attribute-level anchoring effects of product recommendations. *Journal of Retailing, 95*(1), 24-41.

Koivisto, E., & Mattila, P. (2018). Extending the luxury experience to social media–User-Generated Content co-creation in a branded event. *Journal of Business Research.*

Koles, B., et al. (2018). Compensatory consumption and consumer compromises: a state-of-the-art review. *Journal of Marketing Management, 34*(1-2), 96-133.

Korgaonkar, P. K., et al. (2020). Preventing shoplifting: Exploring online comments to propose a model. *Psychology & Marketing, 37*(1), 141-153.

Kornberger, M. (2017). The values of strategy: Valuation practices, rivalry and strategic agency. *Organization Studies, 38*(12), 1753-1773.

Kornberger, M., et al. (2017). Evaluative infrastructures: Accounting for platform organization. *Accounting, Organizations and Society, 60,* 79-95.

Koskinen-Koivisto, E. (2019). Transnational heritage work and commemorative rituals across the Finnish-Russian border in the old Salla region. *Transnational Death, 17,* 200.

Koubaa, Y., Tabbane, R. S., & Hamouda, M. (2017). Segmentation of the senior market: how do different variable sets discriminate between senior segments? *Journal of Marketing Analytics, 5*(3-4), 99-110.

Kreuzer, M., Mühlbacher, H., & von Wallpach, S. (2018). Home in the re-making: Immigrants' transcultural experiencing of home. *Journal of Business Research, 91,* 334-341.

Krishna, A., Herd, K. B., & Aydınoğlu, N. Z. (2019). A review of consumer embarrassment as a public and private emotion. *Journal of Consumer Psychology, 29*(3), 492-516.

Kroll, R. J., & Hunt, S. D. (1980). Consumer-interest study in higher education: A conceptual analysis of an emerging discipline. *Journal of Consumer Affairs, 14*(2), 267-287.

Kronby, M. C. (2010). *Canadian family law.* John Wiley & Sons.

Krueger, A. B., & Mueller, A. I. (2012). Time use, emotional well-being, and unemployment: Evidence from longitudinal data. *American Economic Review, 102*(3), 594-99.

Kubrin, C. E., et al. (2019). Institutional completeness and crime rates in immigrant neighborhoods. *Journal of Research in Crime and Delinquency, 56*(2), 175-212.

Kuhle, S., & Veugelers, P. J. (2008). Why does the social gradient in health not apply to overweight? *Health Reports, 19*(4), 7.

Kuksov, D., & Xie, Y. (2012). Competition in a status goods market. *Journal of Marketing Research, 49*(5), 609-623.

Kumar, A., & Gilovich, T. (2016). To do or to have, now or later? The preferred consumption profiles of material and experiential purchases. *Journal of Consumer Psychology, 26*(2), 169-178.

Kumar, A., Paul, J., & Unnithan, A. B. (2020). 'Masstige' marketing: A review, synthesis and research agenda. *Journal of Business Research, 113,* 384-398.

Kumar, R. (2008). How embarrassing! An examination of the sources of consumer embarrassment and the role of self-awareness. *ACR North American Advances.*

Kumar, V. (2017). Inequality in India: Caste and Hindu Social Order. *Transience, 5*(1), 36-52.

Kumar, V. (2019). Global implications of cause-related loyalty marketing. *International Marketing Review*.

Kuppuswamy, V., & Bayus, B. L. (2018). Crowdfunding creative ideas: The dynamics of project backers. In *The economics of crowdfunding* (pp. 151-182). Palgrave Macmillan, Cham.

Kurtz, Paul. (1977, July). Review of To Have or To Be. Humanist: A Magazine of Critical Inquiry and Social Concern 37, 50.

Kwak, L. E., & Sojka, J. Z. (2010). If they could see me now: immigrants' use of prestige brands to convey status. *Journal of Consumer Marketing*.

Kymlicka, W. (2020). Solidarity in diverse societies: Beyond neoliberal multiculturalism and welfare chauvinism. In *Minorities and Populism–Critical Perspectives from South Asia and Europe* (pp. 41-62). Springer, Cham.

Kyriacou, A. P. (2016). Individualism–collectivism, governance and economic development. *European Journal of Political Economy*, 42, 91-104.

Lachance, M. J., & Legault, F. (2007). College students' consumer competence: Identifying the socialization sources. *Journal of Research for Consumers*, (13), 1.

Ladhari, R., & Tchetgna, N. M. (2017). Values, socially conscious behaviour and consumption emotions as predictors of Canadians' intent to buy fair trade products. *International Journal of Consumer Studies*, 41(6), 696-705.

Lagrée, P., Cappé, O., Cautis, B., & Maniu, S. (2018). Algorithms for online influencer marketing. *ACM Transactions on Knowledge Discovery from Data (TKDD)*, 13(1), 1-30.

Lahelma, E., Pietiläinen, O., Ferrie, J., Kivimäki, M., Lahti, J., Marmot, M., ... & Lallukka, T. (2016). Changes over time in absolute and relative socioeconomic differences in smoking: a comparison of cohort studies from Britain, Finland, and Japan. *Nicotine & Tobacco Research*, 18(8), 1697-1704.

Lai, I. K. W. (2019). Hotel image and reputation on building customer loyalty: An empirical study in Macau. *Journal of Hospitality and Tourism Management*, 38, 111-121

Lambert-Pandraud, R., & Laurent, G. (2010). Why do older consumers buy older brands? The role of attachment and declining innovativeness. *Journal of Marketing*, 74(5), 104-121.

Lambert-Pandraud, et al. (2005). Repeat purchasing of new automobiles by older consumers: empirical evidence and interpretations. *Journal of Marketing*, 69(2), 97-113

Lambert-Pandraud, R., Laurent, G., Mullet, E., & Yoon, C. (2017). Impact of age on brand awareness sets: a turning point in consumers' early 60s. *Marketing Letters*, 28(2), 205-218.

Lambert, C. J. (2019). Consumerism, Violence, and Dehumanization: The Vicious Dynamic Circle. In *Multifaceted Explorations of Consumer Culture and Its Impact on Individuals and Society* (pp. 196-209). IGI Global.

Landberg, J., et al. (2020). The Contribution of Alcohol Use, Other Lifestyle Factors and Working Conditions to Socioeconomic Differences in Sickness Absence. *European Addiction Research*, 26(1), 40-51.

Landis, B., & Gladstone, J. J. (2017). Personality, income, and compensatory consumption: Low-income extraverts spend more on status. *Psychological Science*, 28(10), 1518-1520.

Langlois, Judith H. et al. 2000. Maxims or Myths of Beauty? A Meta-Analytic and Theoretical Review. *Psychological Bulletin* 126(3):390–423.

Langman, L. (2017). Frankfurt School, The. *The Wiley-Blackwell Encyclopedia of Social Theory*, 1-9.

Lareau, A. (2017). Concerted cultivation and the accomplishment of natural growth. In *Childhood Socialization* (pp. 335-344). Routledge.

Lareau, A., & Jo, H. (2017). Commentary: The American Tradition of Inequality: Neighborhoods and Schools. *American Educational Research Journal*, 54(1_suppl), 190S-192S.

Laroche, M., et al. (2012). The effects of social media based brand communities on brand community markers, value creation practices, brand trust and brand loyalty. *Computers in Human Behavior*, 28(5), 1755-1767.

Laroche, M., et al. (2007). How culture matters in children's purchase influence: a multi-level investigation. *Journal of the Academy of Marketing Science*, 35(1), 113-126.

Larrasquet, J. M., & V. Pilnière (2012). Seeking a sustainable future–the role of university. *International Journal of Technology Management & Sustainable Development*, 11(3), 207-215.

Lash, C. L. (2018). Making Americans: Schooling, Diversity, and Assimilation in the Twenty-First Century. *RSF: The Russell Sage Foundation Journal of the Social Sciences*, 4(5), 99-117.

Laterza, V. (2018). Cambridge Analytica, independent research and the national interest. *Anthropology Today*, 34(3), 1-2

Lavalette, M., & Ferguson, I. (2018). Marx: alienation, commodity fetishism and the world of contemporary social work. *Critical and Radical Social Work*, 6(2), 197-213.

Lavy, B. L., et al. (2016). Media portrayal of gentrification and redevelopment on Rainey Street in Austin, Texas (USA), 2000–2014. *City, Culture and Society*, 7(4), 197-207.

Lawrence, D. (2017). Genteel women: empire and domestic material culture, 1840–1910.

Lawson, T. T. (2018). *Carl Jung, Darwin of the mind*. Routledge.

Lazar, A., & Litvak Hirsch, T. (2018). High school multicultural class and the question of films' age appropriateness. *Available at SSRN 3261781*.

Lazer, D.M., et al. (2018). The science of fake news. *Science*, 359(6380), 1094-1096.

Le Meunier-Fitzhugh, K., & Massey, G. R. (2019). Improving relationships between sales and marketing: the relative effectiveness of cross-functional coordination mechanisms. *Journal of Marketing Management*, 35(13-14), 1267-1290.

Lears, J. (2006). The American Way of Debt. *The New York Times Magazine*, 11, 13.

Leary, M. R. (2019). *Self-presentation: Impression management and interpersonal behavior*. Routledge.

Leckie, C., Nyadzayo, M. W., & Johnson, L. W. (2016). Antecedents of consumer brand engagement and brand loyalty. *Journal of Marketing Management*, 32(5-6), 558-578.

Ledikwe, A., et al. (2019). The perceived influence of relationship quality on brand loyalty. *African Journal of Economic and Management Studies*.

Lee, C. K., & Conroy, D. M. (2005). Socialisation through consumption: teenagers and the internet. *Australasian Marketing Journal (AMJ)*, 13(1), 8-19.

Lee, Euehun; Mathur, Anil & Moschis, George P. (1997). Targeting the Mature Market: Opportunities and Challenges. *Journal of Consumer Marketing*, 14, 282-293

Lee, J. (2018). Can a rude waiter make your food less tasty? Social class differences in thinking style and carryover in consumer judgments. *Journal of Consumer Psychology*, 28(3), 450-465.

Lee, J., Hong, J. M., & Cheong, H. J. (2020). Perfect Mothers? The Description of Mothers in Food Advertising. *Journal of Promotion Management*, 1-19.

Lee, K. H., et al. (2018). Relationship between health-related physical fitness, cognitive function and isolation in the elderly. *Journal of the Korea Convergence Society*, 9(4), 285-301.

Lee, L., & Böttger, T. M. (2017). The Therapeutic Utility of Shopping: Retail Therapy, Emotion Regulation, and Well-Being. In *The Routledge Companion to Consumer Behavior*.

Lee, L., et al. (2019). Getting creative in everyday life: Investigating arts and crafts hobbyists' information behavior. *Proceedings of the Association for Information Science and Technology*, 56(1), 703-705.

Lee, M. (2017). A Conceptual Understanding of Inconspicuous Consumption in the Luxury Business Sector. In *The essence of luxury*, 77.

Lee, M. J. (Ed.). (2000). *The consumer society reader*. Wiley-Blackwell.

Lee, M. S., & Ahn, C. S. Y. (2016). Anti-consumption, materialism, and consumer well-being. *Journal of Consumer Affairs*, 50(1), 18-47.

Lee, M., & Lee, S. (2017). Identifying new business opportunities from competitor intelligence: An integrated use of patent and trademark databases. *Technological Forecasting and Social Change*, 119, 170-183.

Lee, S. H. M. (2016). When are frugal consumers not frugal? The influence of personal networks. *Journal of Retailing and Consumer Services*, 30, 1-7.

Lee, S. L., et al. (2000). The effect of family life cycle and financial management practices on household saving patterns. *International Journal of Human Ecology*, 1(1), 79-93.

Lee, S. M., et al. (2017). When sex doesn't sell to men: mortality salience, disgust and the appeal of products and advertisements featuring sexualized women. *Motivation and emotion*, 41(4), 478-491.

Lee, S., Ito, T., Kubota, K., & Ohtake, F. (2018). Noncognitive Traits and Social Preferences Formulated by Elementary School Uniforms: Progress Report. *Journal of Behavioral Economics and Finance*, 11(Special_issue), S22-S26.

Lee, S., Park, J., & Bryan Lee, S. (2016). The interplay of Internet addiction and compulsive shopping behaviors. *Social Behavior and Personality: an international journal*, 44(11), 1901-1912.

Lee, Sun Hwa. (2012). Parental Influence on Children's Achievement from Korea: Types of Involvement, Attributions, Education, and Income. PhD dissertation, Department of Disability and Psychoeducational Studies, University of Arizona.

Leeman, Y., & Pels, T. (2006). Citizenship education in the Dutch multiethnic context. *European Education*, 38(2), 64-75.

Lees, G., Winchester, M., & De Silva, S. (2016). Demographic product segmentation in financial services products in Australia and New Zealand. *Journal of Financial Services Marketing*, 21(3), 240-250.

Leher, R., & Vittoria, P. (2016). The Commodification of Education in Brazil. In *Commodifying Education* (pp. 107-122). SensePublishers, Rotterdam.

Lei, S. S. I., Pratt, S., & Wang, D. (2017). Factors influencing customer engagement with branded content in the social network sites of integrated resorts. *Asia Pacific Journal of Tourism Research*, 22(3), 316-328.

Leiss, W., Kline, S., & Jhally, S. (2009). Two approaches to the study of advertisements. *Mass Communication Research methods*, 2, 106-128.

Leiss, W., Kline, S., Jhally, S., & Botterill, J. (2018). *Social communication in advertising: Consumption in the mediated marketplace*. Routledge.

Leiss, W., Kline, S., Jhally, S., Botterill, J., & Asquith, K. (1990). *Social communication in advertising* (Vol. 2). London: Routledge.

LeMeunier-FitzHugh, K., & Piercy, N. F. (2007). Exploring collaboration between sales and marketing. *European Journal of Marketing*, 41(7/8), 939–955.

Lemke, S. (2016). The Documentary: Barbara Ehrenreich's Nickel and Dimed and David Shipler's The Working Poor. In *Inequality, Poverty and Precarity in Contemporary American Culture* (pp. 61-84). Palgrave Macmillan, New York.

Lena, J. C. (2019). *Entitled: Discriminating tastes and the expansion of the arts*. Princeton University Press.

Lenka, U. (2016). Direct and Indirect Influence of Interpersonal and Environmental Agents on Materialism in Children. *Psychological Studies*, 61(1), 55-66.

Leone, E. C. (2019). *Are older people really happier than younger people?* (Doctoral dissertation).

Leppaniemi, M., & Karjaluoto, H. (2005). Factors influencing consumers' willingness to accept mobile advertising: a conceptual model. *International Journal of Mobile Communications*, 3(3), 197-213.

Lesakova, D. (2016). Seniors and their food shopping behavior: an empirical analysis. *Procedia-Social and Behavioral Sciences*, 220(243-250), 19th.

Leslie, C. A. (2017). Home is what you make it. *International Federation for Home Economics*, 89.

Leslie, D., & Reimer, S. (2003). Gender, modern design, and home consumption. *Environment and Planning D: Society and Space*, 21(3), 293-316.

Letkiewicz, J. C., et al. (2019). Parental Financial Socialization: Is Too Much Help Leading to Debt Ignorance among College Students? *Family and Consumer Sciences Research Journal*, 48(2), 149-164.

Lewis, C., & D'Alessandro, S. (2019). Understanding why: Push-factors that drive rural tourism amongst senior travellers. *Tourism Management Perspectives*, 32, 100574.

Lewis, R. A., & Rao, J. M. (2015). The unfavorable economics of measuring the returns to advertising. *The Quarterly Journal of Economics*, 130(4), 1941-1973.

Lewis, R. A., & Reiley, D. H. (2014). Online ads and offline sales: measuring the effect of retail advertising via a controlled experiment on Yahoo!. *Quantitative Marketing and Economics*, 12(3), 235-266.

Li, C. (2007), "Social technographics", Forrester Research Paper.

Li, Dongjin, et al. (2009). The Influence of Money Attitudes on Young Chinese Consumers Compulsive Buying. *Young Consumers* 10(2):98–109.

Li, M. (2017, November). Innovation and Guarantee Mechanism of Poverty Alleviation Model in Rural Tourism. In *2nd International Conference on Education Technology and Economic Management (ICETEM 2017)*. Atlantis Press.

Li, N. (2016). Multidimensionality of longitudinal data: Unlocking the age-happiness puzzle. *Social Indicators Research*, 128(1), 305-320.

Li, S., et al. (2019). Conceptualising and validating the social capital construct in consumer-initiated online brand communities (COBCs). *Technological Forecasting and Social Change*, 139, 303-310.

Li, Y. J., Haws, K. L., & Griskevicius, V. (2019). Parenting motivation and consumer decision-making. *Journal of Consumer Research*, 45(5), 1117-1137.

Lieberman, H. (2016). Selling sex toys: Marketing and the meaning of vibrators in early twentieth-century America. *Enterprise & Society*, 17(2), 393-433.

Lieberman, H. (2017). Intimate transactions: Sex toys and the sexual discourse of second-wave feminism. *Sexuality & Culture*, 21(1), 96-120.

Light, I., & Isralowitz, R. E. (Eds.). *Immigrant Entrepreneurs and Immigrants in the United States and Israel*. Routledge.

Lightfoot, E. B. (2019). Consumer Activism for Social Change. *Social Work*, 64(4), 301-309.

Lim, S.S., et al. (2018). Measuring human capital: a systematic analysis of 195 countries and territories, 1990–2016. *The Lancet*, 392(10154), 1217-1234.

Lin, C. H., & Shih, L. C. (2016). Effects of different packages on food product contagion: The moderating roles of mood states and product-related information. *Journal of Consumer Behaviour*, 15(2), 163-174.

Lin, C. W., et al. (2019). Investigating the development of brand loyalty in brand communities from a positive psychology perspective. *Journal of Business Research*, 99, 446-455.

Lin, C., Ma, C., Sun, Y., & Xu, Y. (2019). The Telegraph and Modern Banking Development. *Available at SSRN 3483419*.

Lin, L., et al. (2012). Do the Crime, Always Do the Time? Insights into Consumer-to-Consumer Punishment Decisions. *Journal of Consumer Research*, 40, pp. 64-77.

Lin, M., & Zhou, M. (2005). Community transformation and the formation of ethnic capital: Immigrant Chinese communities in the United States. *Journal of Chinese Overseas*, 1(2), 260-284.

Lin, Y. H., & Chen, C. Y. (2012). Adolescents' impulse buying: Susceptibility to interpersonal influence and fear of negative evaluation. *Social Behavior & Personality*, 40(3).

Lincoln, Y. S. (2018). A dangerous accountability: Neoliberalism's veer toward accountancy in higher education. In *Dissident knowledge in higher education*, 3-20.

Lindblad, A. (2019). Political branding through Facebook: A study of party branding during the Swedish general elections 2018.

Linders, A. (2017). Deconstructing Adolescence. In *International Handbook on Adolescent Health and Development* (pp. 15-28). Springer, Cham.

Lindquist, J. D. (2016). Does Social Class Influence Children's Attitudes Toward Advertising on Television and Radio and in Children's Magazines? In *Proceedings of the 1979 Academy of Marketing Science (AMS) Annual Conference* (pp. 370-370). Springer, Cham.

Lindsay, J. (2010). Healthy living guidelines and the disconnect with everyday life. *Critical Public Health*, 20(4), 475-487.

Ling, C., & Kramer, T. (2017). The Effect of Social Exclusion on Consumer Shoplifting. *ACR North American Advances*.

Lingel, J. (2017). *Digital countercultures and the struggle for community*. MIT Press.

Linn, Susan & Courtney L. Novosat (2008). Calories for Sale: Food Marketing to Children in the Twenty-First Century. *ANNALS of the American Academy of Political and Social Science* 615(1), 133-155.

Littler, J. (2011). What's wrong with ethical consumption? In Lewis, T., & Potter, E. (2013). *Ethical consumption: A critical introduction*. Routledge.

Litvin, S,W. et al. (2008). Electronic word-of-mouth in hospitality and tourism management. *Tourism Management*, 458-468

Litvin, S. W., et al. (2018). A retrospective view of electronic word-of-mouth in hospitality and tourism management. *International Journal of Contemporary Hospitality Management*.

Liu, C. Y., Miller, J., & Wang, Q. (2014). Ethnic enterprises and community development. *GeoJournal*, 79(5), 565-576.

Liu, C., & Hogg, M. K. (2017). The interplay of the desired and undesired selves in everyday consumption. In *The Routledge Companion to Consumer Behavior* (pp. 133-146). Routledge.

Liu, K., & Huang, X. (2019, February). Research on Conspicuous Consumption in Travel Behaviors of the College Students. In *2018 International Symposium on Social Science and Management Innovation (SSMI 2018)*. Atlantis Press.

Lizardo, O. (2016). Why "cultural matters" matter: Culture talk as the mobilization of cultural capital in interaction. *Poetics*, 58, 1-17.

Logan, D. (2017). Commerce, Consumerism, and Christianity in America. In *Oxford Research Encyclopedia of Religion*

Loia, D. (2019). Lights of disenchantment: a study of Max Weber's thesis on the 'disenchantment of the world'from the perspective of visual studies. *Visual Studies*, 34(2), 182-200.

Loibl, C., & Hira, T. K. (2016). Financial Issues of Women. In *Handbook of Consumer Finance Research* (pp. 195-203). Springer, Cham.

Lord, K. R., et al. (2019). Ethnic influences on attractiveness and trustworthiness perceptions of celebrity endorsers. *International Journal of Advertising*, 38(3), 489-505.

Lorenzo, Genevieve L., et al. (2010). What Is Beautiful Is Good and More Accurately Understood. *Psychological Science* 21(12):1777–82.

Lou, C., & Yuan, S. (2019). Influencer marketing: how message value and credibility affect consumer trust of branded content on social media. *Journal of Interactive Advertising*, 19(1), 58-73.

Loureiro, S. M. C., Ruediger, K. H., & Demetris, V. (2012). Brand emotional connection and loyalty. *Journal of Brand Management*, 20(1), 13-27.

Lovett, M. J., & Staelin, R. (2016). The role of paid, earned, and owned media in building entertainment brands: Reminding, informing, and enhancing enjoyment. *Marketing Science*, 35(1), 142-157.

Lua, Yan. (2009). Analysis of Culture and Buyer Behavior in Chinese Market. *Asian Culture and History* 1(1b).

Luangrath, A.W., et al. (2017). Textual paralanguage and its implications for marketing communications. *Journal of Consumer Psychology*, 27(1), 98-107.

Lubienski, C. (2007). Marketing schools: Consumer goods and competitive incentives for consumer information. *Education and Urban Society*, 40(1), 118-141.

Lubienski, C., & Lee, J. (2016). Competitive incentives and the education market: How charter schools define themselves in metropolitan Detroit. *Peabody Journal of Education*, 91(1), 64-80.

Lucal, Betsy (2016). Food and Inequalities. *Qualitative Sociology* 39(2), 217-220.

Lucas, P. J., et al. (2017). Preschool and school meal policies: an overview of what we know about regulation, implementation, and impact on diet in the UK, Sweden, and Australia. *Nutrients*, 9(7), 736.

Luedicke, M. K. (2011). Consumer acculturation theory:(crossing) conceptual boundaries. *Consumption Markets & Culture*, 14(3), 223-244.

Luedicke, M. K., et al. (2010). Consumer identity work as moral protagonism: How myth and ideology animate a brand-mediated moral conflict. *Journal of Consumer Research*, 36(6), 1016-1032.

Lumsden, K., & Morgan, H. (2017). Media framing of trolling and online abuse: silencing strategies, symbolic violence, and victim blaming. *Feminist Media Studies*, 17(6), 926-940.

Lunardo, R., & Mouangue, E. (2019). Getting over discomfort in luxury brand stores: How pop-up stores affect perceptions of luxury, embarrassment, and store evaluations. *Journal of Retailing and Consumer Services*, 49, 77-85.

Lung-Amam, W., & Gade, A. (2019). Suburbia reimagined: Asian immigration and the form and function of faith-based institutions in Silicon Valley. *Journal of Urban Design*, 24(5), 738-756.

Luo, H., Han, X., Yu, Y., & Wang, S. (2016, June). An empirical study on the effect of consumer complaints handling on consumer loyalty. In *2016 13th International Conference on Service Systems and Service Management (ICSSSM)* (pp. 1-6). IEEE.

Lury, C. (2002). *Cultural rights: Technology, legality and personality*. Routledge.

Lury, C. (2006). *Brands: The logos of the global economy*. Routledge.

Lury, C. (2008). *Consumer culture*. Rutgers University Press.

Lury, C. (2013). *Prosthetic culture*. Routledge.

Lury, C., & Moor, L. (2010). *Brand valuation and topological culture*. Peter Lang.

Lusardi, A., & Mitchell, O. S. (2011a). *Financial literacy and planning: Implications for retirement wellbeing* (No. w17078). National Bureau of Economic Research.

Lusardi, A., & Mitchell, O. S. (2011b). Financial literacy around the world: an overview. *Journal of Pension Economics & Finance*, 10(4), 497-508.

Lusk, J. L. (2017). Consumer research with big data: applications from the food demand survey (FooDS). *American Journal of Agricultural Economics*, 99(2), 303-320.

Luth (2016), Luth Research Report at https://luthresearch.com/411-marketing-men/

Lyons, S. T., et al. (2019). A dynamic social-ecological model of generational identity in the workplace. *Journal of Intergenerational Relationships*, 17(1), 1-24.

Ma, Y. C., & Cheng, S. H. (2018, March). A Study of Product Anticipant Images of the Elderly. In *KEER2018, Go Green with Emotion. 7th International Conference on Kansei Engineering & Emotion Research 2018, 19-22 March 2018, Kuching, Malaysia* (No. 146, pp. 128-132). Linköping University Electronic Press.

MacGregor, S. (Ed.). (2017). *Routledge Handbook of Gender and Environment*. London and New York: Routledge.

Machado, C. M., & Sousa, J. P. (2019). Stereotypes of Old Age. *Media Studies*, 10(20), 69-88.

Machado, J. C., et al. (2018, May). Design, personality traits and consumer responses to brand logos. Proceedings of the 13th Global Brand Conference.

Mackay, B. (2008). From life insurance to safer sex: Reflections of a marketing man. *Social Science & Medicine*, 66(10), 2168-2172.

Mackenzie, J. M. (2017 [1986]). *Propaganda and empire: The manipulation of British public opinion, 1880–1960*. New York: St. Martin's.

Maclaran, P. (2018). Judith Butler: Gender Performativity and Heterosexual Hegemony. *Canonical Authors in Consumption Theory*, 227-233.

Madigan, R., & Munro, M. (1996). 'House beautiful': Style and consumption in the home. *Sociology*, 30(1), 41-57.

Maglaty, J. (2011). When did girls start wearing pink. *Smithsonian Magazine*, 7.

Maguire, J., & K. Stanway. (2008). "Looking Good: Consumption and the Problems of Self-Production." *European Journal of Cultural Studies* 11(1):63–81.

Makela, J., & Niva, M. (2019). 9.1 Defining proper meals. *Context: The Effects of Environment on Product Design and Evaluation*, 191.

Makkar, M., & Yap, S. F. (2018). The anatomy of the inconspicuous luxury fashion experience. *Journal of Fashion Marketing and Management: An International Journal* 22(1):129-156.

Malcolm, K. (2017). *An Examination of the Influence of an Adopted Uniform Policy on Climate in an Urban Middle School* (Doctoral dissertation, Argosy University, Atlanta).

Maly, I., & Varis, P. (2016). The 21st-century hipster: On micro-populations in times of superdiversity. *European Journal of Cultural Studies*, 19(6), 637-653.

Mandeville, B. (2019). *The Fable of the Bees*. Good Press.

Mandrik, C., Bao, Y., & Wang, S. (2018). A cross-national study of intergenerational influence: US and PRC. *Journal of Consumer Marketing*.

Mann, S., et al. (2019, July). Children's Snacks, their Ads and Consumer Sovereignty. *Forum for Social Economics*, 48(3), 264-280.

Mannarini, T., & Procentese, F. (2018). Identity and immigrant Stereotypes: A study based on the ego-ecological approach. *Identity*, 18(2), 77-93.

Mansfield, P. M., Pinto, M. B., & Parente, D. H. (2003). Self-control and credit-card use among college students. *Psychological Reports*, 92(3_suppl), 1067-1078.

Manzerolle, V. (2010). Mobilizing the audience commodity: Digital labour in a wireless world. *Ephemera: theory & politics in organization*, 10(4), 455.

Manzerolle, V. R., & Kjøsen, A. M. (2012). The communication of capital: Digital media and the logic of acceleration. *tripleC: Communication, Capitalism & Critique. Open Access Journal for a Global Sustainable Information Society*, 10(2), 214-229

Manzerolle, V., & Smeltzer, S. (2011). Consumer databases, neoliberalism, and the commercial mediation of identity: A medium theory analysis. *Surveillance & Society*, 8(3), 323-337.

Marber, P., & Araya, D. (Eds.). (2017). *The Evolution of Liberal Arts in the Global Age*. Taylor & Francis.

Marcella, R., & Chowdhury, G. (2019). Eradicating information poverty: An agenda for research. *Journal of Librarianship and Information Science*, 0961000618804589.

Marcucci, O., & Elmesky, R. (2016). Roadblocks on the Way to Higher Education: Non-Dominant Cultural Capital, Race, and the "Schools are Equalizer" Myth. In *The Crisis of Race in Higher Education: A Day of Discovery and Dialogue*. Emerald Group Publishing Limited.

Marginson, S. (2006). Dynamics of national and global competition in higher education. *Higher Education*, 52(1), 1-39.

Marginson, S. (2018). Public/private in higher education: A synthesis of economic and political approaches. *Studies in Higher Education*, 43(2), 322-337.

Marginson, S. (2019). Limitations of human capital theory. *Studies in Higher Education*, 44(2), 287-301.

Margolis, K. A., et al. (2018). E-cigarette openness, curiosity, harm perceptions and advertising exposure among US middle and high school students. *Preventive Medicine*, 112, 119-125.

Mark, M., & Pearson, C. S. (2001). *The hero and the outlaw*. McGraw-Hill.

Marki, G., & Russo, J. (2019). CUSLI Experts' Roundtable Report on Canada-United States Relations-Looking Forward. *Can.-USLJ*, 43, 296.

Marks, M. J., & Wosick, K. (2017). Exploring College Men's and Women's Attitudes about Women's Sexuality and Pleasure via their Perceptions of Female Novelty Party Attendees. *Sex Roles*, 77(7-8), 550-561.

Marlatt, K. L., et al. (2016). Breakfast and fast food consumption are associated with selected biomarkers in adolescents. *Preventive Medicine Reports*, 3, 49-52

Marowits, R. (2017). Ultra low-cost airline battle heats up as Canada Jetlines prepares to launch. *Financial Post*, 14.

Marques, C. P., & Guia, A. T. B. (2018). Gender, knowledge and motivation for wine purchasing. *International Journal of Wine Business Research*.

Martens, L. (2005). Learning to consume—consuming to learn: Children at the interface between consumption and education. *British Journal of Sociology of Education*, 26(3), 343-357.

Martens, L., & Scott, S. (2017). Understanding everyday kitchen life: Looking at performance, into performances and for practices. In *Methodological reflections on practice oriented theories* (pp. 177-191). Springer, Cham.

Martens, L., et al. (2004). Bringing children (and parents) into the sociology of consumption: Towards a theoretical and empirical agenda. *Journal of Consumer Culture*, 4(2), 155-182.

Martin, T. K., Jr., et al. (2016). Do retirement planning strategies alter the effect of time preference on retirement wealth? *Applied Economics Letters*, 23(14), 1003-1005.

Martín-Santana, J. D., & Beerli-Palacio, A. (2013). Magazine advertising: Factors influencing the effectiveness of celebrity advertising. *Journal of Promotion Management*, 19(2), 139-166.

Martin, B. A., Lee, M. S. W., & Lacey, C. (2011). Countering negative country of origin effects using imagery processing. *Journal of Consumer Behaviour*, 10(2), 80-92.

Martin, C. A. (2013). Examining Children's perceptions of parent-adolescent communication quality, consumption interaction, and shopping enjoyment. *The Journal of Applied Business Research*, 29(2), 327-338.

Martin, C.L., et al. (2017). A dual identity approach for conceptualizing and measuring children's gender identity. *Child Development*, 88(1), 167-182.

Martin, C., Czellar, S., & Pandelaere, M. (2019). Age-related changes in materialism in adults–A self-uncertainty perspective. *Journal of Research in Personality*, 78, 16-24.

Martin, D., Palakshappa, N., & Woodside, A. (2019). Consumer metaphoria: Uncovering the automaticity of animal, product/brand, and country meanings. *Australasian Marketing Journal (AMJ)*, 27(2), 113-125.

Martin, K., & Hill, R. (2011). Life Satisfaction, Self-Determination, and Consumption Adequacy at the Bottom of the Pyramid. *Journal of Consumer Research, 38*, pp. 1155-1168.

Martin, M. (2007). A literature review on the effectiveness of financial education. Federal Reserve Bank of Richmond.

Martin, W. J. (2017). *The global information society*. Taylor & Francis.

Martínez, A. N. G. (2016). The Two Faces of Consumerism: When Things Make Us (In) Human. In *Being Human in a Consumer Society* (pp. 87-104). Routledge.

Marumo, O., & Mabuza, M. L. (2018). Determinants of urban consumers' participation in informal vegetable markets: Evidence from Mahikeng, North West province, South Africa, and implications for policy. *South African Journal of Economic and Management Sciences*, 21(1), 1-9.

Maruna, S., & Copes, H. (2017). Techniques of Neutralization: A Theory of Its Time and Ahead of Its Time. In *Delinquency and Drift Revisited, Volume 21* (pp. 43-58). Routledge.

Marwick, A. E. (2010). *Status update: Celebrity, publicity and self-branding in Web 2.0*. (Doctoral dissertation, New York University).

Mastandrea, S., Wagoner, J. A., & Hogg, M. A. (2019). Liking for abstract and representational art: National identity as an art appreciation heuristic. *Psychology of Aesthetics, Creativity, and the Arts*. Advance online publication. https://doi.org/10.1037/aca0000272

Mathwick, C., et al. (2001). Experiential value: conceptualization, measurement and application in the catalog and Internet shopping environment. *Journal of retailing*, 77(1), 39-56.

Matzler, K., et al. (2016). Brand personality and culture: The role of cultural differences on the impact of brand personality perceptions on tourists' visit intentions. *Tourism Management*, 52, 507-520.

Maulana, I. (2019). Big Brothers Are Seducing You: Consumerism, Surveillance, and the Agency of Consumers. In *Handbook of Research on Consumption, Media, and Popular Culture in the Global Age* (pp. 57-75). IGI Global.

Mavisakalyan, A. (2018). Do employers reward physical attractiveness in transition countries? *Economics & Human Biology*, 28, 38-52.

Mawhinney, T., & Kochkina, S. (2019). Is the Medium the Message? Examining Transactions Conducted via Text in Comparison with Traditional Virtual Reference Methods. *Journal of Library & Information Services in Distance Learning*, 13(1-2), 56-73.

Mazur, E., et al. (2019). The internet behavior of older adults. In *Advanced Methodologies and Technologies in Media and Communications* (pp. 405-416). IGI Global.

McCartney, D. M., & Metcalfe, A. S. (2018). Corporatization of higher education through internationalization: The emergence of pathway colleges in Canada. *Tertiary Education and Management*, 24(3), 206-220.

McClintock, A. (1995). *Imperial leather*. New York: Routledge.

McCluskey, J. J., et al. (2016). Media coverage, public perceptions, and consumer behavior: Insights from new food technologies. *Annual Review of Resource Economics*, 8, 467-486.

McCormick, M. (2009). The effectiveness of youth financial education: A review of the literature. *Journal of Financial Planning and Counselling* 20 (1): 70-83.

McCullough, H. E. (2018). Identity Discounts. PhD diss., University of Tennessee.

McEachern, M. (2019). Pursuing social & ethical capital in the alternative food marketplace. http://usir.salford.ac.uk/id/eprint/40177.

McGregor, S. L. (2008). Conceptualizing immoral and unethical consumption using neutralization theory. *Family and Consumer Sciences Research Journal*, 36(3), 261-276.

McGregor, S. L. (2016). Framing consumer education conceptual innovations as consumer activism. *International Journal of Consumer Studies*, 40(1), 35-47.

McGuigan, L., & Manzerolle, V. (2015). "All the world's a shopping cart": Theorizing the political economy of ubiquitous media and markets. *New Media & Society*, 17(11), 1830-1848.

McKanan, D. (2017). *Eco-alchemy: Anthroposophy and the History and Future of Environmentalism*. Univ. of California Press.

McKendrick, N., J. Brewer and J.H. Plumb (eds.). (1982). *The Birth of Consumer Society*. London: Europa.

McKenzie, H. J., & McKay, F. H. (2017). Food as a discretionary item: The impact of welfare payment changes on low-income single mother's food choices and strategies. *Journal of Poverty and Social Justice*, 25(1), 35-48.

McKenzie, J. S., & Watts, D. (2020). "Things like tinned burgers and tinned macaroni, I ate as a kid—I would not look at it twice!" Understanding changing eating practices across the lifecourse. *Food, Culture & Society*, 23(1), 66-85.

McLuhan, M. (1964). *Understanding media: The extensions of man*. New York: McGraw-Hill.

McMahan, E. A., et al. (2016). Some implications of believing that happiness involves the absence of pain: Negative hedonic beliefs exacerbate the effects of stress on well-being. *Journal of Happiness Studies*, 17(6), 2569-2593.

McMurtrey, M. E., et al. (2011). Seniors and technology: Results from a field study. *Journal of Computer Information Systems*, 51(4), 22-30.

McNeill, L. S., & Douglas, K. (2011). Retailing masculinity: Gender expectations and social image of male grooming products in New Zealand. *Journal of Retailing and Consumer Services*, 18(5), 448-454.

McPherson, M. S., & Purcell, F. B. (2018). The Future of American Undergraduate Education. *International Higher Education*, (95), 33-34.

McQuarrie, E. & Miller, J., & Phillips, B. (2012). The Megaphone Effect: Taste and Audience in Fashion Blogging. *Journal of Consumer Research, 40*, pp. 136-158.

Mead, G. H. (1934). *Mind, self and society* (Vol. 111). University of Chicago Press.: Chicago.

Mead, W. E. (2019). *The English medieval feast* (Vol. 35). Routledge.

Meadows, D. H., et al. (1972). *The limits to growth*. New York: Potomac Books.

Meadows, D., et al. (2004). *Limits to growth: The 30-year update*. Chelsea Green Publishing.

Meek, M. (2017). Lolita Speaks: Disrupting Nabokov's "Aesthetic Bliss." *Girlhood Studies*, *10*(3), 152-167.

Meer, N. (Ed.). (2016). *Multiculturalism and interculturalism: Debating the dividing lines*. Edinburgh University Press.

Meesala, A., & Paul, J. (2018). Service quality, consumer satisfaction and loyalty in hospitals: Thinking for the future. *Journal of Retailing and Consumer Services, 40,* 261-269.

Mehta, R., & Belk, R. W. (1991). Artifacts, identity, and transition: Favorite possessions of Indians and Indian immigrants to the United States. *Journal of consumer Research*, *17*(4), 398-411.

Melbye, E. L., et al. (2016). Adolescent impulsivity and soft drink consumption: The role of parental regulation. *Appetite*, *96*, 432-442.

Melnyk, V., et al. (2009). Are women more loyal customers than men? Gender differences in loyalty to firms and individual service providers. *Journal of Marketing*, *73*(4), 82-96.

Mennell, S. (1996). *All manners of food: eating and taste in England and France from the Middle Ages to the present*. University of Illinois Press.

Merleaux, A. (2015). *Sugar and Civilization: American Empire and the Cultural Politics of Sweetness*. UNC Press Books.

Messerschmidt, J. W. (2019). The salience of "hegemonic masculinity". *Men and masculinities*, *22*(1), 85-91.

Messerschmidt, J. W., & Messner, M. A. (2018). Hegemonic, nonhegemonic, and "new" masculinities. *Gender reckonings: New social theory and research*, 35-56.

Metro-Roland, M. M. (2016). *Tourists, signs and the city: The semiotics of culture in an urban landscape*. Routledge.

Meyrowitz, J. (2019). Medium theory. *The International Encyclopedia of Media Literacy*, 1-7.

Mhurchu, C. N., et al. (2013). Food prices and consumer demand: differences across income levels and ethnic groups. *PloS one*, *8*(10), e75934.

Mihailidis, P., & Viotty, S. (2017). Spreadable spectacle in digital culture: Civic expression, fake news, and the role of media literacies in "post-fact" society. *American behavioral scientist*, *61*(4), 441-454.

Mikeska, J., et al. (2017). A meta-analysis of parental style and consumer socialization of children. *Journal of Consumer Psychology*, *27*(2), 245-256.

Mikkonen, J., & Raphael, D. (2010). *Social determinants of health: The Canadian facts*. Toronto: York University School of Health Policy and Management.

Millan, E., & Wright, L. T. (2018). Gender effects on consumers' symbolic and hedonic preferences and actual clothing consumption in the Czech Republic. *International journal of Consumer Studies*, *42*(5), 478-488.

Millard, Jennifer. 2009. "Performing Beauty: Dove's "Real Beauty" Campaign." *Symbolic Interaction* 32(2):146-168.

Miller, D. (1987). *Material culture and mass consumerism*. Oxford: Basil Blackwell.

Miller, D. (1995). *Unwrapping Christmas*. Oxford University Press

Miller, D. (2008). So, what's wrong with consumerism? *RSA Journal*, *154*(5534), 44-47.

Miller, D. (2017). Christmas: An anthropological lens. *Journal of Ethnographic Theory*, *7*(3), 409-442.

Miller, D. L. (2017). Gender and performance capital among local musicians. *Qualitative Sociology*, *40*(3), 263-286.

Miller, D., & Slater, D. (2001). *The Internet: an ethnographic approach*. Oxford: Berg.

Miller, H. (2018). Veblen online: information and the risk of commandeering the conspicuous self. *Information Research: An International Electronic Journal*, *23*(3), n3.

Miller, T. (2017). *Greenwashing culture*. Routledge.

Mills, C. W. (1981 [1956]). *The power elite*. New York.

Min, P. G. (2017). Korean Immigrants in Los Angeles 1. In *Immigration and Entrepreneurship* (pp. 185-204). Routledge.

Minahan, Stella and Patricia Huddleston. 2010. "Shopping with Mum—Mother and Daughter Consumer Socialization." *Young Consumers* 11(3):170-77.

Minchin, C., & Alpert, F. (2017). Realising Drucker and Kotler's Vision for a Strategic Marketing Department. *Available at SSRN 3069972*.

Minocher, X. (2019). Online consumer activism: Challenging companies with Change. org. *New Media & Society*, *21*(3), 620-638.

Minogue, S. (2017, March 1) 'Inadequate and unsafe' Inuit housing needs national fix, say senators. CBC North.

Mintz, S. W. (1974). *Worker in the cane: a Puerto Rican life history* (Vol. 2). New York: W.W. Norton & Company.

Mintz, S.W. (1986). *Sweetness and power: The place of sugar in modern history*. Penguin.

Mintz, S.W. (2010). *Three ancient colonies: Caribbean themes and variations* (Vol. 8). Harvard University Press.

Mishra, A., et al. (2018). Adolescent's eWOM intentions: An investigation into the roles of peers, the Internet and gender. *Journal of Business Research*, *86*, 394-405.

Mishra, H., et al. (2013). Influence of motivated reasoning on saving and spending decisions. *Organizational Behavior and Human Decision Processes*, *121*(1), 13-23.

Mitchell, A. (1983). *The nine American lifestyles: Who we are and where we're going*. New York: Scribner.

Mitchell, B., & Lucas, J. R. (2017). *An Engagement with Plato's Republic: A companion to the Republic*. Routledge.

Mitchell, E. V. (2019). *Self, Style, and Service: A Qualitative Study of Gender, Labor, and Embodied Cultural Capital in the Tattoo Industry*. M.A. thesis, University of North Carolina, Chapel Hill.

Mitra, A. (2016). The trans-Indian: Perspectives on real vs. virtual identity in the age of the Internet. In *Indian Transnationalism Online* (pp. 67-81). Routledge.

Mittal, B. (2016). Psychographics of comparison shoppers. *Journal of Consumer Marketing*.

Moav, O., & Neeman, Z. (2010). Saving Rates and Poverty: The Role of Conspicuous Consumption and Human Capital. *The Economic Journal* 122(563), 37.

Möbius, M. M. and T. S. Rosenblat. (2006). Why Beauty Matters. *American Economic Review* 96(1): 222–35.

Mocan, N. H., & Tekin, E. (2006). Catholic schools and bad behavior: A propensity score matching analysis. *The BE Journal of Economic Analysis & Policy*, *5*(1).

Mohamedbhai, G. (2008). The contribution of higher education to the millennium development goals. 4th International Barcelona Conference on Higher Education.

Moisander, J. (2007). Motivational complexity of green consumerism. *International Journal of Consumer Studies*, *31*(4), 404-409.

Moisio, R., Arnould, R. & Gentry, J. (2013). Productive Consumption in the Class-Mediated Construction of Domestic Masculinity: Do-It-Yourself (DIY) Home Improvement in Men's Identity Work. *Journal of Consumer Research, 40,* 298-316.

Mokhlis, Safiek. (2016). "Shopping Styles of Female Consumers In A Developing Country." *Actual Problems of Economics* 9(183): 250-257.

Mollick, E. (2014). The dynamics of crowdfunding: An exploratory study. *Journal of Business Venturing*, *29*(1), 1-16.

Monroe, J. S. (2016). Sharing subscriptions is pirating?! Millenials and ethical behaviors. Bachelor of science undergraduate thesis, University of Arizona. https://repository.arizona.edu/handle/10150/613292.

Montgomerie, J. (Ed.). (2017). *Critical methods in political and cultural economy*. Routledge.

Moon, T. H. (2016). Evolution of Limits to Growth Studies and its Implications on Concept and Strategy of Sustainable Development. *Korean System Dynamics Review*, *17*(2), 5-32.

Moore, R. (2019). Digital Reproducibility and the Culture Industry: Popular Music and the Adorno-Benjamin Debate. *Fast Capitalism*, *9*(1).

Moore, R. L., & Moschis, G. P. (1978). Teenagers' reactions to advertising. *Journal of Advertising*, *7*(4), 24-30.

Moore, S. N., Murphy, S., & Moore, L. (2011). Health improvement, nutrition-related behaviour and the role of school meals: the usefulness of a socio-ecological perspective to inform policy design, implementation and evaluation. *Critical Public Health*, *21*(4), 441-454.

Morgan, G. (2016). Transnational governance: the role of communities, networks and private actors. *RAE*, *56*(4), 459-460.

Morgan, K. (1991). Women and the Knife: Cosmetic Surgery and the Colonization of Women's Bodies. *Hypatia, 6(3)*, pp. 25-53.

Morgan, N.A., et al. (2019). Research in marketing strategy. *Journal of the Academy of Marketing Science*, *47*(1), 4-29.

Morgan, S.L., & Sørensen, A. B. (1999). Parental networks, social closure, and mathematics learning: A test of Coleman's social capital explanation of school effects. *American Sociological Review*, 661-681.

Moritz, A., & Block, J. H. (2016). Crowdfunding: A literature review and research directions. In *Crowdfunding in Europe* (pp. 25-53). Springer, Cham.

Moro, S., Pires, G., Rita, P., & Cortez, P. (2018). A cross-cultural case study of consumers' communications about a new technological product. *Journal of Business Research*. [Advanced online publication on 16 August 2018; print publication, *Journal of Business Research*, 121(December 2020), 438-447.]

Moschis, G. P. (1979). Formal consumer education: An empirical assessment. *ACR North American Advances*.

Moschis, G. P. (2017). Research frontiers on the dark side of consumer behaviour: The case of materialism and compulsive buying. *Journal of Marketing Management*, *33*(15-16), 1384-1401.

Moschis, G. P. (2017). The Aging Marketplace: Implications for Food Marketers. In *Food for the Aging Population* (pp. 269-281). Woodhead Publishing.

Moschis, G. P. (2019). *Consumer Behavior over the Life Course Research Frontiers and New Directions*. Springer Nature.

Moschis, G. P. (2019). Contributions to Previous Efforts to Study Consumers over Their Life Span. In *Consumer Behavior over the Life Course* (pp. 133-145). Springer, Cham.

Moschis, G. P., & Moore, R. L. (1978). An analysis of the acquisition of some consumer competencies among adolescents. *Journal of Consumer Affairs*, *12*(2), 277-291.

Moschis, G. P., & Churchill, G. (1978). Consumer Socialization: A theoretical and Empirical Analysis. *Journal of Marketing Research, 15(1)*, pp. 599-609.

Mulvey, L. (1975, 1 October). Visual pleasure and narrative cinema. *Screen* 16(3): 6–18.

Mumper, M. & Freeman, M. L. (2011). The continuing paradox of public college tuition inflation. In *The states and public higher education policy: Affordability, access, and accountability*, pp. 37-60.

Mumper, M., & Freeman, M. L. (2005). The causes and consequences of public college tuition inflation. In *Higher education: Handbook of theory and research* (pp. 307-361). Springer, Dordrecht.

Muñiz-Velázquez, J. A., Gomez-Baya, D., & Lopez-Casquete, M. (2017). Implicit and explicit assessment of materialism: Associations with happiness and depression. *Personality and Individual Differences*, *116*, 123-132.

Muniz, Albert., and Thomas O'Guinn. (2001). Brand Community. *Journal of Consumer Research* 27(4): 412-32

Munnukka, J., Karjaluoto, H., & Tikkanen, A. (2015). Are Facebook brand community members truly loyal to the brand?. *Computers in Human Behavior*, *51*, 429-439.

Murdock, G. P. (1949). *Social structure*. Glencoe, Ill.: Free Press

Murray, D. C. (2020). Selfie consumerism in a narcissistic age. *Consumption Markets & Culture*, *23*(1), 21-43.

Musiał, M. (2019). Disenchanting and Re-enchanting in Modernity. In *Enchanting Robots* (pp. 115-140). Palgrave Macmillan, Cham.

Muyeba, S. (2019). Institutional capital, urban poverty and household wealth in Cape Town. *World Development Perspectives*, *16*, 100139.

Myers, D. G. (2000). The funds, friends, and faith of happy people. *American Psychologist*, *55*(1), 56.

Nabi, N., O'Cass, A., & Siahtiri, V. (2019). Status consumption in newly emerging countries: the influence of personality traits and the mediating role of motivation to consume conspicuously. *Journal of Retailing and Consumer Services, 46*, 173-178.

Nabi, N., Siahtiri, V., & O'Cass, A. (2019). In search of status: Unpacking the relationship of status with individualism-collectivism, counterconformity motivations and life satisfaction. *Journal of Retailing and Consumer Services, 51*, 378-386.

Nadler, A., & McGuigan, L. (2016). Captains of Habit Formation. *Explorations in Critical Studies of Advertising*, 124.

Nash, C. (2009). *The parent child purchase relationship*. M.A. thesis, Technological University Dublin.

Naumov, N. (2016). Cultural Tourism. *European Journal of Tourism, Hospitality and Recreation, 7*(1), 72-73.

Nava, M. (1997) Women, the city and the department store. In Falk, P. and Campbell, C. (eds.), *The Shopping Experience*. London: Sage.

Nayak, A. (2016). *Race, place and globalization: Youth cultures in a changing world*. Bloomsbury Publishing.

Neale, L., Robbie, R., & Martin, B. (2016). Gender identity and brand incongruence: When in doubt, pursue masculinity. *Journal of Strategic Marketing, 24*(5), 347-359.

Neeley, S. M., & Coffey, T. (2007). Understanding the "four-eyed, four-legged" consumer: a segmentation analysis of US moms. *Journal of Marketing Theory and Practice, 15*(3), 251-261.

Neirotti, P., Raguseo, E., & Paolucci, E. (2016). Are customers' reviews creating value in the hospitality industry? Exploring the moderating effects of market positioning. *International Journal of Information Management, 36*(6), 1133-1143.

Nesset, E., Nervik, B., & Helgesen, Ø. (2011). Satisfaction and image as mediators of store loyalty drivers in grocery retailing. *The International Review of Retail, Distribution and Consumer Research, 21*(3), 267-292.

Netburn, D. (2016, 24 August). The aging paradox: The older we get, the happier we are. *Los Angeles Times*.

Netemeyer, R.G., et al. (2016). Graphic health warnings on cigarette packages: the role of emotions in affecting adolescent smoking consideration and secondhand smoke beliefs. *Journal of Public Policy & Marketing, 35*(1), 124-143.

Ni Mhurchu, C., et al. (2013). Monitoring the availability of healthy and unhealthy foods and non-alcoholic beverages in community and consumer retail food environments globally. *Obesity reviews, 14*, 108-119.

Nia, A., & Lynne Zaichkowsky, J. (2000). Do counterfeits devalue the ownership of luxury brands? *Journal of Product & Brand Management, 9*(7), 485-49

Nichols, B. S., Raska, D., & Flint, D. J. (2015). Effects of consumer embarrassment on shopping basket size and value: A study of the millennial consumer. *Journal of Consumer Behaviour, 14*(1), 41-56.

Nimrod, G. (2010). Seniors' online communities: A quantitative content analysis. *The Gerontologist, 50*(3), 382-392.

Nind, M., & Hewett, D. (2018). When age-appropriateness isn't appropriate. In *Whose Choice?* (pp. 48-57). Routledge.

Nishimura, M., & Sasao, T. (Eds.). (2018). *Doing Liberal Arts Education: The Global Case Studies*. Springer.

Nixon, J. (2020). Hannah Arendt (1906–1975): Embodying a Promise in the University. In *Philosophers on the University* (pp. 83-94). Springer, Cham.

Noble, G., & Ang, I. (2018). Ethnicity and cultural consumption in Australia. *Continuum, 32*(3), 296-307.

Noonan, H. W. (2019). *Personal identity*. Routledge.

Norberg, M. M., et al. (2020). Determinants of object choice and object attachment: Compensatory consumption in compulsive buying–shopping disorder and hoarding disorder. *Journal of Behavioral Addictions*, 1-10.

Nunan, D., & Di Domenico, M. (2019). Older consumers, digital marketing, and public policy: A review and research agenda. *Journal of Public Policy & Marketing, 38*(4), 469-483.

Nye, J. S., Jr. (2003). *The paradox of American power: Why the world's only superpower can't go it alone*. Oxford University Press.

Nyhus, E. K., & Webley, P. (2005, September). The inter-generational transmission of future orientation and saving preferences. In *IAREP Conference Proceedings*.

O'Brien, D., et al. (2017). Producing and consuming inequality: A cultural sociology of the cultural industries.

O'Keefe, D. J. (2018). Message pretesting using assessments of expected or perceived persuasiveness: Evidence about diagnosticity of relative actual persuasiveness. *Journal of Communication, 68*(1), 120-142.

O'Neill, R. (2015). Whither critical masculinity studies? Notes on inclusive masculinity theory, postfeminism, and sexual politics. *Men and Masculinities, 18*(1), 100-120.

O'Shea, S. (2016). Avoiding the manufacture of 'sameness': First-in-family students, cultural capital and the higher education environment. *Higher Education, 72*(1), 59-78.

Oakley, A. (1974). *Housewife*. London: Allen Lane.

Oakley, A. (2018 [1970]). *The sociology of housework*. Policy Press.

Odgers, Candice L., Sachiko Donley, Avshalom Caspi, Christopher J. Bates, and Terrie E. Moffitt. 2015. "Living alongside More Affluent Neighbors Predicts Greater Involvement in Antisocial Behavior among Low-Income Boys." *Journal of Child Psychology and Psychiatry* 56(10):1055–64.

Ogle, J. P., & Damhorst, M. L. (2003). Mothers and daughters: Interpersonal approaches to body and dieting. *Journal of Family Issues, 24*(4), 448-487.

Ogle, J. P., & Park, J. (2018). Maternal Experiences of Parenting Girls who are Perceived as Overweight or at Risk for Becoming So: Narratives of Uncertainty, Ambivalence and Struggle. *Children & Society, 32*(4), 325-340.

Ogle, J. P., Reddy-Best, K., & Park, J. (2017). Socializing girls whose bodies may not align with contemporary ideals of thinness: An interpretive study of US mothers' accounts. *Body image, 23*, 13-27.

Ognyanova, K., Foucault-Wells, B., & Gonzalez-Bailon, S. (2018). Rebooting mass communication: Using computational and network tools to rebuild media theory. *The Oxford handbook of networked communication*.

Ojo, T. H., & Shizha, E. (2018). Ethnic Enclaves in Canada: Opportunities and Challenges of Residing Within. In *Living beyond borders: Essays on global immigrants and refugees* (pp.162-179). New York: Peter Lang.

Okrent, A. M., & Kumcu, A. (2016). *US households' demand for convenience foods* (No. 1477-2017-3961).

Okun, S., & Nimrod, G. (2019). Online religious communities and wellbeing in later life. *Journal of Religion, Spirituality & Aging*, 1-20.

Oleschuk, M. (2017). Foodies of color: Authenticity and exoticism in omnivorous food culture. *Cultural Sociology, 11*(2), 217-233.

Oleschuk, M., et al. (2019, June). Maintaining meat: Cultural repertoires and the meat paradox in a diverse sociocultural context. In *Sociological Forum, 34*(2), 337-360.

Ollier-Malaterre, A., Jacobs, J. A., & Rothbard, N. P. (2019). Technology, work, and family: Digital cultural capital and boundary management. *Annual Review of Sociology, 45*

Olsen, J. (2016, February). Melting Pot or Blended Wine: Does Ethnicity Still Matter in Understanding Consumer Wine Behavior?. In *9th Academy of Wine Business Research Conference* (p. 163).

Olson, J., & Rick, S. (2013). A penny saved is a partner earned: The romantic appeal of savers. *SSRN Electronic Journal*.

Opatrny, M. (2018). *Extent of Irrationality of the Consumer: Combining the Critical Cost Eciency and Houtman Maks Indices* (No. 11/2018). IES Working Paper.

Oppenheim, F. E. (2018). Egalitarianism as a descriptive concept. In *The Notion of Equality* (pp. 27-36). Routledge.

Ossewaarde-Lowtoo, R. (2020). Rousseau's Antidote to Egoism. *The European Legacy, 25*(1), 20-37.

Oswald, Laura. R. (1999). Culture swapping: Consumption and the ethnogenesis of middle-class Haitian immigrants. *Journal of Consumer Research, 25*(4), 303-318.

Otnes, C. (2017). Mind, Self and Consumption: George Herbert Mead. In *Canonical Authors in Consumption Theory* (pp. 113-119). Routledge.

Otoo, F. E., & Kim, S. (2020). Analysis of studies on the travel motivations of senior tourists from 1980 to 2017: progress and future directions. *Current Issues in Tourism, 23*(4), 393-417.

Ott, B. L., & Mack, R. L. (2020). *Critical media studies*. John Wiley & Sons.

Paavilainen, H., Ahde-Deal, P., & Koskinen, I. (2017). Dwelling with design. *The Design Journal, 20*(1), 13-27.

Packard, V. (1957). *The hidden persuaders*. New York: McKay.

Page, A. (2017). "How many slaves work for you?" Race, new media, and neoliberal consumer activism. *Journal of Consumer Culture, 17*(1), 46-61.

Page, B., et al. (2019). Using the eyberg child behaviour inventory to investigate pester power. *Journal of Retailing and Consumer Services, 47*, 265-271.

Page, Christine, and Nancy Ridgway. (2001). "The impact of consumer environments on consumption patterns of children from disparate socioeconomic background." *Journal of Consumer Marketing* 18(1), 21-40

Palfreyman, Z., et al. (2015). Parental modelling of eating behaviours: Observational validation of the parental modelling of eating behaviours scale (PARM). *Appetite, 86*, 31-37.

Palmatier, R. W. (2018). Advancing marketing strategy research. *Journal of the Academy of Marketing Science, 46*, 983–986.

Panitch, L., & Leys, C. (Eds.). (2006). *Coming to terms with nature: Socialist register 2007*. New York: NYU Press.

Panwar, Diksha & Patra, Sidheswar. (2017). Localization in Fast Food Industry: A Case Study on McDonald's Strategy in India. *Researcher's World* 8(3), 70-74.

Papadimitriou, D., et al. (2019). The brand personality of professional football teams. *Sport, Business and Management: An International Journal*.

Pappas, I. O., et al. (2017). The interplay of online shopping motivations and experiential factors on personalized e-commerce: A complexity theory approach. *Telematics and Informatics, 34*(5), 730-742.

Paradeise, C., & Thoenig, J. C. (2013). Academic institutions in search of quality: Local orders and global standards. *Organization Studies, 34*(2), 189-218.

Paredes, C. L. (2016). The consumption of out-of-home highbrow leisure by ethnicity and national origin: attendance at museums and live theatres in Houston. *Ethnic and Racial Studies, 39*(7), 1150-1169.

Parisi, D. (2017, October 18). Older consumers just as likely to shop luxury online as millennials. Luxury daily. Retrieved from https://www.luxurydaily.com/older-consumers-just-as-likely-to-shop-luxury-online-as-millennials/.

Parsons, E., Maclaran, P., & Chatzidakis, A. (2017). *Contemporary issues in marketing and consumer behaviour*. Routledge.

Pascual-Miguel, F. J., et al. (2015). Influences of gender and product type on online purchasing. *Journal of Business Research, 68*(7), 1550-1556.

Passell, P., et al. (1976). Economists on the Doomsday Models: A Review of *The Limits to Growth* by Donella H. Meadows et al., and *World Dynamics and Urban Dynamics*, by Jay W. Forrester (pp. 166-173). In *The Economic Approach to Public Policy: Selected Readings*, R. Amacher et al. (eds.). Ithaca, NY: Cornell University

Paterson, M. (2017). *Consumption and everyday life*. Routledge.

Patwardhan, P., Habib, S., & Patwardhan, H. (2019). Managing Change and Finding Identity: A Grounded Analysis of Advertising Agency Leadership. *Journal of Current Issues & Research in Advertising, 40*(3), 315-333.

Pavlou, P. A., & Stewart, D. W. (2000). Measuring the effects and effectiveness of interactive advertising: A research agenda. *Journal of Interactive Advertising, 1*(1), 61-77.

Paxson, P. (2018). *Mass communications and media studies: An introduction*. Bloomsbury Publishing USA.

Pearson, C. S. (2017). Heroic organizations and institutions as secular temples: A personal outlook. *Journal of Genius and Eminence, 2*(2), 126-132.

Pechmann, C., et al. (2005). Impulsive and self-conscious: Adolescents' vulnerability to advertising and promotion. *Journal of Public Policy & Marketing, 24*(2), 202-221.

Peguero, A. A., et al. (2017). Social bonds across immigrant generations: Bonding to school and examining the relevance of assimilation. *Youth & Society, 49*(6), 733-754.

Pelet, J. É., et al. (2017). Don't believe the hype: a grounded exploratory six country wine purchasing study. *Journal of Wine Research, 28*(2), 91-104.

Peluchette, J. V. E., & Karl, K. (2018). 'She's got the look': Examining feminine and provocative dress in the workplace. In *Research Handbook of Diversity and Careers.* Edward Elgar Publishing.

Peluchette, J. V., & Karl, K. (2007). The impact of workplace attire on employee self-perceptions. *Human Resource Development Quarterly, 18*(3), 345-360.

Peluchette, J. V., Karl, K., & Rust, K. (2006). Dressing to impress: Beliefs and attitudes regarding workplace attire. *Journal of Business and Psychology, 21*(1), 45-63.

Peñaloza, L., & Gilly, M. C. (1999). Marketer acculturation: The changer and the changed. *Journal of Marketing, 63*(3), 84-104.

Peñaloza, L., & Price, L. L. (1993). Consumer resistance: a conceptual overview. *ACR North American Advances.*

Percy, L. (2016). *Strategic advertising management.* Oxford University Press.

Pereira, S., & E. Ayrosa. (2012). Between Two Worlds: An Ethnographic Study of Gay Consumer Culture in Rio De Janeiro. *BAR-Brazilian Administration Review* 9(2): 211-228.

Perez, M.E., et al. (2010). Constructing identity through the consumption of counterfeit luxury goods. *Qualitative Market Research, 13*(3), 219-235.

Peris, T. S., & Schneider, B. N. (2017). Obsessive–Compulsive Disorder. In *Clinical Handbook of Psychological Disorders in Children and Adolescents: A Step-by-Step Treatment Manual.*

Perreault, S. 2015. Criminal victimization in Canada, 2014. *Juristat.* Statistics Canada Catalogue no. 85-002-X

Perry, M. (2017). Luxury Lodges New Zealand and prospects for elegant disruption. In *Sustainable Luxury* (pp. 110-129). Routledge.

Perry, P., Barnes, L., & Ye, T. (2020). The Evolution of the Chinese Luxury Fashion Consumer: An Interpretive Study of Luxury Value Perceptions. In *Understanding Luxury Fashion* (pp. 175-202). Palgrave Macmillan, Cham.

Peter, B., & Williams, J. (2019). One Foot in the Rave: Aging Ravers' Transitions to Adulthood and Their Participation in Rave Culture. *Leisure Sciences,* 1-19.

Peterson, G. (2017). An Ecological Application of Kleinian Theory to Political and Social Discourses as a Means to Extend Ecological Modernization Discourse. Chapman University Digital Commons. https://digitalcommons.chapman.edu/cgi/viewcontent.cgi?article=1233&context=cusrd_abstracts.

Peterson, R. (2018). Fed Up with the Personal Responsibility Narrative of Obesity: A Pentadic Analysis. *Kentucky Journal of Communication, 37*(2).

Peterson, R. A. (2005). Problems in comparative research: The example of omnivorousness. *Poetics, 33*(5-6), 257-282.

Peterson, R.A. (1992) Understanding Audience Segmentation: From Elite and Mass to Omnivore and Univore. *Poetics* 21(4): 243–58.

Petery, G., et al. (2019). Age stereotypes and subjective age: Influences and indicators of successful aging? In *34th Annual Conference of the Society for Industrial-Organizational Psychology.*

Petry, N. M., Zajac, K., & Ginley, M. K. (2018). Behavioral addictions as mental disorders: to be or not to be? *Annual review of clinical psychology, 14*, 399-423.

Pettersson, A., et al. (2004). Family life in grocery stores: A study of interaction between adults and children. *International Journal of Consumer Studies, 28*(4), 317-328.

Pettigrew, S., Mizerski, K., & Donovan, R. (2005). The three "big issues" for older supermarket shoppers. *Journal of Consumer Marketing.*

Pettigrew, S., Worrall, C., Biagioni, N., Talati, Z., & Jongenelis, M. (2017). The role of food shopping in later life. *Appetite, 111,* 71-78.

Peyer, M., Balderjahn, I., Seegebarth, B., & Klemm, A. (2017). The role of sustainability in profiling voluntary simplifiers. *Journal of Business Research, 70,* 37-43.

Pham, T. H., Yap, K., & Dowling, N. A. (2012). The impact of financial management practices and financial attitudes on the relationship between materialism and compulsive buying. *Journal of Economic Psychology, 33*(3), 461-470.

Phan, Ly. (2016). Measuring Women's Empowerment at Household Level Using DHS Data of Four Southeast Asian Countries. *Social Indicators Research* 126, 359–378.

Phau, I., & Teah, M. (2009). Devil wears (counterfeit) Prada: a study of antecedents and outcomes of attitudes towards counterfeits of luxury brands. *Journal of Consumer Marketing, 26*(1), 15-27.

Phau, I., et al. (2016). Looking beyond pasta and pizzas: Examining personal and historical nostalgia as travel motives. *International Journal of Culture, Tourism and Hospitality Research.*

Phelps, J. E., et al. (2004). Viral marketing or electronic word-of-mouth advertising: Examining consumer responses and motivations to pass along email. *Journal of advertising research, 44*(4), 333-348.

Phelps, N. A. (2017). *Interplaces: an economic geography of the inter-urban and international economies.* Oxford University Press.

Phua, P., et al. (2020). Examining older consumers' loyalty towards older brands in grocery retailing. *Journal of Retailing and Consumer Services, 52.*

Pich, C., & Newman, B. I. (2019). Evolution of Political Branding: Typologies, Diverse Settings and Future Research. *Journal of Political Marketing,* 1-12.

Pierce, J. P., & Gilpin, E. A. (1995). A historical analysis of tobacco marketing and the uptake of smoking by youth in the United States: 1890–1977. *Health Psychology, 14*(6), 500.

Pierce, J. P., et al. (1991). Does tobacco advertising target young people to start smoking?: evidence from California. *JAMA, 266*(22), 3154-3158.

Pieterse, J. N. (2019). *Globalization and culture: Global mélange.* Rowman & Littlefield.

Pike, A. (2016). Brands and branding. In *International Encyclopedia of Geography: People, the Earth, Environment and Technology: People, the Earth, Environment and Technology,* 1-11.

Pila, E., et al. (2020). Fitness-and appearance-related self-conscious emotions and sport experiences: A prospective longitudinal investigation among adolescent girls. *Psychology of Sport and Exercise, 47,* 101641.

Pilcher, J. M. (2017). *Food in world history.* Taylor & Francis.

Pinto, L. E. (2017). *Financial Literacy Education: Navigating a Paradox.* https://the-learningexchange.ca/wp-content/uploads/2017/09/Financial_Literacy_Education_Navigating_Paradox_en.pdf.

Piontkowski, U., et al. (2000). Predicting acculturation attitudes of dominant and non-dominant groups. *International Journal of Intercultural Relations, 24*(1), 1-26.

Pirenne, H. (2014). *Medieval Cities: Their Origins and the Revival of Trade, Updated Edition.* Princeton University Press.

Pires, G. D., & Stanton, J. (2018). *Ethnic Marketing: Theory, Practice and Entrepreneurship.* Routledge.

Pitman, S. D., Daniels, C. B., & Sutton, P. C. (2018). Ecological literacy and psychographics: lifestyle contributors to ecological knowledge and understanding. *International Journal of Sustainable Development & World Ecology, 25*(2), 117-130.

Pitman, T., et al. (2019). An Australian study of graduate outcomes for disadvantaged students. *Journal of Further and Higher Education, 43*(1), 45-57.

Pitt, C. S., Bal, A. S., & Plangger, K. (2020). New approaches to psychographic consumer segmentation. *European Journal of Marketing* 54(2):305-326

Pitts, M. J., & Gallois, C. (2019). Social Markers in Language and Speech. In *Oxford Research Encyclopedia of Psychology.* https://oxfordre.com/psychology.

Plangger, K., & Montecchi, M. (2020). Thinking Beyond Privacy Calculus: Investigating Reactions to Customer Surveillance. *Journal of Interactive Marketing, 50,* 32-44.

Platt, L., & Parsons, S. (2018). Occupational aspirations of children from primary school to teenage years across ethnic groups. Centre for Longitudinal Studies and the Runnymede Trust.

Poddar, A., et al. (2019). False advertising or slander? Using location-based tweets to assess online rating-reliability. *Journal of Business Research, 99,* 390-397.

Podoshen, Jeffrey S., Lu Li, and Junfeng Zhang. (2010.) Materialism and Conspicuous Consumption in China: a Cross-Cultural Examination. *International Journal of Consumer Studies* 35(1):17–25.

Pointner, F. E. (2018). Chavs: The Clash of Social Classes in Urban Britain. In *Resistance and the City* (pp. 97-111). Brill Rodopi.

Pons, F., & Harris, P. L. (2019). Children's Understanding of Emotions or Pascal's "Error": Review and Prospects. In *Handbook of emotional development* (pp. 431-449). Springer, Cham.

Poole, M., & O'Cass, A. (2003). Personal values: a Comparative study between mall and online shoppers. ANZMAC 2003 Conference Proceedings. Adelaide, Austria.

Poorthuis, A. M., Slagt, M., van Aken, M. A., Denissen, J. J., & Thomaes, S. (2019). Narcissism and popularity among peers: A cross-transition longitudinal study. *Self and Identity,* 1-15.

Posselt, J. R., & Grodsky, E. (2017). Graduate education and social stratification. *Annual Review of Sociology, 43,* 353-378.

Poster, M. (2019). *Critical theory and poststructuralism: In search of a context.* Cornell University Press.

Powell, A., & Shade, L. R. (2006). Going Wi-Fi in Canada: municipal and community initiatives. *Government Information Quarterly, 23*(3-4), 381-403.

Powell, B. (2018). Sweatshop regulation: Tradeoffs and welfare judgements. *Journal of Business Ethics, 151*(1), 29-36.

Powell, H. (2018). Branding, brand value and the hidden persuaders on eBay. In *The Advertising Handbook* (pp. 44-56). Routledge.

Powers, T. L. (2016). History of selling and sales management. In *Routledge Companion to Marketing History* (pp. 225-238). New York: Routledge.

Powers, T. L., et al. (2018). Price And Quality Value Influences On Retail Customer Satisfaction And Loyalty. *Journal of Consumer Satisfaction, Dissatisfaction and Complaining Behavior, 31,* 21-39.

Pracejus, J. W., et al. (2020). Fit in cause-related marketing: An integrative retrospective. *Journal of Global Scholars of Marketing Science, 30*(2), 105-114.

Pradhan, D., Duraipandian, I., & Sethi, D. (2016). Celebrity endorsement: How celebrity–brand–user personality congruence affects brand attitude and purchase intention. *Journal of Marketing Communications, 22*(5), 456-473.

Präg, P., et al. (2019, 26 April). Understanding the marriage–cohabitation gap in income pooling: Evidence from 29 European countries. https://doi.org/10.31235/osf.io/rqzj3.

Prato, G.B. (ed.). (2016). *Beyond multiculturalism: views from anthropology.* Routledge.

Prendergast, G., Paliwal, A., & Chan, K. K. F. (2018). Trust in online recommendations: an evolutionary psychology perspective. *International Journal of Advertising, 37*(2), 199-216.

Priporas, C. V., & Tan, H. (2020). An exploratory study of the upper middle-class consumer attitudes towards counterfeiting in China. *Journal of Retailing and Consumer Services, 53,* 101959.

Puntoni, S., de Hooge, I. E., & Verbeke, W. J. (2015). Advertising-induced embarrassment. *Journal of Advertising, 44*(1), 71-79.

Purkiss, D. (2016). Fractious: Teenage Girls' Tales in and out of Shakespeare. In *Oral Traditions and Gender in Early Modern Literary Texts* (pp. 83-98). Routledge.

Qi, L.E I., & Wand, L.Y. (2017). An Analysis of Materialism and Bandwagon Consumption Influencing on Subjective Well-being. *DEStech Transactions on Social Science, Education and Human Science.*

Qi, L., & Dong, X. Y. (2018). Gender, low-paid status, and time poverty in urban China. *Feminist Economics*, 24(2), 171-193.

Qin, C., Li, C., & Wei, J. (2019). Study on the evaluation of multimedia advertising performance. *Multimedia Tools and Applications*, 1-14.

Quan-Haase, A., et al. (2016). Interviews with digital seniors: ICT use in the context of everyday life. *Information, Communication & Society*, 19(5), 691-707.

Quester, P., et al. (2000). Acculturation and consumer behaviour: The case of Chinese Australian consumers. In *Proceedings of ANZMAC 2000: Visionary marketing for the 21st century: Facing the challenge*, pp. 1019-1024. Gold Coast, Australia: ANZMAC.

Rabie, M. (2018). Market Capitalism and Materialism. In *The Global Debt Crisis and Its Socioeconomic Implications* (pp. 111-124). Palgrave Macmillan, Cham.

Rabinovich, A., & Webley, P. (2007). Filling the gap between planning and doing: Psychological factors involved in the successful implementation of saving intention. *Journal of Economic Psychology*, 28(4), 444-461

Radcliffe-Brown, A. R. (1940). On social structure. *The Journal of the Royal Anthropological Institute of Great Britain and Ireland*, 70(1), 1-12.

Rafaeli, A., & Pratt, M. G. (1993). Tailored meanings: On the meaning and impact of organizational dress. *Academy of Management Review*, 18(1), 32-55.

Rafaeli, A., et al. (1997). Navigating by attire: The use of dress by female administrative employees. *Academy of Management Journal*, 40(1), 9-45.

Rahman, M., et al. (2017). Corporate social responsibility and marketing performance: The moderating role of advertising intensity. *Journal of Advertising Research*, 57(4), 368-378.

Rai, R., et al. (2018). Materialistic values, brand knowledge and the mass media: Hours spent on the internet predicts materialistic values and brand knowledge. *Current Psychology*, 1-9.

Rajagopalan, R., & Heitmeyer, J. (2005). Ethnicity and consumer choice. *Journal of Fashion Marketing and Management: An International Journal*.

Rajendran, S.R., & Chamundeswari, S. (2019). Understanding the impact of lifestyle on the academic performance of middle-and high-school students. *Journal of Sociological Research* 10(2), 67.

Ramírez, L., & Palacios-Espinosa, X. (2016). Stereotypes about old age, social support, aging anxiety and evaluations of one's own health. *Journal of Social Issues*, 72(1), 47-68.

Ramzy, O., et al. (2012). Perceptions of children's influence on purchase decisions: Empirical investigation for the US and Egyptian families. *World Journal of Management*, 4(1), 30-50.

Rao, A. H. (2016). *Unemployed: What Men's and Women's Divergent Experiences Tell Us about Gender Inequality* (Doctoral dissertation, University of Pennsylvania).

Rao, A. H. (2017). Stand by your man: Wives' emotion work during men's unemployment. *Journal of Marriage and Family*, 79(3), 636-656.

Raphael, D. (2017). The State of Health Equity in Ontario. *Population Health in Canada: Issues, Research, and Action*, 90.

Rapoport, R., & Rapoport, R. N. (2019). *Leisure and the family life cycle*. Routledge.

Rappaport, E. (2019). *A Thirst for Empire*. Princeton University Press.

Rattansi, A. (2017). 'Metaphoricity'in Bauman's sociology. In *Bauman and contemporary sociology*. Manchester University Press.

Rauschnabel, P. A., et al. (2016). Brand management in higher education: the university brand personality scale. *Journal of Business Research*, 69(8), 3077-3086.

Ravallion, M., & Chen, S. (2019). Global poverty measurement when relative income matters. *Journal of Public Economics*, 177, 104046.

Ray, D., & Genicot, G. (2019). Aspirations: A review. https://edi.opml.co.uk/wpcms/wp-content/uploads/2019/12/19AspReview09-002.pdf.

Raymond, M. (2018). *Brand Publics and Online Video Game Streaming* (Doctoral dissertation, Concordia University).

Razak, I., et al. (2016). The impact of product quality and price on customer satisfaction with the mediator of customer value. *Journal of Marketing and Consumer Research*, 30(1), 59-68.

Reczek, R.W., et al. (2018). Focusing on the forest or the trees: How abstract versus concrete construal level predicts responses to eco-friendly products. *Journal of Environmental Psychology*, 57, 87-98.

Redhead, D., et al. (2019). On the dynamics of social hierarchy: A longitudinal investigation of the rise and fall of prestige, dominance, and social rank in naturalistic task groups. *Evol. Hum. Behav*, 40, 222-234.

Reed, Americus, Mark R. Forehand, Stefano Puntoni, and Luk Warlop. 2012. "Identity-based consumer behavior." *International Journal of Research in Marketing* 29: 310-321.

Reilly, Andrew, Nancy A. Rudd, and Julie Hillery. 2008. "Shopping Behavior Among Gay Men." *Clothing and Textiles Research Journal* 26(4): 313-326.

Reinarman, C., & Duskin, C. (2017). Dominant ideology and drugs in the media. In *Making Trouble* (pp. 73-88). Routledge.

Reith, G. (2018). *Addictive consumption: capitalism, modernity and excess*. Routledge.

Reny, T., & Manzano, S. (2016). The negative effects of mass media stereotypes of Latinos and immigrants. *Media and Minorities*, 4, 195-212.

Requena, F. (2017). Erotic capital and subjective well-being. *Research in Social Stratification and Mobility*, 50, 13-18.

Rettie, R., Bruchell, K., & Barnham, C. (2014). Social normalization: Using marketing to make green normal. *Journal of Consumer Behaviour*, 13, pp. 9-17.

Reynolds, A. (2019). Review of *Pragmatist Egalitarianism* by David Rondel. *The Pluralist* 14(3).

Rhodes, A., & Wilson, C. M. (2018). False advertising. *The RAND Journal of Economics*, 49(2), 348-369.

Rich, A. (2019). The Accent of Truth: The Hollywood Research Bible and the Republic of Images. *Representations*, 145(1), 152-173.

Richards, C. (2019). Later life learning from experience: the cross-cultural importance of 'life reviews' in seniors' lifelong education and learning. *Zeitschrift für Weiterbildungsforschung*, 42(1), 5-22.

Richins, M. L. (2017). Materialism pathways: The processes that create and perpetuate materialism. *Journal of Consumer Psychology*, 27(4), 480-499.

Riefler, P. (2020). Local versus global food consumption: The role of brand authenticity. *Journal of Consumer Marketing* 37(3): 317–327.

Riello, G. (2017). Things that shape history: material culture and historical narratives. In *History and Material Culture* (pp. 27-50). Routledge.

Riello, G., & Rublack, U. (Eds.). (2019). *The right to dress: sumptuary laws in a global perspective, c. 1200–1800*. Cambridge University Press.

Riesman, D., Glazer, N., & Denney, R. (1953). *The lonely crowd: A study of the changing American character*. Garden City, NY: Doubleday.

Riley, J. (2019). Depictions of Murder in Maine: The Dominant Ideology Thesis. *Deviant Behavior*, 40(4), 417-434.

Riley, S., Evans, A., & Mackiewicz, A. (2016). It's just between girls: Negotiating the postfeminist gaze in women's 'looking talk'. *Feminism & Psychology*, 26(1), 94-113.

Rinallo, Diego. (2007). Metro/Fashion/Tribes of men: Negotiating the Boundaries of Men's Legitimate Consumption, in *Consumer Tribes: Theory, Practice and Prospects*, edited by B. Covas et al. London: Butterworth/Heinemann.

Ringer, F. B., & Anestis, M. D. (2018). Thwarted Belongingness in Relation to Face-to-Face and Online Interactions. *Suicide and Life-Threatening Behavior*, 48(4), 468-480.

Riston, M. (2007). Fakes can genuinely aid luxury brands. *Marketing*, 25 (July), 21–22.

Ritzer, G. (1996). The McDonaldization thesis: Is expansion inevitable? *International Sociology*, 11(3), 291-308.

Ritzer, G. (2017). Theorizing McDonaldization. *The Wiley-Blackwell Encyclopedia of Social Theory*, 1-5.

Ritzer, G. (2018). Rationalization, Bureaucratization, and McDonaldization. *Core Concepts in Sociology*, 247.

Ritzer, G. (2008). Review Essay: Not Consumed Enough. *Journal of Consumer Culture*, 8(1).

Roberto, Christina A., et al. (2010, July). Influence of Licensed Characters on Children's Taste and Snack Preferences. *Pediatrics* 126(1):88-93.

Roberts, Mary Louise. (1998). "Gender, Consumption, and Commodity Culture." *The American Historical Review* 103(3):817.

Robertson, R. (2018). Glocalization. In *The International Encyclopedia of Anthropology*, 1-8. Hoboken, NJ: Wiley-Blackwell.

Robertson, R. (Ed.). (2016). *European Glocalization in Global Context*. Springer.

Robertson, S. (2011). Cash cows, backdoor migrants, or activist citizens? International students, citizenship, and rights in Australia. *Ethnic and Racial Studies*, 34(12), 2192-2211.

Robinson, J., & Godbey, G. (2010). *Time for life: The surprising ways Americans use their time*. University Park, PA: Penn State University Press.

Robinson, R. M. (2018). Friendships of virtue, pursuit of the moral community, and the ends of business. *Journal of Business Ethics*, 151(1).

Rocha, C. (2018). Crowdfunding images of Colombia and Ecuador: International collaborations and transnational circulation in a neoliberal context. In *Contemporary Latin American Cinema* (pp. 153-170). Palgrave Macmillan, Cham.

Rodríguez-Díaz, M., et al. (2018). A model of market positioning of destinations based on online customer reviews of lodgings. *Sustainability*, 10(1), 78.

Rody-Mantha, B. (2017, 27 February). Reader's Digest and the Globe and Mail Top Vividata Rankings. *Media in Canada*, 27.

Rogers, L. O., & Meltzoff, A. N. (2017). Is gender more important and meaningful than race? An analysis of racial and gender identity among Black, White, and mixed-race children. *Cultural Diversity and Ethnic Minority Psychology*, 23(3), 323.

Rogošić, S., & Baranović, B. (2016). Social capital and educational achievements: Coleman vs. Bourdieu. *Center for Educational Policy Studies Journal*, 6(2), 81-100.

Rohlinger, Deana A. 2002. "Eroticizing Men: Cultural Influences On Advertising And Male Objectification." *Sex Roles* 46(3-4):61-74

Rohmann, A., Florack, A., & Piontkowski, U. (2006). The role of discordant acculturation attitudes in perceived threat: An analysis of host and immigrant attitudes in Germany. *International Journal of Intercultural Relations*, 30(6), 683-702.

Rojek, C. (2017). Counterfeit Commerce: Relations of production, distribution and exchange. *Cultural Sociology*, 11(1), 28-43.

Rollwagen, K. (2016). Classrooms for Consumer Society: Practical Education and Secondary School Reform in Post-Second World War Canada. *Historical Studies in Education/Revue d'histoire de l'éducation*.

Roper, S., & La Niece, C. (2009). The importance of brands in the lunch-box choices of low-income British school children. *Journal of Consumer Behaviour*, 8(2-3), 84-99.

Roper, Stuart and Binita Shah. (2007). Vulnerable consumers: The social impact of branding on children. *Equal Opportunities International* 26(7): 713-714.

Rose, G. M. (1999). Consumer socialization, parental style, and developmental timetables in the United States and Japan. *The Journal of Marketing*, 105-119.

Rose, G. M., et al. (2002). Family communication and children's purchasing influence: a cross-national examination. *Journal of Business Research*, 55(11), 867-873.

Rose, J., & Spencer, C. (2016). Immaterial labour in spaces of leisure: producing biopolitical subjectivities through Facebook. *Leisure Studies*, 35(6), 809-826.

Rosen, N. L., & Nofziger, S. (2019). Boys, Bullying, and Gender Roles: How Hegemonic Masculinity Shapes Bullying Behavior. *Gender Issues*, 36(3), 295-318.

Rosenberg, Morris. The self-concept: Social product and social force. In *Social psychology* (pp. 593-624). Routledge, 2017.

Ross, A. (2016). *No respect: Intellectuals and popular culture*. Routledge.

Ross, R. J. (2017). Domhoff, Mills, and Slow Power. In *Studying the Power Elite* (pp. 73-79). Routledge.

Rossiter, H. (2016). She's always a woman: Butch lesbian trans women in the lesbian community. *Journal of Lesbian Studies*, 20(1), 87-96.

Rossiter, J. R., & Percy, L. (2017). Methodological guidelines for advertising research. *Journal of Advertising*, 46(1), 71-82.

Roudometof, V. (2016). Theorizing glocalization: Three interpretations1. *European Journal of Social Theory*, 19(3), 391-408.

Roudometof, Victor (2019). Cosmopolitanism, Glocalization and Youth Cultures. *Youth and Globalization* 1(1), 19-39.

Rountree, J. (2018). Jürgen Habermas and Communication Studies. In *Oxford Research Encyclopedia of Communication*. https://oxfordre.com/communication.

Rouse, M. (2007). What is greenwashing? https://whatis.techtarget.com/definition/greenwashing (accessed January 15, 2019).

Rousseau, G. G. (2018). The impact of longevity on older consumer needs: implications for business. *Journal of Consumer Sciences*, 46.

Rovai, S. (2016). Chinese Outbound Shopping Tourism: A Market-Driven Approach for the Luxury and Fashion Industry. *Symphonya. Emerging Issues in Management* 1, 56-63.

Rowthorn, D. (2019). Is Child Advertising Inherently Unfair?. *Journal of Business Ethics*, 158(3), 603-615.

Royo-Vela, M., & Casamassima, P. (2011). The influence of belonging to virtual brand communities on consumers' affective commitment, satisfaction and word-of-mouth advertising: The ZARA case. *Online Information Review*, 35(4), 517-542.

Royo-Vela, M., & Hünermund, U. (2016). Effects of inbound marketing communications on HEIs' brand equity: the mediating role of the student's decision-making process. An exploratory research. *Journal of Marketing for Higher Education*, 26(2), 143-167.

Rozin, P., Hormes, J., Faith, M. & Wansink, B. (2012). Is Meat Male? A Quantitative Multimethod Framework to Establish Metaphoric Relationships. *Journal of Consumer Research*, 39, 629-643.

Rubinstein, R. (2018). *Dress codes: Meanings and messages in American culture*. Routledge.

Rucker, D. D., Dubois, D., & Galinsky, A. D. (2011). Generous paupers and stingy princes: Power drives consumer spending on self versus others. *Journal of Consumer Research*, 37(6), 1015-1029.

Rucker, D. D., et al. (2012). Power and consumer behavior: How power shapes who and what consumers value. *Journal of Consumer Psychology*, 22(3), 352-368.

Rucker, D. D., et al. (2018). The agentic–communal model of advantage and disadvantage: How inequality produces similarities in the psychology of power, social class, gender, and race. In *Advances in Experimental Social Psychology* (vol. 58, pp. 71-125). Academic Press.

Rughiniș, C., et al. (2016). Three Shadowed Dimensions of Feminine Presence in Video Games. In *Proceedings of 1st International Joint Conference of DiGRA and FDG* (Vol. 13, No. 1).

Russel, Richard, et al. (2018). "Differential effects of makeup on perceieved age." *British Journal of Psychology*. 110(10), 1-191.

Russell, M. A., & Odgers, C. L. (2016). Desistance and life-course persistence: Findings from longitudinal studies using group-based trajectory modeling of antisocial behavior.

Russell, R., et al. (2019). Differential effects of makeup on perceived age. *British Journal of Psychology*, 110(1), 87-100.

Russo, C., & Simeone, M. (2017). The growing influence of social and digital media. *British Food Journal*.

Rustagi, N., & Shrum, L. J. (2017). Conceptualizations of Materialism. *The Routledge Companion to Consumer Behavior*, 9.

Rusu, R. (2018). The Protestant Work Ethic and Attitudes Towards Work. *Scientific Bulletin*, 23(2), 112-117.

Rutherford, P. (1988). The culture of advertising. *Canadian Journal of Communication*, 13(3).

Rutherford, P. (2018). *Adman's Dilemma: From Barnum to Trump*. University of Toronto Press.

Ruvio, A., et al. (2014). When bad gets worse: The amplifying effect of materialism on traumatic stress and maladaptive consumption. *Journal of the Academy of Marketing Science*, 42(1), 90-101.

Ryman-Tubb, N. F., Krause, P., & Garn, W. (2018). How Artificial Intelligence and machine learning research impacts payment card fraud detection: A survey and industry benchmark. *Engineering Applications of Artificial Intelligence*, 76, 130-157.

Saad, G., & Vongas, J. G. (2009). The effect of conspicuous consumption on men's testosterone levels. *Organizational Behavior and Human Decision Processes*, 110(2), 80-92.

Saatcioglu, B. & Ozanne, J. (2013). Moral Habitus and Status Negotiation in a Marginalized Working-Class Neighborhood. *Journal of Consumer Research*, 40, 692-710.

Saatcioglu, B., & Corus, C. (2016). Exploring spatial vulnerability: inequality and agency formulations in social space. *Journal of Marketing Management*, 32(3-4), 230-251.

Sadachar, A., & Fiore, A. M. (2018). The path to mall patronage intentions is paved with 4E-based experiential value for Indian consumers. *International Journal of Retail & Distribution Management*.

Sadowski, B. M. (2017). Consumer cooperatives as an alternative form of governance: The case of the broadband industry. *Economic Systems*, 41(1), 86-97.

Safdar, H., et al. (2018). Consumers' online information adoption behaviour: Motives and antecedents of electronic word of mouth communications. *Computers in Human Behavior*, 80, 22-32.

Sahni, S. P., & Gupta, I. (2019). Novelty Seeking: Exploring the Role of Variety Seeking Behavior in Digital Piracy. In *Piracy in the Digital Era* (pp. 99-113). Springer, Singapore.

Salimath, M. S., & Chandna, V. (2018). Sustainable consumption and growth: Examining complementary perspectives. *Management Decision*. Published online before print July 2018, doi: 10.1108/MD-12-2016-0934.

Salinsky, Eileen, (2006). Effects of Food Marketing to Kids: I'm Lovin' It? *National Health Policy Forum*, Issue Brief No. 814.

Salley-Toler, T. A. (2014). *The formation and examination of the multiethnic consumer identity construct in the context of culture-specific brand attitudes* (Doctoral dissertation, St. Louis University).

Samiee, S. (2019). Reflections on global brands, global consumer culture and globalization. *International Marketing Review* 36(9).

Samper, Adriana, Linyun W. Yang, and Michelle E. Daniels. (2017). Beauty, Effort, and Misrepresentation: How Beauty Work Affects Judgments of Moral Character and Consumer Preferences. *Journal of Consumer Research* 45:126-147.

Sander, W. (2017). Religion, religiosity, and happiness. *Review of Religious Research*, 59(2), 251-262.

Sandikci, Ö., & Ger, G. (2009). Veiling in style: How does a stigmatized practice become fashionable? *Journal of Consumer Research*, 37(1), 15-36.

Sandlin, J.A., & Callahan, J.L. (2009). Deviance, dissonance, and détournement: culture jammersuse of emotion in consumer resistance. *Journal of Consumer Culture*, 9(1), 79-115.

Sandlin, J.A., & Maudlin, J.G. (2012). Consuming pedagogies: Controlling images of women as consumers in popular culture. *Journal of Consumer Culture*, 12(2), 175-194.

Santos, D. B., et al. (2019). Credit card and financial well-being among females. In *Individual Behaviors and Technologies for Financial Innovations*, pp. 97-116. Springer.

Saraneva, A., & Sääksjärvi, M. (2008). Young compulsive buyers and the emotional roller-coaster in shopping. *Young Consumers*.

Sarpong, S. (2018). Sweatshops and a duty of care: to what extent? The case of Bangladesh. *Stakeholders, Governance and Responsibility*, 229.

Scaglioni, S., et al. (2018). Factors influencing children's eating behaviours. *Nutrients*, 10(6), 706.

Scerri, A. (2017). Escape from moral quietism: What might Britain's chav and Australia's bogan offer the US'hillbilly? https://mds.marshall.edu/asa_conference/2017/accepted_proposals/102/.

Schade, M., et al. (2016). The impact of attitude functions on luxury brand consumption: An age-based group comparison. *Journal of business research*, 69(1), 314-322.

Schamel, G. H. (2017). Wine and culinary tourism: Preferences of experiential consumers. In *BIO Web of Conferences* (Vol. 9, p. 03021). EDP Sciences.

Scheibling, C. (2014). *Just For Men: The Representation of Masculinities in Grooming Product Advertising* (Doctoral dissertation, Concordia University).

Schenck-Fontaine, A., & Panico, L. (2019). Many kinds of poverty: Three dimensions of economic hardship, their combinations, and children's behavior problems. *Demography*, 56(6), 2279-2305.

Schilbach, F., Schofield, H., & Mullainathan, S. (2016). The psychological lives of the poor. *American Economic Review*, 106(5), 435-40.

Schimmele, C., & Davidson, J. (2019). *Evolving Internet Use Among Canadian Seniors* (No. 2019015e). Statistics Canada, Analytical Studies Branch.

Schindler, R. M., Lala, V., & Corcoran, C. (2014). Intergenerational influence in consumer deal proneness. *Psychology & Marketing*, 31(5), 307-320.

Schlosberg, D., & Rinfret, S. (2008). Ecological modernisation, American style. *Environmental Politics*, 17(2), 254-275.

Schlosser, A. E. (2020). Self-disclosure versus self-presentation on social media. *Current Opinion in Psychology*, 31, 1-6.

Schmelzer, M. (2010). Marketing morals, moralizing markets: Assessing the effectiveness of fair trade as a form of boycott. *Management & Organizational History*, 5(2), 221-250.

Schmiedeberg, C., & Schumann, N. (2019). Poverty and adverse peer relationships among children in Germany: A longitudinal study. *Child Indicators Research*, 12(5), 1717-1733.

Schnaiberg, A. (1981). Will population slowdowns yield resource conservation? Some social demurrers. *Qualitative Sociology*, 4(1), 21-33.

Scholz, J. K., & Sicinski, K. (2011). *Facial Attractiveness and Lifetime Earnings* (Doctoral dissertation, University of Wisconsin).

Schor, J. (2016). Debating the sharing economy. *Journal of Self-Governance and Management Economics*, 4(3), 7-22.

Schor, J. B. (2014). Born to buy: The commercialized child and the new consumer cult. New York: Simon & Schuster

Schor, J. B., & Fitzmaurice, C. J. (2017). Complicating conventionalisation. *Journal of Marketing Management*, 33(7-8), 644-651.

Schor, J.B. and Attwood-Charles, W. (2017) The 'sharing' economy: labor, inequality, and social connection on for-profit platforms. *Sociology Compass*, 11(8).

Schroeder, S. A. (2016). American health improvement depends upon addressing class disparities. *Preventive Medicine*, 92, 6-15.

Schuch, J. C., & Wang, Q. (2015). Immigrant businesses, place-making, and community development: a case from an emerging immigrant gateway. *Journal of Cultural Geography*, 32(2), 214-241.

Schudson, M. (2013). *Advertising, the uneasy persuasion (RLE Advertising): Its dubious impact on American society*. Routledge.

Schuetze, H. G., & Slowey, M. (2002). Participation and exclusion: A comparative analysis of non-traditional students and lifelong learners in higher education. *Higher Education*, 44(3-4), 309-327.

Schultz, D. (2016). The future of advertising or whatever we're going to call it. *Journal of Advertising*, 45(3), 276-285.

Schumacher, E. F. (2011). *Small is beautiful: A study of economics as if people mattered*. Random House.

Schussman, A., & Soule, S. A. (2005). Process and protest: Accounting for individual protest participation. *Social Forces, 84*(2), 1083-1108.

Schwartz, D. C. (2017). From the lonely crowd to the Strident Society. In *Political Alienation and Political Behavior* (pp. 231-246). Routledge.

Schwarzenberg, S. J., & Georgieff, M. K. (2018). Advocacy for improving nutrition in the first 1000 days to support childhood development and adult health. *Pediatrics, 141*(2), e20173716.

Scott, D. (2017). Why Veblen matters: The role of status seeking in contemporary leisure. In *The Palgrave handbook of leisure theory* (pp. 385-399). Palgrave Macmillan, London.

Scranton, P. (2000). *Endless novelty: Specialty production and American industrialization, 1865-1925.* Princeton University Press.

Searle, B. (2008). *Well-being: In search of a good life?* Policy Press.

Sebastian, R. J., & Ryan, E. B. (2018). Speech cues and social evaluation: Markers of ethnicity, social class, and age. In *Recent advances in language, communication, and social psychology* (pp. 112-143). Routledge.

Segal, B., & Podoshen, J. S. (2013). An examination of materialism, conspicuous consumption and gender differences. *International Journal of Consumer Studies, 37*(2), 189-198.

Segal, J. M. (2017). Alternatives to the Mass Consumption Society *Philosophical Dimensions of Public Policy, 13,* 283.

Seger-Guttmann, T., Vilnai-Yavetz, I., & Rosenbaum, M. S. (2017). Disparate satisfaction scores? Consider your customer's country-of-origin: a case study. *The International Review of Retail, Distribution and Consumer Research, 27*(2), 189-206.

Segev, S. (2014). The effect of acculturation on ethnic consumers' decision-making styles: An empirical analysis of Hispanic consumers. *Journal of International Consumer Marketing, 26*(3), 168-184.

Seginer, R., & Mahajna, S. (2018). Future orientation in cultural transition: Acculturation strategies of youth from three minority groups in Israel. *New Directions for Child and Adolescent Development, 2018*(160), 31-43.

Seifert, A., & Schelling, H. R. (2018). Seniors online: Attitudes toward the internet and coping with everyday life. *Journal of Applied Gerontology, 37*(1), 99-109.

Seiler, S., Yao, S., & Wang, W. (2017). Does online word of mouth increase demand?(and how?) evidence from a natural experiment. *Marketing Science, 36*(6), 838-861.

Seliger, M. (2019). *Ideology and politics* (Vol. 52). Routledge.

Seshadri, S. R., & Ramakrishna, J. (2018). Nutritional Status of School-Going Children: What Do We Know?. In *Nutritional adequacy, diversity and choice among primary school children* (pp. 1-14). Springer, Singapore.

Sethna, Z., Fakoussa, R., & Bamber, D. (2017). The young ones, shopping and marketing channels: What actually shapes their mind?. In *Young Consumer Behaviour* (pp. 155-169). Routledge.

Sevim, H., & Hall, E. E. (2016). Consumer acculturation: perspective of immigrants and tourists. *International Journal of Academic Research in Economics and Management Sciences, 5*(4), 126-139.

Shade, L. R. (2002). The digital divide: From definitional stances to policy initiatives. Department of Canadian Heritage.

Shade, L. R. (2003). Here comes the dot force! The new cavalry for equity? *Gazette* (Leiden, Netherlands), 65(2), 107-120.

Shade, L. R. (2008). Internet social networking in young women's everyday lives: Some insights from focus groups. *Our Schools, Our Selves, 17*(4), 65-73.

Shade, L. R., & Jacobson, J. (2015). Hungry for the job: gender, unpaid internships, and the creative industries. *The Sociological Review, 63*(1_suppl), 188-205.

Shade, L. R., Jones, S., & Rainie, L. (2004). Bending gender into the net. *Society online: The Internet in context,* 57-71.

Shadid, Z., et al. (2020, April 17). [Potential impact of border restrictions due to CO-VID-19 as it relates to the availability of temporary foreign workers during the 2020 growing season.] Retrieved from https://www150.statcan.gc.ca/n1/pub/45-28-0001/2020001/article/00002-eng.htm?HPA=1.

Shane-Simpson, C., Manago, A., Gaggi, N., & Gillespie-Lynch, K. (2018). Why do college students prefer Facebook, Twitter, or Instagram? Site affordances, tensions between privacy and self-expression, and implications for social capital. *Computers in Human Behavior, 86,* 276-288.

Shang, R., Abernethy, M. A., & Hung, C. Y. (2020). Group identity, performance transparency, and employee performance. *The Accounting Review.*

Shannon, R., et al. (2020). Family life cycle and the life course paradigm: A four-country comparative study of consumer expenditures. *Journal of Global Scholars of Marketing Science, 30*(1), 34-44

Shao, C., Ciampaglia, G. L., Varol, O., Flammini, A., & Menczer, F. (2017). The spread of fake news by social bots. *arXiv preprint arXiv:1707.07592, 96,* 104.

Sharaf, R. (2017). The U.S. News Media: Is it News or Opinionated Entertainment? An Exploratory Study. *French Journal for Mass Research 9.*

Sharaievska, I., West, S., & Weddell, M. (2018). The privilege of healthy eating: A qualitative study exploring the local food choices of low-income families from Appalachia. *Journal of Health Disparities Research and Practice, 11*(3), 10.

Sharbatian, Y., & Bagheri, R. (2019). Analyzing Kurdish music and Dancing from the viewpoint of anthropology and its Effect on Attracting Tourists. *Journal of Tourism Hospitality Research, 7*(4), 99-113.

Sharma, A. (2011). Role of family in consumer socialization of children: Literature review. *Researchers World, 2*(3), 161.

Sharma, A., et al. (2016). Role of Children in Purchase of Technical Products. *Researchers World,* 120-127.

Sharma, Piyush and Ricky Y. K. Chan. 2011. "Counterfeit Proneness: Conceptualisationand Scale Development." *Journal of Marketing Management* 27 (5–6): 602–626.

Sharma, Ravi S. & Yang Yi (2013). Trend-Casting in the Interactive Digital Media Industry: Some Results and Guidelines. *Asian Journal of Innovation and Policy* 2(1).

Shavit, Y., et al. (2018). *Emerging Early Childhood Inequality: On the Relationship Between Poverty, Sensory Stimulation, Child Development, and Achievement.* Taub Center.

Shavitt, Sharon, Duo Jiang, and Hyewon Cho. 2016. "Stratification and Segmentation: Social Class in Consumer Behavior." *Journal of Consumer Psychology* 26(4): 583–93.

Shaw, D. (2017). *The Inside Out of the Ageing Self: Identity, Trust, and Friendship of Australian Seniors in an Online Community of Older People* (Doctoral dissertation).

Shaw, G., et al. (2016). A life-course analysis of older tourists and their changing patterns of holiday behaviour. In *The Routledge handbook of health tourism,* 141-152.

Shaw, I., & Aldridge, A. (2003). Consumerism, health and social order. *Social Policy and Society, 2*(1), 35-43.

Shaw, J. (2013). Full-spectrum reproductive justice: The affinity of abortion rights and birth activism. *Studies in Social Justice, 7*(1), 143-159.

Shaykevich, A. (2018). The King of the CASL: Canada's Anti-Spam Law Invades the United States. *Brook. L. Rev., 84,* 1321.

Shephard, Arles, et al. (2016). Media Influence, Fashion, and Shopping: A Gendered Perspective. *Journal of Fashion Marketing and Management* 20(1): 4-18

Sherry, J. F., & Fischer, E. M. (Eds.). (2017). *Contemporary Consumer Culture Theory.* Taylor & Francis.

Shimpi, S. S., & Sinha, D. K. (2010). A factor analysis on product attributes for consumer buying behavior of male cosmetics in Pune city. *International Journal in Multidisciplinary and Academic Research, 2*(2), 28-48.

Shivdas, A., & Chandrasekhar, J. (2016). Sustainability through frugal innovations: An application of Indian spiritual wisdom. *Prabandhan: Indian Journal of Management, 9*(5), 7-23.

Shu, K., Sliva, A., Wang, S., Tang, J., & Liu, H. (2017). Fake news detection on social media: A data mining perspective. *ACM SIGKDD Explorations Newsletter, 19*(1), 22-36.

Sieben, S., & Lechner, C. M. (2019). Measuring cultural capital through the number of books in the household. *Measurement Instruments for the Social Sciences, 2*(1), 1.

Silhouette-Dercourt, V., De Lassus, C., & Darpy, D. (2014). How second-generation consumers choose where to shop: A cross-cultural semiotic analysis. *Journal of Retailing and Consumer Services, 21*(6), 1059-1067.

Silva, J., Raposo, D., Neves, J., & da Silva, F. M. (2019, July). Visual Storytelling-Creative Strategy of Visual Clues Promoted by Archetypal Images. In *International Conference on Applied Human Factors and Ergonomics* (pp. 287-295). Springer, Cham.

Sim, C., & Baker, S. (2016). Where Are the Straight Edge Women?. *Youth Cultures and Subcultures: Australian Perspectives,* 139.

Simmel, G. (1957). Fashion. *American Journal of Sociology, 62*(6), 541-558.

Simmel, G. (1997). Fashion, adornment and style, in *Simmel on culture: Selected writings* (Vol. 903). Sage, London

Simmel, G. (2004 [1907]). *The philosophy of money.* Routledge.

Singer, E. (2017). Reference groups and social evaluations. In *Social psychology* (pp. 66-93). Routledge.

Sirgy, M. J., et al. (2019). The Dual Model of Materialism: Success Versus Happiness Materialism on Present and Future Life Satisfaction. *Applied Research in Quality of Life,* 1-20.

Skandalis, A., Byrom, J., & Banister, E. (2019). Experiential marketing and the changing nature of extraordinary experiences in post-postmodern consumer culture. *Journal of Business Research, 97,* 43-50.

Skivington, K., et al. (2016). Systematic literature review of interventions to improve health, happiness and wellbeing in the transition from adolescence to adulthood.

Slot, P. L., et al. (2018). D5.3. Internet survey among staff working in formal and informal (education) sectors in ten European countries. http://archive.isotis.org/wp-content/uploads/2019/06/ISOTIS_D5.3-Internet-survey-among-staff.pdf.

Smith Maguire, J. (2019). Media representations of the nouveaux riches and the cultural constitution of the global middle class. *Cultural Politics, 15*(1), 29-47.

Smith, A. (2010). *The Wealth of Nations: An inquiry into the nature and causes of the Wealth of Nations.* Harriman House Limited.

Smith, P. H. (2018). "Self-Help," Black Conservatives, and the Reemergence of Black Privatism. In *Without justice for all* (pp. 257-289). Routledge.

Smithers, L. G., Sawyer, A. C., Chittleborough, C. R., Davies, N. M., Smith, G. D., & Lynch, J. W. (2018). A systematic review and meta-analysis of effects of early life non-cognitive skills on academic, psychosocial, cognitive and health outcomes. *Nature Human Behaviour, 2*(11), 867-880.

Śniadek, J. (2006). Age of seniors: A challenge for tourism and leisure industry. *Studies in Physical Culture and Tourism, 13,* 103-105.

So, K.K.F., King, C., Sparks, B. A., & Wang, Y. (2016). The role of customer engagement in building consumer loyalty to tourism brands. *Journal of Travel Research, 55*(1), 64-78.

Sohaib, O., Kang, K., & Nurunnabi, M. (2019). Gender-based iTrust in E-commerce: The moderating role of cognitive innovativeness. *Sustainability, 11*(1), 175.

Somech, A., & Drach-Zahavy, A. (2016). Gender role ideology. *The Wiley Blackwell Encyclopedia of Gender and Sexuality Studies,* 1-3.

Song, M., & Shin, K. S. (2019). Forecasting economic indicators using a consumer sentiment index: Survey-based versus text-based data. *Journal of Forecasting, 38*(6), 504-518.

Song, S. Y., & Kim, Y. K. (2019). Doing Good Better: Impure Altruism in Green Apparel Advertising. *Sustainability, 11*(20), 5762.

Song, W., et al. (2020). Will Buying Follow Others Ease Their Threat of Death? An Analysis of Consumer Data during the Period of COVID-19 in China. *International Journal of Environmental Research and Public Health, 17*(9), 3215.

Sørensen, G. (2017). *The transformation of the state: Beyond the myth of retreat.* Macmillan International Higher Education.

Southerton, D., Warde, A., & Hand, M. (2004). The limited autonomy of the consumer: implications for sustainable consumption. *Sustainable consumption: The implications of changing infrastructures of provision*, 32-48.

Spence, K., & De Beukelaer, C. (2018). Global Cultural Economy: Key Ideas in Media & Cultural Studies.

Spenkuch, J. L., & Toniatti, D. (2016). Political advertising and election outcomes. *Kilts Center for Marketing at Chicago Booth–Nielsen Dataset Paper Series*, 1-046.

Spero, Ian, and Merlin Stone. 2004. "Agents of change: how young consumers are changing theworld of marketing." *Qualitative Market Research* 7, 153–159.

Spicer, R. N. (2017). Extensions and Concentric Circles. *Postphenomenology and Media: Essays on Human–Media–World Relations*, 81.

Spohr, D. (2017). Fake news and ideological polarization: Filter bubbles and selective exposure on social media. *Business Information Review*, 34(3), 150-160.

Spracklen, K., & Spracklen, B. (2018). Goth as Virtual Identity and Virtual Culture Online. In *The Evolution of Goth Culture: The Origins and Deeds of the New Goths* (Emerald Studies in Alternativity and Marginalization) (pp. 123-36). Emerald Publishing Limited.

Springer, S., et al. (Eds.). (2016). *Handbook of neoliberalism*. Routledge.

Sproesser, G., Klusmann, V., Schupp, H. T., & Renner, B. (2017). Self-other differences in perceiving why people eat what they eat. *Frontiers in Psychology*, 8, 209.

Sramova, Blandina. (2014). "Aggressive Marketing, Consumer Kids and Stereotyping of Media Contents." *Procedia Social and Behavioral Sciences* 140:255-259

Stack, Carol B. (1974). *All our Kin: Strategies for Survival in a Black Community*. New York: Harper and Row.

Stanfield, J. R., & Stanfield, J. B. (1980). Consumption in contemporary capitalism: the backward art of living. *Journal of Economic Issues*, 14(2), 437-451.

Starmans, C., & Bloom, P. (2018). Nothing personal: What psychologists get wrong about identity. *Trends in Cognitive Sciences*, 22(7), 566-568.

Steenkamp, J. B. E. (2019). Global versus local consumer culture: theory, measurement, and future research directions. *Journal of International Marketing*, 27(1), 1-19.

Steenkamp, J. B. E., & Fang, E. (2011). The impact of economic contractions on the effectiveness of R&D and advertising: evidence from US companies spanning three decades. *Marketing Science*, 30(4), 628-645.

Stehr, N. (2018). The culture and structure of social inequality. In *Nico Stehr: Pioneer in the Theory of Society and Knowledge* (pp. 181-198). Springer, Cham.

Stein, S., & de Andreotti, V. O. (2016). Cash, competition, or charity: International students and the global imaginary. *Higher Education*, 72(2), 225-239.

Steinert-Threlkeld, Z. C. (2017). Spontaneous collective action: Peripheral mobilization during the Arab Spring. *American Political Science Review*, 111(2), 379-403.

Steinhoff, J. (2019). Critiquing the New Autonomy of Immaterial Labour: An Analysis of Work in the Artificial Intelligence Industry.

Stelzer, A., Englert, F., Hörold, S., & Mayas, C. (2016). Improving service quality in public transportation systems using automated customer feedback. *Transportation Research Part E: Logistics and Transportation Review*, 89, 259-271.

Stephens, Lena D. et al. 2018. "A Qualitative Study of the Drivers of Socioeconomic Inequalities in Men's Eating Behaviours." *BMC Public Health* 18(1):1–12.

Stephens, N. & Swartz, T. (2013). Beliefs of Chinese buyers of pirated goods. *Journal of Consumer Behaviour, 12*, pp. 42-48.

Sterling, C. H., Bracken, J. K., & Hill, S. B. (Eds.). (2016). *Mass communications research resources: An annotated guide*. Routledge.

Stilwell, C. (2016). The public library as institutional capital: Towards measures for addressing social inclusion and combating poverty. *Information Development*, 32(1), 44-59.

Stockburger-Sauer, N. and Teichmann, K. (2011) Is Luxury Just a Female Thing? The Role of Gender in Luxury Brand Consumption, *Journal of Business Research*, 66(7), 889-896.

Stoller, R. J. (2020). *Sex and gender: The development of masculinity and femininity*. Routledge.

Storey, J. (2018). *Cultural theory and popular culture: An introduction*. Routledge.

Strate, L. (2017). Understanding the message of understanding media. *Atlantic Journal of Communication*, 25(4), 244-254.

Strikwerda, Carl. (2016). World War I in the History of Globalization. *Historical Reflections*, 42, 112-132. 10.3167/hrrh.2016.420307.

Strong, C. (1996). Features contributing to the growth of ethical consumerism: A preliminary investigation. *Marketing Intelligence & Planning* 14(5): 5-13.

Suárez-Orozco, C., et al. (2018). An integrative risk and resilience model for understanding the adaptation of immigrant-origin children and youth. *American Psychologist*, 73(6), 781.

Sujatha, R., & Sarada, D. (2016). Knowledge on lingerie selection and usage among adolescent girls. *IJAR*, 2(11), 304-308.

Sullivan, D. (2019). *Education, Liberal Democracy and Populism: Arguments from Plato, Locke, Rousseau and Mill*. Routledge.

Sullivan, O. (2018). The gendered division of household labor. In *Handbook of the Sociology of Gender* (pp. 377-392). Springer, Cham.

Sun, Gong et al. (2016). The Intermediate Linkage Between Materialism and Luxury Consumption: Evidence from the Emerging Market of China. *Soc Indic Res* 132:475-487

Sun, Y., & Zhang, J. (2019). Acquiescence or Resistance: Group Norms and Self-Interest Motivation in Unethical Consumer Behaviour. *Sustainability*, 11(8), 2190

Sung, Y. A. (2017). Age Differences in the Effects of Frugality and Materialism on Subjective Well-Being in Korea. *Family and Consumer Sciences Research Journal*, 46(2), 144-159.

Sutton-Brady, C., et al. (2010). Perceived cultural spaces and cultural in-betweens: Consumption among Korean Australians. *Journal of Consumer Behaviour*, 9(5), 349-363.

Sutton, P. W. (2019). *Explaining environmentalism: in search of a new social movement*. Routledge.

Swan, E. (2010). Commodity diversity: Smiling faces as a strategy of containment. *Organization*, 17(1), 77-100.

Sweeting, H., Hunt, K., & Bhaskar, A. (2012). Consumerism and well-being in early adolescence. *Journal of Youth Studies*, 15(6), 802-820.

Symes, C. (1998). Education for sale: A semiotic analysis of school prospectuses and other forms of educational marketing. *Australian Journal of Education*, 42(2), 133-152.

Symonds, J., Schoon, I., Eccles, J., & Salmela-Aro, K. (2019). The Development of motivation and amotivation to study and work across age-graded transitions in adolescence and young adulthood. *Journal of Youth and Adolescence*, 48(6), 1131-1145.

Tadajewski, M. (2018). Critical reflections on the marketing concept and consumer sovereignty. In *The Routledge companion to critical marketing studies* (pp. 196-224). London: Routledge.

Tal, D., & Gordon, A. (2016). Jacques Ellul revisited: 55 years of propaganda study. *Society*, 53(2), 182-187.

Talonen, A., et al. (2016). Consumer cooperatives: uncovering the value potential of customer ownership. *AMS Review*, 6(3-4), 142-156.

Tam, B., Findlay, L., & Kohen, D. (2017). Conceptualization of family: complexities of defining an Indigenous family. *Indigenous Policy Journal*, 28(1).

Tamari, T. (2018). Modernization and the Department Store in Early-Twentieth-Century Japan: Modern Girl and New Consumer Culture Lifestyles. In *Approaching Consumer Culture* (pp. 237-255). Springer, Cham.

Tambiah, S. J. (2017). Transnational movements, diaspora, and multiple modernities. In *Multiple modernities* (pp. 163-194). Routledge.

Tandoc, E. C., Jr., et al. (2018). Defining "fake news" A typology of scholarly definitions. *Digital Journalism*, 6(2), 137-153.

Tanford, S., et al. (2016). Back to the future: progress and trends in hotel loyalty marketing. *International Journal of Contemporary Hospitality Management*.

Tang-Martínez, Z. (2016). Rethinking Bateman's principles: challenging persistent myths of sexually reluctant females and promiscuous males. *The Journal of Sex Research*, 53(4-5), 532-559.

Tang, Felix, Vane-Ing Tian, and Judy Zaichkowsky. 2014. "Understanding counterfeit consumption." *Asia Pacific Journal of Marketing and Logistics* 26(1):4-20.

Tang, T. L. P., & Sutarso, T. (2013). Falling or not falling into temptation? Multiple faces of temptation, monetary intelligence, and unethical intentions across gender. *Journal of Business Ethics*, 116(3), 529-552.

Tang, T. L. P., et al. (2006). The love of money and pay level satisfaction: Measurement and functional equivalence in 29 geopolitical entities around the world. *Management and Organization Review*, 2(3), 423-452.

Tang, T. L. P., et al. (2018). Monetary intelligence and behavioral economics across 32 cultures: Good apples enjoy good quality of life in good barrels. *Journal of Business Ethics*, 148(4), 893-917.

Tang, T.L.P., Chen, Y. J., & Sutarso, T. (2008). Bad apples in bad (business) barrels: The love of money, Machiavellianism, risk tolerance, and unethical behavior. *Management Decision*, 46(2), 243-263

Taras, H. (2005, August). Nutrition and Student Performance at School. *Journal of School Health*, 75(6).

Tasdemir-Ozdes, A., Strickland-Hughes, C. M., Bluck, S., & Ebner, N. C. (2016). Future perspective and healthy lifestyle choices in adulthood. *Psychology and Aging*, 31(6), 618.

Taylor, C. (2017). How to define secularism. In *Religious Rights* (pp. 541-560). Routledge.

Taylor, C., & Peter, T. (2011). "We are not aliens, we're people, and we have rights." Canadian human rights discourse and high school climate for LGBTQ students. *Canadian Review of Sociology/Revue Canadienne De Sociologie*, 48(3), 275-312.

Taylor, J., Johnston, J., & Whitehead, K. (2016). A corporation in feminist clothing? Young women discuss the dove 'Real beauty' campaign. *Critical Sociology*, 42(1), 123-144.

Taylor, Lesley Ciarula (2009, 30 Jan.). Tamils protest 'genocide'. Thestar.com. N.p., 30 Jan. 2009.

Telling, K. (2018). Selling the liberal arts degree in England: Unique students, generic skills and mass higher education. *Sociology*, 52(6), 1290-1306.

Testa, P., Cova, B., & Cantone, L. (2017). The process of de-iconisation of an iconic brand: A genealogical approach. *Journal of Marketing Management*, 33(17-18), 1490-1521.

Thang, L. L., Lim, E., & Tan, S. L. S. (2019). Lifelong learning and productive aging among the baby-boomers in Singapore. *Social Science & Medicine*, 229, 41-49.

Theodoridis, K., & Miles, S. (2019). Young People and Consumption. In *The Oxford Handbook of Consumption*, 253.

Thomas, K. (2018). The labor market value of taste: An experimental study of class Bias in US employment. *Sociological Science*, 5, 562-595.

Thompson, C. J. (2004). Marketplace mythology and discourses of power. *Journal of Consumer Research*, 31(1), 162-180

Thompson, C. J. (2004). Special Session Summary Beyond Brand Image: Analyzing the Culture of Brands. *ACR North American Advances*.

Thompson, C. J. (2005). Consumer risk perceptions in a community of reflexive doubt. *Journal of Consumer Research*, 32(2), 235-248.

Thompson, C.J., & Arsel, Z. (2004). The Starbucks brandscape and consumers' (anticorporate) experiences of glocalization. *Journal of Consumer Research*, 31(3), 631-642

Thompson, C. J., & Coskuner-Balli, G. (2007). Enchanting ethical consumerism: The case of community supported agriculture. *Journal of Consumer Culture*, 7(3), 275-303.

Thompson, C. J., & Haytko, D. L. (1997). Speaking of fashion: consumers' uses of fashion discourses and the appropriation of countervailing cultural meanings. *Journal of Consumer Research*, 24(1), 15-42.

Thompson, C. J., & Hirschman, E. C. (1995). Understanding the socialized body: A poststructuralist analysis of consumers' self-conceptions, body images, and self-care practices. *Journal of Consumer Research*, 22(2), 139-153

Thompson, C. J., & Tambyah, S. K. (1999). Trying to be cosmopolitan. *Journal of Consumer Research*, 26(3), 214-241.

Thompson, C. J., & Troester, M. (2002). Consumer value systems in the age of postmodern fragmentation: The case of the natural health microculture. *Journal of Consumer Research*, 28(4), 550-571.

Thompson, C. J., et al. (2018). Theorizing reactive reflexivity: Lifestyle displacement and discordant performances of taste. *Journal of Consumer Research*, 45(3), 571-594.

Thompson, C. J., et al. (1989). Putting consumer experience back into consumer research: The philosophy and method of existential-phenomenology. *Journal of Consumer Research*, 16(2), 133-146.

Thompson, C. J., et al. (1990). The lived meaning of free choice: An existential-phenomenological description of everyday consumer experiences of contemporary married women. *Journal of Consumer Research, 17*(3), 346-361

Thompson, M. J. (2016). The domestication of critical theory. *Contemporary Political Theory*, 18(S2), S78-S82.

Thoo, A.C., et al. (2018). Millennials' Attitudes Toward Facebook Advertising. *Advanced Science Letters*, 24(6), 3864-3868.

Thye, S.R., & Harrell, A. (2017). The status value theory of power and mechanisms of micro stratification: Theory and new experimental evidence. *Social Science Research*, 63, 54-66.

Tilly, C. (2019). *Work under capitalism*. Routledge.

Timmermans, S. (2018). Review Essay: Being and Becoming Mead. *American Journal of Sociology* 123(6), 1826-30.

Tinson, J., Nancarrow, C., & Brace, I. (2008). Purchase decision making and the increasing significance of family types. *Journal of Consumer Marketing*, 25(1), 45-56.

Todd, B. M., & Soule, C. A. A. (2020). Fans and brands: Delineating between fandoms, brand communities, and brand publics. In *Global Branding: Breakthroughs in Research and Practice* (pp. 668-684). IGI Global.

Tomić, S., & Leković, K. (2017). Influence of basic demographic characteristics of children consumers on family travel purchase. *Marketing*, 48(3), 161-168.

Tonkin, E., et al. (2016). *History and ethnicity*. Routledge.

Trapido, Joseph. (2011). The political economy of migration and reputation in Kinshasa. *Africa* 81(2):204-225.

Trevisan, E. (2016). *The Irrational Consumer: Applying Behavioural Economics to Your Business Strategy*. Routledge

Triandis, H. C. (2018). *Individualism and collectivism*. Routledge.

Trocchia, P. J., & Janda, S. (2000). A phenomenological investigation of Internet usage among older individuals. *Journal of Consumer Marketing*.

Tsai, C.C., & Chang, C. H. (2007). The effect of physical attractiveness of models on advertising effectiveness for male and female adolescents. *Adolescence*, 42(168), 827.

Tsai, W. H. S., et al. (2019). En-Gendering Power and Empowerment in Advertising: A Content Analysis. *Journal of Current Issues & Research in Advertising*, 1-15.

Turna, J., et al. (2018). Prevalence of hoarding behaviours and excessive acquisition in users of online classified advertisements. *Psychiatry Research*, 270, 194-197.

Tyler, T. (2019). Meanings of Meat in Videogames. In *Literature and Meat Since 1900* (pp. 231-247). Palgrave Macmillan, Cham.

Tynan, C., McKechnie, S., & Chhuon, C. (2010). Co-creating value for luxury brands. *Journal of Business Research*, 63(11), 1156-1163.

Unger, R. M. (2019). *The knowledge economy*. Verso Books.

Uppal, S., & Barayandema, A. (2018, 2 August). Life satisfaction among Canadian seniors. Statistics Canada.

Urakawa, K., Wang, W., & Alam, M. (2020). Empirical Analysis of Time Poverty and Health-Related Activities in Japan. *Journal of Family and Economic Issues*.

Usman, M. (2019). Does constant advertising change consumer attitude? *Journal of Business and Retail Management Research*, 13(4).

Ustuner, T. & Thompson, C. (2011). How Marketplace Performances Produce Interdependent Status Games and Contested Forms of Symbolic Capital. *Journal of Consumer Research*, 38, pp. 796-814.

Üstüner, T., & Holt, D. B. (2009). Toward a theory of status consumption in less industrialized countries. *Journal of Consumer Research*, 37(1), 37-56.

Valadez-Martinez, L. (2019). Decoration makes a home: The role of living room furnishings in achieving a dignified standard of living in urban Mexico. *Emotion, Space and Society*, 32, 100586.

Valkenburg, P. M., & Cantor, J. (2001). The development of a child into a consumer. *Journal of Applied Developmental Psychology*, 22(1), 61-72.

Van Dam, P., & Jonker, J. (2017). Introduction: The rise of consumer society. *BMGN-Low Countries Historical Review*, 132.

Van De Ven, N., Zeelenberg, M. & Pieters, A. (2010). The Envy Premium in Product Evaluation. *Journal of Consumer Research*, 37, pp. 984-998.

Van den Haak, M., & Wilterdink, N. (2019). Struggling with distinction: How and why people switch between cultural hierarchy and equality. *European Journal of Cultural Studies*, 22(4), 416-432.

Van Gennep, A. (2019). *The rites of passage*. University of Chicago Press.

Van Heerde, H. J., & Neslin, S. A. (2017). Sales promotion models. In *Handbook of marketing decision models* (pp. 13-77). Springer, Cham.

Van Laer, T., et al. (2019). What happens in Vegas stays on TripAdvisor? A theory and technique to understand narrativity in consumer reviews. *Journal of Consumer Research*, 46(2), 267-285.

Van Oudenhoven, J.P., et al. (2016). Immigrants and ethnocultural groups. In D.L. Sam & J. W. Berry (Eds.), *The Cambridge handbook of acculturation psychology*, 134-152.

Van Putten, B. J., & Glende, S. (2016). How to improve technology acceptance by seniors. *Journal of Medical Internet Research* 18(5): e98.

Van Rompay, T. J., et al. (2019). Served straight up: Effects of verticality cues on taste evaluations and luxury perceptions. *Appetite*, 135, 72-78.

Van Ruler, B. (2018). Communication theory: An underrated pillar on which strategic communication rests. *International Journal of Strategic Communication*, 12(4), 367-381.

Vanhala, M., et al. (2020). The usage of large data sets in online consumer behaviour: A bibliometric and computational text-mining–driven analysis of previous research. *Journal of Business Research*, 106, 46-59.

Vannini, P., & Williams, J. P. (2016). Authenticity in culture, self, and society. In *Authenticity in culture, self, and society* (pp. 17-34). Routledge.

Veblen, Thorstein (1901 [1899]). *The Theory of The Leisure Class*. MIT Press.

Velasufah, W., & Setiawan, A. R. (2019). *Erotic Capital at a Glance*. MediArXiv.

Veldman, K., et al. (2017). A life course perspective on mental health problems, employment, and work outcomes. *Scandinavian Journal of Work, Environment & Health*, 316-325.

Ventura, T. (2017). *Sugar and Civilization: American Empire and the Cultural Politics of Sweetness*. Chapel Hill, NC: University of North Carolina Press.

Verhoest, P. (2019). Seventeenth-Century Pamphlets as Constituents of a Public Communications Space: A Historical Critique of Public Sphere Theory. *Theory, Culture & Society*, 36(1), 47-62.

Verplanken, B., & Sato, A. (2011). The psychology of impulse buying: An integrative self-regulation approach. *Journal of Consumer Policy*, 34(2), 197-210.

Veugelers, W. (2007). Creating critical-democratic citizenship education: empowering humanity and democracy in Dutch education. *Compare: A Journal of Comparative and International Education*, 37(1), 105-119.

Veugelers, W., & de Groot, I. (2019). Theory and Practice of Citizenship education. In *Education for Democratic Intercultural Citizenship* (pp. 14-41). Brill Sense.

Veugelers, W., & Vedder, P. (2003). Values in teaching. *Teachers and Teaching*, 9(4), 377-389.

Vezich, S., et al. (2017). Women's responses to stereotypical media portrayals: An fMRI study of sexualized and domestic images of women. *Journal of Consumer Behaviour*, 16: 322-331.

Vijaygopal, R., & Dibb, S. (2012). Exploring the role of acculturation in brand choice: A new perspective for targeting Indians living in the United Kingdom. *Journal of Targeting, Measurement and Analysis for Marketing*, 20(1), 47-56.

Villareal, M. A., & Fergusson, I. F. (2017). The North American Free Trade Agreement (NAFTA) (CRS Report R42965). Washington, D.C.: Congressional Research Service.

Visconti, L. & Di Giuli, A. (2014). Principles and levels of Mediterranean connectivity: Evidence from Prada's "Made in Worlds" brand strategy. *Journal of Consumer Behaviour*, 13, pp. 164-175.

Visconti, Luca M., et al. (2014). Consumer Ethnicity Three Decades after: A TCR Agenda. *Journal of Marketing Management* 30(17–18):1882–1922.

Vogler, C., Lyonette, C., & Wiggins, R. D. (2008). Money, power and spending decisions in intimate relationships. *The Sociological Review*, 56(1), 117-143.

Vohra, J., & Soni, P. (2016). Understanding dimensionality of children's food shopping behaviour in retail stores. *British Food Journal*.

Vohs, K. D., et al. (2018). Making choices impairs subsequent self-control: A limited-resource account of decision making, self-regulation, and active initiative. In *Self-regulation and self-control* (pp. 45-77). Routledge.

Vohs, K. D., Mead, N. L., & Goode, M. R. (2006). The psychological consequences of money. *Science*, 314(5802), 1154-1156.

Von Loewenfeld, F., & Kilian, K. (2016). Brand communities as experience drivers: empirical research findings. In *Memorable Customer Experiences* (pp. 107-120). Routledge.

Wade, K. K., & Stafford, M. E. (2003). Public school uniforms: Effect on perceptions of gang presence, school climate, and student self-perceptions. *Education and Urban Society*, 35(4), 399-420.

Wagner, J. (2019). Financial education and financial literacy by income and education groups. *Journal of Financial Counseling and Planning*, 30(1), 132-141.

Walasek, L., & Brown, D. A. (2015). Income Inequality and Status Seeking: Searching for Positional Goods in Unequal U.S. States. *Psychological Science*, 25(4), 527-533.

Walters, T., & Carr, N. (2019). Changing patterns of conspicuous consumption: Media representations of luxury in second homes. *Journal of Consumer Culture*, 19(3), 295-315.

Wan, W.W.N., et al. (2009). Do Traditional Chinese Culture Values Nourish a Market for Pirated CDs? *Journal of Business Ethics* 88(1): 185-196.

Wang, F. (2013). Educational Equity in the Access to Post-Secondary Education: A Comparison of Ethnic Minorities in China with Aboriginals in Canada. *Interchange*, 44(1-2), 45-62.

Wang, F., et al. (2019). Online brand image, luxury value perception and brand equity. *INTI JOURNAL*, 2019(1).

Wang, Fengling and Xu, Shuchan. (2009). Impact of Cultural Values on Consumption Behavior: A Survey of Contemporary Chinese University Students. *Intercultural Communication Studies XVIII*.

Wang, Guozhao, Li Liu, Xuyun Tan, and Wenwen Zheng. (2017). The Moderating Effect of Dispositional Mindfulness on the Relationship between Materialism and Mental Health. *Personality and Individual Differences*107, 131–36.

Wang, J., et al. (2018). Green image and consumers' word-of-mouth intention in the green hotel industry: The moderating effect of Millennials. *Journal of Cleaner Production*, 181, 426-436.

Wang, K. Y., Chih, W. H., & Hsu, L. C. (2020). Building Brand Community Relationships on Facebook Fan Pages: The Role of Perceived Interactivity. *International Journal of Electronic Commerce*, 24(2), 211-231.

Wang, P., et al. (2016, January). Effect of Complex Multimedia Advertising Campaigns: A New Automated Method for Big Data. *SSRN Electronic Journal* DOI: 10.2139/ssrn.2867081.

Wang, R., et al. (2017). Will materialism lead to happiness? A longitudinal analysis of the mediating role of psychological needs satisfaction. *Personality and Individual Differences*, 105, 312-317.

Wang, S.L., et al. (2020). Cultural industries in international business research: Progress and prospect. *Journal of International Business Studies*, 1-28.

Wang, S., & Hernandez, T. (2018). Contemporary Ethnic Retailing: An Expanded Framework of Study. *Canadian Ethnic Studies*, 50(1), 37-68.

Wang, T. & C. Chen. (2014). Impact of fuel price on vehicle miles traveled (VMT): Do the poor respond in the same way as the rich? *Transportation* 41(1):91-105.

Wang, Y. (2017). *Authenticity, creativity and the future: Adidas advertising and contemporary youth culture* (Doctoral dissertation, Maryland Institute College of Art).

Wang, Y., & Griskevicius, V. (2014). Conspicuous consumption, relationships, and rivals: Women's luxury products as signals to other women. *Journal of Consumer Research*, 40(5), 834-854.

Wang, Y., & Vladas Griskevicius. (2014). Conspicuous Consumption, Relationships, andRivals: Women's Luxury Products as Signals to Other Women. *Journal of ConsumerResearch* 40: 834-854.

Wang, Ying, Shaojing Sun, and Yiping Song. (2011). "Chinese Luxury Consumers: Motivation, Attitude and Behavior." Journal of Promotion Management 17(3):345–59.

Wang, Z., Lee, A., & Polonsky, M. (2013). *Perceived egregiousness and boycott intensity: evidence from the BP Deepwater Horizon oil spill.* Working Paper.

Wänke, M. (2016). Primes as hidden persuaders. *Current Opinion in Psychology*, 12, 63-66.

Ward, J. (2017). What are you doing on Tinder? Impression management on a matchmaking mobile app. *Information, Communication & Society*, 20(11), 1644-1659.

Ward, Lester F. (1900, May). The Theory of the Leisure Class. An Economic Study in the Evolution of Institutions. *American Journal of Sociology*.

Ward, S., & Wackman, D. (1974). Consumer socialization: Initial study results. *ACR North American Advances.*

Warde, A. (2014). After taste: Culture, consumption and theories of practice. *Journal of Consumer Culture*, 14(3), 279-303.

Warde, A. (2016). *Consumption: A sociological analysis.* Springer.

Warde, A. (2017). The Development of the Sociology of Consumption. In *Consumption* (pp. 33-55). Palgrave Macmillan, London.

Warde, A. (2018). Changing Tastes? The Evolution of Dining Out in England. *Gastronomica: The Journal of Critical Food Studies*, 18(4), 1-12.

Warde, A., & Southerton, D. (2012). *The habits of consumption* (Vol. 12). Helsinki: Helsinki Collegium in the Humanities and Social Sciences.

Warde, A., et al. (2009). *Culture, class, distinction.* Routledge

Warde, A., Wright, D., & Gayo-Cal, M. (2007). Understanding cultural omnivorousness: Or, the myth of the cultural omnivore. *Cultural Sociology*, 1(2), 143-164.

Warde, Alan. *Consumption, food and taste.* Sage, 1997.

Waskul, D., & Anklan, M. (2019). "Best invention, second to the dishwasher": Vibrators and sexual pleasure. *Sexualities*, 1363460719861836.

Watkins, J. P. (2018). The Stories That Economists Tell: Mainstream, Hyman Minsky, and Institutional Views of Consumer Behavior. *Journal of Economic Issues*, 52(2), 534-540.

Watne, T., & Winchester, T. (2011, January). Family holiday decision making: the knowledge and influence of adolescent children and parents. In *ANZMAC 2011 conference proceedings: Marketing in the Age of Consumerism: Jekyll or Hyde?* (pp. 1-9). ANZMAC.

Watne, T., Lobo, A., & Brennan, L. (2011). Children as agents of secondary socialisation for their parents. *Young Consumers.*

Weale, A. (2019). *The will of the people: A modern myth.* John Wiley & Sons.

Weaver, R. H. (2019). Is Consumer Activism Economic Democracy. *U. Pa. JL & Soc. Change*, 22, 241.

Weber, K., Sparks, B., & Hsu, C. H. (2016). The effects of acculturation, social distinctiveness, and social presence in a service failure situation. *International Journal of Hospitality Management*, 56, 44-55.

Weber, N. (2020). Experience and Perception of Social Mobility: A Cross-Country Test of the Self-Serving Bias. *Available at SSRN.*

Webley, P., & Nyhus, E. K. (2006). Parents' influence on children's future orientation and saving. *Journal of Economic Psychology*, 27(1), 140-164.

Webster, J. (2019). Taste in the platform age: music streaming services and new forms of class distinction. *Information, Communication & Society*, 1-16.

Wei, L. I. (2018). On Bernard Mandeville's Thoughts of Moral Philosophy. *Journal of Social Science of Hunan Normal University* (6), 10.

Weijters, Bert and Maggie Geuens. (2002). Segmenting the Senior Market: Professional and Social Activity Level. In *AP: Asia Pacific Advances in Consumer Research*, Volume 5 (eds. Ramizwick and Tu Ping) (pp. 140-47). . Valdosta, GA : Association for Consumer Research

Weinberger, M. F. (2017). Gifts: intertwining market and moral economies and the rise of store bought gifts. *Consumption Markets & Culture*, 20(3), 245-257.

Weinstein, D. (2017). Rock protest songs: so many and so few. In *The resisting muse: Popular music and social protest* (pp. 3-16). Routledge.

Weinstein, M. (2016). Consumption, identity and young people. In *Rethinking Children as Consumers* (pp. 118-137). Routledge.

Weisfeld-Spolter, S., et al. (2018). Integrating affect, cognition, and culture in Hispanic financial planning. *International Journal of Bank Marketing* 36 (4): 726-743.

Weiss, H. B. (2017). Family support and education programs: Working through ecological theories of human development. In *Evaluating family programs* (pp. 3-36). Routledge.

Wells, P., & Nieuwenhuis, P. (2018). Over the hill? Exploring the other side of the Rogers' innovation diffusion model from a consumer and business model perspective. *Journal of Cleaner Production*, 194, 444-451.

Wen, J., Yu, C. E., Huang, S., & Goh, E. (2020). Perceived constraint and negotiation of Chinese outbound senior tourists. *Anatolia*, 1-5.

Wesley, S. C., Fowler, D. C., & Vazquez, M. E. (2006). Retail personality and the Hispanic consumer. *Managing Service Quality: An International Journal.*

West, Candace and Don H. Zimmerman. (2009). Accounting for Doing Gender. *Gender & Society* 23(1): 112–22

West, E. (2019). Amazon: Surveillance as a Service. *Surveillance & Society*, 17(1/2), 27-33.

West, M. R., et al. (2016). Promise and paradox: Measuring students' non-cognitive skills and the impact of schooling. *Educational Evaluation and Policy Analysis*, 38(1), 148-170.

West, P., et al. (2006). A material paradox: socioeconomic status, young people's disposable income and consumer culture. *Journal of Youth Studies*, 9(4), 437-462.

Wheeler, L., & Suls, J. (2019). A History of Social Comparison Theory. *Social Comparison, Judgment, and Behavior*, 5.

Whiteley, S., & Sklower, J. (2016). *Countercultures and Popular Music.* Routledge.

Whitfield, S. (2018). *Silk, Slaves, and Stupas: Material Culture of the Silk Road.* Univ. of California Press.

Whitmer, J. M. (2019). You are your brand: Self-branding and the marketization of self. *Sociology Compass*, 13(3), e12662.

Wiedmann, K., Hennigs, N., & Siebels, A. (2007). Measuring Consumers' Luxury Value Perception: A Cross-Cultural. *Academy of Marketing Science Review*, 1.

Wilcox, K., Kim, H. M., & Sen, S. (2009). Why do consumers buy counterfeit luxury brands? *Journal of Marketing Research*, 46(2), 247-259.

Williams, A. (2020). The Complex Hegemony of Neoliberalism. In *Political Hegemony and Social Complexity* (pp. 195-232). Palgrave Macmillan, Cham.

Williams, B. (2004). *Debt for sale: A social history of the credit trap.* University of Pennsylvania Press.

Williams, L. A., & Burns, A. C. (2000). Exploring the dimensionality of children's direct influence attempts. *ACR North American Advances.*

Williams, R. M. (2017). Relative deprivation. In *The idea of social structure* (pp. 355-378). Routledge.

Wilson, D. (2017). For richer or poorer in sickness for wealth: what price consumerism? *Integral Ecology and Sustainable Business*, 169-180.

Winant, G. (2018). The Making of Nickel and Dimed: Barbara Ehrenreich and the Exposé of Class in America. *Labor: Studies in Working-Class History*, 15(1), 67-79.

Winkelmann, L., & Winkelmann, R. (2010). Does inequality harm the middle class? *Kyklos*, 63, 301–316.

Winkelmann, R. (2012). Conspicuous consumption and satisfaction. *Journal of Economic Psychology*, 33(1), 183-191.

Wirt, F. M. (2017). *Politics, products, and markets: Exploring political consumerism past and present.* Routledge.

Wise, P. H. (2016). Child poverty and the promise of human capacity: childhood as a foundation for healthy aging. *Academic Pediatrics*, 16(3), S37-S45.

Wisman, J. D., & Baker, B. (2016). *Consequences of Economic Downturn: Beyond the Usual Economics.*

Wisman, Jon D. 2009. Household Saving, Class Identity, and Conspicuous Consumption. *Journal of Economic Issues* 43(1):89–114.

Withers, E. T. (2017). Whiteness and culture. *Sociology compass*, 11(4), e12464.

Wodtke, G. T. (2017). Social relations, technical divisions, and class stratification in the United States: An empirical test of the death and decomposition of class hypotheses. *Social Forces*, 95(4), 1479-1508.

Woelbert, E., & d'Hombres, B. (2019). Pictorial health warnings and wear-out effects: evidence from a web experiment in 10 European countries. *Tobacco Control*, 28(e1), e71-e76.

Wolff, J. (1985). The invisible flâneuse. Women and the literature of modernity. *Theory, Culture & Society*, 2(3), 37-46.

Wolfinbarger, M., & Gilly, M. C. (2001). Shopping online for freedom, control, and fun. *California Management Review*, 43(2), 34-55.

Wood, R. (2017). *Consumer sexualities: Women and sex shopping.* Routledge.

Wood, Rachel. 2016. "You do Act Differently when You're in it": Lingerie and Femininity. *Journal of Gender Studies* 25 (1):10-23.

Woodhouse, B. B. (2017). "Out of Children's Needs, Children's Rights": The Child's Voice in Defining the Family. In *Children's Rights* (pp. 107-127). Routledge.

Woodhouse, K. M. (2018). *The Ecocentrists: A History of Radical Environmentalism.* Columbia University Press.

Woodman, D., & Bennett, A. (Eds.). (2016). *Youth cultures, transitions, and generations: Bridging the gap in youth research.* Springer.

Woodruff, S. J. (2019). Fruit and Vegetable Intake and Preferences Associated with the Northern Fruit and Vegetable Program (2014–2016). *Canadian Journal of Dietetic Practice and Research*, 80(2), 72-78.

Woodruffe-Burton, H., & Eccles, S., & Elliott, R. (2001). Towards a Theory of Shopping: A Holistic Framework. *Journal of Consumer Behaviour*, 1(3), pp. 256-266.

Woodside, M. (2016). The Nineteenth-Century Dime Western, Boyhood, and Empowered Adolescence. *Boyhood Studies*, 9(2), 5-24.

Wooten, D., & Rank-Christman, T. (2019). Stigmatized-identity cues: Threats as opportunities for consumer psychology. *Journal of Consumer Psychology*, 29(1), 142-151.

Wright, D. (2016). Cultural consumption and cultural omnivorousness. In *The Sage*

Handbook of Cultural Sociology (pp. 567-77). London: Sage.

Wu, L. L., & Mattila, A. (2013). Investigating consumer embarrassment in service interactions. *International Journal of Hospitality Management, 33,* 196-202.

Wu, S. (2005). Fatalistic Tendencies: An Explanation of Why People Don't Save. *Contributions in Economic Analysis & Policy, 4*(1).

Wu, Z., et al. (2017). Forms of inconspicuous consumption: What drives inconspicuous luxury consumption in China? *Marketing Theory, 17*(4), 491-516.

Xiao Lu, P., & Pras, B. (2011). Profiling mass affluent luxury goods consumers in China: A psychographic approach. *Thunderbird International Business Review, 53*(4), 435-455.

Xiao, G., & Tessema, K. (2019). Values, Materialism and Life Satisfaction: A Study of Cultural Influence and Gender Differences in China. *Journal of Business Diversity, 19*(5).

Xiao, J. J., Tang, C., & Shim, S. (2009). Acting for happiness: Financial behavior and life satisfaction of college students. *Social Indicators Research, 92*(1), 53-68

Xie, J., & Min, C. (2019). Can embodied cultural capital affect citation impact? *iConference 2019 Proceedings.*

Xing, X., Popp, M., & Price, H. (2020). Acculturation Strategies of Chinese University Students in the United States. *Journal of Advances in Education Research, 5*(1).

Yang, B., & Mattila, A. S. (2020). How rational thinking style affects sales promotion effectiveness. *International Journal of Hospitality Management, 84,* 102335.

Yang, C. C., & Brown, B. B. (2016). Online self-presentation on Facebook and self development during the college transition. *Journal of Youth and Adolescence, 45*(2), 402-416

Yang, Z., et al. (2014). Parental style and consumer socialization among adolescents: A cross-cultural investigation. *Journal of Business Research, 67*(3), 228-236.

Yasin, A. (2019). Impact of celebrities in advertising campaigns. Undergraduate External Publications. Paper 26. https://fisherpub.sjfc.edu/undergraduate_ext_pub/26.

Yeh, H. Y. (2016). Classification of Edibility and Inedibility: Unveiling the Sociomental Logics beneath Food Habits. *Theory in Action, 9*(4).

Yeung, R. (2009). Are school uniforms a good fit? Results from the ECLS-K and the NELS. *Educational Policy, 23*(6), 847-874.

Yodanis, C. (2006). A place in town: Doing class in a coffee shop. *Journal of Contemporary Ethnography, 35*(3), 341-366.

Young-Bruehl, E., & Kohn, J. (2018). What and how we learned from Hannah Arendt: an exchange of letters. In *Hannah Arendt And Education* (pp. 225-256). Routledge.

Yousafzai, A. L. (2019). *Identity Performance Among Muslim International Women: A Narrative Inquiry* (Doctoral dissertation, Virginia Tech).

Yu, C., & Bastin, M. (2017). Hedonic Shopping Value and Impulse Buying Behavior in Transitional Economies: A Symbiosis in the Mainland China Marketplace. In *Advances in Chinese Brand Management* (pp. 316-330). Palgrave Macmillan, London.

Yu, L., Zhou, W., Yu, B., & Liu, H. (2016). Towards a comprehensive measurement of the information rich and poor: Based on the conceptualization of individuals as information agents *Journal of Documentation* 72(4), 614–635. https://doi.org/10.1108/JDOC-03-2015-0032.

Yu, T. K., Lin, M. L., & Liao, Y. K. (2017). Understanding factors influencing information communication technology adoption behavior: The moderators of information literacy and digital skills. *Computers in Human Behavior, 71,* 196-208.

Zalega, T. (2018). Deconsumption in consumer behaviour of Polish seniors. *Zeszyty Naukowe SGGW w Warszawie. Ekonomika i Organizacja Gospodarki Żywnościowej,* (124), 29-49.

Zavestoski, S., & Weigert, A. J. (2016). Mead, interactionism, and the improbability of ecological selves: toward a meta-environmental microsociological theory. In *Microsociological Perspectives for Environmental Sociology* (pp. 114-132). Routledge.

Zelko, F. (2020). The Wild and the Toxic: American Environmentalism and the Politics of Health. By Jennifer Thomson. *Journal of Social History.*

Zerbini, C., Vergura, D. T., & Latusi, S. (2019). A new model to predict consumers' willingness to buy fair-trade products. *Food Research International, 122,* 167-173.

Zhang, C., et al. (2017). Compulsive buying and quality of life: An estimate of the monetary cost of compulsive buying among adults in early midlife. *Psychiatry Research, 252,* 208-214.

Zhang, C., et al. (2018). Extending face-to-face interactions: Understanding and developing an online teacher and family community. *Early Childhood Education Journal, 46*(3), 331-341.

Zhang, J. W., et al. (2016). Living in wealthy neighborhoods increases material desires and maladaptive consumption. *Journal of Consumer Culture, 16*(1), 297-316.

Zhang, K. Z., & Benyoucef, M. (2016). Consumer behavior in social commerce: A literature review. *Decision Support Systems, 86,* 95-108.

Zhang, Lingjing & He, Yanqun. (2011). Understanding luxury consumption in China: Consumer perceptions of best-known brands. *Journal of Business Research.*

Zhang, W. (2020). Consumption, taste, and the economic transition in modern China. *Consumption Markets & Culture, 23*(1), 1-20.

Zhao, X., et al. (2017). Examining advertising intrusiveness on Instagram: Hedonic and utilitarian attributes of brand and sponsored content. In *American Academy of Advertising. Conference. Proceedings (Online)* (p. 243). American Academy of Advertising.

Zhao, Xin and Russell Belk. (2008). "Politicizing Consumer Culture: Advertising's Appropriation of Political Ideology in China's Social Transition." *Journal of Consumer Research* 35(2):231-244.a

Zhou, M., & Cho, M. (2010). Noneconomic effects of ethnic entrepreneurship: A focused look at the Chinese and Korean enclave economies in Los Angeles. *Thunderbird International Business Review, 52*(2), 83-96.

Zhou, Y. R., et al. (2019). Rethinking "Chinese Community" in the Context of Transnationalism: the Case of Chinese Economic Immigrants in Canada. *Journal of International Migration and Integration, 20*(2), 537-555.

Zhu, W., Treviño, L. K., & Zheng, X. (2016). Ethical leaders and their followers: The transmission of moral identity and moral attentiveness. *Business Ethics Quarterly, 26*(1), 95-115.

Žižek, S. (2018). The seven veils of fantasy. In *Key concepts of Lacanian psychoanalysis* (pp. 190-218). Routledge.

Zniva, R., & Weitzl, W. (2016). It's not how old you are but how you are old: A review on aging and consumer behavior. *Management Review Quarterly, 66*(4), 267-297.

Zolkeplee, S. Z., et al. (2018). Determinant Factors of Student's Perception Toward Educational Loan Repayment. *The Journal of Muamalat and Islamic Finance Research, 15*(1), 73-83.

Zuckerman, P., & Shook, J. R. (Eds.). (2017). *The Oxford handbook of secularism.* Oxford University Press.

Zuk, M., et al. (2018). Gentrification, displacement, and the role of public investment. *Journal of Planning Literature, 33*(1), 31-44.

Zuzanek, J. (2005). Adolescent time use and well-being from a comparative perspective. *Loisir et société/Society and Leisure, 28*(2), 379-423.

Sources and References for Boxes

In chapter order. Includes online supplemental boxes.

"Canadian Mail Order Catalogues," Library and Archives Canada. "Canadians Have A Big Appetite for Debt," Debt.ca. (2012). D. Frank, "Working Class History: English Canada," *The Canadian Encyclopedia* (2013). S. Lavertu, "Catalogues and Women's Fashion," A History of Canadian Mail-order Catalogues. Library and Archives Canada, "Mail order catalogues: history, Government of Canada (2019). PayScale, "Average Factory Worker Hourly Pay in Canada," PayScale.com. S. Penfold, A Mile of Make-Believe: A History of the Eaton's Santa Claus Parade Toronto: University of Toronto Press, 2016. C. Sorensen, "What's behind Canada's newfound lust for luxury?" Macleans.ca (2015). "The Winnipeg General Strike," CBC Learning (2001). T. Veblen, The Theory of The Leisure Class (1899). Wang & Griskevicius (2014), "Conspicuous consumption, relationships, and rivals: Women's luxury products as signals to other women," Journal of Consumer Research, 40, 834-854. J. Becker, "Avril Lavigne's clothing line and beyond," Toronto Star (2011). CBC Music, "5 fashion trends we can thank Canadian musicians for" (2019). CBC News, "Stampede celebrates 100th anniversary of Victory Stampede that marked end of WWI" (2019). CBC Radio, "Teacher says she feels 'betrayed' as classes start under Quebec's religious symbols law" (2019). A. Infantry, "Gen Y Canadians splurging on luxury items, despite high unemployment," *The Star* (2012). R. Naidu-Ghelani, "Canada's luxury retail market takes off as brands flock to cities," CBC News (2018). K.M. Ruppenthal and L.N. Bonikowsky, "Automobile," *Canadian Encyclopedia* (2006). A. Smith, "Record-breaking attendance for first full day of 2019 Calgary Stampede," *Calgary Herald* (2019). Valiante, G., "In Quebec, there's no embarrassment in being called a nationalist," *Toronto Star* (2019). "Essential facts about Parenting in Canada," Live & Learn (2015). N. Bohnert, et al., "Living arrangements of children in Canada: A century of change," Statistics Canada (2014). CBC News, "Canadian Parents More Lenient" (2010). B. Dyas, "The Weirdest Parenting Advice We've Tried the Past 100 Years," Good Housekeeping (2017). Family and Community Support Services, "Positive Parenting and Family Functioning," Government of Calgary (2014). Government of Canada, "What Do We Know About Family Influences on Young Children's Development? The Well-Being of Canada's Young Children: Government of Canada Report," (2011). R. Heller, "Childhood, then and now," *Phi Delta Kappan* (2019). A. Modugno, "A spoonful of kerosene: 150 years of parenting advice," Today's Parent (2019). K. Moloney, "Opinion: We need to rethink student loans across this country," National Post (2019). A. Nova, "How student loans are making some people abandon their dreams," CNBC (2019). A. Sagan, "Average student debt difficult to pay off, delays life milestones," CBC News (2014). S. Scott (1993), "From Major to Minor: An Historical Overview of Children's Rights and benefits," *Journal of Law and Sociology*, 9, 222-257. H.G. Watson, "Debt Nation: How the student-loan crisis is putting young Canadians—and their futures—at risk," TVO (2018). K. Bulo, "The Gibson Girl: The turn of the century's 'ideal' woman, independent and feminine," *The Vintage News* (2018). "Global Smart Kitchen Market to Exceed USD 7 Billion by 2020, According to Technavio," Business Wire (2016). L. Carroll, "A lot of families have a hard time: Back-to-school shopping a stressful time for many," Ottawa Citizen (2019). M. Cliff, "H&M launches adorable 'mini-me' collection for mums and daughters just in time for the family holiday—but it's selling out fast," *The Sun* (2019). Ebates Canada, "Canadian parents cite expenses as top back-to-school stressor," Newswire (2019). P. Huddleston et al. (2010), "It's a family affair: mothers, daughters and siblings shopping experiences," Deakin Research Online (2010). A. Kimball, "The Untold Story of the Canadian Kardashians," Toronto Life (2017). LG Electronics Canada, "Survey finds 77 per cent of Canadians are missing out on family memories by not cooking and eating together," Newswire (2019). D. Licorish, "Poll finds most Canadians spend more on back-to-school than on holiday shopping," LowestRates.ca (2017). A. Patel, "How much these Canadians spent on back-to-school shopping," Global News (2019). S. Pappas, "Moms Mimic Teen Daughters' Style," Live Science (2011). Statistics Canada, "Eating Out: How Often and Why?" Government of Canada (2019). J. Wilson, "Moms are copying their teen daughters' style, study says," Toronto Star (2011). M. Abedi, "Lack of financial literacy could hold Canadian millennials back: report," Global News (2017). P. Banerjee, "Should we give up on financial literacy?" *The Globe and Mail* (2019). P. Cain, "University Tuition Fees in Canada Rise 40% in a decade," Global News (2016). P. Cain, "60% more Toronto students have private tutors—in wealthy areas most of all," Global News (2013). "Generation Why!" BMO Wealth Management (2017). S. Fayer et al. (2017), "STEM Occupations: Past, Present, And Future," U.S. Bureau of Labor Statistics. "History of Family Planning in Canada," Canadian Public Health Association. M. McQuigge, "Financial literacy classes welcomed in schools; experts suggest courses start sooner," CTV News (2019). M. Scotti, "Canadians still struggle with basic financial rules, rights: study," Global News (2017). L. Twells, "Current and Predicted Prevalence of Obesity in Canada," *Rehab and Community Care Medicine* (2014). S. Williamson, "Why Reducing Food Waste in School Meal Programs Matters" Healthy Food Choices in Schools (2019). M. Wisenthal, "Section W: Education," Statistics Canada (2014). S. Barker, "The Victory Loans Campaign of 1919," The Albert County Museum & R.B. Bennett Centre. S. Barmak, "Cheerios campaign shares stories of human connection," *Marketing Magazine* (2014). J. Bradburn, "Doing their bit: How Ontarians bought up Victory Bonds for town pride—and to help win the war," TVO.org (2018). P. Bridge, "Canada Social Media 2018: The Platforms Grabbing Social Ad Dollars," *eMarketer* (2018). "Canadian Posters from the First World War—Victory Bonds," Ontario Minister of Government and Consumer Services. C. Cole, "Eaton's Christmas Catalogues," Canadian Museum of History. B. Curry, "Elections Canada cancels influencer campaign after discovering partisan comments," *The Globe and Mail* (2019). J. Glantz, "The surprising origin of 'always a bridesmaid, never a bride,'" *TODAY* (2016). J. Neff, "Top 15 ad campaigns of the 21st century," *AdAge* (2015). P. Suggett, "Advertising Sets Impossible Standards for Women," The Balance: Careers (2019). S. Bruce, "4 cruise ships at once not ideal, says Port Charlottetown," CBC News (2018). "String of record tourism years on PEI comes to an end," CBC News (2019). W. Eileen, "Mary Pickford," *The Canadian Encyclopedia* (2018). S. Fraser, "New Anne of Green Gables series creates P.E.I. tourism interest," CBC News (2017). J. Friesen, "Tim Hortons: How a Brand Became A Part of Our National Identity," *The Globe and Mail* (2018). R. Rocha, "What 35,000 political ads on Facebook reveal about Canada's election-year message battle" (2019). The Canadian Press, "Tim Hortons Poppy Doughnut Causes Social Media Stir," Global News (2017). "Tim Hortons Foundation Camps," Tim Hortons (2019). E. Alini, "Tired of high cellphone and internet bills? This election is full of promise(s)," Global News (2019). M. Biss, "Canada Is Nowhere Close to Ending the Student Debt Crisis," *Huffington Post* (2017). "How 5 Ottawans are dealing with crushing student debt," CBC News (2017). "Student unions, university, college still have 'lots of questions' about what tuition cuts mean," CBC News (2019). M. Draaisma, "High cost of internet access leaving low-income families behind, report finds," CBC (2019). A. Gaviola, "Cancelling Student Debt Could Help Pay Your Rent. What if the Next PM Did It?" *Vice* (2019). J. Gerster and K. Hessey, "Why some First Nations still don't have clean drinking water—despite Trudeau's promise," Global News (2019). Goodyear, S., "Digital divide: Is high-speed internet access a luxury or a right?" CBC (2016). J. Graham, "Sask. reserve to get clean drinking water after more than 5 years," CBC (2017). A. Jones, "Ontario's Tories eliminate free tuition for low-income students," CTV News (2019). "Just the Facts," Canada Without Poverty. J. Ke and L. Ford-Jones, "Food insecurity and hunger: A review of the effects on children's health and behaviour," *Paediatrics & Child Health* 20,2 (2015), 89-91. K. Lane and G Gagnon, "The lack of clean drinking water in Indigenous communities is unacceptable," *The Globe and Mail*, (2019). S. Munroe, "Winnipeg General Strike of 1919," Thought Co (2019). V. Ouellet, "40% of Ontario full-time post-secondary students granted free tuition, CBC analysis shows," CBC News (2019). Public Health Agency of Canada, "Inequalities in children in low income families in Canada," Government of Canada (2019). "Student Debt Crisis—A Generation Buried in Student Debt," Hoyes-Michalos—Debt Relief Experts. "Student Nutrition Programs," Toronto Foundation for Student Success. "The Winnipeg General Strike," CBC News (2001). S. Weale, "Children in Low-Income Families Suffer Shame and Social Exclusion," *The Guardian* (2019). "Winnipeg General Strike," Canadian Museum of History. E. Bedford, "Canadian off-price retailers apparel sales from 2015 to 2019," Statista (2019). Bryce et al., "Inequality Explained: The Hidden Gaps in Canada's Education System," OpenCanada.org (2016). S. Cameron, "Why Canada Goose jackets are so expensive," *Business Insider* (2019). L. Debter, "The Golden Goose: How Dani Reiss Became A Billionaire Turning Canada Goose into A Luxury Brand Powerhouse," *Forbes* (2019). M. Dimon, "The Most Expensive Private Schools in Canada," *University Magazine* (2018). J. Grant, "Nine of Meghan Markle's favourite Canadian brands," *Toronto Life* (2017). B. Grossberg, "5 Major Differences Between Public and Private Schools," Thought Co. (2019). H. Hoffower, "The reasons flying first class can be worth the money have nothing to do with the math," *Business Insider* (2018). "Houses in Canada are too expensive, and it's not just the fault of foreign speculators," *The Globe and Mail* (2019). N. Kalashnikova, "9 of the Richest Neighbourhoods in Canada," *Narcity* (2016). K. Kerr, "Primer on private schools," *The Globe and Mail* (2018). R. Khederian, "Why Gilded Age ocean liners were so luxurious," *Curbed* (2017). S. Leung, "Off-price Retailers: What Wholesalers Need to Know," *Handshake*, (2015). T. Loudenback, "The world's richest people spend $234 billion a year on luxury goods—here's how much they spend on yachts, private jets, wine, and clothes," *Business Insider* (2018). A. Naraghi, A., "Canada's richest communities 2019," *Maclean's* (2019). H. Shaw, "Nordstrom's off-price Rack brand dares to tread where Holt Renfrew failed," *Financial Post*, (2018). D. Slotnick, "How first-class flying has changed over the past 70 years," *Business Insider* (2019). C. Patterson, "Nordstrom Rack Announces 3 Canadian Fall Store Opening Dates," *Retail Insider* (2018). "What is the Future of Canadian Fashion?" *The Kit* (2019). M. Toneguzzi, "Industry Changes See Underwhelming Growth in Apparel Sales in Canada: Expert," *Retail Insider* (2019). S. Treleaven, "Canada Goose takes flight across the globe," *Maclean's* (2018). K. Bueckert, " 'I can be her': Camp encourages Indigenous girls to explore tech careers," CBC News (2018). "Canada's first Inuk cardiac surgeon gets to the heart of the matter," *Globe and Mail* (2019). CBC News, "Women's clothier Aritzia devising new loyalty program to help drive booming sales even higher," CBC (2019). D. D'addario, "Ellen Page on Freeheld and Why She Came Out: 'I was Just Depressed,'" *Time* (2015). T. Deschamps, "American Apparel is staging a comeback with a few twists and a Canadian owner," Toronto City News (2018). "Ellen Page Joins HRCF's Time to Thrive Conference," Human Rights Campaign (2014). S. Elvins, "Review of the book *The Modern Girl: Feminine Modernities, the Body, and Commodities in the 1920s*, by Jane Nicholas," *Canadian Journal of History*, 53(1), (2018): 139-140. J. Ellison, "Jane Nicholas. *The Modern Girl: Feminine Modernities, the Body, and Commodities in the 1920s*," *Urban History Review*, 45(1), (2016):55+. S. Lavertu, "Catalogues and Women's Fashion," Canadian Museum of History (2004). K. Lawler, " 'Natural' trend excludes some women, critics say; no-bra, no-makeup look is easier for those who meet traditional beauty standards," *Times-Colonist* **(2016).** J. Richard, "Canadian women unhappy with their appearance: Study," *Toronto Sun* (2015). L. Thomas, "Men aren't willing to shop online as much as women, survey finds," CNBC (2018). M. Campbell, "Men in compression tights bend gender norms," *Maclean's* (2016). "From 'silly-ass fad' to luxury status symbol: Inside the billion-dollar men's watch industry," CBC Radio (2019). S. Harris, "The best a man can get? Why some men are brushing off Gillette's ad campaign," CBC News (2019). M. Healy, "What makes men show off; study suggests a dose of testosterone increases appetite for luxury products," *Times-Colonist* (2018). T. Keenan, "Keenan: Guys shop differently than girls, sort of," *Calgary Herald* (2018). S. Krashinsky, "Sexism in advertising: What Canadian men and women find unacceptable," *The Globe and Mail* (2018). J. Lin, "A new look: retail clothing sales in Canada," Statistics Canada (2003). D. Lockman, "Opinion: Parenting brings out our most sexist selves," *The Globe and Mail* (2019). D. Parisi, "Men spend more on luxury but shop the same amount as women: report," *Luxury Daily* (2017). A. Sagan, "Lululemon plans to double revenue from men's line, digital sales by 2023," *Toronto Star* (2019). B. Taylor, "The great retail divide between men and women: Some say shopping is a necessary evil for him, while a pastime for her," *Toronto Star* (2012). D. Thomas, "The census and the evolution of gender roles in early 20th century Canada," *Canadian Social Trends*, 89 (2010): 40-46. M. Bain, "National borders can't contain the new phase of global connection," *Quartz* (2017). W. Chevalier et al., "Montreal," Brittanica.com (2020). D. Clément, "1760 British Conquest (Colonial Rule)," Canada's Human Rights History (2017). "Distillery District Heritage Website," The Distillery Historic District. M. Drouin, "Montréal in Time," *Canada's History* (2017) . T. Ford, "eCommerce," International Trade Administration (2019). S. Harris, " 'Very depressing': CIBC staff losing jobs to workers in India, expected to help with training," CBC News (2017). A. Russell, "Canadians Unaware How Many Products Made Using Child Labor: World Vision," Global News (2015). A. Westfield, "How E-commerce is Eroding Retailer Earnings in Canada," *Retail Insider* (2018). "2015 Corporate Social Responsibility Report," Loblaw (2015). M. Abedi, "For some Canadians, it isn't easy to celebrate religious holidays," Global News (2019). A. Borschel-Dan, "First survey of Canadian Jewry shows lower assimilation, intermarriage than US," *Times of Israel* (2019). O. Bowden, "How new Canadians embrace holiday traditions: 'Christmas back home was very different,'" Global News (2019). R. Csillag, "New survey reveals behaviours and attitudes of Canadian Jews," *The Canadian Jewish News* (2019). T. Douglas, "Remittances: $24 billion a year sent home from Canada," *Vancouver Sun* (2014). J. Dunham, "Filipinos in Canada sent more money abroad than any other group in 2017: study," CTV News (2019). W.B. Henderson, "Indian Act," *The Canadian Encyclopedia* (2006). N. Keung, "Canada's ethnic enclaves more diverse than you think, study finds," *Toronto Star* (2015). J.R. Miller, "Residential Schools in Canada," *The Canadian Encyclopedia* (2019). The Royal Canadian Geographical Society, "Redress and Healing," *Canadian Geographic*, (2018). J. Jankovic, "Unprecedented survey of Jews in Canada finds 'exceptional cohesion,' highlights paths for programming and education," University of Toronto (2019). C. Reynolds, "Tech companies helping to bring lower prices, choice to money remittance market," City News (2019). A. Sandeep, "Opinion: Ethnic enclaves no barrier to social inclusion in Edmonton, Calgary," *Edmonton Journal* (2015). "Study on international money transfers 2017," Statistics Canada, (2019). "Timeline: Key dates for Canada's dealings with First Nations," *Toronto Star*, (2012). Bright Horizons Education Team, "Children and Music: Benefits of Music in Child Development," *Bright Horizons* (2019). G. Brockell, "The Dionne quintuplets: The exploitation of five girls raised in a 'baby zoo,'" *The Washington Post* (2019). "First World War (WWI)," *The Canadian Encyclopedia* (2019). History.com. Editors, "The Roaring Twenties History," History.com (2019). "How Marketers Target Kids," MediaSmarts (2019). "Musical Instruments," Indigo (2020). T. Poulton, "'Kidfluence' on family spending strong: YTV Tween Report," *Mediaincanada* (2019). "Social Networking Addiction Facts in Canada—Drug Facts," Drug Facts (2019). A. Thomson, "Most vegans, vegetarians in Canada are under 35: survey," *The Globe and Mail* (2018). J. Anderson, "History of Caring for Our Elders," aPlaceforMom (2015). "Around the World Cruises," Oceania Cruises (2019). C. Bieber, "Is cruise ship living a cheaper option for seniors than assisted living?" *USA Today* (2017). N. Brown, "How the Face of Senior Living in Toronto is Changing," *Toronto Storeys* (2019). "Canada's Seniors and the Positive Impact of Social Media," *Comfort Keepers* (2016). "Canada's population estimates: Age and sex, July 1, 2019," Statistics Canada (2019). R. Carrick, "The Sad Reality of Seniors Discounts," *The Globe and Mail* (2018). J. Davison, "Seniors and social media: more than keeping up with the grandkids," CBC News (2013). Government of Canada, "Seniors Online," Get Cyber Safe (2018). Y. Kim et al., "The relationships among family and social interaction, loneliness, mall shopping motivation, and mall spending of older consumers," *Psychology & Marketing*, 22, (2005), 995-1015. King et al., "Safe, Affordable, Convenient: Environmental Features of Malls and Other Public Spaces Used by Older Adults for Walking," *J Phys Act Health* (2016). R. Marowits, "Older Gen-Xers are starting to qualify for some seniors' discounts," *The Globe and Mail* (2019). "Senior Travel: Reasons to Cruise in Your Golden Years," Dunhill Travel Deals. "Seniors and Travel," *Aging in Place* (2019). "Seniors and the Positive Impact of Social Media," *Comfort Keepers*, (2016). "Smartphone Apps for Seniors," Medical Alert Advice. P. Taylor, "Why Seniors Shouldn't Get Discounts," *Maclean's* (2013). "Technology key to keeping Canadian seniors healthy at home," Telus Health (2018). T. Tyler, "When 'poorhouse' wasn't only an expression," *Toronto Star* (2009). "7 Ways Technology Has Improved Senior Care," Aging.com. B. Boyd and M. Boucher, "Diamond," *The Canadian Encyclopedia* (2012). M. Bush, "How Popular Online Casino is in Canada," Chart Attack (2019). S. Carter, "Get off the Bandwagon of Banning Plastics," BNN Bloomberg (2019). L. Denne et al., "Canada's major grocery chains slow to tackle the mounting problem of plastic waste," CBC (2019). "Retail Therapy: Does It Help?" *Forbes* (2015). "Gen Z stress an opportunity for retail success, finds A.T. Kearney," Consulting.ca. (2019). P. Kozicka, "What to spend and how to save on a diamond ring," Global News (2015). "Legal Canadian Online Casinos," Gamblinginsider. C.

Lemire, "'Confessions of a Shopaholic' feels like a knockoff," CTV News (2009). O. Mosleh, "Alberta rolls the dice on online gambling—but at what cost?" *Toronto Star*, (2019). S. Rick, "In Defense of Retail Therapy," *Psychology Today* (2013). "The History of the Diamond as an Engagement Rings," American Gem Society (2019). M. Aboud and L. Ritchie, "Deferred Prosecution Agreements (DPAs) come into force in Canada," Osler, Hoskin & Harcourt LLP (2018). E. Alini, "SNC-Lavalin: Does 9,000 jobs make it a 'public policy problem'?" Global News (2019). A. Bosse, "Boycott against U.S. food not the best answer to Trump tariffs, economist says," CBC News (2018). "Child Labor, Forced Labor & Human Trafficking," U.S. Department of Labor. T. Cook, "A changed Canada emerged from the First World War," *The Globe and Mail* (2018). "Crowdfunding—Canada: Statista Market Forecast," Statista. L. D'Amato, "First World War ripped away Canada's 'age of innocence,'" *TheRecord.com* (2014). K. Dangerfield, "Boycotting U.S. products? Here is how to buy Canadian during a trade war," Global News (2018). L. Desjardins, "Bamboo fabric may not be all it's cracked up to be," Radio Canada International (2019). "Fairtrade in Canada—A Consumer Perspective," Fairtrade Canada (2017). R. Reints, "Canadians Are Boycotting U.S. Goods in #BuyCanadian Campaign," *Fortune* (2018). R. Rocha, "What 10,000 Kickstarter projects reveal about Canada's entrepreneurs," CBC News (2017). M. Rouse, "Greenwashing, Its Impact and How to Fight it," *Pocket Up* (2019). The Canadian Press, "Health Canada wants further public input in regulating natural health products," CBC News (2019). M. Turcotte, "Ethical Consumption," Statistics Canada (2011). A. Zhu, "Where Canadians Can Buy Ethical and Sustainable Fashion Online," *Terumah* (2019). C. Bateman, "Historicist: Talk by Lightening," *Torontoist* (2016). E. Bedford, "Vegetarianism and veganism in Canada—Statistics and Facts," Statista (2019). A. Bresge, "Dining of the future: Vegan restaurant boom fuelled by meat eaters," City News (2018). Canadian Government, "Communications Monitoring Report 2018," Canadian Radio-television and Telecommunications Commission (2018). H. Chana, "Considering Options for International Business Expansion," BDO Canada (2017). D. Cox, "Is veganism as good for you as they say?" *The Guardian* (2019). CTV Ottawa, "Local stores set to close for global climate strike," CTV Ottawa (2019). R. Flanagan, "More than 3 million Canadians vegetarian or vegan: Study," CTVNews (2018). R. Kanani, "Canadian Prime Minister Justin Trudeau on Climate Change, Cybercrime, and Gender Equality—IMF F&D," International Monetary Fund (2019). S. Little, "MEC, Lush Cosmetics to close stores across Canada on Friday for climate strike," Global News (2019). A. McDowell, "Canadian companies sticking with Chinese growth plans despite trade tensions," *The Globe and Mail* (2019). "Costco chaos proves why more Canadian companies should expand to China," Dailyhive.com (2019). "Paris Agreement—Climate Action," European Commission (2015). T. Rana, "International Trade Implications on Canadian Business," NAOC (2019). S. Shearman, "From tinsel to turkey, shoppers dream of a 'guilt-free' Christmas," Reuters (2019). "Top Reasons for Corporate Global Expansion," Wolters Kluwer (2016). A. Vera, "Canada is Warming at Twice the Global Rate, report says," CNN Health (2019).

Sources for Photographs and Images

Chapter One: Opener: Darko Stojanovic/Pixabay. Golfing: Pexels. Veblin, Orwell: Wikimedia Commons [WC]. Baudrillard: Europeangraduateschool/WC. Lonely Crowd: Mike Chai/Pexels. Wedgewood: Victoria McGlinchey/WC. Galerie Vivienne: Benh Lieu Song/WC. Eaton's: 1923 postcard/WC. Weber: WC.
Chapter Two: Opener: Andrea Piacquadio /Pexels. Massage therapy: Social Butterfly/Pixabay. Car: Dave 7/WC. World Values Survey map, 2017 version: http://www.worldvaluessurvey.org/WVSContents.jsp/WC. Protest: Michael Swan/Flickr. Foodie: Public Co/Pixabay. Calgary Stampede: Provincial Archives of Alberta (https://www.flickr.com/photos/alberta_archives/18965039693/). Tim Hortons cup: GoToVan/Flickr. Drake: Musicisentropy/Flickr.
Chapter Three: Opener: Porapak Apichodilok/Pexels. Head with words: John Hain/Pixabay. Parents with kid, laptop: Andrea Piacquadio/Pexels. Kid with piggy bank: Annie Spratt/Unsplash.
Chapter Four: Opener: Pasja1000/Pixabay. Gibson girl: Charles Dana Gibson, 1891/WC. Farmhouse: Marsden Kemp, Farmhouse and load of pumpkins, 1905 (Archives of Ontario C 130-6-0-12-2). Back to school: VisionPic/Pexels. Bathroom: William LeMond/Pexels. Caruso with phonograph: Library of Congress/Flickr Commons Project. Housewife: Victoria Borodinova/Pixabay. Mother and daughter: Anastasia Gepp/Pixabay.
Chapter 5: Opener: Anastasia Gepp/Pixabay. Peer group: Sammie Vasquez/Unsplash. Woman and money: Gerd Altmann/Pixabay. School uniform: Pixabay/Pexels. School lunch program: U.S. Department of Agriculture. Pop machine: Atlantis Curry/Pixabay. University of Toronto corridor: V.V. Nincic/Flickr. Graduation: Totum Revolutum/Pixabay
Chapter 6: Opener: Joshua Earle/Unsplash. Innis and McLuhan: Library and Archives Canada. CBS ad: WC. Woman with hat: Pera Detlic/Pixabay. Sigmund Freud: Max Halberstadt/WC. Victory Bond posters: Archives of Ontario. Cheerios: Aline Ponce/Pixabay. Online word of mouth: Cottonbro/Pexels. Eaton's parade and catalogue: Archives of Ontario.
Chapter 7: Opener: Pexels/Pixabay. Bovril: 1915 poster, Library of Congress. Bag: LUM3N/Pixabay. McDonald's: Restaurant in 2014. Northwalker/WC. Word of mouth: Gerd Altmann/Pixabay. Tim Hortons: Andrew Scheer/Flickr.
Chapter 8: Opener: Strangelv/WC. Box graphics—Clothing, food: Clker-Free-Vector-Images/Pixabay. . Car: G. Lopez/Pixabay. House: Open Clip-Art Vectors/Pixabay. Dollar sign: Gordon Johnson/Pixabay. Equal sign: Ryan Morrison/Pixabay. Packard plant: Albert uce/WC. Tobacco: CDC. Handbags: Pexels/Pixabay. TTC: Victoria Rokita/Unsplash. Bastille: Anonymous painter/WC.
Chapter 9: Opener: Adriana Calvo/Pexels. Saks Off 5th: Mike Mozart/Flickr. Canada Goose: Gaelen Marsden/WC. Ridley College: ReliableCoaster/WC. Occupy Toronto, 2011: Dan Perl/Flickr. SAS 747: SAS Museet/Flickr. Restaurant: Navin75/Flickr/WC.
Chapter 10: Opener: Pexels/Pixabay. Intersectionality: Jakayla Toney/Unsplash. Woman in mirror: Orna Wachman/Pixabay. Laura Mulvey: Maurius Kubik/WC. Plastic surgery: Joeyy Lee/Unsplash.
Chapter 11: Opener: Daria Usanova/Pexels. Ronald Reagan: National Archives and Records Administration. Ram pick-up truck: Kevauto/WC. Beer: ELEVATE/Pexels. DIY: Bidvine/Pexels. Bentley: Neri Vill/Pixabay. Grilling: Askar Abayev/Pexels.
Chapter 12: Opener: Tim Reckmann/Flickr. COVID-19: Government of Odisha, Twitter account, I & PR Department. Anti-globalization: Sam Fentress/WC. PPE: Whispyhistory/WC. Globe: Apollo 17/NASA. Wallerstein: Alexei Kouprianov/WC. Jasper, Alta.: Provincial Archives of Alberta/flickr. Beijing, 2017: Picrazy2/WC.
Chapter 13: Opener: City of Toronto/Flickr. Western Union office: FoxLad/WC. Mohawk Institute: Anglican Church of Canada. Kim's Convenience: Booledozer/WC. Little Italy, Albert Street, New York: Todd Crusham/WC. Vancouver Chinatown: Xicotencatl/WC. Starbucks: Wikimedia Commons.
Chapter 14: Opener: Naku Mayo/Unsplash. Sunnyside, Toronto, in the 1920s: Toronto Public Library. Woman on wall: Sebastian Pociecha/Unsplash. Tween: Iiona Virgin/Unsplash. Soft drinks: Marlith/WC. Shoes: Thomas B./Pixabay. Smoking: Fotografierende/Unsplash.
Chapter 15: Opener: RODNAE Productions/Pexels. Senior tourists: Vidar Nordli-Mathisen/Unsplash. Wellington County Poor House: Wellington County. James C. Floyd: Jim Floyd/WC. Senior with cup: RODNAE Productions/Pexels. Queen Mary 2: Ken Heaton/WC. Senior on laptop: Andrea Piacquadio/Pexels. Seniors in Thunderbird: Clem Onojeghuo/Pexels. Roulette wheel: Naim Benjelloun/Pexels.
Chapter 16: Opener: David Vives/Pexels. Las Vegas: Pixabay/Pexels. Retail therapy: Gustavo Fring/Pexels. Pirate Bay cartoon: Dylan Horrocks/WC.
Chapter 17: Opener: Jim Killock/Flickr. Nixon: Thomas J. O'Halloran, *U.S. News & World Report*, Library of Congress, Prints and Photographs Division, *U.S. News & World Report* Magazine Collection, reproduction number LC-DIG-ppmsca-19730. Berlin/Kitchener: James J. MacCallum, 1910/Toronto Public Library. Naomi Klein: Moizsyed/WC. Fair trade banana: Bjerkebanen/WC. Zipcar: Zipcar Car Sharing/GoToVan, Vancouver, Canada/WC. Oil spill: Petty Officer 2nd Class Justin Stumberg, U.S. Navy/WC. Habermas: Európa Pont/Habermas10/WC. Arendt: Unknown phoptographer/WC. Consumer in chains: Clker-Free-Vector-Images/Pixabay.
Chapter 18: Opener: Sears closing in Edmonton: Jason Woodhead (jasonwoodhead23)/WC/Flickr. Arctic sea ice: NASA Science Visualization Laboratory. Shopper: Anna Shvets/Pexels. Christopher Wylie: Jwslubbock/WC.

Index